A Cardinal for the Ages

ROBERTO DE MATTEI

A CARDINAL *for the* AGES

Merry del Val and His Enduring Influence on the Church

Translated by Nicholas Reitzug

SOPHIA INSTITUTE PRESS
Manchester, New Hampshire

First published in Italian as *Merry Del Val. Il cardinale che servì quattro papi* © SugarCo; Edizione standard (14 marzo 2024)

Cover by LUCAS Art & Design, Jenison, MI

Cover image: Rafael Merry del Val (Alamy PPCCT3)

Sophia Institute Press
Box 5284, Manchester, NH 03108
1-800-888-9344
www.SophiaInstitute.com

Sophia Institute Press is a registered trademark of Sophia Institute.

paperback ISBN 979-8-88911-336-2

ebook ISBN 979-8-88911-337-9

Library of Congress Control Number: 2025936725

First printing

Thanks

I would like to express my gratitude for the invaluable help of Prof. Alberto Corteggiani of the Central State Archive; to Prof. Alejandro Mario Dieguez of the Vatican Apostolic Archive; to Prof. Daniel Ponziani of the Dicastery for the Doctrine of the Faith; to Prof. Simona Duranti of the Archive of the Dicastery of the Causes of Saints; to Msgr. Marco Agostini and Prof. Emanuele Pressacco of the Historical Archive of the Secretariat of State, Relations with States Section; to Prof. Claudio Maria Mancini of the Historical Archive of the Ministry of Foreign Affairs; to Prof. Maria Lamas of the Merry de Val Archive at the Pontifical Spanish College of San José; to Prof. Pasquale Luca of the Historical Archive of the Diocese of Rome; to Prof. Diane Brunning of the Historical Archive of the Abbey of Downside; to Prof. Rebecca Somerset of the British Jesuit Archives of Farm Street; to the Countess Luisa Maddalena Medolago Albani, of the Medolago Albani Archive; to Prof. Thomas Henderson of the Archive of the Ushaw Library; to Prof. Dianora Citi and engineer Domingo Merry del Val, indefatigable custodian of the memory of his great-uncle, Cardinal Rafael Merry del Val.

December 8, 2023, Feast of the Immaculate Conception

Contents

A Cardinal for the Ages

Introduction

Cardinal Rafael Merry del Val is an extraordinary man of the Church, still little investigated by historians despite having lived and worked in the heart of the ecclesiastical events of his time under four popes: Leo XIII, Pius X, Benedict XV, and Pius XI.

He was born on October 10, 1865, in London, where his father served at the time as Spanish ambassador to Great Britain. In his veins flowed the blood of the various nationalities of his ancestors: illustrious families from Spain, Ireland, England, Scotland, and Holland. He studied in Rome, at the behest of Leo XIII entering the Pontifical Academy of Ecclesiastical Nobles, of which he later became president, and carried out delicate missions in the service of the Holy See, concerning himself in particular with the problem of the validity of Anglican ordinations.

Merry del Val was the secretary of the conclave that elected Pope St. Pius X, who was to name him secretary of state and cardinal when he was only thirty-eight years old. For eleven years he accompanied the pontiff in a profound union of mind and heart, through all the difficult trials of his pontificate, beginning with the battle against modernism. Under Benedict XV, he was the archpriest of the Vatican basilica and secretary of the Holy Office. In this capacity he fought the main errors of the day and, in 1929, he published a revised edition of the *Index librorum prohibitorum,* pointing out the danger to faith and morals represented by the errors propagated by the media. During the conclaves of 1914 and 1922 he nearly missed being elected Pope himself.

His death is still shrouded in mystery. He died in Rome on February 26, 1930, after a botched operation for appendicitis. On his tomb one reads the inscription he desired as his testament: "*Da mihi animas, coetera tolle*" [Give me souls, take away the rest]. His dignity as a prince of the Church was never separated from his profound humility, which found expression in the famous

Litanies of Humility he composed. His process of beatification was begun on February 26, 1953, at which point he received the title Servant of God.

The first biography of the cardinal appeared in January 1933, three years after his death, written by Msgr. Pio Cenci, an archivist in the Vaticans Secret Archive, with a preface by Cardinal Eugenio Pacelli, then secretary of state to Pius XI. This work, although not particularly scientific in its methodology, is of great importance because it constitutes an invaluable source of documents and firsthand testimonies.[1]

In the following years, still valuable biographies of a more apologetical flavor appeared, by Frances A. Forbes,[2] Vigilio Dalpiaz,[3] and Viktor von Hettlingen,[4] as well as the *Notes de direction*[5] edited by Fr. Gillet, the first collection of the cardinal's spiritual writings.

A turning point in the research into Merry del Val came thanks to the introduction of his cause for beatification, strongly desired by Pius XII, who began his ecclesiastical career in the secretariat of state under the cardinal and who remained close to him through esteem and personal devotion. The cause was officially opened on February 26, 1953, at the request of Cardinal Enrique Pla y Deniel, archbishop of Toledo and primate of Spain, and was promoted by the Pontifical Spanish College in Rome, whose rector, Don Jaime Flores, was nominated postulator.[6]

1 Pio Cenci, *Il Cardinale Raffaele Merry del Val*, Roberto Berruti, Turin 1953. Pio Cenci (1876–1955) was a Franciscan priest from Umbria, who worked in the Vatican Secret Archive. According to a police notice of January 3, 1933, the true author of the biography was "Francesco Zanetti, for whom Msgr. Cenci served as an escort" (ACS, Fascicoli Personali. Busta 828. "Merry del Val"), however Msgr. Nicola Canali, personal secretary of Cardinal Merry del Val, and future cardinal, testified that he was the author of the work (*Processus Informativus Ordinarius*, vol. 3, *Sessio* CXIII, pp. 673–674), availing himself of Giuseppe De Mori's help in writing it. On August 20, 1939, in one of his first discourses to the faithful of the Veneto, commemorating the "illustrious figure of Pius X," Pius XII praised "Cardinal Canali who kept alive and ardent the fervor for the memory of Pius X and of his most faithful prime minister and collaborator Cardinal Merry del Val" (*L'Osservatore Romano*, February 27, 1953).

2 *Rafael, Cardinal Merry del Val. A character sketch*, Longman, Green and Co., London 1932, p. 21. Frances Alice Forbes (1869–1936) was the pseudonym of Madre Frances Alice Monica Forbes, RSCJ, member of the Scottish *Society of the Sacred Heart.*

3 *Attraverso una porpora: il cardinale Merry del Val*, L.I.C.E., Turin 1935. The book was translated into English (1937). Vigilio Dalpiaz (1887–1950), professor of religion in Rovereto and then of canon law at the Lateran University, was in 1925 nominated substitute notary to the Congregation for the Doctrine of the Faith [at that time, the Congregation of the Holy Office], at the service of its secretary, Merry del Val.

4 *Raphael Kardinal Merry del Val: ein Lebensbild*, with an introduction by Cardinal Eugenio Pacelli, Benzinger, Köln 1937. Viktor von Hettlingen (1899–1955), of the diocese of Coira, was pastor in the canton of Schwyz, of which he wrote a history (1950).

5 Rafael Merry del Val, *Notes de direction*, Cerf, Paris 1937, with an introduction by Fr. Martin Stanislas Gillet (1875–1951), Master of the Dominican Order from 1929 to 1946, the year in which he was elevated to the episcopate.

6 Following him as postulators were Juan Sanchez, José M. Carda, Ambrogio Esser, Tomas Amable Diez Olano, and Santiago L. De Vega Alonso.

During the ceremony, a petition was read by the Spanish bishops who had been ordained priests by Cardinal Merry del Val, and the members of the Tribunal who were to examine the acts of the informative process were presented. The "ordinary" (diocesan-level) trial was conducted by the Vicariate of the Vatican City State by express will of Pius XII. Msgr. Pietro Canisius van Lierde (1907–1995), vicar general of the Holy Father for the Vatican City, was nominated president of the Tribunal. After three years, the process was closed (1953–1956), and in 1957, the writings of the Servant of God were approved by the Congregation of Rites. But Pius XII, who wanted Merry del Val's canonization to complement that of Pius X [May 29, 1954], died before this goal could be achieved, on October 9, 1958.

A series of books of a more educational character on Merry del Val have appeared in recent years. The first, a work by the Capuchin priest Girolamo Dal-Gal, focuses primarlily on the holiness of the man.[7] As Robert Havard de la Montagne writes in the book's French preface, the Cardinal Secretary of State "concedes pride of place to the ascetic of the mystical life, to the spiritual director, to the apostle. The diplomat and the politician recede into the shadows to highlight the interior man."[8]

Along similar lines, though with different results, are the works of the journalist Hary Mitchell (1956),[9] Maria Cecilia Buehrle (1957),[10] Sr. Mary Bernetta Quinn (1958),[11] and Fr. Javierre (1961).[12]

Joan de Trafford, who founded the Legion of Pius X in 1933 to promote the beatification of Giuseppe Melchiorre Sarto, in 1965 obtained episcopal approval for the establishment of the Legion of Merry del Val on the occasion of

7 *Il Cardinale Raffaele Merry del Val, segretario di Stato del Beato Pio X*, Paulines, Rome 1953. Unless otherwise noted, citations are taken from the English translation, *The Spiritual Life of Cardinal Merry del Val*, trans. Joseph A. McMullin, Benzinger Brothers, New York 1959. Fr. Girolamo Dal-Gal (1875–1968), of the Order of the Franciscan Conventuals, was also the author of a *Vita ufficiale della postulazione per la causa di canonizzazione di San Pio X*, published in 1951. The book was translated into Spanish (1954) and French (1955).

8 Introduction to the French edition of the book by Fr. Dal-Gal, Nouvelles Éditions Latines, Paris 1955, p. 16. Robert Havard de la Montagne (1877–1963), a Catholic historian and journalist, lived in Rome from December 1922 to March 1934, where he founded a newspaper "*d'union catholique et latine*," and the bimonthly *Rome*.

9 *The Cardinal Merry del Val*, Paris-Livres, Paris 1956.

10 *Rafael Cardinal Merry del Val*, The Bruce Publishing Company, Milwaukee 1957. Maria Cecilia Buehrle (1887–1976) was an American writer and author of a lengthy biography on *Saint Maria Goretti* (1950).

11 *Give me Souls: A Life of Raphael Cardinal Merry del Val*, Newman, Westminster 1958. Viola Roselyn Quinn (1916–2003), in religion Mary Bernetta, of the Franciscan Sisters of the Congregation of Our Lady of Lourdes, was author of several literary works, including *Ezra Pound: Introduction to Poetry* (1972).

12 *Merry del Val*, Juan Flors Editor, Barcelona 1965. José María Javierre Ortas (1924–2009) was a Spanish priest of the Hermandad de Sacerdotes Operarios Diocesanos and author of many biographies of the saints.

the centenary of the cardinal's birth. The Legion's untiring representative in Rome was Prof. Robin Anderson.[13]

Despite all this, from 1959 onwards, just when the Promoter General of the Faith, Silvio Romani, published the *Animadversiones,* the cause of Merry del Val's beatification halted, in part because it had been deprived of the support given by Pius XII.[14]

Since that period, no response has been forthcoming to the *Animadversiones,* that is, to the legitimate objections raised in every cause of beatification to verify the solidity of the candidate's virtues before being raised to the altars.[15] The main reason for the dormancy of Cardinal Merry del Val's cause for the beatification, however, is not a lack of response to doubts concerning his exercise of heroic virtues, but the doctrinal and political context of his public activity. If Pope Pius XII opened the cause of beatification of Cardinal Merry del Val in light of the upcoming canonization of Pius X, it is that same light that makes the figure of the Anglo-Spanish cardinal now appear inconvenient: the role he played alongside Pius X, especially in the battle against modernism.

There has been no lack of good texts of an educational nature in recent years, such as that of Don Alberto José González Chaves,[16] and Harriet Murphy's publication *Spiritual Writings* (2009),[17] but historians have continued to give little

13 Robin Anderson, who was born in London in 1913 and died in Rome in 2005, was educated at Marlborough College and studied at the Royal Academy of Dramatic Art in London. Transferred to Rome in 1953, he worked with Radio Vaticana and taught languages. He published books, articles and poetry, and held conferences on religious and cultural topics in numerous countries, including Italy, Enlgand, and the United States. In his private archive and his unpublished *Memoirs* (1994), he documented his organizational efforts for the commemorations of Cardinal Merry del Val held in Rome beginning in 1965, the centenary of the birth of the Servant of God. On that occasion, Cardinals Bacci and Ottaviani spoke, and later Card. Antonio Bacci (1968), Card. Paolo Marella (1969), Msgr. Pietro Canisio Van der Lierde (1971), Card. Egidio Vagnozzi (1972), Msgr. John Patrick Carroll-Abbing (1973 and 1974), Card. John-Joseph Wright (1975), Card. Luigi Ciappi (1978), Card. Giuseppe Caprio (1985), Card. Maximilien de Fürstenberg (1987), and Card. Paul Augustin Mayer (1990).

14 Santiago L. De Vega Alonso, *Estado de la causa de Beatificación del Siervo de Dios Rafael card. Merry del Val*, in *Rafael Merry del Val, 150 anni dalla sua nascita*, ed. Domingo Merry del Val, Editrice Pliniana, Selci-Lama (PG) 2020, pp. 267–270.

15 Frederic Raurell, "Un cardinale e tre conclavi: Merry del Val," in *Laurentianum* 50 (2009), p. 286 (pp. 283–311). The author makes a critical analysis in this article of the *Animadversiones* presented by the Promoter General of the Faith.

16 Don Alberto José González Chaves, *Rafael Merry del Val,* San Pablo, Madrid 2004; then, *Dame almas!: Una biografía del cardenal Merry del Val,* Editorial Ivat SL, Madrid 2022. Cf. the review of the former work by Pablo Martín de Santa Olalla Saludes, "Rafael Merry Del Val," *Estudios Eclesiásticos. Revista de investigación e información teológica y canónica* 82 (2007), pp. 171–173.

17 Harriet Murphy, *The Spiritual Writings of Raphael Cardinal Merry del Val,* Gracewing, Leominster 2009. This work takes up the letters of spiritual direction published in the United States as *The Spiritual*

attention to the figure of Cardinal Merry del Val. Fr. José Maria Muñoz Urbano, whose doctoral dissertation in ecclesiastical history was dedicated to the history of the cardinal's cause, has appropriately called for a documented biography.[18] Fr. Santiago de Vega Alonso, postulator of the Cause, considered the creation of a historical commission necessary for the sake of investigating the numerous and complex questions concerning the cardinal's life. Along these lines, the historian Philippe Roy-Lysencourt has set to work. In his *Aperçu biographique,* published in 2016, he offers us a concise panorama of the questions on the table.[19] The 2015 convention organized in Rome by Domingo Merry del Val, on the 150th anniversary of the cardinal's birth, with the contribution of Roy-Lysencourt, represented an important contribution in this direction.[20]

The pages that follow propose a historical reconstruction of the life and works of Cardinal Merry del Val, based not only on the process of beatification, but on archival sources and a vast bibliography that can be found directly in the footnotes. The Church will have to declare one day whether Cardinal Rafael Merry del Val was a saint only in the private sphere or if, on the contrary, he exercised virtue in a heroic manner in his function as secretary of state, as St. Pius X did in his role as the visible head of the Church.[21] The aim of this work is not merely to fill a historiographic void, but also to display the current relevance of the thought and activity of Rafael Merry del Val in a historical moment in which the Roman Church, which he served with extraordinary dedication, is living a particularly difficult period of its history.

Diary of Raphael Cardinal Merry del Val (1964) and in England under the title *Let God Act,* edited by Sister Paula Fairie, OSB, with an introduction by bishop Pietro Canisius Van der Lierde, then republished by the Carmelite Monastery in Quidenham, Norfolk (1977, 1979, 1986). The text by Harriet Murphy has an interesting introduction. Her work has been translated into Spanish under the title *El ángel del Vaticano: Escritos espirituales del Cardenal Merry del Val,* Ediciones Nueva Eva, Madrid 2021.

18 José María Muñoz Urbano, *El cardenal secretario de Estado Rafael Merry del Val y su proceso de Beatificación, Historia de su causa: problemas, investigaciones de archivos y documentación inédita,* extract of a doctoral dissertation on the history of England, Gregorian Pontifical University, Rome 2008.

19 Philippe Roy-Lysencourt, *Le cardinal Rafael Merry del Val (1865–1930). Aperçu biographique,* Institut d'Étude du Christianisme, Strasbourg 2016.

20 Domingo Merry del Val (ed.), *Rafael Merry del Val, 150 anni dalla sua nascita.*

21 Victor-Alain Berto, "A la mémoire du serviteur de Dieu le cardinal Raphael Merry del Val," in *La Pensée Catholique* 26 (1953), p. 46 (pp. 42–46).

List of Acronyms and Abbreviations Used

Archival Sources

AAV = Vatican Apostolic Archive.

AA.EE.SS. = Archive of the Sacred Congregation of Extraordinary Ecclesiastical Affairs.

ADDF = Archive of the Dicastery (formerly Congregation) for the Doctrine of the Faith.

ACS = Central State Archive, Rome.

Archive of the Dicastery (formerly Congregation) for the Causes of Saints.

Archive of the Postulation (Pontifical Spanish College of St. Joseph, Merry del Val Archive).

Archive of the Spanish Embassy to the Holy See.

ARSI = Archivum Romanum Societatis Jesu.

ASMAE = Historical Archive of the Ministry of Foreign Affairs, Rome.

Farm Street Archive, *Papers Woodlock*, Letters-Cardinal Merry del Val.

Ushaw College Library, *Merry del Val Papers.*

Spoglio Merry del Val = AAV. Secretariat of State. Spogli of Cardinals and Officials of the Curia. Rafael Merry del Val.

Cause of Beatification of Cardinal Rafael Merry del Val

Informative Articles = *Beatificazione e Canonizzazione del Servo di Dio il Cardinale Raffaele Merry del Val Segretario di Stato del Beato Pio X. Articoli per il Processo ordinario informativo*, Tipografia Poliglotta Vaticana 1952.

Processus Informativus Ordinarius = *Romana Beatificationis. Transumptum Processus Ordinarii Informativi super fama sanctitatis vitae, virtutum et miraculorum Servi Dei Raphaelis Merry del Val, Secretarii Status* S. Pii Papae X, 6 vols., Vatican City 1956.

Super scriptis = *Romana Beatificationis et Canonizationis Servi Dei Raphaelis Merry del Val, S.R.E. Cardinalis Summarium ex officio super scriptis,* Typis Polyglottis Vaticanis 1956.

Informatio = *Romana Beatificationis et Canonizationis Servi Dei Raphaelis card. Merry del Val, Secretarii Status Sancti Pii Papae X. Informatio - Tabella testium - Summarium - Litterae postulatoriae super causae introductione et summarium ex officio super scriptis,* Typis Polyglottis Vaticanis, Vatican City 1957.

Animadversione = *Romana Beatificationis et canonizationis Servi De Raphaelos card. Merry del Val, Secretarii Status Sancti Pii Papae X. Animadversiones Promotoris Generalis Fidei,* Typis Polyglottis Vaticanis 1959.

Printed Works

AAS = *Acta Apostolicae Sedis.*

Acta Pii X = *Acta Pii X P.M.,*Vols. I-V, Romae 1905–1914 (Reprint, Graz 1971).

ASS = *Acta Sanctae Sedis.*

Bullarium romanum = *Bullarium diplomatum et privilegiorum sanctorum romanorum pontificum,* S. and H. Dalmezzo, Turin 1860.

DBC = *Dictionnaire biographique des cardinaux du XIX siècle. Contribution à l'histoire du Sacré Collège sous les pontificats de Pie VII, Léon XII, Pie VIII, Grégoire XVI, Pie IX et Léon XIII, 1800–1903,* edited by Jean Le Blanc, Wilson and Lafleur, Montreal 2007.

DBI = *Dizionario Biografico degli Italiani,* Istituto dell'Enciclopedia Italiana, Rome 1960.

DDC = *Dictionnaire de Droit Canonique,* Letouzey and Ané, Paris 1935–1958 (7 vols.).

DENZ = Heinrich Denzinger, *Enchiridion Symbolorum definitionum et declarationum de rebus fidei et morum,* edited by Peter Hünermann, bilingual edition, EDB, Bologna 1995.

DHGE = *Dictionnaire d'Histoire et de Géographie Ecclésiastiques,* Letouzey and Ané, Paris 1912.

DIP = *Dizionario degli Istituti di Perfezione,* Paoline, Rome 1965 (10 vols.).

DSMC = *Dizionario storico del Movimento Cattolico in Italia,* edited by Francesco Traniello and Giorgio Campanini, Marietti, Turin 1981 (3 vols. in 5 tomes).

DSp = *Dictionnaire de Spiritualité,* Beauchesne, Paris 1937–1994 (16 vols.).

DSP = *Dizionario Storico del Papato,* Bompiani, Milan 1996 (2 vols.).

DTC = *Dictionnaire de Théologie Catholique,* edited by A. Vacant and E. Mangenot, Letouzey and Ané, Paris 1909–1972 (33 vols.).

EC = *Enciclopedia Cattolica,* Sansoni, Florence 1949–1954 (12 vols.).

Enchiridion = *Enchiridion delle Encicliche,* bilingual edition, EDB, Bologna 1995–1999.

EI = *Enciclopedia Italiana,* 36 vols., Istituto della Enciclopedia Italiana, Rome 1949–1952.

EP = *Enciclopedia dei Papi,* vol. III, Istituto della Enciclopedia Italiana, Rome 2000.

Pii X Disquisitio = *Disquisitio circa quasdam obiectiones modum agendi Servi Dei respicientes in modernismi debellatione una cum Summario additionali ex officio compilato,* Typis Polyglottis Vaticanis, Rome 1950.

Pii Papae X. Positio = *Positio super introductione causae* (Report on the introduction of the Cause, i.e.) compilation of evidence, testimonies, and the life story of the Servant of God, collected during the diocesan inquiry, and presented to the Dicastery for the Causes of Saints. Typis Polyglottis Vaticanis, Rome 1941.

Pio XII, Discorsi e Radiomessaggi = Pio XII, *Discorsi e Radiomessaggi,* Tipografia Poliglotta Vaticana, Vatican City 1959 (21 vols.).

1

From London to Rome

A Spanish Family in London

The nomination of Msgr. Nicholas Wiseman[22] in 1850 as archbishop of the new diocese of Westminster and his elevation to the cardinalate during the pontificate of Pius IX[23] constituted an extraordinary event in the history of England. The reestablishment of the Catholic hierarchy and the influx of illustrious converts from the Oxford Movement and from the ranks of the aristocracy gave the English Church a previously unheard-of vitality, a thrust of warm and profound piety, and sincere attachment to the Roman primate.[24]

Blessed Domenico Barberi,[25] who had arrived in England from Italy in 1845, received into the Catholic Church the future Cardinal Newman,[26]

22 Nicholas Wiseman (1802–1865), rector of the English College in Rome, from 1848 the apostolic vicar in London, promoted the renewal of the Enlgish hierarchy, which took place on September 29, 1850, when Pius IX, with the bull *Universalis Ecclesia*, nominated him archbishop of Westminster and member of the consistory, and in the days following made him a cardinal. He is also renowned for his historical novel *Fabiola* (1854). Cf. Wilfrid Ward, *The Life and Times of Cardinal Wiseman*, Longmans Green, New York 1897, 2 vols.; Sydney W. Jackman, *Nicholas Cardinal Wiseman: a Victorian Prelate and His Writings*, University Press of Virginia, Charlottesville, VA 1977.

23 Giovanni Maria Mastai Ferretti (1792–1878) reigned as Pope Pius IX from June 16, 1846, until his death. John Paul II proclaimed him blessed on September 3, 2000. Cf. Giacomo Martina, *Pio IX*, Università Gregoriana Editrice, 3 vols., Rome 1986; Roberto de Mattei, *Pio IX*, Cantagalli, Siena 2012.

24 Martina, *Pio IX*, vol. 2, pp. 384–385. Cf. also J. Derek Holmes, *More Roman than Rome: English Catholicism in the Nineteenth Century*, Burns & Oates, London 1978, pp. 55–110; Edward Norman, *The English Catholic Church in the Nineteenth Century*, Clarendon Press, Oxford 1984, pp. 110–157; Madeleine Beard, *Faith and Fortune*, Gracewing, Leominster 1997.

25 Domenico Barberi (1792–1849), Passionist, carried out his apostolate in England, receiving the conversion to the Catholic Church of the future Cardinal John Henry Newman and of hundreds among the Anglo-Saxon clergy and laity. He was proclaimed blessed by Paul VI in 1963. Cf. P. Federico dell'Addolorata C.P., *Il B. Domenico della Madre di Dio Passionista*, Postulazione dei Padri Passionisti, Isola del Liri 1963.

26 John Henry Newman (1801–1890), Anglican minister, converted to Catholicism in 1845 and was created cardinal by Leo XIII in 1879. He was beatified by Benedict XVI in 2010 and canonized by Pope Francis in 2019. Cf. José Morales Marín, *John Henry Newman: la vita (1801–1890)*, Italian translation, Jaca Book, Milano 1998; Christopher Dawson, *The Spirit of the Oxford Movement and Newman's Place in History*, Saint Austin, London 2001; Ian Ker, *John Henry Newman: a Biography*, Oxford University Press, New York 2010.

previously an Anglican minister. Newman, along with Fr. Frederick Faber,[27] was one of the protagonists of the great movement of conversions that had its epicenter in the Birmingham and London houses of the Congregation of the Oratory.

Among the converts of Fr. Domenico was George Spencer, who became a Passionist, taking the name Ignatius of St. Paul.[28] In September 1851 he obtained from Pius IX an indulgence for whomever would pray three Hail Marys for the conversion of England. Other illustrious converts included the Oxford student Gerard Manley Hopkins (1866),[29] who entered the Society of Jesus and became one of England's most important poets; the Marquess of Bute (1868),[30] who after having left Oxford allocated most of his fortune to the founding and reconstruction of churches and monasteries, and the Marquess of Ripon (1874),[31] formerly the Grand Master of Freemasonry and later a key personality in the British Catholic world.

The prophecy of St. Paul of the Cross regarding the conversion of England seemed to be coming to pass.[32] Msgr. Talbot,[33] one of the "secret chamberlains" of Pius IX stated in 1865: "There is no other diocese in the Christian world in which religion has made as much progress as in London in the past twelve years."[34]

The Catholic enclave in London had its center in the church of St. James in Spanish Place where, from 1676 to 1679, in a city openly hostile to the Roman Church, Fr. Claude de la Colombière preached as chaplain to the Duchess of

27 Frederick William Faber (1808–1892) converted to Catholicism in 1845, entered the Congregation of the Oratory, and was one of the most widely read religious writers of the late nineteenth and early twentieth centuries. On him, see Ronald Chapman, *Father Faber*, Burn and Oates, London 1961.

28 Ignazio di San Paolo (Giorgio Spencer: 1799–1864), born into an Anglican family of the English upper nobility, was converted by Fr. Barberi and entered the Passionists in 1846. He was proclaimed venerable in 2021.

29 Gerard Manley Hopkins (1844–1889), converted to Catholicism in 1866, entered the Society of Jesus, taught at the University of Dublin, and was to become one of the greatest English poets of his time.

30 John Patrick Crichton-Stuart, III Marquis of Bute (1847–1900), Scottish, was buried in a little chapel on the Island of Bute, although his heart was buried on the Mount of Olives in Jerusalem.

31 George Robinson, I Marquis of Ripon (1827–1909), was viceroy of the Indies (1880–1884) and first Lord of the Admiralty under Gladstone (1886).

32 Paolo Giuseppe of the Immaculate Conception, *Vita di S. Paolo della Croce, fondatore della Congregazione de' Chierici Scalzi della SS. Croce e Passione di N. S. Gesù Cristo*, Tipografia Salviucci, Rome 1867, pp. 215–218. Paul of the Cross (1694–1775), born Paolo Francesco Danei, founder of the Congregation of the Passion of Jesus Christ and of the Passionist cloistered nuns, was canonized by Pius IX in 1867.

33 Monsignor Gilbert Chetwynd Talbot (1816–1896), son of Lord Charles Chetwynd-Talbot, II Earl Talbot.

34 Martina, *Pio IX*, vol. 2, p. 385.

York.[35] Not far from Spanish Place lived the Spanish family Zulueta, whose sitting room was a fulcrum of Catholic life in London.

Don Pedro José de Zulueta y Madariaga,[36] Count of Torre Diaz, of Basque ancestry, had moved to London, where he founded the bank Zulueta & Co. and in 1836 married Sofia Josefa Wilcox y van der Gutch, the daughter of a Scottish father and a Dutch mother. Their marriage was celebrated according to the Evangelical rite,[37] to which the Wilcox family belonged; but when the wife converted to Catholicism, she turned their home into an active religious center of Catholicism under the prompting of Cardinal Nicholas Wiseman.[38] The eldest daughter of the Count of Torre Diaz, Josefa, recalls from her infancy, "when she and her brothers and sisters were frequent visitors at the Cardinal's house, and his companions in seaside excursions," saying of him, "He was at home with us Spaniards.... He was like a Spaniard himself, and we understood each other."[39]

Josefa, or Josefina,[40] met and married a young Spanish diplomat in Madrid on February 3, 1863, Rafael Carlos Merry y del Val,[41] who was sent to

35 Claudio de la Colombière (1641–1682), Jesuit, was superior of the house of Paray-le-Monial, where he was the spiritual director of St. Margaret Mary Alacoque. He was canonized by John Paul II in 1992. Involved in the pseudo "papal Plot" in 1678, he was imprisoned for weeks in the King's Bench Prison of Southwark, but thanks to his position in court and to his French citizenship, his life was spared. He was expelled from England in 1679.

36 Pedro José de Zulueta y Madariaga (1809–1882), second Count of Torre Diaz, was a banker and senator from 1858 to 1868. He was implicated but later absolved in a trial concerning the slave trade. Cf. "The Trial of Pedro Jose de Zulueta in London for Trading in Slaves," in Hugh Thomas, *The Slave Trade: The Story of the Atlantic Slave Trade: 1440–1870*, Simon & Schuster, London 1999.

37 Don Pedro de Zulueta returned to the Catholicism which he had temporarily left, and his marriage to Sofia Wilcox was celebrated again in the Catholic rite.

38 José M. Javierre, *Merry del Val*, Juan Flors Editor, Barcelona 1965, pp. 4–6.

39 Ward, *The Life and Times of Cardinal Wiseman*, vol. 2, pp. 171–172, 175.

40 Josefa Sopfia de Zulueta y Wilcox (1839–1925), daughter of Pedro José Zulueta y Madariaga and Sofia Wilcox y van der Gutch, the first of four siblings, married Rafael Carlos Merry y del Val in 1863, with whom she had five children: Alfonso (1864–1946); Rafael (1865–1930); Maria Ana (1868–1934); Pedro (1867–1958), an engineer who died in Tangiers, married to Dolores García-Zapata; and Domingo (1870–1935), a mechanical engineer and viticulturist who died in Santiago del Cile, married to Emma Ramilla Rojas, all of them with abundant progeny spread throughout Latin America, Spain and Italy. Emma Merry de Val dedicated the final years of her life to the needy in a hospital in Santiago del Cile and died in sanctity.

41 Rafael Carlos Merry y del Val (1831–1917) was the secretary of a Spanish legate in Madrid, then in the Embassy in London, and later plenipotentiary minister in Belgium (1876–1887), the extraordinary envoy and minister in Vienna to the Austro-Hungarian Empire (1887–1893), and Spanish ambassador to the Holy See (1893–1901). He was a member of the Real Academia de Jurisprudencia y Legislación and the Real Academia de la Historia; doctor *honoris causa* at the University of Oxford and Cambridge; and a Gentleman of the Chamber to the sovereigns Isabella II, Alfonso XII, and Alfonso XIII. Cf. José Pablo Alzina, *Embajadores de España en Londres. Una guía de retratos de la Embajada de España*, Ministerio de Asuntos Exteriores, Madrid 2001. Cf. also the entries dedicated to him in *Dicionario Biografico Español*, Real Academia de la Historia, Madrid

London in 1865 as the secretary to the Legation of Spain to the English Royal Court. Spain was experiencing a period of historical confusion under Queen Isabella II,[42] whereas England under the long reign of Queen Victoria[43] was living through an age of industrial progress and colonial expansion that reached its apex in the proclamation of the sovereign as Empress of the Indies.

Rafael Carlos Merry y del Val was the son of Rafael Merry y Gayté and Maria de la Trinidad del Val y Gómez. The name Merry came from a family in County Waterford, Ireland; they had moved to Seville at the end of the 1700s to escape English laws limiting the rights of Catholics.[44] The del Val were an ancient Aragonite family from Saragossa and could count as one of their ancestors a young martyr.[45] The name Rafael Carlos Merry y del Val, associating the paternal name with the maternal name, was later legalized as the paternal name Merry del Val.

The Spanish diplomat was an ardent monarchist who took an active role in the political life of his country. Since his mother was a lady in waiting to the queen, he spent his youth in the palace of Queen Isabella, becoming friends with the Countess Eugenia Maria de Montijo, the future empress of the French.[46] The turbulent period of the dynastic wars between partisans of Don

2009, vol. 34, pp. 776–777; *Diccionario Crítico de Juristas Españoles, Portugueses y Latinoamericanos*, Universidad de Málaga, Zaragoza-Málaga 2012, vol. 3, p. 367.

42 Quinn, *Give me Souls*, p. 4.

43 Victoria (1819–1901), daughter of the Duke of Kent, Edward, fourth son of King George III and Princess Victoria of Saxe-Coburg, was queen of the United Kingdom of Great Britain and Ireland from June 20, 1837 and empress of India from 1876 until her death.

44 *Algunos modestos apuntes referentes a la familia de Su Eminencia el Cardinal Merry del Val, y a los primeros anos de su vida*, edited by Domingo Merry del Val, the cardinal's brother, in Archive of the Postulation, n. 1035. The family name was originally O'Hoolachan and they lived in a little village in County Connaught, Ireland. In the eighteenth century, to escape persecution, the O'Hoolachans took the name Merry that has the same meaning as the Irish word.

45 Dominguito del Val, son of the notary of the Cathedral of Zaragoza, at the age of seven, was kidnapped and tortured by a Jewish rabbi. Miraculously, his body was found in the River Ebro and his veneration spread immediately throughout Aragon. The little martyr was canonized on July 9, 1808, by Pius VII and his remains taken to the cathedral of Zaragoza. He was one of the thirty-three medieval saints (among whom St. Christopher, St. George, and St. Valentine) whose veneration was suppressed when the new liturgy came into effect in 1969. Elena Mazzini has written in opposition to this veneration: "La sopravvivenza di una pratica liturgica in età post-conciliare. Il culto locale di San Domenichino del Val," in Maria Paiano (ed.), *Chiesa italiana, politica e società. Studi in onore di Bruna Bocchini*, Aracne, Rome 2019, pp. 133–144. The Merry del Val family has a chapel in honor of the martyr, with his relics, in the parish church of San Nicola in Seville (Javierre, *Merry del Val*, p. 3).

46 Quinn, *Give me Souls*, p. 4. Countess Eugenia de Montijo (1826–1920) was empress of the French from 1853 to 1870 thanks to her marriage to Napoleon III.

Carlos[47] and those faithful to Queen Isabella[48] concluded in September 1868, in a revolution known as the September Revolution or the Glorious Revolution, which led in 1870 to the sovereign's abdication and the crowning of Amadeo of Savoy, Duke of Aosta.[49] Opposition by Carlos's supporters and Republicans forced Amadeo to abdicate just two years into his reign, leaving space for an ephemeral republic that lasted until December 29, 1874, when the Bourbon monarchy was restored.

From 1870 to 1874, the Spanish diplomat traveled frequently from London to Paris to assist his exiled queen with his counsel. Isabella's son Alfonso, the heir to the throne, was studying at the military college of Sandhurst, and in his free time in England he reported to the Merry del Val family home.[50]

Josefina Merry del Val y Zulueta, educated by the Ladies of the Sacred Heart in the city of San Sebastian, was a pious woman and generous in coming to the aid of the poor and needy of all types. Her spiritual director was the Dominican priest Fr. Giacinto Maria Cormier.[51] She took direct care of the education of her five children, with the help of her brother, Fr. Francisco de Zulueta, a learned Jesuit, author of a multiple-volume work entitled *Letters on Christian Doctrine,* in which he expounded Catholic doctrine on the Ten Commandments and the Sacraments.[52]

In London, the young couple lived in the heart of the aristocratic neighborhood of Marylebone. It was here, in their residence on Portman Square,

47 The Carlists were partisans of Don Carlos of Bourbon-Spain (1788–1855) who, refusing the abrogation of the Salic Law carried out by Ferdinand VII in 1833, proclaimed himself king of Spain with the title Carlo V, and entered into war with the new Queen Isabella II. The Carlist Wars ended in 1875 with the defeat of Carlo VII (1848–1909).

48 Isabella II of Bourbon (1830–1904), daughter of Ferdinand VII, king of Spain, and of Maria Cristina of the Two Sicilies, his fourth wife, exiled in 1868, lived the rest of her life in France, while her son took the throne as Alfonso XII.

49 Amedeo I of Savoy (1845–1890), son of the king of Italy, Vittorio Emanuele II, was king of Spain from January 2, 1871, to February 11, 1873, and first Duke of Aosta, progenitor of the Savoy-Aosta branch.

50 Alfonso XII (1857–1885), son of Isabella II and Francesco d'Assisi of Bourbon, was king of Spain from December 19, 1874, until his death.

51 Giacinto Maria Cormier (1832–1916), a French religious with the Order of Preachers, was the Master General of the Order from 1904 to 1916. He was beatified by John Paul II on November 20th, 1994.

52 Francisco de Zulueta (1853–1937) joined the Society of Jesus in 1871 and resided in Roehampton until his death. He was the author of books and musical compositions, including a Mass in honor of the English Martyrs. Cf. *Letters on Christian doctrine,* R & T. Washbourne, London 1914 (1905), 3 vols.

Gloucester Place, that their firstborn son, Alfonso, was born in 1864.[53] A year later, their second son, Rafael, was born on October 10, 1865, and baptized the following day in the church of Spanish Place.[54]

Rafael Carlos Merry y del Val likely imagined that his firstborn, Alfonso, was destined to have a brilliant diplomatic career.[55] As it turned out, following in his father's footsteps, Alfonso was in fact for many years the Spanish ambassador in London. But Rafael certainly could not have foreseen that his second-born would become an archbishop, Vatican secretary of state, cardinal, and finally a candidate to the glory of the altars.

Many lines of convergence exist between Cardinal Wiseman and the future Cardinal Merry del Val. Wiseman was born in Seville in 1802 to an Irish family from Waterford that settled in Spain in the eighteenth century. He died in London on February 15, 1865, eight months before the birth of Rafael Merry del Val. Their respective families hailed from the same county in Ireland, but Wiseman was an Englishman born in Seville, while Merry del Val was a Spaniard born in London. The former studied and lived in Rome, but carried out his mission in England, while the latter studied in England and spent his life in Rome. Both were cardinals and both died relatively young, Wiseman at sixty-three and Merry del Val at sixty-five. What they had in common was their strong "Roman spirit" and an ardent longing for the conversion of England, for which they would gladly have given their lives.[56]

53 Portman Square, which takes its name from Henry William Portman, is a large eighteenth-century square next to Gloucester Place, in which modern buildings have today replaced the older ones. Memory of the past remains only in the Portman Gardens in the center of the Square. Cf. Edward Walford, *Old and New London*, Petter & Galpin, London 2019 (1878).

54 The Vatican Apostolic Archive preserves an autographed note by Rafael Carlos Merry y del Val, who wrote: "My second son was born in London at 10:08 a.m. on October 10, 1865, at Number 33 Gloucester Place. He was baptized the following day by the canon Hearn in the chapel of the Spanish Embassy and was given the name Rafael, Maria, José, Pedro, Francisco de Borja, Domingo del Val, Gerardo de la Santisima Trinidad, Merry del Val y Zulueta. His godfather was his maternal grandfather Don Pedro José de Zulueta, Count of Torre Diaz, and his godmother was his paternal grandmother Donna Maria Trinidad del Val de Merry" (AAV, *Spoglio Merry del Val,* busta 3, n. 2).

55 Alfonso Merry del Val y Zulueta (1864–1946), after having begun his career in Belgium, was plenipotentiary minister in Tangiers (1908) and ambassador in London from 1913 to 1931. In 1936, when the civil war broke out, he returned to London and in 1938, as unofficial representative of General Franco, negotiated with British authorities the recognition of the Burgos government. On August 15, 1925, Alfonso XIII bestowed on him the title of Marquis Merry del Val, which he transmitted to his two sons Alfonso and Pablo. The son of the latter, Rafael Merry del Val y Melgarejo, inherited the title in 1979, which he transmitted at his death in 2005 to his son Rafael Merry del Val y Roca de Togores, Count of the Valle de San Juan and fourth Marquis Merry del Val.

56 Cf. Harriet Murphy, "Cardinal Merry del Val and the Conversion of England," *Christian Order* 47 (December 2006), pp. 12–21; *Christian Order* 48 (January 2007), pp. 27–36.

Studies in England and in Belgium

Rafael Merry del Val's education took place in a family setting imbued with strong political and religious principles. His younger brother Pedro recalled, "Rafael inherited from our father rectitude, integrity, diplomacy, and the greatest discretion. From our mother, profound piety and a solid and well-rooted religious education."[57]

Together with his brother Pedro, Rafael attended the first two classes of elementary school at Baylis House, in Slough, in the heart of Buckinghamshire in southeastern England.[58] This institute was opened in 1830 and closed its doors definitively in 1907. It was set in an ancient seventh-century building and was considered the "Catholic Eton." The last survivor of the family that directed it, Miss Cecilia Magdalen Butt, gave an interview in August 1957 when she was eighty years old, recalling that the school was nestled amid a property of ninety acres and had sixty students with twenty staff members. It was "like a village, with its own brewery, bakery, wash house, dairy, scalding-house for pans, apple-house, and potato house," and the students even had their own pack of beagles, like the boys of Eton College, who would come to Baylis House on Sundays for cricket, since it was not allowed on Sundays in their college.[59] The canon Edwin Burton, in his history of the institute, recalls, "Baylis House was always much more than a school; it was a center from which, for many long years, flowed charity and help for the spiritual and corporal needs of the scattered flock of Christ which in that neighbourhood held to the ancient faith."[60]

It was in this college that the little Rafael received the Sacrament of Confirmation, followed by First Communion, which he received on August 29, 1875, in the church of the Jesuits in Bournemouth, the town where the Merry del Val family lived during the years of the Spanish Republic, in the house of Josefina's grandfather, Don Pedro de Zulueta.[61]

57 In Isabel Flores de Lemus, *El fulgor de una purpura. El cardenal Rafael Merry del Val*, El perpetuo socorro, Madrid 1956, p. 178.

58 Canon Edwin Burton, *Baylis House, Salt Hill, Slough: Catholic School and Catholic Centre, 1830–1907*, Luff & Sons, Slough 1923. The school was founded by the brothers William Henry Butt (1787–1878) and James Palmer Butt (1789–1873) in Richmond in 1823 and was transferred to Salt Hill, near Slough, in 1830, until it closed in 1907.

59 Maxwell Fraser, *The History of Slough*, Slough Corporation, Slough 1980, p. 91 (pp. 91–92). The chaplain of the school from 1880 was the Italian priest Giuseppe Maria Clemente (1845–1918). Maxwell Fraser was the pseudonym of Dorothy Phillips (d. 1980), who was born in London but moved with her family to Slough at the age of six or seven and attended St. Joseph's Convent School..

60 Burton, *Baylis House*, p. 18.

61 Cf. AAV, *Spoglio Merry del Val*, busta 3, nn. 45–62 containing the correspondence received on that occasion from relatives and friends.

On March 11, 1875, in the Hotel Mirabeau in Paris, Don Rafael Carlos Merry del Val and the Duke of Santoña attended the encounter of young Alfonso XII with the Carlist general Ramon Cabrera, during which the general recognized the seventeen-year-old son of Isabella II as the legitimate king of Spain.[62] Alfonso thereafter succeeded in returning to his homeland and ascending to the throne in January 1875, after a coup d'état carried out by the army.[63] With the restoration of the monarchy on October 11, 1875, the Spanish diplomat was rewarded with an appointment as plenipotentiary minister to Brussels, and the family followed him to Belgium. After spending a year in the College of Notre-Dame de la Paix in Namur, young Rafael entered the College Saint-Michel of Brussels where he studied until 1883.

After the cardinal's death, Jesuit Fr. Leone Morel, director of the College, collected the judgments and impressions of the old student's classmates. The replies bear witness to the high esteem his companions and classmates cultivated toward him. Rafael is described as "a most pious student, serious and very studious," uniting "a nearly angelic sweetness to surprising energy." He was "a thin boy, pallid in complexion, with a straight nose, beautiful eyes, and a sweet tone of voice," and "was distinguished for the nobility of his visage, the fineness of his manners, the southern expression of his eyes, the perfection of his pronunciation, and his knowledge of both English and Spanish."[64] His distinction and piety merited him the honor of serving the Solemn Mass in the Royal Parish of St. James for the First Communion of the two sons of Prince Philippe of Belgium and Princess Marie of Belgium.[65]

"It was in this northern country," observes one of his biographers, "that he acquired his intense understanding of the simple, robust type of English Catholic," for here, "religion is lived like the strong, virile thing that Catholicism is."[66] Sporting activities were part of the formation of every aristocratic child of that age. The young Rafael was keen on every type of physical exercise. He played tennis and cricket, was an able swimmer, shot with the rifle, and excelled in

62 Ramón Cabrera (1806–1877) was a Carlist general during the first and second Carlist Wars (1833–39, 1846–1849).

63 Leo XIII disapproved the division of Spanish Catholics and later invited them to support Alfonso XII. Cf. Encyclical *Cum multa sint* of December 8, 1882, *On the Current conditions of the Church in Spain*, ASS, vol. 15 (1882–1883), pp. 241–246.

64 Cenci, *Merry del Val*, pp. 14–21. The testimony of the classmates of the college are preserved in the Archive of the Postulation, pp. 1137–1154.

65 Testimony of Enrichetta of Belgium, Duchess of Vendôme (1870– 1948), in Arch. MdV, H, 10.

66 Buehrle, *Merry del Val*, p. 15.

fencing and in horse riding. Nevertheless, during his stay in Brussels, the youth's dominant concern was the choice of his state of life. According to the statements of his brother Pedro and his sister Maria, it seems he was at first inclined toward undertaking a military career, but at the College St. Michel he felt the first inklings of a vocation to the ecclesiastical state.[67]

The priestly vocation is a call that occurs by means of interior inspirations that progressively urge a youth toward this great supernatural goal. The nature of this inclination must first be verified to resolve any doubts. Prudence requires that in order to embrace the priesthood one must demonstrate that the vocation is sure and motivated by proper intentions. Otherwise, it would not be correct to undertake this great step.[68] With good reason was Rafael attentively examining his interior impulses in that period, for, after having expressed his idea to his family, he encountered scarce enthusiasm in his father, who preferred that he pursue a military career. But the young man had learned that the ultimate criteria of his every choice was God and His will. His brother Pedro recalled that one day their father said to Rafael, "How are you going to be a priest when you are so in love with sports and horseback riding?" The boy quickly replied, "For God one should and one can sacrifice everything."[69]

From Ushaw to Rome

In 1883, having overcome the last of his family's resistance, Rafael entered the seminary at eighteen to undertake the itinerary of formation that prepared him for the great step of becoming a priest. He began his ecclesiastical studies at the historical college of Ushaw, in County Durham. The institute was founded in 1808 by a group of students from the English College in Douay, having escaped France after the Revolution.[70] Among the priests and laymen who had

67 Flores de Lemus, *El fulgor de una purpura*, p. 181.

68 Msgr. Pier Carlo Landucci, *La Sacra Vocazione*, Edizioni Paoline, Rome 1960, pp. 233–234.

69 Buehrle, *Merry del Val*, 17; Cenci, *Merry del Val*, p. 23; Flores de Lemus, *El fulgor de una purpura*, pp. 185–186.

70 Ushaw was the main Roman Catholic seminary for the formation of Catholic priests in the north of England, closed definitively in 2011 due to a lack of vocations. Cardinal Merry del Val suggested in 1908 that Pius X bestow on it the title of Pontifical College, thus making it St. Cuthbert's Pontifical College, Ushaw. Cf. Edwin Bonney, "Ushaw College," in *The Catholic Encyclopedia*, Robert Appleton Company, New York 1912, vol. 15, pp. 233–235; David Milburn, *A History of Ushaw College*, The Ushaw Bookshop, Ushaw 1964; William James Campbell (ed.), *Ushaw College 1808–2008, A Celebration*, St Cuthbert Society, Durham 2008. Cf. also J. Derek Holmes, "Cardinal Raphael Merry del Val: An Uncompromising Ultramontane: Gleanings from His Correspondence with England," *The Catholic Historical Review* 60, n. 1 (April 1974), pp. 55–56.

studied at Ushaw, Merry del Val recalled in a letter in 1894 the names of Cardinal Wiseman and Julian Watts-Russell, the eighteen-year-old Pontifical Zouave "who fell at Mentana while defending the rights and independence of the Holy Church."[71] These two figures — the archbishop of Westminster and the papal soldier, fallen on the battlefield in the defense of Pius IX — were expressions of the same militant spirit that characterized "ultramontane" Catholics of that period.[72] Cardinal Manning, who succeeded Cardinal Wiseman as archbishop of Westminster, was the new champion of this spirit of ardent attachment to the Church of Rome.[73]

Two years later, on October 5, 1884, in the church of St. Cuthbert in Ushaw, Rafael received the tonsure and the four minor orders from Msgr. Bewick, bishop of Hexham and Newcastle; these enrolled him officially and canonically into the "ecclesiastical state."[74] Among his fellow disciples at Ushaw were Arthur Hinsley, the future cardinal archbishop of Westminster,[75] and Msgr. Joseph Broadhead, with whom he was bound in the closest of friendships.[76] In the seminary, he proved to be a very vivacious and playful youth, quite disorderly, something which, as observed Cardinal Vagnozzi, could not be said of him by those who knew him as a cardinal.[77] His manners were always those of a gentleman, however. Msgr. Alberto Serafini testified, "He had an exuberant nature,

[71] Ushaw Archive, Letter of Merry del Val to Bishop Thomas William Wilkinson, October 10, 1894. Julian Watts-Russell (1850–1867), educated at Ushaw, belonged to a Catholic family from Staffordshire. He was the youngest Papal Zuave killed at Mentana on September 3, 1867. The Requiem Mass for him was celebrated by the rector of the English College in Rome, Msgr. Henry O'Callaghan (1827–1904). Merry del Val contributed to the construction of a monument to him in the church of St. Thomas of Canterbury in the English College. Cf. Valeriano Cardella, *Giulio Watts Russell zuavo pontificio. Memorie*, Tip. Salviucci, Roma 1868. The book was translated in London in 1896.

[72] In the nineteenth century, the term *ultramontane* ("beyond the mountains") referred to a tendency to look to Rome for guidance in matters of doctrine and governance, as contrasted to Gallicanism and other movements that favored greater authority for national churches or local civil power.

[73] Henry Edward Manning (1808–1892), pastor in the Anglican church, converted to Catholicicm and was ordained a priest in 1851 by Cardinal Wiseman, whom he succeeded in 1865 as archbishop of Westminster. He participated in the First Vatican Council and was made a cardinal on March 15, 1875, by Pius IX.

[74] AAV, *Spoglio Merry del Val*, busta 3, n. 117.

[75] Arthur Hinsley (1865–1937) was consecrated bishop on November 30, 1926, by Cardinal Merry del Val. He was archbishop of Westminster from 1935 to 1943. Leo XIII made him a cardinal on December 13, 1937.

[76] Joseph Broadhead (1860–1929) became vice-rector of Ushaw College, where he had studied. The college library preserves 102 letters he wrote to Merry del Val until his death, one year before that of the cardinal.

[77] Card. Egidio Vagnozzi, *Il cardinale Merry del Val, Pastore di anime*. A discourse given at the Association of the Sacred Heart of Jesus in Trastevere on March 6, 1976, typewritten. Cardinal Vagnozzi (1906–1980) was ordained on December 22, 1928, by Cardinal Merry del Val.

which he knew how to master completely. It was his Spanish character enveloped by his entirely English education."[78] One of his classmates of his same age wrote, "He was humble and unassuming. One felt at home with him at once. He was my ideal of a perfect gentleman, never obtruding his rank, but simply one of us."[79] And another classmate recalled, "Everyone who had anything to do with him loved him. He had a wonderful power of attraction and of making lifelong friends."[80]

At the end of Rafael's seminary training, Msgr. Herbert Vaughan, bishop of Salford and close to the Merry del Val family, advised his parents to have the young man finish his ecclesiastical studies in Rome at the Pontifical Scottish College.[81] The proposal was well received, in part because Denis Sheil,[82] a relative and dear friend of Rafael, was also studying at the Scottish College.[83] Everything was agreed upon and a room was already prepared.

Meanwhile, after his mission in Brussels, Rafael Carlos Merry y del Val was now assigned as the Spanish plenipotentiary minister in Vienna. In autumn 1885, he asked to meet the Holy Father in order to present the young seminarian to him, entrusting his request to a collegue, the Marquiss di Molins, ambassador of Spain to the Holy See.[84] Leo XIII gladly conceded a private audience in the Vatican to the diplomat and his son.

The pontiff received them affectionately and meticulously interrogated the young man about his studies and his vocation and asked the Spanish diplomat

[78] Msgr. Alberto Serafini, *Processus informativus ordinarius,* vol. 2, *Sessio* LII, p. 388. Alberto Serafini (1879–1962) was the apostolic protonotary and canon of St. Peter's and the author of a biography on Pius IX, used at the cause for beatification.

[79] Forbes, *Merry del Val,* p. 21.

[80] Buehrle, *Merry del Val,* p. 15; Forbes, *Merry del Val,* p. 22..

[81] Herbert Alfred Vaughan (1832–1903), nominated bishop of Salford in 1872, was promoted to the Metropolitan See of Westminster on April 8, 1892, and made a cardinal in 1893. Cf. John George Snead-Cox, *The Life of Cardinal Vaughan,* Burns & Oates, London 1910, 2 vols.; Arthur McCormack, *Cardinal Vaughan,* Burns & Oates, London 1966; Robert O'Neil, *Cardinal Herbert Vaughan: Archbishop of Westminster, Bishop of Salford, Founder of the Mill Hill Missionaries,* Burns & Oates, London 1997.

[82] Denis Florence Sheil (1865–1962), son of the Irish official and diplomat Sir Justin Sheil (1803–1871), entered the Scottish College in Rome in 1884. He was ordained in 1889 and was received by Cardinal Newman into the Birmingham Oratory, of which he was superior from 1923 to 1932. His sister Laura Sheil married Pedro Juan de Zulueta y Wilcox (1847–1908), the secretary of the Spanish embassy in London.

[83] Buehrle, *Merry del Val,* pp. 8–11.

[84] Don Mariano Roca de Togores (1812–1889), Minister of the Economy and for several terms of the Navy, received from Queen Isabella the marquisate of Molins, collaborated in the restoration of Alfonso XII, and was ambassador in Paris and later to the Holy See from 1884 to 1886.

why he had chosen the Scottish College. At the end of the audience, he stated clearly that he wished for Rafael to continue his studies not at the Scottish College but at the Pontifical Academy of Ecclesiastical Nobles. He himself would give the suitable orders to the Msgr. President so that the young man could doubtless be admitted as a student. Both father and son were taken aback by this unexpected decision of the pope. The father dared to offer several objections delicately, but Leo XIII was unmovable in the face of all observations: he confirmed his decision and excused them after having given his paternal blessing to the young man, placing his hand on his head. And he dismissed the father saying, "I will remain the father of your son!"[85] The pope's resoluteness unsettled the ambassador who was, however, obliged to write with his own hand the request for his son's admission to the Academy.

On November 20, 1885, just as he turned twenty, Rafael Merry del Val entered the Pontifical Academy of Ecclesiastical Nobles. He was the youngest among the students and the only one who was not an ordained priest.

[85] Cenci, *Merry del Val*, p. 31.

2

In the Service of Leo XIII

Leo XIII, the "Diplomatic Pope"

Leo XIII was seventy-five at the time and, despite his apparent fragility, emanated great energy.[86] Émile Zola, during his trip to Rome, described him as "a waxen figure, with a diaphanous whiteness like an alabaster lamp illuminated from within, with a large nose that accentuated his physiognomy."[87]

Gioacchino Pecci had administered the diocese of Benevento (a papal province) as apostolic delegate, had gained strong diplomatic experience as the nuncio to Brussels, and had governed the Archdiocese of Perugia for thirty years before being raised to the papal throne with the name Leo XIII on February 20, 1878. The pontificate afforded him an opportunity to manifest his qualities as a diplomat and to make use of diplomacy to restore authority and prestige to the papacy. One historian observed, "In the eyes of Leo XIII, diplomacy was the sovereign science, the supreme art form. He held that mild words, wise counsel, pleasant manners, legitimate and opportune concessions would always have positive results. 'There is no one,' he would repeat, 'from whom one cannot obtain something by making him understand the language of reason.'"[88]

The preservation of the pontifical monarchy and the reaffirmation of its rights constituted the primary objective of Pope Leo XIII. This political agenda could be carried out only by a man who commanded all the power needed to lead it to a successful outcome. And this man could only be the Roman pontiff,

[86] Gioacchino Pecci (1810–1923) became pope with the name Leo XIII on February 20, 1878. On his pontificate cf., among others, Charles T'Serclaes, *Pape Léon XIII, sa vie, son action religieuse, politique et sociale*, Desclée de Brouwer, Bruges 1894, 2 vols.; Louis Teste, *Léon XIII et le Vatican*, C. Forestier, Paris 1880; Henri des Houx, *Histoire de Léon XIII. Joachim Pecci (1810–1878)*, Librarie Paul Ollendorff, Paris 1900, 3rd ed.; Edoardo Soderini, *Il pontificato di Leone XIII*, Mondadori, Milan 1933, 3 vols.

[87] Émile Zola, *Il mio viaggio a Roma 31 ottobre—15 dicembre 1894*, Italian translation, Intra Moenia, Naples 2013, p. 80.

[88] Édouard Lecanuet, *L'Église de France sous la troisième République*, Librarie Félix Alcan, Paris 1930–1931, vol. 2, pp. 7–8.

supreme leader of the Church by divine right. He moved on two fronts: on one side a strong Magisterium that could reaffirm in all fields the fundamental principals of Catholic doctrine; on the other side, political activity that was malleable and realistic and could restore to the Holy See the role of protagonist on the international scene, leaving behind the isolation in which it found itself. The first point was developed by Leo XIII through an imposing doctrinal corpus that had its architrave in the encyclical *Aeterni Patris.*[89] The second point, which sought to establish political and diplomatic relations with the leading European powers, had its central moment in the policy of *ralliement* with the French Third Republic. As a historical episode, *ralliement* became in fact a pastoral paradigm and a form of ecclesiastical governance with profound, though unhappy consequences.[90]

The instruments for Leo XIII's diplomatic activity were the pontifical nuncios, his ambassadors to European governments. These were trained at the Academy of Ecclesiastical Nobles, where Leo himself had studied and which he intended to develop. We can assume he was quite impressed by the angelic innocence of the young Rafael, but also by his talents and his diplomatic education, and that he thought of making him into a future nuncio in some great European capital. What is certain is that the decision was the pope's alone. There is no truth to imagining some sort of "intrigue" on the part of a father to launch his son into the prestigious institution, because at that moment the Spanish diplomat was entirely ignored by pontifical Rome where, eight years later, he was to represent his government.

The Academy of Ecclesiastical Nobles

The Academy of Ecclesiastical Nobles[91] was established in 1701 and, after various reorganizations, flourished once again during the pontificate of Leo

89 Leo XIII, *Aeterni Patris,* August 4, 1879, in ASS, 12 (1879), pp. 97–115.

90 Regarding the ecclesiastical politics of Leo XIII, cf. R. de Mattei, *Il ralliement di Leone XIII. Il fallimento di un progetto pastorale,* The Letters, Florence 2014; Martin Dumont, *Le Saint-Siège et l'organisation politique des catholiques français aux lendemains du ralliement 1890–1902,* Honoré Champion, Paris 2012; Crispolto Crispolti and Guido Aureli, *La politica di Leone XIII da Luigi Galimberti a Mariano Rampolla su documenti inediti,* Bontempelli e Invernizzi Editori, Rome 1912; Domenico Ferrata, *Mémoires,* Rome 1920 (3 vols.), later published as *Ma nontiature en France,* Action Populaire, Paris 1922.

91 The Academy of Ecclesiastical Nobles, still functioning today under the name Ecclesiastical Academy, is an institute of higher studies for the formation of diplomats for the Holy See. Four pontiffs have come out of its doors thus far: Clement XIII (1758–1769), Leo XII (1823–1829), Leo XIII (1878–1903) and Benedict XV (1914–1922). Cf. Ferdinando Procaccini di Montescaglioso, *La Pontificia Accademia dei nobili ecclesiastici,* Tip. A. Befani, Rome 1889; *La Pontificia Accademia Ecclesiastica (1701–1951),* Tip. Poliglotta Vaticana, Vatican City 1951, pp. 157–158; Roberto Regoli, "Merry del Val e l'Accademia dei nobili ecclesiastici," in Domingo Merry del Val (ed.), *Rafael Merry del Val. 150 anni dalla sua nascita,* pp. 135–150.

XIII, who made it a privileged place for the formation of an ecclesiastical leadership class from various countries, with the ages of its members ranging from eighteen to twenty-five.[92] Its defining characteristic throughout the 1800s and the first part of the 1900s was "membership in the elite."[93] Its president was Msgr. Luigi Sepiacci (cardinal from 1891), who directed it for just one year before being substituted by Archbishop Francesco Satolli, who remained its president until 1896, when he was made a cardinal. Entering the Academy in 1885 along with Merry del Val were the noble Giovanni Tacci Porcelli, made a cardinal in 1921, and the Neapolitan Marquiss Settimio Caracciolo, the future bishop of Alife and then of Aversa. The following year, Ferdinando Procaccini of the Counts of Montescaglioso entered, destined to become the Academy's historiographer, and in 1887 a future apostolic nuncio and cardinal, Count Raffaele Scapinelli of Léguigno.

The young Merry del Val resided at the Academy and studied first at the Gregorian, then in Palazzo Borromeo in Via del Seminario, where, thanks to the impulse of Leo XIII, the number of students grew from 415 in 1880 to over 1000 by the end of his pontificate. They represented some twenty different nationalities, and Leo XIII declared he was "quite satisfied" with the "solid and profound teaching" being given by the pontifical institute.[94] Merry del Val had illustrious professors who often held important positions in the Roman Curia, among whom were Fr. Michele De Maria (1836–1913), general prefect of studies from 1886; Gennare Bucceroni (1841–1918); Pio De Mandato (1850–1914); Louis Billot (1846–1931); and Emilio De Augustinis (1829–1899). At the Gregorian he obtained a doctorate in philosophy (1886),[95] a doctorate in theology (1890),[96] and a license in canon law (1891).[97] With some of his professors, like the future Cardinal Billot, he would have a long acquaintance over the years.

92 Between 1885 and 1891, the Academy welcomed thirty young men, of whom fourteen were Italians, four from the United Kingdom, three Germans, three French, two Spanish (including Merry del Val), one Maltese, one Swiss, one Czech, and one Brazilian (Regoli, "Merry del Val e l'Academia dei nobili ecclesiastici," p. 141).

93 Regoli, *Merry del Val e l'Accademia dei nobili ecclesiastici*, p. 138.

94 Pietro Pirri, "L'Università Gregoriana del Collegio romano dal 1824 al 1924," in *L'Università Gregoriana del Collegio Romano nel primo secolo della restaurazione, 1553–1824–1924*, Tipografia Cuggiani, Rome 1924, p. 36 (pp. 1–44).

95 AAV, *Spoglio Merry del Val*, busta 3, n. 116.

96 Ibid, n. 138.

97 Ibid, n. 145.

In the autumn, the young man spent his vacations with his family in Vienna, but his life remained always recollected and reserved. Finding himself in Vienna, on September 29, 1887, he received the subdiaconate in Prague, at the altar of St. John Nepomuk in the cathedral of St. Vito, at the hands of Cardinal Franzikus von Paula Schönborn, the city's archbishop and intimate friend of the Merry del Val family.[98] His devotion to the Infant Jesus in royal dress and with the insignia of a sovereign in the act of blessing, as portrayed by the statue in the sanctuary of St. Mary of Victory in Prague, was part of his spiritual life from that time on.[99] When, in 1924, he went to Arenzano near Genoa to crown the Holy Infant of Prague venerated in that sanctuary, he recalled that "a sweet tie bound him to that devout homage since it was in this city and under the auspices of that celestial Image that he had consecrated himself to the Lord receiving the order of the subdiaconate, and thus that solemn coronation recalled in him a dear personal memory."[100]

While knowing that the Academy destined its students to diplomatic careers, the young Merry del Val longed to pursue a missionary apostolate, perhaps in England. During those years, he wrote several verses preserved by his mother:

What is there that I can call my own that has never been yours?
On earth my all, in heaven my crown.
Yes, nothing but sin is mine.
From now on, Sweet Lord, the world's glory will have no part of me.
Like you, I shall seek a crown of thorns.[101]

MISSION IN LONDON

Leo XIII had long desired to reestablish diplomatic relations between the Holy See and Great Britain, interrupted by the Act of Supremacy of Queen Elizabeth in 1559.[102] With Gladstone's third term as prime minister in 1886, the possibility

98 Franziskus von Paula Schönborn (1844–1899) was consecrated bishop by Leo XIII in 1883 and appointed by Emperor Franz Josef to the See of Prague on May 21, 1885. He received the pallium on July 30, 1885.

99 Murphy, *Spiritual Writings*, pp. 20–21.

100 Cenci, *Merry del Val*, p. 270.

101 Flores de Lemus, *El fulgor de una purpura*, p. 194.

102 Cf. Massimo de Leonardis, "Appunti per una storia delle relazioni anglo-vaticane," *Nova Historica* 1 (2002), 3, pp. 27–45; idem, "Le relazioni diplomatiche tra la Gran Bretagna e la Santa Sede negli ultimi due secoli," *Miscellanea Storica dell'Accademia Olubrense* 2 (1995), pp. 17–36; Umberto Castagnino Berlinghieri, "Le relazioni tra Santa Sede e Regno Unito dal Venti Settembre allo scoppio della Grande Guerra," in M. de Leonardis (ed.), *Fede e diplomazia. Le relazioni internazionali della Santa Sede nell'età contemporanea*, EDUCatt, Milan 2014, pp. 51–68.

of a liaison between the British government and the Holy See presented itself, and the queen's Golden Jubilee in June of 1887 offered the occasion.

Despite the power of the British Empire, court life was more modest than that of other European courts. After the death of the Prince Consort Albert in 1861, the queen began a long period of mourning, retreating to her residences in Windsor, Balmoral, and Osborne. She was rarely seen in public until 1887, when she left her isolation for the occasion of the solemn celebration of the fiftieth year of her reign.

Leo XIII decided to send to London an extraordinary envoy in the person of the prince, Msgr. Luigi Ruffo Scilla, the titular Archbishop of Petra.[103] His mission was to congratulate the queen on the occasion of the fiftieth anniversary of her ascension to the throne. Rafael Merry del Val was chosen as secretary to the Pontifical Mission and on June 8 was nominated his Holiness' supernumerary secret chamberlain.[104] Added to this role was the title of Monsignor, which the young man received even before becoming a priest. At twenty-two, he entered the pontifical court, wearing the red cape during papal functions.

By instruction of Secretary of State Cardinal Mariano Rampolla del Tindaro, the pontifical envoy was to praise the United Kingdom because, though officially Anglican, it did not hinder Catholic worship throughout its dominions and because it demonstrated deference "toward the Catholic Church especially in the Missions in Canada and in the East Indies." Msgr. Ruffo Scilla had the role of expressing the pope's full gratitude to the British government, but was to avoid any discussion of the delicate question of Irish nationalism. Nevertheless, if he was asked about this issue, he was to say that the Holy See had always recommended moderation to the Irish bishops and reprimanded "the illegitimate and criminal means of which some Irish made use in the defense of their cause," and that it was also ready to repeat the counsel of moderation "if the need of its intervention were to become manifest."[105]

103 Luigi Ruffo Scilla (1840–1895) was nominated in 1877 archbishop of Chieti and consecrated on January 6, 1878, by Cardinal Fabio Chigi. On May 23, 1887, he resigned as archbishop of Chieti and was transferred to the titular see of Petra. He was later sent to Bavaria as apostolic nuncio. Leo XIII made him a cardinal on December 17, 1891.

104 AAV, *Spoglio Merry del Val*, busta 3, n. 119. Supernumerary secret chamberlains were pontifical dignitaries who, dependent on the Master of Chamber, served in turns in the papal antechamber with the task of entertaining guests awaiting to be received in audience by the Holy Father, participating as well in all the functions celebrated by the pontiff.

105 AA.EE.SS., *Inghilterra, 1886–1888,* Pos. 111, fasc. 45, London 1887, *Istruzioni per Mons. Ruffo Scilla Incaricato dal S. Padre a complimentare la Regina d'Inghilterra per il 50° anniversario della sua esaltazione al trono*, ff. 39–41. The dossier contains instructions to Msgr. Ruffo Scilla (June 7, 1887) and the Letter to Card. Manning to Leo XIII on the outcome of the mission (July 3, 1887).

Along the route from the royal palace to Westminster Abbey, the queen was acclaimed by a multitude of enthusiasts. In the Abbey, where the invited parliamentarians and diplomats awaited her, the sovereign in her magnificent vestments was received by the hymn "God Save the Queen" and a solemn overture of Handel. The splendor of the ceremony made a strong impression on the illustrious visitors and on the English people proud of their sovereign.[106]

"The good and most faithful Duke of Norfolk," wrote Cardinal Manning to Leo XIII on July 3, 1887, "displayed the most delicate hospitality. Our faithful came in throngs to the Cathedral on the Day of the Jubilee, when Msgr. Ruffo Scilla did me the favor of celebrating in a most solemn manner the Pontifical Mass. Our Queen showed every hint of veneration toward the person of Your Sanctity at the Palace in London and at Windsor Castle, and respect and benevolence toward the Envoy.... Nearly 400 of the most important Catholics were gathered at the Archbishopric to pay their respects to Msgr. Envoy."[107]

In fact, the Master of Ceremonies gave precedence to Msgr. Ruffo Scilla and his companions, Msgr. Ladislas Zaleski and Msgr. Rafael Merry del Val, even over the representatives of the Great Powers; precedence which, if it was the norm in Catholic countries, for Anglican England was probably justified by the fact that the pope had no permanent ambassador at the time.[108] Queen Victoria thanked Leo XIII in a public and formal manner, sending to the Holy See as her special envoy the most representative personality of English Catholic aristocracy, the Duke of Norfolk, who was received by Leo XIII in the Throne Room on December 17, 1887.[109]

On January 1, 1888, Leo XIII also celebrated a jubilee, the fiftieth anniversary of his priesthood, with a solemn Mass in St. Peter's in the presence of fifty cardinals and two hundred bishops and a throng of the faithful calculated at around fifty thousand people.[110] When he appeared on the *sedia gestatoria*, the

106 Roland Marx, *La regina Vittoria et il suo temps*, Il Mulino, Bologna 2001, pp. 273–281.

107 Card. Manning to Leo XIII, July 3, 1887, in AA.EE.SS., *England*, 1886–1888, f. 47.

108 Castagnino, "Le relazioni tra Santa Sede e Regno Unito," p. 63.

109 Henry Fitzalan-Howard (1847–1917), Count of Surrey, of Arundel, and of Norfolk, peer of the United Kingdom, Earl Marshal of England, heir (in the Howard family), was XV Duke of Norfolk. In 1895, he received the appointment of private counsellor to Queen Victoria and was nominated Postmaster General of the United Kingdom.

110 Cf. Jean-Marc Ticchi, "Le Jubilé pontifical de 1888. Un exemple de l'interaction entre Question romaine, diplomatie vaticane et dévotion de masse au Pape," in Vincent Vianae, *The Papacy and the New World Order: Vatican Diplomacy, Catholic Opinion and International Politics at the Time of Lèon XIII (1878–1903)*, Leuven University Press, Leuven 2005, pp. 225–248.

basilica resounded to the acclamation: "*Viva il Papa! Viva il Papa Re!*" (Long live the pope! Long live the pope King!). The pontiff had on his head the miter sent by the German Kaiser and on his finger a *bague* offered by the Ottoman Sultan. The Leonine pontificate had reached its zenith. The encyclical *Libertas*, promulgated on June 20, crowned the magisterial tryptic composed of *Diuturnum* (1881) on the origins of political power and *Immortale Dei* (1885) on the Christian constitution of States.

Msgr. Galimberti and Cardinal Rampolla del Tindaro

On February 28, 1887, Leo XIII's secretary of state Cardinal Ludovico Jacobini died.[111] In the intermediate period before the nomination of a new secretary of state, matters of foreign policy were handled by Msgr. Luigi Galimberti, who had assumed the role of secretary of the Congregation of Extraordinary Ecclesiastical Affairs on July 31, 1885,[112] becoming the main architect of the Holy See's foreign policy, above all as concerned the policy of détente between the Holy See and Bismarck.[113]

In May 1887, Msgr. Galimberti carried out a mission to Berlin, obtaining the end of the *Kulturkampf*, which for fifteen years had set Germany against the Church of Rome. "Returning from the Congress of Vienna, Cardinal Consalvi was not draped in greater glory than Msgr. Galimberti after Berlin." Thus, the newspapers, even those antagonistic, commented on the Roman prelate's journey to the Prussian capital and the result of his mission.[114] Behind the Bronze

111 Ludovico Jacobini (1832–1887) was titular archbishop of Thessalonica and nuncio in Vienna from 1874 to 1880. He was made cardinal by Leo XIII on September 9, 1879, and was secretary of state from December 16, 1880, until his death on February 28, 1887.

112 Luigi Galimberti (1836–1896), born in Rome, after completing his studies at the Roman Seminary and at the Apollinare, was ordained a priest in 1860 and nominated professor of Ecclesiastical History at the college of Propaganda Fide. He was chosen by Leo XIII as secretary of Extraordinary Ecclesiastical Affairs, and later made titular archbishop of Nicaea and nuncio in Vienna (1887). Elevated to the cardinalate on January 16, 1893, he succeeded Cardinal Hergenröther as prefect of the Vatican Archive. Cf. the entry under Maria Franca Mellano, in DBI, vol. 5, pp. 492–494; Crispolti and Aureli, *La politica di Leone XIII*, passim; Soderini, *Il pontificato di Leone XIII*, passim.

113 Otto, Prince of Bismarck (1815–1898), was a German statesman and diplomat who oversaw the unification of Germany and served as its first Chancellor, 1871–1890. Cf. Massimiliano Valente, *Diplomazia pontificia e Kulturkampf: la Santa Sede e la Prussia tra Pio IX e Bismarck (1862–1878)*, Studium, Rome 2004; idem (ed.), *Vatikanische Akten zur Geschichte des deutschen Kulturkampfes, Edition der Sitzungsprotokolle der "Sacra Congregazione degli Affari Ecclesiastici Straordinari," 1880–1884*, Deutsches Historisches Institut in Rom, Rome 2009; Ronald Ross, *The Failure of Bismarck's Kulturkampf. Catholicism and state power in imperial Germany, 1871–1887*, The Catholic University of America Press, Washington 1998.

114 Crispolti and Aureli, *La politica di Leone XIII*, p. 140.

Door of the Apostolic Palace, everyone was convinced that Leo XIII would entrust to Galimberti, currently acting as pro-secretary of state, the direction of all the affairs of the Holy See, calling him to succeed in name as in deed, the deceased Cardinal Jacobini.

Instead, on June 1, 1887, Leo XIII appointed as his new secretary of state Mariano Rampolla del Tindaro.[115] Galimberti, for his part, was sent to Vienna as nuncio with the title of Archbishop of Nicaea. He left the Vatican Palaces so hastily that he opted for Vienna instead of Rome as the place of his episcopal consecration. "I don't like his type," said Galimberti of Rampolla. "I consider him duplicitous and now that the pope has nominated me bishop, sending me to Vienna to replace the nuncio Serafino Vannutelli, off I go."[116]

Mariano Rampolla del Tindaro, born into a family of the Sicilian lower nobility, was forty-four years old at the time. After having led the Extraordinary Ecclesiastical Affairs office for two years, he was sent by Leo XIII to Madrid as apostolic nuncio, distinguishing himself for the support given to the young King Alfonso XII against the Carlists and intransigent Catholics.[117] During the consistory of March 14, 1887, the pope raised him to the cardinalate and on June 3 officially nominated him secretary of state. In the act of nomination, a long letter was added in which the pontiff laid out the program for his future activity.[118]

Cardinal Aloisi Masella,[119] in his unpublished *Memoires,* described Rampolla del Tindaro as "a well-prepared and versatile man of brilliance, good

[115] Mariano Rampolla del Tindaro (1843–1913), born in Polizzi Generosa, near Palermo, was ordained a priest on March 17, 1866, and was trained at the Academy of Ecclesiastical Nobles. Pius IX appointed him as counsellor in charge of affairs at the nunciature in Madrid, where he returned as apostolic nuncio and titular archbishop of Eraclea in October 1882. On May 27, 1887, Leo XIII made him a cardinal and on June 1, named him secretary of state. For biography, see Gian Pietro Sinopoli di Giunta, *Il card. Mariano Rampolla del Tindaro,* Tip. Poliglotta Vaticana, Rome 1923; Calogero Cerami (ed.), *La figura e l'opera del cardinale Mariano Rampolla del Tindaro,* Salvatore Sciascia, Caltanissetta 2006. See also J.–M. Ticchi, "Avec lui, il n'y en a que pour la France! Remarques sur la contribution du cardinal Rampolla à la politique de Léon XIII," *Mélanges de l'École française de Rome, Italie et Méditerranée* (2004), pp. 199–241.

[116] Cit. in Benny Lai, *Affari del Papa, Storia di Monsignori, nobiluomini e faccendieri nella Roma dell'Ottocento,* Laterza, Rome-Bari 1999, p. 114.

[117] Laura Civinini, "Rampolla e la Spagna: il caso della Nunziatura di Madrid (1876–1877)," in Cerami (ed.), *La figura e l'opera del cardinale Mariano Rampolla,* pp. 51–80. Cf. also V. Cárcel Ortí, *Leon XIII y los católicos españoles. Informes vaticanos sobre la Iglesia en España,* Eunsa, Pamplona 1988.

[118] Sinopoli Di Giunta, *Il card. Mariano Rampolla,* pp. 85–96.

[119] Gaetano Aloisi Masella (1826–1902), born in Pontecorvo, to a noble family, entered the diplomatic service of the Holy See and in 1877 was consecrated titular Archbishop of Neo-Caesarea in Porto and was nuncio in Bavaria (1877–1879) and in Portugal (1879–1883). Made a cardinal in the consistory of 1887, he was the prefect of various congregations. Cf. Luigi Casatelli, *Il cardinale Gaetano Aloisi Masella, vescovo e diplomatico,* Grafiche Ponticelli, Castrocielo 2002.

memory, great erudition, with a character generally so calm that he makes you forget that he is a Sicilian, with courteous and refined manners and, above all, the most profound piety, which makes one overlook whatever errors of judgment he may have made in the weighty events in which the Holy See participated, sometimes in ways that one may not have entirely approved."[120]

Rampolla and Galimberti represented in that moment two opposite visions of the Holy See's foreign policy: the former in favor of a convergence with republican France, the latter of an agreement with the empires of Germany and Austria-Hungary, which in 1882 had established the Triple Alliance with the Kingdom of Italy.[121]

The so-called Roman Question, which commenced after the invasion of the Papal States and the Italian occupation of Rome in 1870, constituted the terrain on which the two adversaries "fought mutely but tenaciously . . . the most bitter struggle; one was in favor of the Triple Alliance; the other of France."[122] Early on, Leo XIII opted for the "German strategy" that consisted in exercising, through the courts of Berlin and Vienna, strong political pressure on the temporal governments to reach a possible reconciliation with the Holy See and obtain the pope's sovereignty over a territory, however minimal.[123]

With the advent of Rampolla this strategy mutated.[124] The political project on which the new secretary of state worked after his nomination set three strategic objectives, as the historian Giorgio Rumi has observed: "the dismantling of the Triple Alliance, the alignment of France and Austria, and the isolation of

[120] Gaetano Aloisi Masella, *Memorie inedite*, in AAV, Instr. Misc. 8562, p. 2803.

[121] The Triple Alliance (uniting the Central Powers) was stipulated on May 20, 1882, in Vienna as a defensive military pact between the German and Austro-Hungarian Empires and the Kingdom of Italy. Cf. the broad study by Holger Afflerbach, *Der Dreibund: europäische Grossmachtund Allianzpolitik vor dem Ersten Weltkrieg*, Böhlau, Wien 2002. In World War I, this alliance was opposed to the Triple Entente of Great Britain, Russia, and France, also known as the Allies.

[122] Crispolti and Aureli, *La politica di Leone XIII*, p. 186.

[123] Luciano Trincia, *Il nucleo tedesco. Vaticano e Triplice Alleanza nei dispacci del nunzio a Vienna Luigi Galimberti, 1887–1892 [The German Nucleus. Vatican and Triple Entente in the Dispatches of the Nuncio in Vienna Luigi Galimberti]*, Morcelliana, Brescia 2001; idem, "Galimberti e il nucleo tedesco. Un potere parallelo? in Les secrétaires d'État du Saint-Siège," *Mélanges de l'École française de Rome, Italie et Méditerranée* 16 (2004), p. 257 (pp. 255–279). At that time, one spoke of a "Quartet" that sought to facilitate the courting of the Holy See by the Triple Alliance. It was composed of Msgr. Galimberti; the pro-secretary of Extraordinary Ecclesiastical Affairs Msgr. Antonio Agliardi (1832–1915); Msgr. Johannes Montel von Treuenfest (1831–1910), auditor of the Roman Rota; and Baron Kurt von Schlözer (1822–1894), plenipotentiary of the Court of Berlin to the Holy See.

[124] The bishop of Cremona, Msgr. Geremia Bonomelli, stated, "To me, it's always been a mystery whether Rampolla guided Leo or if Leo pulled along Rampolla. History will provide the solution to this enigma." Cited in Trincia, *Il nucleo tedesco*, p. 35.

the liberal Italy of the Savoys,"[125] foreseeing, according to another historian, "the collapse of the Italian national state by means of diplomatic or military intervention of a coalition of European powers."[126]

Rampolla considered a European war to be imminent and during the years 1888–1889 aired to the French government a scenario that envisaged, as a consequence of a military event, the collapse of the Savoy monarchy in Italy, the disintegration of Italian unity, the restitution of the temporal domains of the pope and, finally, the establishment of an Italian Republic with which the Holy See would reach an agreement.[127] In this scenario, France was called to be an ally of the Holy See due to the reciprocal advantage of both parts. According to Luciano Trincia, "Just as the Second Republic had brought Pius IX back to Rome in 1848, so now the Third Republic, reconciled with the Holy See and allied with the papacy, could take advantage of the international crisis looming on the horizon to support the Vatican's claims and better exploit the subsequent loss of Austro-Germanic hegemony over Italy."[128]

Crispolto Crispolti and Guido Aureli pinpoint the year 1888 as the beginning of the decadence of Leo XIII's pontificate due to the deviation made in the Holy See's policies, which passed from the pro-German attitudes of Msgr. Galimberti to the pro-French policy of Cardinal Rampolla del Tindaro. Luigi Galimberti and Mariano Rampolla, they write, are "two men and two ideas" which, together with Leo XIII, "form the tryptic of this drama which was tragic because of the broken dream, the energies accumulated and dispersed, the heights to which the Church seemed destined to rise and the abyss into which it was dragged."[129] This was certainly a diplomatic reversal, which Trincia documented in his publication of nuncio Galimberti's dispatches between 1887 and 1892.[130] The "German nucleus" was progressively dismantled and the policy of reconciliation between Germany and Italy was confined to the nunciature in

[125] Giorgio Rumi, "Austria e Santa Sede. Da Leone XIII a Benedetto XV, nella crisi dell'Impero," in *Storia religiosa dell'Austria,* Centro Ambrosiano, Milan 1997, p. 499 (pp. 489–516).

[126] Trincia, *Il nucleo tedesco*, p. 273. Cf. idem, "Il primato della politica: il progetto della Santa Sede del Cardinale Mariano Rampolla del Tindaro," in Cerami (ed.), *La figura e l'opera del cardinale Mariano Rampolla*, pp.15–33.

[127] Trincia, "Il primato della politica," p. 23; J. M. Ticchi, *La politica francese del cardinale Rampolla e la preservazione degli interessi della Santa Sede,* in Cerami (ed.), *La figura e l'opera del cardinale Mariano Rampolla*, pp. 35–50.

[128] Trincia, "Il primato della politica," p. 22.

[129] Crispolti and Aureli, *La politica di Leone XIII,* p. 41.

[130] Trincia, *Il nucleo tedesco,* pp. 12–13.

Vienna entrusted to Galimberti. The political project of Leo XIII identified itself with that of his secretary of state, who was both its executor and author.

Mission to Berlin

It was in this context that, in March 1888, the second mission to Berlin by the nuncio in Vienna, Msgr. Galimberti, took place. The aim was to present to Kaiser Friedrich III, in the name of the Holy Father, condolences for the death of his father Wilhelm I, and at the same time congratulate him for his succession to the imperial throne of Germany.[131]

In fact, three kaisers would ascend to the German throne in 1888. Wilhelm I, the first kaiser of the new German Reich, passed away after a brief illness on March 9. He was followed by the ninety-nine-day reign of his son Friedrich III, who died of cancer of the larynx on June 15, 1888. That same day, Wilhelm II, at the age of twenty-nine, became the new emperor of Germany.[132]

Msgr. Galimberti and Msgr. Merry del Val reached Berlin after a stop in Munich toward midnight on March 18, taking up lodgings at the British Hotel. There they found a letter in which Bismarck announced to them that the following Tuesday the emperor would receive them at Charlottenburg Castle. On the day of the visit, the entire imperial antechamber was awaiting the two prelates at the castle. The emperor and empress came to meet them. They were presented then to the imperial prince, Friedrich III. All the main personalities of the court competed in showing their deference to the two Italian *Monsignori*. On March 24, Msgr. Galimberti met with Bismarck, whom he found "very tired and worried."[133] During his colloquy with the chancellor, Galimberti followed the indications of Rampolla, who had suggested he raise the theme of the

[131] On the mission of Msgr. Luigi Galimberti to Berlin see AA.EE.SS., *Stati ecclesiastici*, 1887–1888, Pos. 1083, fasc. 355, Berlin–1888, containing the confidential and personal instructions of Card. Rampolla to Msgr. Galimberti and the report of Msgr. Galimberti summarizing his mission. Cf. also Crispolti and Aureli, *La politica di Leone XIII*, pp. 326–353, which publishes the "Secret Instructions of Card. Mariano Rampolla del Tindaro, secretary of State, of March 14th, 1888 to Msgr. Luigi Galimberti, apostolic nuncio in Vienna, extraordinary envoy to Berlin" (pp. 419–425) and the report-diary of the extraordinary mission to Berlin written on March 26, 1888 by Msgr. Galimberti (pp. 432–444, above all pp. 442–444).

[132] Wilhelm I (1797–1888) was the first emperor of modern Germany from January 18, 1871, to his death on March 9, 1888. He was succeeded by his son Friedrich III of Prussia (1831–1888). At the latter's death on June 15, his son Wilhelm II ascended the throne (1859–1941), the third and last German Emperor, who reigned from 1888 to 1918.

[133] The report of Msgr. Galimberti to Card. Rampolla, in AA.EE.SS., *Stati ecclesiastici*, 1887–1888, ff. 54–55.

religious question in Germany and the Roman Question: "Regarding the former issue you must speak as commanded by Rome; regarding the latter, as you see fit."[134] Galimberti raised the problem of the Roman Question, which he knew was dear to Leo XIII, but Bismarck repeated that "*il faut savoir attendre*." "I do not understand," said the Prince, "what the Holy See would gain by the triumph of schismatic Russia and republican France." "But if France were to wage war on Italy with the aim of restoring the independence of the Holy See would Catholic Austria oppose them?" "First it must think of existing," replied the Prince, "then of being Catholic."[135]

The following year, in a reserved document with the title *Considerations on the Alliance between Germany and Italy*, which reached the pope without the knowledge of Rampolla, Galimberti proposed to Leo XIII a strategic plan based on the recognition of the existence of Savoy Italy.[136] Today, this project seems more realistic than that of Rampolla because it would have been easier to imagine a concession on the part of Crispi to the pressure of his allies than to the threats of his enemies.[137]

War with France did not frighten Crispi precisely because of the support he received from Vienna and Berlin. The political line chosen by Leo XIII and Secretary of State Rampolla, meanwhile, saw in France an ally and in Savoy, Italy, usurpers of the Papal State, the main enemy.

The familiarity that Merry del Val had with Msgr. Galimberti constituted for him an important diplomatic experience. In this phase of his life, Merry del Val earned many confidences from Galimberti for sure, whose sympathies toward the Triple Alliance were likely shared by the young Anglo-Spanish prelate. This was reinforced by his stay in Vienna, where his father had carried out his mission as extraordinary envoy of the Kingdom of Spain, and by friendly

134 Rampolla to Galimberti, confidential personal correspondance of March 14, 1888, ibid, f. 44.

135 Crispolti and Aureli, *La politica di Leone XIII*, pp. 331–332.

136 The document is reproduced in its entirety in Trincia, *Il nucleo tedesco*, pp. 204–209. According to Galimberti's report: "There are two systems or two agendas: one of them takes as its point of departure for the restitution of pontifical sovereignty the distribution, or dismemberment of Italy as it currently stands; the other prefers the existence of a sensible and moderate Italy, which gives heed to the rights of the Holy See, in its own interest. The former school considers Italian unity incompatible with the real independence of the Holy See; the latter believes the existence of both to be possible."

137 Francesco Crispi (1818–1901) was an Italian patriot and statesman. He was among the main protagonists of Italian unification in 1860 and served as Italy's prime minister 1887–1891 and 1893–1896.

relations with the House of Austria. Archduchess Elisabeth of Austria[138] was the mother of Queen Maria Cristina,[139] who in 1879 had married Alfonso XII and, after his death on November 25, 1885, was Regent for her newborn son Alfonso XIII until he reached maturity.[140]

The young Monsignor had been to Vienna many times, and not only to see his family. He was the message bearer for the pope of a gift to the Emperor Franz Josef and returned to Austria in June 1893 to deliver the red biretta to Cardinal Lőrinc Schlauch.[141]

Sacerdos in Aeternum

On Sunday, May 27, 1888, feast of the Most Holy Trinty, Rafael Merry del Val received the order of the Diaconate in the church of the Daughters of St. Anne in Via Merulana, at the hands of Cardinal Lucido Maria Parocchi, the vicar of Rome.[142] That same year, on December 30, Cardinal Parocchi ordained him a priest; this time the ceremony took place in Parocchi's private chapel in the ancient palace of the Vicariate in Via della Scrofa. Merry del Val was the only one to be ordained on this occasion, having been given the apostolic dispensation authorizing it despite his tender age.

Among the books that had formed him was Cardinal Manning's *The Eternal Priesthood,* recalling how each priest offers to the Father, day after day, the eternal oblation of Jesus Christ, but in that action he must also offer himself: "When he says, *Hoc est corpum meum,* he ought to offer his own body; when he says, *Hic est calix sanguinis mei,* he ought to offer his own blood; that is, he ought to offer himself as an oblation to his Divine Master, in body, soul and spirit, with all his faculties, powers, and affections, in life and unto death."[143]

[138] The archduchess of Austria Elisabeth (1831–1903) was the wife of Archduke Carl Ferdinand von Hapsburg-Teschen (1818–1874).

[139] Maria Cristina (1858–1929), archduchess of Austria, royal princess of Hungary and Bohemia, was the regent of the Spanish throne until 1902, when Alfonso XII came of age and was proclaimed king. From that moment on she dedicated herself to works of charity and to family life, and after 1906, when Alfonso married Victoria Eugenia von Battenberg, used the title "Queen Mother."

[140] Alfonso XIII (1886–1941), posthumous son of Alfonso XII, was king of Spain from 1906 to 1931, when the Spanish Second Republic was proclaimed. After that he lived and died in Rome.

[141] Lőrinc Schlauch (1824–1902), Hungarian, bishop of Satu Mara (1873) and archbishop of Great Varadin (1887), was made a cardinal in the consistory on June 12, 1893 with the title of St. Jerome of the Croatians.

[142] Lucido Maria Parocchi (1833–1903), bishop of Pavia (1871), was made a cardinal in the consistory of June 22, 1877. From 1884 to 1889 he was the cardinal vicar of Rome, to which was added in 1896 the role of secretary of the Holy Office.

[143] Henry Edward Manning, *The Eternal Priesthood,* Burns & Oates, London 1884, p. 5.

The spirit of sacrifice and oblation without reserve that the offering of the body and blood of Christ demands of each priest was a constant in the spirituality of Merry del Val. At the end of the Mass, Cardinal Parocchi held a lofty discourse for the newly ordained priest, illustrating the Gospel of the day: "This child is set for the fall and the rising of many in Israel, and for a sign that is spoken against" (Lk 2:34). These words were to be prophetic of the many trials that the young priest was destined to suffer throughout his life.

On January 1, 1889, Msgr. Merry del Val celebrated privately his first Mass in the "little rooms" of St. Ignatius at the Church of the Jesuits, assisted only by his parents and a few friends, among whom were his companions at the Academy, Msgr. Luigi Misciattelli,[144] Msgr. Ladislao Zaleski,[145] and Francis Augustus MacNutt,[146] an ambitious youth who was to embrace a quite different destiny. "I was profoundly impressed," records the latter. "The joy that radiated from his mother's face when she received Holy Communion from her son's newly consecrated hands seemed supernatural."[147]

On January 25, the president of the Academy of Ecclesiastical Nobles entrusted the newly ordained priest with the spiritual guidance of the youth of the Pontifical Popular School run by the Christian Brothers in Piazza Mastai in Trastevere, nominating him "Regulator of the Sunday Congregation."[148] Merry del Val turned especially to the youngest of the youth who wandered about that Roman neighborhood, often without any guidance, and invited them to meet as often as possible at the school where they found instruction, assistance, and recreation.

The Pious Association of the Sacred Heart of Jesus, founded in 1890, was located in Via delle Fratte in Trastevere, near the Church of San Francesco a

144 Luigi dei Marchesi Misciattelli (1861–1918) was a student at the Capranica College and of the Academy of Ecclesiastical Nobles. Merry del Val was one of his best friends and later became the spiritual director of his sister Aurora. Ordained a priest in 1884, he was sent as a legate to France in June 1886. A participating secret chamberlain of Leo XIII, he was nominated a canon of St. Peter's on December 20, 1891, and vice-prefect of the Apostolic Palaces on December 14, 1905, by Pius X who entrusted him with the supervision and safeguarding of the Vatican's artistic goods. Benedict XV confirmed these roles and promoted him to be a palatine prelate on September 7, 1914.

145 Ladislao Michele Zaleski (1852–1925), Lithuanian-Polish, after having studied at the Academy of Ecclesiastical Nobles and at the Gregorian, was a diplomat of the Holy See and apostolic delegate to the East Indies. Benedict XV appointed him as Latin patriarch of Antioch in 1916.

146 Francis Augustus MacNutt (1863–1927), after having studied at the Academy of Ecclesiastical Nobles, abandoned the religious vocation to enter the diplomatic corps of the United States.

147 *A Papal Chamberlain. The Personal Chronicle of Francis Augustus MacNutt*, Longmans, Green & Co., London 1936, p. 148.

148 AAV, *Spoglio Merry del Val*, busta 3, n. 127.

Ripa. The young priest went there on foot every Saturday, passing through the rubble of the homes demolished for the opening of the Viale del Re (King's Avenue), constructed in 1889 to connect the center with the new Trastevere train station. He would return home as night was falling, with the rare petroleum-lit streetlamps dimly illuminating the treacherous streets. Sunday mornings he returned early to hear the last confessions and to celebrate Holy Mass, accompanied by religious instruction.[149]

From then on, the worship of the Sacred Heart began to have a central role in the piety of Merry del Val.[150] This ancient devotion had received a great impulse from the revelations in 1673 to St. Margaret Mary Alacoque, a Visitation nun in the monastery of Paray-le-Monial.[151] In an epoch of decadence and spiritual decline such as was the second half of the seventeenth century, this devotion relit in souls the love for Jesus. "Behold the Heart that has so loved men that It spared nothing, even going so far as to exhaust and consume Itself," Jesus said to St. Margaret Mary, promising her then, "And I promise that My Heart shall dilate to pour out abundantly the influences of its love on all that will render it this honor." In the nineteenth and twentieth centuries, devotion to the Sacred Heart developed in the Church thanks to the Jesuit Fathers François-Xavier Gautrelet[152] and Henri Ramière[153] and to mystical souls such as Blessed Maria of the Divine Heart.[154] Leo XIII's encyclical *Annum sacrum* (May 25, 1899) confirmed the devotion, promulgating the litanies to the Sacred Heart and a formula of consecration to recite to the Most Sacred Heart of Jesus.

On March 1, 1889, Msgr. Merry del Val enrolled his school children in the Apostolate of Prayer, officially encouraging among his youth devotion to the

149 Cenci, *Merry del Val*, p. 305.

150 Cf. Francesco Olgiati, "Il cardinal Merry del Val e la devozione al Sacro Cuore," *Rivista del Clero Italiano* 14, no. 6 (June 1933), pp. 347–349. On the devotion to the Sacred Heart, cf. Augustin Hamon S.J., *Histoire de la dévotion au Sacré-Cœur*, Beauchesne, Paris 1923–1940, 5 vols.

151 St. Margaret Mary Alacoque (1647–1690), Visitandine nun in the convent of Paray-le-Monial, was canonized by Benedict XV in 1920.

152 François-Xavier Gautrelet (1807–1886), a Jesuit, founded in 1844 the *Apostolat de la prière* and is author of *Manuel de la dévotion au Sacré Cœur* (Lyon 1850) which was reworked by Fr. Henri Ramière in his book *L'apostolat de la prière* (Lyon 1861).

153 Henri Ramière (1821–1884), a Jesuit, inherited in 1861 from Fr. Gautrelet the *Apostolat de la prière*, spreading it throughout the world, especially through the monthly journal *Le Messager du Cœur de Jésus*, which he founded and directed until his death.

154 Maria of the Divine Heart (Maria Droste zu Vischering: 1863–1899), a German nun of the Congregation of the Sisters of Our Lady of the Charity of the Good Shepherd, promoted the consecration of the world to the Sacred Heart of Jesus, which was carried out by Leo XIII in 1899. She was beatified by Paul VI on November 1, 1975.

Sacred Heart of Jesus. He later formed among the more fervent youth a "Little Group of the Sacred Heart," from which the Pious Association of the Sacred Heart of Jesus would later arise.[155] Among its aims was reparation for offenses against the Sacred Heart in the Sacrament of the Altar, by reciting the litany of the Sacred Heart every Sunday before Eucharistic Benediction."[156]

In his recollections on the end of the month of June 1892, one of the boys in Trastevere, fifteen at the time, wrote, "Our director said that humility is not that of the child who bows his head when daddy or mommy yells at him, nor does it consist in denying the good work one has done when people praise him for it. Humility is when, for all that we do well and others praise us, we say: 'What I did is a gift of God and so may the Lord be praised.'"[157]

These counsels are rich in theological wisdom. The right knowledge of oneself forms the root and measure of humility, which does not consist in denying the gifts one has received from God, but in rendering to Him the honor that is due to Him alone.[158] Humility is the presupposition and foundation of the supernatural edifice, because it removes all the obstacles that impede the soul from rising up to God.[159] Rafael Merry del Val, immersed in the Vatican environment where it was easy to loose this virtue, observed it his entire life, composing the famous *Litanies of Humility* that are present in one of his manuscripts bearing the date February 24, 1895.[160]

Merry del Val's affiliation with the Sodality of the Third Order of the Servites of Mary, whose Seven Holy Founders were canonized with great solemnity in 1888, dates to at least 1900. The Sodality's register in the church of San Marcello al Corso contains an entry dated July 2, 1900, recording the consecration and vesting of Msgr. Rafael Merry del Val as titular Archbishop of Nicaea [on May 6, 1900].[161] The same register tells us that on January 8,

155 Antonello Blasi, "Il cardinal Merry del Val e l'Associazione del Sacro Cuore di Trastevere," in Domingo Merry del Val (ed.), *Rafael Merry del Val. 150 anni dalla sua nascita*, pp. 81–106.

156 Cenci, *Merry del Val*, p. 320. The existence of the Pious Association of the Sacred Heart of Jesus appears in the minutes of the meetings at least beginning on November 3, 1901 (p. 85).

157 Ibid., p. 307.

158 Viktor Cathrein, *L'umiltà cristiana*, Morcelliana, Brescia 1931, pp. 31–48.

159 Antonio Royo Marin O. P., *Teologia della perfezione cristiana*, Edizioni Paoline, Rome 1964, pp. 736–737.

160 Cf. Archive of the Postulation, f. 2823; Cenci, *Merry del Val*, p. 438. The text was published innumerable times. Cf. for example, *Pensieri ascetici del Servo di Dio Card. Merry del Val, segretario di Stato di San Pio X [Ascetical Thoughts of the Servant of God Card. Merry del Val, Secretary of State of St. Pius X]*, Pontifical Spanish College, Rome 1953, pp. 123–125.

161 *Processus Informativus Ordinarius*, vol. 1, Doc. 91, p. 259.

1904, the young bishop's profession in the Third Order was received by Fr. Alessio Lépicier, later a cardinal.[162]

In the following years, Cardinal Merry del Val had the opportunity to establish and maintain lively contacts with the Servites of Mary: not only with the Superior General, the Procurator General, and the Confessor of the Pontifical family, but also with the simple friars of the Convents of San Marcello in Via del Corso and Santa Maria in Via al Tritone.[163] The young Monsignor understood the specific focus that distinguished the Servites' veneration of the Mother of God: Mary suffering together with her Son for love of men. The Passion of Christ, which according to St. Thomas Aquinas was "the greatest of all pains,"[164] is reflected in the liveliest way, as in the clearest of mirrors, in the soul of Mary,[165] venerated as Our Lady of Sorrows. From that time, the young Merry del Val recited daily not only the normal Rosary, but also the Crown of Sorrows of Our Lady, making use of a long rosary with large beads which, after his death, were wrapped around his hands. The sufferings of Jesus and His Blessed Mother Mary were the favorite theme of the Monsignor's reflections and of his homilies during Mass. He meditated on the hours that followed the burial of Jesus: Our Lady alone, no longer in the company of her Son; the Desolate Lady, as he loved to call her, although he did not like the images of Our Lady of Sorrows painted in a soppy and sentimental attitude.[166] Thus, as soon as he was allowed to have his own chapel, he had painted above the altar a portrait of the Lady of Sorrows according to his own indications. In it we see Our Lady standing with joined hands and next to her, lying on a table, the scourges, the crown of thorns, and the nails used to torment Jesus. Her face expresses immense pain and supreme abandonment to the will of God. This was the dominant note in Merry del Val's

162 Alexis-Henri-Marie Lépicier (1863–1936), of the Order of Servites of Mary, was a professor and then novice master in England. Leo XIII later called him to Rome to entrust him a chair in Thomistic theology at the Urbanianum. A consultor to various dicasteries, he was also the author of numerous publications on theological, biblical, ascetical, and apologetical themes. Provost and then prior general of the Servites, he was sent by the pontiffs on delicate missions in Europe, Asia, and Africa, and was granted the cardinalate by Pius XI in the consistory of December 19, 1927.

163 P. Fernando Luigi Barbieri, "Il Servo di Dio Cardinale Raffaele Merry del Val membro del Terz'Ordine dei Servi di Maria," Il Servo di Maria 2–3 (February–March 1977), p. 8 (pp. 3–11). Cf. *Regola e Manuale dei Fratelli e Sorelle del Terz'Ordine dei Servi di Maria [Rule and Manual of the Brothers and Sisters of the Third Order of the Servites of Mary]*, Tipografia Poliglotta, Rome 1895.

164 Thomas Aquinas, *Summa Theologiae*, III, q. 46, a. 6.

165 Gabriele M. Roschini O. S. M., *Dizionario di Mariologia*, Studium, Rome 1961, p. 13.

166 As testified by Sr. Clara Vasquez of the Servants of Mary in *Informatio*, Typis Polyglottis Vaticanis, Vatican City 1957, p. 15.

priestly life, which evolved in a manner quite different from how he would have desired.

The *Ralliement* of Leo XIII

In 1890, the pope addressed the theme of a possible *ralliement* (accord) with the French Third Republic. The discussion took place over the course of six audiences involving Cardinal Rampolla and a number of French prelates. Leo XIII had desired an accord with republican France from the very beginning of his pontificate. Cardinal Rampolla convinced him that this reconciliation could resolve the conflict that, since 1870, opposed Italy to the Holy See. Cardinal Archbishop of Algeri, Msgr. Lavigerie, who had begun to play a primary role under the pontificate of Leo XIII, was chosen by the pope as an "authorized intermediary" between Paris and the Vatican, completing along with Cardinal Rampolla and Msgr. Ferrata, the "triptych" of prelates to whom Leo XIII entrusted the realization of *ralliement*. On February 17, 1892, *Le Petit Journal* published an unexpected interview with Leo XIII in which the pope declared, "I am of the opinion that all citizens must unite on legal grounds; each can maintain their own intimate preferences; but in the arena of activity there is no other government than that which France has come up with. The Republic is a form of government just as legitimate as any other." There followed a eulogy of the Republic of the United States of America where the Catholic Church was free and prosperous.

The interview opened the path for an official document, already signed on February 16, and made public on the twentieth: the encyclical *Au milieu des sollicitudes*, which officially endorsed the new policy of *ralliement* of the Holy See.[167] Drafted in French, it was addressed "to the archbishops, the bishops, the clergy, and all Catholics in France."

Merry del Val was of monarchist sentiments as a family heritage and by doctrinal choice. For the same reasons that would lead him into conflict with Pius XI in the case of *Action Française*, he presumably nourished reservations toward the *ralliement* of Leo XIII toward Republican France. However, he was too young and respectful of pontifical authority to assume a position of dissent on this delicate point. The split between his position and that of Secretary of

[167] Leo XIII, Encyclical *Au milieu des sollicitudes*, February 16, 1892, in ASS, vol. 24 (1891–1892), pp. 519–529.

State Rampolla del Tindaro dates from that period and would continue under Cardinal Gasparri.[168]

"I return to Rome," he wrote in October 1890 to his friend Denis Sheil, "perplexed and without enthusiasm, and neither does the perspective of canon law encourage me, because I have entered so fully into accord with theology and philosophy that I would gladly start all over. Even if I thought that a year of canon law might be useful to me, I hope that this will be my last course here in Rome and that it might serve as a preparation for my next 'mission.' I cannot remember if I told you that I sent the Holy Father a petition, praying him to let me go and explaining the reasons why I am convinced that my vocation does not lie in entering in what we might call 'public life,' whether in the Vatican or not. My desire for apostolic work, in spite of myself and of the opinion of others, has become so strong day by day that I cannot aspire to anything more perfect. If the pope replies by telling me I must take another path, I will obey, but I feel that it would be too much for my soul and that our Lord and God would remove me from the world rather than leave me where it seems it is not His will that I remain. The Holy Father has not yet responded: this could be a positive sign or a negative one. We shall see. Pray for me."[169]

A short time later, Leo XIII sent for him to ask if he was willing to obey the pope and to serve the Church. "In everything that Your Holiness commands," replied Rafael. "Well then!" exclaimed the pope, without communicating that he already had a very precise idea concerning the young prelate's future.

Merry del Val's parents did not spend their summers in Austria in 1891 and 1892, but in San Sebastian in the north of Spain, where the Spanish sovereigns were sojourning as well. Queen Maria Cristina asked Rafael to join them in order to prepare the young King of Spain Alfonso XIII for his First Communion.[170] The young Monsignor lived with his family and every

[168] Pietro Gasparri (1852–1934), ordained in 1877, was professor of canon law at the *Institut Catholique* in Paris from 1880 to 1897. He was then archbishop of Caesarea (1898) and apostolic delegate to Bolivia, Peru, and Ecuador until 1901, when he was nominated secretary of the Congregation for Extraordinary Ecclesiastical Affairs. He was made a cardinal in 1907. He was secretary of state (1914–1930) under Benedict XV and Pius XI. About his life, cf. the extensive entry by Romeo Astorri-Carlo Fantappié, DBI, 52 (1999), pp. 500–507.

[169] Javierre, *Merry del Val*, p. 34.

[170] Buehrle, *Merry del Val*, p. 48; Charles Petrie, *King Alfonso XIII and His Age*, Chapman & Hall, London 1963, p. 49. In a letter to Cardinal Merry del Val, sent from the royal palace in Madrid on January 6, 1906, Queen Maria Cristina expressed her *"muy grato recuerdo de tantos y buenos servicios of"* that the Monsignor had offered her and her sons in the past, assuring him *"l'afecto verdadero en que lo tengo de muy antiguo y que en esta ocasion le reitero muy gustosa"* (AAV, *Spoglio Merry del Val*, busta 3, n. 1).

morning went to the palace to instruct Alfonso. In October 1891, returning to Italy with his father, they stopped in Venice, staying at the Grand Hotel, whose windows opened onto the church of Santa Maria della Salute. They visited the Basilica of San Marco, admiring the "Golden Ball," and in the evening were struck by the gondolas, "all black" with "a melancholy appearance." "I do not know what will happen to me, nor do I know if I shall ever see the fulfillment of my desire to work for the conversion of England as a religious," wrote Rafael on October 31 to his mother, "but wherever I shall be, I hope always to fulfill my duty for the greater glory of God. I shall have this possibility if you, kneeling on the Mount of your Virtues, will hold high your arms in prayer for me, while I, down below, combat the enemy."[171]

On December 31, 1891, Leo XIII called for Msgr. Merry del Val to be his secret chamberlain, admitting him to his direct service in the pontifical antechamber.[172] This decision frustrated the young man's desire to return to England as a simple priest and dedicate himself exclusively to the care of souls and the conversion of schismatics. Msgr. Merry del Val now officially entered the pontifical household (at that time known as the Papal Court), which comprised the vast complex of persons who assisted the pontiff in his daily work and his sacred functions.[173] Two cardinals were part of the family, the apostolic datary and the secretary of state, as well as a great number of other high-ranking clergy and prominent lay persons associated with the Noble Secret Antechamber (private apartments where the pope could conduct private business, receive dignitaries, and engage in confidential discussions). The very day Merry del Val was appointed, Cardinal Serafino Vannutelli sent news to the young man's father with an affectionate letter, announcing the nomination so sought after by all young prelates, "but not by Rafael who has no other ambition than to serve God and His Holy Church."[174]

171 AAV, *Spoglio Merry del Val*, busta 3, n. 139.

172 AAV, *Spoglio Merry del Val*, busta 3, n. 146.

173 Cf. Rufo Ruffo della Scaletta, "La Famiglia Pontificia," in Giovanni Fallani and Mario Escobar (eds.), *Vaticano*, Sansoni, Florence 1946, pp. 159–190.

174 AAV, *Spoglio Merry del Val*, busta 3, n. 147.

The Spanish College of St. Joseph

Under the pontificate of Pius IX, the Latin American College and the French Seminary were both established. But this initiative did not especially flourish under the direction of the Spanish bishops, unfortunately. As soon as he was elected Pope, Leo XIII became interested in the question. Don Manuel Domingo y Sol, a priest born in Tortosa, Tarragona, had founded a certain number of seminaries in his country, all dedicated to St. Joseph, and was convinced of the necessity of planting one in Rome as well.[175] By complete chance, Domingo y Sol happened to cross paths near the Piazza Navona in Rome with a young Monsignor and countryman of his, Rafael Merry del Val, who had just been nominated president of the Pontifical Ecclesiastical Academy. Merry del Val helped him, opening one door after another.[176]

April 1, 1892, is considered by historians the date on which the College of St. Joseph was founded. The tenacious priest settled the first eleven seminarians in Via Giulia, in a building attached to the Spanish national church. Several months later, the number of young men had grown to forty-two and, a year later, the Spanish colony moved to the first floor of Palazzo Altieri in Piazza del Gesù, thanks to the intervention of Leo XIII who offered to pay the rent. It was also Leo XIII who found a definitive location for the College of St. Joseph, conceding the use of Palazzo Altemps, an old and lovely building in Piazza Sant'Apollinare, near Piazza Navona. The concession was made official on October 25, 1893 with the letter *Non mediocri cura,* in which it was established that the direction of the College would be entrusted to the priests of Don Manuel Domingo y Sol. Msgr. Merry del Val, nicknamed by Don Manuel "St. Rafael of the College," was designated from the first day the spiritual director and confessor of the students.[177]

The arrival in February 1893 of Msgr. Rafael's father, Rafael Carlos Merry del Val, as the Spanish ambassador to the Vatican signified a powerful help for

175 Manuel Domingo y Sol (1836–1909), after being ordained a priest in Tortosa, where he was born in 1883, founded the Fraternity of Diocesan Working Priests of the Sacred Heart and on April 1, 1892, the Spanish College in Rome. He was proclaimed Blessed by John Paul II on March 29, 1987. Cf. Francisco Martín Hernández, Lopez Rubio Parrado, *Vida de Manuel Domingo y Sol,* Ediciones Sigueme, S. A., 2014 (Salamanca 1978).

176 Javierre, *Merry del Val,* pp. 41–46; Juan de Andres Hernansanz, *Pontificio Colegio Español de San José, Cien años de Historia,* Rome 1992, pp. 15–21; Vicente Cárcel Ortí and Lopez Rubio Parrado, *Pontificio Colegio Español de San José de Roma. Aproximación a su historia,* Pontificio Colegio Español, Rome 2010, pp. 45–60.

177 Javierre, *Merry del Val,* p. 44.

the College. As seminarians from all the dioceses in Spain began to arrive, scholarships began to arrive as well. During the papacy of Pius X, thanks to the good graces of Merry del Val who had become secretary of state in the meantime, the College was even given the title "Pontifical." During his episcopal career, Merry del Val ordained more than four hundred priests from the college and many bishops.[178]

The Question of Anglican Ordinations

Monsignor Merry del Val had become Leo XIII's right hand man for all that concerned England. His friendship with the archbishop of Westminster, Cardinal Herbert Vaughan, and with other prelates, made him the ideal intermediary between Rome and London. Beyond ecclesiastical relations, Merry del Val had profound knowledge of the psychology, the customs, and the habits of the English people and the best way of relating with them. One delicate English question, the case of Anglican ordinations, revealed the strong personality of the young collaborator of Leo XIII.

The problem had been raised by the English bishops, who asked Rome for clear guidelines on a point that was controversial at the time: the validity or nullity of priestly and episcopal ordinations that dated back to the Anglican schism. During the reign of Henry VIII (1534–1547), all ordinations were made according to the Roman rite and all were considered valid. The same occurred during the first three years of the reign of Edward VI, from 1547 to 1550. But in 1550, the *Book of Common Prayer* took effect, mandating that the Roman Pontifical was to be substituted by the new Edwardian Ordinal.[179] This Ordinal, suffering from defects in both form and intention, not only denied the Sacrament of Orders, but eliminated from the Mass, now referred to simply as the Supper, any idea of sacrifice and of consecration of bread and wine into the Body and Blood of Jesus Christ.

During the reign of Mary Tudor (r. 1553–1558), the priestly ordinations that took place under the reign of Edward were examined by Cardinal Reginald Pole, pontifical legate to England, and declared invalid due to defect in form and

[178] Ortí and Parrado, *Pontificio Colegio Español,* pp. 45–47.

[179] A pontifical is a compendium of liturgical rites that only bishops can perform, such as the ordination of priests.

intention.[180] Queen Elizabeth (r. 1558–1603) subsequently renewed the schism and, as Cardinal Pole's successor as archbishop of Canterbury, chose Matthew Parker, who had previously been chaplain to her mother, Anne Boleyn, and had been ordained a bishop according to the Edwardian Ordinal, and thus invalidly.[181] Parker then consecrated other Anglican bishops; all these consecrations followed the Ordinal of Edward VI and were therefore invalid. The Anglican episcopate derived from them through successive consecrations.

In 1889, while convalescing on the island of Madera, two persons met and became friends who were destined to have an important role in the so-called ecumenical movement: Lord Halifax, secretary of the English Church Union,[182] and the French Lazarite priest Fr. Fernand Portal.[183] They proposed to work for the unity of the two Churches to which they belonged, though without any official role assigned to them from their respective hierarchies. The suitable theme, in their opinion, was the issue of Anglican ordinations. They hoped that the Roman position on the invalidity of Anglican ordinations could be modified. In December 1893, Fr. Portal set the discussions in motion by publishing a brochure on *Les ordinations anglicanes* under the pseudonym Fernand Dalbus.[184] Leo XIII called Fr. Portal to Rome and received him benevolently in September 1894. Lord Halifax came to Rome as well and, on March 21, 1895, was received amicably by the pope.[185] Meanwhile in London, Cardinal Vaughan, who had succeeded Cardinal Manning as

180 Cardinal Reginald Pole (1500–1558), made a cardinal in 1536, in 1545 served as the papal legate at the Council of Trent. With the coronation of Mary Tudor, he was consecrated archbishop of Canterbury (1556) and became the main counsellor to the queen in matters of religious politics. Accused of heresy, he was sent to the tribunal of the Inquisition, but died before the end of the trial. Cf. Paolo Simoncelli, *Il caso Reginald Pole. Eresia e santità nelle polemiche religiose del Cinquecento*, Edizioni di Storia e Letteratura, Rome 1977; Thomas F. Mayer, *Cardinal Pole, Prince & Prophet*, Cambridge University Press, Cambridge-New York 2000.

181 Matthew Parker (1504–1575), former chaplain to Anne Boleyn, headed the archdiocese of Canterbury from 1559 until his death. He was one of the authors of the *Thirty-Nine Articles* of the Anglican church.

182 Charles Lindley Wood, Viscount of Halifax (1839–1934), was secretary from 1868 of the *English Church Union*, an Anglo-Catholic association composed of laity and clergy. Cf. John Gilbert Lockhart, *Charles Lindley Viscount Halifax*, Geoffrey Bless, London 1935–36, 2 vols.

183 Fernand Portal (1885–1926), of the Congregation of the Mission of the Lazarists, abandoned his post as superior of the University Seminary of Saint-Vincent de Paul in 1908, under suspicion of modernism. Cf. *Refaire l'Église de toujours,* Textes présentés par Régis Ladous, Nouvelle Cité, Paris 1977; R. Ladous, *Monsieur Portal et les siens (1855–1926)*, Cerf, Paris 1985.

184 Fernand Dalbus, *Les ordinations anglicanes*, Sueur-Charruey, Arras 1894.

185 Viscount Halifax, *Leo XIII and Anglican Orders*, Longmans, Green and Co., London 1912, pp. 194–201.

the Archbishop of Westminster in 1892, along with all the Catholic hierarchy in England, expressed their deep perplexity to the pope about this initiative, asking for a papal declaration to clarify in a definitive manner whether ministers ordained according to the rite of the Anglican Church were true priests and true bishops, on a par with the bishops and priests of the eastern schismatics.[186]

The Theological Debate in Rome

During the debate over the issue, Msgr. Rafael Merry del Val played an important role in the drafting of the apostolic letter *Ad Anglos* (April 14, 1895). In this letter, Leo XIII prayed "for the return of Christian nations now divided from us to the unity of former days."[187] The theme of religious unity was dear to Leo XIII, and he had already dealt with it in his encyclical *Praeclara gratulationis* to the sovereigns and peoples of all the world on June 20, 1894.[188] He returned to the same issue in the encyclical *Satis cognitum* on the unity of the Church, promulgated on June 29, 1896.[189] His thesis was that the rediscovery of religious unity in Christendom, without the conversion of the errant, would be a reunion without true unity. The Catholic Church, in fact, is not a merely human institution, but a supernatural society called to the eternal salvation of souls.[190]

The letter *Ad Anglos* was received with interest and deference by the English public, although it continued to leave open the question of ordination. Merry del Val followed attentively all that happened in England, at times bypassing Cardinal Rampolla in the information he gave to the Holy Father. In a letter sent shortly before *Satis cognitum* was promulgated and reserved to Leo XIII's personal secretary, Msgr. Rinaldo Angeli,[191] he wrote, "While the Holy

[186] Cf. Alejandro Cifres Giménez, *La validez de las ordenaciones anglicanas. Los documentos de la comisión preparatoria de la bula "Apostolicae Curae," II. Los documentos de 1896* (Fontes Archivi Sancti Officii Romani, 2), LEV, Rome 2012; idem, "Mons. Merry del Val y las ordenaciones anglicanas," in Domingo Merry del Val (ed.), *Rafael Merry del Val. 150 anni dalla sua nascita*, pp. 199–226; Giuseppe Rambaldi, *Ordinazioni anglicane e sacramento dell'ordine nella Chiesa: aspetti storici e teologici: a cento anni dalla bolla* Apostolicae curae *di Leone XIII*, Pontificia Università Gregoriana, Rome 1995.

[187] Leo XIII, Apostolic letter *Amantissimae voluntatis, Ad Anglos regnum Christi in fidei unitate quaerentes*, April 14, 1895, https://www.papalencyclicals.net/leo13/l13amantissima.htm.

[188] Leo XIII, Encyclical *Praeclara gratulationis*, June 20, 1894, ASS, vol. 26 (1893–1894), pp. 705–717.

[189] Leo XIII, Encyclical *Satis cognitum*, June 29, 1896, ASS, vol. 28 (1895–1896), pp. 708–739.

[190] Murphy, "Cardinal Merry del Val and the Conversion of England," pp. 28–29.

[191] Rinaldo Angeli (1851–1914), ordained a priest in 1864 by Msgr. Gioacchino Pecci, then bishop of Perugia, was called to Rome by Leo XIII eight months after his election as his personal secretary. He assisted the pope until his death and published his *Political Testament*.

Father yearns to make the true concept of the Church better known, Portal, playing the game of Halifax, who is leading him in all things, takes it upon himself to diminish the effect of the Encyclical by advancing the most modern heretical poison concerning the constitution of the Church."[192] "I believe we would do well to recall the Holy Father's attention to the most recent, in my humble opinion, scandalous number of the *Revue Anglo-Romaine*,"[193] he added, flagging the journal that appeared on December 7, 1895, which Leo XIII would later condemn.[194]

The policy followed by Merry del Val was different on this occasion from that of Cardinal Rampolla, but also from that of the hesitating Leo XIII, as can be seen in the many letters sent between 1895 and 1896 to Msgr. Angeli, as well as to the newly created Cardinal Herbert Vaughan, Angeli's old friend.

On July 24, 1895, Msgr. Merry del Val wrote Cardinal Vaughan a long letter in which he stated regarding Secretary of State Rampolla, "The Cardinal is an earnest upholder of H. He has to my mind been completely hoodwinked by him and he evidently has no grasp of the situation in England.... I am alone entirely and I am nobody, he is the Card. Secretary and has numberless Italian and French Portals to back up his impressions.... I am not at all sure that things will turn out as easily as we hoped. I see a growing conviction on the part of the Holy Father and of course of Card. R. that any concession that could be made on the point of Anglican ordinations would be a step toward reunion and help on conversions!!"[195]

On August 29, 1895, Msgr. Merry del Val wrote Msgr. Angeli, "It is entirely necessary now that the question be discussed and decided once more in Rome: it can only be for the best; and if Anglican ordinations are condemned again, as is likely, many Ritualists are ready to abandon the Anglican Church and heresy, and this will be a step forward for many conversions."[196]

192 AAV, *Spoglio Merry del Val*, busta 3, n. 160. Numbers 154–212 contain the exchange of letter with Msgr. Rinaldo Angeli from August 12, 1895, to July 24, 1902.

193 Ibid.

194 ASS, vol. 29 (1896–1897), pp. 664–665. Cf. G. Rambaldi, "Una lettera del card. Richard sulla fine della *Revue Anglo-Romaine*," *Archivum historiae pontificiae* 18 (1980), pp. 403–410.

195 Merry del Val to Cardinal Vaughan, July 24, 1895. Complete text in John Jay Hughes, *Absolutely Null & Utterly Void—An Account of the 1896 Papal Condemnation of Anglican Orders*, Sheed and Ward, London and Sydney, 1968, pp. 296–297.

196 Merry del Val to Msgr. Rinaldo Angeli, August 29, 1895, reproduced in Cenci, *Merry del Val*, p. 59. The term *ritualist* denotes persons in favor of reintroducing a range of Roman Catholic liturgical practices to the Church of England.

Ever more concerned about the ambiguous work of Halifax, later that year on December 15, Merry del Val again wrote Msgr. Angeli, "I pray that you place in the Holy Father's hands this important letter from Halifax, published in Anglican newspapers a moment ago. I believe that His Holiness will be persuaded that many months ago I was right in saying that those who believed and affirmed that Halifax admits the primacy and infallibility of the pope were deceived. I am well acquainted with his doctrine, in all its complexity, and it is shared by a minority at any rate; he can speak like a Catholic and easily deceive those who do not know him."[197]

In October, the pope instructed his nuncio in Paris to have Prof. Louis Duchesne[198] "compose a dissertation on Anglican ordinations, gathering all that he knows and can find regarding news of this subject."[199] Duchesne taught ecclesiastical history at the *Institut Catholique* and was known for his publication of the *Liber Pontificalis,* the second volume of which had just been printed. The *Institut* was already becoming a hothouse for modernist tendencies, and Duchesne was not a paragon of orthodox doctrine.[200]

Duchesne openly argued for the validity of Anglican ordinations and was followed along these lines, albeit in a more nuanced way, by another professor at the *Institut Catholique* consulted by Leo XIII: Msgr. Pietro Gasparri. Gasparri had published a small volume earlier that year under the title *De la Valeur des ordinations anglicanes,* in which he stated that Anglican ordinations should be considered "doubtful" and therefore to be repeated *sub condicione.*[201] Also consulted by Leo XIII was a professor of dogmatic theology at the Gregorian, Emilio De Augustinis, who responded in August 1895 with a "vote" in favor

197 Merry del Val to Msgr. Rinaldo Angeli, December 15, 1895, in AAV, *Spoglio Merry del Val,* busta 3, n. 173.

198 Louis Duchesne (1843–1922), professor at the *Institut Catholique* in Paris from 1877 to 1885, was later director of the *École française* of Rome (1895–1922). His *Histoire ancienne de l'Église* in 3 volumes (1906–1910) was placed on the Index (1912). Cf. the entry of Fr. d'Espezel, DHGE, 14, col. 965–984 (which tried to exonerate him of the accusation of heterodoxy) and the Acts of the Convention *Monseigneur Duchesne et son temps,* École française de Rome, Rome 1975; Brigitte Wache, *Monseigneur Louis Duchesne (1843–1922),* École française de Rome, Rome 1992.

199 Rambaldi, *Ordinazioni anglicane,* p. 50.

200 Maurice La Sage d'Hauteroche d'Hulst (1841–1896), created the *Institut Catholique* of Paris of which he was rector from 1881 until his death. Cf. Alfred Baudrillart, *Vie de Mgr d'Hulst,* 2 vols., Librairie Poussielgue, Paris 1912–1914; Claude Bressolette (ed.), *Monseigneur d'Hulst, fondateur de l'Institut Catholique de Paris,* Beauchesne, Paris 1998.

201 Pietro Gasparri, *De la valeur des ordinations anglicanes,* F. Levé, Paris 1895, p. 52.

of the validity of the ordinations.[202] On March 31, 1896, Fr. Portal wrote Lord Halifax that "no condemnation is to be feared.... This is the opinion of Duchesne and Gasparri."[203] In London, however, opposite conclusions were reached at about the same time after a meticulous study by a commission convoked by Cardinal Vaughan.[204] Three highly qualified scholars were part of it: Canon James Moyes,[205] Benedictine historian and later cardinal Aidan Gasquet,[206] and Franciscan theologian David Fleming.[207]

On April 3, 1896, Fr. Gasquet told of his long walk with Halifax. "We spoke, of course, on religious questions a good deal, and my impression is that his belief is not Catholic (I mean our) belief on many essential matters. For instance, I do not think he believes as I do about the Blessed Eucharist and the Sacrifice of the Mass, although I had previously thought he did. It was rather a revelation to me, what I understood him to say with regard to his belief in the Sacrifice."[208]

The two future cardinals, Gasquet and Merry del Val, were convinced (and facts were to bear them out) that the capable diplomat Halifax sought to deceive Leo XIII and Cardinal Rampolla, hiding his true positions on the nature of the sacraments. Fr. Portal, who certainly did not ignore the English politician's ideas, was playing his game.

"My conviction," wrote Merry del Val on February 17, 1896, "is more and more confirmed by the facts, namely that the devil's primary maneuver is to lead the Holy See to some form of recognition of Anglicanism and their Orders,

202 Emilio De Augustinis S. J. (1829–1899) was professor of theology at the Jesuit House of Studies in Woodstock (Maryland) from 1872 to 1885 and then, from 1887 to 1897, professor of dogmatic theology at the Gregorian University, of which he was also rector (1891–1895).

203 Halifax, *Leo XIII and Anglican Orders*, p. 284.

204 Merry del Val, after having met with Cardinal Vaughan in Rome, reported to Msgr. Angeli in a letter of August 29, 1895. Cf. AAV, *Spoglio Merry del Val*, busta 3, n. 165.

205 James Moyes (1851–1927), an English priest educated at Bede College in Rome, was a general canon at the Chapter of Salford (1891) and of Westminster (1895). Director of the *Dublin Review* until 1903, he was the author of a vast array of theological polemical works.

206 Aidan Gasquet O. S. B. (1846–1929) was abbot and president of the English Benedictine Congregation (1900); president of the Commission for the Review of the Vulgate (1906), cardinal (1914), librarian and archivist of the Holy Roman Church (1919). He wrote *Edward VI and the Book of Common Prayer: An Examination into Its Origin and Early History with an Appendix of Unpublished Documents*, Hodges, London 1891. See also *Leaves from My Diary. 1894–1896*, Burns & Oates, London 1911.

207 David Fleming, O. F. M. Oss. (1851–1915), Irish Franciscan and provincial of the new province of Friars Minor in Great Britain (1891), was a consultor to the Holy Office (1897–1915) and vicar general (1901–1903) of his order.

208 Gasquet, *Leaves from My Diary*, p. 27.

not perhaps a formal recognition, but sufficient for keeping people in heresy."[209] In that same month, Leo XIII created a pontifical commission to study the question of Anglican ordinations.[210] Duchesne, De Augustinis, and Gasparri were appointed to discuss and compare their results with those of the three theologians and erudite Englishmen, Gasquet, Moyes, and Fleming. Two members were later added to the study group: Thomas Scannell,[211] a parish priest from Kent in favor of validity; and Capuchin José de Calasanz Vives y Tutó[212] (also known as José de Calasanz de Llevaranes), a future cardinal, of the opposite opinion. Cardinal Camillo Mazzella[213] was nominated president of the commission and Msgr. Merry del Val its secretary.[214] The latter, consulting his notes, recalled, "My impression is that they were as follows: Gasquet, Moyes, David [Fleming], and Llevaranes voted for invalidity; Duchesne and De Augustinis for the validity; Gasparri and Scannell for a doubtful validity and therefore a *sub condicione*."[215] The powers were balanced, but Mazzella and Merry del Val successfully swayed the majority vote in support of invalidity.

The commission was an entirely technical organism lacking authority to decide on the delicate matter. Its members met twelve times from March 24 to

209 Letter of February 17, 1896, in AAV, *Spoglio Rafael Merry del Val*, busta 3, n. 176.

210 Cf. Giménez Cifres, *La validité des ordinations anglicanes. Les documents de la commission préparatoire à la lettre "Apostolicae Curae,"* 1.—*Les dossiers précédents. Introduction, transcription et notes par A. F. von Gunten O.P.*, Florence 1997; and the article by G. Rambaldi, "Leone XIII e le ordinazioni anglicane. Dal rito di conferimento al sacerdozio conferito," *La Civiltà Cattolica* 148 (1997), pp. 250–263.

211 Thomas Bartholomew Scannell (1854–1917), after studying at the Gregorian, was professor of philosophy at St. Edmund's College in England and a parish priest. He was director of the *Catholic Dictionary* and collaborated on the *Dublin Review*.

212 José de Calasanz Vives y Tutó, O.F.M. Cap. (1854–1913), entered the Order of Capuchins in 1869, and thanks to his theological preparation was called to Rome by Leo XIII as consultor to the Holy Office (1887) and to the Congregations of Rites (1889), Propaganda Fide (1893), the Council (1894), and Extraordinary Ecclesiastical Affairs (1895). He was made a cardinal in the consistory of June 9, 1899, and was a member of various pontifical congregations until Pius X appointed him prefect of the Congregation of Religious in 1908. F. Raurell, *L'antimodernisme y el cardenal Vives y Tutó*, Ed Facultad de Teologia de Catalunya, Barcelona 2000; Fra' Valenti Serra de Manresa, O.F.M. Cap., "El capuchino José de Calasanz de Llavaneres, cardenal Vives y Tutó (1854–1913). Su actuación durante los pontificados de León XIII y Pío X," *Archivum historiae pontificiae* 44 (2006), pp. 173–205.

213 Camillo Mazzella S.J. (1833–1900) entered the Society of Jesus in 1857, taught at Georgetown and Woodstock, and was called by Leo XIII in 1878 to teach at the Gregorian University to restore Thomism. He was made a cardinal in 1886 (despite opposition from the General of the Jesuits) and in 1897 consecrated bishop of Palestrina. He was a resolute adversary of the tendencies of Americanism and collaborated with Leo XIII on several encyclicals such as *Rerum novarum* and *Satis cognitum* on Church unity.

214 Two Anglican theologians were also called to Rome, T.A. Lacey and F.W. Puller, both as private experts and not as official representatives of the Anglican church, to provide the members of the commission with information they needed.

215 Merry del Val to Canon Moyes, in Hughes, *Absolutely Null*, p. 302.

May 7, 1896, and presented the final report to the consultors of the Congregation of the Holy Office. On July 6, 1896, the cardinals of the Holy Office judged unanimously that there was no reason to reconsider the negative judgment that Rome had expressed over the course of the last three centuries on the issue.[216]

Although the cardinals had come out unanimously against the validity of the ordinations, the decision had no juridical value until Leo XIII pronounced his final verdict, intervening with the full weight of his authority as supreme pontiff.

The Encyclical *Apostolicae Curae*

With the letter *Apostolicae curae et caritatis* of September 3, 1896, Leo XIII confirmed and renewed the decrees of his predecessors, declaring and pronouncing that, due to defect of form and defect in intention, "ordinations carried out according to the Anglican rite have been, and are, absolutely null and utterly void."[217] The decisions and dispositions of this letter, he added, "are and shall be always valid and in force and shall be inviolably observed both juridically and otherwise, by all of whatsoever degree and preeminence, declaring null and void anything which, in these matters, may happen to be contrariwise attempted."[218]

Leo XIII, influenced by Cardinal Rampolla, was more inclined to the undecided approach, but the position taken by Msgr. Merry del Val, after having studied attentively the dossier, convinced Leo XIII of the necessity of confirming the perennial Magisterium of the Church. Msgr. Merry del Val was, along with Fr. Gasquet, one of the main draftors of the text of the encyclical, which was well received in England, even by the *Times*, to the surprise of Cardinal Vaughan himself.[219]

Msgr. Merry del Val's thorough study of this subject resulted in an article entitled "Concerning the Anglican Ordinations," composed in 1897 by order of

216 Cf. G. Rambaldi, "Relazione e voto del P. Raffaele Pierotti O. P. Maestro del S. Palazzo Apostolico sulle ordinazioni anglicane. Note introduttive ed edizione del testo," *Archivum historiae pontificiae* 20 (1982), pp. 337–388; idem, "Come Leone XIII arrivò a pubblicare la bolla *Apostolicae curae*," *La Civiltà Cattolica* 140 (1989), pp. 227–237 and 462–477.

217 Leo XIII, Apostolic letter *Apostolicae curae de ordinationibus anglicanis*, September 13, 1896, no. 36, https://www.papalencyclicals.net/leo13/l13curae.htm.

218 Ibid., no. 40. The authority of *Apostolicae curae* was reiterated by Cardinal Gianfranco Ghirlanda in his work *The Significance of the Apostolic Constitution Anglicanorum Coetibus* of November 9, 2009. In this essay, approved by the Congregation for the Doctrine of the Faith, Ghirlanda commented that "the ordination of ministers coming from Anglicanism will be absolute, on the basis of the Bull *Apostolicae curae* of Leo XIII of September 13, 1896."

219 McCormack, *Cardinal Vaughan*, p. 254.

Leo XIII. The author explained how within the variegated Anglican world three parties were fighting among themselves, though they were united in their aversion to the Church of Rome: the "High Church," which was "in dialogue" [with Catholicism]; the "Broad Church," which in its tolerance of all beliefs counted the largest number of followers; and the "Low Church," which represented the most coherent form of continuity with old Protestantism. The "Ritualists," an active and restless minority, inheritors of the Oxford Movement, constituted in turn "a hybrid middle way between old Protestantism and the Catholic Church," although "always stubbornly maintaining their refusal to recognize the existence of a divinely constituted center of teaching and governance."[220]

Halifax presented himself as the spokesman for the "Ritualists," but Merry del Val knew that within the Anglican world, many who were inclined to pass over to Catholicism would do so only if they were certain of the invalidity of Anglican apostolic succession. The principal goal of Anglicans, on the contrary, was to obtain recognition of their ordinations to reinforce the theses of the separated churches and to keep the Ritualists within them. Merry del Val wrote: "Just as the word *reunion* in the mouths of Anglicans has never had the meaning of *conversion* or *submission,* so too the word *valid,* applied to their ordinations, does not mean for the vast majority of them that the Edwardian Rite is *valid* in its effect of conferring the power to offer the sacrifice [of the Mass], a sacrificing priesthood, which is Catholic priesthood." In fact, Anglicans "pretend to possess *the valid and legitimate ministry as instituted by Christ,*" but they continue to refute the Catholic doctrine of sacrifice. "In a word, with such assertions and considerations one is implicitly asking the pope to admit that the powers of true sacrifice are not essential to Catholic priesthood, as instituted by Christ."[221]

According to Régis Ladous, Merry Del Val's victory over Rampolla depended on the convergence of support given by the English episcopate and by members of the Roman Curia who looked with suspicion on the new historical-critical method launched by Duchesne.[222] Nevertheless, it would be a profound error to reduce such an important decision to Anglo-Roman political

220 "A proposito delle Ordinazioni anglicane. Un documento inedito sulla situazione religiosa in Inghilterra," *La Civiltà Cattolica* 63, no. 3 (1912), pp. 82–83. Added to this document was Rafael Merry del Val's *The Truth of Papal Claims,* Sands & Company, London 1902, a concise and vigorous confutation of the pamphlet *The Validity of Papal Claims,* by theologian Nutcombe Oxenham, (1829–1888), in favor of Anglican ordinations.

221 "A proposito delle Ordinazioni anglicane", p. 95.

222 Ladous, *Monsieur Portal et les siens,* pp. 109–110.

maneuvers. The truth is that the historical-critical method employed by Duchesne belied the learned Frenchman's own conclusions, especially after Fr. Gasquet found in the *Regesta* of Pope Paul IV the Bull *Praeclara carissimi* and the papal brief *Regimini* of 1555, in which the pontiff qualified the English ordinations as invalid because they had not been administered *rite et recte*.[223]

From this period date the divergences destined to intensify over the years between Merry del Val and the future Cardinal Gasparri, about whom he had written to Cardinal Vaughan on June 2, 1895: "Gasparri is simply an emissary of Portal's, full of Portal's ideas and I must say honestly at times hardly orthodox. I don't know where he has learnt or unlearnt his theology.'"[224]

At the time, Gasparri was forty-three and had been designated by Leo XIII to occupy the chair of canon law at the *Institut Catholique* in Paris. His volumes *Tractatus de matrimonio* (1892) and *De sacra ordinatione* (1893–1894) were appreciated for their synthesis and the clarity of their exposition. In 1898, Leo XIII nominated him titular archbishop of Caesarea in Palestine and apostolic delegate to the Republic of Peru, Bolivia, and Ecuador, forcing him to abandon the scholarly life he had led up to that point and take up the diplomatic life. His mission in America lasted three years. On April 23, 1901, he was nominated secretary of the Sacred Congregation of Extraordinary Ecclesiastical Affairs, where two years later he found Merry del Val, whom he did not love, as his superior.

What guided Merry del Val in this complex matter was above all his apostolic zeal. "His entire spiritual life was guided by his desire for the propagation of the Faith, for the conversion of heretics; this was the aim of his life," as one of his spiritual daughters testified.[225] The encyclical *Ad Anglos* concluded with a prayer that most think was inspired by Msgr. Merry del Val and that is worth quoting in its entirety:

> *O Blessed Virgin Mary, Mother of God and our most gentle Queen and Mother, look down in mercy upon England thy "Dowry" and upon us all who greatly hope and trust in thee. By thee it was that Jesus our Saviour*

[223] Vatican *regesta* are bound volumes containing collections of papal letters and official documents, usually organized in chronological order.

[224] Merry del Val to Cardinal Vaughan, June 2, 1896, AAV, cit. in Holmes, *More Roman than Rome*, p. 221.

[225] *Dichiarazione della Marchesa Aurora Misciattelli nata Contessa Boutourline*, in AAV, *Spoglio Merry del Val*, busta 9, n. 1982, p. 2.

and our hope was given unto the world; and He has given thee to us that we might hope still more.

Plead for us thy children, whom thou didst receive and accept at the foot of the cross. O sorrowful Mother! intercede for our separated brethren, that with us in the one true fold they may be united to the supreme Shepherd, the Vicar of thy Son.

Pray for us all, dear Mother, that by faith fruitful in good works we may all deserve to see and praise God, together with thee, in our heavenly home. Amen.[226]

There certainly did seem to be new cause of hope for the Catholic Church in England during these years. On April 2, 1889, the cause of beatification was opened in Rome for Fr. Dominic of the Mother of God. The construction in London from 1880 to 1884 of the "Brompton Oratory" in the style of Roman Baroque, as well as the Cathedral of Westminster from 1895 to 1903, and finally, the restoration in 1897 of the historic sanctuary of Our Lady of Walsingham, constituted a visible expression of the rebirth of the English Church, to which the encyclical of Leo XIII offered an important contribution.

Apostolic Delegate in Canada

On March 10, 1897, Leo XIII nominated Msgr. Merry del Val as apostolic delegate in an extraordinary mission to Canada.[227] The young priest, who up to that moment had not exercised direct responsibility in his journeys, was now designated the personal representative of the pope to communicate to the Canadian bishops and clergy the will and directives of the Holy See. To grant him greater authority, Leo XIII nominated him domestic prelate of the Pontifical House on March 13.[228]

Canada, which had become a unified state in 1867, was already an immense nation, extending from the coasts of the Atlantic to those of the Pacific, with ten million square kilometers in between. The tensions between its two souls — the French-speaking Catholic one concentrated in Quebec, and the

226 *Ad Anglos,* https://www.papalencyclicals.net/leo13/l13amantissima.htm; Archive of the Postulation, ff. 89–90.

227 AAV, *Spoglio Merry del Val,* busta 3, n. 214.

228 Ibid., n. 216.

English-speaking Protestant one dominant in Ontario — had yet to be resolved. One local case went national when, on March 31, 1890, the government of Manitoba approved the *Manitoba School Act,* legislation that mandated the use of English only in the Province and the abolition of public financing for Catholic schools.[229] In the elections of July 1896, Conservatives, who defended the rights of Catholics in Quebec but were more ambivalent on the matter in anglophone Canada, were defeated by the Liberals, led by the Catholic Wilfrid Laurier.[230] In the same year, newly elected Prime Minister Laurier and the premier of Manitoba, Thomas Greenway, settled upon a compromise that gave some concessions for religious instruction and teaching in French.[231] The bishops of Quebec did not like the agreement, however, and guided by Msgr. Louis-Philippe-Adélard Langevin, asked for a new federal law that would unambivalently guarantee the linguistic and religious rights of the francophone minority.[232] To neutralize the opposition of the bishops, Premier Laurier sent to Rome a priest close to him, Fr. Jean-Baptiste Proulx, who convinced some of the Roman prelates of the goodness of the accord.[233]

Leo XIII was perplexed, and entrusted to Msgr. Merry del Val the task of resolving the thorny question and reestablishing religious peace in Canada. The pope's decision to entrust this task to a simple, thirty-two-year-old prelate was proof of the trust the pontiff placed in him, though this did arouse no little

229 The bibliography on the issue of the *Manitoba School Act* is incredibly vast. Cf. Louis-Philippe Audet, "Le projet de ministère de l'instruction publique en 1897," *Mémoires de la société royale du Canada* 1 (June 1963), pp. 133–161; Robert Perin, *Rome in Canada. The Vatican and Canadian Affairs in the Late Victorian Age,* University of Toronto Press, Toronto 1990; Stephen T. Rusak, "The Canadian Concordat of 1897," *Catholic Historical Review* 77, 2 (April 1991), pp. 209–234; Matteo Sanfilippo, *L'affermazione del cattolicesimo nel Nord America. Élite, emigranti e Chiesa cattolica negli Stati Uniti e in Canada (1750–1920) [The Affirmation of Catholicism in North America. Elite, Emigrants and Catholic Church in the United States and Canada],* Sette Città, Viterbo 2003.

230 Sir Henri Charles Wilfrid Laurier (1841–1919) was the seventh prime minister of Canada from July 11, 1896, until October 5, 1911.

231 Thomas Greenway (1838–1908) was premier of the Canadian Province of Manitoba from 1888 to 1900.

232 Louis-Philippe-Adélard Langevin (1855–1915), founder of the Sœurs missionnaires oblates du Sacré-Cœur et de Marie Immaculée, was Archbishop of Saint-Boniface in Manitoba from January 8, 1895, until his death. Fr. Elie-J. Auclair defined him "*le lutteur par excellence, le champion qui ne faiblit pas, et, bien souvent, le dominateur qui magnétise et subjugue*" (*Figures Canadiennes,* Éditions Albert Lévesque, Montréal 1933, p. 157). Cf. Robert Choquette, "Adélard Langevin et les questions scolaires du Manitoba et du Nord-Ouest, 1895–1915," *Revue de l'Université d'Ottawa* 46 (1976), pp. 324–344.

233 Fr. Jean-Baptiste Proulx (1846–1904) was the author of *Documents pour servir à l'intelligence de la question des écoles du Manitoba,* Befani, Rome 1896, and *Dans la ville éternelle pendant que se discutait au Canada la question des écoles du Manitoba (Journal de voyage),* Granger-Fils, Montréal 1897.

surprise among Canadian Catholics. These latter were divided on the issue of the accord, some rejecting it entirely and others considering that the compromise was the best that could be obtained under the circumstances. Laurier, for his part, held that the main aim of Merry del Val's presence in Canada was to bring an end to the "inappropriate" clerical interference in political affairs. The more intransigent bishops hoped that the Holy See's envoy would denounce the compromise, convinced, as Msgr. Langevin's close collaborator Fr. Paul Benoit wrote, that the position of the liberal party on the school question could be attributed to English Freemasonry.[234]

The faithful were agitated, and the pontifical delegate, besieged from both sides, defined his presence as a mission of peace, destined, God-willing, to restore unity among Catholics in Canada, to ensure the prestige of the bishops, to consolidate the obedience of the faithful, and to obtain from the government an acceptable solution for everyone. "The Holy Father has placed me under obedience," he wrote to his friend Msgr. Broadhead on the eve of his journey, "and I go with a broken heart, but, I hope, determined to do God's will at any cost. There are moments when I feel the very life going out of me. I consider myself more than incompetent to deal with the critical and passionate situation existing in Canada; the responsibility and the anxiety of the question are enormous."[235] Before arriving in Canada, Merry del Val stopped in New York for several days, a guest of Archbishop Corrigan.[236] When he reached Montreal on the evening of April 1, 1897, the platform at the train station was packed with an enthusiastic crowd, desiring to express their warmest welcome to the pope's representative.[237] "I remember as if it were only yesterday," writes Fr. Auclair,[238] "the arrival of the Papal Delegate in Montreal. A great crowd of people awaited him at the station, foremost among

[234] Dom Paul Benoît (Joseph-Paul-Augustin, 1850–1915), of the Regular Canons of the Immaculate Conception, born and died in France, carried out a missionary apostolate in Canada, collaborating as parish priest of Notre-Dame of Lourdes, with Msgr. Langevin. In 1899, in *L'anglomanie au Canada. Resumé historique de la question des écoles du Manitoba,* he tied the educational dilemma in Manitoba due to the position of the liberal party, in power at that time in Canada, to the work of Freemasonry. He was the author of *La cité antichrétienne au XIXe siècle* (Société générale de librairie catholique, Paris 1885–86, 4 vols.).

[235] Cit. in Buehrle, *Merry del Val*, p. 51; Cenci, *Merry del Val*, p. 78; Forbes, *Merry del Val*, p. 49.

[236] Michael Augustine Corrigan (1839–1902), bishop of Newark in 1873, was named titular archbishop of Petra and coadjutor of New York on October 1, 1880. On October 10, 1885, he became the archbishop of the same See.

[237] Buehrle, *Merry del Val*, p. 52.

[238] Élie-J. Auclair (1866–1946) was a Canadian historian and theologian.

them being the highest ecclesiastical and civil dignitaries of the city. The door of the carriage opened, and he appeared — tall, slim, very handsome, apparently very young, but with a certain air of distinction and gravity which compelled respect."[239]

Merry del Val stayed three and a half months in Canada, welcomed by the political and religious authorities with great kindness and deference. During his stay, a train was even placed at his disposal to visit all the great cities that were diocesan sees. In Montreal, the apostolic delegate convoked the first assembly of bishops and listened to them all with attention. The University of Ottawa conferred on him a doctorate in letters *honoris causa*.[240]

During a formal banquet at the Château Frontenac, in the center of Quebec, a conservative parliamentarian, Louis-Philippe Pelletier,[241] addressed the apostolic delegate in these terms, "Monsignor, you find yourself facing Heaven (the blue of the conservative party) and Hell (the red of the liberal party). Which do you prefer? Could there be any doubt as to your choice between Heaven and Hell?"[242]

The question was clever, but even more astute was the reply by the young prelate who wittily said, "I have not yet had the pleasure of seeing Heaven; I hope never to have the extreme misfortune of seeing the color of Hell; but what I know with certainty is that between Heaven and Hell there is Purgatory and it is precisely in Purgatory that I find myself thanks to your thorny question."[243]

A parish priest present at the banquet, Fr. Joseph Placide Desrosiers,[244] testified, "I can still hear the clear and musical voice with which he answered everyone with equal facility, in French, English, and in Italian. He expressed himself grateful for the welcome extended to him — a welcome which he knew was really given to honour the Pope, whose representative he was. His mission to Canada, he said, was a mission of peace; he felt that he could count beforehand on the good will of all concerned."[245]

239 Buehrle, *Merry del Val*, p. 52.

240 On his journey in Canada, cf. Perin, *Rome in Canada*, pp. 81–88, 113–120. Merry del Val found staunch opposition in Msgr. Louis-Nazare Bégin (1840–1925), archbishop coadjutor (1891) and then archbishop of Québec (1898), made a cardinal by Pius X on May 25, 1914.

241 Louis-Philippe Pelletier (1857–1921) was a Canadian lawyer, journalist, and politician; he was a member of the legislative assembly of Québec from 1888 to 1904.

242 Cit. in Cenci, *Merry del Val*, p. 86.

243 Ibid.

244 Joseph Placide Desrosiers (1869–1934) was parish priest of the Church of St. Brigid in Montréal.

245 Buehrle, *Merry del Val*, pp. 52–53; Cenci, *Merry del Val*, p. 87.

Catholics in Quebec were known for their loyalty to Rome. During the pontificate of Pius IX, a group of Pontifical Canadian Zouaves had fought to defend the borders of the Papal State and for the rights of the Holy See. Merry del Val counted on this "ultramontane" spirit, which he shared. Before entering into the details of the complex political and religious situation, he asked the Canadian bishops and laity to recognize in him the pope's representative and to respect that authority, whatever his decision might be.

The task was arduous. In a report to Rampolla of April 3, 1897, Merry del Val wrote, "It is quite true that the bishops are unanimous on the foundations of the issue, but are absolutely divided on the way of proceeding. They produce the most extraordinary anomalies and exaggerations which cannot be defended ... The state of souls is such at this moment that any word of mine or word from the bishops with my approval would only ignite the passions and would become, to use a vulgar expression, a political 'platform' in the coming elections."[246]

Due to the excessive workload and nervous tension, Merry del Val fell seriously ill toward the end of his mission with a high fever. He was cared for in the great hospital of the *Soeurs Grises*, the Sisters of Charity of Montreal, of which he was to become cardinal protector.

Returning to Rome, finally, the pontifical delegate delivered to Leo XIII his Report on Canadian Affairs.[247] On the basis of the information he received, Leo XIII published the encyclical to the Canadian bishops *Affari vos*, on December 8, 1897.[248] In this document, the pope criticized the law concerning education approved by the State of Manitoba and reiterated the need to guarantee young Catholics religious education in conformity with Catholic doctrine, but urged the Canadian bishops to accept the compromise and to seek to improve it. The Holy See praised Catholic resistance against the education law of Manitoba, but lamented the divisions among Catholics and invited them to act "with zeal and prudence." Concerning the concessions, he argued that, "wherever the law or administration or the good dispositions of the people offer some means of lessening the evil and of warding off some of the dangers, it is absolutely expedient and advantageous that they should make use of them and derive all the benefit possible from them."[249]

[246] Archive of the Postulation, ff. 6944–6950.

[247] Report of Msgr. Delegato, in AA.EE.SS., 1897, 100.

[248] Leo XIII, Encyclical *Affari vos*, December 8, 1897, https://www.vatican.va/content/leo-xiii/en/encyclicals/documents/hf_l-xiii_enc_08121897_affari-vos.html. Cf. also AAV, *Epistolae ad Principes. Positiones et Minutae*, vol. 133, ff. 222r-273v; vol. 138; and vol. 141, fasc. B.

[249] Leo XIII, *Affari vos*, nos. 8–9.

In the encyclical, furthermore, Leo XIII stated that the apostolic delegate he had nominated with the instruction to "make a careful survey of the situation and to report upon it to us, he has with fidelity and ability fulfilled the task we imposed upon him"[250] As Fr. Javierre observed, "No one failed to note the importance of the praise for the management on the part of the apostolic delegate included in the text of Leo XIII's encyclical. The trust and approval expressed by the pope were profligate."[251]

The political approach of Leo XIII, unlike that of Pius IX, was to privilege relations with nation states rather than with the local episcopate. The excessive interference by Canadian clergy in politics rendered relations between Rome and Ottawa difficult, and the pope's recommendation to Catholics was to accept the compromise. Msgr. Merry del Val's visit had as one of its immediate consequences the establishment of a permanent apostolic delegation to the Holy See in Canada, although the situation remained tense. On August 3, 1899, Leo XIII named Msgr. Diomede Falconio as successor to Merry del Val.[252] His task was to sooth disagreements between the bishops and the political authorities of Canada. Unfortunately, the new delegate was unsuccessful in securing the educational rights of Catholics, in particular those of French speakers, and in 1902 was sent instead to the United States, while the burning issue of Catholic education in Canada would return to the desk of a new secretary of state under the pontificate of Pius X.

President of the Academy of Ecclesiastical Nobles

During his mission in Canada, Msgr. Merry del Val proved not only his diplomatic abilities, but above all his fidelity to the indications received by the pontiff. Leo XIII entrusted him with another delicate task in 1898, appointing him to inspect the Pius College in Rome, which had been founded in 1852 at the behest of Pius IX to welcome converts from Anglicanism and English priests.[253] Based on Merry del Val's report, Leo XIII decided to reconstitute the college for all aspirants to the priesthood of Anglo-Saxon origins, entrusting it henceforth to the patronage

250 Ibid., no. 3.

251 Javierre, *Merry del Val*, p. 68.

252 Diomede Falconio (1842–1917), archbishop of Gaeta (1893) and later of Acerenza (1895), was named apostolic delegate in Canada on August 3, 1899, and on September 30, 1902, apostolic delegate to the United States. Pius X made him a cardinal on November 27, 1911.

253 Mary Mechtilde, "The Beda," *American Catholic Historical Society* 57, no. 4 (December 1946), pp. 222–234.

of the Venerable Bede, the great English saint whom Leo XIII was about to proclaim a Doctor of the Church in a *motu proprio* of December 29, 1898.[254] Merry del Val was a contributing editor to the document.

On July 6, 1898, the pope appointed Merry del Val as consultant to the Congregation of the Index.[255] This prominent dicastery had universal authority in the review and eventual condemnation of books to be inserted into the catalog of books whose reading and possession were prohibited.[256] In his capacity as consultant, Monsignor Merry del Val urged the condemnation of Fr. Isaac Thomas Hecker's[257] "Americanism," which advocated a general evolution of faith and the Church's accommodation to the demands of modernity.[258] In a letter to Cardinal Vaughan of July 5, 1899, Merry del Val denounced "Americanism," "to use the name which Mr. O'Connell has given it, tho' it is no more American than English, French, German and Italian."[259]

The young prelate also contributed to the drafting of the *Joint Pastoral Letter on the Church and Liberal Catholicism* by Vaughan and the bishops of the Westminster province.[260]

In the correspondence he had in those years with Archbishop Vaughan, Merry del Val criticized the scientist George Mivart[261] and the writer and journalist Wilfrid Ward.[262] "In some respects I consider Ward's action more harmful

254 The Venerable Bede (673–735) was an Anglo-Saxon monk and historian who lived in the Benedictine monastery of St. Paul in Wearmouth, England, and in Jarrow, Northumberland. On November 13, 1899, Leo XIII decreed that the feast of St. Bede the Venerable with the title of *Doctor Ecclesiae* should be celebrated by the entire Catholic Church on May 25. The college dedicated to his honor would henceforth bear the name *Pontificio Collegio Beda*.

255 AAV, *Spoglio Merry del Val*, busta 3, n. 222.

256 The Congregation of the Index was established in 1571 by St. Pius V to examine suspicious works, with the aim of safeguarding the sacred deposit of Catholic faith and morals. In 1917, its duties passed entirely to the Holy Office.

257 Thomas Isaac Hecker (1819–1888), born to German immigrants, a Protestant convert, after entering the Redemptorists, left the order in 1858 to establish the Missionary Society of St. Paul the Apostle in New York state, of which he was the superior from 1871. Cf. Joseph McSorley, *Father Hecker and His Friends*, Herder Book, St. Louis 1952.

258 Merry del Val to Vaughan, April 2, 1896, in Gary Lease, *"Odd Fellows" in the Politics of Religion. Modernism, National-Socialism and German Judaism*, De Gruyter, Berlin-New York 1995, p. 56.

259 Merry del Val to Vaughan, July 5, 1899, in Lease, *Odd Fellows*, p. 57.

260 David G. Schultenover, *A View from Rome. On the Eve of the Modernist Crisis*, Fordham University Press, New York 1993, pp. 138–143.

261 George Jackson Mivart (1827–1900), English biologist and naturalist, convert to Catholicism in 1844, accepted most of Darwin's theories on evolution. He was later excommunicated. Cf. John Root, "The Final Apostasy of St. George Jackson Mivart," *The Catholic Historical Review* 71, no. 1 (1985), pp. 1–25. Cf. Merry del Val to Vaughan, January 10–11, 1900, in Lease, *Odd Fellows*, p. 57.

262 Wilfrid Ward (1856–1916) was an English journalist and biographer, director of the *Dublin Review* from 1906 to 1915. Together with his friend Friedrich von Hügel, they are is defined as "the two

than Mivarts, because it steadily weakens all the screws and prepares the way for many more Mivarts in the future."[263] He confided to a friend that Ward taught "an unhealthy doctrine, but nonetheless is always able to wriggle away saying that he is reproposing the doctrine of Newman whom he represents." Despite this, he always treated the Englich journalist cordially, avoiding direct controversy with him.

In September 1899, the young prelate was in Bedfordshire, England, in the country home of his uncle, Count Torre Diaz. He was asked to write a few lines in an album, where Cardinal Vaughan had responded to the same request in these simple words, *The best will do*.[264] Msgr. Merry del Val wrote after him:

The best will do, if best it be.
What is the best? Can you define?
Others call best what you think worst—
Which shall prevail, your best or mine?
While thus our views of what is best
Do ever change, a voice divine
The real best to us declares,
God is the best, your best and mine.

Thoughts about his future, in which he always envisaged himself tied to the apostolate in England, assailed the mind of Rafael Merry del Val, for whom Leo XIII had other plans. During that same summer, the president of the Academy of Ecclesiastical Nobles, Msgr. Castracane degli Antelminelli, passed away.[265] Leo XIII immediately thought of naming Merry del Val as his successor and, on October 23, 1899, the young prelate left the Vatican to reenter the institution he had left eight years earlier as a student, now as its president.[266]

According to the practice followed at that time, the president of the Academy was bestowed with episcopal dignity. Hence, Merry del Val, six months after his nomination, was nominated titular archbishop of Nicaea on April 19,

leading lay English Catholic thinkers of their generation" (Michael de la Bedoyère, *The Life of Baron von Hügel*, J. M. Dent, London 1951, p. 292).

263 Merry del Val to Vaughan, June 17, 1900 in Lease, *Odd Fellows*, p. 59.

264 Buehrle, *Merry del Val*, p. 62; Forbes, *Merry del Val*, p. 55.

265 Filippo Castracane degli Antelminelli (1851–1899) was named titular archbishop of Edessa of Osroene in 1895, and president of the Pontifical Ecclesiastical Academy.

266 AAV, *Spoglio Merry del Val*, busta 3, n. 230.

1900.[267] Soon afterward, on May 6, he received episcopal consecration through the hands of Cardinal Secretary of State Rampolla del Tindaro in the Spanish national church of Santa Maria in via Monserrato.[268] Various archbishops and bishops were present, as well as the diplomatic corps to the Holy See and a large representation of the Roman aristocracy and of the Pontifical Academy of Ecclesiastical Nobles. His parents attended the ceremony in tears, seated in the front row. On March 8, 1899, he wrote to an English nun who had been unexpectedly transferred to another house of her order, "I could not fail to remember the words you so aptly quoted to me: '*Je suis où Dieu veut que je sois, je fais ce que Dieu veut que je fasse,*' ['I am where God wishes me to be, I do what God wishes that I do.'] and I prayed for you as you had done for me. We must indeed hope that, with God's grace, the latter words of the quotation may be true of both of us in every way."[269]

The young man carried out without enthusiasm but with extreme diligence the unexpected task that the pope had entrusted to him. Under Merry del Val, the Academy underwent a formative modernization, but also a thorough plan of pastoral commitment and spiritual renewal.[270] The new president instituted a two-year course of diplomatic studies that included ecclesiastical diplomacy, history of relations between Church and State, international law, political economy, diplomatic style, and languages.[271] The formation of students was not limited, however, to diplomatic specialization. Some were sent to chapels around the Roman countryside to celebrate Mass, hear confessions, and teach catechism. Others went to educational institutions to celebrate Mass, teach catechism, and preach the spiritual exercises.[272]

The president of the Academy was the first to observe scrupulously the rule of the community. In the morning, the students always found him first in the chapel, and it was Msgr. Merry del Val who read the meditation points, choosing texts with the greatest spirit and piety. Under his presidency, the young Marquis

[267] Ibid., n. 235.

[268] Cardinal Rampolla del Tindaro was aided by Edmond Stonor, titular archbishop of Trabzon, and by Guglielmo Pifferi O. S. A., titular bishop of Porfireone and assistant to the Pontifical Soglio.

[269] Forbes, *Merry del Val*, p. 53. The quote is from St. Claude de la Colombière and appears often in the words of Cardinal Merry del Val. Cf. also Forbes, *Merry del Val*, pp. 32–133.

[270] Regoli, "Merry del Val e l'Accademia dei nobili ecclesiastici," pp. 146–147.

[271] *Regolamento per gli studi speciali della Pontificia Accademia de' Nobili Ecclesiastici*, op cit. in AA.EE. SS., *Stati ecclesiastici*, Pos. 1232, fasc. 391, Rome 1900, f. 29r-v. The rule was approved by Leo XIII on June 12, 1900.

[272] Cenci, *Merry del Val*, p. 103; Regoli, "Merry del Val e l'Accademia dei nobili ecclesiastici," p.147.

Nicola Canali of Rieti was admitted.[273] On his behalf, Merry del Val requested Msgr. Angeli, the pope's personal secretary, to grant him a reduction of the monthly board.[274] From that time on, the young Nicola Canali was thoroughly devoted to his superior, displaying throughout his life an absolute fidelity.

Msgr. Beniamino Nardone later recalled that Msgr. Merry del Val had a "very familial" way of directing the Academy. "He was exemplary in communal activities, from which he never absented himself, and he even participated in recreation with us. We were taken by the benevolence he indiscriminately showed to all. He loved sports, played billiards with us, and was always the best shot."[275] At times he would take the young men horseback riding, confiding to Nardone, who marveled at his abilities, that he used to ride often.

The Conquest of Souls

The demands on the new president of the Academy were intense and, mainly, they seemed a distraction from the missionary vocation he still hoped to pursue; he was still young, and it was not too late for his life to take a pastoral turn. Meanwhile, as of 1893, his father was in Rome as Spain's ambassador. The Roman nobility at the end of the century was divided between the "black" aristocracy, faithful to the pope, and the "white" aristocracy, which sided with the House of Savoy. These positions were reflected in social life as well. The Lancellotti princes, faithful to the Church, closed the doors of their palace until the signing of the Lateran Accords, while other families threw them open to the new sovereigns. All, however, white, black, and gray, gathered for the evening stroll in their carriages along the main avenue to Piazza del Popolo and the Pincian Hill, in an exhibition of rivalry and livery.

In Rome, the aristocracy was still a landed class with immense holdings peppered with villas and estates, and many of its members allowed themselves

273 Nicola Canali (1874–1961) was ordained priest on March 31, 1900. He concluded his training at the Academy of Ecclesiastical Nobles, and became secretary to Card. Merry del Val and member of the personnel of the Secretariat of State on September 1, 1903. He was promoted to substitute for General Affairs on March 21, 1908 and domestic prelate of His Holiness on the following March 23. He was only a priest when Pope Pius XI raised him to the rank of cardinal in the consistory on December 16, 1935. In 1940, he was named cardinal protector of the Equestrian Order of the Holy Sepulcher in Jerusalem and Grand Master on December 25, 1949, until his death. He was the last cardinal never to have been a bishop, before Pope John XXIII issued the motu proprio *Cum gravissima* on April 15, 1962, declaring that all cardinals must first receive episcopal consecration.

274 AAV, *Spoglio Merry del Val*, busta 3, n. 249.

275 *Informatio*, p. 214.

to be tempted by the idea of easy gains. The Italian authorities had undertaken a policy of urbanization with the aim of constructing new public buildings. New neighborhoods arose, new roads, new buildings, furnished with all the conveniences, while all sorts of speculators descended upon Rome from the north.

In 1866, Prince Rodolfo Boncompagni Ludovisi, owner of the splendid Villa Ludovisi, struck a deal with the City of Rome and the *Società Generale Immobiliare* to subdivide the entire terrain of his villa, involving in the speculation his brother-in-law, Prince Paolo Borghese; Prince Emilio Altieri, commander of the Pontifical Noble Guards[276]; and the Marquis Gerolamo Theodoli, brother of Cardinal Augusto Theodoli.[277] "A financial crisis struck Rome in 1899," recalled the Marquis Alberto Theodoli, "and swept away the fortunes of the Borghese and Boncompagni with whom my father and his brothers had collaborated.... As a result, France closed the line of credit for Italian banks and the latter were no longer able to help the Roman noblemen, who had begun their venture with such audacity and courage. They had the misfortune of belonging to the black aristocracy, against which the anticlerical parties waged relentless war. And so the Borghese, Boncompagni, and Theoldi were ruined. But they paid their debts to the last cent. Meanwhile, profiteering developers descended on Rome from every part of Italy and made vast fortunes after the crash of the Roman Bank."[278]

The Altieri family which, as the young calvary official Hubert Lyautey recalled, was a "black world, the center and fulcrum of papal fidelity," was one of the families engulfed in this affair.[279] Among the most assiduous participants in the whilst games every Friday at Palazzo Altieri in Piazza del Gesù were Cardinal Serafino[280] and Cardinal Vincenzo Vannutelli,[281] Roman diplomats and aristocrats.

276 Prince Emilio Altieri (1819–1900), married to Beatrice Archinto, was the father; Paolo Altieri (1849–1901) was husband of Princess Matilde von Urach; and his two sisters were Laura, wife of Ugo Bonocompagni, and Cristina, wife of Girolamo Theodoli.

277 Augusto Theodoli (1819–1892), of the Roman noble family, was made a cardinal in the consistory of June 7, 1886.

278 Alberto Theodoli, *A cavallo di due secoli*, La Navicella, Rome 1950, p. 23. Senator Alberto Theodoli (1873–1955) was the son of Gerolamo Theodoli and Cristina Altieri.

279 *Lettres de jeunesse*, Grasset, Paris 1931, p. 370. Hubert Lyautey (1854– 1934), officer in the colonial troops, was War Minister during the First World War, marshall, and member of the French Academy.

280 Serafino Vannutelli (1834–1915), alumnus of the Academy of Ecclesiastical Nobility, was made titular archbishop of Nicaea in 1869 and then sent to Central and South America as apostolic delegate. Leo XIII then sent him as nuncio to Brussels (1875) and Vienna (1880) and made him a cardinal on March 14, 1887. He was later the prefect of the Congregation of the Index (1893), prefect of the Congregation of Bishops (1896), and secretary of the Holy Office (1903–1908).

281 Vincenzo Vannutelli (1836–1930), brother of the above, was also an alumnus of the Academy of Ecclesiastical Nobles. In 1875, he was named pro-substitute and in 1876 substitute for the secretary

Also in regular attendance was the father of our Monsignor, the representative of the Spanish government to the Holy See. Maria Theodoli recalls, "The Spanish ambassador Merry del Val was charming, refined, and brilliant, and he deplored the life of perfect recluse that his son the priest was leading, at the time director of the Academy of Ecclesiastical Nobles. My grandmother was saddened not to have met him and insisted that his father bring him along. One evening, I can still see it, the Monsignor accompanied his family. The father gestured as if to take him by the collar, saying, 'See, princess, how this hermit must be led!'"[282]

This testimony dispels any notion one might have of an inclination toward worldliness in the young Monsignor who, given his father's position and his own innate refinement, had ample opportunity to make a splendid appearance in the Roman salons frequented by so many prelates. Msgr. Merry del Val never once took part at the sumptuous receptions given by his father at the embassy, and never once did he leave the refectory of the Academy at mealtime to dine with his family at Palazzo di Spagna, despite the insistence of his parents.[283] Those who knew him during this period testified, "He lived only for his work and was never to be seen in the receptions of high society, unless there was good to be done. Even at functions hosted by his father, the Spanish ambassador to the Holy See, he was rarely to be seen, and this, only to obey the desire of the pope, whom he so loved; from his demeanor it was easy to perceive that he attended reluctantly, finding himself a fish out of water."[284]

Msgr. Merry del Val's lifelong aspiration was to win souls, to work for their eternal salvation. On his horizon, reminisced his brother Pedro, "one sun alone was resplendent: zeal for the salvation of souls."[285] The Monsignor's social life was wholly guided by his apostolic spirit, mainly focused on the English and American residents or visitors of Rome. In a memoir compiled after his death, we find the names of forty non-Catholics of English background who were

of state. Titular archbishop of Sardi (1880), he was sent as nuncio to Lisbon (1883) and made a cardinal on June 23, 1890. He was later prefect of numerous congregations.

282 Maria Theodoli de Luca, *Mi ricordo … ho visto*, Garzanti, Milan 1939, p. 75.

283 Cenci, *Merry del Val*, p. 102.

284 Mother Maria de Raymond di S. Veronica Giuliani, "Memorie del fruttuoso apostolato esercitato dal venerato e santo compianto Em.mo Cardinale Merry del Val nel monastero di Santa Maria Riparatrice in Roma dal 1893 al 1903, scritte il 28 marzo 1930" [Memories of the fruitful apostolate exercised by the venerable and holy deceased Eminence Cardinal Merry del Val, in the convent of Santa Maria Riparatrice in Rome from 1893 to 1903, written on March 28th, 1930] in Cenci, *Merry del Val*, p. 392 (pp. 391–406).

285 Flores de Lemus, *El fulgor de una purpura*, p. 192.

patiently instructed, baptized, and received into the Church by him over a period spanning just ten years, from 1894 to 1904.[286]

In 1877, Mary Potter founded the Little Company of Mary to care for the sick and assist the dying.[287] The foundress took as her model Mary at the foot of the Cross on Calvary. The name of the institute, the Little Company of Mary, was inspired by Potter's devotion to St. Louis Marie Grignon de Montfort. Beginning in 1893, these English sisters, known familiarly as the Blue Sisters, enjoyed the religious and spiritual assistance of the young Monsignor, who gave them conferences many times, led them in spiritual exercises, and received the vows of some of them.[288] One religious of this institute recalled him preaching in English during Lent in 1895, in the church of San Silvestro in Capite: "His sermons were always set on highly spiritual subjects; his preaching on the Passion of Our Lord and on the Most Holy Virgin of Sorrows was often very moving."[289] When the archbishop fell gravely ill with typhoid in July 1901 and was bedridden for about a month in the Spanish embassy, he was assisted by two sisters of the Little Company of Mary, who were edified by his patience to which they attributed his recovery, by God's grace.[290]

Other religious sisters, too, benefited from the spiritual assistance of the young Monsignor. Among these were the English sisters belonging to the Institute of the Poor Handmaids of the Mother of God, founded by Maddalena of the Sacred Heart,[291] who had opened a house in 1886 in Via San Sebastianello next to Piazza di Spagna, at the foot of the Spanish Steps.

Another field of his apostolate during these years was in the convent of Santa Maria Riparatrice in Via dei Lucchesi.[292] Mother Maria de Raymond of St.

286 Cenci, *Merry del Val*, p. 378.

287 Mother Mary Potter (1847–1913), English woman, founded the Sisters of the Little Company of Mary, also known as the Blue Sisters, in 1877. She died in Rome on April 9, 1913, after having received from Cardinal Merry del Val a special blessing from Pope Pius X. She was proclaimed venerable on February 8, 1988. Her remains were transferred in 1997 to the cathedral of Nottingham.

288 Cenci, *Merry del Val*, p. 383.

289 Ibid., pp. 384–385.

290 Ibid., p. 474.

291 Frances Margaret Taylor (1832–1900), in religion Mother Magdalen of the Sacred Heart, born in England of Anglican parents, after her conversion founded the Poor Servants of the Mother of God in 1868. She was proclaimed venerable on June 12, 2014. Their generalate is still in Via S. Sebastianello.

292 The Congrégation des Soeurs de Marie Réparatrice was founded by the Belgian noble lady Emilie d'Oultremont d'Hooghvorst (1818–1878), in religion Mother Maria of Jesus, with the mission of "consecrating themselves totally to Mary for the reparation of offenses against God and the evil men cause through their sin." The foundress was beatified by John Paul II on October 12, 1997, and her remains lie in the Church of Santa Croce and Bonaventura, annexed to their convent in Via dei Lucchesi, Rome.

Veronica Giuliani,[293] a religious in this institute who knew Merry del Val from London, recalled how he began his mission in their house in Via degli Artisti in 1893, teaching the Protestant men and women of English and American colonies who wanted to embrace the Catholic religion.[294] "Many are the conversions that the grace of God worked through him, especially between 1893 and 1903, for in this period, being at the Pontifical Academy of Ecclesiastical Nobles, he lived near our new convent in Via dei Lucchesi: this allowed him to come even daily to give the necessary instruction to the Protestants preparing for the abjuration."[295]

In 1896, the Methodist Episcopal Church opened a branch in Rome in Via Venti Settembre and distributed invitations to its meetings.[296] In 1899, at the urging of Leo XIII, Fr. Pio De Mandato founded the Work of the Preservation of the Faith, with the declared objective of combating Protestant propaganda in Rome.[297] He was aided in the development of this initiative by Merry del Val. Another institution of which Merry del Val was the cornerstone was the Work of Christian Doctrine, founded in 1901 in Prati di Castello by Evangelina Caymari. This endeavor, officially approved by Piux X in 1905, focused on the religious education of children by means of a group of lay catechists involved in preparing children for the sacraments in parishes.[298] Merry del Val would remain Caymari's confessor until his nomination as secretary of state.

Among the many converts accompanied by Merry del Val was a minister of the Anglican Church, Arthur Stapylton Barnes, who made his abjuration in 1895

293 Gwendaline de Raymond (1853–1932), in religion Mother Maria di Santa Veronica Giuliani, born in Florence of an Irish noble family, met Msgr. Merry del Val in 1887 during his journey to London, where the sisters had a house. After returning to Rome in 1890 until her death on January 28, 1932, (and not March 28, 1930, as Dal-Gal writes), she saw him for spiritual direction. Her brother, Msgr. Reginald de Raymond, who died in 1925, was a canon in St. Peter's and apostolic protonotary.

294 Madre Maria de Raymond di S. Veronica Giuliani, "Memorie," in Cenci, *Merry del Val*, pp. 391–394.

295 Ibid., p. 392. Abjuration of heretical or schismatic beliefs was part of the process of being restored to communion with the Catholic Church; see Code of Canon Law of 1917, c. 2314.

296 Pio De Mandato, *Errori spacciati per le vie di Roma dai protestanti metodisti e da altri pretesi evangelici. Osservazioni di D.M.P. [Errors Passed Off on the Streets of Rome by Methodist Protestants and by Other So-Called Evangelicals. Observations by D. M. P.]*, Tipografia Giachetti, Prato 1896.

297 In 1881, the apostasy of the priest Enrico Campello (1831–1903) was confirmed, who presumed to have founded an Italian National Church with the support of English Protestants. In 1902, Campello was reconciled with the Church. Cf. the entry by Mario Themelly, DBI, vol. 17, pp. 479–481; Maria Paiano, "Combattere con tutti i mezzi l'eretica setta straniera: antiprotestantesimo e questione nazionale nell'Opera per la Preservazione della Fede in Roma" [Combat by All Means the Heretical Foreign Sect: Anti-Protestantism and the National Question for the Preservation of the Faith in Rome], *Rivista di Storia e Letteratura religiosa* 51, no. 2 (2015), pp. 275–305.

298 Cf. Evangelina Caymari, *Sinite parvulos: nel XXV dell'Opera del Catechismo ai fanciulli delle Parrocchie di Roma — 1901-1925*, Arti Grafiche Pompeo Sansaini, Rome 1926.

in the presence of Msgr. Merry del Val, received his First Communion from Leo XIII, and later became a priest.[299] There was also William Lucas-Shadwell, an English conservative received into the Catholic Church along with his wife in 1902, in the private chapel of a Roman convent.[300] There were Mildred Haseltine and Ethel Bronson, wives respectively of the two brothers, princes Ludovico and Giambattista Rospigliosi.[301] Some years later, it was Mary Gayley, an American who had married Count Giulio Senni and settled in Rome.[302]

Among the names not to be forgotten is that of the Swedish Lutheran Maria Elisabeth Hesselblad, who converted to Catholicism and arrived in Rome in 1904, gravely ill, to offer her life like St. Bridget for the conversion of Sweden, separated from the Roman Church.[303] She was miraculously healed and founded the Order of the Most Holy Savior of St. Bridget. She was assisted in this by Cardinal Merry del Val, who defined her "the most extraordinary woman in Rome."[304]

In 1898, Merry del Val journeyed to Newnham Paddox in Warwickshire, the ancestral house of the Count of Denbigh and of the Feilding family, to be

299 Arthur Stapylton Barnes (1861–1936), minister in the Anglican church, educated at Eton, converted in 1895 in the hands of Cardinal Merry del Val and received his First Communion from Leo XIII. In 1898, he was ordained a Catholic priest and in 1904 made chaplain to Pius X. He was the author of erudite works on the tomb of St. Peter and of a collection of documents concerning Anglican ordinations, *The Popes and the Ordinal* (1897). He was the first priest to be Catholic chaplain at the universities of Cambridge and Oxford. His successor was Msgr. Ronald Knox. His niece was the writer Mary Barnes Hutchinson (1889–1977); his nephew James Strachey Barnes (1890–1955), also a Catholic convert in 1914, became general secretary of the *Centre international d'études sur le Fascisme* (Cinef) based in Lousanna, on which, cf. Claudio Maria Mancini, *La vita e le carte del maggiore James Strachey Barnes R.F.C.*, Vecchiarelli Editore, Manziana (Rome) 2022.

300 William Lucas-Shadwell (1852–1915) was a conservative English politician and member of parliament from 1895 to 1900.

301 Mildred Haseltine (1879–1946), wife of Prince Ludovico Rospigliosi (1881–1917); and Ethel Bronson (1870–1924), wife of Prince Giambattista Rospigliosi (1877–1955). "I understood from my mother and from my aunt Ethel Bronson that the main cause of their conversion was the attraction that the Servant of God exercised through his life shrouded in a aura of holiness and above all that special charity and understanding that at times Protestants do not find in others," (Deposition of Prince Guglielmo Rospigliosi in *Informatio*, p. 228). Ludovico Rospigliosi, commander of the Pontifical Guard, Lieutenant of the 4th Cavalry Squadron of Genoa, died in Pozzuolo del Friuli in 1917.

302 Mary Gayley (1884–1972), daughter of a steel magnate, married Count Giulio Senni in 1907 in New York. The couple settled in Grottaferrata. The Rose Garden on the Aventine Hill in Rome is attributable to Mary Gayley, inaugurated in 1932.

303 Mary Elisabeth Hesselblad (1870–1957), a Swedish Lutheran, nurse and later director of the Roosevelt Hospital in New York, after travelling in Belgium in 1901, converted to Catholicism and, falling gravely ill, decided to await her death among the Carmelite nuns living in the home where St. Bridget of Sweden died on July 23, 1375, in Piazza Farnese, Rome. Recovering, she obtained from Pius X the commission of renewing the ancient Order of the Sisters of the Most Holy Savior, founded by St. Bridget. She was proclaimed blessed by John Paul II on April 9, 2000. Cf. Marguerite Tjader, *La donna più straordinaria di Roma*, Tip. Poliglotta Vaticana, Rome 1975.

304 Ibid, p. 5.

present at the ordination of the young Basil Feilding, of whom he had been the confessor and spiritual director in Rome.[305] Msgr. Merry del Val nourished great hopes for the young cleric, whose father had turned his house into a fervent center of Catholic life, but the English priest died prematurely at the age of thirty-three.

The Conversion of Sir Esmé Howard

Another important conversion was that of a young English diplomat, Sir Esmé Howard, belonging to an Anglican branch of the most illustrious English Catholic family, that of the Dukes of Norfolk.[306] In spring 1898, Howard came to Rome to ask the hand of Lady Isabella, daughter of Prince Sigismondo Giustiniani Bandini,[307] whom he had met three years earlier, but to whom he had never dared to express his sentiments.[308] He was received in the "red sitting room" of their prestigious palace in Corso Vittorio Emanuele, where Lady Isabella, after having heard his proposal of marriage, replied that she would gladly marry him but only on condition that he converted, because her religion was the most important thing in the world to her and represented the foundation of family unity.

Esmé Howard was not a practicing Anglican and the young princess suggested he resolve his doubts with Msgr. Merry del Val, who had studied in England and was "a special favourite" of Pope Leo XIII.[309] Howard recounts in his memoirs that he met the prelate in the Vatican where "he lived in two rooms on the top floor of the Vatican Palace, commanding a most magnificent view over the city of Rome and the campagna beyond to the Alban hills on the south and the Sabine mountains on the east and northeast."[310] Merry del Val listened in silence to Howard's

305 Basil Feilding (1873–1906) was the son of Rudolph Feilding (1823–1892), VIII Earl of Denbigh, a convert to the Catholic Church in 1850. One of his sisters, Sr. Clare Feilding (1868–1895), a Sister of Charity, died a missionary in China. On the Feilding family, cf. Beard, *Faith and Fortune*, pp. 63–75.

306 Esmé William Howard (1863–1939), I Baron Howard of Penrith, was British ambassador to the United States from 1924 to 1930. His grandfather was Lord Henry Howard-Molyneux-Howard, younger brother of Bernard Howard, XII Duke of Norfolk. Cf. vol. 1 of his autobiography, *Theatre of Life, 1863–1905*, Hodder and Stoughton, London 1935; and B. J. C. McKercher, *Esmé Howard: A Diplomatic Biography*, Cambridge University Press, Cambridge 1989, revised ed. 2006.

307 The Giustiniani Bandini were among the Roman families whose ancestors had married English aristocracy. Prince Sigismondo Giustiniani Bandini (1818–1908) was, on his mother's side, Count of Newburgh, Viscount Kynnaird, Baron Levingstone, and equal heir of Scotland.

308 Esmé Howard, "A Roman Courtship," *The Atlantic Monthly* 156 (September 1935), pp. 257–266; reprinted in *Theatre of Life*, pp. 233–244.

309 Howard, *Theatre of Life*, p. 235.

310 Ibid, p. 236.

lengthy remonstrances with the Catholic Church and patiently, that day and the following days, responded to every question and clarified every doubt.[311]

> My lessons, if I can call them so, covered a period of three or four weeks, generally lasting an hour in the morning.
>
> As soon as, with Monsignor Merry del Val's help, I had gone over all the well-known texts in support of the doctrine of the real Body and Blood of Our Lord actually being in the bread and wine of the Eucharist in accordance with His promise to remain with His Church on earth for ever; after I had studied the sacrifice of the Mass and seen how this differed from the purely human services of other churches, I felt that this was the loadstone that would draw me irresistibly into the arms of the Church. Surely nothing so spiritual and at the same time so genuinely tangible could have been " invented " by any mere man....
>
> So at Mass, which I began now to attend frequently, these thoughts filled my mind; I worshipped there the presence of Jesus the Son of God and rejoiced to think that I was about to be privileged to be one of the millions who could so worship Him, all in the same way and with the same words, no longer a member of a mere national Church, dependent on questions of latitude and longitude for what I was to hold as truth.
>
> I look back to that time as the happiest of my life, and to those hours spent with Monsignor Merry del Val as undoubtedly the most supremely useful I have ever passed.
>
> For him I have always felt the liveliest gratitude and affection. His was a really wonderful personality, combining nearly all the most essential qualities of a Christian priest and an entirely human hearted man with a keen mind and much erudition. He had a quite exceptional charm of manner and a great gift for various languages—Spanish and English were his father and mother tongues. He spoke also perfect Italian and French and, I believe, excellent German, so that he was well equipped for his post when, some years later, Pius X appointed him his Cardinal Secretary of State at an unusually early age. He desired no honours; indeed, he most of all wished to be a parish priest in some poor district in England.
>
> When the time came for me to return to England, I told both Monsignor Merry and my fiancée, for matters had by now proceeded so far between us that I could call her so, that I would but read a few

311 Ibid, pp. 237–243.

more books recommended to me by the Monsignor and then make my "submission" to the Church.[312]

The Death of Leo XIII

On December 24, 1899, Leo XIII inaugurated in St. Peter's Basilica the Holy Year that would open the new century.[313] The pope decided to render the event even more solemn through the celebration of two moments of Eucharistic adoration: the first during the night of 1899 that closed the nineteenth century and the second during the night of 1900 that inaugurated the twentieth century, extending the Jubilee indulgence also to those not able to come to Rome on pilgrimage.

On March 2, 1900, Leo XIII celebrated his ninetieth birthday. The French painter Benjamin Constant was asked to paint a portrait.[314] He came to the Vatican for an entire week during which the pope, between audiences, posed docilely, telling him, "Above all, don't make me look too old; don't paint too many wrinkles!"[315]

The end of an era was coming, however. On July 29, 1900, King Umberto I of Savoy was assassinated, shot with a revolver in Monza by an anarchist. His son Vittorio Emanuele III ascended to the throne,[316] accompanied by his wife Princess Elena of Montenegro.[317] Six months later, on January 22, 1901, Queen Victoria of England died in Osborne House on the Island of Wight, with her entire family at her bedside and Kaiser Wilhelm II, her grandson, holding her pillow. Thanks to the marriages of her many children and grandchildren, she had become "the Grandmother of Europe," with descendants who sat on the thrones of an ever-growing number of European kingdoms. On that same day, the Prince of Wales ascended to the throne, taking the name Edward VII.[318] His

312 Ibid, pp. 257–244.

313 Cf. Rosario F. Esposito S. S. P., *L'enciclica Tametsi futura e la notte eucaristica del secolo*, San Paolo, Rome 2000.

314 Jean-Joseph Constant, called Benjamin Constant (1845–1902), not to be confused with the famous historian, was one of the most famous portrait artists of the late nineteenth century.

315 François D. Mathieu, *Les derniers jours de Léon XIII et le conclave de 1903, par un témoin*, Victor Lecoffre, Paris 1904, p. 6.

316 Vittorio Emanuele III of Savoy (1869–1947) reigned from 1900 to 1946, when he abdicated and was succeeded by his son Umberto II, the last king of Italy. Cf. Gioacchino Volpe, *Vittorio Emanuele III. Dalla nascita alla corona d'Albania [Vittorio Emanuele III. From his Birth to the Albanian Crown]*, with an introduction by Domenico Fisichella, Marco Editore, Lungro di Cosenza 2000.

317 Elena di Montenegro (1873–1952) was the queen consort of Italy until the abdication of Vittorio Emanuele III, on May 9, 1946.

318 Edward VII (1841–1910), king of Great Britain and Ireland and emperor of the Indies, was the first-born son of Queen Victoria and Prince Albert of Saxe-Coburg. Cf. Gordon Brook-Shepherd, *Lo zio d'Europa Edoardo VII [The Uncle of Europe Edward VII]*, Rizzoli, tr. Milano 1977.

coronation as King of the United Kingdom and of the British Empire took place in Westminster Abbey on August 9, 1902. The ceremony had been set for June 26 but was postponed due to the urgent operation the king had to undergo, afflicted by an abdominal abscess. All England held its breath for three days, and when danger had passed, Msgr. Merry del Val, who had been appointed on June 3 as papal representative to the coronation,[319] intoned a solemn *Te Deum* at the Brompton Oratory. Many important personages at that moment in London attended, including the Canadian prime minister, Sir Wilfrid Laurier.[320]

Msgr. Merry del Val did not love these assignments and continued to aspire to a quite different apostolate. On December 18, 1901, in a letter posted from the Ecclesiastical Academy to Leo XIII, Merry del Val asked, "Most Blessed Father, prostrate at the feet of Your Holiness, and with sentiments of filial submission, I come bearing the intimate desire of my heart and asking in this moment a grace that, to my eyes, is the greatest I could obtain from Your Holiness' paternal benevolence toward the most humble of his sons. To date I have asked nothing for myself from Your Holiness, and behold the first grace, and perhaps the last that I implore: I would like Your Holiness to grant me the faculty of renouncing the office I occupy, however unworthily, in the Ecclesiastical Academy, and to allow me to return to Trastevere or any other neighborhood in Rome; where, free from any other responsibility, I might consecrate myself entirely to the priestly ministry among the people, and at the same time, work for the spiritual good of foreigners in Rome, and especially those of the English language."[321]

The Holy See still needed his help, however. In April 1903, King Edward VII came as guest to the King of Italy at the Quirinale,[322] asking for an audience with the aged Leo XIII, now in the twilight of his existence. In view of this, a private audience was arranged between the British ambassador to the Quirinale, Sir Francis Bertie, and Msgr. Merry del Val.[323] Ambassador Rennell Rodd tells in his memoirs that, thanks to the friendship between the diplomat Esmé

319 AAV, *Spoglio Merry del Val*, busta 3, n. 264.

320 Javierre, *Merry del Val*, p. 77.

321 Cenci, *Merry del Val*, p. 107; Archive of the Postulation, ff. 305–306.

322 The Quirinale Palace was built in 1583 by Pope Gregory XIII as a papal summer residence. It served as the location for several papal conclaves and housed the central offices responsible for the civil government of the Papal States until September 1870 (when these latter were occupied militarily and annexed to the Kingdom of Italy), at which point the palace became the official residence of the kings of Italy and, afterwards, of the presidents of the Italian Republic.

323 Sir Francis Bertie (1844–1919), First Viscount Bertie of Thame, was British ambassador to Italy (1903–1905) and then to France during the First World War.

Howard (personal friend of Edward VII) and Msgr. Merry del Val, they were able to resolve all the difficulties that hindered the sovereign's visit in the Vatican.[324] On the English side, every precaution was taken to avoid any indiscretion toward the pope. For example, the offer by the Italian government to grant King Edward an escort of cuirassiers along the route from his embassy to the Vatican was refused, since an escort by the Kingdom of Italy "would have rendered the visit too official and also offensive to the pope." Thus, the king limited himself to going to the Apostolic Palace in a closed carriage without any escort.

Meanwhile, on March 3, 1902, the twenty-fifth anniversary of his coronation, Leo XIII opened a Jubilee Year with a solemn Mass celebrated in St. Peter's in the presence of more than fifty thousand people and representatives from all the European powers.[325] According to the expression of Cardinal Gibbons, the pontiff appeared to be "the most popular man in Europe."[326] The pope, whose reign was the second longest in history, was at the apex of his prestige, but his death was approaching. On March 19, he published the encyclical *Annum ingressi* to raise a hymn of thanksgiving to God for the many years of his pontificate.

After retracing the centuries-old history of the wars waged against the Church by anti-Christian forces, the pope raised a heartfelt protest against the stripping of the Church's temporal sovereignty, which had been to him the object of so much affliction and concern.[327]

The discourse pronounced by Prime Minister Combes of France,[328] on March 21, 1903, was a sort of ultimatum to the Holy See in light of the coming breach of the Concordat.[329] The last politician Leo XIII received, by an exceptional favor, at the end of June, was former French prime minister, Jules Méline,

[324] Sir James Rennell Rodd, *Social and Diplomatic Memories, 1902–1919,* Edward Arnold & Co., London 1925, pp. 27–28. James Rennell Rodd (1858–1941) was ambassador to Rome from 1908 to 1919.

[325] T'Serclaes, *Le pape Léon XIII,* pp. 408–414.

[326] Cit. in Aubert, "Leone XIII: tradizione e progresso," in Augustin Fliche and Victor Martin (eds.), *Storia della Chiesa,* 36 vols., vol. 22/1, trans., Edizioni Paoline, Cinisello Balsamo (Milano), p. 104.

[327] Leo XIII, Apostolic letter *Annum ingressi,* March 19, 1902, ASS, vol. 34 (1901–1902), pp. 513–532, https://www.tfp.org/annum-ingressi-apostolic-letter-of-pope-leo-xiii/.

[328] Émile Combes (1835–1921) was a seminarian in Albi, but in 1862 lost his faith, married, and was intitiated into the Lodge *Les Amis réunis* of the Grand Orient, of which he became Master, then entered militant politics. Elected to the French Senate in 1885, he became its vice-president (1893) and the following year, succeeded Waldeck-Rousseau as prime minister, Interior Minister and Minister of Worship, from June 7, 1902, to February 24, 1905. In "*Le combisme, apogée de l'anticléricalisme français,*" cf. Alec Mellor, *Histoire de l'anticléricalisme français,* Mame, Tours 1966, pp. 381–407. "*Émile Combes, au pouvoir, c'est tout le programme élaboré de longue date dans les Convents du Grand Orient qui se déclenche*" (ibid, p. 385).

[329] Leo XIII, *Annum ingressi,* ASS, vol. 34 (1901–1902), p. 666.

to whom he said, "I have sincerely attached myself to the Republic, but this has not stopped the current government from disregarding my clearly expressed sentiments. It has unleashed a religious war that I deplore and that does more harm to France than to religion."[330]

Leo XIII continued to handle the administrative and political affairs of the Church right to the end of his life. On July 3, 1903, he was stricken with pleurisy that gradually worsened. Despite this, he continued working and receiving members of the Sacred College. His extraordinary memory and iron will supported his weakening body.

For sixteen days, wrote Georges Goyau, "in the Church and outside the Church, throughout Christendom and outside Christendom, the august twilight that lingered on the hills of the Vatican held everyone in suspense; for sixteen days, men woke up and observed in that direction, between heaven and earth, the white ghost that wanted to die standing."[331]

On July 17, the pontiff received Extreme Unction, though he remained lucid, so much so that he called for Msgr. Rinaldo Angeli, to whom he had asked to oversee the printing of verses he had composed in honor of St. Anslem of Aosta, the glory of the Benedictine order, and thereafter to deliver his composition to the abbot primate of St. Anselm, Fr. Ildebrando of Hemptinne.[332]

The pope's sickness worsened over the following days, and on July 20, his closest collaborators were called to his bedside. After a long agony, at a quarter to four in the afternoon, the pontifical head physician, Giuseppe Lapponi, indicated to Cardinal Serafino Vannutelli to begin recitation of the prayers for the dying. At 4:02 p.m., as the prayers were ending, Leo XIII breathed his last. He was ninety-three years old, and twenty-five of those years were spent as pope. The official news of the Roman pontiff's death was declared by the Vatican at 7:30 p.m. that same evening. Half an hour later, at 8:00 p.m., the Foreign Ministry of the Austro-Hungarian Empire sent its ambassador to the Holy See, Count Nikolaus Szécsen, a coded telegram containing instructions for the conclave, suggesting the "veto" of Cardinal Mariano Rampolla del Tindaro.[333]

330 Lecanuet, *L'Église de France*, vol. 4, p. 486.

331 Georges Goyau, *Le Pape Léon XIII*, Perrin, Paris 1903, p. 8.

332 Adriano Pierconti, *Da Leone XIII a Pio X. Diario dal giorno 3 luglio al 9 agosto 1903 [From Leo XIII to Pius X. Diary from July 3rd to August 9th, 1903]*, Cooperativa Poligrafica Editrice, Rome 1904, p. 121.

333 Friedrich Engel-Janosi, *Oesterreich und der Vatikan*, Styria Verlag, Graz 1960, II, p. 25. Count Nikolaus Szécsen von Temerin (1857–1926) was the Austrian ambassador to the Holy See from 1901 al 1911.

3

Secretary of State Under Pius X

Msgr. Merry del Val, Secretary of the Sacred College

Leo XIII expired at four in the afternoon on Monday, July 20, 1903. The Cardinal Chamberlain Luigi Oreglia di Santo Stefano,[334] called in to verify his death, pronounced the traditional formula: *Vere Papa mortuus est* (The pope is truly dead). Oreglia, the last survivor of the cardinals created by Pius IX, accumulated in his person the offices of Chamberlain of the Holy Roman Church and Dean of the Sacred College. It fell to the chamberlain to preside over the period of the *Sede vacante* and to the dean of cardinals to convene the new conclave.

On July 16, while Leo XIII lived his final hours, Msgr. Alessandro Volpini died suddenly, struck by apoplexy.[335] The pope had just named him (on July 9) secretary of the Sacred College. In this function, Volpini would have become secretary of the conclave upon the death of the pontiff.[336] The cardinals now had to choose his successor.

334 Luigi Oreglia of the Barons of Santo Stefano (1828–1913) was consecrated bishop in 1866 and sent as apostolic nuncio first to Belgium and then to Portugal. Pius IX made him a cardinal on December 22, 1873. He was chamberlain from March 27, 1885 until his death and on November 30, 1896, became dean of the College of Cardinals.

335 Msgr. Alessandro Volpini (1844–1903), rector of the seminary of Montefiascone, became secretary of Latin Letters in 1884 and then of Letters to Princes. In this role, he was the writer of Leo XIII's most important acts, among which those regarding the school question in Canada and on Anglican ordinations.

336 On the conclave of 1903, there are many contemporary documents, among which the reports of Msgr. Merry del Val, secretary of the conclave, published by Luciano Trincia, in *Conclave e potere politico. Il veto a Rampolla nel sistema delle potenze europeo (1887–1904)* [*Conclave and Political Power. The Veto against Rampolla in the System of European Powers (1887–1904)*] Studium, Roma 2004, pp. 249–280; the diary of Fr. Maurice Landrieux, "Le conclave de 1903. Journal d'un conclaviste," *Études* 299 (Oct–Dec 1958), pp. 157–183. Also Cardinal Mathieu, hidden behind the pseudonym "un témoin," had published in *Revue des Deux Mondes* on March 5, 1904, a report on the events under the title "Les derniers jours de Léon XIII et le conclave de 1903" (pp. 241–285). The French diplomatic correspondence was used by Hubert Néant, "Diplomatie et conclave à la veille de l'élection de Pie X (1897–1903)," *Revue d'histoire diplomatique* 16 (1963), pp. 97–111; while for the German diplomacy of Prince Bernhard von Bülow, cf. "Denkwürdigkeiten: vom Staatssekretariat bis zur Marokko (1930–1931)" and Austrian diplomacy by F. Engel-Janosi, "L'Autriche au conclave de 1903," *Revue belge de philologie et d'histoire* 29, fasc. 4 (1951), pp. 1119–1141. Among the best reconstructions are: Carlo Snider, *I tempi di Pio X*, vol. 2: *L'episcopato del cardinale Andrea*

Msgr. Alberto Serafini later certified what Cardinal Oreglia had said to him, also confirmed by Cardinal Agliardi, "The Most Eminent Cardinals, in the first gatherings held, were divided into two equal camps in favor of two candidates," both chosen in 1901 by Secretary of State Rampolla del Tindaro, as his direct collaborators: Msgr. Giacomo della Chiesa[337] and Msgr. Pietro Gasparri; the former who had been his personal secretary in Spain and had nominated him substitute to the secretary of state; the latter who had three years of experience as apostolic delegate in the Republics of Ecuador, Peru, and Bolivia and who was secretary of the Congregation of Extraordinary Ecclesiastical Affairs.[338] "Unfortunately, despite the efforts made by Card. Oreglia, they remained intractable in their positions, without foreseeing the possibility of a change in the voting in one direction or the other. At that point, it came to Card. Oreglia's mind to propose the provisional choice of someone outside the circle of traditional candidates for the office, leaving the future pontiff free to confirm the chosen prelate or to nominate another."[339]

The name proposed by Cardinal Oreglia was that of Msgr. Rafael Merry del Val, who obtained the approval of those present. When the Cardinal Chamberlain quietly communicated to Merry del Val his intention of proposing his name to the Sacred College as secretary of the future conclave, the Monsignor, dismayed, tried to dissuade him, arguing his need to leave Rome for health reasons. But Oreglia was impassible and, during the first plenary congregation after the pope's death, the cardinals welcomed his proposal by a large majority and elected Msgr. Merry del Val secretary of the conclave.[340]

C. Ferrari, Neri Pozza, Vicenza 1982, pp. 1–129, based on the *Secret Report* of Card. Ferrari; and Christian-Philippe Chanut, *L'élection de saint Pie X*, Sicré Éditions, Paris 2003.

337 Giacomo della Chiesa (1854–1922) was ordained in 1878 and, after studying at the Academy of Ecclesiastical Nobles, followed Msgr. Rampolla del Tindaro to Spain as his personal secretary where he was later sent as nuncio. When Rampolla was named secretary of state, Della Chiesa became his minute keeper and in 1901 the substitute to the secretary of state. Pius X named him archbishop of Bologna and in 1914 made him a cardinal. On September 3, 1914, he was elected Pope with the name Benedict XV. He governed the Church until January 22, 1922. For a summary, cf. the entries by Gabriele De Rosa, EP, vol. 3, pp. 608–617, DBI and vol. 8 (1966), pp. 408–417.

338 Cf. R. Regoli, "Congrégation pour les Affaires ecclésiastiques extraordinaires," in Christophe Dickès (ed.) *Dictionnaire du Vatican et du Saint-Siège*, Robert Laffont, Paris 2013, pp. 309–312; idem, "Decisioni cardinalizie ed interventi papali. Il caso della Congregazione degli Affari Ecclesiastici Straordinari," in Laura Pettinaroli (ed.), *Le gouvernement pontifical sous Pie XI. Pratiques romaines et gestion de l'universel*, École française de Rome, Rome 2013, pp. 481–501.

339 Testimony of Msgr. Alberto Serafini in *Processus Informativus Ordinarius*, vol. 2, *Sessio* LIII, pp. 395–396.

340 Cenci, *Merry del Val*, pp. 115–116. The candidacy of Della Chiesa and Gasparri having failed, Card. Oreglia proposed three possibilities: Msgr. Merry del Val, Msgr. De Lai, and Msgr. Giustini. Merry del Val was elected with twenty votes in favor and eight against.

The office he assumed was demanding, all the more because twenty-five years had passed since the last conclave in which Leo XIII had been elected, and it was necessary to review the complex organization of the event. Merry del Val enjoyed widespread esteem, even though it was not easy to pigeonhole him. The weekly *Illustrazione Italiana*, defining him a "Rampollian creation," described him thus: "He has great commitment and an iron will, knows the main languages perfectly, and is very courteous, almost suave, insinuating; he is agile, terse, swarthy of complexion and hair, and quick-sighted; he is a perfect portrait, in physique and morals, of his protector Mariano Rampolla del Tindaro."[341]

In reality, the nomination of Merry del Val appeared to many as a first defeat of the Rampollian coalition and a clear signal to the former secretary of state of Leo XIII, too self-sure of his own papal aspirations.[342] On the other hand, Cardinal Oreglia's opposition to Leo XIII's politics and to the views of his secretary of state was no secret to anyone. It was said that in his first act as Chamberlain, namely that of officially recognizing the death of the pope, calling him three times by his baptismal name, and three times tapping the deceased with a silver hammer on his forehead, Oreglia called him in a barely intelligible voice and struck him very lightly on the forehead, responding to those who asked him about his manner of proceeding saying, "I feared he might reawaken!"[343]

Great Maneuvers in the Vatican

Cardinal Oreglia, who had spent his entire life in the Curia, did not have a preferred candidate. His only goal was to bar the way to Rampolla del Tindaro, who appeared as the great favorite because his partisans were the most organized, and he enjoyed strong political support. As early as March 25, 1899, French Foreign Minister Delcassé[344] had sent a coded telegram to his ambassador in Rome, writing, "We must support the candidacy of Rampolla in the most effective way possible."[345] The

341 *Ilustrazione Italiana*, November 1, 1903, p. 363.

342 Jean de Bonnefon, special envoy of the French journal *L'Éclair*, arrived in Rome at the beginning of July, 1903. He judged the nomination of Merry del Val as "*un échec personnel pour le cardinal Rampolla*" (*L'Éclair*, July 27, 1903, cit. in Chanut, *L'élection de saint Pie X*, p. 128).

343 Francesco Zanetti, *Da un Papa all'altro. Il conclave*, Istituto Editoriale S. Michele, Rome 1939, p. 18.

344 Théophile Delcassé (1852–1923) was French foreign minister from 1898 to 1905.

345 Cited in Pierre Blet, "La diplomatie française et l'élection de Pie X," in *Pro Fide et Iustitia. Festschrift für Agostino Kard. Casaroli zum 70. Geburtstag*, Duncker und Humblot, Berlin 1984, p. 552 (pp. 549–562).

French government, recalled Fr. Landrieux, a "conclavist"[346] of Cardinal Langénieux,[347] "is working actively for Rampolla. All the French cardinals were invited by Delcassé to confer with him before departing. Russia supports this."[348]

Even earlier, in a report addressed to Chancellor Hohenlohe on April 8, 1896, the Prussian ambassador, Bernhard von Bülow, wrote that within the Curia, in light of a conclave, two alignments were facing off: the first, pro-French, guided by Cardinal Rampolla, and the second, pro-German, directed by Cardinal Galimberti.[349] But not long after, on May 7, 1896, after a sudden illness, Luigi Galimberti had died in his Roman residence in Via dei Prefetti, perhaps poisoned as some thought.[350] "At the conclave," wrote Raffaele De Cesare, "Galimberti would have had a notable part to play, perhaps the most important."[351]

What is certain is that Galimberti's death weakened the anti-Rampollian party in light of a future conclave, and consensus around the former secretary of state — to whom cardinals created in the previous sixteen years under Leo XIII owed their nomination — broadened. During the conclave of 1903, Rampolla presented himself with the support of five Spanish cardinals,[352] seven French,[353] ten or so cardinals of the Curia, and a good number of Italians, especially from central and southern Italy.

346 Conclavists were the secretaries and the servants, either ecclesiastics or laity, usually in pairs, whom each cardinal had the faculty of bringing to the conclave.

347 Benoît-Marie Langénieux (1824–1905), bishop of Tarbes in 1873, was promoted the following year to the See of Reims, governing for over thirty years. In 1886, Leo XIII made him a cardinal.

348 Landrieux, "Le conclave de 1903," p. 161; Blet, "La diplomatie française et l'élection de Pie X," pp. 556–557.

349 Bülow a Hoenlohe, April 6, 1896, in Christoph Weber, "Italien, Deutschland und das Konklave von 1903. Eine Studie zur Kirchenund Bündnispolitik der Dreibundmächte," *Quellen und Forschungen aus italienischen Bibliotheken und Archiven* 57 (1977), p. 245 (pp. 199–260).

350 Arturo Carlo Jemolo, "Italia, Francia e Vaticano," *Rassegna storica toscana* 13 (1967), p. 82 sgg. (pp. 81–89).

351 Raffaele De Cesare, "La politica di Leone XIII e i cardinali Rampolla e Galimberti," *La Rassegna Nazionale* 2 (1912), p. 198 (pp. 193–203).

352 The five Spanish cardinals were Salvador Cassanas y Pagés, bishop of Barcellona; José María Martín Herrera y de la Iglesia, archbishop of Santiago di Compostella; Sebastián Herrera y Espinosa de los Monteros, archbishop of Valenza; Ciriaco María Sancha y Hervás, archbishop of Toledo and patriarch of the West Indies; José de Calasanz Félix Santiago Vives y Tutó, cardinal of the Curia.

353 The seven French cardinals were Pierre Hector Coullié, archbishop of Lyon; Guillaume-Marie Labouré, archbishop of Rennes; Benoît-Marie Langénieux, archbishop of Reims; Victor-Lucien Lecot, archbishop of Bordeaux; François-Désiré Mathieu, cardinal of the Curia, former archbishop of Toulouse; Adolphe-Louis Perraud, bishop of Autun; François-Marie Richard de la Vergne, archbishop of Paris.

On the opposite front, besides Cardinal Oreglia and the brothers Serafino and Vincenzo Vannutelli, inveterate anti-Rampollians, were the cardinals of the Central Empires,[354] coordinated by Cardinal Georg von Kopp, president of the German bishops.[355] In effect, Rampolla's tenure as secretary of state had marked one of the lowest moments in relations between the Holy See and Austria and Germany. Count Revertera,[356] imperial ambassador to the Holy See, wrote that Rampolla, "pious, severe with himself, diffident, hidden and extremely violent in his sentiments, represents with all the defects of the Sicilian character, the ascetic type of Prince of the Church."[357] The Sicilian Cardinal was not welcome in Vienna because he was accused of favoring schismatic Russia, especially in the Balkans, to the harm of the Danubian Monarchy, and of encouraging republican democracy to the detriment of European monarchies.[358]

The archbishop of Capua, Cardinal Alfonso Capecelatro,[359] of great repute, was convinced that the clash would occur not between two political currents, but between two lines, "one political, the other exclusively religious."[360] Archbishop of Milan Andrea Carlo Ferrari[361] shared this opinion, writing in his diary in those days, "The pope we need now needs to have a more clearly pastoral tone than a political one, and this cannot be Card. Rampolla, or at least it can be found much better in Card. Sarto."[362]

354 The Austrian cardinals were Anton Josef Gruscha, archbishop of Vienna; Johannes Baptist Katschthaler, archbishop of Salzburg; Jan Kniaz Puzyna, prince-bishop of Krakow; Lev Skrbensky-Hriste, prince-archbishop of Prague; Kolos Ferenc Vaszary von Vaszar, archbishop and primate of Hungary; the Germans were Antonius H. Fischer, archbishop of Cologne; Georg von Kopp, prince-bishop of Breslau; Andreas Steinhuber, prefect of the Congregation of the Index.

355 Georg von Kopp (1837–1914), bishop of Fulda (1881), later prince-bishop of Bresau (1887), made a cardinal by Leo XIII on January 19, 1893, was a member of the Chamber of Lords of Prussia (from 1886) and of the Diet of Austrian Silesiaria ca, 1914.

356 Count Friedrich Revertera von Salandra (1827–1904) was the Austro-Hungarian ambassador to the Holy See from 1888 to 1901.

357 Engel-Janosi, "L'Autriche au conclave de 1903," p. 1128.

358 Ibid, pp. 1129–1130.

359 Alfonso Capecelatro (1824–1912) was named archbishop of Capua by Leo XIII (1880) and later made a cardinal at the consistory of July 27, 1885. From 1890 he was the head of the Vatican Apostolic Library.

360 *Le Constitutionnel*, July 31, 1903, in Chanut, *L'élection de saint Pie X*, pp. 94–95.

361 Andrea Carlo Ferrari (1850–1921), of the diocese of Parma, made bishop of Guastalla in 1890 and transfered to the See of Como in 1891, was made a cardinal in 1894 by Leo XIII and named archbishop of Milan. Cf. the entry by Giuseppe Pignatelli, DBI, vol. 46, pp. 506–512; and the biography by Snider, *I tempi di Pio X*, vol. 2.

362 Snider, *I tempi di Pio X*, vol. 2, pp. 88–89.

Leo XIII had confided to the historian Ludwig von Pastor, "Gotti or Sarto will be my successor."[363] Rather than Sarto, on the eve of the conclave there was more talk about Cardinal Girolamo Maria Gotti, an austere Carmelite monk, prefect of the Congregation for the Propagation of the Faith.[364] The Austro-Germanic cardinals had decided to converge their votes on him, and he enjoyed the support of Cardinal Oreglia as well. Cardinal Serafino Vannutelli was also a possible candidate, favored by the Italian government but not in the good graces of Vienna. The match was set, and the election of Rampolla was not a foregone conclusion. Nine general congregations were held before the conclave in the Consistory Hall, allowing the cardinals arriving in Rome time to get to know each other.

During one of these congregations, Cardinal Lecot,[365] archbishop of Bordeaux, asked Cardinal Sarto in French, "Of which diocese are you the bishop, Your Eminence?" "I do not speak French," replied the patriarch of Venice. The archbishop of Bordeaux repeated his question in Latin. Cardinal Sarto replied, "*Sum patriarca Venetiae.*" Lecot thought it pertinent to add, "*Non loqueris gallice? Ergo non es papabilis, siquidem papa debet gallice loqui*" (You do not speak French? Therefore, you are not *papabile,* because a pope must speak French). Cardinal Sarto's reply was ready, as if relieved of a burden: "*Verum est, Eminentissime Domine, non sum papabilis. Deo gratias*!" (True, Most Eminent Lord, I am not papabile. Thanks be to God!)"[366]

The Opening of the Conclave of 1903

The opening of the conclave was set for 8 p.m. on July 31, 1903. Prince Mario Chigi Albani,[367] Hereditary Marshal of the Holy Roman Church, was invited to

363 Ludwig Freiherr von Pastor, *Tagebücher, Briefe Erinnerungen*, ed. Wilhelm Wühr, F. H. Kerle Verlag, Heidelberg 1950: "Gotti oder Sarto wird mein Nachfolger sein" (p. 421).

364 Girolamo Maria Gotti (1834–1916), a Discalced Carmelite, was the provost and Superior General of his order from 1881 to 1899. Leo XIII nominated him titular archbishop of Petra (1892) and made him a cardinal at the consistory of November 29, 1895. «Le cardinal Gotti a été appelé par un de ses amis le "cardinal de marbre, parce qu'il a du marbre le froid, le poli et la solidité." Devant sa candidature, il s'est montré de glace" (Mathieu, *Les derniers jours de Léon XIII et le conclave de 1903*, p. 271).

365 Victor Lecot (1831–1908), bishop of Dijon (1886) and then archbishop of Bordeaux (1890), along with Cardinal Lavigerie, was one of the most ardent defenders of *ralliement*. He was made a cardinal by Leo XIII in 1893.

366 Mathieu, *Les derniers jours de Léon XIII et le conclave de 1903*, p. 267.

367 Prince Mario Chigi Albani (1832–1914), who married Princess Antonietta Sayn Wittgenstein in 1857, participated as Hereditary Marshal of the Holy Roman Church in the conclave of Leo XIII as well as that of Pius X. He was forced, however, to renounce participating in the conclave of 1914 due

appear at 5 p.m. with his court in gala livery in the Sistine Chapel to assume their function as custodians of the conclave.[368] It was his task to ensure that the cloister of the cardinals would in no way be violated, employing the security services of the Swiss Guards, the Palatine Honor Guard, and the Pontifical Gendarmerie. The term conclave is derived from the Latin *cum clave*, indicating a closed space and the severe seclusion imposed on the cardinals with its prohibition of communicating with the outside world until the election has been finished.

At the established hour, the Marshal of the Holy Roman Church, in the traditional black velvet costume of a Roman patrician, escorted by a squadron of Swiss Guards and the commanders of the Pontifical Armed Corps, arranged for the external closure of the doors of the conclave. At 5 p.m., the chamberlain intoned the *Veni Creator* in the Pauline Chapel, to which the cantors responded under the direction of Maestro Fr. Lorenzo Perosi.[369] The procession of cardinals set off toward the Sistine Chapel, while the Noble Guard, under the command of Prince Rospigliosi, rendered them military honors.[370] On both the long sides of the Sistine Chapel, seventy-four chairs stood, all but one of them topped by canopies tapestried in violet. Only the chair of the chamberlain-dean, whose cardinalate pre-existed the reign of the deceased pope, did not bear the symbols of mourning. In front of each chair was a small table and writing instruments. At one end was the altar before the backdrop of Michelangelo's fresco; in the middle were the tables and chairs for the scrutineers.

The cardinals possessing the right to vote were sixty-four.[371] Two were absent due to impediments: the Australian (though born in Ireland) Patrick Moran, archbishop of Sydney, who had not arrived in time;[372] and ninety-year-old Pietro

---

to an illness that would lead to his death soon thereafter. The permanent titular marshals were the princes of Savelli, until the extinction of their house. In 1712, the privilege passed to the Chigi and remained in their possession until 1975, when Paul VI disbanded the role *de facto*. Cf. Niccolò Del Re, *Il Maresciallo di Santa Romana Chiesa custode del conclave*, Istituto Nazionale di Studi Romani, Rome 1962.

368 AAV, Segreteria di Stato, *Morte di Pontefici e Conclavi. Conclave di Pio X*, scatola 14b, n. 3933.

369 Lorenzo Perosi (1872–1956), ordained a priest in 1895, was a prolific composer and, from 1902 until his death, was the director of the Sistine Chapel.

370 Prince Camillo Rospigliosi (1850–1915), commander of the Pontifical Noble Guard, married Elena of the Giustiniani Bandini princes. The titles of this family, after the death of the firstborn Sigismondo, entered the patrimony of the Rospigliosi family.

371 AAV, Secretariat of State, *Morte di Pontefici e Conclavi. Conclave di Pio X*, scatola 14, n. 3917. *Elenco dei cardinali presenti in conclave [List of Cardinals Present in Conclave].*

372 Francis Patrick Moran (December 1830–1911), an Australian, after his priestly ordination in Rome, was named bishop of Ossory in 1872, and archbishop of Sydney in 1885. That same year he was made a cardinal by Leo XIII, Australia's first.

Celesia from Palermo, who was gravely ill.[373] Thus, there were sixty-two electors: seven were French, five Spanish, five Austro-Hungarian, three German, one Portuguese, one Irish, and one Belgian. The only non-European, James Gibbons, the archbishop of Baltimore, came from the United States.[374] The Italian cardinals, thirty-eight of them, made up almost two-thirds of the Sacred College. Since a two-thirds majority was necessary, forty-two votes were needed for election.

On the morning of Saturday, August 1, after Cardinal Oreglia had read the prescriptions of the conclave, each cardinal took the oath: "I call as my witness Our Lord Jesus Christ that I elect him whom before God I think should be elected, and that I will do so also in the *accessus*."[375] After having sworn the oath, each cardinal placed his ballot in the chalice, bowed before the cross, greeted the scrutineers, and returned to his seat.

Cardinal Mathieu[376] noted, "There was an incontestable solemnity to this oath, under the gaze of Michelangelo's terrible Judge, near the abyss into which the painter had cast the despotic cardinals."[377] Cardinal Oreglia, with his powers as Chamberlain, refused the practice of requesting an *accessus*, which would have favored Rampolla. "It was not even used in the last conclave," he said. "It is a manner of voting that is too complicated and gives way to surprises."[378] "In this conclave, there was no *accessus*," wrote Msgr. Merry del Val in his report. "Some cardinals would have preferred this, but His Excellency the Dean and others were opposed, and not without reason. In fact, this form of scrutiny presents serious drawbacks, and it seems that in the future it will have to be abandoned."[379]

373 Pietro (Michelangelo) Celesia (1814–1904), bishop of Patti in exile (1860– 1866), after having participated in the First Vatican Council, was named archbishop of Palermo in 1871 and made a cardinal by Leo XIII in 1884.

374 James Gibbons (1834–1921), born in Baltimore of Irish parents, consecrated bishop in 1869, was named by Pius IX bishop of Baltimore in 1877 and made a cardinal by Leo XIII in 1886. He participated in the foundation of Catholic University in Washington D. C., of which he was the Grand Chancellor in 1897.

375 By the term *accessus* is meant a method of voting within the conclave that allows one to change one's vote after the scrutiny, giving it to one of the candidates that had received at least one valid vote. The *accessus* was abolished in 1904 by Pius X, together with the *ius exclusivae*. Pius X decreed that the *accessus* be substituted with a second vote to be held immediately after the morning and afternoon ballots, creating in this manner two votes in the morning and two in the afternoon.

376 François-Desiré Mathieu (1839–1908) was bishop of Angers (1893), archbishop of Toulouse (1896), and cardinal with the title of Santa Sabina (1899). In 1906, he was elected a member of the Académie française. Cf. E. Renard, *Le cardinal Mathieu, 1839–1908, Angers, Toulouse, Rome. La dernière crise de l'Église concordataire*, de Gigord, Paris 1925.

377 Mathieu, *Les derniers jours de Léon XIII et le conclave de 1903*, p. 274.

378 Mathieu, *Les derniers jours de Léon XIII et le conclave de 1903*, p. 275.

379 Trincia, *Conclave e potere politico*, p. 195.

Destiny had it that the first scrutineer was precisely Cardinal Rampolla del Tindaro. When everyone had submitted his vote and after checking that the number of votes corresponded to the number of voters, the Sicilian cardinal extracted the first ballot, showed it to his two assessors, and read out loud: Cardinal Gotti. It was the first name that rang out in the Sistine Chapel, and it was repeated that morning seventeen times. Cardinal Rampolla read his own name twenty-four times, without betraying any emotion in his voice.[380] Cardinal Sarto, the patriarch of Venice, received five votes. Turning to one of the electors behind him, he said, "The cardinals are having fun behind my back."[381] Cardinal Serafino Vannutelli, for whom his brother Vincenzo had carried out an intense but disastrous propaganda campaign, received only four votes.

Saturday evening, during the second scrutiny, Rampolla received twenty-nine votes, Gotti sixteen, Sarto ten, two each for Richelmy, Capecelatro, and Serafino Vannutelli, and one each for Cardinals Segna and Di Pietro. Rampolla was still far from victory, which required forty-two out of sixty-four electors. "Beginning on Saturday," Mathieu remarked in his notes, "one can see two camps forming, dividing the Sacred College almost equally; one is either for or against Rampolla. Truth be told, there is no other debate."[382]

Prince-Bishop of Breslau Cardinal Kopp reports that, at this point, Cardinal Agliardi,[383] one of Gotti's electors, but above all an adversary of Rampolla, came to him to discuss this impasse and to recommend the candidacy of Sarto.[384] That same evening, Merry del Val wrote in his report, "Card. Puzyna, seeing the majority of votes taken by Card. Rampolla and perhaps troubled by rumors, albeit somewhat exaggerated, considering his election to be certain, decided to act."

380 Vatican Apostolic Archive contains fourteen lists of votes obtained by the cardinals in the conclave of 1903. Cf. Secretariat of State, *Morte di pontefici e conclavi. Appendice*, scatola 39, fasc. 1, busta 8760, ff. 2r-15r. Cf. also scatola 14a, n. 3898, ff. 235r-238r. The first count had the following results: Rampolla 24 votes, Gotti 17, Sarto 5, Serafino Vannutelli 4, Oreglia 2, Capecelatro 2, Di Pietro 2, Agliardi 1, Richelmy 1, Segna 1, Ferrata 1, Cassetta 1, Portanova 1.

381 Ernesto Vercesi, *Tre Papi. Leone XIII. Pio X. Benedetto XV*, Edizione Athena, Milan 1929, p. 171.

382 Mathieu, *Les derniers jours de Léon XIII et le conclave de 1903*, p. 277.

383 Antonio Agliardi (1832–1915), titular archbishop of Caesare and apostolic delegate in the Indies (1885), pro-secretary (1887–1888) and later secretary of the Congregation of Extraordinary Ecclesiastical Affairs (1888–1889), apostolic nuncio in Munich (1889–1893), on May 6, 1893, replaced Galimberti in the nunciature in Vienna. He was later extraordinary envoy in Moscow for the coronation of Nicholas II (1896) and upon his return was made a cardinal.

384 Bülow, "Denkwürdigkeiten," p. 621.

Cardinal Rampolla "Vetoed"

The *ius exclusivae*, or "right to veto," indicated the ancient privilege of some European Catholic sovereigns, exercised numerous times over the course of history, to prohibit the election to the papacy of a candidate displeasing to them.[385] On the eve of the conclave, Cardinal Kopp had gone to Cardinal Rampolla to inform him that the government of Vienna opposed his election and that it was willing, as a last resort, to exercise this privilege against him.[386] But Rampolla, according to Kopp, "evidently hoped he would be elected and considered it to be so certain that he gave no credence to his words."[387]

Cardinal Jan Pawel Puzyna,[388] Bishop of Krakow, had received from the Austrian government the text of Emperor Franz Josef in opposition to Cardinal Rampolla, with the task of reading it in the chapel. Saturday evening, the Archbishop of Krakow, urged by Cardinal Kopp,[389] went to the secretary of the Sacred College, Merry del Val, asking him to announce the imperial decision to the cardinals himself, but the prelate refused vigorously. Puzyna insisted, attempting to place in his hand the text of the declaration. Merry del Val pulled

385 During the conclave of 1681, which elected Pope Innocent XII, French Cardinal Toussaint de Forbin-Janson (1631–1713) spoke openly for the first time of an exclusive right of the crowns of France, Spain, and Austria. H. Néant defined it a privilege that these powers "more in virtue of its use than through a formal act that recognized it" (*Diplomatie et conclave à la veille de l'élection de Pie X*, p. 107). This privilege was abolished by Pius X with the constitution *Commissum nobis* of January 20, 1904.

386 According to Snider, this was not an official veto, but rather a "vote" that left the possibility of retracting a candidacy, making any declaration of exclusivity superfluous (*I tempi di Pio X*, vol. 2, pp. 82–86). Others, like Alberto Belletti, hold that regardless of the more or less official form one might use, it must be considered for all intents and purposes an exercise of *jus exclusivae* (*Veto al conclave. Lo ius exclusivae austro-ungarico contro il cardinal Rampolla [Veto at the Conclave, Ius exclusivae of the Austro-Hungarian Emperor Against Cardinal Rampolla]*, Erreci edizioni, Bologna 2010, pp. 43–44). Cf. also Matteo Lamacchia, "*Ius exclusivae* e conclave: il diritto di veto delle potenze cattoliche nella storia delle elezioni pontificie" ["*Ius exclusivae* and Conclave: The Right to Veto by Catholic Powers Throughout the History of Papal Elections"], *Eunomia. Journal of Studies of Peace and Human Rights* 2 (2018), pp. 105–130.

387 Bülow, "Denkwürdigkeiten," p. 623.

388 Jan Kniaz Puzyna von Kolzielsko (1842–1911), born in Galizia of a Ruthenian noble family, was named titular bishop of Memphis in 1866 and auxiliary Latin archbishop in Lvov. On January 25, 1895, he was promoted to the See of Krakow as prince-bishop and on April 15, 1901, was made a cardinal by Leo XIII. He belonged to the Chamber of Lords in Vienna and to the Diet of Galizia, in Lemberg. Regarding the conduct of Card. Puzyna, cf. also Eduard Winter, *Rußland und die slawischen Völker in der Diplomatie des Vatikans*, Akademie Verlag, Miroslaw Lenart; idem, "Il cardinale Jan Puzyna, un discusso protagonista del conclave del 1903, alla luce della documentazione polacca," in R. Regoli (ed.), *San Pio X. Papa riformatore di fronte alle sfide del nuovo secolo [Cardinal Jan Puzyna, a Controversial Protagonist at the Conclave of 1903, in Light of Polish Documentation]*, Acts on the occasion of the centenary of the death of Pius X (1914–2014), Libreria Editrice Vaticana, Vatican City 2016, pp. 49–63.

389 Bülow, "Denkwürdigkeiten," pp. 621–622.

back his hand, allowing the paper to fall to the ground, which Puzyna was forced to pick up himself.[390] Cardinal Dean Oreglia also refused to communicate the imperial veto to the cardinals.

On the morning of Sunday, August 2, at the start of the third scrutiny, while all were writing their votes, Cardinal Puzyna asked to speak and, in broken Latin, made the following declaration: "It is my honor, being called to this office by a high order, to beg most humbly Your Eminence in the quality of Dean of the Sacred College and Chamberlain of the Holy Roman Church to know and to be informed, and to declare officially in the name of and by the authority of His Apostolic Majesty Franz Josef, Emperor of Austria and King of Hungary, that desiring to make use of an ancient right and privilege, His Majesty pronounces the veto of exclusion against my Eminent Lord Cardinal Mariano Rampolla del Tindaro."[391]

Not everyone understood what Puzyna had said. Cardinal Gibbons later told how Rampolla, seated nearby, asked him, "What did he say?"[392] The Cardinal of Krakow was asked to repeat the reading of his message, which was clearly understood only after Cardinal Cavagnis read it with a clear and firm voice.[393] Amid the general murmur, under Michelangelo's fresco of the Last Judgment, Cardinal Oreglia stood up in turn and made the following declaration: "This communication cannot be accepted by the conclave either officially or unofficially, and it will not be taken into account."

Cardinal Rampolla asked to speak and, with a grave tone of voice and pale countenance, protested in these terms: "I deplore that such a grave offense be brought, not against my person, but insofar as it constitutes a grave attack on matters of a papal election, against the freedom of the Church and the dignity of the Sacred College, by a secular power, and I therefore vigorously protest. As concerns my humble person, I declare that nothing more honorable and more entertaining could have befallen me."[394] Exiting the Sistine Chapel, some of the cardinals remonstrated with the Archbishop of Krakow, saying *puteat te* (shame on you) and the cardinal responded *honor meus.*

390 Pastor, *Tagebücher*, p. 696.

391 The text is found in numerous sources, among which Trincia, *Conclave e potere politico*, p. 275.

392 Engel-Janosi, *L'Autriche au conclave de 1903*, p. 1139.

393 Felice Cavagnis (1841–1906) was rector of the Roman Pontifical Seminary (1888), pro-secretary of the Sacred Congregation of Extraordinary Ecclesiastical Affairs (1896), and cardinal on April 5, 1901.

394 Mathieu, *Les derniers jours de Léon XIII et le conclave de 1903*, p. 281; Landrieux, "Le conclave de 1903," pp. 174–175.

Puzyna came from a Ruthenian princely family that had come into the Latin Rite generations earlier and since 1895 occupied the See of Krakow, an immense diocese that included about 770,000 Catholics. He had been made a cardinal by Leo XIII in the secret consistory of April 15, 1901, but had never concealed his opposition to the Russophile politics of the pope and Cardinal Rampolla.[395] According to the historian Luciano Trincia, the use of the *jus exclusivae,* which the Polish cardinal pronounced on behalf of Emperor Franz Josef, constituted a weapon by means of which the Polish intended to put an end to the ecclesiastical politics of Leo XIII's secretary of state.[396] Puzyna revendicated having acted for the good of the Church, confiding, "My conscience dictated that I not allow the election of Cardinal Rampolla and for this reason I took recourse to the privilege of the 'veto' as the final licit and legal means for blocking his election. I had at heart only the future of the Church, the currents and the direction within the Church. It was I who made use of Austria, and not Austria of me."[397]

The Polish cardinal was indignant at the behavior of Rampolla, whom he characterized as a "little man."[398] Rampolla made it seem that he was surprised by the Archbishop of Krakow's intervention, keeping silent about the fact that he had been informed by him of the matter beforehand, not only of his intention to present the veto, but also of the reasons for this initiative. "Such behavior," comments Miroslaw Lenart, "must have seemed somewhat pathetic and lacking in honor in the eyes of Puzyna."[399]

Puzyna, on the other hand, was described, in the ever-contemptuous tone of Gasparri, as a "poor man," ignorant in Latin.[400] Gasparri did not participate in the conclave, but he belonged to the Rampollian current and could not forgive Puzyna for having paved the way for the election of Pius X, something the Polish cardinal boasted of against his detractors.[401] The rumor according to which

395 A secret (or ordinary) consistory is a formal meeting in which only the pope and cardinals participate, as distinguished from public and semi-public consistories.

396 Trincia, *Conclave e potere politico,* pp. 214–216.

397 Lenart, "Il cardinale Jan Puzyna," p. 60.

398 Ibid, 57.

399 Ibid, p. 59.

400 *Il cardinale Gasparri e la questione romana (con brani delle memorie inedite) [Cardinal Gasparri and the Roman Question (With Passages from Unpublished Works)],* ed. Giovanni Spadolini, Le Monnier, Florence 1972, p. 91. Snider called this judgment "against truth and justice," defining Puzyna "a good bishop truly pious and very zealous" (Snider, *I tempi di Pio X,* vol. 2, pp. 91–92). A reevaluation of his figure was competently made by Msgr. Walerian Meysztowicz, in *La Pologne dans la chretienté. Coup d'oeil sur mille ans d'histoire (966– 1966),* Nouvelles Éditions Latines, Paris 1966, pp. 134–139.

401 Lenart, "Il cardinale Jan Puzyna," p. 54.

Franz Josef had given his veto because of Cardinal Rampolla's affiliation with Freemasonry appears to be unfounded.[402] On the other hand, compromising correspondence with exponents of modernism was discovered among the papers of Leo XIII's secretary of state after his death, as was later made known by Pius X to Baron Ludwig von Pastor on May 30, 1914.[403]

In an extremely tense atmosphere, the cardinal electors decided to proceed with the voting, with the following results: Rampolla twenty-nine votes, Sarto twenty-one, Gotti nine. Rampolla was not increasing, Gotti was decreasing, while Sarto gained ground thanks to the votes of the anti-Rampollian block. At the beginning of the afternoon proceedings, after the recital of the *Veni Creator*, Cardinal Perraud,[404] on behalf of his French colleagues, read a resonating protest against the veto of Puzyna.[405] Perraud's intervention, according to Carlo Snider, "was no less inopportune and regrettable than the Austrian one," because, after the statement of Rampolla, and another by Oreglia, it appeared as a pressing attempty by the French bishops to gain the majority of votes for Rampolla.[406] "His voice fell and was extinguished by the silence of all," writes Cardinal Mathieu's biographer.[407] After Perraud, Cardinal Sarto took the floor to implore his colleagues not to give him their votes; he would never accept the papacy, for which he felt too unworthy.[408]

During the afternoon scrutiny, Rampolla received thirty votes, while Sarto climbed to twenty-four. Neither the veto of Puzyna, nor the protest of Perraud had drawn the majority behind Leo XIII's secretary of state. At this point, the reality of Cardinal Sarto's candidacy began to impose itself on the cardinals, who still had to convince the patriarch of Venice to accept the papacy, however. Cardinal Ferrari, archbishop of Milan, bound to him by old ties of friendship,

402 Equally improbable was the news according to which the Sicilian cardinal had belonged to the O. T. O., a lodge of initiation founded by the "Black Magician" Aleister Crowley. For an overview of the situation, cf. H. Murphy, "Cardinal Rampolla and the 1903 Papal conclave," in *Christian Order* 48 (2007), pp. 52–68; F. Ricossa, "Il cardinale Rampolla era massone? [Was Cardinal Rampolla a Freemason?], *Sodalitium* 33, 1 (February 2007), pp. 5–36.

403 Pastor, *Tagebücher*, p. 598.

404 Adolphe Perraud (1828–1908), ordained in 1855 in the Oratory in France, professor of Church History at the Sorbonne (1865), was bishop of Autun (1874) and cardinal in 1893 (the nomination was made public in 1895). In 1883 he was received into the French Academy. At his death, his position was assigned to Cardinal Mathieu.

405 Perraud, *Journal*, pp. 60–62.

406 Snider, *I tempi di Pio X*, vol. 2, pp. 90–92.

407 Renard, *Le cardinal Mathieu*, p. 400.

408 Mathieu, *Les derniers jours de Léon XIII et le conclave de 1903*, pp. 282–283; Landrieux, "Le conclave de 1903," p. 176; Snider, *I tempi di Pio X*, vol. 2, p. 93.

was put in charge of the work of persuading Cardinal Sarto. In his *Secret Summary of the Conclave*, published by Snider, Cardinal Ferrari recalled the arguments he submitted to Cardinal Sarto to convince him to accept the candidacy. The election of Rampolla, he said, was to be prevented because, in his foreign policy, he would have led Italy into international isolation, and no other candidate besides Sarto seemed suitable to assume the papacy. Cardinal Sarto replied that he felt inadequate for such a burden, but Ferrari pressed him, "If this is the way things stand, how is it you accepted to be a bishop and then patriarch and cardinal? We all say the '*Domine non sum dignus*' everyday and truthfully. And if Your Excellency distrusts his own judgment, why should he distrust the judgment of others?"[409]

At this point, the meeting took a turn that might be defined prophetic. Cardinal Sarto seemed already to foresee what would be the first characteristic of his pontificate, which took place essentially in a climate of incomprehension, if not of deaf hostility among ecclesiastical circles. Responding to Ferrari, he said, "But I shall have my first enemies among those closest to me; the same ones who brought me there I know well, they cannot be benevolent."[410] "Close enemies," replied Ferrari, "we shall always have in plenty, and they shall be the most terrible, because they shall feign benevolence to our face and use the most affectionate courtesy; they shall never wound us in our chest but plant their daggers in our back; and we who are bishops, do we not know this?" The bishop of Milan reminded him of the example of Jesus with Judas in the Cenacle and in the Garden, and with heartfelt words added, "I have not come to beg you, to implore you through the effect of that benevolence with which you have always been so generous to me, without any merit on my part; only love for the Church makes me speak like this, and I speak on behalf of others as well."[411]

Cardinal Giuseppe Sarto did not change his mind and Ferrari left him with "a glimmer of hope and nothing more."[412] That evening, at a meeting of cardinals held in the First Loggia, the archbishop of Milan reported all that Cardinal Sarto had told him but was invited to insist upon his request. The following morning, Monday, August 3, after having celebrated Mass at 5:30 in the Pauline

409 Snider, *I tempi di Pio X*, vol. 2, pp. 99–100.
410 Ibid., p. 100.
411 Ibid., pp. 101–104.
412 Ibid., p. 103.

Chapel, Ferrari returned to Sarto for another attempt at persuasion, but found him even more convinced of his intention, with that "tranquil firmness which can be conquered only with great difficulty."[413]

The Election of Pius X

During the morning session, Rampolla's thirty votes the preceding evening had decreased to twenty-four, while Sarto rose to twenty-seven, placing him at the top of the table. At this point, the seven French electors, seeing the difficulty of having their candidate prevail, as he was clearly regressing, sent to Rampolla a deputation composed of Cardinals Richard, Perraud, and Mathieu, begging him to find the determination to "withdraw nobly and leave them an open field for a practical maneuver. Because, according to his best friends, it is finished."[414] Leo XIII's secretary of state replied that above and beyond his person, there was the question of principle to be sustained, and considered it his duty to maintain his candidacy, also because Cardinal Sarto had made known that he would refuse the pontificate.[415] The French were left with no other option but to insist on Rampolla's candidacy.

Meanwhile, the dean of the cardinals had appointed Msgr. Merry del Val to ask Cardinal Sarto if he wished to persist in his reluctance in accepting the pontificate. He found him in the Pauline Chapel, kneeling on the bare pavement, in front of an image of Our Lady of Good Counsel, holding his head in his hands and crying bitterly. "When I asked if the Cardinal Dean should declare to the Sacred College that he was immovable in his refusal of the pontificate, he replied, 'Tell the Cardinal Dean to do me this favor.'"[416] Msgr. Merry del Val still remembered, "The only words I had the strength to pronounce, and which came spontaneously to my lips were: 'Eminence, take courage, the Lord will help you.' The cardinal stared at me intently with his profound gaze which later, through an admirable disposition of Providence, I would come to know so well, and added simply, 'Thank you, thank you!'"[417] Merry del Val never told anyone

413 Ibid., p. 104.

414 Landrieux, "Le conclave de 1903," p. 178. "On ne comprend pas la conduite de Rampolla. Il n'a rien fait; il a retenu inutilement durant quatre scrutins une trentaine de voix sur son nom; il n'a ni su ni voulu donner aucune direction à ceux qui se sont dévoués pou lui" (p. 179).

415 Snider, *I tempi di Pio X*, vol. 2, pp. 108–109; Trincia, *Conclave e potere politico*, pp. 20–21.

416 *Pii Papae X*, p. 183.

417 Card. Merry del Val, *San Pio X. Un santo che ho conosciuto da vicino [St. Pius X. A Saint I Knew Intimately]*, Fede & Cultura, Verona 2016, p. 7.

that he had been the person to convince the pope, but his role had certainly been decisive and in that moment, at the feet of Our Lady of Good Counsel, a tacit pact was established between the cardinal and the young Monsignor.[418]

This took place around noon on Monday. In the afternoon, there was an intervention on the part of Cardinal Francesco Satolli,[419] formerly a close collaborator with Leo XIII, who said to Cardinal Sarto, "Eminence, one who resists the Holy Spirit compromises his soul. And you who are resisting the voting of the cardinals are resisting the Holy Spirit."[420] Satolli's authority as a theologian renowned for the solidity of his doctrine certainly had an influence on the future pontiff, who probably had already made his decision after his encounter with Merry del Val.

During the scrutiny in the evening of Monday August 3, Sarto's votes went from twenty-seven to thirty-five; those for Rampolla diminished from twenty-four to sixteen; and only six remained for Gotti. At this point, the atmosphere had changed. Everyone knew, as Merry del Val noted, "that Card. Sarto had succumbed to their insistency, and from that moment his election was considered certain, even though that evening he still did not have the majority of votes required by the sacred canons." Cardinal Satolli gave the announcement to the cardinals ready to proceed with the scrutiny, in these words: "Cardinal Sarto, succumbing to the insistency of his colleagues, entrusts his election to Providence."[421]

Rampolla remained obstinate until the end in maintaining his candidacy, but the French cardinals abandoned him and Cardinal Langénieux communicated to Sarto that his confreres, "*sans arrière pensée*," had decided to grant him the seven votes needed to ensure the quota of forty-two necessary for election.[422] During the seventh scrutiny, the votes in favor of Cardinal Sarto were fifty against Rampolla's ten and two for Gotti. The Church had a new pope.[423]

418 Harriet Murphy highlights the supernatural importance that the miraculous image, venerated in the sanctuary in Gennazzano south of Rome, had on the first encounter Cardinal Merry del Val had with Pius X. (*Spiritual Writings*, p. 11).

419 Francesco Satolli (1839–1910) was named archbishop by Leo XIII in 1888, apostolic delegate to the United States in 1893, and cardinal on November 29, 1895. Regarding his actions at the conclave of 1903, cf. Chanut, *L'élection de saint Pie X*, pp. 212–214.

420 Snider, *I tempi di Pio X*, vol. 2, p. 11.

421 Mathieu, *Les derniers jours de Léon XIII et le conclave de 1903*, p. 283.

422 Snider, *I tempi di Pio X*, vol. 2, pp. 115–116.

423 Giuseppe Melchiorre Sarto (1835–1914), ordained in 1858, bishop of Mantua in 1884, was created a cardinal and promoted to the Patriarchal See of Venice by Leo XIII in 1893. He governed the Church as Pius X from 1903 to August 20, 1914. About him cf. among others: P. Girolamo

Cardinal Oreglia asked Cardinal Sarto the ritual question: "*Acceptasne electionem de te canonice factam in Summum Pontificem?*" The Patriarch of Venice, with his eyes full of tears, responded, "*Quoniam calix non potest transire, fiat voluntas Dei*" ["If this chalice can not pass from me, God's will be done," cf. Matt. 26:42]. This was not the response foreseen in the ceremonial, and the Cardinal Chamberlain repeated his question, to which Sarto finally replied, "*Accepto.*" To the second ritual question, "*Quo nomine vis vocari*?" the newly elected replied in Latin, "Confident of the divine protection and that of the holy apostles Peter and Paul and of the holy pontiffs who have been called with the name Pius, above all those who throughout the centuries have fought against sects and the spreading errors, I assume the name Pius X."[424]

Msgr. Merry del Val accompanied him into the Sistine Chapel where the new pope was dressed in the papal habit. The chamberlain left the Sistine Chapel to go to the door of the conclave where Prince Chigi and his men were occupying the great parlor that led to the Royal Hall. The Marshal opened the locks with the symbolic keys, then at the head of a military procession, through corridors flooded with sunlight, he reached the Sistine Chapel where he knelt before the throne of Peter. Pius X invited him to rise and Marshal Chigi gave him the military salute, raising his sword, as did all the high officers of the Pontifical Guard: Prince Rospigliosi, commander of the Noble Guard; Baron Meyer de Schaunsée, commander of the Swiss Guard; Count Camillo Pecci, commander of the Palatine Guard; and Knight Commander Tagliaferri, commander of the Pontifical Gendarmerie.

Dal-Gal, *Pio X il Papa santo*, Libreria Editrice Fiorentina, Florence 1960; Yves Chiron, *Saint Pie X. Reformateur de l'Église*, Courrier de Rome, Versailles 2000; Giampaolo Romanato, *Pio X. Alle origini del cattolicesimo contemporaneo*, Lindau, Torino 2014; Oscar Sanguinetti, *Pio X. Un pontefice santo alle soglie del "secolo breve" [Pius X. A Holy Pontiff on the Threshold of the "Brief Century"]*, Sugarco, Milano 2014; Cristina Siccardi, *San Pio X. Vita del Papa che ha ordinato e riformato la Chiesa, [St. Pius X. Life of the Pope who Reordered and Reformed the Church]*, San Paolo, Rome 2014, with an introduction by Card. Raymond Leo Burke. Of particular interest are the studies by A. M. Dieguez, *L'archivio particolare di Pio X. Cenni storici e inventario [The Particular Archive of Pius X. Historical Notes and Inventory]*, Vatican Secret Archive, Vatican City 2003; A. M. Dieguez and Sergio Pagano, *Le carte del "Sacro tavolo." Aspetti del pontificato di Pio X dai documenti del suo archivio privato [The Papers of the "Sacred Tablet" Aspects of the Pontificate of Pius X from the Documents of his Private Archive]*, 2 vols., Vatican Secret Archive, Vatican City 2006; A. M. Dieguez, *Carte Pio X. Scritti, omelie, conferenze e letture di Giuseppe Sarto. Cenni storici, inventario e appendice documentaria [Papers of Pius X. Writings, Homilies, Conferences and Readings of Giuseppe Sarto. Historical Notes, Inventory and Documentary Appendix]*, Vatican Secret Archive, Vatican City 2010; and Regoli (ed.), *San Pio X Papa riformatore*, cit.

424 Landrieux, "Le conclave de 1903," p. 182.

After this first act of homage by the Sacred College, the secretary of the conclave asked the newly elected pope if he wished to give the solemn blessing outside or inside the basilica. Pius X asked what the opinion of the Sacred College would be. Merry del Val replied that in a congregation held before the conclave, the cardinals had expressed the opinion of following the example of Leo XIII, while leaving full liberty to the new pontiff. Pius X nodded to this response and, at the suggestion of Merry del Val, immediately gave the blessing from the balcony within the Vatican Basilica.[425]

It was Tuesday, August 4, and the basilica was packed with an enthusiastic crowd that shouted, "*Evviva il Papa!* Long live the pope!" Fr. Landrieux described the scene as follows: "When Sarto appeared in the Loggia, serious, emotional and as if crushed under the weight of the burden which he had sought three times to shake from his shoulders, the acclamations doubled. Then, at a signal, the crowd quieted down and, in religious silence, bowed their heads and a strong voice resounded: '*Benedicat vos*!' It was Pius X who, for the first time, blessed his people."[426]

Pope Pius XII recalled, "We who were then at the beginning of our priesthood, already in the service of the Holy See, can never forget our intense emotion, when, in the afternoon of that August 4, 1903, from the Loggia of the Vatican Basilica, the voice of the Cardinal Dean announced to the multitude that the conclave — so noteworthy for many reasons! — had placed its choice in the Patriarch of Venice, Giuseppe Sarto. The name Pius X was then pronounced for the first time before the world's attention. What would that name signify for the papacy, for the Church, for humanity? While today, after nearly half a century, we review in spirit the succession of momentous and complex occurrences that have filled it, our forehead bows and our knees bend in admiring devotion to the divine counsels, whose mystery is slowly unveiled to human eyes as it is gradually fulfilled over the course of history."[427]

Cardinal Merry del Val recounted the following: "I went to him once again that evening to carry out the last act as secretary of the conclave, to obtain his signature of the letters of participation at his election to be sent to the sovereigns. I entered begging to excuse myself for importuning him at such a late hour, when he must have been quite exhausted by the emotions of the day. I found him reciting

425 *Pii Papae X. Positio*, p. 184.

426 Landrieux, "Le conclave de 1903," p. 181.

427 Pius XII, Discourse on June 3, 1951, in *Discorsi e Radiomessaggi*, vol. 13, p. 128.

the breviary in his cell, for the pontifical apartments were still sealed. And as I stated my concern for his tiredness, he looked at me with great sweetness and said, 'Yes, yes, and you, Monsignor, are you not tired? I saw how much you exerted yourself in these days.' And I, quite moved by this attention, replied that this was not important. After this, he asked me how he should sign the letters; and I replied that he must sign with the formula 'Pius Papa X,' and so he did. As I gathered the papers, I kneeled to take my leave, having terminated my office as secretary of the conclave, asking for his blessing. Then he turned to me and exclaimed, 'Monsignor, do you wish to abandon me?' 'No, Holy Father,' I replied, 'but I have terminated my task.' Then he added, 'Remain with me: I have not yet decided anything. I do not know what I shall do; for the moment I have no one. Remain with me as pro-secretary of state: then we shall see. Do me this favor.' And a little later he sent me his autographed photo, on which he gave me this title of Pro-Secretary of State."[428]

Secretary of State

One of the first and most significant decisions of the new pontiff would be the choice of the new secretary of state. Would he confirm Mariano Rampolla? Or would he choose some cardinal of the "Rampollian" line, like Cardinal Domenico Ferrata?[429]

The newly elected Giuseppe Sarto was anything but a poor country parish priest. "Governing capacity, knowledge of men, experience of the Church, mastery of the issues, cultural assurance, albeit of a conservative kind (lived culture, rather than culture learned in a library), made him without a doubt one of the loftiest figures of the episcopate of that time, although little known by the public."[430]

428 *Pii Papae X. Positio*, p. 185. Cf. also Merry del Val, *San Pio X*, pp. 10–11.

429 Domenico Ferrata (1847–1914), after a diplomatic experience in Paris (1879), was nominated undersecretary of Extraordinary Ecclesiastical Affairs (1883), president of the Pontifical Academy of Ecclesiastical Nobles, nuncio in Brussels (1885), and titular archbishop of Thessalonica. In 1889, he was named secretary of Extraordinary Ecclesiastical Affairs and in July 1891 nuncio in France, contributing in a decisive manner to *ralliement*. He was made a cardinal on June 22, 1896, and went on to direct the prefecture of the Congregations of Indulgences, Rites, Bishops, Sacraments, and, at the start of 1914, the Holy Office. Benedict XV, upon his election to the papacy, named him secretary of state, but Ferrata died after only one and a half months, on October 10, 1914. Cf. Carlo Salotti, *L'opera diplomatica e sacerdotale del card. Domenico Ferrata [The Diplomatic and Priestly Work of Card. Domenico Ferrata]*, Artigianelli S. Giuseppe, Rome 1915; Soderini, *Il pontificato di Leone XIII*, II, pp. 40–485; and above all the entries of R. Aubert, DHGE, vol. 16, col. 1229– 1234; and G. Fagioli Vercellone, DBI, vol. 46, pp. 755–760.

430 Romanato, *Pio X*, p. 388.

Merry del Val knew that his name had been suggested to Pius X by Cardinal Oreglia and by other cardinals. Msgr. Giuseppe Pinchetti Sammarchi, a prelate from Mantua who knew well the new pope, testified that Merry del Val had asked him to give the following communication to the pope: "Tell the Holy Father in my name that I know what is being said to him about my being nominated secretary of state. Bring to his attention that I am an outsider and am too young for such a post and that he ought thus to consider someone else." Pinchetti Sammarchi recalled that not only did he deliver the commission, but even tried to "make the pope understand that in the common estimation of all the most sensible people, Cardinal Domenico Ferrata would be the most acceptable as secretary of state," adding that this was also his opinion. "The pope then observed that he knew well the various tendencies of the Sacred College and that if he were to nominate one, he would offend the other, that if he were to nominate Ferrata, he would lead them to think he was continuing the French policy. And taking pause for a moment, with interrogatory emphasis, he suddenly came out with this expression: 'But has Msgr. Merry del Val not been nominated by all the cardinals in concord as secretary of the Sacred College?' I then pointed out to him the immense difference between secretary of the conclave and secretary of state, that the Sacred College would never have nominated him to that position if it had foreseen that he would then proceed to becoming secretary of state and that finally the nomination would be a solemn insult to the entire Sacred College, which would be greatly offended by it. To this strong observation, the pope did not pursue the issue and concluded by saying that he had not yet decided the matter, that there was still time and that he would think about it."[431]

On October 18, 1903, at the end of the daily audience he had with the pope, Rafael Merry del Val received an envelope containing his nomination as secretary of state and the raising to the cardinalate. The cardinal himself remembers the moment:

> That Sunday morning, October 18, 1903, as usual, I was with the Holy Father for about an hour to carry out affairs and, when I rose to take my leave, he handed me a large envelope addressed to me in his own hand and telling me, as if he were referring to something he had

[431] Cenci, *Merry del Val*, pp. 127–128.

nearly forgotten: "Ah, Monsignor! This is for you!" On other occasions as well he had done this and, more than once, had given me sealed envelopes containing documents of special importance. Placing the envelope among my other papers, I replied simply, "Very good, Holy Father, I shall see to it tomorrow and refer back to you."

Passing through the loggia as I returned to my apartment, I met Cardinal Mocenni, who gave me the impression of having seen the Holy Father that same morning and formed a suspicion of what was about to happen.[432] His Eminence had always been very cordial and kind to me during the eight years I had spent in the Vatican in the service to Leo XIII, and he usually treated me with great familiarity. "Well," he said to me with his usual manner, a bit coarse and swift, "who is to be the new Cardinal Secretary of State?" "I can assure you, Eminence, that I do not know; the Holy Father has never spoken of this to me." The cardinal inclined his head, then raised it in a gesture of surprise and said, "What?! Come to my room." I followed him into his study, where he had me sit down and began to press me with questions, saying that it was impossible that I knew nothing about the decision taken by His Holiness. I repeated my assurances that nothing exceptional had marked my audience with the pope; that not even one word was said about the future Cardinal Secretary of State and that I was dismissed, as usual, with my papers and an envelope of documents His Holiness had given me. "An envelope!" he exclaimed. "Why have you not opened it?"

I immediately opened it and gave a quick perusal of the letter contained inside. Needless to say, I was dismayed and shocked by its contents.

The cardinal looked upon me with a smile, as of one who knew all along, and gave me an affectionate pat on the back. Along with the signed letter there was a notable sum of money and this explained the volume of the envelope. His Holiness, in his paternal goodness, wanted me to accept this gift, for to that moment I had not received any compensation and because he wanted to contribute to the expenses I would have for my promotion."[433]

432 Mario Mocenni (1823–1904), of Montefiascone, after a long career as a diplomat, was made a cardinal by Leo XIII on January 16, 1893.

433 Merry del Val, *San Pio X*, p. 18.

The letter expressed the following:

> Illustrious, Most Reverend Monsignor, your election by the Eminent Cardinals who chose you as secretary of the conclave, the goodness with which you accepted to sustain in this period the cares of secretary of state and the scrupulous fidelity with which you have carried out this most delicate office, oblige me to beg you to assume in a stable manner the office of my secretary of state. To this end, and to satisfy a need of my heart and giving you a little sign of my profound gratitude, during the next consistory this coming November 9, I shall have the pleasure of creating you a Cardinal of the Holy Roman Church. I can assure you to your great comfort that, in doing so, I shall do something most gratifying to the greater part of the Eminent Cardinals who, with me, admire the outstanding qualities with which the Lord has endowed you, and by which you will certainly render the Church your fine services. And in conclusion, I impart on you with particular affection my apostolic blessing.
>
> The Vatican, October 18, 1903. PIUS PP. X"[434]

After having recovered from the shock, Merry del Val returned to the pope, who welcomed him affectionately but did not allow him to challenge his decision. "He had made his resolution, so he assured me, and I had to bend myself to the will of God, as he too had to do before me."[435]

With surprise and wonder in the Vatican Court, Rafael Merry del Val became the youngest secretary of state and the first non-Italian to hold the office. His term corresponded precisely to the pontificate of Pius X: from 1903 to 1914. Philippe Roy-Lysencourt rightly observed, "The nomination of Rafael Merry del Val was atypical for his young age, his geographical background, and the exact synchronicity of his term with the pontificate of the pope who nominated him."[436] Pius X, during an interview with Cardinal Mathieu on October 20, 1904, explained his decision saying, "I chose Archbishop Merry del Val because he is a polyglot: he speaks fluently five or six languages. Born in England, raised in Belgium, a diplomat in Vienna, Spanish by

434 AA.EE.SS., *Stati Ecclesiastici 1903–1904*, Pos. 1267, fasc. 429.

435 Merry del Val, *San Pio X*, p. 19.

436 Roy-Lysencourt, *Merry del Val*, pp. 35–36.

nationality, knowledgeable in the affairs of many countries.... He comes here every morning and tells me the news from all over the world. I give him my opinion and he ventures not one observation."[437]

Once he accepted his election, Pius X had to contemplate his choice of a new secretary of state, the most important man in the Church after him. The new pope had great pastoral experience, but unlike his predecessor and then his successor, he did not have diplomatic practice and knowledge of languages. He certainly saw in Rafael Merry del Val the traits that he lacked, traits that would make him indispensable. It would be belittling to imagine, however, that the reason for his choice of Merry del Val was solely due to his diplomatic abilities. Cardinal Nasalli Rocca,[438] Archbishop of Bologna, in a letter to Cardinal Canali dated October 29, 1949, wrote that on October 18, 1903, he was received by Pius X who asked, 'Have you seen that I made Msgr. Merry del Val the new secretary of state? Do you know him?' 'Very well,' I replied, 'He was my president at the Ecclesiastical Academy.' 'I wanted,' the pope added, 'to choose one who could worthily succeed Card. Rampolla, especially for his piety and priestly spirit.'"[439]

The young Anglo-Spanish archbishop spoke fluently the main European languages and knew the mechanisms of chanceries, the lifestyle in the great courts, and the language of politics and administration. But what he had in common with Giuseppe Sarto was a profound spiritual life, a vast apostolic horizon, a supernatural spirit that translated into a disposition of the soul opposed to the modernist one. Between these two great souls, above and beyond a working collaboration, there was born and developed an intimate and constant spiritual union. For eleven years, from 1903 to 1914, they truly formed one heart and one soul. Merry del Val was neither the passive and subdued executor of Pius X's will, nor the one who inspired his intransigence. Between the pope and his secretary of state there was an uncommon harmony, both doctrinal and spiritual.

Baron d'Erp,[440] the Belgian ambassador to the Holy See, in his report of April 8, 1905, after having met Merry del Val, wrote, "The way in which the

437 Reported by Renard, *Le cardinal Mathieu*, p. 411.

438 Giovanni Battista Nasalli Rocca (1872–1952), among the main founders and reorganizers of Catholic Action in Italy, was archbishop of Bologna from 1921 to his death and, in 1923, was named cardinal by Pope Pius XI. In 1904, he was named apostolic visitor in Rome for Pius X, receiving the same charge for the dioceses of Ancona, Penne and Atri, Recanati and Loreto, Teramo and Fermo, Bojano and Campobasso, and various Italian seminaries.

439 AAV, *Spoglio Merry del Val*, busta 9, n. 1354, f. 16.

440 Baron Maximilien d'Erp (1847–1946) was Belgian ambassador to the Holy See from February 1896 to February 1915.

Cardinal Secretary of State expresses himself reflects the most intimate thought that His Holiness manifests in all his conduct: being unshakable in principles and extremely affable in all of his actions."[441] Pius X, recalled Plinio Corrêa de Oliveira, was an excellent psychologist, and many of the people who spoke with him had the impression that he could read their hearts. His serene, lucid gaze seemed to scrutinize with incredible clarity, painfully but also courageously, a much deeper horizon covered with dark clouds.[442] The same melancholy and firmness was present in the eyes of Rafael Merry del Val, "a fighter who was under no illusions about the world, who had taken a definitive position toward it, and was ready for all the battles that life presented him."[443]

Nomination to the Cardinalate

During the consistory on November 9, 1903, Pius X announced to the cardinals the elevation of his secretary of state to the honors of the sacred *porpora* [the cardinalate], highlighting "the excellent gifts of soul and intelligence, no less than his uncommon prudence in treating affairs of the Church."[444] Two days later, on Wednesday, November 11, in the Hall of the Consistory, imposing the cardinal's biretta on him, and granting him the titular church of Santa Prassede, Pius X gave Merry del Val another unusual compliment: "The fine scent of Christ, Lord Cardinal, which you have spread in all places, even in your temporary dwelling, and the multiple works of charity to which you have continuously dedicated yourself in your priestly ministry especially in this our city of Rome, have acquired for you universal admiration and esteem."[445]

The neo-cardinal turned to Pius X, risen to his throne, to thank him also on behalf of his colleague, the cardinal of Padua, Giuseppe Callegari,[446] in these words: "Holy Father, as high as the concept that we must have and indeed do have of the honor conferred on us today by the goodness of Your Holiness, as

441 Légation de Belgique n. 132/38 in R. Aubert, "Documents relatifs au mouvement catholique italien," *Rivista di Storia della Chiesa in Italia* 12 (1958), pp. 242–243.

442 Plinio Corrêa de Oliveira, "Significação essencial de um grande pontificado," *Catolicismo* 47 (November 1954), pp. 1–2.

443 Id. "A Altivez é harmonioso complemento da humildade," *Catolicismo* 44 (August 1954), p. 7.

444 ASS, vol. 36 (1903–1904), pp. 193–198, 276. Cf. *Spoglio Merry del Val*, n. 271, November 9, 1903. Card communicating his elevation to the dignity of the cardinalate.

445 ASS, vol. 36 (1903–1904), p. 280; Cenci, *Merry del Val*, p. 138.

446 Giuseppe Callegari (1841–1906), bishop of Treviso (1880), then of Padua (1883), was among the first and most active organizers of the Catholic Associations. He was made a cardinal on October 9, 1903, together with Cardinal Rafael Merry del Val. Cardinal Sarto had served as his clerk in Treviso from 1880 to 1882.

glorious as the ministry entrusted to us appears in our eyes, we understand all too well that in our times and in the difficult circumstances at large, this sublime dignity imposes on us not only grave responsibilities but the constant sacrifice of all that is ours, not excluding our lives, to procure the glory and the triumph of the Holy Church."[447]

From that day and hour, Rafael Merry del Val, observed Fr. Girolamo Dal-Gal, "for eleven years, without interruption and without uncertainty, praying and fighting, identified his name and his work with the name and work of Pius X in an intimate and profound unity of thought and aspirations, with but one goal, with the same faith and with the same courage."[448]

The following day, Cardinal Merry del Val was nominated member of the Sacred Congregation of the Roman and Universal Inquisition, and of the Congregations of the Council, Rites, and Extraordinary Ecclesiastical Affairs.

The cardinals were referred to as "created" by the pontiff who had elevated them to the *porpora*. Cardinal Merry del Val was the first "creation" of the new pontiff. This earned him the privilege every year of celebrating Mass in the Sistine Chapel on the occasion of the anniversary of the coronation of the Pontifex Maximus. Camille Bellaigue, the renowned music critic, remembering how the Cardinal Secretary of State received his guests in the halls of the Borgia Apartment, under the vaulted ceilings which Pinturicchio decorated for Pope Alexander VI, describes him entering the corner of the hall, to the back on the left: "The light of the day shines on his noble and handsome Spanish face."[449]

Pius X did not hide his deep satisfaction over this nomination of his, repeating to many people that he "could not thank God enough for having given me such a precious collaborator."[450] Other important nominations were made in the first days of the pontificate. Every new pope carefully chooses his collaborators. Pius X nominated four private secretaries who enjoyed his close trust, forming the so-called *Segreteriola,* a particular administrative office different

447 Cenci, *Merry del Val*, p. 137.

448 Dal-Gal, *Merry del Val*, p. 79.

449 *Pie X et nous. Notes et souvenirs (1903–1914),* Nouvelle Librairie Nationale, Paris 1916, p. 50. Camille Bellaigue (1858–1930) was a French music critic, author of numerous books, among which a biography on Giuseppe Verdi (1913).

450 Cenci, *Merry del Val*, pp. 139–140.

and distinct from the "secretariat downstairs" (as Pius X called the secretary of state, from the vantage of his third-floor Vatican apartments).[451]

The head and coordinator of this modest, but efficient, office was his secretary from Mantua, Fr. Giovanni Bressan,[452] who had followed him to Venice and then to the conclave and who served him faithfully for his entire pontificate. Msgr. Bressan, testifying at the cause for beatification of Pius X, recalled,

> The Servant of God, as soon as he was elected pope, created the particular secretariat. It was composed by me, Msgr. Pescini, Msgr. Gasoni, Msgr. Bianchi, and Msgr. Ungherini. The latter oversaw the opening of correspondence, which was divided according to the respective dicasteries and offices. The pope's personal correspondence was collected by me and presented within a file. Some of the less important matters I reported to him orally. The more serious matters were considered personally by the pope; he gave his personal attention to each of them and at times handled the entire issue. Other times, for very serious matters, he would hand me his response in a sealed envelope. All the outgoing letters, including those sent to the Congregations, were protocoled. The pope's personal correspondence, that is, those he had written by hand, had a special protocol with Msgr. Gasoni. Msgr. Pescini, assisted by two nuns, oversaw the distribution of vestments and sacred vessels, which under the pontificate of the Servant of God was quite vast. I kept a special register for the donation of money. Every month, all the paperwork was archived, distributed in units of ten. Furthermore, every morning, around eleven, I received the people who wanted to express some desire to the pope (requests for autographs, offers of books, etc.). All of this I gave account of to the Holy Father.[453]

451 The *Segreteriola* included Msgr. Bressan; Msgr. Francesco Gasoni (1843–1926), a priest from Mantua, founder of the Catholic newspaper *Il Vessillo* and director of what was to become *Il Cittadino* of Matua, named secret chaplain by Pius X on December 23, 1903; Msgr. Giuseppe Pescini (1875– 1950), collaborator with Sarto in the patriarchy of Venice and his private chaplain from December 1903; Fr. Attilio Bianchi (1869–1951), of Como, nephew and formerly secretary of Msgr. Giovanni Battista Scalabrini; and Msgr. Vincenzo Maria Ungherini (1853–1927), canon of St. Maria in Trastevere, who was responsible for the elaboration of various protocols of the *Segreteriola* and inventor of the archival method they used.

452 Giambattista Bressan (1861–1950), Venetian priest, who met Giuseppe Sarto while attending seminary in Treviso and who accompanied him from 1885 onward. He was named personal secretary on August 6, 1903; he later became the supernumerary apostolic pro-notary on May 26, 1904. After the death of Pius X, he was counted among the pontifical masters of ceremony.

453 *Pii X Disquisitio*, pp. 16–17.

The files of the *Segreteriola* show, against any insinuation, that Pius X was "assisted but never fooled by his personal secretaries,"[454] over whom he exercised attentive control. "The members of the little secretariat," as the cardinal of Palermo, Ernesto Ruffini, testified at the cause of Pius X's beatification, "did not act of their own will, but on the orders of the Servant of God. I can surely testify to the full devotion of the members Msgr. Bressan, Msgr. Pescini, and finally also Msgr. Bianchi, who were convinced they were working for a saint."[455]

On August 4, 1903, when the cardinal patriarch of Venice, Giuseppe Sarto, was elevated to the papal throne, the Barnabite priest Giovanni Semeria[456] received the news from Fr. Salvatore Minocchi,[457] who was with him in Batum, Russia, on the Black Sea. "Whom did they make pope?" he asked. "Sarto," replied Minocchi, "with the name Pius X."

"A reactionary! We're finished!" replied Semeria, who frequented modernist circles.[458] The modernist candidate was Rampolla, as Fr. Johannes Wehrlé confessed to Maurice Blondel in a letter on August 8, 1903, entrusting himself to the Holy Spirit: "If Austria has excluded our candidate, we firmly believe that the Holy Spirit has given victory to His: His tastes must be as good as ours."[459]

In reality, the "reactionary" Pius X "was at the same time one of the greatest reformer popes in history," as Roger Aubert rightly underscores.[460] His program of restoration of Christian society implied, beyond the firm defense of the orthodoxy of the Church, undermined by modernism, a vast program of pastoral initiatives and reforms as well, beginning with that of the Pontifical Curia.

454 A. M. Dieguez, "La mentalità giuridica di Pio X nelle carte del suo Archivio particolare" [The Juridical Mentality of Pius X in the Papers of His Personal Archive], in Arturo Cattaneo (ed.), *L'eredità giuridica di san Pio X*, Marcianum Press, Venice 2006, p. 107. Cf. also C. Siccardi, *San Pio X*, pp. 248– 251; Romanato, *Pio X*, pp. 396–404.

455 *Pii X Disquisitio*, p. 17.

456 On Giovanni Semeria (1867–1931), Barnabite preacher and lecturer, close to modernist circles, cf. the bibliographical notes in the appendix by Virginio M. Colciago to the collection of Semeria's writings, *Saggi clandestine [Clandestine Essays]*, Edizioni Domenicane, Alba 1967, pp. 377–500.

457 Salvatore Minocchi (1869–1943), professor of Hebrew language and literature at the University of Florence (1901–1909) and later in Pisa (1909–1922), was suspended *a divinis* in 1907 and was defrocked the following year; he later contracted a civil marriage in 1912. Cf. Attilio Agnoletto, *Salvatore Minocchi. Vita e opera*, Morcelliana, Brescia 1964; and, by Minocchi as well, *Memorie di un modernista*, Vallecchi, Florence 1974. In the same year, Minocchi and Semeria made a long journey through Russia, Siberia, and Manciuria, sending articles to *Il Giornale d'Italia*.

458 Minocchi, *Memorie di un modernista*, p. 78.

459 Letter of Maurice Blondel to Fr. Johannes Wehrlé, August 5, 1903, in M. Blondel and J. Wehrlé, *Correspondance*, Aubier-Montaigne, Paris 1969, vol. 1, p. 204.

460 R. Aubert, "Pio X tra restaurazione e riforma," in Fliche and Martin (eds.), *Storia della Chiesa*, vol. 22/1, p. 137.

The Reform Work of the Pontificate

The Roman Curia is distinct from the Pontifical Family. The former comprises all the ecclesiastical dicasteries that have arisen throughout the centuries. These dicasteries — commonly called Roman Congregations, Tribunals, and Offices — have undergone various reforms over the course of centuries.[461] Pius X's apostolic constitution *Sapienti consilio* (June 29, 1908) was the third reform of the Roman Curia in the history of the Church,[462] after those of St. Gregory VII and Sixtus V,[463] and was one of the most important acts of his pontificate. It sought to rationalize the jurisdiction of the distinct organs of the Roman Curia, henceforth organized into eleven congregations, three tribunals, and six offices, and suppressed the organs not directly ecclesiastical.[464] The Congregation of the Holy Inquisition took the name of "Congregation of the Holy Office," which was distinguished from the others by the fact that its head was not a cardinal but the pope himself. Pius X placed the Secretariat of State among the offices instead of the congregations, with three sections subordinate to it: the Section for Relations with States (which continued to be called the Congregation for Extraordinary Ecclesiastical Affairs), the Section for General Affairs, and the Section for Apostolic Briefs. The first section was presided over by the its own secretary, the second by the substitute to the secretary of state, and the third by the chancellor of the apostolic briefs.

The reason why the Secretariat of State assumed vast importance *de facto* was due to the perfect coincidence of views and orientation that always existed between Pius X and its president, Cardinal Merry del Val, more than to the

461 Felice Cappello, *La Curia romana secondo la sapiente riforma di Pio X [The Roman Curia According to the Wise Reform of Pius X]*, Marietti, Turin 1910, pp. 6–8.

462 Pius X, Apostolic constitution *Sapienti consilio*, in ASS, vol. 41 (1908), pp. 425–440; Apostolic constitution *De Romana curia*, in AAS, vol. 1, n. 1 (1909), pp. 7–19.

463 With the Apostolic Constitution *Immensa Aeterni Dei*, January 22, 1588, Sixtus V established permanent congregations of cardinals, giving to the hierarchical structure of the Church the appearance it preserves in part still today.

464 Cf. François Jankowiak, *La Curie romaine de Pie IX à Pie X. Le gouvernement central de l'Église et la fin des États pontificaux*, École française de Rome, Rome 2007, pp. 535–539; Giovanni Battista Varnier, "La riforma della Curia," in Gianni La Bella (ed.), *Pio X e il suo tempo*, Il Mulino, Bologna 2003, pp. 275–310; Giovanni Vian, "Convergenze e divergenze nella Curia romana di Pio X" [Convergences and Divergences in the Roman Curia of Pius X], in idem, pp. 481–522; Paolo Valvo, "Da Roma al mondo: l'agenda del nuovo papa. Situazione della Chiesa e prospettive di riforma all'alba del pontificato di Pio X" [From Rome to the World: the Plan of the New Pope, Situation in the Church and Prospects for Reform under Pius X], *Rivista della Storia della Chiesa in Italia* 67, no. 2 (July–December 2013), pp. 521–541.

importance of the office itself.[465] The issues it dealt with were numerous, but they concerned above all the complex relations between church and state. In 1907, after nominating Cardinal Merry del Val as secretary of state, Pius X dismissed both Cardinal Rampolla's protégés, Giacomo della Chiesa and Pietro Gasparri; the former was replaced by Msgr. Nicholas Canali, the latter by Msgr. Raffaele Scapinelli di Léguigno.[466]

These two thus became the close collaborators of Cardinal Merry del Val: Msgr. Canali, as substitute to the secretary of state, to whom was entrusted the Section on General Ecclesiastical Affairs; and Msgr. Scapinelli, as secretary of the Congregation of Extraordinary Ecclesiastical Affairs.[467]

After Merry del Val's nomination there followed the nomination of Msgr. Gaetano De Lai as secretary of the Congregation of the Council on November 11, 1903.[468] De Lai was created cardinal deacon by Pius X during the consistory of December 16, 1907, and was nominated secretary of the Congregation for Consistories on October 20, 1908. In the following consistory on November 27, 1911, relieved of his duties as deacon of St. Nicola in Carcere, De Lai chose the diocese of Sabina outside Rome and was consecrated bishop by Pius X on December 17, 1911. Also in 1911, he became president of the financial office of the ecclesiastical dicasteries and enlarged his influence over the Curia by

465 Romanato, *Pio X*, p. 442. The centrality that the Secretariat of State holds today in Church governance is due to the reform of the Curia under Paul VI with the constitution *Regimini Ecclesiae universae*, August 15, 1967.

466 Raffaello Scapinelli di Léguigno (1858–1933) was called by Pius X in 1908 to replace Msgr. Pietro Gasparri as secretary of the Congregation for Ecclesiastical Affairs. In 1912, he was nominated apostolic nuncio to the Austro-Hungarian Empire and titular archbishop of Laodicea in Syria, receiving episcopal consecration from Cardinal Merry del Val. He was made a cardinal by Benedict XV in 1915 and in 1918 prefect of the Congregation for Religious.

467 When in 1914, after the death of Pius X, Merry del Val left the direction of the Secretariat of State, the prelates proposed to the three sections — General Affairs, Extraordinary Affairs, and Apostolic Briefs — were Msgr. Nicola Canali, Msgr. Eugenio Pacelli (future Pope Pius XII), and Msgr. Federico Tedeschini.

468 Gaetano De Lai (1853–1928), of Vicenza, was ordained in 1876 and entered the Congregation of the Council where he was first an auditor and then under-secretary (1891) and finally secretary (1903). Made a cardinal deacon in 1907, with the reform of the Curia in 1908, he was named secretary of the Congregation of the Consistory, receiving episcopal consecration from Pius X on December 17, 1911. Cf. Giovanni Azzolini, *Gaetano De Lai "l'uomo forte" di Pio X. Cultura e fede nel primo Novecento nell'esperienza del cardinale vicentino [Gaetano De Lai, "Strong Man" of Pius X. Culture and Faith in the Early 1900s in the Experience of the Cardinal from Vicenza]*, Accademia Olimpica, Vicenza 2003; G. Vian, "Gaetano De Lai, zelante collaboratore di Pio X nella repressione antimodernista" [Gaetano De Lai, Zealous collaborator of Pius X in the Anti-Modernist Repression], in Hubert Wolf and Judith Schepers (eds.), *In wilder zügelloser Jagd nach Neuem. 100 Jahre Modernismus und Antimodernismus in der katholischen Kirche*, , Schöningh, Paderborn 2008, pp. 453–473.

entering the Congregations of the Holy Office, of Religious, of Extraordinary Ecclesiastical Affairs, of Seminaries and Universities, and of Ceremonies.

The Catalan cardinal, José Vives Y Tutó, confessor of the new pontiff, became prefect of the Congregation of Religious from 1908 to 1912, and was a trusted consultant of the Holy Office. Vives Y Tutó, a man of great culture and piety, had embraced since his youth the ideas of the Spanish theologian Félix Sardá y Salvany.[469]

According to Cardinal Gasparri, Pius X "placed his trust in three cardinals in particular: Vives y Tutó, Merry del Val, and De Lai."[470] In his deposition, Cardinal Augusto Silj confirmed, "When making important decisions he took counsel especially with Cardinals Vives y Tutó, Merry del Val and De Lai."[471] But to those who accused him of being influenced by this triad, Pius X responded, "Those going around divulging that three cardinals are in command (Vives, Merry, and De Lai) are among those unqualifiable beings who are never lacking in the Church, who, seeking to avoid dutiful obedience, want to remove any obligation in their conscience by thinking it is not the pope who is in control."[472]

Certainly, Vives y Tutó was among the main collaborators of the pope in theological matters and De Lai in the discipline of the clergy. Merry del Val applied the pontiff's directives in the field of politics and diplomacy and, of the three, was the closest to Pius X. Twice a week, on Tuesdays and Thursdays, the secretary of state received ambassadors. On other days, he was in direct meetings with the pope. In the evenings he was available to meet anyone who wished to speak with him of anything considered useful for the Holy Father to know. A frequentor of the Vatican in that period stated, "No European minister has greater access than any other to the secretary of the pope; every foreigner who presents his calling card is easily admitted to these evening receptions."[473] The

469 Valenti Serra de Manresa, *El capuchino José de Calasanz de Llavenares*, pp. 185–186. Félix Sardá y Salvany (1844–1916) was considered an exemplary priest for the firmness of his principles and the charity of his apostolic works. On him, cf. *Le libéralisme est un péché. Suivi de la lettre pastorale des Evêques de l'Equateur sur le libéralisme*, Nuova edizione, Pierre Téqui, Paris 1910, p. 11. The Holy Congregation of the Index declared this work to be worthy of praise on January 10, 1887, "since it expounds and defends healthy doctrine on the above-mentioned material with solid arguments developed with order and clarity, without offense to anyone."

470 *Pii Papae X. Positio*, p. 456.

471 Ibid, p. 276.

472 Letter to Fr. Ciceri, December 18, 1912, in *Pii Papae X. Positio*, p. 2.

473 Comte Ludovic de Colleville (1855–1918), *Pie X, intime*, Librairie Félix Juven, Paris 1908, p. 241; Alberto De Angelis, "Accanto alla Tiara. Il collaboratore di Pio X Merry del Val" [Next to the Tiara. Pius X's Collaborator Merry del Val], *Noi e il Mondo*, p. 90.

Count of Colleville, secret chamberlain "of sword and cloak" to Pius X, who knew Merry del Val well, described him in the following way: "He is tall and well-built, with a broad forehead, a kindly smile on his mouth and big black eyes that give to his physique a certain sweetness and sincerity. His entire person emanates the perfume of exquisite distinction, a calmness in his manner that seduces; the tone of his voice is harmonious, and his witty conversation very fascinating. He is a consummate man of the world."[474]

The French scholar Henry Bordeaux, arriving in Rome in 1910, before being introduced in the Vatican, was placed on guard against Pius X and his secretary of state by Ambassador Barrère, and above all by Msgr. Duchesne, director if the Ecole Français of Rome.[475] During his meeting with Merry del Val, which lasted an hour, Bordeaux was impressed by his noble figure: "To give a portrait of Cardinal Merry del Val one would need a Van Dyck or a Velasquez. He speaks many languages with marvelous precision. The exquisite amiability of his words, the aristocratic courtesy of his manners, his appearance so full of *gravitas* and decorum strikes the visitor, who quickly discovers himself in the presence of a man of great nobility, gifted with a firm, determined will in pursuing the good of the Church."[476]

After the reform of the Curia, there followed that of the Vicariate. With his constitution *Etsi nos*,[477] Pius X provided for the reorganization of parishes of the Diocese of Rome and the establishment of new parishes in the periphery. At the same time, greater powers were given to the Cardinal Vicar (vicar general of the diocese of Rome) who acted on behalf of the pontiff.

These reforms were part of wider legislative work by Pius X. With his motu proprio *Arduum sane munus* of March 19, 1904, the pope began preparations for the *Code of Canon Law*, destined to put into order the many norms and laws approved over the course of history.[478] According to the testimony of the

474 Colleville, *Pie X, intime*, p. 243.

475 Henry Bordeaux (1870–1963) was a French literary figure, the author of numerous novels and essays, and member of the French Academy (1919). Cf. Anne-Christine Feitrop, "Il letterato diplomatico Henry Bordeaux in Roma," *Strenna dei Romanisti*, Editrice Roma Amor, Rome 1980, pp. 197–212.

476 H. Bordeaux, *Images romaines*, Plon, Paris 1950, pp. 110–111.

477 Pius X, Apostolic constitution *Etsi nos de vicariato urbis*, January 1, 1912, in AAS, vol. 4 (1912), pp. 5–22.

478 Pius X, motu proprio *Arduum sane munus de Ecclesiae legibus in unum redigendis*, March 19, 1904, in ASS, vol. 36 (1903–1904), pp. 549–551. "A great historian of canon law, Stickler, summarized quite nicely in six points the problems afflicting canon law in the Church before this codification: the great number of laws (*multitudo legum*), the disorder of the laws (*inordinatio legum*), the form of the laws (*forma legum*), the uncertainty of the dispositions in force (*incertitudo legum*), the continued

Cardinal Archbishop of Cologne, Hartmann,[479] this intention dated from the first night after his election.[480] The decision, as Merry del Val recalled, was born of strictly pastoral needs, "because more than once, Pius X realized the impossibility of governing well with decrees that admitted different interpretations, complex and antiquated laws, and a heap of dispositions that were far from harmonious and often not very befitting under the new circumstances."[481]

On April 4, the pope nominated Msgr. Gasparri secretary of the Pontifical Commission for the Codification of Canon Law. Beginning on April 17, 1904, the work continued at a constant pace for eight years. In 1912, Gasparri communicated the outlines voted on by the commission to the Latin episcopates, to the territorial abbots, and to the superiors general of religious orders for a wide consultation. In 1914, the editing of the final book of the *Codex iuris canonici* was completed and the draft was prepared for its promulgation.[482]

Pius X nurtured the hope that he would see this reform finished before the end of his life, and during the preparatory studies, Merry del Val heard him exclaim, "We must make haste because I am growing old and wish to see it finished."[483] This aspiration did not come to pass and the *Code of Canon Law* was promulgated in 1917 by Benedict XV, who recognized in his predecessor the author of this impressive work.

Divergent ideas existed concerning the reform of canon law. The Jesuits of the Gregorian University advocated maintaining the order of the Decretals,[484] while the school of Apollinare, from which Gasparri took inspiration, supported the need for a centralized codification modeled on the Napoleonic Code,

presence of norms that had become useless (*inutilitas legum*), the gaps in the system (*lacunae legum*)." Giuseppe Dalla Torre, "Il codice di diritto canonico," in La Bella (ed.), *Pio X e il suo tempo*, p. 317, which refers to Alfonso M. Stickler, *Historia iuris canonici latini*, vol. 1, Augustae Taurinorum 1950, pp. 371–374. Cf. also Carlo Fantappié, "Chiesa romana e modernità giuridica," vol. 2, in *Codex iuris canonici (1917)*, Giuffré, Milan 2008; Sanguinetti, *San Pio X*, pp. 144–150; Siccardi, *San Pio X*, pp. 269–276.

479 Felix von Hartmann (1851–1919), archbishop of Münster (1911) and later of Cologne (1912), was made a cardinal by Pius X on May 25, 1914.

480 Fantappié, *Chiesa romana e modernità giuridica*, vol. 2, pp. 643–644.

481 Merry del Val, *San Pio X*, p. 53.

482 Cf. Giorgio Feliciani, "La codificazione del diritto canonico e la riforma della curia romana" [The Codification of Canon Law and the Reform of the Roman Curia], in Fliche and Martin (eds.), *Storia della Chiesa*, vol. 22/2, *La Chiesa e la società industriale (1878–1922)*, pp. 293–310.

483 Merry del Val, *San Pio X*, p. 54.

484 Decretals were letters written by popes (or occasionally cardinals) on specific legal or disciplinary matters in the Catholic Church. Originally intended to provide clarification or arbitration in an individual case, their influence grew as they began to be applied to other similar cases. They were grouped together in various collections, beginning with the *Decretum Gratiani* of the twelfth century.

thus following secular legal thought.[485] Ultimately, the *Corpus iuris canonici* was constructed from the whole of the official collections (*Decretum Gratiani, Liber Extra, Liber VI, Clementiae, Extravagantes Ioannis XXII, Extravagantes communes*) and was enriched bit by bit with further normative interventions from pontifical and conciliar sources, as well as from decrees of the Roman Congregations and jurisprudence from the Roman Rota.

The legal historian Carlo Fantappié highlighted the parallelism between the program of unification of the laws of the Church and those of the unification of sacred music, and generally of all liturgy and sacred art, undertaken by Pius X.[486] Four months before beginning the codification of canon law, Pius X published the motu proprio *Tra le sollecitudini,* for the "restoration of sacred music," by which he reestablished in the Church the excellence and the supremacy of Gregorian Chant, calling for a "juridical code for sacred music."[487] Merry del Val, who collaborated closely with Pius X in all of these reforms, was musically talented, and even composed motets with Latin texts in polyphony accompanied by the organ, presenting a perfect fusion between words and music, which according to the renowned French music critic Jaques Chailley, surpass in beauty the greatest composers of that time.[488]

This work of canonical and liturgical codification was connected to the promulgation of a unified catechism of the Church, born of the same pastoral exigencies. One of the first encyclicals of Pius X, *Acerbo nimis,*[489] of April 15, 1905, was dedicated precisely to the teaching of Christian doctrine. The *Compendium of Christian Doctrine,* known also as the *Catechism of St. Pius X,* dates

485 Cf. Giuseppe Sciacca, *Nodi di una giustizia. Problemi aperti del diritto canonico [Points of Contention of Justice. Open Problems in Canon Law]*, Il Mulino, Bologna 2022, pp. 250–251.

486 Fantappié, *Chiesa romana e modernità giuridica,* vol. 2, p. 928.

487 Pius X, motu proprio *Tra le sollecitudini,* November 22, 1903, intro, https://www.papalencyclicals.net/pius10/tra-le-sollecitudini. John Paul II referred to this text, defining it "a sort of code of law for sacred music," in *Chirografo per il centenario del motu proprio "Tra le sollecitudini" sulla musica sacra [Chirograph on the Centenary of the Motu Proprio "Tra le sollecitudini" on Sacred Music],* of November 22, 2003, written with the intention of reaffirming the norms promulgated a century earlier by his predecessor. (A chirograph is a papal decree whose circulation is limited to the Roman Curia.)Pius X decided that the Vatican Edict would be based on the *Graduale di Solesmes* which had been circulating for thirty years, rather than take a risk with the "archaeological" edition of Dom Mocquereau. Cf. Pierre Combe, *Histoire de la restauration du chant grégorien d'après des documents inédits,* Solesmes 1969, p. 344.

488 Filippo Delpino, "Composizioni sacre del Cardinal Merry del Val" [Sacred Compositions of Merry del Val], *Una Voce* 108–109 (January–May 1994), p. 19. Most of these motets remained unpublished until 1970, for the occasion of the fiftieth anniversary of his death.

489 Pius X, Encyclical *Acerbo nimis,* April 15, 1905, in *Enchiridion/Pio X,* pp. 108–129.

from 1905, and was republished on October 28, 1912, as the *Catechism of Christian Doctrine.*[490]

The *Code of Canon Law,* the liturgical codification, articulated in both the Latin and the Eastern Rites, and the universal catechism with one sole Creed, presented a Church renewed in unity and universality in its essential dimensions, opposed to every form of individualism. "The profound wellspring of the legislative work of Pius X," said Pius XII after his canonization, "is to be found in his personal sanctity, in his intimate persuasion that the reality of God, perceived by him in a constant communion of life, is the origin and foundation of all order, of all justice, of every law in the world."[491] Pius XII also affirmed the central role the Eucharist had in his predecessor's life, which is why the latter had extended Eucharistic communion to children and promoted even daily communion. "In his profound vision of the Church as a society, Pius X recognized in the Eucharist the power essentially to nourish his inner life and to elevate it far above all other human associations."[492]

On this point once again, the soul of Pius X was in perfect harmony with that of his secretary of state, who on July 14, 1902, had written this offering:

> At your feet, my Jesus, I prostrate myself and offer you the repentance of my contrite heart which plunges into its nothingness in your presence. I adore you in the Sacrament of Love, the unspeakable Eucharist; I desire to receive you in the poor abode that my soul offers you. As I await the happiness of sacramental Communion, I want to possess you in spirit. Come to me, that I might come to you, O my Jesus, and may your love inflame my entire being in life and in death. I believe in you; I hope in you; and I love you. Amen.[493]

Instaurare Omnia in Christo

This program was solemnly announced in Pius X's very first encyclical, *E supremi apostolatus,*[494] on October 4, 1903, in which the new pope declared that his only

490 Luciano Nordera, *Il Catechismo di Pio X. Per una storia della catechesi in Italia (1896–1916) [The Catechism of Pius X. A History of Catechesis in Italy (1896–1916)],* LAS, Rome 1988.

491 Pius XII, Discourse, May 29, 1954, for the canonization of Pius X, in *Discorsi e Radiomessaggi,* vol. 16, p. 32 (pp. 31–37).

492 Ibid, p. 35.

493 AAV, *Spoglio Merry del Val,* Autograph of July 14, 1902, busta 8, f. 1057.

494 Pius X, Encyclical *E supremi apostolatus,* October 4, 1903, in *Enchiridion/Pio X,* pp. 21–39.

aim was to *instaurare omnia in Christo* (Eph 1:10), namely, to draw all things to unity in Christ. *Instaurare omnia in Christo.* With this motto-program, Msgr. Giuseppe Sarto had begun his episcopate in Mantua in 1885. With the same motto, he presented himself as Cardinal Patriarch in Venice in 1894. Pius X's perspective was that of Christ's "social kingship," later more explicitly developed by Pius XI in his encyclical *Quas primas,*[495] but already present in Catholic thought. In this, Pius X's thought was greatly influenced by the teaching of Cardinal Pie,[496] of whom he declared, "I have read everything Cardinal Pie has written; he is my master."[497]

In his first allocution in the consistory of November 9, 1903, before the cardinals who constituted the supreme senate of the Church, Pius X took up the theme in these words:

> Restoring all things in Christ: such we have affirmed to be our purpose, for Christ is the truth. We must uphold above all the magisterium and the proclamation of the truth.... Ours is a sublime mission because it is something that transcends these transient goods of the earth, extending unto eternity; which, not constrained by local boundaries, embraces all the nations of the earth; which includes the defense of the Gospel in all fields, even in that eventful field of politics; which urges our solicitude not only toward the faithful, but to all men for whom Christ died.[498]

Pius X reiterated these concepts even more solemnly in his encyclical *Jucunda sane* on March 12, 1904, on the occasion of the thirteenth centenary of the pontificate of St. Gregory the Great.

> Yet there is no salvation for the world but in Christ: "For there is no other name under heaven given to men whereby we may be saved"

495 Pius XI, Encyclical *Quas primas,* December 11, 1925, in *Enchiridion/Pio XI,* pp. 158–193.

496 Édouard-Louis Pie (1815–1880) was bishop of Poitiers from September 28, 1849, until his death, and cardinal from May 12, 1879. He was considered the leader of militant French Catholics united around the *Univers* of Louis Veuillot. Cf. *Oeuvres de Monseigneur l'Evêque de Poitiers* (10 editions, the last by J. Ledars, Paris 1890–94, 10 vols.). Cf. Étienne Catta, *La doctrine politique et sociale du cardinal Pie,* Nouvelles Éditions Latines, Paris 1959; Théotime de Saint-Just, *La royauté sociale de Notre-Seigneur Jésus-Christ, d'après le cardinal Pie,* Editions Sainte Jeanne d'Arc, Chiré-en-Montreuil 1988; Alfred Saenz, *El cardinal Pie; lucidez y coraje al servicio de la verdad,* Ediciones Nihuil, Buenos Aires 1987.

497 Cited in René Bazin, *Pie X,* Éditions du Trident, Paris 2011 (1928), p. 41.

498 Pius X, Address to the Consistory *Primum vos,* November 9, 1903; in ASS, p. 195 (pp. 193–197).

> (Acts iv. 12). To Christ then we must return.... Men have once more attempted to work here below without Him, they have begun to build up the edifice after rejecting the corner stone, as the Apostle Peter rebuked the executioners of Jesus for doing. And lo! the pile that has been raised again crumbles and falls upon the heads of the builders, crushing them. But Jesus remains for ever the corner stone of human society, and again the truth becomes apparent that without Him there is no salvation: "This is the stone which has been rejected by you, the builders, and which has become the head of the corner, neither is there salvation in any other" (Acts iv. 11, 12).[499]

The same program resurfaced with great clarity in the encyclical *Il fermo proposito* of June 11, 1905, dedicated to establishing guidelines for the political action of Catholics in Italy.

> "To restore all things in Christ" has always been the Church's motto, and it is especially Our Own during these fearful moments through which we are now passing. "To restore all things" — not in any haphazard fashion, but "in Christ"; and the Apostle adds, "both those in the heavens and those on the earth" (Eph. 1:10). "To restore all things in Christ" includes not only what properly pertains to the divine mission of the Church, namely, leading souls to God, but also what We have already explained as flowing from that divine mission, namely, Christian civilization in each and every one of the elements composing it.[500]

The pope reiterated, therefore, that "The civilization of the world is Christian. The more completely Christian it is, the more true, more lasting and more productive of genuine fruit it is. On the other hand, the further it draws away from the Christian ideal, the more seriously the social order is endangered."[501]

499 Pius X, Encyclical *Jucunda sane,* March 12, 1904, no. 20. https://www.vatican.va/content/pius-x/en/encyclicals/documents/hf_p-x_enc_12031904_iucunda-sane.html.

500 Pius X, Encyclical *Il fermo proposito circa l'istituzione e lo sviluppo dell'Azione Cattolica in Italia,* June, 11th, 1905, no. 6, https://www.vatican.va/content/pius-x/en/encyclicals/documents/hf_p-x_enc_11061905_il-fermo-proposito.html. Cf. also Luis Cano, "Restaurar en Cristo la sociedad civil. Algunas reflexiones en el centenario de la encíclica *Il fermo proposito* (1905) de san Pío X," in Cattaneo (ed.), *L'eredità giuridica di san Pio X,* pp. 93–105.

501 Pius X, *Il fermo proposito,* no. 4.

Pius X's vision of history was no different from that expressed by Leo XIII on March 19, 1902, celebrating the twenty-fifth anniversary of his pontificate shortly before his death in the apostolic letter *Annum ingressi,* known also as *Pervenuti all'anno vigesimo quinto,* in which Plinio Corrêa de Oliveira saw a compendium of counterrevolutionary philosophy of history.[502] The same philosophy of history was amply expressed by Msgr. Henri Delassus in 1904, in the book *The Problem of the Present Moment,* introduced by a letter from Cardinal Merry del Val, imparting the apostolic blessing of Pius X on the author.[503] In 1904, Pius X elevated Delassus to the papal household and in 1911, to apostolic protonotary.[504] In 1910, the French Monsignor's masterpiece appeared, *The Anti-Christian Conspiracy,*[505] an admirable, systematic exposition of Catholic counterrevolutionary thought of the nineteenth century, of which, as his biographer writes, Delassus was "the universal inheritor on the threshold of the twentieth century."[506]

The work bears a preface by Cardinal Merry del Val, who on October 23, 1910, wrote,

> The Holy Father Pius X welcomed with paternal interest the book entitled *The Anti-Christian Conspiracy,* which you asked me to present to him in your name. His Holiness congratulates you affectionately for having successfully completed the composition of this important and impressive work, after a long series of studies that do honor to your zeal and your ardent desire to serve the cause of God and His Holy Church. The guiding ideas of your fine book

502 Plinio Corrêa de Oliveira, "Il secolo della guerra, della morte e del peccato [The Century of War, Death and Sin," Italian translation in *Rivoluzione e Contro-Rivoluzione,* Sugarco, Milano 2009, pp. 209–217.

503 The main works of Msgr. Henri Delassus (1836–1921) are: *L'Américanisme et la conjuration antichrétienne* (Paris 1899) and *Le problème de l'heure présente: Antagonisme de deux civilisations* (Paris 1904, 2 vols.), later reelaborated in *La conjuration antichrétienne: le temple maçonnique voulant s'élever sur les ruines de l'Église catholique* (Paris 1910, 3 vols., with an introductory letter by Cardinal Rafael Merry del Val); *La mission posthume de la Bienheureuse Jeanne d'Arc et le Règne social de Notre Signeur Jésus Christ* (Paris 1914); *Les pourquoi de la guerre mondiale* (Paris 1919–1922, 3 vols.).

504 For his priestly jubilee, on June 14, 1912,Msgr. Delassus received a letter of praise from Pius X, which the pope presented as a "well-deserved act of benevolence… for your devotion to our person as well as for the unequivocal testimony of your zeal, both towards Catholic doctrine that you defend, as for the ecclesiastical discipline which you observe, as well as for all the Catholic works which you support and of which our age has such great need." (*Actes de Pie X,* Maison de la Bonne Presse, Paris 1936, vol. 7, p. 238.)

505 H. Delassus, *La conjuration antichrétienne: le temple maçonnique voulant s'élever sur les ruines de l'Église catholique,* Desclée de Brouwer, Lille 1910, 3 vols.

506 Louis Medler, *Mgr Delassus (1836–1921),* Éditions Le Sel de la Terre, Avrillé 2005, p. 6.

> are those that inspired the great Catholic historians: the action of God in the events of this world, the event of Revelation, the inauguration of the supernatural order and the resistance that the spirit of evil poses to the work of Redemption. You display the abyss opened by the antagonism between Christian civilization and the so-called retrograde civilization which leads to paganism. How right you are to affirm that social renewal can be obtained only by proclaiming the rights of God and of the Church!"

On October 22, 1913, for the centenary of the birth of Louis Veuillot,[507] Pius X presented the ultramontane French journalist as "a champion of the sovereignty of Jesus Christ" and of his "social kingship."

> He understood that a society's strength resides in the full and complete recognition of the social kingship of Our Lord and in the unconditional acceptance of the doctrinal supremacy of the Church.... His entire illustrious career is worthy of being presented as a model to those who fight for the Church and for holy causes, and who are subject to the same contradictions and the same explosions of passion.[508]

A Eucharistic Congress was convened in Lourdes on July 22–26, 1914, presided over by the pontifical legate, Cardinal Granito Pignatelli di Belmonte. It was to bring to completion the voting adopted by the congresses in London, Montreal, and Madrid to arrive at the public proclamation of Jesus Christ King of the Universe. But that very same week, Europe plunged into war.[509]

Concerning the French Republic

The first test case for Pius X and his secretary of state Merry del Val was the religious and political situation in France, where the failure of Leo XIII's *ralliement* had provoked devastating consequences. An attentive Catholic writer, Msgr. Justin Fèvre, welcoming the election of Pius X, wrote, "The policy of timing, of

507 Louis-François Veuillot (1813–1883) converted in 1838 during a trip to Rome and dedicated all his energies to the defense of the papacy, in his books and in his columns in the Catholic periodical *L'Univers*. His *Oeuvres complètes*, Lethiellieux, Paris 1924–1940, fill twenty volumes. Cf. Eugene Tavernier, *Louis Veuillot, l'homme, le lutteur, l'écrivain*, Plon, Paris 1913.

508 Brief by Pius X, October 22, 1913, in AAS, V (1913), pp. 513–515.

509 Yves de la Brière, *Les Luttes Présentes de l'Église*, 2nd series, Beauchesne, Paris 1916, pp. 463–500.

meekness, of conciliatory optimism, proposed by Leo XIII has evidently failed; it could not have done otherwise. Against blind and ferocious anticlericalism, the battle standards must now be unfurled."[510]

When, in 1895, Léon Bourgeois had formed the first entirely anticlerical cabinet of the Republic, France was more than ever under the control of Freemasonry.[511] The Grand Orient exercised its will over parliament "imposing on its followers, who are members of parliament, the duty to carry out the masonic program through their voting; requiring the candidates in elections to adhere to this program; convoking members of parliament belonging to the Order to dictate conduct."[512]

The secularization of education and the dissolution of religious congregations were the primary objectives of the Grand Orient's policy. *Resistance ou soumission* is the title of the long chapter that Card. Ferrata dedicated to the problem that arose after the approval, on April 16, 1895, of the government tax on the property of religious congregations. "From the beginning," he wrote, "there emerged two different opinions, not only among the congregations but also among Catholics. The first was that of submitting to the law, taking advantage of its favorable dispositions and seeking to make as light as possible the less favorable ones.... The second was that of considering the law null and void.... This system was called passive resistance."[513]

The discussion grew heated and divided French Catholics over the following years. The cardinal archbishop of Reims, Langénieux, in agreement with Cardinal Richard and with the support of Catholic newspapers such as *La Croix* and *La Vérité* as well as the monarchist press, began organizing resistance among a large number of superiors of congregations. Along different lines, the "authorized" congregations set to work as their superiors met at the Seminary of Saint-Sulpice. They leaned toward "collaboration" with political authorities.

The nuncio of Leo XIII in Paris at the time, Msgr. Ferrata, sought to dissuade the religious from their passive resistance against the unjust law, fearing that the policy of *ralliement* might risk being jeapordized by the resistance of the

510 P. Justin Fèvre, *Pie X Pontife et souverain*, Arthur Savaète, Paris 1903, p. 125.

511 "Le Grand Orient — wrote André Combes — peut s'enorgueiller de la formation du ministère Léon Bourgeois, en novembre 1895, qui passe, à juste titre, comme 'le ministère des Loges' avec sept Maçons" (André Combes, *Histoire de la franc-maçonnerie au XIX siècle*, 2 vols., Éditions de Rocher, Paris 1998–1999, vol. 2, p. 259.)

512 Paul Nourisson, *Un siècle de politique maçonnique*, Éditions Spes, Paris 1929, p. 72, quoting the directives of the *Bulletin du Grand Orient*, 1891, 1892 and 1897.

513 Ferrata, *Mémoires*, vol. 3, p. 109 (pp. 105–155).

religious congregations. In a long report sent to Rome on April 16, he made it clear that he was in favor of submission, although observing "that it would be very delicate and full of problems for the Holy See to decide in favor of either resistance or submission."[514]

Leo XIII himself did not advise submission, "but this submission," as noted Card. Aloisi Masella, "was counseled by those who spoke on behalf of the pope. What was said in Rome, was repeated with even greater zeal in Paris, where Msgr. Ferrata supported the conciliatory dispositions of his superior even more than it behooved him."[515]

Leo XIII recalled Msgr. Ferrata to Rome but wanted to elevate him to the cardinalate first during the secret consistory of June 22, 1896. The new president of the Republic, Émile Loubet,[516] succeeding Félix Faure,[517] chose as his prime minister Pierre Waldeck-Rousseau,[518]whose administration was the longest of the Third Republic: from June 22, 1899, to June 7, 1902. Waldeck-Rousseau, born into a Protestant family in Nantes, was not a Freemason but took inspiration for his political action from the Grand Orient.[519] On November 14, 1899, he submitted a bill that would suppress the congregations altogether, who in his opinion were guilty of inculcating in French youth a counterrevolutionary spirit and of forming a state within the state.

On July 1, 1901, the so-called Association Contract was promulgated, which in reality was a law against the congregations and, in particular, against religious education entrusted to them.[520] This law subjected religious

514 Ferrata, *Mémoires,* vol. 3, p. 122.

515 Aloisi Masella, *Memorie inedite,* vol. 7, p. 3877.

516 Émile Loubet (1838–1929) was prime minister from February 27 to December 6, 1892, and president of the French Republic from February 18, 1899, to February 18, 1906.

517 François-Félix Faure (1841–1899) was president of the Republic from January 17, 1895, until February 16, 1899, when he died suddenly at the Eliseo while amusing himself with his mistress Margherite Steinhell.

518 Pierre Marie Ernest Waldeck-Rousseau (1846–1904) was prime minister, Interior Minister, and Minister of Worship from June 22, 1899, to June 7, 1902.

519 Cf. Philippe Girard, "La maçonnerie et l'enseignement 1879–1914," in *Le Sel de la Terre* 76 (Spring 2011), pp. 20–41.

520 There is a vast bibliography on the persecutions against the congregations. Cf. Guy Laperrière, *Les congrégations religieuses. De la France au Québec (1880–1914),* Presses de l'Université de Laval, Sainte-Foy 1996–1999, 2 vols.; Jean-Paul Durand, *La liberté des congrégations religieuses en France,* Cerf, Paris 1999; Christian Sorrel, *La République contre les congrégations. Histoire d'une passion française (1899–1904),* Cerf, Paris 2003; André Lanfray, *Sécularisation, séparation et guerre scolaire. Les catholiques français et l'école (1901–1914),* Cerf, Paris 2003; Maurice Larkin, *L'Église et l'État en France, 1905: la crise de la Séparation,* Privat, Toulouse 2004 (1974); Jean Sévillia, *Quand les catholiques étaient hors la loi,* Perrin, Paris 2005.

congregations to a tyrannical regime, requiring from each of them a special authorization not only in order to possess juridical status, but simply to have the right to exist. Article 13 of Title III specified that "no religious congregation can establish an institute without a decree issued by the executive branch."[521]

In 1901, France had about 128,000 religious women and nearly 30,000 religious men. Altogether, 158,000 men and women were harshly chastised by this secular law. The alternative for the congregations was either to submit to this arbitrary act or to be dissolved.[522]

About five hundred religious congregations placed their request for authorization. Others, like the Jesuits, requested and obtained permission from the pope to be relinquished from their vows, abandoned their houses, and entrusted their colleges to lay people or to diocesan priests. Still others, such as the Benedictines, Carmelites, and Cistercians took the path of exile. Among these religious who left France, many went to distant lands, from the Far East to Latin America, from the United States to China.[523]

The elections of 1902 brought a politician to the presidency who was little known to the wider public, Émile Combes. He had been a seminarian at Albi and had received the tonsure and minor orders, but then got married and, after exercising the medical profession, went into politics among the republican ranks. Elected senator in 1885, he became Minister of Public Education and of Religion in the Bourgeois administration. When he in turn became president, he also assumed the role of Interior Minister and Minister of Religion, to be sure to bring to fulfillment unhindered his "mission" of "de-Catholicizing" France. He had affiliated himself with the Grand Orient.

The anti-religious program of Freemasonry was, the same as always, based on three points: the struggle against religious congregations, the abolition of

[521] Text of the *Loi relative au contrat d'association* of July 1, 1901, in Daniel Moulinet, *Genèse de la laïcité. À travers les textes fondamentaux de 1801 à 1959*, Cerf, Paris 2005, pp. 138–141.

[522] Cf. Sarah A. Curtis, "Persécution et résistence, les congrégations enseignantes face à la loi sur les associations de 1901," *Revue d'histoire de l'Église de France* 88 (2002), 1, pp. 175–195; Patrick Cabanel and Jean-Dominique Durand (eds.), *Le grand exil des congrégations religieuses françaises 1901–1914*, Cerf, Paris 2005; P. Cabanel, *Lettre d'exil (1901–1909). Les congrégations françaises dans le monde, après les lois laïques de 1901 et 1904*, Brépol, Turnhout (Belgique) 2008.

[523] In 1900, there were in France 1,865 congregations: 154 for men (of which only 5 were legally authorized) and 1,511 for women (of which 905 were legally authorized). After the passing of the law of July 1, 1901, 89 male congregations and 211 female ones disbanded to avoid requesting authorization; 60 male congregations and 395 female ones made the request for authorization (Sévillia, *Quand les catholiques étaient hors la loi*, pp. 135–136).

religious instruction and, as their final objective, the separation of church and state. From 1880 to 1886, only a part of this program had been carried out. Combes was to bring it to completion. To those who said to him, "You cannot limit the politics of a great nation to the fight against the congregations," Combes replied, "I have come to power only for this reason."[524]

On July 7, 1902, a decree of his administration ordered the closing of twenty-eight hundred unauthorized free schools, opened before the law of 1901, concerning which Waldeck-Rousseau had reassured the pope and his bishops that the law would not be applied. By means of a simple ministerial newsletter, Combes ordered prefects to close them within eight days.[525] Just as Pius X was ascending to the papal throne, French anticlericalism had reached its zenith and Freemasonry the height of its power.[526]

THE VISIT TO ROME OF PRESIDENT LOUBET

On December 23, 1903, Pius X wrote to French President Loubet to denounce the fact that the secular laws aimed not only at the complete separation of the state from the Church, but also and even, if it were possible, to remove from France the Christian stamp that had rendered it glorious in past centuries. Loubet's response was to announce a visit to Rome, which had the hint of provocation.[527] Despite the pope's interdiction to Catholic heads of state to make visits to Italian sovereigns (subsequent to Italy's military occupation of the Papal States from 1859 to 1870), the French President was received in Rome by Vittorio Emanuele III on April 24, 1904. The king processed ostentatiously past the Vatican walls in an open carriage that he himself drove and in which he led his guest on a visit of the capital. Alessandro Guiccioli, in his *Diary*, defined it "a great masonic revelry."[528] In a formal note of April 28, Cardinal Merry del Val communicated to the French ambassador to the Holy See,

[524] Adrien Dansette, *Histoire religieuse de la France contemporaine*, Flammarion, Paris 1965, vol. 1, p. 575.

[525] Louis Caperan, *L'invasion laïque. De l'avènement de Combes au vote de la séparation*, Desclée de Brouwer, Paris 1935, pp. 27–28.

[526] Mellor, *L'anticlericalisme*, pp. 373–374.

[527] Cf. AA.EE.SS., *Francia, 1903–1904*, Pos. 906, fasc. 503–505. *Visita in Roma del Sig. Loubet, Presidente della Repubblica francese*; M. Larkin, "Loubet's Visit To Rome And The Question Of Papal Prestige," *The Historical Journal* 4, no. 1 (1961), pp. 97–103.

[528] Diary of Alessandro Guiccioli in *Nuova Antologia*, January 1, 1943, pp. 10 and 15 and January 16, 1943, p. 86. The Marquis Alessandro Guiccioli (1843–1922) was a diplomat who held the post of mayor of Rome during the years 1888–1889. In 1900, he became a senator.

Nisard,[529] "the profound bitterness" of the pope in the face of this "grave offense" elevating "his highest and most explicit protest."[530] In response, the French government recalled its ambassador from Rome and stripped the nuncio in Paris of his diplomatic passport. On July 29, 1904, France broke off relations with the Holy See.[531]

In May 1904, foreseeing what was about to happen, Merry del Val began preparations for a "documented presentation regarding the separation" of church and state, shedding light on the responsibilities of the French government in the breach of the Concordat of 1801.[532] Thus came to birth the *Livre blanc* on *La separation de l'Eglise et de l'Etat en France,* presented on November 30, 1905, by Cardinal Merry del Val to the ministers and ambassadors. Barely a week later, December 9, 1905, the total separation of church and state in France, presaged by the diplomatic rift of 1904, was officially proclaimed in the *Loi concernant la Séparation des Eglises et de l'Etat,*[533] known as the "Combes Law," even though it was approved by the administration of his successor Maurice Rouvier.[534]

The law of separation suppressed all financing and public recognition of the Church and established that ecclesiastical property would be confiscated by the state, while the places of worship were entrusted free of charge to *associations cultuelles* elected democratically by the faithful, without the approval of the Church. The Concordat of 1801, which had regulated relations between France and the Holy See for a century, was shattered. The separation was the natural outcome of the anticlerical legislation developed by the Third Republic over the course of twenty-five years, but also marked the definitive failure of the policy of *ralliement* of Leo XIII.

[529] Armand Nisard (1841–1925) was French ambassador to the Holy See from 1898 to 1904. Diplomatic relations were renewed only in 1920, with the extraordinary embassy of Gabriel Hanoteaux for the beatification of Joan of Arc.

[530] Note of Merry del Val to Nisard, April 28, 1904, in AA.EE.SS., *Francia. Pio X,* Pos. 968, fasc. 503, 1903–1904, ff. 67–68, and, more generally, fasc. 503–505.

[531] AA.EE.SS., *Francia, Pio X,* Pos. 963, fasc. 501, 1903–1904 and 987, fasc. 21, 1904–1905.

[532] *Exposé documenté de la rupture des relations diplomatiques entre le Saint-Siège et le gouvernement français,* Imprimerie du Vatican, 1904–1906. The work was carried out by Msgr. Pietro Gasparri, who attended to it during the summer of 1905, profiting from the collaboration of the young Msgr. Eugenio Pacelli.

[533] Cf. the text of the "Loi de suppression de l'enseignement congréganiste" of July 7, 1904, in Moulinet, *Genèse de la laïcité,* pp. 152–166.

[534] Maurice Rouvier (1842–1911), Republican deputy from 1871, prime minister in 1887, was affiliated with the Grand Orient just like his predecessor.

Msgr. Beniamino Nardone recalls that on the evening of the rupture of the concordat between the Holy See and France, he found himself in the antechamber of Card. Merry del Val, when he saw the French ambassador Nisard leaving his room. "Did you see who came out?" said Merry del Val. "Yes, Eminence, the ambassador just left." "Well, know that this evening the breach of the concordat between the Holy See and France will be published. Half an hour ago, I saw the Holy Father have his final word concerning the issue. The pope, calm and serene, told me, 'Let us look to the Crucifix. The Crucified One tells us: *non possumus*.' And so, Your Eminence, tell the French ambassador: *non possumus*."[535]

On February 11, 1906, Pius X published *Vehementer nos*, the first of three strident encyclicals against the French Third Republic. In this document, the pope solemnly reprimanded and condemned the law passed in France regarding the separation of church and state

> as deeply unjust to God whom it denies, and as laying down the principle that the Republic recognizes no [worship]. We reprove and condemn it as violating the natural law, the law of nations, and fidelity to treaties; as contrary to the Divine constitution of the Church, to her essential rights and to her liberty; as destroying justice and trampling underfoot the rights of property which the Church has acquired by many titles and, in addition, by virtue of the Concordat. We reprove and condemn it as gravely offensive to the dignity of this Apostolic See, to Our own person, to the Episcopacy, and to the clergy and all the Catholics of France. Therefore, We protest solemnly and with all Our strength against the introduction, the voting and the promulgation of this law, declaring that it can never be alleged against the imprescriptible rights of the Church. [536]

The Condemnation of the *Associations Cultuelles*

The rejection of the law of separation by the French bishops was nearly unanimous; however, many of them thought that the *associations cultuelles* proposed

535 *Processus Informativus Ordinarius*, vol. 2, Sessio LXXXIX, pp. 549–550.

536 Pius X, Encyclical *Vehementer nos de Ecclesiae in Gallia asperrima conditione*, February 11, 1906, no. 13, in *Enchiridion/Pio X*, pp. 164–165 (pp. 146–171). https://www.vatican.va/content/pius-x/en/encyclicals/documents/hf_p-x_enc_11021906_vehementer-nos.html.

by the government represented the only possibility for worship in France.[537] The archbishop of Besançon, Marie-Joseph Fulbert-Petit,[538] suggested to the Holy See that there might be room for agreement with the governement, if the *associations cultuelles* were replaced by *associations fabriciennes* with a sort of canonical-legal status.[539] Meanwhile, Ferdinand Brunetière,[540] a writer and member of the French Academy, along with a group of secular personalities called the "*cardinaux verts*," sponsored a letter to the French episcopate endorsing the promotion of the *associations cultuelles*, supported in Rome by some prelates. In the general assembly of French bishops, which opened in Paris on May 30, 1906, the line conciliatory toward the government prevailed with fifty-six votes against and eighteen in favor of the Fulbert-Petit proposal.

This was not, however, the position of the pope and his secretary of state. On February 27, 1906, Cardinal Merry del Val sent a confidential letter to Msgr. Montagnini,[541] the Holy See's representative in Paris, asking him to advise Cardinal Richard[542] with the utmost secrecy, "not to believe that the Holy Father

537 "Nommés sous Léon XIII, pape du Ralliement, et habitués au Concordat, les prélats ne cherchent pas l'affrontement" (Sévillia, *Quand les catholiques étaient hors la loi*, p. 215).

538 Marie-Joseph Fulbert-Petit (1832–1909) was ordained in 1857, bishop of Puy-en-Velay in 1887, then archbishop of Besançon from 1894 until his death.

539 *Associations fabriciennes*, established under the Concordat, managed the finances and material resources of Catholic parishes in France. They were comprised of the parish priest and lay members of the parish.

540 Ferdinand Brunetière (1849–1906), literary critic and secretary, then from 1894 director of the *Revue des Deux Mondes*, in 1900 announced his unequivocal return to Catholicism. Member of the French Academy, he was a promoter of a *Supplique aux évêques*, made public by *Le Figaro* on March 26, 1906, in which twenty-three signatories called "*les cardinaux verts*," since they were members of the *Académie Française*, of the *Institut de France* and of other prestigious institutions, expressed their support for the *associations cultuelles.*

541 Carlo Montagnini (1863–1913), diplomat of the Holy See when the nuncio Msgr. Lorenzelli was recalled to Rome, was kept in Paris by Msgr. Merry del Val "to safeguard the archives of the Nuciature, or to carry out whatever the Holy See might need." On November 11, 1906, the government had the Nunciature, at 10 Rue de l'Elysée, confiscated, sequestering the archives. The Holy See protested against this violation of international law, while the so-called scandal of the "fiches" which supposedly involved the Vatican Nunciature, came to nothing. Montagnini was expelled from France and later became apostolic delegate in Colombia in 1912 and titular archbishop of Larissa in March 1913. He died six months later, still young, in Berlin. Cf. *Les Fiches Pontificales de Monsignor Montagnini*, Librairie Critique, Paris 1908, in which some of the files are reproduced of ecclesiastical personalities and French politicians; Olivier Poncet, *La Nonciature de France (1819–1904) et ses archives*, Vatican Secret Archive, Vatican City 2006, pp. 284–288; Gilles Ferragu and Hervé Jannou, "Une nonciature sans nonce: Mgr Montagnini en France, sa mission et son expulsion (1904–1906)," *Mélanges de l'École française de Rome* 119, no. 1 (2007), pp. 109–120.

542 François-Marie-Benjamin Richard de la Vergne (1819–1908) was bishop of Belley in 1872; in 1879 he became coadjutor to Cardinal Joseph Guibert, archbishop of Paris, whom he succeeded in 1886. In May 1889, he was made a cardinal.

actually wants or believes he will accept the formation of the Associations, giving credence to those in the liberal and masonic press of the world who are saying that the protest is simply doctrinal and platonic and that the pope, after having blustered hot words, in practice will accept everything. This opinion has its advocates here too, even among us, under the influence of the school of Brunetière, and they work to attain their goal.... I am very concerned because I clearly see that we are at a '*tournant de l'histoire*' for the universal Church. France finds itself at this moment in the front lines of this struggle with all the forces of evil, with international Freemasonry against the Church. What will be done in France will give an example for everyone and therefore the decision is of greatest importance."[543]

Pius X had no illusions when, on July 12, 1906, he convoked a meeting of the Congregation of Ecclesiastical Affairs to discuss this important topic. When the assembly began, Cardinal Rampolla spoke in support of the thesis of compromise with the French government. Leo XIII's secretary of state compared the situation to that in England in the sixteenth century, when Henry VIII prepared for schism, and with that of France at the end of the same century when the Catholic League put up stiff resistance to the succession of Protestant Henry IV of Navarre. "Now," he insisted, "Clement VII lost England due to excessive severity and Sixtus V saved France, despite his advisers, thanks to the timely compliance toward Béarnais."[544]

Cardinal Ferrata intervened along the same lines and Cardinal Mathieu, the only French cardinal present at the meeting, took up the argumentation he and Rampolla had developed in favor of the compromise with the Third Republic. Cardinal Merry del Val, on the other hand, expressed an opinion decidedly contrary to the formation of the *associations cultuelles*, stating that they would have a disastrous effect on religion in France. "The best Catholics will be discouraged. The wider public will interpret such a concession as acceptance of the law despite all the explanations and all the cautions."[545]

543 "Highly confidential" letter from Card. Merry del Val to Msgr. Montagnini of February 27, 1906, in AAV, *Nunziatura Parigi*, 361, 3, 68, reproduced in Cesare Silva, *La separazione dello Stato dalla Chiesa in Francia del 1905*, Pontificia Università Gregoriana, Rome 1920, p. 265.

544 Renard, *Le cardinal Mathieu*, p. 467.

545 The opinion of Card. Merry del Val at session 1077 of the Sacred Congregation of Extraordinary Ecclesiastical Affairs of July 12, 1906, in Silva, *La separazione dello Stato dalla Chiesa in Francia del 1905*, p. 276 (pp. 275–277).

Pius X adjourned the session until July 19. During the second meeting, Card. Mathieu presented an opinion claiming that the prohibition of the *associations cultuelles* "would lead the Holy See to incur enormous responsibility without an evident need to do so; the considerable ecclesiastical patrimony would be completely lost and the churches closed for worship; public worship would be prohibited with an irreparable loss of faith among the masses; in effect, it would be the ruin of the Church in France, for which public opinion would hold the Holy See responsible."[546]

Merry del Val replied, recalling that "Bonapart and the Directory had wanted to obtain from Pius VI a favorable stance toward the Civil Constitution of the Clergy; then too the pope was counseled to avoid the accusation of having provoked conflicts disastrous for religion, and they employed threats and all sorts of tricks to bend the Holy See, and many bishops invoked calm. But the Holy See replied to Bonapart opposing force with constancy in its principles and with trust in God. The result of this attitude, after a number of years of easily predictable suffering, was the signing of the Concordat and a century of religious peace in France. Such was the policy of the Holy See at that time (if it can be called a policy). And today?"[547]

The pope secretly prescribed a triduum of prayer in monasteries and convents, but did not leak the decision he had made. This was publicized only on August 10, 1906, when with the encyclical *Gravissimo officii*,[548] the Pontifex Maximus opposed with a firm *non possumus* not only the *associations cultuelles* imposed by the law of separation, but also the compromise proposed by Bishop Fulbert-Petit, with the "canonical-legal" associations.

When the deadline established by the law on separation expired on December 11, 1906, the anticlerical measures were brutally approved by the Third Republic. The Church in France lost a patrimony equal to 450 million Francs, an amount ten times greater that the annual budget for worship.[549] Besides this, the Church was stripped of every form of juridical status and

546 Ibid, p. 281. The opinion of Card. Mathieu at the session of the Sacred Congregation of Extraordinary Ecclesiastical Affairs of July 19, 1906.

547 Ibid, p. 281 (pp. 279–281). The opinion of Card. Merry del Val at the session of the Sacred Congregation of Extraordinary Ecclesiastical Affairs of July 19, 1906.

548 Pius X, Encyclical *Gravissimo officii de Ecclesiae in Gallia*, August 10, 1906, in *Pii X Acta*, vol. 3, pp. 181–185.

549 Martin Grichting, *Pio X e la separazione tra Chiesa e Stato in Francia*, in Cattaneo (ed.), *L'eredità giuridica di san Pio X*, pp. 259–260 (pp. 253–266).

stood before the law as an illegal entity. The French cabinet and parliament were convinced that the Church would have to concede defeat in the face of such a depravation.

Cardinal Mathieu's biography reports his sentiments of sadness and disappointment due to the strong position taken by the pope: the Church and the French government "were by now officially antagonists."[550] But when reproached by those who observed that rejecting the worship associations meant depriving French dioceses of all material sustenance, and that the archbishop of Paris, stripped of home and income, could no longer exercise his ministry, the pope responded that in that event he could always appoint to that office a Franciscan, obliged by his Rule to live by begging, in absolute poverty.[551]

While receiving the Assumptionist Fathers Baudouy and Bertoye on December 23, 1906, Merry del Val stated: "Ah, if only the resistance had begun twenty years ago! The Church in France would have found itself in superb condition! But we have made too many holes in the levee and today the flood is overwhelming us.... If only we had met six years ago, when it had become clear that the enemy was preparing his most furious attack.... The struggle is much more difficult today because we are in the midst of the ruins of the bastion. Everything has been demolished and everything must be rebuilt. But the battle is not lost. But to win it we must first be united and second, act."[552]

The dramatic events in France made evident the distance between the position of Pius X and his secretary of state, on the one hand, and of Leo XIII and Cardinal Rampolla, on the other. Giovanni Spadolini observes that Pius X's attitude toward the French Republic was just the contrary of what Leo XIII's would have been: "As he became aware of the impossibility of an honorable and

550 Renard, *Le cardinal Mathieu*, p. 472. Among the prelates who were closest to him in this moment, Renard recalls Msgr. Gasparri and Msgr. Della Chiesa, heirs of the spirit of Rampolla (p. 473). In the *Positio* of St. Pius X, Cardinal Canali dwells on the difference of positions between Pius X and Msgr. Gasparri as concerned the conflict between the Holy See and France, especially concerning the laws on worship associations: Gasparri, in favor of accepting the laws out of fear of losing the Ecclesiastical patrimony, was decidedly opposed to Pius X (*Pii Papae X. Positio*, pp. 360–364).

551 Vittorio Emanuele Orlando, among others, dealt with this in *Miei rapporti di governo con la Santa Sede [My Governance Relationship with the Holy See]*, Garzanti, Milano 1944, pp. 13, 24.

552 Audience of Cardinal Merry del Val with Fathers Baudouy and Bertoye on December 20, 1906, cited in Emmanuel Tawil, *Le Cardinal Merry del Val et la France: La défense de la liberté de l'Église*, text presented at the convention on October 1, 2015, not published in the acts. Ernest Baudouy (1862–1923) was assistant and General Provost of the Assumptionists from 1904 to 1923; François d'Assise (Georges) Bertoye (1857–1929), Assumptionist, directed *La Croix* from 1901 to 1927.

decorous agreement for the Church, he preferred to leave the diplomatic and political fields and place the entire issue on the religious level."[553]

Msgr. Pescini told how one evening he went to the pope and alerted him that some cardinals, whose names he mentioned, were concerned about his resistance toward France, accusing him of not having fully understood the gravity of the situation. "The Servant of God was writing. Without in the least losing his composure (and smiling) he looked at me and said, 'I know all this. I know that they say I do not understand a thing. This does not concern me!' Then pointing the pen in his hand toward the Crucifix in front of him, he added, 'I have but one path ... one point of view.... You see, I am going straight toward Him.'"[554]

On January 6, 1907, the pope promulgated the encyclical *Une fois encore*, in which he reiterated, "The whole world now knows that if peace of conscience is broken in France, that is not the work of the Church but of her enemies. Fair-minded men, even though not of our faith, recognize that if there is a struggle on the question of religion in your beloved country, it is not because the Church was the first to unfurl the flag, but because war was declared against her. During the last twenty-five years she has had to undergo this warfare. That is the truth and the proof of it is seen in the declarations made and repeated over and over again in the Press, at meetings, at Masonic congresses, and even in Parliament, as well as in the attacks which have been progressively and systematically directed against her. These facts are undeniable, and no argument can ever make away with them."[555]

Pius X Consecrates New Bishops "Born for War"

On February 25, 1906, a few months after the Combes law was adopted but before it took effect, a touching and memorable ceremony was held in secret in Rome in which the pope consecrated at the Altar of the Chair in St. Peter's Basilica fourteen bishops "born for war," the first in the history of France to be nominated without the agreement of civil authorities. At 8 a.m., Pius X made his entrance into St. Peter's on foot, accompanied by his escort, the papal guards, and the fourteen new bishops, as the Choir of the Sistine Chapel intoned Lorenzo

553 G. Spadolini, *L'opposizione cattolica*, Vallecchi, Florence 1961, p. 656.

554 *Pii Papae X. Positio*, p. 107.

555 Pius X, Encyclical *Une fois encore sur l'Église catholique de France*, January 6, 1907, no. 8, https://www.vatican.va/content/pius-x/en/encyclicals/documents/hf_p-x_enc_06011907_une-fois-encore.html.

Perosi's *Tu es Petrus*.[556] The bishops prostrated themselves face down during the litany of saints, then they stood up and the pope laid his hands on them, anointed them, and gave each the crosier and ring. Msgr. Erminio Jasoni, who was present at the ceremony, recalled, "I had a feeling, a shudder of joy that I'll never forget and that I might never feel again in my life. The Altar of the Chair seemed to me as radiant that morning as it was in the Cenacle that marked the dawn of the nascent Church: next to the Successor of Peter, humble, peaceful, was Cardinal Merry del Val, absorbed in prayer, emotional yet serene, and satisfied with his duty done after unimaginable struggles."[557]

Two days later, Pius X received the newly consecrated bishops in his private library where he gave them a moving exhortation. Cardinal Merry del Val, the only one present in the library next to the pope, reported the text, which the Holy Father, contrary to his custom, had committed to memory, but read from his manuscript with a solemn tone, pronouncing each word to give greater importance to what he was saying.

> I have been anxious to see you all together to give you a word of confidence and affection, despite the seal of secrecy; to tell you I esteem the great sacrifice you have made in exposing yourselves to poverty, to privation, and even to being, God forbid, not only misunderstood in your authority, but even persecuted. You shall receive today instructions on how to maintain yourselves upon your imminent return to, and recovery of, the dioceses entrusted to you. I shall not advise you to be punctilious in carrying out what shall be said, because this would offend your sentiments of obedience and reverence to all the instructions of the Apostolic Holy See. In time you shall be invited to take part in the general assembly of all the bishops of France to express your judgment, after the rules concerning the laws of separation will be published: if and under what conditions it behooves us to suffer it; if and how it will be licit to resist it. It is not improbable that, finding yourselves in Rome during these days, you have heard talk about it or have even received suggestions concerning the issue. I counsel you not to heed this,

556 Bazin, *Pie X*, pp. 132–133.

557 *Il ven. Servo di Dio Card. Raffaele Merry del Val "come lo vide Mons. Erminio Jasoni,"* ed. Msgr. Prof. Gustavo Tulli, Tip. Linograf, Rome 1954, p. 13. Msgr. Erminio Jasoni (1866–1941), of Parma, was director of the Roman Hospice Tata Giovanni, and director of the General Archive of the Vicariat until 1933, when he was named domestic prelate.

because the pope, who hitherto has manifested to no one his judgment on the matter, before pronouncing the final word wants to hear the opinion of all the bishops, free in manifesting their opinion on what shall be for the greater glory of God, for the good of souls, for the decorum of the clergy and for the security of religion in France. I recommend only that in the future conference of bishops, when giving your vote to the questions you shall be asked, that you:

1. Conform yourselves to the spirit of Jesus Christ, *quacumque humana affectione postposita* [setting human affections aside].
2. Remember that we are born for war: *Non veni pacem mittere, sed gladium* [I did not come to bring peace, but a sword; Matt. 10:34].
3. Take into account, as you form your opinion, the spirit of the true Catholics of your Nation.
4. Consider that you were called to safeguard the absolute principles of justice and to defend the rights of the Church, which are the rights of God.
5. Keep present not only the judgment of God, but also that of the world that is watching you, if ever your dignity were to falter and the duties which it imposes on you.

And I conclude here by telling you that I envy your fate, that I would like to come with you to share your pains, your anxieties, to remain always by your side to comfort you. But if I am far in body, I shall always be with you in spirit and every day we shall meet in the divine sacrifice of the Mass, before the holy tabernacle, from which flows the strength to combat and the sure means of victory.[558]

On April 18, 1909, Pius X testified to his love for France by beatifying Joan of Arc, the French national heroine.[559] The following day, the pope received forty thousand

558 Merry del Val, *San Pio X*, pp. 28–29. Cf. also AAV, *Spoglio Merry del Val*, busta 4, n. 332.

559 Cf. Msgr. Henri Delassus, *La mission posthume de la Bienheureuse Jeanne d'Arc et le Règne social de Notre Signeur Jésus Christ*, Desclée De Brouwer, Lille 1914. Joan of Arc (1412–1431) was proclaimed blessed by Pius X on April 18, 1909, and canonized by Benedict XV on July 10, 1920. During his pontificate, Pius X also raised to the honors of the altar the holy Cure of Ars, Jean-Marie Vianney; the Carmelites of Compiègne, victims of the French Revolution; Marie-Madeleine Postel, foundress of the Daughters of Mercy; Madaleine-Sophie Barat, foundress of the Society of the Sacred Heart of Jesus; and Jean Eudes, apostle of the Sacred Hearts of Jesus and Mary.

French pilgrims in St. Peter's. During the ceremony, from his *sedia gestatoria*, the pope drew toward him the hem of a French flag and kissed it. This gesture aroused a wave of enthusiasm among the thousands of pilgrims present, among whom was the French music critic Camille Bellaigue.[560] Cardinal Merry del Val later said, "This was not the case of a spectacular and calculated demonstration, because the Holy Father did not know that he would have a French standard next to him. The spontaneity of his outpouring merely emphasized the sense and meaning of it."[561]

Among the pilgrims present was Robert Havard de la Montagne, who was delighted. In his memoirs, he recals the words that Cardinal Merry del Val some weeks later wrote to Colonel Keller, who advocated that Catholicism was the only terrain that could unite the French. "Your words respond completely to the thoughts and desires of the Sovereign pontiff, who is happy to give you his full and total approval.... The Holy Father hopes that this plan of action, so clear and fruitful, will be adopted by all the good French people."[562]

Pius X never had anti-French sentiments. On the evening of November 29, 1911, during his allocution to the cardinals upon whom he had imposed the biretta, he stated, "The day shall come, and let us hope not very far now, in which France, like Saul on the Road to Damascus, will be surrounded by a light from above and shall hear a voice repeating to her, '*O daughter, why are you persecuting me?*' When she responds, '*Who are you, Lord?*' the voice will add, 'I am Jesus whom you are persecuting; it is a hard thing for you to go against the goad, because through your obstinacy you destroy yourself.' And shaking and stunned she will reply, 'Lord, what would you have me do?' And he: 'Rise up, wash away the filth that pollutes you, and awaken in your breast the slumbering sentiments and the pacts of our alliance and go, firstborn daughter of the Church, predestined nation, elected vase, and take as in the past my name before all peoples and kings of the earth.'"[563]

The Pope? He Was the Only One Who Saw Clearly

In the face of the intransigence of the Holy See, the Third Republic did not dare to carry out to the bitter end the persecution, so as to avoid creating martyrs,

[560] Camille Bellaigue, *Pie X et Rome. Notes et souvenirs 1903–1914*, Nouvelle Librairie Nationale, Paris 1916, p. 124.

[561] Hary Mitchell, *Pie X et la France*, Éditions du Cèdre, Paris 1954, p. 101.

[562] Robert Havard de la Montagne, *Chemins de Rome et de France. Cinquante ans de souvenirs*, Nouvelles Éditions Latines, Paris 1956, p. 99.

[563] The text of the discourse is reported in Dieguez (ed.), *Carte Pio X*, pp. 457–458.

and renounced its plan to close the churches and imprison priests. Pius X's unbending policies, judged "daring" by many moderates, showed themselves to be farsighted. The law of separation was never strictly applied and the pope's appeal contributed to a widespread rebirth of Catholicism in France on the eve of the First World War.

On May 13, 1904, in a dispatch to his government, the French ambassador to Italy, Camille Barrère, referred to a meeting he had had with Cardinal Agliardi, considered to be the foremost expert among the cardinals of the Curia on international relations.[564] Agliardi had harshly criticized Pius X and his secretary of state Merry del Val for their "disastrous break with France." According to Agliardi, Pius X had granted blind trust to a man who was too young and inexperienced like Merry del Val, with whom he was infatuated, and deceived himself in thinking that the break with France would cause greater independence for the Church.[565]

Agliardi's accusations, which evidently reflected those of the entire Rampollian ecclesiastical current, were unjust, but above all, they were refuted by the facts. As the historian Anthony Rhodes observed, "The result of this persecution was, paradoxically, somehow to the Church's advantage."[566] The Holy See, free to choose its own bishops, created in a very short time a strong and independent French episcopate. Pius X took advantage of the conflictual situation to nominate sixty-three bishops in France over the course of his pontificate, no longer needing the recognition of the State.

The consequences of the separation were catastrophic not for the Church, but for the French government, which since the nineteenth century had relied on the missionary work of its priests to expand its political and cultural influence around the world. In 1875, of the six thousand missionary priests throughout the world, forty-five hundred were French, and France was considered by Rome as the protecting power of all Catholics, of any nationality, throughout those lands.[567]

[564] Camille Barrère (1851–1940) was the French ambassador to Rome from 1899 to 1924. Cf. Jules Laroche, *Quinze ans à Rome avec Camille Barrère (1898–1913)*, Plon, Paris 1948; Enrico Serra, *Camille Barrère e l'intesa italo-francese*, Giuffrè, Milan 1950.

[565] Quai d'Orsay, C. P. *Politique Etrangère, Saint-Siège*, Tome 22, *Relations avec la France*, January-June 1904, Dispatch of M. Barrère on May 13, 1904, cited in Anthony Rhodes, *The Power of Rome in the Twentieth Century*, Sidwick & Jackson, London 1983, pp. 205–206.

[566] Ibid., p. 209.

[567] Ibid., pp. 210–211.

French clergy, persecuted by the Third Republic, deprived France of the influence and prestige that it once had, above all in the Far East, as Foreign Minister Delcassé had foreseen, in a message to Combes on February 10, 1904.[568] Furthermore, neither Combes nor his successors understood the importance of having an official representative in the Vatican, in situations such as the world war that broke out in 1915. The Vatican, in continual contact with bishops and nuncios throughout the world, was in fact an extraordinary center of information, of which the nations accredited with the Holy See could take advantage, though not France, which had renounced its diplomatic representative.[569]

This explains the words of Aristide Briand,[570] one of the promoters of the law of separation, who was later to confess with reference to Pius X, "The pope? He was the only one who saw clearly.... There was only one man who saw clearly, only one whose policies were coherent and who worked for the future, for the coming age! The pope."[571] The judgment of the liberal Vittorio Emanuele Orlando follows the lines of Briand: "For the first time in centuries, the papacy could fully regain its supremacy over the Gallican clergy. And this occurred under Pius X."[572]

"The break that took place with France," testified Cardinal Tommaso Boggiani during the cause for beatification, "revealed in my opinion that the pontificate of the Servant of God was one of the strongest of the Church, and that it was animated by the liveliest faith. And for this reason, I consider that act the most splendid of his pontificate."[573]

568 Memo of M. Delcassé to the Prime Minister, February 10, 1904, in Rhodes, *The Power of Rome*, pp. 211–212.

569 Ibid, p. 214.

570 Aristide Briand (1862–1932) was prime minister eleven times and twenty times a minister. About him, cf. Georges Suarez, *Briand, sa vie, son œuvre avec son journal et de nombreux documents inédits*, Plon, Paris 1938–1952, 6 vols.

571 Sevilla, *Quand les catholiques étaient hors la loi*, p. 265.

572 V. E. Orlando, *Miei rapporti di governo con la S. Sede*, Garzanti, Milano 1944, p. 14. Vittorio Emanuele Orlando (1860–1952) was professor of law in various Italian universities, a minister several times, prime minister (1917–1919) and president of the Chamber of Deputies (1919–1920), head of the Italian delegation at the Conference of Versailles (1919), deputy of the Constitutional Assembly (1946–1947), and senator for life of the Republic. Cf. V. E. Orlando, *Memorie (1915–1919)*, ed. Rodolfo Mosca, Rizzoli, Milan 1960.

573 *Pii Papae X. Positio*, p. 79.

4

Against Modernism and Other Battles

Pius X, Merry del Val, and Italy

When Pius X was elected to the papal throne, Vittorio Emanuele III reigned in Italy and Giovanni Giolitti dominated the political scene.[574] Giolitti governed directly or indirectly from February 1901 to March 1915. The Age of Giolitti coincided directly with the period of Pius X, who from the moment of his election found himself dealing with the problems unleashed by the Roman Question, regulated by the Law of the *Guarentigie,* namely, the "guarantees" assured in 1871 by the Kingdom of Italy to the Church, but rejected by Pius IX and by his successors.[575]

Secretary of State Merry del Val had to deal not only with diplomatic relations with the Italian state, but also with the movement *Azione Cattolica* (Catholic Action) that developed after the foundation of the unified Kingdom of Italy. The *Opera dei Congressi,* or Work of the Congress, was the main Catholic organization within this movement, established in Venice in 1874.[576] Its aim was to unite

574 Giovanni Giolitti (1842–1828) was Minister of the Treasury (1889–1890) and of the Interior (1901–1903) and prime minister on various occasions from 1892–1914 and from 1920–1921. Cf. G. Spadolini, *Giolitti e i cattolici (1901–1914),* Le Monnier, Florence 1960; Giovanni Ansaldo, *Il ministro della buona vita. Giovanni Giolitti e i suoi tempi [The Minister of the Good Life. Giovanni Giolitti and His Times],* Le Lettere, Florence 2002, with an introduction by Francesco Perfetti.

575 Law n. 214 of May 13, 1871, called the Law of the *guarentigie,* was a legislative provision of the Kingdom of Italy that regulated relations between the Italian State and the Holy See until 1929, when the Lateran Pacts were signed. It was rejected by Pius IX with the Encyclical *Ubi nos,* May 15, 1871. Cf. the criticism of the law made at the start of Pius X's pontificate by Fr. Salvatore Brandi (1852–1915) in "La dotazione della Santa Sede secondo la legge delle guarentigie" [The Provisioning of the Holy See according to the Law of the Guarentigie], *La Civiltà Cattolica* 55, no. 4 (1904). For an overview: Arturo Carlo Jemolo, *Chiesa e Stato in Italia dalla unificazione ai giorni nostri [Church and State in Italy from Unification to Our Days],* Einaudi, Turin 1991 (1948).

576 Cf. Marco Invernizzi, *Il movimento cattolico in Italia dalla fondazione dell'Opera dei congressi all'inizio della Seconda guerra mondiale (1874–1939) [The Catholic Movement in Italy of the Foundation of the Work of the Congress at the Beginning of the Second World War],* 2nd revised ed. Mimep-Docete, Pessano (Milan) 1995; and *L'Opera dei Congressi (1874–1904). Con i profili dei principali protagonisti,* D'Ettoris, Crotone 2022. National presidents of the Work of the Congress were Giovanni Acquaderni (1875–1878), Scipione Salviati (1878–1884), Marcellino Venturoli (1884–1889), Giovanni Battista Paganuzzi (1889–1902), and Giovanni Grosoli Pironi (1902–1904).

Catholics and their associations in order to create common action in defense of the rights of the Church and in defense of the religious and social rights of Italians affected by the *non expedit* (the prohibition by which the ecclesiastical hierarchy had forbidden the faithful to participate in political elections, so as not to endorse the new status quo).[577] The essential structures of the Work were parish committees, and the fundamental moment of its activity were the congresses that met nineteen times over the course of thirty years. Within the movement there existed a more intransigent wing whose stronghold was in Veneto, and a more moderate wing, especially in Lombardy. But its equilibrium was overturned in the last decade of the century when some Catholics became convinced that the Church ought to be reconciled with the political and social gains of modernity.

In France, the ideas of Lamennais,[578] who had theorized the necessity of Catholicizing the French Revolution, were reproposed by Fr. Jules Lemire,[579] the first "Christian Democrat" priest, or perhaps "Christian Socialist" (the media vacillated between the two expressions).[580] The same ideas were being agitated in Italy by Fr. Romolo Murri,[581] who sought to transform the spirit and methods of the Work of the Congress, under the presidency of Count Giovanni Grosoli Pironi.[582]

577 The expression *non expedit*, used for the first time by the Holy See in 1868, was a disposition which prohibited Italian Catholics from participating in national elections (thought not local elections) within the Kingdom of Italy. This order was officially repealed by Benedict XV in 1919. Cf. Cesare Marongiu Buonaiuti, *Non expedit. Storia di una politica (1866–1919) [Non expedit. The History of a Policy (1866–1919)]*, Giuffrè, Milan 1971; Saretta Marotta, "Il non expedit," in Alberto Melloni (ed.), *Cristiani d'Italia. Chiese, società, Stato (1861–2011) [Christians of Italy. Church, Society, State]*, Istituto della Enciclopedia Italiana (Treccani), Rome 2011, vol. 1, pp. 215–235.

578 Félicité de Lamennais (1782–1854) founded in 1830 the newspaper *L'Avenir*, condemned by Gregory XVI in 1832 for its liberal ideas. After further condemnations, Lamennais abandoned the Church in 1834 and died on February 27, 1854, refusing the sacraments. Cf. The historical reconstruction of Fr. Paul Dudon S.J. (1859–1941), *Lamennais et le Saint-Siège, 1820–1834*, Perrin et Cie, Paris 1911.

579 Fr. Jules Lemire (1853–1928) was a deputy of parliament from 1893 to 1914 as an exponent of the "republican" clergy. Cf. Jean-Marie Mayeur, *Un prêtre démocrate. L'abbé Lemire. 1853–1928*, Casterman, Paris-Tournai 1968; Jean Pascal Vanhoye, *L'abbé Lemire*, Le Maras du Livre, Herzebrouck 2013; Robert Havard de la Montagne, *Histoire de la démocratie chrétienne. De Lamennais à Georges Bidault*, Amiot-Dumont, Paris 1948, pp. 153–158.

580 Mayeur, *Un prêtre démocrate, l'abbé Lemire*, p. 43.

581 Romolo Murri (1870–1944), excommunicated in 1909, married Ragnhild Lund in April 1912, daughter of the president of the Norwegian senate. He adhered, as did many modernists, to fascism, only to return just before his death to the embrace of the Church. About him, cf., among others, Maurilio Guasco, *Romolo Murri e il modernismo*, Cinque Lune, Rome 1968; idem, *Il caso Murri dalla sospensione alla scomunica [The Case of Murri from the Suspension to the Excommunication]*, Argalia, Urbino 1978; Lidia Pupilli, *Intellettuale nel regime. L'altra vita di Romolo Murri [An Intellectual in the Regime. The Other Life of Romolo Murri]*, Marsilio, Venice 2019.

582 Count Giovanni Grosoli Pironi (1859–1937), named by Leo XIII in 1902 president of the Work of the Congress, was removed in 1904 by Pius X. Later he was a senator (1920) and among the founders of the Popular Party.

In his encyclical *Graves de communi*, of January 18, 1901, Leo XIII had clarified in what way the term Christian Democracy could be used.[583] But in November 1905, Murri founded in Bologna the National Democratic League, non-confessional and left-leaning, which insisted on having full autonomy from ecclesiastical hierarchy. Mariano Rampolla, secretary of state under Leo XIII, had displayed a certain benevolence toward this new orientation. Cardinal Aloisi Masella wrote in his *Memoires* that the birth of Christian Democracy in Italy was favored by Cardinal Rampolla, "who even hoped it would develop into something quite damaging to the Savoy government."[584] According to Murri, the secretary of state had declared to him in 1900, "Every day the appeals pour in from the bishops against you; but go forward with prudence and we will give you our support."[585]

Here too, the policy of Pius X was different from that of his predecessor. Murri's claim to autonomy stood in open contrast with the recommendations of Pius X that they should align with the orientations of the Holy See to avoid the doctrinal deviations that were arising in the Catholic movement.

The pontiff did not limit himself to halting the action of Murri, but proposed to reformulate the orientation of the Catholic movement. The motu proprio *Fin dalla prima*,[586] published on December 18, 1903, was the first document in which Pius X confronted in an organic manner the issue of the Catholic social apostolate.[587] In this text, also defined as the "Social syllabus," the pope expounded in nineteen articles a sort of "code" and "practical guide" for Catholics. On July 14, 1904, Count Grosoli Pironi, who was leaning toward Murri's positions, was invited to resign from the presidency of the Work of the Congress, and on July 28, a letter from Cardinal Merry del Val to the Italian bishops announced the suppression of the Catholic institution.

On July 28, 1906, Pius X condemned the Democratic League and prohibited priests from taking part in it. Murri was suspended *a divinis* in 1907 and excommunicated in 1909, after his election to parliament with the support of the radical-progressive party.

The reorganization of the Catholic movement was carried out through the encyclical *Il fermo proposito* of June 11, 1905, which replaced the Work of the

583 Leo XIII, Encyclical *Graves de Communi*, January 18, 1901, in ASS, vol. 33 (1900–1901), pp. 385–396.

584 Aloisi Masella, *Memorie inedite*, vol. 8, pp. 4649–4650.

585 R. Murri, *Dalla democrazia cristiana al partito popolare italiano [From Christian Democracy to the Italian Popular Party]*, Battistelli, Florence 1920, p. 72.

586 Pius X, Motu proprio *Fin dalla prima*, December 18, 1903, in ASS, vol. 37 (1904–1905), pp. 17–23.

587 Sanguinetti, *San Pio X*, pp. 119–124.

Congress with three unions: the Popular Union, the Social Economic Union, and the Electoral Union.

Pius X needed solid ground to stand on within the movement and found it in Count Stanislao Medolago Albani of Bergamo, highly regarded by Merry del Val.[588]. Under his direction, the Social Economic Union made a lasting impact, even after the other two unions eventually dissolved. Meanwhile, in 1904, a letter by Card. Merry del Val entrusted to the Catholic Youth, a movement under the direction of Paolo Pericoli,[589] the role of aggregating all youth activities present in the Work of the Congress.[590] In 1905, Pius X called Pericoli, as well as Stanislao Medolago Albani and Prof. Giuseppe Toniolo,[591] to form a commission to organize the reform of the statutes of Catholic Action. The objective was to bring the entire organization of Catholic laity into hierarchical relation with the Holy See,[592] requiring its members to make a firm profession of faith and seek authentic personal sanctity.

On March 4, 1906, Merry del Val sent to this triumvirate a letter in which he thanked them for the work they had done and communicated the pope's invitation to translate into practice his plans, "directed solely to defend Christian society, and toward a healthy reawakening of old and new energies in the common interest of the Church and the homeland, for the salvation of souls."[593]

Thus, under the presidency of Giuseppe Toniolo, the Popular Union among Catholics in Italy was born, called more succinctly the Popular Union, defined by the pontifical document as an "institution of a general character,

588 Count Stanislao Medolago Albani (1851–1921), son of Gerolamo and Benedetta de Maistre, earned his degree in theology and philosophy at the Gregorian University. Cf. Paolo De Töth, *Stanislao Medolago Albani soldato di Cristo. Profilo biografico fino al 1904*, ed. Paolo Borsotti, Publimedia, 2019.

589 Paolo Pericoli (1859–1942) was a member and later president (1900–1922) of Catholic Youth. Cf. *La "Gioventù cattolica" dopo l'unità. 1868–1968*, ed. Luciano Osbat, F. Piva, Rome 1972; and the two essays by Liliana Ferrari, "Appunti sulla Gioventù cattolica d'inizio secolo. La presidenza di Paolo Pericoli" [Notes on Catholic Youth at the Beginning of the Century. The Presidency of Paolo Pericoli], *Rivista di storia e letteratura religiosa* 26, no. 2 (1990), pp. 266–297; and "La Gioventù cattolica italiana nella seconda fase della presidenza Pericoli (1910–1922)" [Italian Catholic Youth in the Second Phase of the Pericoli Presidency], *Rivista di storia e letteratura religiosa* 27, no. 2 (1992), pp. 533–589.

590 Letter of Merry del Val, March 22, 1904, in ASS, vol. 36 (1903–1904), pp. 604–605.

591 Giuseppe Toniolo (1845–1918), professor of political economy from 1878 in Pisa, was beatified by Benedict XVI on April 29, 2012. His compete works were published in twenty volumes, from 1942 to 1953, by the Libreria Editrice Vaticana. Cf. Domenico Sorrentino, *Giuseppe Toniolo. Una Chiesa nella storia*, Edizioni Paoline, Cinisello Balsamo, Milan 1987; Fiorella Manzalini, *Elementi di economia politica in Giuseppe Toniolo*, Cantagalli, Siena 2009.

592 Francesco Malgeri, "Il Papa dell'Azione Cattolica," in La Bella (ed.), *Pio X e il suo tempo*, pp. 453–480.

593 Letter of Merry del Val, March 1st, 1906, in AAS, vol. 38 (1905–1906), pp. 3–8.

aimed at gathering Catholics of all social classes, but especially the great masses of people, around one common center of doctrine, advocacy, and social organization." Initially, the fields in which they committed themselves were above all the campaigns against divorce, blasphemy, and anticlericalism and in defense of religious instruction and the freedom of schools.

After Toniolo, Antonio Boggiano Pico (1909) and Ludovico Necchi (1910–1912) took turns at being president, until Pius X nominated Count Giuseppe dalla Torre to this position on October 2, 1912.[594] The pope had learned to appreciate Torre when this latter, just twenty years old, was in charge of the Catholic Federation of Padua. But in the meantime, Pius X and Cardinal Merry del Val had to face the problem of Italian political elections.

The Attack of Freemasonry

A radical-progressive alliance, including left-liberals, radicals, republicans, and socialists, won the administrative elections in Rome on June 30, 1907, and on the following November 25, elected Ernesto Nathan mayor of the capital.[595] Nathan, English by birth and Jewish by religion, had been the Grand Master of Italian Freemasonry and did not delay in manifesting his aggressive anticlericalism, encouraged by the French Third Republic, which sought to heighten the tension between the Vatican and the Italian state.

In a discourse on September 20, 1910, at Porta Pia, Mayor Nathan juxtaposed "the Rome that my office is honored to represent, avenger of freedom of thought, which entered here with the Tri-color flag through this breach in the walls" with "another Rome, prototype of the past, that closes itself within the narrow perimeter of the walls of Belisarius,[596] with the intent of

594 Count Giuseppe Dalla Torre del Tempio di Sanguinetto (1885–1967), founder and later director of the daily newspaper *La Libertà* of Florence (1910), was the president of the Popular Union among Catholics of Italy (1912), and later president of the central committee of Catholic Action (1915–1920). From 1920 to 1960 he directed *L'Osservatore Romano* and from 1930 to 1938 *L'Illustrazione vaticana.*

595 Ernesto Nathan (1845–1921) was Grand Master of the Grand Orient of Italy from 1896 to 1903 and from 1917 to 1919, and mayor of Rome from 1907 to 1913. Cf. Aldo Alessandro Mola, "Un Gran Maestro "mazziniano." Ernesto Nathan e il Grande Oriente d'Italia," in M. Novarino (ed.), *L'Italia delle minoranze. Massoneria, protestantesimo e repubblicanesimo nell'Italia contemporanea [Italy of the Minorities. Freemasonry, Protestantism and Republicanism in Contemporary Italy]*, Edizioni L'Età dell'Acquario, Turin 2003, pp. 29–56.

596 The Byzantine general Belisarius repaired and strengthened the Aurelian Wall during his defense of Rome in A. D. 537–538 against the Ostrogoths. The Aurelian Wall encloses an area of 5.3 square miles and defined the boundaries of the city until the nineteenth century. The wall was breached in the September 20, 1870 capture of the city by the Kingdom of Italy.

constricting their thoughts to a most limited circuit, in the fear that, like the embalmed cadavers in Egypt of old, their contact with the free air might reduce them to dust."[597]

Pius X, in a rescript to Cardinal Vicar Pietro Respighi on September 22, 1910, reacted with indignation: "Two days ago, a public functionary in the exercise of his duties, not content to recall solemnly the anniversary of the day on which the sacred rights of papal sovereignty were trampled, raised his voice to hurl against the doctrines of the Catholic Faith, against the Vicar of Christ on earth and against the Church herself, derision and insult ... taking direct aim at our own spiritual jurisdiction, to the point of denouncing with impunity to the contempt of the public even the actions of our apostolic ministry."[598]

Secretary of State Merry del Val sent an encoded telegram to the apostolic nuncios in which he asked them to bring to the attention of their respective governments Nathan's speech and Pius X's response.[599] It was a head-on clash, but Freemasonry, of which Nathan was at that moment a standard bearer, did not back off from its program.

In 1911, for the celebration of the fiftieth anniversary of Italian unification, Nathan entrusted to new architects and city planners his project for a "Third Rome," destined to substitute papal Rome through the construction of public buildings, squares and monuments such as the Vittoriano Complex, intended as the expression of a new *Patria di Marmo* (Marble Fatherland).[600] The Masonic administration planned the urban plan of the new Prati neighborhood in such a way that none of the streets would have as its backdrop the dome of St. Peter's. All the street names were dedicated to historical personalities of pagan Rome and to the heroes of the *Risorgimento*.[601]

The plan took direct aim at Catholics and the symbols of Catholicism. The anticlericalism of that period, writes a historian of Freemasonry, Rosario

597 Alessandro Levi, *Ricordi della vita e dei tempi di Ernesto Nathan*, Maria Pacini Fazzi Editori, Pisa 2006, p. 236.

598 AAV, Segr. Stato, 1911, rubr. 66, fasc. 1, f. 5.

599 Ibid. Mario Sanfilippo gathered the international reactions to the speech of the Mayor of Rome: "La Santa Sede, Ernesto Nathan e le ripercussioni internazionali delle celebrazioni per il 20 settembre 1910" [The Holy See, Ernesto Nathan and the International Repercussions of the Celebrations on September 20, 1910], *Archivio della società romana di storia patria* 113 (1990), pp. 347–360.

600 Cf. Marcello Venturoli, *La Patria di marmo (1870–1911)*, Nistri-Lischi, Pisa 1957, pp. 467–504. The monument was inaugurated in 1911, together with the Justice Palace, the Vittorio Emanuele Bridge, Risorgimento Bridge, the Zoo, the Gallery of Modern Art at Valle Giulia, and the National Stadium.

601 Roberto Quarta, *Roma massonica*, Mediterranee, Rome 2014, pp.156–160.

Esposito, was "vulgar and criminal."[602] The assassination attempts of cardinals in Rome and in the Castelli Romani, the profanation of churches, the disturbances during processions, all became daily news events. Merry del Val himself, while at leisure in Castel Gandolfo, was the victim of an ambush organized against him in August 1907 by several anticlerical fanatics from the town of Marino. Several hundred people were gathered along the road that the cardinal's carriage was to travel, planning to assault it, but his carriage managed to escape the ambush. "No measures were taken to repress such ignominies," wrote senator Guiccioli in his *Diary*. "The Government trembles before a few scoundrels who in twenty-four hours could be called to account."[603] Baron d'Erp reported that Cardinal Merry del Val had told him that the watchword of the anticlerical campaign had come from the French lodges. "He added that he had proof of this in hand: emissaries were sent from France all over Italy, providing money to carry out their sad task, which unfortunately obtained all too much success."[604]

Maria Cristina Giustiniani Bandini

As in France, so too in Italy, Freemasonry and anticlerical movements sought the total abolition of religious instruction in public schools and the total separation of church and state. In February 1908, an intense discussion took place in the Chamber of Deputies on the motion of Hon. Leonida Bissolati, a socialist and Freemason, to abolish religious instruction in elementary schools.[605] The discussion opened within the parliament as well as in the Grand Orient of Palazzo Giustiniani. A more moderate masonic current, led by the Methodist pastor Saverio Fera, the *Gran Commendatore* of the Scottish Rite, founded the Grand Lodge of Italy, better known under the name of the site of its headquarters in Piazza del Gesù, Rome.

602 R. F. Esposito, *La massoneria e l'Italia. Dall'800 ai nostri giorni [Freemasonry and Italy. From the 1800s to Our Days]*, Edizioni Paoline, Rome 1979, p. 318.

603 Alessandro Guiccioli, *Diario di un conservatore [Diary of a Conservative]*, Il Borghese, Rome 1973, p. 329.

604 Esposito, *La massoneria e l'Italia*, p. 318.

605 Leonida Bissolati (1857–1920) was one of the founders of the Italian Socialist Reformist Party. In 1908, he presented a motion to the Chamber of Deputies to abolish religious instruction in elementary schools, and during the annual meeting of the Grand Lodge of the Grand Orient of Italy, the Grand Master Ettore Ferrari proposed to censure those parliamentarians adhering to Freemasonry who refused to vote in favor of the motion. The Sovereign Grand Commendator, Saverio Fera placed a formal veto against this proposal of censure, setting off a clash that led to internal division and to the birth of the Ancient and Accepted Scottish Rite on June 24, 1908.

April 20–30, 1908, the First National Congress of Italian Women took place, with a strong suffragist respresentation.[606] When the Congress pronounced against religious instruction in the schools, the Catholic delegation, guided by Princess Maria Cristina Giustiniani Bandini, left the assembly and proposed to react against Freemasonry and nascent Italian feminism.[607]

Received by Pius X on July 4, 1908, Cristina Giustiniani Bandini expounded to him the proposal of founding "Female societies of cultural and Catholic activities" in defense of Christian women. "The Holy Father," she recalled, "showed his opposition to all female organizations and, with his typical benevolence, added in his characteristic Venetian dialect, '*La donna che la piasa, che la tasa, che la staga a casa*' (The woman who is pleasant is silent and stays at home). I replied that this was certainly more comfortable, but when women are targeted, as revealed by the interests of the sect in their preparation for that first congress and by statements to this effect by well-known Freemasons, it became a duty for us Catholics to defend ourselves, and not only that, but also to save our imprudent and endangered sisters. And I added, 'If we were to remain silently at home and the enemy in the meantime has invaded the battlefield, then it will be too late to call us to duty. We must at all costs preserve the women of the Church and not allow them to become the instruments and the prey of Freemasonry.'"[608]

At these words, the Holy Father remained perplexed and absorbed in his thoughts for a moment, although he did not yet seem convinced. The Princess insisted on the project of the foundation of female societies, showing him an

[606] Claudia Frattini, *Il primo congresso delle donne italiane. Roma 1908 [The First Congress of Italian Women]*, Biblink, Roma 2008.

[607] Maria Cristina of the Princess Giustiniani Bandini (1866–1959) guided the Union of Catholic Women of Italy from 1909 to 1917. In his discourse on July 2, 1958, for the fiftieth anniversary of the Women's Union of Catholic Action Italy, Pius XII praised "the chosen soul of the first President, Maria Cristina of the Giustiniani Bandini Princes, a woman of strong Christian mettle, prudently daring and open to the issues of her time" (*Discourses and Radio Messages*, vol. 20, p. 220). The princess was present, despite her frail health and ninety-two years. It was the rare case of the praise of a Pope to a living person. Cf. Paola Gaiotti de Biase, "La nascita dell'organizzazione cattolica nelle lettere di Maria Cristina Giustiniani Bandini a Toniolo" [The Birth of the Catholic Organization in the Letters of Maria Cristina Giustiniani Bandini to Toniolo], *Ricerche per la storia religiosa di Roma* 3 (1979), pp. 225–271; Cecilia Dau Novelli, "Alle origini dell'esperienza cattolica femminile: rapporti con la Chiesa e altri movimenti femminili (1908–1912)" [The Origins of the Catholic Women's Experience: Relations with the Church and Other Women's Movements], *Storia contemporanea* 12 (1981), pp. 667–711; idem, "Il fondo Cristina Giustiniani Bandini," *Bulletin of the historical archive on the history of the Catholic social movement in Italy* 20 (1985), pp. 141–152.

[608] Maria Cristina Giustiniani Bandini, *Il Beato Pio X e l'Associazione cattolica femminile [Blessed Pius X and the Catholic Women's Association]*, Rome 1951 (in particular, regarding the adage of Pius X on women, p. 12).

outline of her program, which consisted in fighting sectarian feminism through a movement of Catholic ladies. Pius X, after having read this, said, "I like it. Leave this with me. If there is anything to add, I shall add it; if there is anything to remove, I shall remove it. I want to think about it."[609]

On July 16, the pope approved the program and on April 21, 1909, with his full approval, the Union of Catholic Ladies of Italy was born, of which Giustiniani Bandini was nominated president and Fr. Vincenzo Bianchi Cagliesi the assistant general.[610]

Giustiniani Bandini's objective was to form a true army of women to combat not only everything that was anti-religious and anti-Christian in the field of the feminine, but also everything that was neutral. "We wanted to save the woman whom Freemasonry had decided to tear away from the Church and from the family to serve its tenebrous aims. But for this objective we had to fight Catholic feminists as well, who often, in good faith, held that a position of compromise with our adversaries was possible. The secret of success was contained in the motto we had chosen: *Fortes in fide*."[611]

The Union succeeded in mobilizing nearly thirty thousand women, operating in every region in Italy and involving them in civic campaigns, such as the fight against divorce and in defense of religious instruction in elementary schools.

Secretary of State Merry del Val was the intermediary between Giustiniani Bandini and Pius X. Testifying at the process of beatification, the Princess recalled that the cardinal "always displayed his desire to enter and understand the thought of Blessed Pius X and to execute his august wishes," even though, due to her character, she found it easier to speak with the pope than with the secretary of state, "who seemed too solemn and majestic and whom I certainly was not able to appreciate as much as he deserved."[612] Giustiniani Bandini's impulsive character at times clashed with that of the prudent cardinal whom she accused of being too "diplomatic," without comprehending that this was precisely the function he was carrying out with the pope's explicit mandate. Merry del Val, for that matter, had a great love for simplicity and candor. Cardinal Canali recalled that, having heard

609 Ibid, p. 17.

610 Vincenzo Bianchi Cagliesi (1873–1950), nephew of Pius IX, ordained priest in 1899, collaborated with the journal *Rivista Internazionale di scienze sociali* of Msgr. Salvatore Talamo (1854–1932) and held the post of assistant general of the Union of Catholic Women until 1915.

611 M. C. Giustiniani Bandini, *Alcuni appunti sulla storia della nostra Unione 1907–1917*, Rome 1934, manuscript in Fondo Giustiniani Bandini.

612 *Processus Informativus Ordinarius*, vol. 1, *Sessio* XIII, p.120.

it said one day that the Lord will have to judge liars with great indulgence because in certain positions the truth cannot always be told, "a bolt of indignation lit up his face; it was the natural accent of his loyal and sincere soul."[613]

THE CATHOLIC ELECTORAL UNION

On September 10, 1874, the year the Work of the Congress was founded, the Sacred Penitentiary had repeated its prohibition against Catholics participating in elections and, in general, in the political life of the Italian State.[614] Thirty years later, on May 31, 1904, Secretary of State Merry del Val wrote a private letter to Count Medolago communicating to him that "His Holiness maintains the dispositions of his August Predecessors in the fullness of their extension, confirming the authoritative interpretation which was given to the word *non expedit* by the Sacred Tribunal, which explained it as *non licet*."[615]

Nevertheless, Pius X united doctrinal intransigence with great flexibility on his political and pastoral program and, although not formally revoking the *non expedit*, allowed the entrance of Catholics into political life in the case of special circumstances as recognized by the bishops. This was expressed in the encyclical *Il fermo proposito* of 1905. While confirming the valid reasons why Pius IX and Leo XIII had "prohibited in Italy the participation of Catholics in legislative power," the pope recalled the "equally serious reasons, derived from the supreme good of society," that led him to concede to individual bishops the possibility of allowing Catholics in their respective dioceses to participate in political elections as candidates or as electors, for the sake of fostering and promoting among all the institutions "those which above all propose to discipline properly the multitudes against the invasive predominance of socialism." To this end, to coordinate the electoral activity of Italian Catholics in the various dioceses, the Italian Catholic Electoral Union (UECI) was established.[616] This union was "destined to gather

[613] Deposition of Card. Nicola Canali, in *Processus Informativus Ordinarius, Sessio* CXII, vol. 3, p. 685.

[614] Filippo Tamburini, "Il *non expedit* negli atti della Penitenzieria apostolica" [The *non expedit* in the acts of the Apostolic Penitentiary], *Rivista di Storia della Chiesa in Italia* 41 (1987), pp. 128–151.

[615] Merry del Val to Medolago, in *Archivio Medolago*. The Medolago Archive also preserves seventh-two letters sent by Pius X to Medolago from July 11, 1904, to July 31, 1914.

[616] The UECI was established in 1906 and disbanded in 1919, when the Italian Popular Party was founded. Its presidents were: Filippo Tolli (1906– 1910), Ottorino Gentiloni (1910–1916), Carlo Santucci (1916–1918), and Giorgio Montini (1918–1919). Cf. M. Invernizzi, *L'Unione Elettorale Cattolica Italiana. 1906–1919. Un modello di impegno politico unitario dei cattolic [The Catholic Electoral Union of Italy. 1906–1919. A Model of United Political Commitment Among Catholics]*, Cristianità, Piacenza 1993.

Catholics of all social classes but especially the great multitude of people around one common center of doctrine, of advocacy, and of social organization," characterized by the fact that adhesion to it was on a personal basis, while the Work of the Congress had been a federation of associations.

In July 1909, Pius X designated president of the Electoral Union, Count Vincenzo Ottorino Gentiloni.[617] In 1911, accompanied by a letter of Cardinal Merry del Val, the new statute and rules of the UECI were made known. The instructions given to Italian bishops by the secretary of state said that the conditions to which the Holy See subordinated its waiver of the *non expedit* were summarized "in the need to permit Catholics access to the political ballot boxes to impede serious harm to the Church; in the moral certainty of a happy outcome; and in the fact that the preferred candidate among Catholics not intend to present himself as the Catholic candidate as if to form a political party, and much less to offer the creation of a Catholic center in parliament, which the Holy Father does not want in Italy."[618]

Pius X in no way desired a Catholic party, but rather an alliance among Catholics and liberal conservatives, in order to form an "organized block" against the socialist, anticlerical left.[619] The formula *cattolici deputati, ma non deputati cattolici,* according to Cardinal Canali, was coined by Cardinal Merry del Val with Pius X's approval.[620]

The Letter of Card. Merry del Val to Card. Maffi

The two cardinals who caused Pius X the most suffering were the archbishops of Milan, Andrea Ferrari, and of Pisa, Pietro Maffi,[621] especially as concerned the issue of Catholic journalism.

During the moments of most intense controversy, Pius X manifested his sympathy and benevolence toward intransigent journalists whom he subsidized,

617 On Count Vincenzo Ottorino Gentiloni (1865–1916), cf. the biography by Augusto Grossi Gonda, *Il conte Vincenzo Ottorino Gentiloni,* Industria Tipografica Romana, Rome 1927.

618 Cenci, *Merry del Val,* pp. 158–159.

619 Cf. Romanato, *Pio X,* pp. 486–493.

620 *Pii Papae X. Positio,* p. 355. "Pius X does not want Catholic deputies but rather, deputies who happen to be Catholics," affirmed Cardinal Hergenröther (Rhodes, *The Power of Rome,* p. 190). In other words, that Catholics have an influential role in the national assembly, but not as as members of a Catholic party.

621 Pietro Maffi (1858–1931), of the diocese of Pavia, rector and professor of physics and natural sciences in the seminary of Pavia, was made titular bishop of Caesare and named auxiliary of Ravenna on June 9, 1902. Promoted to the metropolitan see of Pisa on June 22, 1903, he was made a cardinal by Pius X in the consistory of April 15, 1907.

as recalled by his personal secretary Msgr. Pescini, that they might combat modernism,[622] such as the daily *L'Unità Cattolica*[623] and the journal *La Riscossa* of the Scotton Brothers,[624] in which Paul Sabatier saw "an even more perfect mirror of the personal thought of Pius X."[625]

Cardinal Maffi and Cardinal Ferrari belonged to the episcopal current that criticized the intransigent press, holding that an openly Catholic press would distance unbelieving readers to whom they must instead offer "penetrating newspapers," edited with conciliatory tones and open to the suggestions of the times, as did the "Trust," i.e., the *Società Editrice Romana* (SER) founded in 1907 by Count Grosoli Pironi, which published *Il Momento* in Turin, *L'Avvenire d'Italia* in Bologna, and *Il Corriere d'Italia* in Rome.[626]

Pius X did not share this idea and, with a specific *Avvertenza* (warning missive) appearing on December 1, 1912, in the *Acta Apostolicae Sedis,* stated that the Holy See does not recognize the publications of the SER as "in conformity with pontifical directives and the norms in the letter of His Holiness to the episcopate of Lombardy."[627]

[622] *Pii Papae X. Positio,* p. 109.

[623] The daily *L'Unità Cattolica,* founded in Turin in 1863 by Fr. Giacomo Margotti (1883–1887), later transferred to Florence in 1892 and entrusted to the direction of Giuseppe Sacchetti (1845–1906), was the most important intransigent daily newspaper of the age and the closest to Pius X. It was directed by two young priests, Fr. Paolo De Töth (1881–1965) and then Fr. Alessandro Cavallanti (1879–1917). Cf. Lorenzo Bedeschi, "Note e documenti per la storia dell'antimodernismo. De Töth e Cavallanti alla direzione dell'Unità Cattolica," *Nuova Rivista Storica* 55, nos. 1–2 (1971), p. 90–132; idem, *L'antimodernismo in Italia,* San Paolo, Rome 2000, pp. 53–68; Maurizio Tagliaferri, *L'Unità Cattolica. Studio di una mentalità,* Pontificia Università Gregoriana, Rome 1993.

[624] The journal *La Riscossa. Per la chiesa e per la patria* of the brothers Jacopo (1834–1909), Andrea (1838–1915), and Gottardo (1845–1916) Scotton, hailed from Breganze, in the diocese of Vicenza, from 1890 to 1915. Cf. G. Azzolini, *Gli Scotton. Prediche, battaglie, imboscate. Tre fratelli Monsignori, papi, cardinali e vescovi tra liberalismo e modernismo dall'Unità d'Italia al primo Novecento [The Scotton Brothers. Sermons, Battles, Ambushes. Three Monsignor Brothers, Popes, Cardinals, and Bishops Between Liberalism and Modernism from the Unity of Italy to the Early 1900s],* La Serenissima, Vicenza 1998.

[625] Paul Sabatier, *Les modernistes : notes d'histoire religieuse contemporaine,* Fischbacher, Paris 1909, p. 224. "These writers of the Periodical are wrong (wrote Pius X on March 28, 1911 to Cardinal Ferrari, who was under attack by the Scotton Brothers) when they allowed their passions to get the better of them, when in particular cases, they draw general conclusions, when they stoop to personal attacks, but they also have an extenuating circumstance to their guilt, knowing the evil before which they find themselves with people who obstinately deny it and work to defend themselves with the same weapons they are being struck with." (*Pii X Disquisitio,* p. 178).

[626] An interesting record of Italian newspapers, including those of the SER trust, edited by Msgr. Umberto Benigni in 1912, was published by Msgr. S. Pagano, in "Documenti sul modernismo romano dal fondo Benigni," *Ricerche per la storia religiosa di Roma* 8 (1990), pp. 280–281 (pp. 223–300).

[627] AAS, vol. 4 (1912), p. 695.

On December 14, 1907, the newspaper *L'Unione* began circulation in the diocese of Cardinal Ferrari, under the direction of Filippo Meda.[628] This aroused the disapproval of Pius X, who three times arranged for apostolic visits in his diocese. "No other struggle between a pope and a cardinal was fought with greater acrimony, but at the same time with greater circumspection. The scandal to the public was immense. This was the reason why the Vatican hesitated and did not adopt provisions of a radical disciplinary nature. Pius X would often say, 'Archbishop Ferrari gave me more displeasure than all the bishops of Christianity together.'"[629] Speaking with Fr. Giacomo Pastori, Pius X defined him in the Venetian dialect: "*Busiaro, busiaro e gnente altro che busiaro*" [Liar, liar and nothing but a liar].[630]

On August 5, 1912, Cardinal Pietro Maffi addressed Card. Merry del Val concerning two interconnected issues: that of the forthcoming political elections and that of Catholic journalism.

Several days later, on August 13, Merry del Val wrote Cardinal Maffi, "Your Eminence knows well that the pope has no desire whatsoever for these so-called insightful newspapers, which are in the end nothing but a pernicious and progressive adaptation: as an illustrious French bishop recently wrote me, '*C'est parfait d'acclamer le Saint Père, Il serait bien plus parfait de Lui obéir, au moins à peu près*' [It's all very well to acclaim the Holy Father, but it would be far more perfect to obey him, at least more or less]."[631]

The secretary of state then touched on the electoral issue, stating that, as far as this was concerned, "the line of conduct indicated by the encyclical *Il fermo proposito* is perfectly clear. It is now widely known that the Holy Father desires in no way (for those lofty reasons which Your Eminence understands well) the formation of a Catholic political party in Italy, and for this reason the candidacy of 'Catholic politicians' as such remains excluded."[632]

628 Filippo Meda (1869–1939), director in 1898 of the daily *Osservatore Cattolico* of Milan, then of *Unione*, which later became *Italia*, was one of the greatest exponents of liberal Catholicism, in favor of reconciliation between church and state. A deputy from 1909, he was among the founders of the Popular Party. Minister of Finance (1916–1919) and of the Treasury (1920–1921), he remained in the Chamber until 1924.

629 Giacomo Pastori, *Il Cardinal Ferrari*, Modernissima, Milan 1919, p. 31.

630 Ibid, p. 40.

631 Citing Msgr. Gilbert, bishop of Arsinoe. *Pii X Disquisitio*, p. 100.

632 Ibid., p. 99.

Pius X and his secretary of state clearly condemned the project of a "Catholic Party" being developed at that time by Hon. Filippo Meda and Don Luigi Sturzo.[633]

Instructions for the Elections of 1913

The Italian elections in autumn of 1913 were the first with universal male suffrage, with the number of voters increasing from three to eight million. As Giovanni Spadolini observed, it should be doubted that the wary Giolitti would ever have conceded such a vast extension of the vote, without having the certainty of being able to count on Catholic support on the national level,[634] but thanks to the conditions imposed, it was Catholics who "harnessed" the liberals, and not vice versa.[635]

Giovanni Giolitti, the right hand man of the Savoy monarchy, knew the political and administrative apparatus of the state government like none other and used it in an unscrupulous manner to maintain his power. Pius X, intransigent in the sphere of principles, was flexible in the sphere of events, but his pragmatism, contrary to that of Giolitti, was entirely supernatural, guided by his surrender to Providence and by his efforts to discern God's interest and that of the Church in the present moment. Between the Head of the Church and the Piedmont statesman, a *de facto* alliance was created in light of the election of 1913.

In this manner, the so-called Gentiloni Pact was established, wrongly presented as an understanding between the Catholic Electoral Union and the Italian government. It was rather a document in seven points proposed to any candidate aspiring to gain Catholic votes: To defend religious rights, to respect the family, its unity, the equality of workers' organizations, the free school, justice in social relations, and the renewal of economic strength. As recalled by Count Giuseppe dalla Torre, "The candidate would have to sign a declaration that admitted all this, even if he did not believe he would speak explicitly about it in his propaganda. This was not a 'pact'; it was a personal agreement."[636]

633 Don Luigi Sturzo (1871–1959), deputy mayor of Caltagirone (1905–1920), in 1919 founded the Italian Popular Party, of which he assumed the role of secretary. Forced to resign upon the rise of fascism, he was persuaded by Cardinal Gasparri to leave Italy. He lived in London and then in New York, until his return in 1946.

634 G. Spadolini, *Il Tevere più largo. Da Porta Pia ad oggi*, Longanesi & C., Milan 1970, p. 130.

635 Ibid., p. 135.

636 Giuseppe dalla Torre, *Memorie*, Mondadori, Milan 1967, p. 29.

Thanks to the Gentiloni Pact that won them Catholic support, the liberal conservatives were able to obtain 51 percent of the vote, with 228 candidates elected.[637] The following year, in the administrative elections of June 14, 1914, a coalition of Catholics, nationalists, and liberals brought to the Campidoglio [the mayor's office in Rome] Prince Prospero Colonna, bringing an end to the masonic administration.[638]

The Catholic deputies did not constitute a proper group but, in general, supported the ministerial majority against the radical left. Parallel to this political collaboration, Catholics carried out the work of a profound revision of the myths of the *Risorgimento*. On December 7, 1907, Pius X initiated the process of beatification of Pius IX,[639] while studies of historical revisionism found their greatest exponent in the Jesuit priest Ilario Rinieri.[640]

By the time Pius X died, the great organizations of Italian Catholic Action were the Popular Union among Catholics of Italy; the Economic-Social Union; the Electoral Union; Catholic Youth; and the Union among Catholic Women, presided over respectively by Count Giuseppe dalla Torre, Count Stanislao Medolago Albani, Count Ottorino Gentiloni, Sir Paolo Pericoli, and the Princess Cristina Giustiniani Bandini.

The Constantinian Celebrations

From 1912 to 1913, at the behest of Pius X, the extraordinary jubilee of the sixteen-hundredth anniversary of Emperor Constantine the Great was solemnly celebrated. At the direct impulse of Secretary of State Merry del Val and working closely with him, an organizational committee was created;[641] its president was Prince

637 Cf. Luigi Ganapini, *Il nazionalismo cattolico. I cattolici e la politica estera in Italia dal 1871 al 1914 [Catholic Nationalism. Catholics and Foreign Policy in Italy from 1871 to 1914]*, Laterza, Bari 1970; F. Perfetti, *Il movimento nazionalista in Italia (1903–1914)*, Bonacci, Rome 1984; Adriano Roccucci, *Roma capitale del nazionalismo (1908–1923)*, Archivio Guido Izzi, Rome 2001; Hartmut Ullrich, *Le elezioni del 1913 a Roma. I liberali fra massoneria e Vaticano [The Elections of 1913 in Rome. The Liberals Between Freemasonry and the Vatican]*, Editrice Dante Alighieri, Rome 1972.

638 Prospero Colonna of the Princes of Paliano (1858–1937) was a deputy, senator, and twice mayor of Rome from 1899 to 1919.

639 Fabrizio Cannone, *Giovanni Maria Mastai Ferretti: Papa Pio IX, la fama di santità e il processo di canonizzazione [Giovanni Maria Mastai Ferretti: Pope Pius IX, The Fame of Sanctity and the Process of Canonization]*, Ares, Milan 2012.

640 Ilario Rinieri S.J., *Il Padre Francesco Pellico e i suoi tempi*, 5 vols., Artigianelli, Pavia 1934.

641 Cf. Letter of Cardinal Merry del Val, January 24, 1912, on the Constantinian Feasts, to Cardinal Francesco di Paola Cassetta (1841–1919), prefect of the Congregation for Studies, in AAS, vol. 4 (1912), pp. 131–132.

Mario Chigi and its secretary, archaeologist Orazio Marucchi.[642] The commemoration concerned two great events: the victory of Constantine over Maxentius at the Milvian Bridge (October 28, 312) and the proclamation of the Edict of Milan (May 313). Pius X announced the celebration with an apostolic letter *Universis Christi fidelibus* on March 8, 1913, enriching the jubilee with special indulgences.[643]

Over the course of the Jubilee, the city of Milan was chosen as the place for the eighth annual "Social Week" of the Popular Union, which took place from November 30 to December 6, 1913, on the theme of Catholic civil liberties. On behalf of Pius X, Cardinal Merry del Val addressed a letter to Count Giuseppe dalla Torre, president of the Italian Popular Union, in which he highlighted the importance of the anniversary. The archbishop of Udine, Antonio Anastasio Rossi,[644] gave the opening report on "The Constantinian Centenary and the Freedom of the Church." Reiterating the primacy of jurisdiction of the Roman pontiff, Msgr. Rossi raised the possibility of resolving the Roman Question outside of a civil principality, hinting that what interested the Holy See was not insisting on temporal power, but guaranteeing its spiritual authority.

The discourse of Count Dalla Torre affirmed that it was always within the constitutional powers of the state to welcome the legitimate aspirations and requests of the Holy See. This was seen and approved by Cardinal Merry del Val.[645]

Among the initiatives promoted for the anniversary was the construction of the two Roman churches of Sant'Elena outside Porta Maggiore and Santa Croce al Flaminio, near the Milvian Bridge, on the spot where Constantine's troops gave the signal that the battle had been won, according to tradition. Pius X entrusted

642 Orazio Marucchi (1852–1931) was director of the Vatican Egyptian Museum and the Lateran Museum, secretary of the Pontifical Commission of Sacred Archaeology, professor of Christian archaeology at the University of Rome. On his tomb in Campo Verano, he wanted the simple epigraph to be placed, which summarized his archaeological apostolate: "Orazio Marucchi: enthusiast of the martyrs."

643 Francesco Tacchi, "Il XVI Centenario Costantiniano del 1913. Cronaca e significati di un evento" [The 16th Constantinian Centenary of 1913. The News and Significance of an Event], *Italian Archive for the History of Piety* 27 (2014), pp. 243–280; Matteo Sanfilippo, *Dal giubileo al centenario. Strategie di comunicazione politico-religiosa tra il Trecento e il primo Novecento [From the Jubilee to the Centenary. Strategies of Political-Religious Communication from the 14th Century to the 20th Century]*, Settecittà, Rome 2016, pp. 109–131.

644 Antonio Anastasio Rossi (1864–1948) was named archbishop of Udine on January 8, 1910. On December 19, 1927, he was promoted to Latin patriarch of Constantinople and prelate *nullius* of Pompei.

645 Deposition of Count Giuseppe Dalla Torre, in *Processus Informativus Ordinarius, Sessio* XXVII, vol. 1, p. 198.

the project for the church to Aristide Leonori, considered a "holy architect" for his intense work in sacred buildings.[646] In this way, sacred city planning was developed in contrast to the masonic endeavors of the Nathan administration.

Furthermore, Pius X continued the great program of rediscovery of the Christian heritage in Rome begun under the impulse of Pius IX by the archaeologist Giovanni Battista De Rossi and continued by his disciple Marucchi, to bring to renewed flourishing the cult of the martyrs, especially at the tombs in the ancient Christian cemeteries.[647] Work in the catacombs of Santa Priscilla, permitted by Vittorio Emanuele III, owner of the Villa Savoia above it, was entirely and personally financed by Cardinal Merry del Val.[648]

Foreign Policy of the Holy See

Pius X and his secretary of state, Merry del Val, carried out an intense activity of foreign policy in those years, without ever considering appeasements or transactions that might move religious issues into the sphere of politics. Pius X, writes Giovanni Spadolini, "although very involved as he was in the duel with France, although exposed to the attacks of resurging anticlericalism in Spain, Portugal, and South America, never thought of yielding to Germany and Austria but, when necessary, engaged in bitter conflict with Berlin over the nomination of the archbishop of Posen[649] and maintained a vibrant controversy with the Court of Vienna and Minister Aerenthal over the Wahrmund Affair.[650] Nor did he hesitate to accentuate discord and misunderstanding with Russia by insisting on all Catholic claims concerning oppressed Poland."[651]

Pius X's attitude was religious rather than political, and it was shared by his secretary of state. A clear example of this is revealed in what is known as the

[646] Aristide Leonori (1856–1928) was an engineer and architect who designed churches and religious buildings throughout the world. His process of beatification is underway. Cf. Galileo Venturini, *Un ingegnere santo, Aristide Leonori*, Soc. Tip. Macioce e Pisani, Isola del Liri 1931; and the entry by Fabrizio Di Marco, *Aristide Leonori*, DBI, vol. 64, Rome 2005.

[647] On Giovanni Battista De Rossi (1822–1894), founder in 1897 of the *Collegium Cultorum Maryrum*, along with Mariano Armellini and Enrico Stevenson, cf. Antonio Baruffa, *Giovanni Battista De Rossi. L'archeologo esploratore delle catacombe*, Acts of the 13 International Congress of Christian Archaeology, Libreria Editrice Vaticana, Vatican City 1994.

[648] Massimiliano Ghilardi, *Gli arsenali della fede [The Arsenals of Faith]*, Aracne, Rome 2006, pp. 139–140.

[649] Cardinal Mieczyslaw Ledochowski (1822–1902), archbishop of Gniezno and Posen in 1862, was expelled from the diocese by Emperor Wilhelm II.

[650] Ludwig Wahrmund (1860–1932), Viennese canon lawyer, was removed from the Catholic University of Innsbruck in 1908 due to a pamphlet on *Katholische Weltanschauung und freie Wissenschaft* considered offensive to the faith.

[651] Spadolini, *L'opposizione cattolica*, p. 658.

"Roosevelt Case." In 1910, having finished his term as president of the United States of America, Theodore Roosevelt set off on a two-month journey throughout Europe and among the many destinations was, of course, Rome.[652] Merry del Val met with Roosevelt's secretary John Callan O'Laughlin,[653] who expressed the former president's desire to have an audience with the pope, but made clear that he would not accept any restrictions, meeting with whomever he wanted and wherever he wanted. Roosevelt had programmed, in fact, a meeting in the Methodist church of Rome, in Via Venti Settembre, a setting of aggressive anti-Catholic propaganda.

Merry del Val pointed out to him that it was an elementary question of fittingness and decorum, concluding that, while he would arrange to receive Mr. Roosevelt cordially, the pope had every right to ask that he abstain from giving his support to the inveterate enemies of the Catholic religion and of the pope, such as Methodists and Freemasons. "Throughout Mr. O'Laughlin's entire reply, he continuously repeated that Mr. Roosevelt would do whatever he pleased and that, if as he left the pontifical antechamber, he wished to go directly to 'Giordano Bruno' he would do so."[654]

At the end of the conversation, as O'Laughlin took his leave, he warned of catastrophic consequences for the Catholic Church in America. "And I," recalled Merry del Val, "ended by saying that I was ready to accept the judgment of American public opinion once it had been well instructed on how things had gone. My literal words were: 'I am ready to respect the verdict of American public opinion when matters have come to light.' Events later gave witness that it was not the Church, but Mr. Roosevelt, who suffered the sad consequences."[655]

Merry del Val firmly rejected every ideological expression contrary to the Church, but this did not hinder the Holy See from maintaining good relations

652 Theodore Roosevelt Jr. (1858–1919) was the twenty-sixth president of the United States. Initiated into Freemasonry at Matinecock Lodge No. 806 in the Orient of Oyster Bay, New York, he was later an honorary member of numerous lodges in the United States, participating in many masonic ceremonies among which, in 1907, was the groundbreaking ceremony of the masonic temple in Washington D.C. (cf. Cécile Révageur, in *Encyclopedie de la Franc-Maçonnerie*, p. 756). He won the Nobel Peace Prize in 1906.

653 John Callan O'Laughlin (1873–1949), journalist and politician, accompanied Theodore Roosevelt as his secretary during his travels in Europe in 1909.

654 Cenci, *Merry del Val*, p. 167; Javierre, *Merry del Val*, pp. 366–368. Giordano Bruno was burned at the stake in 1600 by the Roman Inquisition for heresy.

655 Ibid. The president's version of this conversation is found in *Theodore Roosevelt and His Time, Shown in His Own Letters*, ed. Joseph Bucklin, Charles Scribner & Sons, New York 1920, pp. 196–198.

with personalities such as the English sovereigns, who were heads of the Anglican Church, and Freemasons. For the coronation of George V as King of England in June of 1911,[656] Pius X decided to send to London a special mission guided by Msgr. Gennaro Granito Pignatelli di Belmonte, made a cardinal in November the same year. Also in attendance were Count Stanislao Medolago Albani;[657] Msgr. Eugenio Pacelli, the undersecretary of Extraordinary Ecclesiastical Affairs;[658] and Count Francesco Bezzi Scali, a Noble Guard.[659]

The Pontifical Mission reached London on June 19. Pius X's envoy was the object of particular regard by the Court and was invited to occupy a place of honor among the guests. The year before, Edward VII had deleted from the formula of the royal coronation oath any possible reference to hostility toward the Roman Church.

The members of the papal mission were then received by the sovereigns, and on June 22 they had a place of honor in the royal cortege going to Westminster Abbey. The pope's representatives avoided participating, however, in the religious function in which the king publicly reaffirmed his Protestant faith.

The participation of the Holy See at the coronation of the English Sovereign was a diplomatic gesture, though not an "ecumenical" one. The following day, the members of the mission also participated, wearing their gala livery, in the second spectacular royal "procession" through the streets of the capital. In his report on the mission, envoy Granito di Belmonte wrote, "What most characterized the affectionate and kindly welcome we received was the manifest will of the sovereigns to honor the person of the Holy Father in his representatives, which they did through public and extraordinary expressions, praised and approved by a large number of the foreign princes, who were happy to follow the

656 George V (1865–1936) was king of Great Britain and Ireland and the British Dominions overseas, as well as emperor of India from May 6, 1910, as successor to his father Edward VII, until his death.

657 Cf. Antonio Medolago Albani, "Un Bergamasco membro della missione pontificia a Londra, per l'incoronazione di Re Giorgio V d'Inghilterra" [A Man from Bergamo, Member of the Papal Mission in London for the Coronation of King George V of England], in *Acts of the Athenaeum of Sciences, Letters and Arts* 40, Bergamo, years 1976–1977 and 1977–1978; idem, *Missione a Londra. Diario di un cameriere segreto del Papa. Stanislao Medolago Albani [Mission in London. Diary of the Pope's Secret Chamberlain, Stanislao Medolago Albani]*, ed. Luisa Maddalena Medolago Albani, D'Ettoris, Crotone 2022.

658 Eugenio Maria Giuseppe Giovanni Pacelli (1876–1958) was elected pope Pius XII on March 2, 1939, on the eve of World War II. Prior to this, he served as secretary of Extraordinary Ecclesiastical Affairs (1914–1917); papal nuncio to Bavaria (1917–1925), Germany (1920–1930), and Prussia (1926–1929); and cardinal secretary of State (1930–1939).

659 Count Francesco Bezzi Scali (1869–1949) was in mission in Rodez with bishop Msgr. Bourret (1893) and in London for the coronation of King George V (1911).

example of the English sovereigns.... One might say that this was done for political motives, to do something appreciated by their Catholic subjects."[660]

Zionism and Antisemitism

Another delicate issue that Pius X and his secretary of state had to confront was the birth of Zionism, the movement founded by Theodor Herzl to create a homeland in Palestine for the Jews dispersed throughout the world.[661] On January 25, 1904, Herzl obtained an audience with Pius X and, before their encounter, on January 22, was received by Secretary of State Merry del Val, who described him in his diary as "tall and thin, with big, brown, serious eyes that questioned but were not irreligious, in a face still young though already serious."[662] Herzl told him he was in Rome to obtain "the benevolence" of the Holy See toward his cause, adding that, in his project, the Holy Sites would remain extra-territorial. For his part, Herzl reports that Merry del Val replied that he could not see how the Holy See could have taken any initiative in this field: "As long as the Jews deny the divinity of Christ, we cannot declare ourselves in their favor. We are not ill disposed toward them. On the contrary, the Church has always taken them under its protection. For us, they are the necessary witnesses to the event of the presence of God on earth. But they deny the divinity of Christ. Now, how can we declare to consent that they return to possess the Holy Land, without sacrificing our supreme principles?"[663]

On January 25, Herzl was received by Pius X.[664] Their meeting, also reported in Herzl's diary, had as its outcome a polite, though firm, rejection by the pontiff to support the Zionist movement's objectives. Pius X confirmed

660 Tiziana Di Maio, "Pio X e la Gran Bretagna," in La Bella (ed.), *Pio X e il suo tempo*, p. 608.

661 Theodor Herzl (1860–1904) was author of the work *Der Judenstaat* (1896), in which he welcomed the construction of a Jewish society within its own state, and was the founder of the Zionist movement. The audience was organized by Count Berthold Dominik Lippay (1864–1919), an Austrian portrait artist whom Herzl had met in Venice.

662 Sergio I. Minerbi, *Il Vaticano, la Terra Santa e il Sionismo*, Bompiani, Milano 1988, p. 149 (pp. 148–153).

663 Theodor Herzl, *Briefe und Tagebücher*, vol. 3, *Zionistisches Tagebuch (1899–1904)*, Propyläen, Berlin-Frankfurt-Wien 1983, pp. 644– 647.

664 In his letter to Felice Ravenna in September 1903, Herzl explained the reasons for which he so desired to confer with the pope: "Les lieux saints doivent être extraterritorialisés pour toujours, *res sacrae extra commercium* du droit des gens. Cette proposition je veux la faire accepter et protéger par le Pape, comme le Souverain spirituel respecté et reconnu même par le chrétiens des autres églises." Cf. Umberto Nahon, "Le lettere di Teodoro Herzl a Felice Ravenna (Il viaggio di Herzl a Roma nel gennaio 1904)," *The Monthly Report on Israel*, p. 242 (pp. 235–256). Neither *La Civiltà Cattolica* nor *L'Osservatore Romano* published an account of the two meetings.

what his secretary of state had already expressed: "We cannot promote this movement. We can not hinder the Jews from going to Jerusalem, but promote it we also could never do. The land of Jerusalem, if it were not always holy, was sanctified through the life of Jesus Christ (he does not pronounce Jesus, but Yesu, in the Venetian manner). I, as head of the Church, cannot tell you otherwise. The Jews have not recognized Our Lord, thus we cannot recognize the Jewish people."[665]

On July 6, 1904, a telegram arrived from Vienna informing the Vatican of the death of Herzl on July 3 (of heart sclerosis), asking that the pontiff be informed. Merry del Val told the nuncio that "it does not seem fitting to respond directly to this telegram so as not to seem to attribute to the said Committee the importance and authority that no government has wished to grant it, and even less so that the supreme pontiff can grant it."[666]

Several months after Herzl's visit in the Vatican, Merry del Val said in an interview with "*Die Welt*": "How can we cede the land of our Redeemer to a people of a different faith? Nevertheless, the Church would do nothing to hinder the efforts of the Zionists to obtain a home in Palestine guaranteed by public law."[667]

Pius X's reservations toward Zionism had nothing to do with antisemitism, which was developing in those same years in neo-pagan settings in Germany.[668] For the Catholic Church, in fact, the Jewish people, "favored, not for its current state, but for its initial election," remains "the prodigal son most awaited by divine mercy."[669] For this reason, in the Letter *Poloniae populum*, Pius X denounced among "the heinous actions" that were committed in 1905, "the public massacre of the Jews, massacres detested and condemned by the

665 Herzl, *Briefe und Tagebücher*, vol. 3, p. 655.

666 AAV, Secr. Stato, 1904, rubr. 247, fasc. 3, ff. 144–145. Cf. the reconstruction of R. Perin, *L'atteggiamento della Santa Sede verso ebrei e protestanti da Pio X a Pio XI [The Attitude of the Holy See toward the Jews and Protestants from Pius X to Pius XI]*, doctoral thesis, School of Doctoral Studies in History, Geography, Religious History, ciclo XXII, University of Padova, 2010, pp. 19–21. More generally, Giovanni Miccoli, "Santa Sede, questione ebraica e antisemitismo fra Otto e Novecento" [Holy See, the Jewish Question and Antisemitism at the Turn of the 19th and 20th centuries], in Corrado Vivanti (ed.), *Storia d'Italia*, Annali 11/2, *Gli ebrei in Italia*, Einaudi, Turin 1997, pp. 1369–1574.

667 "Die Welt," April 1, 1904, cited in Minerbi, *Il Vaticano, la Terra Santa e il Sionismo*, p. 151.

668 Msgr. Antonino Romeo, "Antisemitismo," in *Enciclopedia Cattolica*, vol. 1 (1948), col. 1494–1505.

669 Msgr. Pier Carlo Landucci, "La véritable charité envers le peuple juif," *La Pensée Catholique* 207 (1983), pp.13–31; Denis Judant, *Judaisme et Christianisme, Dossier patristique*, Éditions du Cèdre, Paris 1969. Consider also the apostolate of the Lémann Brothers, Augustin and Joseph, Ashkenazi Jewish twins (1836–1909/1915) who, after their conversion, became priests, theologians, and Monsignors by the will of Pius X.

law of the Gospel, which demands that we love everyone indistinctly."[670] Pius X intervened to condemn the "pogroms" against the Jews in Russia, just as he had intervened to defend Catholics persecuted by the Czarist authorities.[671]

On March 20, 1911, the body of a thirteen-year-old boy was found riddled with wounds and lifeless in a Jewish workshop on the outskirts of Kiev. In July, Mendel Beilis was arrested, the Jewish foreman of the furnace where the cadaver had been found. Beilis was accused of having committed, along with other accomplices, a "ritual homicide," the ancient accusation against the Jews of murdering Christian children to use their blood in the preparation of *matzoth*.[672] The accusation made use of the theological consultation of a Catholic priest, Justinus Elisejevitch Pranaitis, professor of Hebrew in St. Petersburg.[673]

On October 7, 1913, Lord Leopold Rothschild sent an urgent letter by means of the Duke of Norfolk to Cardinal Merry del Val.[674] Rothschild explained to the secretary of State that in the affidavit of Pranaitis, the same arguments were proposed in support of the accusation of ritual homicide that were rejected in the past by theologians such as Card. Lorenzo Ganganelli, later Clement XIV, when he was consultor to the Tribunal of the Holy Office. The English lord, wishing to clarify the matter, asked Cardinal Merry del Val that the

670 Pius X, Letter *Poloniae populum*, in *Enchiridion/Pio X*, vol. 4, p. 763 (pp. 759–771).

671 On the diplomatic relations between the Vatican and Russia in those years, see Z. P. Jakhimovic, "Russia e Vaticano: problemi nelle relazioni diplomatiche tra XIX e XX secolo (materiali d'Archivio di politica estera dell'Impero russo)" [Russia and Vatican: Problems in the Diplomatic Relations in the 19th and 20th Centuries (Material from the Archive of Foreign Policy of the Russian Empire], in *Santa Sede e Russia da Leone XIII a Pio XI*, Acts of the Symposium organized by the Pontifical Committee of Historical Sciences and by the Institute of Universal History of the Academy of Sciences of Moscow, Moscow June 23–25, 1998, Libreria Editrice Vaticana, Vatican City 2002, pp. 62–82.

672 In 1906, Prof. Joaquín Girón y Arcas declared in the book *La cuestión judáica en la España actual y en la Universidad de Salamanca*, (Andrés Iglesias Impr., Salamanca 1906), that he was convinced that the crucifixion of Christian children was confirmed by history, citing the case of "*Santo Dominguito del Val, inmolado en Zaragoza en 1250 y la di Juan di Pasamontes (llamado el Niño de la Guardia)*" (*La cuestión judáica*, p. 125). In the book by Ariel Toaff, *Pasque di sangue. Ebrei d'Europa e omicidi rituali [Easter in Blood. The Jews of Europe and Ritual Homicides]* (Il Mulino, Bologna 2007), the author argues that among the German Ashkenazi communities of the Late Middle Ages there were groups that actually practiced ritual homicide, provoking a wide debate that caused his book to be removed from the shelves and forcing him to present a second edition furnished with an afterward by the author in which he attempted to explain his intentions more clearly.

673 Elisejevitch Pranaitis (1861–1917) was a Lithuanian Catholic priest in charge of a parish in Tashkent (Uzbekistan today), professor of Hebrew at the Catholic Theological Academy in St. Petersburg, and author of *Christianus in Talmudae Judaeorum*, Off. Tip. Academiae Cesarae Scientiarum, Petropoli 1992.

674 Lord Leopold Rothschild (1845–1917) was a high-profile English banker of the famous family and protector of the international Jewish community, on behalf of which he intervened in the matter.

verdict of Card. Ganganelli of 1758 and a papal bull of Pope Innocent IV of July 3, 1247, exonerating the Jews of the accusation of ritual homicide, be confirmed by the Holy See.[675]

The secretary of state replied to Rothschild on October 18, confirming the authenticity of the documents, though without exploring the issue.[676] Merry del Val's letter was not officially received by the Kiev tribunal, but the trial ended with the acquittal of Beilis of the accusation of homicide, though without an explicit denial of the fact that a ritual homicide had been committed. According to some scholars such as Andrew Canepa, the Beilis case constituted a historical shift because, after decades of campaigns against Jewish ritual homicide, a pope, Pius X, finally rose up in their defense.[677] Meanwhile, according to others such as David I. Kertzer, "neither the pope nor his secretary of state made use of the occasion to make a public declaration to confute the accusations of ritual homicide made against the Jews."[678] The most important documents for the interpretation of the Vatican's position in the Beilis case, as observes Kertzer, were the two articles in which the Jesuit priest Paolo Silva reconstructed the case in *Civiltà Cattolica*, certainly with the approval of the Holy See.[679] In these articles, Lord Rothschild was accused of acting in bad faith for having sought to exclude historical evidence of ritual homicide by emphasizing documents that confirmed the benign attitudes that the Holy See always had toward the people of Israel.

Be this as it may, Merry del Val's letter elicited expressions of thanksgiving from various Jewish communities in Italy: in Venice, by way of a letter from Rabbi Giuseppe Bassi; in Innsbruck; and in Livorno.[680] Cardinal Merry del Val would return to this delicate and controversial theme, as we shall see, in his role as secretary of the Holy Office.

675 AAV, Segr. Stato, October 18, 1913, rubr. 66, fasc. unico, ff. 44–47.

676 Ibid., f. 43.

677 Andrew Canepa, "Pius X and the Jews. A reappraisal," *Church History*, 61 (1992), pp. 362–372.

678 David I. Kertzer, *I Papi contro gli ebrei. Il ruolo del Vaticano nell'ascesa dell'antisemitismo moderno [The Popes Against the Jews. The role of the Vatican in the Rise of Modern Antisemitism]*, Italian translation, Garzanti, Milano 2023, pp. 264–265.

679 Cf. (Paolo Silva) "Raggiri ebraici e documenti papali. A proposito di un recente processo" [Jewish Frauds and Papal Documents. Regarding a Recent Trial], *La Civiltà Cattolica* 65 (1914), II, pp. 196–215; 330–344. *La Civiltà Cattolica* marks the publication in that same year of the volume by Albert Monniot, *Le crime rituel chez les juifs*, Pierre Téqui, Paris 1914.

680 AAV, Secr. State, October 18, 1913, rubr. 66, fasc. unico, ff. 37–38; 53; 55. The district court in Kiev refused to accept the document, stating that it could have been taken as evidence only if Merry del Val had sent it directly to the Court.

The Holy See, Spain, and Portugal

One of the primary concerns of Leo XIII and Pius X was the unity of the political action of Spanish Catholics who, ever since the restoration of the monarchy, were divided on the dynastic question as well as on doctrinal issues, and spefically, on the question of the supposed "lesser evil": whether it was permissible to vote for candidates not entirely coherent in order to avoid the election of worse candidates.[681] In May 1901, upon solicitation by the archbishop of Seville, Cardinal Spinola,[682] the *Liga Catòlica* was created with the aim of disseminating Catholic media and supporting the election of authentically Catholic candidates. Pius X encouraged the initiative in a letter to the archbishop on June 27, 1905, while maintaining dynastic neutrality and counseling unity in the defense of religious interests in Spain. Spanish Catholics were in fact divided into a conservative pro-liberal side supporting the monarchy of Alfonso,[683] and an anti-liberal side that included the Carlists[684] and the supporters of the *Integrista* Party founded in a split with the Carlists. The support of one part of the *Liga* in favor of liberal candidates was the occasion for a heated controversy between the Jesuits of *Razon y Fe* and the newspaper *El siglo futuro* of Ramon Nocedal,[685] who opposed the political unity of Catholics.[686] On February 20, 1906, on the occasion of the elections, Pius X approved the doctrine of the "lesser evil" supported by the periodical *Razon y Fe,* in his letter *Inter catholicos Hispaniae,*[687] admitting that in the face of the danger of radical or anarchic socialism, it was licit to vote for a candidate not wholly Catholic, so long as he gave guarantees of respecting the nation and religion.

681 Josè Luis Llaquet de Entrambasaguas, "El Cardenal Merry del Val y la política religiosa española," in Domingo Merry del Val (ed.), *Rafael Merry del Val, 150 anni dalla sua nascita*, pp. 167–198. Cf. also José Andrés Gallego, *La Politica religiosa en España*, national edition. Nacional, Madrid 1975; and Cristóbal Robles Muñoz, "Frente a la supremacía del Estado. La Santa Sede y los católicos en la crisis de la Restauración (1898–1912) (I)," *Anthologica* 34 (1987), pp. 189–305.

682 Marcelo Spínola y Maestre (1835–1906) was consecrated archbishop of Seville in 1881. Pius X made him a cardinal in the consistory of December 11, 1905.

683 The leader of the conservatives was Alejandro Pidal y Mon (1846–1913), who supported the liberal monarchy.

684 From 1893 to 1918 Juan Vázquez de Mella y Fanjul (1861–1928) was the main leader in parliament and ideologue of the Carlista movement together with Juan Víctor Pradera y Larumbe (1873–1936).

685 Ramón Nocedal y Romea (1842–1907), the most visible figure among the Integrista movement, directed the daily *El Siglo futuro* (1875–1936). For a distinction between Carlism and Integrism, cf. Melchor Ferrer, *Historia del tradicionalismo español,* Editorial Católica Española, Sevilla 1959, XVIII/1, pp. 283–285.

686 Regarding the controversy, cf. Gabriel Alférez Callejón, "El mal menor en politica," *Verbo* 269–270 (November–December 1988), pp. 1327–1358; V. Cárcel Ortí, "San Pío X, los jesuitas y los integristas españoles," *Archivum historiae pontificiae* 27 (1989), p. 301 (pp. 249–355).

687 Pius X, *Inter catholicos Hispaniae,* February 29, 1906, in AAS, vol. 39 (1906), pp. 75–76.

The *Integristas* accepted begrudgingly, observing that the thesis of the moralists on the legality of tolerating a lesser evil was probable, but not absolutely certain and therefore not obligatory. The new nuncio Antonio Vico was involved in this controversy, accused by the liberal-leaning monarchists of having supported the fundamentalists.[688] The secretary of state defended the impartiality of the Holy See's representative, who in 1911 was elevated to the cardinalate.[689] In the *Instrucciones* to Nuncio Vico in December 1907, Merry del Val stated that relations between the Holy See and the monarchy were cordial and recommended that he seek unity among the bishops, clergy and Catholic faithful of different convictions.[690] Meanwhile, Cardinal Vives y Tutó was appointed to negotiate with the *Integrista* movement.[691]

After the *Instrucciones* of 1907, there followed the *Normas para la acciòn politica de los catolicos espanoles* of April 20, 1911.[692] This was a text of great significance, because it went beyond the Spanish case, explaining clearly the position of Pius X and Merry del Val toward the political struggles that were inaugurating the twentieth century and that faced the Catholic Church with difficult and, at times, complex decisions. In the first of the twelve norms in the document, the principle was established that "in Spain one can always affirm, as in fact many do affirm nobly, the Catholic thesis and with it the reestablishment of religious unity." The second norm stated that "the existence of political parties is in itself legitimate and honest on condition that their doctrines and actions do not oppose religion and morality. The Church, however, must not in any way identify with or confuse itself with any of them, nor should it presume to

688 Antonio Vico (1847–1929) was consecrated a bishop by Leo XIII in 1898 and made a cardinal by Pius X on November 27, 1911. After having been nuncio in Belgium from 1904 to 1907, he was nuncio in Spain from 1907 to 1911.

689 Llaquet de Entrambasaguas, "El Cardenal Merry del Val," p. 185.

690 In the *Istruzioni per Monsignor Antonio Vico arcivescovo titolare di Filippi nunzio di Spagna* of 1907 Card. Merry del Val noted "the different relationship in which the two governing parties find themselves currently in Spain. While up to 1899, there existed almost no other distinction between them than the protagonists of the two factions, today there exists a substantial difference. The conservative tends explicitly towards the extreme right, while the liberal towards the extreme left, and the line that demarcates the profound division is that which is commonly called the 'religious question,' when in fact, there should be no reason whatsoever for the existence of this question." Cit. in V. Cárcel Ortí, "Instrucciones de Merry del Val a Vico en 1907 y relación final del nuncio en 1912," *Revista Española de Derecho Canónico* 49 (1992), p. 571 (pp. 567–612).

691 Llaquet de Entrambasaguas, "El Cardenal Merry del Val," pp. 194–195.

692 "Normas dadas por encargo de Pio X, firmadas por el Secretario de Estado Merry del Val el 20 de abril 1911, y comunicadas en Madrid por el nuncio el 3 de mayo, para la acción política de los católicos españoles," in *Boletín Oficial del Obispado de Pamplona*, June 1, 1911. The text is reproduced in Alférez Callejón, "El mal menor en politica," pp. 1354–1358.

intervene in the interests and controversies of the parties to favor one over another." The third point said that "it is lawful for no one to accuse or combat as neither good nor authentic Catholics those who, for a legitimate reason and with a right aim, without ever abandoning the defense of the principles of the Church, desire to belong and do belong to the political parties currently existing in Spain." The following point clarified the exact concept of liberalism condemned by the Church, attributing to it the meaning that Leo XIII had given it in the encyclical *Libertas* of July 20, 1888, and in other documents of the Holy Office.[693]

There were many who found it difficult to define the position of Pius X's secretary of state. For example, "The French liberals lamented that Merry del Val would be an *Integrista*; the Spanish *Integristas* lamented that Merry del Val might be a liberal," wrote Fr. Javierre.[694] His policies coincided in reality with that of Pius X: neutrality with regard to the dynasty, commitment to a fully Catholic society, application of tolerance of the lesser evil on the level of electoral choices. For Merry del Val, the destiny of the Catholic Church in Spain was tied to that of the Bourbonic monarchy, for which he demanded respect because it was the legitimately constituted power. The secretary of state did not approve of the anti-Alfonsian policy of the Carlists and fundamentalists, nor their opposition to the electoral union among Catholics, but recognized that these groups were the most active in mobilizing in defense of the interests of the Catholic Church in Spain. In this regard, he insisted that Bishop Salvador y Barrera[695] redress their honor that he had unjustly sullied[696] and, in 1911, arranged a papal audience for the Carlist aspirant Don Jaime, successor to Don Carlos.[697]

While Catholic Spain was rendering homage to Christ the King at the twenty-second International Eucharist Congress being held June 25–30, 1911, in Madrid, the new government in Portugal (established after the assassination of King Carlos[698] and the proclamation of the Republic) decreed the

693 Alférez Callejón, "El mal menor en politica," pp.1354–1356.

694 Javierre, *Merry del Val*, p. 383.

695 José Maria Salvador y Barrera (1851–1919) was bishop of Tarragona (1901) and later of Madrid Alcalá (1905–1917), and then archbishop of Valencia from 1916 until his death.

696 Llaquet de Entrambasaguas, "El Cardenal Merry del Val," p. 197.

697 Don Jaime Pío Juan Carlos di Borbone (1870–1931) from 1909 was the Carlist aspirant to the throne of Spain, bearing the title of Duke of Madrid with the name Jaime III, as well as the legitimist pretender to the throne of France and Navarre, bearing the title of Duke of Anjou with the name Jacques I.

698 Carlos I of Braganza (1863–1908) was king of Portugal from October 19, 1889, until his death on February 1, 1908, at the hands of two republican terrorists. His son Manuel succeeded him, who was the last king of Portugal before the proclamation of the Republic on October 5, 1910.

suppression of all monasteries and all religious institutions. All religious were expelled from the Republic and their possessions were confiscated. This was followed by a quick succession of anti-Catholic laws, among which the legalization of divorce and the suppression of religious instruction in schools.

Pius X reacted with a letter in January 15, 1911, in which he congratulated the bishops for their valorous opposition. On April 20 of the same year, the republican government issued the Law of Separation which copied the French law of 1905. Pius X protested in the encyclical *Iamdudum in Lusitania* of May 24, 1911, in which he solemnly affirmed:

> We by our apostolic authority denounce, condemn, and reject the Law for the Separation of Church and State in the Portuguese Republic. This law despises God and repudiates the Catholic faith; it annuls the treaties solemnly made between Portugal and the Apostolic See; it oppresses the liberty of the Church, and assails her divine Constitution; it injures and insults the majesty of the Roman pontificate, the order of bishops, the Portuguese clergy and people, and so the Catholics of the world. And whilst we strenuously complain that such a law should have been made, sanctioned, and published, we utter a solemn protest against those who have had a part in it as authors or helpers, and, at the same time, we proclaim and denounce as null and void, and to be so regarded, all that the law has enacted against the inviolable rights of the Church."[699]

The "Borromean" Encyclical and Germany

On May 26, 1910, St. Pius X published the encyclical *Editae saepe,* written for the third centenary of the canonization of St. Charles Borromeo. In this document, he pointed to the archbishop of Milan as a "model for both clergy and people in these days. He was the unwearied advocate and defender of the true Catholic reformation, opposing those innovators whose purpose was not the restoration, but the effacement and destruction of faith and morals." [700] In the sixteenth century, as at the beginning of the twentieth,

699 Pius X, Encyclical *Iamdudum in lusitania,* May 24, 1911, https://www.vatican.va/content/pius-x/en/encyclicals/documents/hf_p-x_enc_24051911_iamdudum.html.

700 Pius X, Encyclical *Editae saepe. De S. Caroli Borromaei apostolica activitate et doctrina,* May 6, 1910, no. 5, https://www.vatican.va/content/pius-x/en/encyclicals/documents/hf_p-x_enc_26051910_editae-saepe.html.

> A continual battle was being waged against errors. Human society, going from bad to worse, was rushing headlong into the abyss. Then those proud and rebellious men came on the scene who are "enemies of the cross of Christ. Their god is the belly ... they mind the things of earth" (Phil. 3:18–19). These men were not concerned with correcting morals, but only with denying dogmas. Thus they increased the chaos. They dropped the reins of law, and unbridled licentiousness ran wild. They despised the authoritative guidance of the church and pandered to the whims of the dissolute princes and people. They tried to destroy the Church's doctrine, constitution and discipline....
>
> God, however, brought forth real reformers and holy men to arrest the onrushing current, to extinguish the conflagration, and to repair the harm caused by this crowd of seducers.... In these circumstances God provided a pleasing consolation for the Church in the outstanding zeal and sanctity of Charles Borromeo.[701]

The clear target of Pius X's encyclical was not Protestantism, but modernism, which proposed "universal apostasy even worse than the one that threatened the age of Charles. It is worse, we say, because it stealthily creeps into the very veins of the Church."[702] Pius X opposed it with an authentic reform that had its essence in the conservation and transmission of Catholic truth.

The primary and most important duty of pastors is to guard everything pertaining to the integral and inviolate maintenance of the Catholic Faith, the faith which the Holy Roman Church professes and teaches, without which it is impossible to please God ... With Charles we must be mindful of the supreme zeal and excelling diligence which the bishop must exercise in combating the crime of heresy.[703]

Pius X's encyclical, destined to highlight the duties of Catholic bishops and of their faithful in the presence of heresies and doctrinal errors, was instrumentalized as an aggression against Protestant Churches, not only in German-speaking countries, but throughout the world, arousing bitter controversies. The German government prohibited the publication of the papal

701 Ibid, nos. 9–10.

702 Ibid, no. 19.

703 Ibid, no. 21, citing.

document in Germany in reaction to what seemed an offense against the Protestant majority of the nation.[704]

Thus began a dense correspondence between the apostolic nuncio in Munich, Msgr. Andreas Frühwirth,[705] and the secretary of state. On June 2, the nuncio wrote a letter to Merry del Val to inform the Holy See that the encyclical had "awakened in the liberal Protestant press a downright eruption of hatred and rancor against the Church and against the August Pontiff" for the offensive expressions used toward Protestantism, going so far as to call the papal document "the most insulting document imaginable."[706]

Merry del Val responded: "The aim of that encyclical has been entirely twisted, given that it was mainly directed against modernists, to whom you should attribute at least in part this agitation, seeing that they are the same ones arousing the discontent and uproar, hoping to displace attention from themselves and hide behind the new assaults they are making against the Catholic Church and its August Head. Likewise involved in this agitation lies a certain political maneuver to detach conservative Protestants from the center and create a radical, anti-Catholic block."[707]

When, on August 1, 1897, Leo XIII had promulgated the encyclical *Militantis ecclesiae* addressing the bishops of Austria, Germany, and Switzerland, on the occasion of the third centenary of the death of Blessed Peter Canisius, he expressed a judgment on the Protestant Revolution as equally forceful as that of Pius X. He recalled what had been "the face of Germany at the beginning of the Lutheran revolt," when "the poison spread to most of the provinces and infected all classes. Many considered the cause of religion in that realm to be desperate and doubted that any remedy remained to be tried. Indeed, it is clear that all would have been lost if God had not intervened with powerful aid." And yet Leo XIII's encyclical had not provoked the controversy aroused by the "Borromean" one. The reasons for the growing aversion toward Pius X and his secretary of state were to be attributed to the war they were waging against modernism.

704 Y. de la Brière, *Le luttes présentes de l'Église. Première série 1909–1912*, Éditions des *Questions actuelles*, Paris 1913, pp. 3–25.

705 Andreas (Franz) Frühwirth (1845–1933), a Dominican friar, Master General of his order (1891), was made titular archbishop of Heraclea and nuncio in Bavaria (1907–1916), cardinal (1915), Major Penitentiary (1925), and chancellor of the Holy Roman Church (1927).

706 AAV, Segr. Stato, 1911, rubr. 48, fasc. 1, f. 71.

707 Ibid, ff. 78–79.

A Campaign of Calumny

Around the turn of the twentieth century, in the decadent climate of the *Belle Epoque*, ancient and new forms of moral transgression were spreading. In England, within the Anglo-Catholic movement, the "Uranian" culture developed.[708] One of its exponents was the writer Frederick Rolfe (the self-declared "Baron Corvo"), former seminarian at the Scottish College who cloaked his dissolute life in a thin veil of religiosity.[709] In this period, private accusations and public scandals were taken advantage of by the political and ideological enemies of Pius X to unleash a defamation campaign against the pope and his collaborators.

It is a pity that some of these calumnious voices found an echo in the American journalist Randy Engel, the author of a voluminous book dedicated to the infiltration of homosexual culture and practice within the Catholic Church in the twentieth century.[710] Unfortunately, not all her sources are reliable, especially when she gives credit to the anonymous accusations behind a judicial dispute from 1910 to 1911 that involved a number of noblemen tied to the Holy See.[711] In this period, the Curia received a series of anonymous letters in which various people in the Vatican were accused of homosexuality. One of those defamed was Valentin Emanuel Patrick MacSwiney, former secret chamberlain during Leo XIII's pontificate, who accused another former chamberlain of Leo XIII, Marquis Fernando del Fierro, of having written the letters.[712] Sued

708 The "Uranians" were British writers who, between 1870 and 1930, composed works of a homosexual character, often religiously ambiguous and aimed at adolescents. The term "Uranism" was first used at the beginning of the twentieth century to indicate homosexual practice. Cf. David Hilliard, "Unenglish and Unmanly: Anglo-Catholicism and Homosexuality," *Victorian Studies* 25 (1982), pp. 181–210.

709 The English writer and photographer Frederick Rolfe (1860–1913), called "Baron Corvo," former seminarian at the Scottish College in Rome (1889–1890), was expelled due to his immoral conduct but was protected by the Duchess Caroline Shirley and her husband Lorenzo Sforza Cesarini. He sought to cloak his homosexuality in religious garb. He died in Venice on October 25, 1913, and was buried on the island of San Michele. Fr. Francesco Ricossa, in his review of the essay by Luca Fumagalli, *Baron Corvo, il viaggio sentimentale di Frederick Rolfe,* Edizioni Radio Spada, (Cermenate CO) 2017, brought to light the eccentric and ambiguous environment around the English writer; *La vergogna della traduzione [The Shame of Translation],* Centro Librario Sodalitium, Verrua Savoia 2018.

710 Randy Engel, *The Rite of Sodomy: Homosexuality & the Roman Catholic Church,* New Engel Publishing, Export 2006, pp. 620–622, 716–718.

711 Engel, "Lo scandalo della Corte vaticana in Pretura. Due camerieri di cappa e spada l'un contro l'altro" [The Scandal of the Vatican Court in Pretura. Two Chamberlains of Cloak and Sword Fighting Each Other], *La Stampa,* February 7, 1911. The content of the anonymous letters was reproduced in "Der Homosexuelle Skandal am Papsthofe," *Nord und Süd* 136 (March 1911), pp. 429–430.

712 Valentin Emanuel Patrick MacSwiney (1871–1945), of Irish origins, named by Leo XIII in 1896 Marquis of Mashanaglass and participating secret chamberlain, married and then separated from the Portuguese Marquiss Stella Cavalcanti de Albuquerque and authored several historical-juridical monographs.

by MacSwiney, del Fierro defended himself by accusing a third secret chamberlain of His Holiness, the Baron Léon du Mesnil, as guilty of the operation.[713]

On April 25, 1911, during the trial for defamation, Baron du Mesnil (along with Count Ferruccio Pasini-Frassoni) was sentenced to pay the expenses and damages he had caused Marquis Fernando del Fierro by the anonymous letters that had been sent to MacSwiney.[714] It turned out to be an internal squabble among several members of the Papal Court, with whom Cardinal Merry del Val had had nothing to do, despite the fact that his name appeared in some of the letters. The star of these litigious personalities, as the *Corriere della Sera* wrote on January 10, 1911, had risen under Leo XIII, but was declining under Pius X and his secretary of state Merry del Val, "who displayed a certain most prudent composure toward them."[715] Among Leo XIII's secret chamberlains there were unblemished gentlemen, but also several unscrupulous social climbers of dubious moral character. Pius X and his secretary of state cleaned house, removing all those who were blemished by a hint of any scandal.

This was evident in another case that struck Merry del Val painfully because it involved his old companion from the Academy and good friend. This was the so-called MacNutt case, alluded to by the French writer Jules Romains in a novel entitled *Mission in Rome*, published in 1937.[716]

Romains imagined that, in 1913, the French president Raymond Poincaré had appointed a priest-spy, Fr. Mionnet, to carry out a confidential investigation into the secretary of state of Pius X, considered viscerally Francophobic.[717] The

713 The trial was exclusively for defamation and, finally, on April 25, 1911, Baron Léon du Mesnil de Saint-Front and Count Ferruccio Pasini-Frassoni were condemned to pay expenses and damages caused to the Marquis Fernando del Fierro as authors of the anonymous letters (*Gazzetta Ufficiale del Regno d'Italia*, April 26, 1911, p. 1202). Count Ferruccio Pasini-Frassoni (1861–1928), founder of the *Rivista Araldica* in 1903, was an eminent scholar of noble law.

714 The anonymous letters were also reproduced by the German publisher Maximilian Claar (1873–1938), author of the article "Das Staatssekretariat Merry del Val (1903–1914)," *Zeitschrift für Politik* 20 (1931), pp. 30–42.

715 "Rivalità e gelosie in Vaticano tra due ex camerieri di cappa e spada" [Rivalry and Jealousy in the Vatican between Two Former Chamberlains of the Cloak and Sword], *Corriere della Sera*, January 10, 1911.

716 Jules Romains, *Missione a Roma*, Italian translation, Parenti, Novara 1958, pp. 281–296. Jules Romains, born Louis Henri Jean Farigoule (1885–1972), was a novelist and writer of comedy, member of the *Académie Française*.

717 In this novel, according to a fellow disciple of Jules Romains, "la scène entre Mionnet et Merry del Val me semble, dès maintenant, l'un des points culminants (comme elle en est, au milieu des vingt-sept tomes, le point central) de l'œuvre entière." Lettre d'André Cuisenier, December 29, 1937, in Anne Angremy, *Le dossiers préparatoires des "hommes de bonne volonté,"* Texts of de Jules Romains, Flammarion, Paris 1985, p. 60.

novel was part of a series of episodes, *Hommes de bonne volonté*, that the author pretended to base on historical documentation. However, Romains was ignorant of ecclesiastical matters and drew from questionable sources, like *Les Paroles françaises et romaines*, an entirely disreputable magazine by the pamphleteer Jean de Bonnefon,[718] and collected malevolent voices spread by the modernist abbot Lambert Beauduin,[719] whom he met in Rome to be introduced into the "*milieu très fermé*" of the Roman ecclesiastical world.[720] These voices perfidiously insinuated doubts about the morality of Pius X's secretary of state, based on reports of relations he had had with Francis MacNutt, disguised in the novel under the pseudonym of "Mac Wrenth."

Francis MacNutt was a brilliant and capable personality, born in Richmond in 1863 into a wealthy American family. He had studied in the United States and Europe and, in the end, entered the Academy of Ecclesiastical Nobles in Rome, directed at the time by Cardinal Satolli, where he became friends with Rafael Merry del Val. After two years spent in the Academy (1887–1889), he left his ecclesiastical vocation and returned to America, where he was named by President Benjamin Harrison secretary of the Legate to Constantinople. In 1897, he married Margaret Van Cortland Ogden, a rich heiress, thirteen years older than himself.[721] The following year, the couple moved to Rome where they were warmly received by Leo XIII, who honored the thirty-five-year-old MacNutt with the title of marquis and nominated him papal chamberlain. The MacNutt couple rented a stately apartment in Palazzo Doria Pamphili in Piazza Navona (today the offices of the Brazilian embassy) where they received the best of Roman high society, offering sumptuous receptions. Baron von Pastor recalls a reception of the MacNutts in the magnificent halls of Palazzo Doria Pamphili, "perhaps even more splendid

718 Jean de Bonnefon (1866–1927), a journalist who defined himself an "anticlerical Catholic," was renowned for having bitterly criticized the miracles of Lourdes (*Lourdes et ses Tenanciers*, Louis Michaud, Paris 1905, in which he pretends to write a "*histoire inconnue du mensonge de Lourdes*"). He was also the author of a modest periodical, *Les Paroles françaises et romaines*, that wrote about Roman scandals and gossip.

719 Lambert Beauduin (1873–1960), a Belgian Benedictine in the Abbey of Mont-César, near Louvaine (1907), founded the Monastery of the Union in Amay (Liegi), and later transferred to Chevetogne, in the Province of Namur. He was a professor at Sant'Anselmo in Rome from 1921 to 1925. About him, cf. the biography of Raymond Loonbeek-Jacques Mortiau, *Un pionnier: dom Lambert Beauduin (1873–1960). Liturgie et unité des chrétiens*, Louvain-la-Neuve, Chevetogne 2001, 2 vols.

720 Angremy, *Le dossiers préparatoires*, pp. 106–107.

721 Cf. *New York Times*, December 27, 1897. Margaret Van Cortland Ogden (1849–1936) was the descendant of a wealthy family from New York, of Dutch origins.

than that of our ambassador Count Szécsen."[722] Twice a year, the MacNutt couple gave a grand ball and at least once every winter a reception for the cardinals, foreign dignitaries, and diplomatic corps tied to the Vatican. But the life of the American diplomat took a sudden turn on May 16, 1905, when he was arrested and then condemned to three months parole for immoral decorum.[723]

When the scandal broke, Merry del Val, in agreement with Pius X, imposed banishment from Rome on MacNutt, who was stripped of the pontifical titles that Leo XIII had granted him. MacNutt, who always declared his innocence, considered this a betrayal and, in his *Memoires*, recalled how after being isolated by Merry del Val, was received with the benevolence of "an old friend" by Benedict XV. The young American then purchased a picturesque castle in Brixen ("Schloss Ratzötz"), where he retired to compose exquisite historical works.[724] Merry del Val, in a letter to Cardinal O'Connell in 1927, commented that looking back, regardless of the sad things that happened to MacNutt, he believes he did his "painful duty."[725]

> I am much grieved over pour MacNutt's death.[726] Such a brilliant and attractive man, of whom I was fond and who was a friend of long-standing. He was the object of envy and attack on the part of many, who had every reason to be grateful to him. I stood by him until it became impossible and I had a painful duty to accomplish which I could not betray, even if it had been a question of my own father. He

722 "Der Empfang, bei Mr MacNutt am selben Abend in den herrlichen Räumen des Palazzo Doria Pamphili, war vielleicht noch glänzender als der bei unseres Botschafter Graf Szecsen." (Pastor, *Tagebücher*, p. 404).

723 Cf. *Boston Globe*, July 19, 1905, where this news is reported.

724 Among these, *Bartholomew de Las Casas: His Life, His Apostolate, and His Writings* (1909), *Fernando Cortes and the Conquest of Mexico, 1485–1547* (1909), and *Fernando Cortes: His Five Letters of Relation to the Emperor Charles V, 1519– 1526* (1908).

725 Merry del Val to Cardinal O'Connell, March 16, 1928, cit. in Leasy, *Odd Fellows*, p. 86. In Cardinal Merry del Val's correspondence with Cardinal O'Connell, one finds 125 letters and telegrams, from 1901 to 1929 (*The O'Connell Papers, General correspondence*, Archives of the Archdiocese of Boston, boxes 7–10).

726 Francis McNutt died December 30, 1927, in Schloss Ratzötz, and was buried in the habit of the Franciscan Third Order in the cemetery of St. Mary am Sand in Millan, near Brixen. In 1926, the year before his death, he wrote his autobiography in two volumes which was later edited by Fr. John Donovan and published in 1936 by Longmans, Green and Co. under the title *A Papal Chamberlain: The Personal Chronicle of Francis Augustus MacNutt*. The preface was written by G. K. Chesterton and Cardinal Patrick Joseph Hayes, archbishop of New York, who defined him "a most capable and inflexible defender of Catholic truth" (p. vi).

> had cut the ground from under his feet, poor fellow; morally speaking it was suicide. He misjudged my action in his despair and expected from me what I could not give. In his *Memoirs* he is often mistaken as to the facts and unfair to me: he did not take all into account or realize his position. I kept silence lest it should become worse and this he could not understand. It is all very sad, for he might have played a great part and rendered immense service."[727]

Merry del Val felt human pity, but always deplored the loss of the religious vocation of his young friend, with whom he had but a few formal encounters after he abandoned the Ecclesiastical Academy.

In any case, the insinuations hurled against Merry del Val after his death by Jules Romains lacked all foundation and deserve to be removed from any serious historical investigation. In a letter of May 26, 1953, to an unkwown destinaire, Jules Romains sought to justify the accusations against Merry del Val made in the novel *Mission in Rome*, based on a photograph that he claims captured the Cardinal in an ambiguous attitude toward MacNutt.[728] The photograph, which only he had ever seen, if it exists at all, was most certainly doctored, as Romains himself admits in the last lines of his novel in which the priest-spy Mionnet states, "Naturally, the document was as false as a plug Nickle.... We had a fine nose not to fall for it."[729]

Romains's book was constructed then upon a forgery with ignoble precedents, such as the photomontage that reached the desk of Pius IX in February of 1862, in which Queen Maria Sofia of the Two Sicilies, the younger sister of Sisi (Elisabeth of Bavaria, wife of Emperor Franz Josef I of Austria), exiled in Rome with her husband Francesco II, was represented in obscene photos. Within a month, on March 6, 1862, its authors were arrested: two photographers, Antonio Diotallevi and Costanza Vaccari Diotallevi.

The thesis of Jules Romains is presented upside down, furthermore. The existence of a doctored photograph would confirm the existence of a campaign of defamation against the cardinal, in which many protagonists had an interest, from masonic France to Protestant Germany. It was not difficult to add a few

727 Merry del Val to Cardinal O'Connell, January 21, 1928, cit. in Leasy, *Odd Fellows*, p. 86.

728 Angremy, *Le dossiers préparatoires*, pp. 345–348.

729 Romains, *Missione a Roma*, p. 320. "Quant à l'histoire de la photo, elle a couru à Rome, avec persistance. La photo, truquée ou non, a certainement existé" (Angremy, *Les dossiers préparatoires*, p. 346).

photomontages to the gossip and malicious voices cleverly disseminated. Romains's book, which came out in 1937 with the aim of revealing to the wider public these authentic "events," narrated in a novelistic form, was lacking in historical validation and was likely part of an operation to discredit the conservative wing in the Vatican, during the years in which Cardinal Eugenio Pacelli had inherited Merry del Val's role at the summit of the Secretariat of State, before being elected pope in 1939.

The lives, not only of the saints, but also of many eminent men, are often surrounded by attempts at defamation which the historian has the duty to register and evaluate. Under the pontificate of Pius X, Cardinal Merry del Val was the target of every form of slander. Nevertheless, if in that calumny there had been just one grain of truth, it would have emerged at the cardinal's process of beatification in which there was no lack of voices contrary to him. Not only did this not occur, but it suffices to recall that in the years of the supposed scandals he was accused of having been involved in, Merry del Val lived in daily contact with a saint like Pius X, who had the gift of discernment of souls and who would certainly have removed him if any shadow of a doubt had arisen. Furthermore, Merry del Val continued to guide many souls throughout this period who testified to his profound spiritual life.

His life, filled with so many responsibilities, continued to be humble and recollected. During his morning offering, which he recited daily before celebrating Mass, the cardinal prayed,

> I am willing, O my God, to accept from Your hands, in the manner pleasing to You, health or sickness, wealth or poverty, long life or short life, honors or dishonor, friendship or aversion, and so with everything else, choosing only what is most in conformity with Your glory. And if You are so good as to call me to imitate You more closely and intimately in poverty, in ignominy, and in suffering, O dear Jesus, behold I am ready: speak, for Your servant is listening, but help my weakness. I so desire to love You, my Master, and lower myself in humility and obedience before You, that I would prefer not only any affliction, including death, to mortal or venial sin, but to prefer that loss or that affliction whenever Your glory and honor are thereby promoted.[730]

[730] Cenci, *Merry del Val*, p. 433.

THE BATTLE AGAINST MODERNISM

The most difficult trial Pius X would have to face in his pontificate was undoubtedly the fight against "modernism,"[731] which occupied essentially the entire period of his governance.[732] In this struggle, as well with others, the pope found in his secretary of state, Merry del Val, a loyal and invaluable collaborator. The historian Giovanni Vian is not wrong in writing, "During the years of Pius X's pontificate, the Secretariat of State under Merry del Val was a diligent promoter of anti-modernism, safeguarding the Roman magisterium and ecclesiastical institutions. His communion with the concerns fostered by Pius X seems to have been complete in the expression of ideas and orientations that were considered seriously damaging to correct Catholic doctrine."[733] It must be added that modernism represented a profound wound to Catholic faith and, precisely in combating its errors, Pius X and Merry del Val carried out a decisive role in defending the Holy Roman Church.

Commemorating Cardinal Merry del Val as a "strenuous defender of the faith," Msgr. Ernesto Ruffini, who had been one of his collaborators, stated, "There have always been heretics from the beginning of the age of the Church; never until that time, however, had they reached the point of challenging the very foundations of the Faith with the alleged intention of defending it. Dogmas were no longer absolute truths to be believed according to the traditional teaching of the Holy Church, but simple moral symbols; religion was reduced to mere sentimentalism, stripped of any supernatural and objective base; the hierarchy of the Church was considered to have derived through human evolution from the need for governance in the Christian community; the Bible

731 The term *modernism* was coined by the Belgian Catholic economist Charles Périn (1815–1905) in his volume dedicated to *Le modernisme dans l'Église. D'après des lettres inédites de Lamennais* (Victor Lecoffre, Paris 1881). Merriam-Webster defines it as "a tendency in theology to accommodate traditional religious teaching to contemporary thought and especially to devalue supernatural elements."

732 On modernism there exists a limitless bibliography. For an introduction, cf. the synthesis by M. Guasco, *Modernismo. I fatti, le idee, i personaggi, [Modernism. The Facts, Ideas, Personalities]*, San Paolo, Cinisello Balsamo, Milan 1995; Claus Arnold, *Kleine Geschichte des Modernismus*, Herder, Freiburg i. B. 2007; G. Vian, *Il modernismo. La Chiesa cattolica in conflitto con la modernità*, Carocci, Rome 2012. These works express a positive evaluation of modernism, but it must be said that authors of the opposite tendency often do not grasp the importance of the modernist question, as observed by Vian in "El cardenal Merry del Val y la crisis modernista," *Investigaciones Históricas, época moderna y contemporánea* 41 (2021), p. 819 (pp. 815–844). Cf. also, AA.VV., *Vecchio e nuovo modernismo. Radici della crisi nella Chiesa*, ed. R. de Mattei, Edizioni Fiducia, Rome 2020.

733 Vian, "El cardenal Merry del Val y la crisis modernista," p. 825.

was stripped of its divinity and biblical inspiration lowered to the level of poetic inspiration; in this manner, one sought to overturn everything, destroy everything by men from within the Church for the most part.... This was the great battle that Pope Pius X and his faithful minister prepared to fight in the name of God."[734]

In his discourse on June 3, 1951, in honor of Pius X and reflecting above all on the case of modernism, Pius XII said,

> Now that the most detailed examination has scrutinized to the depths all the acts and vicissitudes of his pontificate, now that we know what has come of those events, no hesitation, no reservation is possible any longer, and one must recognize that even in the most difficult, most bitter periods heavily laden with responsibility, Pius X, assisted by his magnanimous and most faithful secretary of state, Cardinal Merry del Val, gave proof of that enlightened prudence that was never lacking in the saints, even when contrasted in its application, painful and inevitable, by the deceitful postulates of human, earthly prudence.[735]

The detailed examination to which Pius XII referred was the historical *Disquisitio* of the Congregation of Rites, published in 1950 for the process of canonization of Pope Pius X.[736] This document, desired by Pius XII, accurately responded to the criticism aimed at Pius X in his struggle against modernism, even by important figures like that of Cardinal Gasparri.

Merry del Val had no fear in taking up arms at the pope's side. On December 30, 1906, he wrote to his friend Fr. Joe Broadhead,

> The struggle is simply and only the struggle for Christianity, for God, and for religion throughout the world. There is not the least iota of politics in the Holy See's attitude, but we have come to blows with godlessness and blasphemy, and we must combat it.... The times are

734 Cenci, *Merry del Val*, p. 752.

735 Pius XII, Discourse in Honor of Pius X, June 3, 1951, in *Discorsi e Radio- messaggi* 13 (March 2, 1951 — March 1, 1952), p. 131 (pp. 127–136).

736 Cf. *Pii X Disquisitio*, pp. 53–100. The *Disquisitio* was entrusted by Pius XII to the Franciscan theologian Msgr. Ferdinando Antonelli (1897–1993), later cardinal. The main objections to Pius X concerning his struggle against modernism were his overly severe attitude toward Cardinal Ferrari and toward the moderate Catholic press, and his attitude, considered to be too indulgent, towards the *Sodalitium pianum* of Msgr. Umberto Benigni.

> filled with sadness among those who fight for the Lord, but we are not discouraged, and your poor old friend who has been forced to take this prominent position on the battlefield shall carry out his duty to the bitter end, and Ushaw will have no reason to be ashamed of one of its devoted sons.[737]

"Unfortunately, there exists in England as in France, Germany, the United States and here," he wrote to Broadhead in 1908, "a group of traitors in our camp, and it would be better if they would leave as quickly as possible 'from among us' because they are not 'ours.'"[738] And the following year: "The times are evil and my mission is a long and hard fight for the Faith and the rights of the Holy Church."[739]

Modernism, broadly speaking, was a group of theological, philosophical, and exegetical errors that branched out within the Catholic Church under the pontificate of Leo XIII, in the name of a Christianity open to the demands of the contemporary world. "Considered under its most general form," wrote one of the protagonists of the movement, "modernism can be defined as the desire to adapt religion to the intellectual, moral, and social exigencies of its time."[740]

The origins of modernism can be found in "Americanism," condemned by Leo XIII with the apostolic letter *Testem benevolentiae* of January 22, 1899;[741] in liberal Protestantism;[742] and, more remotely, in the "liberal-Catholic" schools inspired by Fr. Félicité de Lamennais. In France, the movement had its cultural birth in the *Institut Catholique* in Paris, where Fr. Alfred

737 *Merry del Val/Broadhead Papers*, Ushaw College Archives, Letters of Merry del Val to Broadhead, December 30, 1906.

738 Ibid, letter, January 17, 1908.

739 Ibid, letter, October 27, 1909.

740 Albert Houtin, *Histoire du Modernisme catholique*, Nourry, Paris 1913, p. 88. Albert Houtin (1867–1926), ordained a priest in 1891, later adhered to modernism and was apostate from the Church in 1912. About him, cf. also *Une vie de prêtre. Mon expérience (1867–1912)*, Rieder, Paris 1926 ; and *Mon expérience II. Ma vie laïque (1912–1926). Documents et souvenirs*, Rieder, Paris 1928.

741 Leo XIII, Letter *Testem benevolentiae de americanismo*, January 22, 1899, in ASS, vol. 31 (1898–1899), pp. 470–479.

742 Modern Protestantism found among its intellectuals in France the two Sabatiers: Auguste (1839–1901) and Paul (1858–1928), the latter the student of the former in the Theology department in Paris, although no family tie existed between them (cf. Émile Poulat, *Modernistica. Horizon, Physionomies, Débats*, Nouvelles Éditions Latines, Paris 1982, pp. 106–109).

Loisy[743] took the historical-critical method of his master Louis Duchesne to its extreme consequences.[744]

In the same years, Maurice Blondel, developing the foundational theme of his doctoral thesis *L'Action*, proposed a new form of apologetics that presumed the immanent orientations of modern thought.[745] In Italy, the appearance in Florence in January 1901 of the journal *Religious Studies* marked the "birthday" of the new philosophical and exegetical tendencies.[746] The journal was founded and directed for seven years (1901-1907) by the biblical scholar Fr. Salvatore Minocchi,[747] with the collaboration of Barnabite Giovanni Semeria;[748] Fr. Giovanni Genocchi, superior of the house in Rome of the Missionaries of the Sacred Heart;[749] Fr. Umberto Fracassini, rector (later removed from office) of the seminary in Perugia;[750] and, beginning in 1904, Fr. Ernesto Buonaiuti, professor of Church history at the Seminary of Apollinare, destined to become the most noteworthy figure in the movement,

743 Alfred Loisy (1857–1940), professor of Biblical Studies at the *Institut Catholique* in Paris, according to his *Mémoires* (vol. 1, p. 154), began to distance himself from the Church as early as 1886. Excommunicated on March 7, 1908, contrary to other modernists, he officially renounced Christianity. His *Mémoires* were placed on the Index in 1932 and in 1938 the censure of all his works followed. His biography was published by Émile Poulat in his edition of the volume by Albert Houtin and Félix Sartieu, *Alfred Loisy. Sa vie, son œuvre*, Éditions du CNRS, Paris 1960. Cf. also Claus Arnold and Giacomo Losito, *La censure d'Alfred Loisy. Les documents des Congrégations de l'Index et du Saint-Office*, Fontes Archivi Sancti Officii Romani, Vatican City 2009.

744 A third personality, Fr. Marcel Hébert (1851–1916), translated the ideas of Loisy and Duchesne into the philosophical field. These three priests, two of whom were to fall into apostasy, exercised in France a decisive influence, according to Fr. Emmanuel Barbier, on the orientation of young clergy and young lay Catholics during the years spanning from 1880 to 1893. *Histoire du catholicisme libéral et social en France du Concile du Vatican à l'avènement de SS. Benoît XV (1870–1914)*, Cadoret, Paris 1923–1924, vol. 2, p. 199.

745 Maurice Blondel (1861–1949) was professor in Aix-en-Provence from 1897 to 1927. Cf. René Virgoulay, *"L'Action" de Maurice Blondel. 1893. Relecture pour un centenaire*, Beauchesne, Paris 1992. An accurate critique of his doctrine was made by Fr. Joseph de Tonquédec S.J., in *Immanence. Essai critique sur la doctrine de M. Maurice Blondel*, Beauchesne, Paris 1933; idem, "Pourquoi j'ai critiqué Maurice Blondel," *Revue Tomiste* 3 (1949), pp. 563–580.

746 Ernesto Buonaiuti, *Modernismo cattolico*, Guanda, Modena 1943, p. 133.

747 On Fr. Salvatore Minocchi (1869–1943), Cf. also n. 451 and the text *Memorie di un modernista*, Vallecchi, Florence 1974.

748 On the Barnabite Giovanni Semeria (1867–1931), cf. the entry by Antonio M. Gentili, DSMCI, II, pp. 596–602 and the introductory essay by A. Gentili and Annibale Zambarbieri for the paper Semeria-Vigorelli, "Il caso Semeria," *Fonti e Documenti* 4 (1975), pp. 54–216.

749 On Fr. Giovanni Genocchi (1890–1926), Superior General of the Roman the Missionaries of the Sacred Heart, cf. Francesco Turvasi: *Padre Genocchi, il Sant'Uffizio e la Bibbia*, Dehoniane, Bologna 1971; and *Giovanni Genocchi e la controversia modernista*, Storia e Letteratura, Rome 1974.

750 On Msgr. Umberto Fracassini (1862–1950), cf. the entries by M. Guasco, DHGE 17 (1971), col. 1367–1369; and R. Cerrato, DBI 49 (1997), pp. 541–543.

who defined it "much more and much better as an attitude of the soul, than as a system and a religious confession."[751]

The person who, along with Buonaiuti, gave the theological framework to modernism was the Irish priest George Tyrrell.[752] A convert from Calvinism to Anglicanism and from there to Catholicism, he entered the Society of Jesus in 1880 and was ordained a priest in 1891, upon which he was sent to the Jesuit church in Farm Street, London. There, he discovered the works of Loisy and Blondel through his collaboration with the Jesuit publication *The Month*. In this journal in 1899, he published the article "On the Relation of Theology to Devotion," later reprinted under the new title "*Lex orandi, lex credendi*" in the collection *Through Scylla and Carybdis* of 1907, which offered a compendium of his "nouvelle théologie." Tyrrell identified revelation with the vital experience (religious experience) made in the conscience of each person, and for this reason it is the *lex orandi* that dictates the norms of the *lex credendi* and not vice versa. "Revelation," he said, "cannot be put into us from outside; it can be occasioned, but it cannot be caused, by instruction."[753]

Tyrrell's God, like that of Blondel, was immanent to the conscience that recognizes it in its own religious experience. It is not truth that determines my experience, but experience that constitutes the supreme criterion of the truth. For Tyrrell, religion is a union of heart with God that can do without the truths of dogmas. The Magisterium of the Church is substituted with the subjective reinterpretation of dogma. In this way, modernism launched a double attack on the sources of Revelation: against Scripture, through the exegetical rationalism of Loisy, and against Tradition, through the theological evolutionism of Tyrrell.

751 Ernesto Buonaiuti (1881–1946), priest in 1903, directed various journals of a modernist orientation, though he managed to avoid ecclesiastical censure until 1921. Excommunicated *vitandus* (1926), he never reconciled with the Church. Cf. the entry by Fausto Parente, DBI 15 (1972), pp. 112–122 with bibliography. His autobiography remains fundamental, *Pellegrino di Roma. La generazione dell'esodo [Pilgrim of Rome. The Generation of the Exodus]*, Editori Laterza, Bari 1964.

752 George Tyrrell (1861–1909), Irish convert to Catholicism from Anglicanism and ordained a priest in the Society of Jesus (1891), was expelled by the Jesuits in 1906 and deprived of the sacraments in 1907. Important documents for comprehending his thought are the *Autobiography and Life of George Tyrrell*, Edward Arnold, London 1912, edited by Maude Petre, and the *Lettres de Georges Tyrrell à Henri Brémond*, Aubier-Montaigne, Paris 1971, a correspondence of which we have the replies by Tyrrell but not the letters of Brémond, which seem to have been lost. The bibliography of Tyrrell's works can be found in Thomas Michael Loome, *A Bibliography of the published writings of George Tyrrell*, pp. 280–314; and idem, *A Bibliography of the printed works of George Tyrrell: supplement*, pp. 161–164. About him, cf. among others: Oliver P. Rafferty, *George Tyrrell and Catholic modernism*, Four Court Press, Dublin 2010.

753 George Tyrrell, *Through Scylla and Charybdis*, Green and Co., London 1907, pp. 305–306.

The "liaison" of Italian, French, and English modernism was Baron Friedrich von Hügel.[754] His father Austrian and his mother Scottish, Hügel was the "*liaison officier*,"[755] "the intermediary link between English-German society and Italian society,"[756] thanks to his social prestige and cosmopolitan condition. Hügel's daughter married a Noble Guard of Pius X, Count Francesco Salimei,[757] and Hügel himself spent the winter months in Rome where he introduced Loisy and Tyrrell to his little group of friends, laymen, and priests, who met periodically in his villa in Via Ludovisi.

The Encyclical Pascendi

In May 1906, Merry del Val wrote his friend Sheil, "I should not be at all surprised if, sooner or later, the Holy Father does denounce the modernist heresies, which are doing incalculable harm, and utterly destroying the faith right and left."[758] In fact, the young secretary of state contributed actively to its condemnation. In the face of the new movement that was developing in an aggressive and clandestine manner, Pius X reacted with the encyclical *Pascendi* on September 8, 1907,[759]

754 Baron Friedrich von Hügel (1852–1925) was the son of an Austrian ambassador in Florence, where he was born. He studied in England and there married the daughter of Lord Herbert of Lea, with whom he had three daughters. He became a naturalized British subject at the beginning of the First World War. Cf. Maurice Nédoncelle, *La pensée religieuse de Friedrich von Hügel*, Vrin, Paris 1935, p. 14. Cf. also John J. Heaney, *The Modernist Crisis: von Hügel*, G. Chapman, London 1969; Bernard Holland (ed.), *Baron Friedrich von Hügel: Selected Letters, 1896–1924*, Dent, London 1928; Lawrence F. Barmann, *Baron Friedrich von Hügel and the Modernist Crisis in England*, Cambridge University Press, New York 1972.

755 Friedrich Heer, *Europa madre delle rivoluzioni [Europe Mother of Revolutions]*, Italian translation, Mondadori, Milano 1968, vol. 2, p. 338.

756 Giuseppe Prezzolini, *Cos'è il modernismo [What is Modernism?]*, Treves, Milan 1908, p. 75.

757 Count Francesco Salimei (1875–1947), Noble Guard under Leo XIII and Pius X, was a city counsellor in Rome during the period of nascent Christian Democracy, from 1902 to 1907. Tied to Roman modernist circles, in 1907, he married Gertrude von Hügel (1877–1915), daughter of the Baron Friedrich, who died at thirty-eight of tuberculosis in Rome. On May 26, 1910, he resigned from the Noble Guard for having accepted a position as assessor in Rome in the Nathan government. Contrary to what some have written of him, he was not reintegrated by Benedict XV into the Noble Guard (cf. Giulio Patrizi di Ripacandida, *Quell'ultimo glorioso stendardo. Le guardie nobili pontificie dall'11 maggio 1801 al 15 settembre 1970 [That Last, Glorious Banner. The Pontifical Noble Guard from May 11, 1801, to September 15, 1970]*, Edizioni Musei Vaticani, Vatican City 1994, p. 64). On him, cf. *Frammenti di vita [Fragments of a Life]*, Tip. Consorzio nazionale, Rome 1954.

758 Buehrle, *Merry del Val*, p. 126; Forbes, *Merry del Val*, p. 96.

759 Pius X, Encyclical *Pascendi Dominici gregis*, September 8, 1907, in AAS, vol. 40 (1907), pp. 596–628. C. Arnold, "Antimodernismo e Magistero romano: la redazione della Pascendi," *Rivista di Storia del Cristianesimo* 5, no. 2 (2008), pp. 345–364.

which among all his works remains, as Fr. Cornelio Fabro writes, "the most illustrious monument of his pontificate."[760]

In the draft signed by Pius X and used by Vincenzo Sardi for the editing of *Pascendi*, the pope wrote,

> The implacable enemy of the human race never sleeps; according to the events of the age and the production of those events he changes his tactical language, but is always ready for the fight, in fact the more error, hounded by the truth, is condemned to hide itself, the more it is to be feared for the dangerous ambushes behind which it hastens to reestablish its always deadly artillery. Thus we can never surrender ourselves to a false security without incurring those anathemas hurled against the false prophets that announced peace where there was no peace, and sang victory songs when everything was calling us into combat. And if this has been necessary throughout all times, it is all the more so in this age in which the great conspiracy formed directly against our Lord Jesus Christ, against his supernatural and revealed religion, against His Church and His Priesthood, has reached the point at which false teachers are arising in the spirit of the nations saying that good is evil and evil is good, *vocantes tenebras lucem et lucem tenebras*, seducing many minds that bend to every wind of doctrine. For this reason we believe the *tempus loquendi* has come.[761]

Collaborating in the editing of the encyclical, in what concerned theology, was Fr. Joseph Lemius[762] with the help of Cardinal Billot, and in what concerned juridical and practical matters, Cardinal Vives y Tutó. Cardinal Merry del Val was involved in the entire process of final editing and translation.[763]

760 Cf. Cornelio Fabro, *Modernismo*, in EC, vol. 8, col. 1190.

761 AAV, Ep. ad Princ., *Positiones et minutae* 157, fasc. 35A, cit. in C. Arnold, "Pius X, Merry del Val and the cases of Alfred Loisy and George Tyrrell," in Giovanni Vian (ed.) *Le pontificat romain dans l'époque contemporaine*, Ca' Foscari, Venice 2018, p. 21.

762 Joseph Lemius (1851–1938), French, General Provost of the Missionary Oblates of Mary Immaculate, cousin of Fr. Giuseppe Lemius (1860–1932), lived for forty-five years in Rome and was a consultor to many congregations.

763 C. Arnold, "Absage an die Moderne? Papst Pius X und die Entstehung der Enziklika Pascendi (1907)," *Theologie und Philosophie* 80 (2005), pp. 201–224; idem, Antimodernismo e Magistero romano: la redazione della Pascendi," pp. 345–363; "La documentazione archivistica relativa all'enciclica *Pascendi*" [The Archival Documentation Relative to the Encyclical *Pascendi*], in C. Arnold and G. Vian (eds.), *La redazione dell'Enciclica Pascendi. Studi e documenti sull'antimodernismo di Papa Pio X [The Editing of the Encyclical Pascendi. Studies and documents on the antimodernism of Pope Pius X]*,

The nucleus of modernism, according to St. Pius X, did not consist so much in opposition to one or another truth of revealed faith, but in the radical change of the very notion of "truth," through the acceptance of the philosophical principle of "immanence" that presumes experience to be absolute and excludes every transcendent reality. Faith is no longer the intellect's adhesion to a truth revealed by God, but a religious exigency that is unleashed from the obscure depths (subconscious) of the human soul. The formulas of dogma, according to modernists, do not contain absolute truths: they are "symbols," images of the truth that must adapt themselves to religious sentiment and to the "interior experience" of the believer.

In this sense, modernism takes up once more the attempt of Gnosticism to embrace all truths through one sole principle, the subjectivity of the truth and the relativity of all its formulas.[764] According to Pius X, "in fact, the immanence of the modernists desires and admits that every phenomenon of conscience is born of man *qua* man. Therefore, as a legitimate consequence we deduce that God and man are the same thing: and for this reason, it is pantheism."[765]

As Émile Poulat highlighted, *Pascendi* was the logical outcome of the orientation vigorously affirmed by Pius IX about half a century earlier in the *Sillabus* (1864): "Pius IX denounced the errors *ad extra* (from outside the Church) that were circulating in the world; Pius X, on the contrary, struck at the phenomenon *ad intra* (within the Church), striking those same errors that had infiltrated the Church, where they were taking shape and setting roots."[766]

The Condemnation of Alfred Loisy

The spark that set the movement ablaze, after a decade of smoldering, was the controversy aroused by the appearance in 1902 of the little volume by Alfred Loisy, *L'Evangile et l'Eglise*,[767] in response to the interpretation of Christianity by

---

Anton Hiersemann Verlag, Stuttgart 2020, pp. 1–23; also G. Vian, "Una complessa elaborazione testuale. I passaggi finali della redazione della *Pascendi*" [A Complex Textual Elaboration. The Final Steps in the Redaction of *Pascendi*], in ibid., pp. 25–89.

764 Fabro, *Modernismo*, col. 1191.

765 Pius X, *Pascendi*, n. 228.

766 Poulat, *Modernistica*, p. 25.

767 On the debate over the small book by Loisy, cf. E. Poulat, *Storia, dogma e critica nella crisi modernista [History, Dogma and Criticism in the Modernist Crisis]*, Italian translation, Morcelliana, Brescia 1967, pp. 38–78, 85–122, with all the relative bibliography.

the German exegete Alfred von Harnack.[768] Applying the new "historical-critical" method to the field of exegesis, Loisy denied and crippled the revealed character of the Old and New Testaments, the divinity of Christ, the institution of the Church, the hierarchy, and the sacraments.

As consultant to the Congregation of the Index, an office to which he had been appointed in 1898, Merry del Val had a relevant part to play in the decision that led to the condemnation of five works by Loisy on December 4, 1903: besides *L'Evangile et l'Eglise,* they included *Religion d'Israel, Etudes évangeliques, Autour d'un petit livre,* and *Quatrième Evangile.*

The judgment of Cardinal Merry del Val on *Religion d'Israel,* like that of Cardinal Billot on *L'Evangile et l'Eglise,* was the most severe. The Loisy case was discussed in the Congregation of the Index and then passed to the Sacred Inquisition. The vast majority was in favor of placing Loisy's books on the Index, and the Capuchin Pie de Langogne authored the concluding *Relatio* for the Inquisition.[769] Msgr. Louis Duchesne, writing to Loisy on November 17, 1903, used a sarcastic tone, "What could we expect from those who declared to be authentic the verse of the three witnesses?[770] Now they have been reinforced by Msgr. Merry del Val who would be more inclined to believe that the whale was swallowed by Jonah than to place the contrary in doubt."[771]

According to Claus Arnold, who reconstructed the affair, "The person who had rendered Loisy's destiny irrevocable"[772] was precisely Merry del Val, who

[768] Adolf von Harnack (1851–1930) was a Protestant theologian who taught at the Universities of Leipzig, Gießen, Marburg, and Berlin. Cf. Guglielmo Forni, *"Essenza del Cristianesimo." Il problema ermeneutico nella discussione protestante e modernista (1897–1940) [The Hermeneutical Problem in the Protestant and Modernist Debate],* Il Mulino, Bologna 1992.

[769] Pio da Langogne (1850–1914), at birth Armand Sabadel, a Capuchin friar, in Rome from 1880 as consultor of many Roman congregations, consecrated by Pius X titular archbishop of Corinth (1911), was a close collaborator with his confrere Cardinal José de Calasanz Vives y Tutó.

[770] This refers to the decree of the Holy Office on January 12, 1897, on the authenticity of the so-called verse of the "Three Witnesses" (1 John 5:5–9), considered by most modern exegetes to be a gloss added at some later date. In this passage, whose authenticity was contested by Loisy, St. John seeks to prove that Jesus Christ is truly the Son of God through the triple testimony of the Spirit, the water, and the blood.

[771] Louis Duchesne to Alfred Loisy, November 17, 1903, in Bruno Neveu, "Lettres de Monseigneur Duchesne, directeur de l'École française de Rome, à Alfred Loisy (1896–1917) et à Friedrich von Hügel (1895–1920)," *Mélanges de l'École française de Rome. Moyen Age, Temps modernes* 84, 2 (1972), p. 299.

[772] C. Arnold, *Introduction* to Arnold-Losito, *La censure d'Alfred Loisy,* p. 46, with reference to the *votum* by Merry del Val on the book by Loisy, *La religion d'Israel.* The text is reproduced in its entirety, ibid., pp. 325–332.

exercised pressure on the Holy Office to bring about his rapid excommunication.[773] One can certainly not find fault with Pius X's secretary of state for this resolute intervention. In retrospect, Loisy declared he had wanted "an essential reform of biblical exegesis, of all theology, and even of Catholicism in general."[774] The horizon he was disclosing was that of a transformation of Christianity into a nebulous "religion of humanity." "Historically speaking," Loisy was to reminisce, "I did not admit that Christ had founded the Church and the sacraments; I professed that dogmas were formed gradually and that they were not immutable; I admitted the same as concerns ecclesiastical authority, which I turned into a ministry of human education. I did not stop at criticizing Harnack. I alluded discretely, though effectively, to a substantial reform of Catholic exegesis, of official theology, and of ecclesiastical governance in general."[775] His ecclesiastical protectors were equally ingenuous, if not deceitful.

In a letter of December 19, 1903, in which he communicated the condemnation to Archbishop Richard of Paris, Merry del Val wrote that the books of the French exegete "regurgitate the gravest of errors," concerning essentially "the primitive revelation, the authenticity of the events and teachings of the Gospels, the divinity and knowledge of Christ, the Resurrection, the divine institution of the Church, and the sacraments."[776]

A few months later, at the end of March 1904, Loisy wrote in his diary, "It seems sufficiently clear to me, if I believe in anything, that I do not believe in what the Church teaches, and that the Church is not willing to teach what I believe.... The entire Catholic system, doctrine, and discipline is contrary to reason and to life. It is not supernatural, it is logically deduced lunacy.... Pius X, who is the head of the Catholic Church, would excommunicate me with the utmost decisiveness if he only knew that to me creation is a purely metaphysical symbol, that the virginal conception and resurrection of Christ are purely moral symbols, and that the whole Catholic system is a tyranny executed in God's

773 *La condanna del modernismo. Documenti, interpretazioni, conseguenze [The Condemnation of Modernism. Documents, Interpretations and Consequences]*, ed. C. Arnold and G. Vian, Viella, Roma 2010, p. 77.

774 Alfred Loisy, *Choses passées*, Nourry, Paris 1913, p. 246.

775 A. Loisy, *Mémoires pour servir à l'histoire religieuse de notre temps,* Nourry, Paris 1930–1933, 3 vols. Citing vol. 2, vol. 2, pp. 168–169.

776 Arnold and Losito, *La censure d'Alfred Loisy*, p. 61. "Pour mettre M. Loisy au pied du mur" wrote Msgr. Montagnini to Merry del Val in April of 1907, "il faudrait exiger de lui la reconnaissance formelle que les paroles de l'institution eucharistique ont été prononcées par le Christ historique" (*Les Fiches pontificales de Monsignor Montagnini*, pp. 99–100).

name and in Christ's name against God himself and against the Gospel."[777] Although he was aware of having a vision of Christianity that had nothing to do with that of the Church, Loisy suffered the promulgation of *Pascendi* as an act of violence. On September 29, 1907, he wrote Cardinal Merry del Val a letter in which he protested "with his whole soul" against the interpretation of the modernist ideas proposed by the encyclical,[778] and his *Memoires* exude hatred toward Pius X's secretary of state. "The despotic, intransigent, inquisitorial Church without viscera, that makes use of orthodoxy as an instrument of domination and that believes it can permit anything that would ensure the reign of its absolutism appears to me in its natural state in Merry del Val."[779] Loisy repeatedly refused the invitations to submit to the Church received from the bishop of Langres, Msgr. Sébastien Herscher,[780] and Cardinal Merry del Val communicated Loisy's reply to the Holy Office on February 28, 1908, writing, "It seems useless to hope that one might change the awful dispositions of this priest who has lost the faith and has done so much incalculable damage to souls in every nation in the world."[781]

Merry del Val acted in close accord with Pius X, and the excommunication arrived on March 7, 1908, with a decree published in *L'Osservatore Romano* and posted in all the main churches in the diocese of Langres.[782] Despite the efforts of various prelates to sustain his orthodoxy, Loisy continued his work of demolishing the dogmas of the Church until his death in 1940.

Merry del Val and Tyrrell

George Tyrrell was an Irish priest of the Society of Jesus, whose theological and spiritual teaching Cardinal Merry del Val had absorbed from his youth. It is no wonder that he followed attentively the young rebellious Jesuit.[783] As early as 1900, he had alerted Cardinal Vaughan, stating that it was necessary "not to be afraid to

777 Loisy, *Mémoires*, vol. 2, p. 387.

778 ADDF, S.O., *Loisy* (S50),1, fasc. 1, ff. 69–71.

779 Loisy, *Mémoires*, vol. 1, p. 250.

780 Sébastien Herscher (1855–1931) was bishop of Langres from 1900. In 1911, he was nominated archbishop *in partibus* of Laodicea.

781 ADDF, S.O., *Loisy* (S50),1, fasc. 2, f. 91.

782 Cf. ASS, vol. 36 (1903–1904), p. 353. ASS, 41 (1908), pp. 141–142. Cf. also E. Poulat, *Alfred Loisy*, pp. 141–155; *Lamentabili sane exitu (1907). Les documents préparatoires du Saint Office*, ed. C. Arnold, G. Losito, Libreria Editrice Vaticana, Rome 2011, pp. 75–89.

783 G. Lease, "Merry del Val and Tyrrell: a Modernist Struggle," *Downside Review* 102 (April 1984), pp. 133–156; reprinted in *Odd Fellows*, pp. 55–76; Schultenover, *A View from Rome*; Arnold, *Pius X, Merry del Val and the Cases of Alfred Loisy and George Tyrrell*, pp. 22–27.

enter into conflict with Fr. Tyrrell, who is quoted as the leader of thought of the other side."[784] Even earlier, in October 1899, in a letter to his friend and confrere Denis Sheil of the Oratory in Birmingham, Merry del Val stated that he had been "very unfavourably impressed by portions of Tyrrell's Lecture V, on the abuse of external aids in religion. I have not yet read the whole series, but my attention was called to that lecture. Even if not pronounced to be explicitly unsound theology, it seems to me that it must be granted that the teaching is so confusedly and incompletely expressed as to leave an unsound impression upon the reader's mind — one which savours of semi-Pelagianism.... There also appears to me to be a strange ignoring of the difference between the natural and the supernatural."[785] It is interesting to note that the confusion between the natural and supernatural orders that Merry del Val attributed to Tyrrell characterized the theology of his Jesuit confrere, later to become cardinal, Henri de Lubac.[786] De Lubac, like Tyrrell, posited in man's conscience the possibility of encountering God by his own power, confusing the fundamental distinction between the natural and supernatural orders.[787]

In the summer of 1904, Tyrrell wrote an anonymous *Letter to a University Professor*, of which several extracts were published in Italy in the *Corriere della Sera* on January 1, 1906. The Superior General of the Jesuits, Luis Martin, asked Tyrrell if he had authored the text and, upon confirmation, forced him to retract it.[788] Tyrrell refused, and on February 7, 1906, was expelled from the Society of Jesus. A journalistic "network of protection" immediately reacted to defend the English priest from Vatican censure. In its Vatican Notes, on July 12, 1906, the *Corriere della Sera* dedicated a frontpage article to "Doctrinal Terrorism," violently attacking the "Spanish Jesuitical regime that currently prevails in the Vatican,"[789] with evident reference to Secretary of State Merry del Val.

784 Letter of Merry del Val to Vaughan, June 30, 1900, in Lease, *Odd Fellows*, p. 67.

785 Buehrle, *Merry del Val*, pp. 124–125; Forbes, *Merry del Val*, p. 95.

786 Henri de Lubac (1896–1991), Jesuit, was an expert at the Second Vatican Council and made a cardinal by John Paul II in 1983. "I cannot share his sympathy for the thought of Blondel and that of Teilhard de Chardin," his friend the philosopher Étienne Gilson wrote on June 21, 1941. (*Un dialogo fecondo. Lettere di Étienne Gilson a Henri de Lubac*, Marietti, Genoa 1990, p. 61).

787 Cardinal Giuseppe Siri, in *Getsemani. Riflessioni sul Movimento Teologico Contemporaneo [Gethsemane. Reflections on the Contemporary Theological Movement]*, Fraternità della Santissima Vergine, Rome 1980, broadly refuted these theological errors. Pius XII, in his encyclical *Humani generis* (1950), condemned the theses of de Lubac and the other exponents of progressive *Nouvelle théologie*.

788 Luis Martín García (1846–1906), Spanish, was Superior General of the order from October 2 until his death. Tyrrell wrote that Merry del Val and Martin were "as identical as any two persons of the Trinity" (*Autobiography and Life*, vol. 2, p. 243).

789 "Terrorismo dottrinale," *Corriere della Sera*, July 12, 1906.

Cardinal Mercier,[790] who was willing to incardinate Tyrrell in the Diocese of Malines, wrote Merry del Val asking him to turn his "benevolent attention" "to poor George Tyrrell who has recently left the Society of Jesus," and "suffers greatly due to his moral isolation," claiming he was sure he would accept not to publish anything else. [791] Merry del Val made it known, in turn, to Mercier through Cardinal Ferrata, that "Tyrrell is dangerous not only for what he can publish in the press, but also for the epistolary correspondence he loves to pursue especially with young students."[792]

During those years, Tyrrell was a constant guest of Sr. Maude Petre, who offered him hospitality in a cottage on her estate in Storrington, Sussex.[793] After having met the Jesuit during a spiritual retreat given to the Society of the Daughters of Mary, of which she was the provincial superior at the time, Sr. Maude was released from her vows to follow him as his disciple, willing to do anything, as she herself recalled: "For the first time in my life, I felt so committed to a person as to be ready to risk everything to have his company."[794] According to Ellen Leonard, citing passages taken from Petre's diary and correspondence, reading between the lines, it seems that Maude was willing to sacrifice her own religious vocation to marry Tyrrell: "This relationship opened to Petre a new and exciting intellectual world, as well as arousing in her a depth of love she had never experienced before."[795] During the same period, Henri

790 On Desiré Mercier (1851–1926) archbishop of Malines and primate of Belgium (1906), and cardinal (1907), cf. R. Aubert, *Le cardinal Mercier (1851–1926). Un prélat d'avant-garde*, ed. Jean-Pierre Hendrickx, Jean Pirotte, and Luc Courtois, Presses Universitaires de Louvain, Louvain-la-Neuve 1976.

791 AAV, Secr. Stato, 1910, rubr. 9, fasc. 3, ff. 7–8.

792 Merry del Val to Ferrata, June 14, 1906, in AAV, Secr. Stato 1910, rubr. 9, fasc. 3, fol. 6.

793 Maude Petre (1863–1947), of an English noble family, made vows in the Society of the Daughters of Mary, of which she became the superior in London in 1896 and from 1900 to 1906 became provincial for England and Ireland. She published the *Autobiography* of Tyrrell (1912), which was immediately placed on the Index, and her own autobiography (*My Way of Faith*, J. M. Dent and Sons, London 1937). Cf. Ivana Dolejsove, "A Sketch of Divine Love: An Account of the Friendship Between George Tyrrell and Maude Petre," *Month* 32, 11 (1999), pp. 431–436; Ilaria Biagioli, "Petre 'versus' Petrus: la crisi modernista di una cattolica credente" [Petre vs. Peter: the Modernist Crisis of a Believing Catholic], in Alfonso Botti and Rocco Cerrato (eds.), *Il modernismo tra cristianità e secolarizzazione [Modernism Between Christianity and Secularization]*, Quattro Venti, Urbino 2000, pp. 487–509.

794 Petre, *My Way of Faith*, p. 271.

795 Ellen Leonard, *Unresting Transformation: Theology and Spirituality of Maude Petre*, University Press of America, Lanham 1991, p. 25. Maude wrote to a friend in December 1903: "[Tyrrell is] ready to throw it all up — and God knows how gladly I would do so to be with him always — know that our union and our cause are one, and can never be separated and that to forsake the latter for the former would be to drop a treasure in order to find it. But how I love him! & how I long to be with him! — we must persevere" (*Unresting Transformation*, p. 35).

Brémond, also a Jesuit impatient with discipline and the Society's teachings, and suffering from a crisis of neurasthenia, confided to Tyrrell his desire to leave the Jesuits to go and live with a lover.[796] His ideal, he wrote, would have been that of a "non-dogmatic clerical life." Tyrrell responded to his confrere to be prudent and not to abandon the Society of Jesus and rush into matters. "She (Petre)," Tyrrell wrote his friend, "seems to think it would be quite simple for us to live together if I leave the Society, and she cultivates fantasies like Paul and Virginia, Costa Azzurra and moon light."[797]

For his part, Baron von Hügel was acting as the "prompter" behind the scenes. He advised Tyrrell to feign submission, keeping silent or, in the case of a reaction, hiding behind figures like that of the deceased Cardinal Newman, whose complete orthodoxy Pius X had decreed in 1908.[798]

A long article titled "The Blessed Excommunicated," written by Tyrrell in May 1904, but remaining unpublished, unexpectedly appeared in the *Grande Revue* on October 10, 1907. In this article, Tyrrell held that excommunication can be a path toward salvation and that excommunication in the current age had lost the physical, social, and economic terror with which it had been applied in preceding ages.

Cardinal Merry del Val wrote the archbishop of Westminster, Francis Bourne,[799] asking him if he had seen Tyrrell's article in the *Grande Revue* of October 10, under the title "Blessed Excommunication"? "It is shocking and heretical. I think you ought to see it. Tyrrell has many more correspondents and sympathizers than is generally believed ... as Fr. Bampton told me last year, the

[796] Henri Brémond (1865–1933) left the Society of Jesus in 1904. He then lived in the world, pursuing a literary career that led to his admittance in the *Académie Française*. His *Histoire littéraire du sentiment religieux en France (1920–1936)* in 12 volumes, which earned him the inheritance of Duchesne in the *Académie Française*, summarizes in the title the modernist theses: faith reduced to poetic intuition, experience of mystical life that nullifies all dogmatic truth. Cf. E. Poulat, *Une œuvre clandestine, d'Henri Brémond. Sylvain Leblanc: un clerc qui n'a pas trahi. Alfred Loisy d'après ses mémoires, 1931, Édition critique et dossier historique*, Edizioni di Storia e letteratura, Rome 1972; André Blanchet, *Henri Brémond 1865–1904*, Aubier Montaigne, Paris 1975.

[797] Letter of Tyrrell to Brémond, May 26, 1907, in *Lettres de Georges Tyrrell à Henri Brémond*, p. 209.

[798] Pius X promulgated the verdict on the orthodoxy of the Oratorian cardinal in his letter of March 10, 1908, with which he approved the booklet *Card. Newman and the Encyclical "Pascendi"* by Msgr. Edward Thomas O'Dwyer, bishop of Limerick, on the writings of Newman: "Profecto in tanta locubrationum eius copia quidpiam reperiri potest, quod ab usitata theologorum ratione alienum videatur: nihil potest, quod de ipsius fide suscipionem afferat" (cf. ASS, vol. 41 (1908) p. 201) and the entry by Msgr. Antonio Piolanti in EC, vol. 8, col. 1800–1806.

[799] Francis Bourne (1861–1935), bishop of Southwark (1897–1903), on September 11, 1903, was named archbishop of Westminster by Pius X, even though at first he thought to nominate Merry del Val to this prestigious episcopal See. He was made a cardinal on November 27, 1988.

Jesuit superiors in England had no idea what was going on and what they learned afterward of Tyrrell's doings astonished them."[800]

Cardinal Bourne's attitude remained ambiguous and Merry del Val did not hide his reservations toward the archbishop, who, after the publication of the decree *Lamentabili* and after the promulgation of the encyclical *Pascendi,* had told the Apostolic See that English Catholicism was only marginally impaired in its doctrinal integrity by modernist suggestions.

On October 12, 1907, the Bishop of Southwark, Msgr. Peter Amigo,[801] concerned by the fact that Tyrrell might continue to receive Communion in his diocese, denounced to Cardinal Gotti, Prefect of the Congregation for the Propagation of the Faith, the two articles that had appeared in the English newspaper *The Times* on September 30 and October 1, 1907, in which the former Jesuit criticized "in disrespectful terms" the encyclical *Pascendi.* "A large number of Catholics have been scandalized, and perhaps they will be even more so if they find out that in my diocese, he receives Holy Communion every morning."[802]

Gotti turned to Merry del Val, who gave Msgr. Amigo these indications: "His Holiness, having turned his attention to what Your Excellency expounded, has entrusted me to tell you his will that you should make known to the aforementioned Mr. Tyrrell that he is deprived of participation in the sacraments and should at the same time inform him that his case is reserved to the Holy See."[803] Merry del Val took this action himself, but the final decision came from Pius X.

This same was confirmed on October 22, 1907, when Tyrrell was formally excommunicated for having openly criticized the encyclical *Pascendi.* Msgr. Amigo wrote a letter announcing that the Vatican had decided on Tyrrell's exclusion from the sacraments, reserving his case to Rome.[804] Amigo clarified that the condemnation was made due to the articles in the *Times,* that the case was submitted to the Holy See and that the pope himself had decided on the excommunication. Merry del Val wrote Msgr. Amigo as well, expressing his solidarity "in the trouble you have had, and perhaps may still have,

800 Merry del Val to Bourne, October 17, 1907, in Lease, *Odd Fellows,* p. 67.

801 Peter Emmanuel Amigo (1864–1949) was consecrated bishop of Southwark by Cardinal Francis Bourne on March 25, 1904. Cf. Michael Clifton, *Amigo: Friend of the Poor,* Gracewing, Leominister 2006.

802 AAV, Secr. Stato, 1910, rubr. 9, fasc. 3, f. 15.

803 AAV, Secr. Stato, 1910, rubr. 9, fasc. 3, f. 17.

804 Amigo to Tyrrell, October 22, 1907, in Petre, *Autobiography and Life of George Tyrrell,* II, p. 34.

with Tyrrell, but I think you have acted exceedingly well in the matter, tho' you seem to have had to act almost alone."[805]

The canon James Moyes of the Archdiocese of Westminster wrote a long article in the *Tablet*, criticizing the analyses of *Pascendi* Tyrrell made in the *Times*. Merry del Val rejoiced over this excellent confutation and bestowed upon Moyes a special blessing from the pope.[806]

On April 7, 1909, Tyrrell wrote to Hügel, "I feel that if the Roman Church cannot be reformed it will remain a permanent threat to civilization and religion; that those who leave the stage are in reality helping what is contemptible in it to consolidate and reorganize, a process which their presence hinders; and therefore, if Babylon is incurable, the 'modernizing' effort is the most secure and solid to destroy it and to save the greatest number of people possible from the shipwreck before the ship goes under."[807]

Three months later, on July 6, 1909, the former Jesuit became gravely ill. He died in the cottage of Ms. Petre on July 15.[808] Due to his state of excommunication, he was denied a Catholic funeral and was buried in the Anglican cemetery in Storrington, accompanied by Maude Petre, von Hügel, and Brémond. Fr. Brémond, who blessed his grave, was immediately suspended *a divinis* by the bishop of Southwark.[809]

On July 30, Merry del Val wrote a confidential letter to Bishop Peter Amigo lamenting that "the conduct of Maude Petre, von Hügel, and the others was abominable and only with difficulty can be called Catholic. One must ask if (given the real and public scandal) they should not be denied the sacraments in their respective dioceses."[810]

805 Merry del Val to Amigo, December 18, 1907, in Lease, *Odd Fellows*, p. 69.

806 F. Barmann, *Baron Friedrich von Hügel and the Modernist Crisis*, pp. 199–200.

807 M. D. Petre, *Von Hügel and Tyrrell. The Story of a Friendship*, J. M. Dent & Sons, London 1937, p. 201.

808 Cf. Robert Boudens, "George Tyrrell: Last Illness, Death and Burial," *Ephemerides Theologicae Lovanienses* 6, no. 4 (December 1985), pp. 340–354.

809 On November 14, 1909, *L'Osservatore Romano* published the retraction of Brémond, thanks to which the suspension *a divinis* came to an end. "Dans des sentiments de pleine et sincère soumission à l'Autorité ecclésiastique et par l'entremise de Sa Grandeur Monseigneur l'Évêque de Southwark, l'abbé Brémond déclare regretter et condamner tout ce qu'il a fait et dit de repréhensible au moment des funerailles du père Tyrrell. Il declare en outre adhérer sans reserve à toutes les doctrines de l'Église et notamment aux enseignements contenus dans le décret *Lamentabili* et dans l'encyclique *Pascendi*" (copy of the text in AAV, Secr. Stato, 1910, rubr. 9, fasc. 3, f. 1621).

810 Lease, *Odd Fellows*, p. 249. Along the same lines, the letter by Merry del Val to Broadhead, on January 17, 1908, Merry del Val/Broadhead Papers, Ushaw College Archives, 11.

Hügel, the great instigator, was able to escape the condemnation, although Loisy wrote that "Ms. Petre was not wrong when she defined him 'a *modernist* and *arch-modernist'* and not merely a culprit behind the modernists with whom he was friends."[811] The Protestant writer Paul Sabatier defined Hügel the "secular bishop of modernists,"[812] and Tyrrell presented him to his friend Henri Brémond as their "secular pope." "Our program," he wrote sarcastically, "is a perfectly acceptable religion and will be welcomed with open arms by most Anglican and Protestant confessions; and when the papacy is utterly confused and discredited, we shall march on the Vatican and install the baron (von Hügel) on the chair of Peter as the first secular pope."[813]

After Tyrrell 's death, his work was continued by Maude Petre. In a "confidential" letter to Msgr. Cahill, bishop of Portsmouth, in May of 1910, Merry del Val wrote:

> Miss Petre is notoriously in rebellion against the Holy See, respecting neither the teaching nor the decisions of the Church. She has notoriously identified herself with the position of Tyrrell and set herself publicly and notoriously in a stance of defiance to the Holy See. Her position has become even more serious than ever following the publication of some of Tyrrell's letters. The most recent of these appeared in the latest editions of the *Revue international des modernists* and reveal that Tyrrell had long been a formal heretic. Miss Petre finds herself then, in the position of a public sinner giving public scandal. She should be treated accordingly.[814]

The Condemnation of Sillon

Pascendi was preceded by the decree *Lamentabili*[815] and followed on August 25, 1910, by the letter *Notre charge apostolique*,[816] in which Pius X condemned *Sillon*,

811 Loisy, *Mémoires*, vol. 3, p. 471.

812 Sabatier, *Les modernistes*, p. li.

813 *Lettres de Georges Tyrrell à Henri Brémond*, p. 280.

814 AAV, Secr. State, 1910, rubr. 9, fasc. 3, fol. 17. f. 132.

815 Decr. S. Officii *Lamentabili* of July 3, 1907, in AAS, vol. 40 (1907), pp. 470–478. Cf. "*Lamentabili sane exitu" (1907). Les documents préparatoires du Saint Office*, ed. C. Arnold and G. Losito, Libreria Editrice Vaticana, Vatican City 2011; C. Arnold, "*Lamentabili sane exitu* (1907). Il magistero romano e l'esegesi di Alfred Loisy," in Arnold and Vian (eds.), *La condanna del modernismo*, pp. 45–81; G. Losito, "La preparazione del decreto Lamentabili e la sua immediata ricezione in Francia" [The Preparation of the Decree *Lamentabili* and Its Immediate Reception in France], *Cristianesimo nella storia* 30 (2009), pp. 781–836.

816 Pius X, Letter *Notre charge apostolique*, August 25, 1910, in AAS, vol. 2 (1910), pp. 607–633.

the liberal-leftist movement created by Marc Sangnier,[817] which opened the path to the social modernism of "Christian Democracy."[818] As Antonio Gramsci wrote, "Modernism, in political terms, means Christian Democracy."[819]

Sillon developed through a series of congresses held in France between 1902 and 1904. Although Cardinal Rampolla had written a letter to Sangnier on December 17, 1902, on the occasion of the first congress in Paris, writing that "the objective and the tendency of *Sillon* were most pleasing to His Holiness," when the national congress was held in 1905, the new secretary of state Merry del Val sent the archbishop of Paris a letter in which he invited the association to clarify several points in its program and to step in line with the teaching of the Church. The following year, Fr. Barbier published a two-volume study dedicated to the errors of *Sillon*, shedding light on the ambiguities of the new movement.[820] After the encyclical *Pascendi*, Barbier also highlighted the close relation between the theological modernism condemned by Pius X and the social modernism of *Sillon*: "In virtue of the affinity between modernism and democracy, the vital immanence that is at the center of the modernist thesis passes from the religious order to the social order, and then once more from the social order to the religious order."[821]

According to Msgr. Alberto Serafini, the condemnation of *Sillon* must be ascribed mainly to Merry del Val.[822] "In its actions as well as in its doctrine," the pope wrote, "*Sillon* does not give satisfaction to the Church.... The beneficiary of this cosmopolitan social action, can only be a Democracy which will be neither Catholic, nor Protestant, nor Jewish. It will be a religion (for *Sillonism*, so the leaders have said, is a religion) more universal than the Catholic Church,

817 Marc Sangnier (1873–1950), born in Paris to a family of the upper bourgeois, Bonapartist, founded in 1894 the journal *Sillon*, from which derived the movement's name, which sought to reconcile Catholic faith with democratic and republican ideas. After the condemnation by Pius X, Sangnier submitted, dedicating himself to politics as a republican deputy and activist for pacifism.

818 Cf. Jeanne Caron, *Le Sillon et la démocratie chrétienne 1894–1910*, Plon, Paris 1966; Hugues Petit, *L'Église, le Sillon et l'Action française*, Nouvelles Éditions Latines, Paris 1998; *Marc Sangnier en 1910. La lettre "Notre charge apostolique" et ses suites*. Actes de la journée d'études du 29 septembre 2000, Institut Marc Sangnier, Paris 2002.

819 Antonio Gramsci, *Quaderni dal carcere*, Einaudi, Torino 1975, vol. 2, p. 1305.

820 On the errors of *Sillon* and of Christian Democracy, cf. Emmanuel Barbier, *Les idées du Sillon. Étude critique*, Lethielleux, Paris 1906; idem, *Histoire du catholicisme libéral*, vol. 4, pp. 393–398; idem, *Les démocrates chrétiens et le modernisme*, Lethielleux, Paris 1907; and Msgr. Henri Delassus, *Vérités sociales et erreurs démocratiques*, Desclée de Brouwer, Lille 1909.

821 Barbier, *Les démocrates chrétiens*, p. 367.

822 *Processus Informativus Ordinarius, Sessio* LXV, vol. 2, p. 428.

uniting all men become brothers and comrades at last in the "Kingdom of God." "We do not work for the Church, we work for mankind."[823]

In the same document, Pius X reminded that "civilization is not something yet to be found, nor is the New City to be built on hazy notions; it has been in existence and still is: it is Christian civilization, it is the Catholic City. It has only to be set up and restored continually against the unremitting attacks of insane dreamers, rebels and miscreants. *Omnia instaurare in Christo* (Eph 1:10)."[824]

Between the encyclicals *Il fermo proposito* of 1905 and *Notre charge apostolique* of 1910, respectively addressing Italian Catholics and French bishops, there lay the program of restoration of Christian civilization which had its concrete application in ecclesiastical politics and in the pastoral action conducted by Pius X over the course of eleven years, with the help of his most loyal secretary of state.

The anti-modernist work of St. Pius X was crowned by the motu proprio *Sacrorum antistitum* of September 1, 1910, and the oath that it imposed.[825] "This oath, without adding anything essential to preceding acts, is a sort of solemn resume."[826] It constituted a positive and direct reaffirmation of Catholic doctrines to which the modernist heresies were opposed.

A "Secret Society" Within the Church?

Pius X understood that he was not dealing with a philosophical school but with a political party, and in the motu proprio *Sacrorum antistitum,* by which he imposed the anti-modernist oath, he also advanced the hypothesis that modernism constitutes an actual "secret society" within the Church.[827]

In Rome, on the main avenue Corso Vittorio Emanuele, in the house of Fr. Ernesto Buonaiuti, a little group of friends and disciples met secretly every Friday afternoon.[828] Buonaiuti explained, "Until today, some have sought to reform

823 Pius X, *Notre charge apostolique,* August 25, 1910, https://www.papalencyclicals.net/pius10/p10notre.htm.

824 Ibid.

825 Pius X, Motu proprio *Sacrorum Antistitum*, September 1, 1910, in ASS, vol. 2 (1910), pp. 669–672.

826 René Latourelle, *Theology of Revelation,* Alba House, New York 1966, p. 286.

827 Pius X, *Sacrorum Antistitum*, p. 655.

828 L. Bedeschi, *Il modernismo italiano. Voci e volti*, San Paolo, Cinisello Balsamo (Milan) 1995, p. 109. The zealots were Fr. Mario Rossi, Fr. Nicola Turchi, Fr. Antonino De Stefano, Fr. Ottorino Coppa, Fr. Luigi Piastrelli, and Fr. Gustavo Verdesi. The latter, following a spiritual crisis, was forced to reveal everything to his confessor, Fr. Carlo Bricarelli (1857–1931), a Jesuit of *La Civiltà Cattolica,* who obliged him to denounce it to the pope.

Rome without Rome, or perhaps even against Rome. One must reform Rome with Rome; make it such that the reform passes through the hands of those who must be reformed. This is the true and infallible method; but it is difficult. *Hic opus, hic labor*."[829] In light of this, modernism proposed to transform Catholicism from within, leaving intact, insofar as it was possible, the exterior trappings of the Church. "Exterior worship," continued Buonaiuti, "will always perdure, as will the hierarchy, but the Church as the master of its sacraments and its orders, shall modify the hierarchy and worship according to the times: she will render the former more simple, more liberal, while the latter more spiritual; and along this path, she will become a form of Protestantism; but a gradual, orthodox Protestantism, and not a violent, aggressive, revolutionary insubordinate one; a Protestantism that shall not destroy the apostolic continuity of the ecclesiastical ministry nor the essence of worship."[830]

Among the adherents to the Buonaiuti circle was the figure of Giovanni Pioli,[831] vice-rector of the Pontifical Urban College for the Propagation of the Faith (*Collegium Urbanum*) until January 11, 1908, when a few months later he abandoned the Church and drifted into non-confessional religious liberalism not very different from that professed by Italian heretics of the 1500s, as emerges from the biography that he later dedicated to Fausto Socino. The analogy between the modernists and the Italian heretics of the 1500s can be observed in the method of dissemblance, for which Delio Cantimori coined the term "Nicodemism."[832] "Knowing how to conceal one's own artillery is one of the essential principles of modern warfare. It was also one of the distinctive traits of the modernist movement, that of associating to the direct attack against dogmas the most extreme variety of subterfuges," Rivière observed,[833] recalling the death-bed counsel given by Fogazzaro in *The Saint*: "Never publish writings concerning difficult religious issues in order to sell

829 Buonaiuti, *Modernismo cattolico*, p. 128.

830 Ibid, p. 130.

831 On Giovanni Pioli (1877–1969), cf. AA.VV., *Dal modernismo al liberalismo religioso: G. Pioli [From Modernism to Religious Liberalism: G. Pioli]*, ed. Francesco Sciuto, Dall'Oglio, Milan 1970; Poulat, *Modernistica*, pp. 161–168 and the entry by F. Malgeri, DSMCI, vol. 3/2, pp. 668–669.

832 Delio Cantimori, *Umanesimo e religione nel rinascimento [Humanism and Religion in the Rennaissance]*, Einaudi, Turin 1975, pp. 207–208; R. de Mattei, *A sinistra di Lutero [Left of Luther]*, Città Nuova, Rome 1999, pp. 84–85.

833 Jean Rivière, *Le modernisme dans l'Église*, Letouzey et Anè, Paris 1929, pp. 484–485.

them, but distribute them according to prudence and never affix your name to them."[834]

A witness from "the inside," Albert Houtin, described the plan of modernism to be that the innovators would not have abandoned the Church, not even in the event they lost their faith, but that they would remain as long as possible to propagate their ideas.[835] "It is in this sense that it was agreed in 1903 (and was still being argued in 1911), that no true modernist, layman or priest, could leave the Church or the cloth, because otherwise they would in that instant cease to be a modernist in the elevated sense of the term."[836]

Msgr. Benigni and the "Roman Correspondence"

Fighting modernism alongside Pius X and his secretary of state Merry del Val, another personality took the field, controversial for his methods as well as for the intransigence of his positions: Msgr. Umberto Benigni.[837]

Born in 1862 in Perugia where he completed his ecclesiastical studies, Umberto Benigni began a double activity: in the historical field and in journalism, in the newsroom of an intransigent daily paper called *l'Eco d'Italia* (The Echo of Italy) in Genoa, of which he was the editor in chief. In the meantime, he had formed a plan for a *Social History of the Church*, on which he had begun to work in the final years of Leo XIII's pontificate, while teaching ecclesiastical history at the Pontifical Roman Seminary. As Count Dalla Torre recalled, it was Msgr. Gasparri who proposed Benigni to Cardinal Merry del Val as undersecretary of

834 Antonio Fogazzaro, *Il Santo*, Mondadori, Milano 1941, p. 282. Fr. Gioacchino Ambrosini (1857–1923), in a book that appeared in 1907 on the topic of *Occultismo e Modernismo* (Tipografia arcivescovile, Bologna 1907), shed light on the analogy between the modernist novel *The Saint* by Antonio Fogazzaro (1842–1911) and the ideas of theosophy.

835 Houtin, *Histoire du Modernisme catholique*, pp. 116–117.

836 Ibid, p. 122.

837 On the figure of Msgr. Umberto Benigni (1862–1934), the two fundamental works are the volumes by Émile Poulat, *Intégrisme et catholicisme intégral. Un réseau secret international antimoderniste: La Sapinière (1909–1921)*, Casterman, Tournai 1969 ; and *Catholicisme, démocratie et socialisme. Le mouvement catholique et Mgr. Benigni de la naissance du socialisme à la victoire du fascisme*, Castermann, Bruxelles-Paris 1977 ; for a biographical-bibliographical synthesis, cf. the entry by the same Poulat in DSMCI and the one by Pietro Scoppola in DBI 8 (1966), pp. 506–508. See, moreover, that by Msgr. Sergio Pagano, *Il Fondo di mons. Umberto Benigni dell'Archivio Segreto Vaticano* e *Documenti sul modernismo romano [The Patrimony of Msgr. Umberto Benigni in the Vatican Secret Archive and Documents on Roman Modernism]*, pp. 223–300, 347–402. Also important is the work carried out by Claudio Maria Mancini on the papers of the Farnesina: *Il Fondo Benigni dell'Archivio storico del Ministero degli Affari Esteri [The Benigni Patrimony of the Historical Archive of the Ministry of Foreign Affairs]*, Ministry of Foreign Affairs and of International Cooperation, Rome 2011.

the Congregation for Ecclesiastical Affairs.[838] In his *Memoires*, Cardinal Pietro Gasparri regretted having been the one, at the time secretary of the Congregation for Extraordinary Ecclesiastical Affairs of the Secretariat of State, to have nominated Benigni as undersecretary of his office. Gasparri explained that Cardinal Merry del Val had asked his opinion on the choice of the new undersecretary, to which he suggested Benigni, then professor of ecclesiastical history at the Roman Seminary and the *Collegium Urbanum*, describing him thus: "He had sharp intelligence, a good memory, sufficient knowledge of languages, constancy in his work, but at the same time he was a stutterer, of fragile health and not in the least physically attractive; thus, he seemed suitable for the job of undersecretary, not to be promoted any further. On the other hand, finding himself overworked and underpaid, he insisted that I find him a better job. I spoke with the Cardinal Secretary of State, who in essence responded justly and more or less along the lines: 'I do not know him, but if you do know him, nominate him under your own responsibility.'"[839]

On May 24, 1906, Cardinal Merry del Val proposed that Pius X nominate Msgr. Gasparri as domestic prelate to His Holiness. The press office and information service of the Holy See was entrusted unofficially to Benigni, which his direct superior Gasparri would not be able to concern himself with due to the enormous work on the *Code of Canon Law* that absorbed his time. Msgr. Pagano notes how "his appointment to this high post in the Secretariat of State (practically the fifth spot in the internal hierarchy) was in some ways dictated by projects that the prelate as well as the cardinal secretary of state, and perhaps even the pontiff, had secretly discussed, and whose execution was 'covered' by the official nomination and the perfectly functional objectives of the office."[840]

Thanks to his knowledge of languages and his international connections, Benigni concerned himself with the press office of the Holy See in particular, carrying out for the first time in history a role that made him the precursor of what was to become the Vatican Press Office.[841] Among the first initiatives was the publication of the bulletin of religious information, *Corrispondenza Romana*,

[838] *Informatio*, p. 69.

[839] Spadolini, *Il cardinale Gasparri e la questione romana*, pp. 109–117. Cf. also Nina Valbousquet, "Gasparri, Benigni et les catholiques intégraux. Autorité du Saint-Siège et opposition intégrale, de Pie X à Pie XI," in L. Pettinaroli and M. Valente (eds.), *Il cardinale Pietro Gasparri segretario di Stato (1914–1930)*, Heidelberg University Publishing, Heidelberg 2020, pp. 35–56.

[840] Pagano, *Documenti sul modernismo romano*, pp. 232–233.

[841] Bedeschi, *L'antimodernismo*, pp. 49–50.

whose first number appeared on May 23, 1907.[842] Two years later, the agency became *Correspondance de Rome* and continued to appear until December 31, 1912, publishing 1,282 editions and carrying out the informative work much appreciated and encouraged by the Holy See. The historian Ludwig von Pastor, in a note of July 9, 1907, recalls having read a "noteworthy article" (*bemerkenswerten Artikel*) about "a secret international League against the Congregations of the Index and of Culture," based on documentation that Cardinal Merry del Val told him was in his possession.[843]

Hary Mitchell, a young French journalist, described an audience he had had in those years with the Cardinal Secretary of State Merry del Val. During the meeting, they spoke about the information agency *Corrispondenza Romana*, among other things.[844] "It had been presented as a document on the presumed clandestine activities of the Holy See! In reality, it was exclusively an organ of information whose aim was that of establishing the facts in their rigorous exactitude and clarifying the directives considered indispensable to Catholic thought."[845] The publication was the object of every sort of calumny and insinuation.[846] "Among the means of communication that had the gift of exasperating the distilleries of false and tendentious news, the cultivators of misunderstanding, the cenacles of the modernists of every color ... *Correspondance de Rome* occupied the first place."[847] It constituted "an organization of defense and resistance."

In the summer of 1910, Benigni submitted to the pope, by the hands of Merry del Val, a memo in which he asked to be relieved from his post to be able to dedicate himself more freely to the work of information at the service of the Holy See.[848] Cardinal Merry del Val replied that both the pope and he appreciated the reasons for his memorandum but would for the moment postpone his

[842] The first edition of *Corrispondenza romana* appeared on May 23, 1907, first as a mimeograph, then printed; from the edition on October 2, 1909, the title changed to *La Correspondance de Rome* and ran until December 31, 1912. The chief director, Giovanni Grandi, and the manager were laymen. Émile Poulat reconstructed and reproduced a collection of all its editions that is nearly complete (Feltrinelli Reprint, Milan 1971, 3 vols.).

[843] Pastor, *Tagebücher*, p. 475.

[844] H. Mitchell, *Le cardinal R. Merry del Val, Secretaire d'État de Saint Pie X*, Paris-Livres, Paris 1956, pp. 99–109.

[845] Ibid., p. 102.

[846] Ibid., p. 61.

[847] Ibid., p. 160.

[848] "Concerning this memo," wrote Msgr. Benigni in one of his confidential notes in 1931, "the witnesses still alive today are Msgr. Canali, then substitute of the secretary of state, and Card. Pacelli, then dean of the minute keepers in the office where Benigni worked and to which Msgr. Pacelli would be the immediate successor." (ASMAE, *Fondo Benigni*, Serie D, 52, 838.

resignation, which was accepted on March 7, 1911, when Benigni was substituted by Msgr. Eugenio Pacelli.[849]

Whatever the reasons were for Benigni's exit from the Secretariat of State, he left with honor, as observed by the fact that Pius X created for him *ex novo* the post of an eighth participatory apostolic protonotary, whereas that College had never had more than seven members. He was therefore not disgraced, nor was he disowned by Pius X. He simply, as observed in his biography, changed his role, being released in part from the *Sodalitium* of the Secretariat of State and transferring to the Consistorial of Cardinal De Lai, but always at the orders of Pius X and with the support of his *segreteriola.*[850]

From that moment, free of ties to any office, Benigni dedicated himself with all his energy to the struggle against modernism. In 1912, just a few months before the closure of *Corrispondenza,* a second information agency opened, the Agency International Rome, with its daily bulletin *Rome et le monde* and the weekly *Quaderni Romani* (Roman Notebooks), which came out in a French edition as well. In 1913, the "Anti-Sectarian Group of St. George" was established, a private accord among friends whose objective was to fight the sect that was enemy of religion and society.[851]

Beginning in 1909, Benigni left his Vatican apartment and opened in Via del Corso the *Casa San Pietro,* the center of his activities. It was there that the *Sodalitium pianum* was born, or *Sodality of St. Pius V* (1909), under the patronage of the pope who had instituted the Holy Office and obtained the great victory at Lepanto against the Turks (1571).

The *Sodalitium Pianum*

In his deposition on March 28, 1928, at the Roman Ordinary Tribunal, Cardinal Gasparri manifested his opposition to the beatification of Pius X, stating (among

849 Msgr. Pacelli succeeded Benigni on March 7, 1911, as undersecretary of the Congregation for Extraordinary Ecclesiastical Affairs of which he was named pro-secretary (1912) and secretary (1914) before being sent as nuncio to Bavaria (1917) where the attorney Alphonse Jonckx visited him, stating: "Mons. Pacelli est un élève et fidèle ami de nos amis" (Poulat, *Intégrisme et catholicisme intégral,* p. 258). On the collaboration of Msgr. Pacelli with Benigni, cf. Pagano, *Documenti sul modernismo romano,* p. 259.

850 Don Francesco Ricossa, "In difesa di mons. Umberto Benigni," *Sodalitium,* special edition 74 (June 2023), p. 18 and, more broadly, pp. 1–18. The author rebuts in a more than convincing manner the theses expressed by Fr. Curzio Nitoglia in the journal *Sì Sì No No,* which sought to dissociate the figure of Msgr. Benigni from that of St. Pius X and Cardinal Merry del Val.

851 ASMAE, Fondo Benigni, busta 2, ff. 71–72. "Notice that we say 'anti-sectarian' and not 'anti-masonic,' because Freemasonry is not the entire sect, but only the noisiest part of the sect."

other things) that "Pius X approved, blessed, and encouraged a hidden association of espionage above and beyond the hierarchy, and even spied on the very members of the hierarchy, even on eminent cardinals; he approved, blessed, and encouraged a sort of Freemasonry within the Church, something never seen before in the history of the Church."[852]

To this grave accusation that directly involved Cardinal Merry del Val as well, and that had been put forth many times since the waning years of Pius X's pontificate, the *Disquisitio* of the historical section of the Sacred Congregation of Rites formed by Pius XII responded with a profusion of documentation. It shed abundant light on the role and the work of Msgr. Umberto Benigni, the information agency *Corrispondenza Romana*, and the *Solidalitium pianum*, highlighting how all these initiatives were promoted in agreement with Pius X and his secretary of state.

On July 5, 1911, the *Sodalitium pianum* (Society of St. Pius V) received from the pope its first signed approval for its activities.[853] On July 8, 1912, Pius X sent a second signed approval[854] and, on July 6, 1914, a third papal acclamation.[855] Msgr. Benigni continued to receive a regular annual contribution of a thousand Lire per month from the pope's personal secretary, Msgr. Bressan.[856]

Contemporary historiography has reconsidered the accusations of "informing" and "espionage" hurled earlier by the modernists against the Roman prelate. Benigni was accused of being, in a word, "the sin of Pius X."[857] There was need, however, to oppose the "manifold and fervent secret workings"[858] of

852 *Pii X Disquisitio*, p. 6.

853 Ibid., p. 239.

854 Ibid., p. 240.

855 Ibid., p. 268. Among the cardinals who esteemed the *Sodalitium pianum* and made use of it, we should recall, besides Merry del Val and De Lai, the Capuchin José Vives y Tutó, prefect of the Congregation of Religious; the Dominican Tommaso Pio Boggiani, assessor of the Consistorial and later archbishop of Genoa and chancellor of the Holy Roman Church; Girolamo Gotti, prefect of Propaganda; the Redemptorist Wilhelmus Van Rossum, prefect of Propaganda; and Hector-Irenée Sevin, archbishop of Lyon (*Pii X Disquisitio*, p. 234).

856 Cf. ASMAE, Fondo Benigni, busta 2, ff. 71–72. A. M. Dieguez, "Una specie di massoneria nella Chiesa. Lo scioglimento del *Sodalitium pianum*" [A Sort of Freemasonry within the Church. The Disbanding of the *Sodalitium Pianum*], in Giovanni Cavagnini and Giulia Grossi (eds.), *Benedetto XV. Papa Giacomo della Chiesa nel mondo dell' "inutile strage"* [*Benedict XV. Pope Giacomo della Chiesa in the World of the "Useless Slaughter"*], Il Mulino, Bologna 2017, vol. 1, p. 446.

857 The formula was used by one of its defenders, Fr. Jules Saubat, in *Pii X Disquisitio*, p. 34. "Ceux qu'il combattit sont unanimes à voir en lui leur pire ennemi; en même temps qu'un produit typique et repoussant de ce catholicisme intégral qui leur apparaissait comme l'inversion du vrai catholicisme. Pour eux, il aura été sans contexte le péché de Pie X, un péché qui a retardé la canonisation en cours du Pontificat après avoir failli l'arrêter" (Poulat, *Catholicisme, démocratie et socialisme*, pp. 39–40).

858 L. Bedeschi, *Interpretazioni e sviluppo del modernismo cattolico [Interpretations and Development of Catholic Modernism]*, Bompiani, Milan 1976, p. 86.

modernism, which were being carried out, as wrote Fr. Bedeschi, by an "elusive and variegated network" spread throughout the main Italian cities.[859] French Protestant theologian Paul Sabatier, in particular, was responsible for much of "the diffusion of Vatican and modernist misinformation" by means of an efficacious connection with correspondents of authoritative organs of information in European capitals — from *The Times* to the *Journal des Débats*, from *Temps* to *Le Siècle*, from the *Daily News* to the *Morning Post*[860] — employing methods, it must be said, not unlike those of the "espionage" attributed to his adversary.[861]

Around Msgr. Benigni and the *Sodalitium pianum* an outright "dark legend" was created in such a way as to impede any objective judgment regarding the person who had a difficult, though intense, character,[862] as wrote Cardinal Antonelli in the *Disquisitio*, "placing himself, his manifold intellectual qualities, his vast experience, above all in the historical-cultural and sociological fields, at the service of the Church."[863] The *Disquisitio*, basing its examination on the important dossier of the Consistorial Congregation, came to the following conclusions:[864]

1. The *Sodalitium pianum*, considered as such and on the basis of its statute and program, was a good organization aimed at a good end.
2. The *Sodalitium pianum* sought to be an organ of *penetration* (the exemplary life of its members in conformity with all papal directives: a "coherent" Catholic life) and of *information* (personal, rapid, and secure

859 Ibid., pp. 86–87.

860 Ibid., p. 85.

861 Thus, in 1907, Sabatier, looking for information on Benigni to refer to the journalist Maurice Pernot, turned to the Oratorian Mattia Federici to learn about the past life in Genoa of the director of *Corrispondenza Romana* (Cf. Carteggio Federici-Sabatier, *Fonti e Documenti* 5–6 (1977), p. 58).

862 *Pii X Disquisitio*, pp. xxii-xxv and 237.

863 Ibid, p. 199; pp. 48–49.

864 The *Disquisitio* took the statute and program of the *Sodalitium pianum* from the files of the Consistorial Congregation in Autumn of 1913, defining it a document of "capital importance" (p. 261). In it one reads: "We are integralist Roman Catholics. As this word indicates, the integral Roman Catholic accepts integrally the doctrine, discipline, and direction of the Holy See and all of its legitimate consequences for the individual and for society. It follows the 'papal line,' and is 'clerical,' antimodernist, antiliberal, anti-sectarian. It is therefore integrally counter-revolutionary since it is adverse not only to the Jacobin Revolution and sectarian radicalism, but equally adverse to religious and social liberalism" (p. 262). Cf. also the documents drawn from the Benigni Patrimony in the Vatican Secret Archive (59, ff. 288–289, cited by Pagano in *Documenti sul modernismo romano*, pp. 233–234).

gathering of news on all aspects of religious, political, social, and cultural life) at the service of the Roman Curia.

3. The *Sodalitium pianum,* in Benigni's original conception, was to be a sort of "lay" ecclesiastical institute subject to the Consistorial Congregation, just as religious Institutes live and act under the Holy Congregation of Religious.

In fact, the *Sodalitium pianum* served the Holy See, offering regular information and making use at times of its own code to guarantee the security of the correspondence. A long letter of June 21, 1910, from Msgr. Benigni to Cardinal Secretary of State Merry del Val, published by Msgr. Pagano, offers a clear framework of the informative work Benigni was providing for the benefit of the Holy See.[865]

Fr. Charles Maignen,[866] correspondent of *Sodalitium pianum* for the north of France and Belgium remembered him in these words: "It was through Cardinal Merry del Val, then secretary of state under Pius X, that I was placed in contact with Msgr. Benigni, who was at that time undersecretary of the Commission for Extraordinary Affairs. I had just been nominated representative to Rome of the *Société d'Education et d'Enseignement,* presided by Émile Keller. I was going to a meeting with Cardinal Merry del Val, who had approved my nomination and who I occasionally visited over the previous two years. Since my new tasks would place me in frequent contact with the Secretariat of State, I asked to whom I was to refer in matters concerning questions that did not seem to require his personal intervention. The cardinal replied, 'You should speak with Msgr. Benigni. I will inform him and will tell him to see you.'"[867]

"Msgr. Benigni," continued Maignen, "was a man of extraordinary activity and operational power. He wanted to equip the Holy See with an organ of information and intelligence conceived according to the methods of a modern press

865 A long letter of June 21, 1910, from Msgr. Benigni to Cardinal Secretary of State Merry del Val, published by Pagano in *Documenti sul modernismo romano,* pp. 230–232, offers a clear overview of the informative activity of Benigni for the benefit of the Holy See; cf. *Pii X Disquisitio,* pp. 48–49.

866 Charles Maignen (1858–1937), of the Congregation of the Frères de Saint-Vincent-de-Paul, published in 1898 *Le Père Hecker est-il un saint?* against the new tendencies of the *abbés democratiques* and in 1903 denounced the works of Loisy: *L'Évangile et l'Église* and *Autour d'un petit livre.* He was twice the superior of his congregation from 1904–1907 and from 1914–1932 and, from 1917, an aid to the Holy Office.

867 "Notes pour servir à l'histoire de l'Institut des FF de St Vincent de Paul 1907–1917–1937," Unpublished mimeograph, in de Mattei, *Il Ralliement di Leone XIII,* p. 340.

agency. With very limited means and resources, he was able to construct a notable collection of newspaper articles, reviews, and unpublished documents on all the political and ecclesiastical movements of the time. A catalog of names and subjects allowed him to find quickly the elements of a vast dossier on people and affairs. This permitted the Holy See to intervene in a timely manner on more than one occasion and to foil more than one plot. *Inde Irae* [hence, wrath]. This explains the ferocious war waged against him and the *Sodalitium*."[868]

Even Fr. Jules Saubat, superior of the Betharram Fathers,[869] who became the secretary of the *Sodalitium pianum*, recalled being sent to Msgr. Benigni by Cardinal Merry del Val, who exhorted him "to be advised by him and to allow myself to be directed by him."[870] He testified that "never during this struggle were illicit or dishonest means employed; but all the human arts, even those most cunning, were placed at the service of the truth."[871] But Saubat testified, "Not a spy: a spy is evil at the service of evil and for evil's sake. Here there was vigilance through sufficiently honest human means, for the good. Otherwise, one would have to say: 'the nuncios were spies charged with informing; the secretary of state was a spy whom the pope would ask every morning: *Custos quid de nocte?*' The secretary of state entered by the royal staircase, whereas Benigni passed through the service staircase: therein lies the only difference."[872]

"In conclusion, and considering matters objectively," stated Card. Antonelli in the *Disquisitio*, "the secretiveness and the codes were in a certain way necessary means, or at least useful ones, certainly not immoral, since Benigni did not

868 Ibid., pp. 842–843.

869 Fr. Jules Saubat (1867–1949), Superior General of the Betharram Fathers, was secretary of the *Sodalitium pianum*. Cf. Poulat, *Intégrisme et catholicisme intégral*, pp. 419–421.

870 *Pii X Disquisitio*, pp. 31–32.

871 Ibid, p. 32. Also, Fr. Henri Jeoffroid (1880–1961), Superior General of the Congregation of the Brothers of St. Vincent de Paul, testified that "the Sodalitium was promoted with entirely upright intentions, aiming to inform the Holy See about the often subtle movements of erroneous tendencies" (*Pii X Disquisitio*, p. 43).

872 *Pii X Disquisitio*, p. 37. Fr. Paolo De Töth recalled, "The Sodalitium rendered the Holy See an exceptional service, and the secretary of State made extensive use of it, and in this way was able to learn about certain men and certain plots of the Christian Congress of Berlin, it acquired important information about the state of Catholics in Russia, and other most sensitive information. Certainly, to attain these results, there were codes and men had to act secretly; but I deny that it was a secret society, as has been falsely said, that they acted with systems of espionage or anything illicit. It was necessary to counter the use of certain systems by our adversaries with similar means with the aim of foiling many hidden dangers" (ibid., pp. 48–49).

have any secrets toward the competent authority of the Holy See with whom he maintained contact."[873]

After the death of Pius X, Msgr. Benigni disbanded the *Sodalitium* in the summer of 1915, but reestablished it "on the simple basis of a friendly agreement,"[874] with the approval of the Consistorial Congregation of Cardinal De Lai. Its definitive termination occurred, at the behest of Benedict XV, on November 25, 1921.[875] Benigni continued his activity in other ways, though without exercising any official post besides teaching, from that moment until his death on February 26, 1934.

After the definitive termination of the *Sodalitium pianum,* Benigni created the *Agenzia urbs,* whose activities continued until 1928, managing the publication of the weekly bulletin *Veritas* and then the monthly *Romana*. In 1933, one year before his death, he published through the editor Vallardi the last volume of his *Social History of the Church,* the first volume of which had appeared in 1907. "He died a poor man," recalled Fr. Paolo De Töth, "and this is one of his greatest glories and the most significant proof of his honesty and loyalty."[876]

The documents published by Msgr. Pagano confirm that Pius X's support of Msgr. Benigni was never lacking. "Merry del Val, and Pius X along with him, wanted more prudence, more tact, greater nuance of tones in the controversy, a more patient and subtle way of proceeding, altogether less impetuosity, but Benigni was not capable of this."[877] Between Cardinal Merry del Val and Msgr. Benigni there were differences of temperament, and above all, of strategy.[878] The former played an institutional role, at the summit of the Holy See, the latter moved freely, at times unscrupulously, but their objectives were the same. And if Benigni called Merry del Val "*La Peur,*" over the following years his judgment was ever more positive, considering him the most likely choice for the papacy in the conclave of 1922.

[873] Ibid., p. 231.

[874] ASMAE, Fondo Benigni, 2, ff. nn.

[875] Dieguez, "Una specie di massoneria nella Chiesa," pp. 437–449.

[876] *Pii X Disquisitio*, p. 48.

[877] Pagano, *Documenti sul modernismo romano*, pp. 239–240.

[878] "Observation capitale: ce n'est pas dans la compréhension des événements, dont ils ont l'un et l'autre une vue identique, mais sur la conduite des affaires que leur divergence s'est affirmée" (Poulat, *Intégrisme et catholiques intégral*, p. 77).

Don Orione During the Modernist Years

The figure of St. Luigi Orione, founder of the Sons of Divine Providence, can help illuminate from within the debate over modernism and anti-modernism in the age of Pius X.[879] The relationship between Don Orione and Cardinal Merry del Val dated back to 1903. The very day on which the latter had received the *porpora*, he went up to Don Orione's agricultural community on the hillside overlooking Rome with some close relatives and would later return there often.[880]

Don Orione wrote in that period, "This week we welcomed here (to the Colony of Monte Mario) three times Card. Merry del Val. He comes here to walk and stays with us for some hours."[881] Cardinal Merry del Val loved the Monte Mario hillside, where he could breath fresh air and, over the coming years, would accept the hospitality offered to him in the villa of Count Bernardo Blumenstihl.[882] The esteem and friendship between the new secretary of state and Don Orione began precisely in that discrete, rustic environment conducive to confidentiality.

The general of the Sons of Divine Providence, Carlo Maria Pensa, recalled the visits the secretary of state made to their country house on Monte Mario, and stated that Don Orione and his confreres considered Merry del Val a saint, like the pope, a reputation that "was spontaneous and emanated from his virtuous life."[883]

One document in particular reveals the accord between Don Orione and Cardinal Merry del Val. Written below a little image-memento of Pius X, dated October 23, 1914, not long after the death of the pontiff, Don Orione wrote, "Received today from the hands of His Eminence Cardinal Merry del Val, who shed tears with me speaking of the Holy Father Pius X; immediately, as soon as

[879] Don Luigi Orione (1872–1940) was canonized by John Paul II on May 16, 2004. Cf. the entry "Orione" by Giovanni Battista Proja, in *Biblioteca Sanctorum*, vol. 10, col. 1234–1238. Cf. Michele Busi, Roberto de Mattei, Antonio Lanza, and Flavio Peloso, *Don Orione negli anni del modernismo [Don Orione During the Years of Modernism]*, Jaca Book, Milan 2002.

[880] F. Peloso, "Una rete di rapporti" [A Network of Relationships], in *Don Orione negli anni del modernismo*, p. 97.

[881] Don Orione, *Scritti [Writings]*, Archive of Divine Providence, Tortona s.d., vol. 54, p. 8.

[882] Bernardo Blumenstihl (1822–1921) was of the Alsatian nobility who came to Rome in 1857 after having fought in the Crimean War. He entered the Pontifical Army as a colonel and was made a count by Pius X. His son Paolo married a marquise of the Malvezzi, whose family still owns the villa on Monte Mario.

[883] *Processus Informativus Ordinarius, Sessio* LXXXVII, vol. 2, pp. 541–542; *Informatio*, p. 212. Cf. also F. Peloso, *Don Orione negli anni del modernismo*, pp. 96–99.

he saw me, he began crying. It was the first time I saw the Cardinal alone after the death of the Holy Father Pius X."

In the correspondence with Don Orione are preserved many letters he sent to Merry del Val, in which he often mentions his frequent visits to the Secretariat of State. Their relationship and correspondence continued even afterward, when the cardinal left the Apostolic Palace and moved to the Holy Office.[884] Concerning the period Don Orione spent as the pope's vicar in Messina, ten of his letters to Merry del Val are preserved, testifying to the close collaboration between them in the tempestuous years of modernism.

The earthquake that destroyed the coasts of Calabria and Sicily on December 28, 1908, aroused an immediate and generous mobilization not only by civil authorities, but also by the Holy See. Pius X immediately expressed his earnest concern, not only for the material situation, but also for the moral and spiritual conditions of the survivors, especially that of the many orphans, and nominated Don Orione as his vicar in Messina. The choice was not due only to the spirit of abnegation of which the priest from Tortona was famously prodigious, but also to his proven fidelity to papal directives and to his diplomatic abilities, necessary in a situation as confused as was that of the Sicilian city after the earthquake. The logic of Don Orione, expressed in a letter to Merry del Val on July 14, 1911, was that of a man of faith who embodied the stance of Pius X: *fortiter in re, suaviter in modo*. "If, in my way of doing things, I seek to use prudence and charity, I do not do so to the detriment of principles; and, in matters of doctrine, discipline, Church, pope, the Church's freedom, obedience, and union in all things with the pope, I have always gloried in being an intransigent and could not imagine how a priest and a Catholic who presumes to be one, could think or do otherwise."[885]

In the month of March 1910, Don Orione learned of the formation of a National Association for the Moral and Economic Interests of Southern Italy, of which Hon. Leopoldo Franchetti was president.[886] The association's nucleus was formed of a group of modernists from Milan tied to Antonio Fogazzaro, in

884 Don Orione wrote to Fr. Sterpi: "I received the order to go to the Cardinal secretary of state, who was not well, but gave the order for me to announce it and pass it on" (Don Orione, *Scritti*, vol. 10, p. 220); on June 22, 1909: "I went to the cardinal secretary of state" (Ibid., p. 223). On January 29, 1910, again to Fr. Sterpi: "This evening I will see Card. Merry del Val" (Ibid., vol. 11, p. 13).

885 Don Orione, *Scritti*, vol. 1, p. 107.

886 Baron Leopoldo Franchetti (1847–1917), senator from 1909 and famous for his investigations into the conditions in southern Italy, was involved in numerous initiatives of a philanthropic nature.

other words the group directing the journal *Rinnovamento* which, after having incurred excommunication on December 24, 1907, had ceased publication in December 1909.[887]

Pascendi and the successive condemnation of *Rinnovamento* had forced modernism in Lombardy to perform a metamorphosis of which the Association of Southern Italy had become an expression. Antonio Aiace Alfieri[888] and Tommaso Gallarati Scotti[889] had begun work in Reggio Calabria, arousing the alarm of Don Orione. Convinced that the association posed a serious threat to the Church especially in Calabria, he informed the Secretariat of State in a letter on March 15, 1910, sent to the substitute Nicola Canali, who spoke personally about the matter to Cardinal Gaetano De Lai, Prefect of the Consistorial.[890] Immediately after this, perhaps at the suggestion of these authorities, Don Orione raised the alarm in the press as well, inviting Fr. Alessandro Cavallanti, director of *Unità Cattolica* to publish three articles on the situation in Messina, without mentioning him by name.

Don Orione's correspondence was published on April 19 and 29, 1910 and again on May 19, 1910. "The infamous modernists are at work," he wrote in the May letter. "They go from town to town, seeking to form groups of friends in every area of Calabria, and extend a vast network of associates and affiliates. Those whom they can trust the most are united more closely."[891]

On April 10, 1910, Don Orione updated Cardinal Merry del Val on the situation: "Count Gallarati Scotti was here twice. Yesterday, Engineer Alfieri was with him. They did not say anything about wanting to make religious propaganda, but I don't think they want to exclude it; religious propaganda in a Protestant sense, certainly very hostile to the Church, even if they do not say so."[892] After this

887 About Antonio Fogazzaro (1842–1911) and the "Fogazzariani," cf. Giovanni Casati, *I libri letterari condannati dall' "Indice," [Literary Books Condemned by the Index]*, Ghirlanda, Milan 1921, pp. 359–404; and Bedeschi, *Il modernismo italiano*, pp. 114–133.

888 Antonio Aiace Alfieri (1880–1962), engineer, was among the founders of the modernist journal *Rinnovamento* in Milan.

889 On Duke Tommaso Gallarati Scotti (1878–1966) and the matter of *Rinnovamento*, cf. L. Bedeschi, *Modernismo a Milano*, Pan editrice, Milan 1974, pp. 31–70.

890 Letter of March 15, 1910, in *Scritti*, vol. 107, p. 76. In a draft of this letter one reads: "It seems to me sufficient to constitute a serious danger, especially for Calabria. It consists of men of various religions, and is presided by Baron Franchetti, a Jew, although morally he seems to be guided by Fogazzaro" (*Scritti*, vol. 107, p. 76; vol. 84, p. 24).

891 *L'Unità Cattolica*, May 19, 1910. "I myself have conducted in *Unità Cattolica* the campaign against the modernists who have descended on Calabria, and the published articles were sent here (Messina) although they bear the stamp of Reggio" (*Scritti*, vol. 73, p. 28).

892 Don Orione, *Scritti*, vol. 84, p. 291; vol. 96, p.137.

information given by Don Orione, the Secretariat of State placed the Calabrian bishops on guard by means of a confidential circular letter.

One year later, in a letter to Merry del Val on July 14, 1911, Don Orione responded to the accusations of contact with modernist exponents made against him by the archbishop of Messina D'Arrigo,[893] defending himself by insisting on his merit of having "conducted in *Unità Cattolica* the fight against the modernists making the rounds in Calabria" and of having "warned the Holy See, which sent a confidential circular to the bishops of Calabria."[894]

Another of Don Orione's initiatives during his period in Messina was in 1911, when he notified the secretary of state of the arrival in Messina of the Countess Gabriella Spalletti Rasponi.[895] "The primary reason for which I felt it was appropriate to inform Your Eminence, for the good of the Church and of souls, is this: the countess Spalletti said that, in Reggio, she will build an institute for orphans and led us to believe that she would call Fr. Semeria to direct it. In fact, I had the impression that arrangements have already been made. This would be serious, and I have not hidden this from you." Don Orione did not conceal his opposition to such a possibility, remarking sarcastically, "Fr. Semeria is the last thing we need."[896]

Fr. Semeria and the Interdict on Genoa

Some Barnabite historians have tried to offer a defense of their confrere Giovanni Semeria,[897] whom Cardinal Merry del Val followed with great suspicion.

893 Letterio D'Arrigo Ramondini (1849–1922) was, from 1898 until his death, metropolitan archbishop of Messina.

894 Cit. in De Mattei, "Modernismo e antimodernismo nell'epoca di Pio X," in *Don Orione negli anni del modernismo*, p. 78.

895 Countess Gabriella Spalletti Rasponi (1853–1931) was president of the Association of Italian Women, which was counterposed to the Association of Catholic Women, founded by Lady Cristina Giustiniani Bandini with the mandate of Pius X. Struck by the personality of Don Orione, Rasponi became close friends with him and received the Last Sacraments from him in 1931. Cf. Antonio Lanza, "Don Orione e la contessa Spalletti Rasponi," *Messaggi di Don Orione* 32 (2000), pp. 51–57.

896 Don Orione, *Scritti*, vol. 107, pp. 48, 61. The *Disquisitio* of Pius XII recalled the words of Pius X to Semeria: "You open your doors to bring in those who are outside while you let out those who are inside" (p. xxviii).

897 Giovanni Semeria, *Anni terribili. Memorie inedite di un "modernista" ortodosso (1903–1913) [The Terrible Years. Unpublished Memoires of an Orthodox Modernist]*, ed. A. Gentili and A. Zambarbieri, San Paolo, Cinisello Balsamo, Milan 2008. Cf. also S. Pagano, "The 'Semeria Case' in the Documents of the Vatican Secret Archive," *Barnabiti Studi* 6 (1989), pp. 7–175; A. Gentili, "The Trial of P. Semeria in the Unpublished Documentation of the Former Holy Office (1909–1919)," *Barnabiti Studi* 25 (2010), pp. 187–260.

Semeria's *Memoires*, published in 2008 by Fr. Gentili and Fr. Zambarbieri, confirm how, in this case as well, the cardinal's judgment was well founded.

For example, regarding the relic of the Holy Shroud, the most important in Christendom, Semeria shared the sacrilegious theses of Fr. Ulysse Chevalier[898] and attacked "the legend" of Turin.[899] He described the God of Lourdes as "sovereignly capricious and despotic" because "at Lourdes there is health for the few sick who can make it there, and for the few among those few"[900] and rebelled against the miracle of the blood of St. Januarius of Naples, wondering why God does not spend his energies more fruitfully. He asked why ecclesiastical discipline is inclined toward tolerating carnal sins, while it is so severe toward "sins of idealism, those which are often the most straightforward exercise of honest scientific freedom"; he considered the formalism of observances in certain religious institutes "pedantry and posturing" and rejoiced at the director of a girls' boarding school who "tells gladly of those she sent off to get married. She does not aspire to manufacture nuns! What a good sister!" And again, "In the wake of juridical Christianity ... I can sense the coming of ethical, truly evangelical Christianity.... I immerse myself in this ethical Christianity to be saved by it." Semeria's "ethical Christianity," wholly lacking the transcendent dimension, was that of his declared masters Duchesne and von Hügel. The Barnabite kept silent, however, about his collaboration with Buonaiuti, who admitted in a letter to Hügel his "debt to Semeria" for his own work, having followed in his *Program of the Modernists* a plan suggested by the Barnabite.[901]

It is no wonder that the anti-modernist newspaper *La Liguria Popolo* directed by Fr. Giovanni Boccardo,[902] in complete agreement with papal directives,

[898] Ulysse Chevalier (1841–1920) was a priest and learned Frenchman who, in a number of controversial studies, placed in doubt the authenticity of the Shroud of Turin and of the Holy House of Loreto. His theses were vigorously refuted by the Jesuit historian Ilario Rinieri (*La Santa Casa di Loreto*, 2 vols., Tipografia Pontificia, Turin 1910–1911).

[899] Semeria, *Anni terribili*, p. 94 (pp. 90–94).

[900] Ibid, pp. 310–311.

[901] Buonaiuti, *Pellegrino di Roma*, pp. 88–89. A decree of the vicariate of Rome (ASS, vol. 40, 1907, p. 720) imposed excommunication on those who had written or in any way taken part in the realization of the work. On the relationship between Buonaiuti and Semeria, cf. also A. Zambarbieri, in *Fonti e Documenti* 1 (1972), pp. 411–440.

[902] Giovanni Boccardo (1877–1956), director of *La Liguria del Popolo* from 1908 to 1915, was a member for a time of the *Sodalitium pianum*. Cf. Poulat, *Intégrisme et catholicisme intégral*, pp. 582–583.

entrusted a series of articles against Semeria to an erudite priest, Fr. Arturo Colletti,[903] who enjoyed the trust and the support of Cardinal Merry del Val.

Fr. Semeria, quite close to the House of Savoy, exercised a strong influence over the diocese of Genoa. When Pius X, in 1911, nominated as archbishop of Genoa an anti-modernist prelate, Msgr. Andrea Caron,[904] the Giolitti government considered denying him the *exequatur*.[905] Pius X did not accept this imposition. On November 29, 1912, he ordered the suspension of all pontifical functions of the bishop in the archdiocese, including the administration of Confirmation and Priestly Ordination, while the Barnabites were transferred to Brussels.

In April 1914, the Holy See nominated Msgr. Tommaso Pio Boggiani as apostolic administrator of the archdiocese of Genoa. After the death of Pius X, however, an agreement between the Holy See and the Italian government was reached. In August 1915, *L'Osservatore Romano* published a declaration of the Minister of the Interior that reintegrated Msgr. Caron and received the request of *exequatur*. Archbishop Caron, tired and ill, wrote a letter renouncing the post; in the meantime, Msgr. Luigi Gavotti, bishop of Casale Monferrato, was nominated.[906]

The battle against modernism was thus conducted with no holds barred, but the pontificate of Pius X was coming to an end.

903 Arturo Colletti (1875–1951), Genovese, entered the Congregation of the Oratory in 1900 and was for nearly a decade the most intransigent adversary of Fr. Giovanni Semeria in the city of Genoa. Expelled from Genoa in 1906 and leaving his congregation, he went first to Perugia (until 1909) and then entered the ranks of the clergy of Spoleto, assuming in 1911 the role of professor in the local seminary. Under his own name and under the pseudonyms *Arcturus* and *Spoletanus* he continued to combat the works and the thought of Semeria.

904 Andrea Caron (1848–1927) was designated archbishop of Genoa by Pius X on April 24, 1912, but was not able to take possession of his See, for the Italian government denied the exequatur to his nomination. He then retired to Montecassino, where he died. Cf. Antonio Duranti, *Monsignor Andrea Caron e un periodo critico di storia genovese [Monsignor Andrea Caron and a Critical Period of Genovese History]*, Scuola Grafica Don Bosco, Genoa 1966.

905 The *exequatur* was the state recognition needed for several acts of the Holy See according to the Law of the *Guarentigie*. The authorization was granted by royal decree upon proposal of the minister of Justice, having heard the State Counsel in general assembly and the Council of Ministers. This institution came to an end with the Concordat of February 11, 1929.

906 Luigi Gavotti (1868–1918), bishop of Casale Monferrato (1903), was transferred to the archbishopric of Genoa in January 22, 1915.

5

From Pius X to Benedict XV

Archpriest of St. Peter's Basilica

On September 7, 1913, while murmuring the prayer "Jesus, Mary, and Joseph, I give you my heart and my soul," the "Holy Cardinal" Capuchin Vives y Tutó died in Monteporzio Catone. He had been one of the most eminent figures of St. Pius X's pontificate.

On December 16 of the same year, another great protagonist of Church life would leave the scene, Cardinal Mariano Rampolla del Tindaro, who after three terms at the pinnacle of the Secretariat of State had spent the last ten years of his life in dignified silence in Santa Marta in the Vatican. With his death, the roles he had filled were made vacant: Chamberlain, Secretary of the Holy Office, Grand Prior of the Order of Malta, Church Librarian, and archpriest of St. Peter's Basilica. On January 14, 1914, the pope assigned the role of archpriest of the Basilica and Prefect of the Fabric of St. Peter's to Cardinal Rafael Merry del Val.[907]

The Italian State press corps followed attentively what was happening in the Vatican.[908] The police chief of the Borgo, Cesare Bertini,[909] in his report to

[907] AAV, *Spoglio Merry del Val*, busta 4, n. 396, January 12, 1914. According to the apostolic constitution *Praedicate evangelium* (March 19, 2022), "The Fabric of Saint Peter's deals with everything that concerns the Papal Basilica of Saint Peter, which preserves the memory of the martyrdom and the tomb of the Apostle, including the conservation and decorum of the building and the internal discipline of its employees and of pilgrims and visitors, in accordance with its proper norms" (n. 244). On the role of archpriest, cf. Fr. Michele Basso, *I privilegi e le consuetudini della Rev.da Fabbrica di San Pietro in Vaticano, sec. XV–XX [The Privileges and the Customs of the Fabric of St. Peter's in the Vatican]*, Tipografia Poliglotta Vaticana, Rome 1987.

[908] Giuseppe Manfroni (1835–1917) directed the state police station in the Borgo (just outside the Vatican walls) from 1870 to 1901. The information he provided was valuable for the first Italian administrations after unification. Cf. the memoires collected by his son Camillo, *Sulla soglia del Vaticano, 1870–1901 [On the Doorstep of the Vatican]*, Nicola Zanichelli, Bologna 1920, 2 vols.

[909] Cesare Bertini (1872–1951) was a police functionary who directed the police station in the Borgo from 1914 to 1919. Police commissioner in Rome from 1920 and prefect from 1923, in May 1925 he was transferred to Piacenza and from there to Ferrara until retirement. Cf. Cesare Bertini, *Ai tempi delle guarentigie. Ricordi di un funzionario di polizia (1913–1918) [In the Days of the Guarentigie. Memories of a Police Functionary]*, Cremonese, Rome 1932.

the Interior Minister on January 13, 1914, insinuated that Merry del Val "would have to leave the Secretariat of State as soon as Pius X died, since with the appointment as archpriest of St. Peter's he was protecting him from being sent out of the Roman Curia and from Rome."[910] The commissary was perhaps ignoring the fact that the greatest longing of the cardinal was precisely that of leaving the Vatican to return to dedicating himself to the apostolate.

As emerged in the testimonies during the process of beatification, it was due to the express desire of Pius X that Merry del Val accepted this office, which he tried in vain to evade.[911]

The new cardinal archpriest donated to the Treasury of St. Peter's an ornate golden chalice that he had received as a gift from the pope, wanting to begin the execution of his role with an act of filial homage to the Most Holy Virgin, setting the day of his investiture on the feast of the Purification, February 2, 1914. From that moment, he did everything in his power to make Christianity's highest temple radiant in the fullness of its magnificence and adornment, demanding that the sacred functions be always celebrated with the solemnity and precision which divine worship demands. He himself carried out with faultless exactitude all the ceremonies and rites demanded of a cardinal archpriest, from the beginning of his charge until the last chapter he attended on February 2, 1930.[912]

On May 25, 1914, Pius X created thirteen new cardinals.[913] The journalist Crispolto Crispolti in *L'Illustrazione Italiana* on May 31, 1914, reviewing the personalities, left for last "those who, perhaps, should have been placed at the top of the entire list of new cardinals: Msgr. Giacomo della Chiesa, archbishop of Bologna," a "capable and sharp diplomat," "who was more than just a collaborator, but a friend even of Mariano Rampolla, and who remained

910 ACS, *Min. Interno, Dir. Gen. Pubblica Sicurezza, Ufficio riservato*, 1914, busta 34, fasc. H 5.

911 Testimony of Msgr. Beniamino Nardone (1877–1963), canon of the Basilica of St. Peter, secretary of the Congregation of the Ceremonial, in *Processus Informativus Ordinarius* vol. 2, p. 553, and of Card. Nicola Canali, Ibid., *Sessio* CXII, p. 708.

912 Dal-Gal, *Merry del Val*, pp. 82–84.

913 The thirteen cardinals created by Pius X in the consistory in May were: Louis Bégin, archbishop of Québec; Franz de Bettinger, archbishop of Munich and Freising; Johann Csernoch, archbishop of Strigonia; Giacomo della Chiesa, archbishop of Bologna; Aidan Gasquet, president of the English Benedictines; Filippo Giustini, secretary of the Congregation of the Sacraments; Victoriano Guisasola y Menéndez, archbishop of Toledo; Felix Hartmann, archbishop of Cologne; Michele Lega, canon vicar of Sant'Eustachio; Antonio Mendez y Bello, patriarch of Lisbon; Gustav Piffl, archbishop of Vienna; Domenico Serafini, archbishop of Spoleto; Scipione Tecchi, canon of the Lateran Basilica. From 1903 to 1914, Pius X created fifty cardinals in seven consistories.

faithful to Leo XIII's secretary even in his hours of misfortune and in exile in Santa Marta." According to Crispolti, "Giacomo della Chiesa will take his place in the ranks of the 'opposition to His Holiness,' he is a declared adversary of Merry del Val, and certainly, when the time comes to elect the future pope, his voice will be heard."[914]

In the address *Il grave dolore* of May 27, 1914, by which he imposed the biretta on the new cardinals, Pius X said to them, "The prerogatives of piety, doctrine, and zeal by which you are distinguished, and furthermore your devotion which you profess to this Holy Apostolic See, reassure me that you will be an effective help in keeping intact the deposit of Faith, in safeguarding ecclesiastical discipline, and in resisting the subtle assaults aimed at the Church not so much by declared enemies, but especially by her own sons."[915]

There could be no misunderstanding the pope's words. On May 30, receiving in a private audience the historian Ludwig von Pastor, Pius X said, "I spoke clearly, taking my stand alongside the hardliners, placing the accent explicitly on *integrata fide*." The following day, Pastor wrote in his diary, "The discourse of May 27 is a clear warning to all the bishops who have spoken against the *integrist* tendency. There is not the least doubt about the pain they cause the Holy Father and about the damage that will come from them for the Catholic cause. The discourse was also an energetic manifestation in favor of an *integrist* and intransigent press."[916]

At the end of 1913, Pius X had a severe bout of influenza, but soon recovered his strength. Merry del Val recalled, "He had never been as ill as the people were generally led to believe from the exaggerated voices of the daily press, and was so full of life during the entire period of his illness and convalescence that no one could persuade him to stay idle."

"If it weren't for these excellent doctors I could do as I wish, and I would now be on my feet and moving!" the pope repeated in jest during the days he spent in bed. "Often," wrote Merry del Val, "I would see him pull himself up from his pillow energetically to sign some document I presented him, and holding out his hand exclaimed smiling, 'Eminence, see how my hand is not trembling!' And went on to affix his signature with his usual firmness. When he resumed his usual life, he seemed much better than we had seen him for many

914 *L'Illustrazione Italiana*, May 31, 1914, p. 25.

915 Pius X, Discourse *Il grave dolore*, May 27, 1914, in AAS, vol. 6 (1914), n. 8, pp. 260–262.

916 Pastor, *Tagebücher*, p. 599.

years. His activity increased. He seemed to have acquired new powers, as if he had been lightened of the burden of age."[917]

The secretary of state continued giving his attention to every issue, also in his role as prefect of the Apostolic Palaces. The administrative functioning of the Vatican depended on him, including the organization of the military corps. The restoration of the historical uniform of the Swiss Guard was decided by Merry del Val, together with the commander of the corps, Jules Repond, who reported to him every week on the affairs of the corps and was struck to find in him a knowledge of military matters quite rare in ecclesiastics.[918] After having spoken of the reform of the corps established by Pius X and of the substitution of the old arms with new Mauser rifles, Merry del Val accepted Repond's proposal of bringing back the military uniforms of the Swiss Guard to the tradition of the sixteenth century, based on the project of Raffaello.

"This was a true historical problem," recalled Repond, "the solution to which was due to the perspicacity and aesthetic sense of Cardinal Merry del Val."[919]

The Outbreak of the First World War

As the sun rose on January 1, 1914, Europe was immersed in the tranquil opulence of the *Belle Epoque* and still trusted in the radiant march of human progress. The twentieth century had opened in the naive presumption of having left behind forever the evils and errors that have afflicted humanity ever since the Fall. Few could have imagined that the assassination of the Austrian Archduke Franz Ferdinand in Sarajevo would have inaugurated an age of death and destruction on a global scale.[920] Nearly nine million men were no more by the end of this global conflagration.[921]

917 Merry del Val, *San Pio X*, p. 63.

918 Jules Repond (1853–1933), from Freiburg, commanded the Swiss Guard from 1910 to 1921.

919 Cenci, *Merry del Val*, p. 229.

920 Archduke Franz Ferdinand of Austria-Este (1863–1914) became heir to the Austro-Hungarian throne after the death of his cousin Rudolf von Mayerling (1889). His marriage with Sophie Chotek von Chotkowa, duchess of Hohenberg (1868–1914), was "morganatic." That is, because she was not of one of the imperial families of Europe, she could not share his title, and their descendants would not have dynastic rights or privileges in any of the Habsburg realms.

921 For some of the best and most recent works on the First World War, cf. Niall Ferguson, *La Verità taciuta. La Prima guerra mondiale: il più grande errore della storia moderna*, Italian translation, Corbaccio, Milano 2002; Jean-Jacques Becker, *1914. L'anno che ha cambiato il mondo*, Italian translation, Lindau, Turin 2014; Christopher Clark, *I sonnambuli. Come l'Europa arrivò alla Grande Guerra*, Italian translation, Laterza, Bari-Rome 2016. Cf. also the excellent chapter dedicated to "The First World War" by François Furet, in *Il passato di un'illusione. L'idea comunista nel XX secolo*, Mondadori, Milano 1995, pp. 44–74.

In his recollections on Pius X, Merry del Val attests that the pope had repeatedly announced the outbreak of the Great War in Europe, long before the storm was to be unleashed.[922] "Matters are going poorly," the pontiff often stated, "the 'Great War' [*Guerrone*] is coming! I'm not speaking about this war (the Italian military expedition in Libya and the conflict in the Balkans). Not this, but the Great War: the '*Guerrone.*'"[923] The Balkan Wars from 1912-1913 had made Pius X very restless.[924] He expressed to Baron Ritter, the Bavarian minister to the Holy See, his deep concern about the advance of Serbians in territories inhabited in part by Catholics. The pope knew that Serbia was supported by Russia and he feared the frenzied proselytism of the Orthodox, to the point of saying, "Better the Turks once more than the Russians."[925]

Moved by these concerns, on June 24, 1914, Merry del Val signed the concordat between the Holy See and the Kingdom of Serbia, according to which an ecclesiastical province was established composed of the archdiocese of Belgrade and the diocese of Skopje, with the aim of safeguarding the religious interests of Catholics in the Kingdom of Serbia.[926] Four days later, in Serbia, the heir to the Austro-Hungarian throne Franz Ferdinand and his wife Sofia, Duchess of Hohenberg, were assassinated by the revolver shots of Gavrilo Princip, a Bosnian affiliated with the terrorist organization "Black Hand."[927]

922 Merry del Val, *San Pio X*, pp. 20–22.

923 Ibid, p. 21. Cf. also *Pii X Positio*, p. 980.

924 The First Balkan War (October–December 1912, then February–April 1913) pitted Turkey against Bulgaria, Greece, and Serbia. The winners, failing to reach an accord, provoked the Second Balkan War (May–August 1913), this time pitting Bulgaria against Turkey, Greece, Romania, and Serbia. The latter increased its territory by a third.

925 Francis Latour, *La Papautè et les problèmes de la paix pendant la première guerre mondiale*, L'Harmattan, Paris 1996, pp. 21–22.

926 The concordat between the Holy See and the Kingdom of Serbia was signed by Card. Merry del Val and Milenko R. Vesnitch (1863–1921), extraordinary envoy and plenipotentiary minister of the King of Serbia, Peter I (1844–1921). Present at the signing were Msgr. Eugenio Pacelli, secretary of the Congregation of Extraordinary Ecclesiastical Affairs, and Nicola Canali, substitute of the secretary of state. Cf. Anna Rigoni, "Il concordato serbo-vaticano del 1914," *Italian Historical Archive* 133, nos. 1–4 (1975), pp. 159–178; M. Valente, "I rapporti tra Santa Sede e Serbia nella Prima Guerra Mondiale," in Lorenzo Botrugno (ed.), *Inutile strage. I cattolici e la Santa Sede nella Prima Guerra Mondiale ["Useless Slaughter." Catholics and the Holy See in the First World War]*, Libreria Editrice Vaticana, Vatican City 2016, pp. 493–513.

927 The assassination was organized by the leader of Black Hand, Dragutin Dimitrijević (1876–1917), alias Apis, who in 1903 had assassinated the Serbian King Alessandro Obrenovich and his wife Draga and who occupied since 1913 a key role as head of the secret services of Serbian Military. Cf. David MacKenzie, *Apis: the congenial conspirator. The life of Colonel Dragutin T. Dimitrijevic*, Columbia University Press, New York 1989.

The assassination had an enormous emotive impact in Austria, since Franz Ferdinand represented the future of the dynasty and the empire. On July 23, Austria sent the government of Belgrade a memorandum asking Serbia to accept the collaboration of Austrian functionaries investigating the crime and to repress the subversive movement militating against the territorial integrity of the monarchy. The Serbian government refused the ultimatum and decreed the mobilization of its army. On July 28, the Austro-Hungarian Empire officially declared war against Serbia, with the conviction that the conflict would remain localized.

Austria wanted to teach Serbia a lesson, but the latter was supported by Russia which, after the meeting between Czar Nicholas II[928] and the French president Poincaré, knew it could count on France.[929] Poincaré was certain that Vienna and Berlin would never risk challenging the Franco-Russian Alliance, supported by Great Britain, which in turn was conducting secret negotiations with Russia against the Turks. Austria and Germany, on the other hand, were convinced that England had no interest in allowing themselves to be dragged into a war brought about by a Russo-Austrian conflict in the Balkans.

The English historian Niall Ferguson reminds us that on the eve of the conflict, numerous descendants and other relatives of Queen Victoria were sitting on European thrones. "Despite the imperial rivalry of prewar diplomacy, the personal relationships among these monarchs had remained cordial, even friendly: the correspondence between George, Willy, and Nicky testifies to the protraction of the existence of a royal, cosmopolitan, polyglot elite with a certain sense of their common interest."[930]

The Italian scholar Alberto Lumbroso published for his part the *Imperial and Royal Correspondence* in which he gathered the telegrams exchanged among European sovereigns during the "tragic week" that closed the month of July and began that of August in 1914. On July 31, Kaiser Wilhelm II addressed a final appeal to his cousin Nicholas II: "European peace can be saved only by you, if Russia decides to stop the military measures that threaten Austria-Hungary."[931]

[928] Nicholas II Romanov (1896–1918) was the last Czar of Russia. Nicholas was the first cousin, on his mother's side, of George V of the United Kingdom (the mothers of the two sovereigns, Princesses of Denmark, were sisters). His wife, Alice of Hesse, like Kaiser Wilhelm II, was the grandchild of Queen Victoria of the United Kingdom and Albert of Saxe-Coburg.

[929] President Raymond Poincaré (1860–1934), along with the Prime Minister René Viviani (1863–1925), consolidated the reciprocal commitments of the two countries during an official visit to St. Petersburg on July 20-23.

[930] Ferguson, *La Verità taciuta*, p. 559.

[931] Alberto Lumbroso, *Carteggi Imperiali e Reali 1870–1918*, Bompiani, Milan 1931, p. 322.

The day before, the Czar had allowed his generals to talk him into giving the order for a general mobilization, which in the vision of that age was the equivalent of a declaration of war against Austria. The mobilization of Russia, writes Christopher Clark, was one of the most momentous decisions during the crisis of July. It was in fact the first mobilization to be enacted, after that of Serbia, and it came at a time when Germany had not even declared a state of "the danger of war" (*Kriegsgefahrstand*), which corresponded to the preparatory period of war.[932]

In the face of Russia's refusal to halt its mobilization, Germany declared war on August 1. A few minutes earlier, France had issued the order of general mobilization. On August 3, Germany declared war on France, and German troops invaded Belgium and Luxemburg. That same day, British Foreign Minister Sir Edward Grey[933] appeared before parliament to announce that the violation of Belgium's neutrality forced Great Britain to enter the war against Germany. On August 6, Austria-Hungary declared war on Russia. On the 11 and 12 of August, France and England in turn declared war on Austria-Hungary. An inexorable dynamic had overwhelmed European heads of state and political leaders. The voice of canons began to thunder from one end of Europe to another.

All were convinced that the war would be over by Christmas, or at the most by Spring 1915. No one imagined that it would last five years, with millions dead, and that it would be unlike every previous war due to the mobilization of the masses and the ideological hatred that characterized it from the very beginning. Begun as an ordinary war, the First World War ended, according to the Hungarian historian François Fejtö, as an ideological mass war whose aim was "to republicanize and de-Catholicize Europe" and to carry out, on the national and international level, the work of the French Revolution that had been interrupted.[934]

The Italian foreign minister Antonio di San Giuliano,[935] who enjoyed King Vittorio Emanuele III's complete trust, intuited the possible catastrophic outcomes of the conflict and suggested maintaining neutrality. The Vatican

932 Clark, *I sonnambuli*, p. 241.

933 Sir Edward Grey, viscount of Fallodon (1862–1933), foreign minister of Great Britain from 1905 to 1916, promoted the Anglo-Russian Accord of 1907 which, in fact, gave life to the Triple Entente.

934 François Fejtö, *Requiem per un impero defunto. La dissoluzione del mondo austro-ungarico [Requiem for a Defunct Empire. The Dissolution of the Austro-Hungarian World]*, Italian translation, Mondadori, Milan 1990 (1988), pp. 316–333. According to Fejtö, by means of the destruction of the Austrian Empire, the objective of an intimate circle of politicians affiliated with Freemasonry was "to extirpate from Europe the last vestiges of clericalism and monarchism" (p. 320).

935 Antonino Paternò-Castello, marquis of San Giuliano (1852–1914), was foreign minister from 1905 to 1906 and from 1910 to 1914.

followed the development of events with extreme concern, while the health of Pius X was rapidly declining.

One of Pius X's secretaries confided to an Austrian friend that the pope, solicited to intervene in favor of peace, had said, "The only sovereign to whom I could offer my service is Emperor Franz Josef, who has always shown his loyalty and fidelity toward the Holy See. But I am simply not capable of intervening upon him because what Austria-Hungary are undertaking is a just war."[936]

Despite the pope's private sympathies for the Austro-Hungarian Empire, the Holy See immediately took a position of impartiality. After the war, Count Pálffy accused the secretary of State Merry del Val of having instigated Austria to declare war, but the cardinal, who had preserved his notes recording every word of the meeting held on July 27, 1914, with the then adviser to the Austrian embassy, clarified that he had never expressed the desire for Austria to take up arms, however convinced he might have been that it had the right to solemn reparations for the horrendous massacre in Sarajevo.[937]

The cardinals in Rome and abroad tended to be divided according to their respective nationalities. On August 17, Cardinal Merry del Val wrote to the cardinals, binding them to the pontifical secret: "In light of the most grievous events that have suddenly upset all of Europe, and which threaten the future with the most frightening of unknowns," the pope recommended that the components of the Sacred College "impose upon themselves the most attentive circumspection and caution with regard to their exterior conduct, and avoid in their eventual social contacts engaging in conversations or expressing approval and judgments relative to all that is occurring among the European Powers."[938]

Eighteen days before his death, Pius X addressed "*ad universos catholicos*" the exhortation *Dum Europa fere omnis*. To "the people of Europe, almost all dragged into the vortex of a most pernicious war, whose dangers, massacres, and consequences no one can contemplate without feeling oppressed by affliction and fright," the pope exhorted "to raise souls to the One from whom comes our help, Christ the Prince of Peace and most powerful mediator between God and

936 R. Aubert, "Pio X tra restaurazione e riforma" [Pius X Between Restoration and Reform], in Fliche and Martin (eds.), *Storia della Chiesa,* vol. 22/1, p. 152.

937 AAV, *Spoglio Merry del Val,* busta VI, n. 685–687, January 18, 1926. *Relazione della conversazione col conte Pálffy* (cf. also ibid, n. 398). Count Moritz von Pálffy (1869–1948) represented the Austro-Hungarian Empire and then the Austrian Republic to the Holy See between 1911 and 1920.

938 AAV, Secr. State, *Guerra 1914–1918,* rubr. 244 (A1), f. 63 (Neutrality), ff. 117–118, Rafael Merry del Val to the members of the Sacred College, n. 72926, August 17, 1914.

men" and asked the clergy to proclaim in their respective parishes, "public prayers that God, moved to pity, might free us as soon as possible from the tragic phases of war and inspire the highest leaders of the nations with thoughts of peace and not of affliction."[939]

The Last Illness and the Death of Pius X

Pius X continued to work until August 1914. "The horror and the laceration he felt when the conflict broke out were very deep," recalled Merry del Val. "Day and night the tremendous spectacle of the terrifying struggle tormented his mind, to which there was added a clear vision of the sufferings and anguish that were inevitably to come from this catastrophe. The invasion of Belgium and the news of the first battles filled him with the most bitter pain. He awaited anxiously the documented proof of the facts to be able to set the trajectory of his own action and be able to raise his authoritative voice without fear in defense of the sacrosanct principles of justice and peace."[940]

After the feast of the Assumption on August 15, the Holy Father showed signs of slight indisposition. But neither he nor those surrounding him attributed much importance to a minor illness that seemed mostly due to the excessive heat in those days.[941] Because of the war already underway, Merry del Val had not yet left the Vatican to take a period of rest on the estate of Palo degli Odescalchi or in the villa of Count Blumenstihl on Monte Mario.

The morning of Tuesday, August 18, 1914, Merry del Val was invited by Msgr. Giovanni Bressan to go up to the third floor to be received by His Holiness. This was to be the last conversation between the pope and his secretary of state. During the audience, which lasted about half an hour, the cardinal reported on several of the more urgent matters, but left concerned about the Holy Father's state of health.[942] When the secretary of state asked his blessing for the

939 Pius X, Exhortation *Dum Europa fere omnis* to all Catholics throughout the world, August 2, 1914, in *Enchiridion/Pio X*, pp. 960–961.

940 Merry del Val, *San Pio X*, p. 63.

941 AAV, Secr. State, *Morte di pontefici e conclavi [Death of Pontiffs and Conclaves]*, scatola 25, fasc. 2, n. 7491, ff. 29r-77r. "Bollettini medici sulle condizioni di salute di Pio X che ne segnalano la grave infermità tra il 9 aprile 1913 e il 19 agosto 1914" [Medical Bulletins on the Health Condition of Pius X Signaling His Serious Illness from April 9, 1913 to August 19, 1914].

942 Cenci, *Merry del Val*, pp. 236–237.

Jesuit General Franz Xavier Wernz,[943] gravely ill, Pius X gave it exclaiming: "It shall be the last!"

"What occurred during the night," recalled Merry del Val, "none of us can say. Msgr. Bressan, the pope's devout chaplain who slept in a room attached and communicating with his, noticed only that the Holy Father was quite sleepless that night and nothing else. But given that the pope had not risen that morning at his usual hour, Msgr. Bressan went to him and found him feverish and suffering. The doctors were immediately called, and they found the Holy Father's lungs congested and himself therefore gravely ill."[944]

Merry del Val immediately understood the gravity of the situation and was terrified. At 10 a.m. on August 19, Pius X suffered a heart attack. The cardinal rushed to his bedside and found him breathing with great difficulty. The Holy Father clasped his hand tightly: "Eminence, Eminence!" was all that he said. After receiving the sacraments, his last words were, "I abandon myself completely." After this, he lost the faculty of speech, but perfectly conscious, he looked at each one in turn, showing clearly that he was aware of his condition.[945]

"Even though incapable of speaking," continued Merry del Val, "he recognized perfectly well those who surrounded him and, every now and then, made the sign of the cross slowly. The long summer day seemed interminable, as we, stricken with grief, lingered in the adjoining room to leave the air to circulate as much as possible. The hours never passed and we, watchful, were awaiting his passage into eternity."[946]

Around 11:30 p.m., Cardinal Merry del Val entered the pope's room. "Immediately he turned toward me, following me with his penetrating gaze as I moved to place myself at the foot of his bed. He raised his arm as if to greet me and, when I sat down closer to him, he took my hand and clasped it with so much strength that I was dumbfounded. He gazed at me intensely and his eyes seemed to be within mine. How strongly I desired to be able to read his thoughts at that moment and to hear his voice! We both gazed at each other and spoke with our eyes. What did he wish to tell me with that look? Was he perhaps recollecting the long years that I had spent in familiar relation with him

943 Franz Xavier Wernz (1842–1914), illustrious scholar of canon law, was Superior General of the Society of Jesus from 1906. At midnight on August 19, Merry del Val received the urgent call from the Jesuit House notifying him of the death of Fr. Wernz.

944 Merry del Val, *San Pio X*, p. 64.

945 Ibid, p. 65.

946 Ibid, p. 67.

and of all that we had faced together? Did he want to comfort me in that moment with a last message, in my distress that I was trying to hide?

"He held me thus as if enthralled for more than forty minutes. Once in a while he loosened his grip to caress me, returning then to take my hand with strength. In the end, he rested his head on the pillow and his eyes closed. It seemed that Pius X had told me farewell!"[947]

Msgr. Pescini, from the *segreteriola,* confirmed, "I saw the Holy father hold tightly the hand of Cardinal Merry del Val for a long time. At times, the Servant of God (Pius X) tried to speak to him, though without being able to make himself understood."[948]

Cardinal Merry del Val wrote, "I will never forget that supreme scene of our separation! It is alive in my mind even today, just as it was on that memorable night when he seemed to repeat the words of St. Lawrence that we had read in the Breviary just a few days before: "*Quo progrederis sine filio, Pater? Quo, Sacerdos sancte, sine Ministro properas*?" (Where are you going, O Father, without your son? Where, holy Priest, without your Minister?).

"Suddenly, the profound peals of the big bell of St. Peter's echoed through the air, sounding the *Pro Pontefice agonizzante* and, at that signal, exposition of the Blessed Sacrament with special prayers began in the patriarchal basilicas. The suffocating *scirocco* of that day, the murmur of the crowd that rose from St. Peter's square below, the hushed whispers of the prelates and other people and the mournful sound of the bell gave the impression of a most sorrowful dream."

With immense sadness, Merry del Val concluded his narration: "Toward midnight, I retired to take a brief rest, with the assurances that His Holiness would survive for many hours still. Only an hour later I was called with great haste, but before I could arrive to Pius X's room, he quietly expired and his beautiful soul was with God."[949]

It was 1:20 a.m. on August 20, 1914. That same day, German troops entered Brussels.

On September 27, Cardinal Merry del Val, stricken at the loss of Pius X, wrote his friend Msgr. Broadhead, "The blow has been a terrible one for me,

947 Merry del Val, *San Pio X*, p. 63; cf. also *Pii Papae X. Positio*, pp. 205–206.

948 *Pii Papae X. Positio*, p. 119.

949 Merry del Val, *San Pio X*, p. 68. Giuseppe Sarto was proclaimed blessed on June 3, 1951, and after the recognition in February of the two required miracles, was canonized by Pius XII on May 29, 1954.

and my heart is fairly broken. You see, I loved him with every fibre of my soul; he was more like a father to me, and I feel as though I could not live without him. He was indeed a saint."[950] Fr. Albin de Cigala, chaplain of the marshal of the conclave, Chigi Albani della Rovere, who met Pius X every year from 1907 to 1914, wrote, "Leo XIII gave me the impression of a great man; Pius X gave me the impression of a saint."[951] Pius XII confirmed the reputation for sanctity that surrounded Pius X immediately after his death, elevating him to the glory of the altars on June 3, 1951. "For more than two centuries," said Pope Pius XII before the coffin of Blessed Pius X, "such a splendid day for the Roman papacy has not dawned.... The world that acclaims him today among the blessed in glory knows that he walked, with a faith that moves mountains, the path that Providence had assigned to him, with unshaken hope, even in the darkest and most uncertain hours, with a charity that urged him to vow himself to every sacrifice in the service of God and the salvation of souls."[952]

Three years later, on May 29, 1954, Pius XII canonized Pius X during a solemn ceremony in the vestibule of the Vatican Basilica. Presenting him as the "undefeated champion of the Church and providential saint for our times," Pius XII said that "his firmness toward error might still be a stumbling stone; in reality, it is the extremity of charitable service rendered by a saint, as head of the Church, to all humanity."[953]

The conclave to elect Pius X's successor was convoked for August 31, 1914. The struggle between the modernist party and its opposers festered in the background of the transition from one pontificate to another. On August 22, Msgr. Benigni communicated to Cardinal De Lai, "on behalf of the assembly of the *Sodalitium pianum*, the decision they have taken at this moment is to disband our modest organization. Circumstances require this and Your Eminence will not find it difficult to agree."[954] On August 29, Filippo Crispolti wrote to his wife, "The fearsome personal secretariat has been dispersed; Bressan and Pescini are hated by all and insults are being heaped upon them."[955]

950 Buehrle, *Merry del Val*, p. 174; Forbes, *Merry del Val*, p. 113.

951 *Vie intime de Sa Sainteté le Pape Pie X, par l'abbé Albin de Cigala*, Lethielleux, Paris 1926, p. 232.

952 Pius XII, Discourse on June 3, 1951, cit., pp. 127, 130.

953 Pius XII, Discourse on May 29, 1954, cit., pp. 33, 34.

954 ASMAE, *Fondo Benigni*, busta 11, f. 114.

955 Cit. in Poulat, *Intégrisme et catholicisme intégral*, p. 461.

The Conclave of 1914

Pius X's body lay in state in the Blessed Sacrament Chapel of St. Peter's as the cardinal chamberlain Francesco Salesio della Volpe organized the conclave.[956] One of Pius X's first acts was to abolish the *jus exclusivae* that granted several Catholic nations the right to veto, as had occurred in the conclave of 1903 that had elected him. Pius X's decree inflicted the most severe excommunication against present and future cardinals who would accept in any way to be vehicles of secular intrusion in the conclave.[957]

Rafael Merry del Val had just turned forty-nine. It was the second conclave he would participate in, but if in the first one he assisted as a simple secretary, now, after eleven years, he participated not only as an elector, but as a potential candidate. Everyone agreed on the need to conclude the proceedings quickly, whether to enable the cardinals from war zones to return urgently to their own nations, or to demonstrate to the world that the Church was extraneous to political interests and the passions of the contenders.[958]

The cardinal of Brussels, Mercier, arrived in Rome on August 24, 1914, and the cardinal of Vienna, Friedrich Gustav Piffl, the following day.[959] We owe to both men, belonging to the most liberal wing of the Sacred College, the detailed information on what went on behind the scenes of the conclave. In his first contacts in Rome, Mercier perceived that there was a general "anti-integralist" mood that united the sympathizers of modernism with those who, for various reasons, wanted a discontinuity with the previous pontificate. Piffl wrote that Card. Agliardi spoke of the necessity "of electing a pope who would give bishops authority in their own dioceses, in other words an anti-integralist pope."[960]

956 Francesco Salesio Della Volpe (1844–1916), made a cardinal by Leo XIII in 1899, was in charge of the Vatican Secret Archive and, from 1911, prefect of the Congregation of the Index. On May 25, 1914, Pius X named him chamberlain of Holy Roman Church.

957 This norm was promulgated in the most solemn form on January 20, 1904, in the constitution *Commissum nobis*. Cf. Jürgen Jamin, "Civile veto cive exclusivam omnino reprobamus: La Costituzione *Commissum nobis* di Pio X alla vigilia della prima codificazione," *Ius Ecclesiae* 29, no. 3 (2017), pp. 591–609.

958 Carlo Falconi, *I Papi del ventesimo secolo [The Popes of the 20th Century]*, Feltrinelli, Milan 1967, pp. 110–111.

959 Friedrich Gustav Piffl (1864–1932), of the Canons Regular of St. Augustine, was elected archbishop of Vienna in 1913 and made a cardinal in the consistory of May 25, 1914. He participated in the two conclaves that elected Benedict XV and Pius XI, keeping a secret diary that he ordered to be incinerated when he died, but was published by the archivist Max Liebmann, allowing the public to learn of the behind the scenes reality of the conclaves. Cf. "Les conclaves de Benoît XV et de Pie XI. Notes du cardinal Piffl," *La Revue Nouvelle* 38 (1963), pp. 34–52.

960 "Notes du cardinal Piffl," p. 37.

Mercier noted in turn: "Certainly, the great figure of the pope will dominate in history, but currently, the language of criticism has been unleashed,"[961] adding, "Cardinals De Lai, Pompili, and Merry del Val have executed with severity, often with brusqueness, the august plans of the good Pius X and have aroused a wind of unpopularity around his memory."[962]

The evening of Friday, August 28, Mercier visited Card. Bourne, archbishop of Westminster, "who has expressed to me, laconically though clearly, the same thoughts about Vatican diplomacy, about the 'relief' produced by the death of Pius X."[963] The battle lines were drawn in this manner. A compact, though minority group was made up of cardinals who were faithful to the memory and inheritance of Pius X and wanted a pope who would ensure continuity with the previous pontiff. The two leaders of this group who were disparagingly called "integralists," but who could have been better defined as the "Pius party," were Cardinals De Lai and Merry del Val. De Lai, considered the "strongman" of Pius X's pontificate, was unpopular and had no chance of being elected. Merry del Val, given his human qualities and his cultural and moral depth, was the one who could have best taken up the legacy of Pius X, but his close ties to Pius X were, paradoxically, his shortcoming.

The party opposing the "Pius party" was not homogeneous, united only by the will to create a fracture with the previous pontificate. In this party, cardinals Maffi, Ferrata, Agliardi, and Della Chiesa stood out. The newly created English cardinal Aidan Gasquet shared the liberal-leaning positions of the cardinal of Pisa, Maffi, and wanted him as pope: "I have never met anyone who was so sympathetic to me," he wrote.[964] But on August 28, Piffl met with a group of Austro-German cardinals who expressed the opinion that "Maffi must be discarded because he is *Italianissimo* and modernizing."[965] Cardinal Maffi, as observed Carlo Falconi, had an Achilles heel in his overly intimate relations with the House of Savoy, of which he was considered the "chaplain."[966]

961 "Notes du cardinal Mercier," in R. Aubert, "Le cardinal Mercier aux conclaves de 1914 et 1922," *Bulletin de la Classe des Lettres et des Sciences morales et politiques* 11 (2000), p. 211 (pp. 164–236).

962 Ibid., p. 212.

963 Ibid.

964 Ibid., p. 235.

965 "Notes du cardinal Piffl," pp. 39–40. Prince Schönburg communicated to the Austrian government the names of the nine *papabili*: Ferrata, Della Chiesa, Van Rossum, Merry del Val, Agliardi, Vincenzo Vannutelli, Pompili, Serafini, Giustini (ibid., pp. 37–38).

966 Falconi, *I Papi del ventesimo secolo*, p. 111.

The political divisions provoked by the war were interwoven with the diversity of attitudes on doctrinal themes. Mercier and Gasquet supported the Entente, but the general sentiment of the Sacred College was in favor of the Triple Alliance, also because the cardinals perceived behind the war the hand of Freemasonry. From the very first, Gasquet realized that "the entire sentiment of ecclesiastical Rome was decidedly pro-German."[967] "I have had long conversations with many cardinals and Roman ecclesiastics," the English cardinal recalled, "but nothing prevailed in dissuading them from the idea that it was English and French Freemasonry responsible for the European conflagration."[968] When, on August 29, the news reached Rome of the "Sack of Louvain" by the German troops invading Belgium, Gasquet wrote, "Cardinal Mercier is suffering terribly for the lack of sympathy. The general opinion is that of deploring the actions but of considering them as an inevitable incident of war."[969]

For his part, Cardinal Piffl noted in his diary, "True, the candidates have been nominated, but it is not possible to distinguish a clear preference for one or another of the *papabili*."[970] Despite their haste to conclude the conclave, uncertainty reigned. On August 20, Cardinal Merry del Val declared to Belgian Minister d'Erp that "the conclave might last a long time still, given that no candidate seems sufficiently designated by the votes of his colleagues."[971]

At 4 p.m. on August 31, 1914, the day the conclave began, all the cardinals passed in their carriages along Via della Fondamenta, while the Royal Carabinieri and the agents of public security honored them with a military salute, overseen by Commander of the Borgo Bertini.[972] At 6 p.m. the Mass of the Holy Spirit was celebrated in the Pauline Chapel by Cardinal Domenico Ferrata. Then the cardinals processed two-by-two into the Sistine Chapel singing the *Veni Creator*. "I and my neighbor to my right, Cardinal Gasparri," recalled Mercier, "have the same words on our lips at the same moment: a spectacle of this nature can be seen only in the Catholic Church."[973]

967 Shane Leslie, *Cardinal Gasquet. A Memoir,* Burns & Oates, London 1953, p. 234.

968 Ibid., p. 235.

969 Ibid.

970 Ibid., p. 39.

971 Letter of d'Erp to Davignon of August 25, 1914, cit. in Aubert, "Le cardinal Mercier aux conclaves de 1914 et 1922," p. 176.

972 Bertini, *Ai tempi delle guarentigie*, p. 230 and following.

973 "Notes du cardinal Mercier," p. 219. Piffl also described in his memoires the entrance into the Sistine Chapel as "*un spectacle très impressionant*" ("Notes du cardinal Piffl," p. 41).

The doors of the chapel were opened and Prince Ludovico Chigi Albani della Rovere, Marshal of the Conclave, entered to pronounce the ritual oath on his knees.[974] Governor Msgr. Misciattelli swore the oath as well, and then the St. Damasus bell rang giving the signal that the doors were closed. On Tuesday morning, before the voting, Cardinal Vincenzo Vannutelli celebrated the Mass of the Holy Spirit to implore divine assistance for the assembly. Mercier recalled, "I saw all the cardinals with such great devotion kneel down during the Creed of the Mass when the celebrant said *Et incarnatus est* and at the final Gospel, *Et verbum caro factum est*!"[975]

At the end of the Mass, the cardinals recited on their knees the *Veni Creator* and the prayer *Pro eligendo pontifice*. Then roll was called and each of the *porporati* took his own canopied seat in the Sistine Chapel, covered with red velvet and gold, with a little table before them on which were provided paper, pen, and ink. There were fifty-seven cardinals, of whom twenty-six were foreigners and thirty Italians. According to the new constitution of Pius X, there were to be two votes in the morning and two in the afternoon.

The strategy of the "Pius" party can be easily reconstructed by the voting that comes down to us through Cardinal Piffl. The group's leaders knew they did not have two-thirds of the vote necessary to elect the pope, and to enlarge their consensus, they divided their votes in the first round between Cardinals Merry del Val and Basilio Pompili,[976] whom Msgr. Benigni, in his *Notes en vue du prochain conclave*, of August 27, 1913, defined as "very kind to us."[977] Their back-up candidate was the Benedictine Domenico Serafini, assessor of the Holy Office, an erudite and pious man who, like Della Chiesa, had been created a cardinal just three months earlier, but who had

[974] Ludovico Chigi Albani della Rovere, Prince of Farnese (1866–1951), the son of Prince Mario Chigi, was Hereditary Marshal of the Holy Roman Church and the Sacred Conclave. He participated in three papal elections. After the death of his wife Anna Aldobrandini (1874–1898), he entered as a Knight of Justice, with the vote, in the Sovereign Military Order of Malta, of which he became the seventy-sixth Grand Master on May 14, 1931. As Marshal of the Conclave he was succeeded by Prince Sigismondo Chigi Albani, nominated by Pius XII on February 20, 1952, the last to hold this office.

[975] "Notes du cardinal Mercier," p. 220.

[976] Basilio Pompili (1858–1931), of Spoleto, ruler of the Sacred Penitentiary (1893), auditor of the Sacred Rota (1894), secretary of the Congregation of the Council (1908), was made a cardinal by Pius X on November 27, 1911, and titular archbishop of Philippi (1913). From April 7, 1913, until his death he was Vicar of His Holiness for the city of Rome and his district. Cf. Elio Venier, *Preti di Roma [Priests of Rome]*, Istituto Salesiano, Rome 2006, pp. 67–74.

[977] Poulat, *Intégrisme et catholicisme intégral*, p. 330.

been residential bishop in Spoleto for more than ten years and a diplomat of the Holy See.[978]

The "anti-integralist" party, for its part, discarded overly assertive personalities like Gasparri and Ferrata, and instead bet on a cardinal who expressed change in a more sober and less explicit manner. The ideal candidate was found in Giacomo della Chiesa, he too elevated to the *porpora* just months earlier, but bearing a wealth of experience as a diplomat, Curia official, and archbishop of Bologna.

From the eve of the conclave, in a meeting held in the church of Santa Maria dell'Anima near Piazza Navona, the Austro-Hungarian cardinals had decided to direct their votes toward Della Chiesa from the first scrutiny and arrange matters from there.[979] The Pius party would have to organize itself.

In the first ballot, Maffi obtained twelve votes as did Della Chiesa, nine went to Pompili, seven to Merry del Val, and four to Serafini, while Ferrata and Gasparri obtained only two each. In the second ballot, Maffi and Della Chiesa continued their deadlock. Piffl's diary reports that Cardinal Agliardi invited the Germans and Austrians to "vote for Maffi, who has superior intelligence, whereas Della Chiesa is a *mediocris homo*, a good bureaucrat,"[980] but the "mediocrity" of Della Chiesa was also his strength since he had fewer enemies than his rivals. In the afternoon, Della Chiesa received eighteen votes in the third ballot and twenty-one in the fourth, whereas Maffi had sixteen and fourteen respectively.

Della Chiesa began a slow but progressive rise beginning in the third ballot. In the fourth scrutiny, he rose to twenty-one, while Maffi lost two votes. The evening of September 1, Cardinal Hartmann, Archbishop of Cologne, attempted to divert the German cardinals' votes from Della Chiesa, stating that "we can not let Della Chiesa be elected because: 1) his election would be interpreted as an affront to Pius X; Della Chiesa was, in fact, Rampolla's undersecretary and afterward continued to work in his spirit, and for this reason was transferred to Bologna; 2) he has a strong character; 3) he is not representative."[981]

978 Domenico Serafini (1852–1918), Benedictine, was elected Abott General of his order in 1896 and in 1900 was nominated by Leo XIII bishop of Spoleto. Pius X, in 1904, sent him as apostolic delegate to Mexico and made him a cardinal on May 25, 1914. He was later prefect of Propaganda Fide (1916–1918).

979 "Notes du cardinal Piffl," pp. 39–40.

980 Ibid., p. 43.

981 Ibid., pp. 43–44.

The cardinals from the Central Empires continued however to vote for Della Chiesa, who decreased slightly to twenty votes in the fifth ballot, the first of the morning, but came back at the second, rising to twenty-seven, while Maffi decreased to thirteen and then seven.

In the face of Della Chiesa's advance, Pompili and Merry del Val, who together collected about fifteen votes, at the fifth ballot decided to divert them to Cardinal Serafini, who was not able to rise beyond a maximum of twenty-two votes during the ninth ballot, while beginning with the seventh ballot, Della Chiesa exceeded thirty. On September 2, during the sixth ballot, Della Chiesa advanced to twenty-seven, then thirty-one in the seventh, and thirty-two in the eighth, still far from the thirty-eight votes needed.

It seemed that the conclave had arrived at a stalemate. Cardinal Gasparri recounted that on the morning of the third day, before gathering in the Sistine Chapel, Cardinal Della Chiesa took him into his cell and said more or less the following: "The Eminent Cardinals are divided and only with difficulty will they come to a hasty agreement as the needs of the Church demand; I have the intention to read this exhortation at the start of the session [in it, he exhorted their Eminences to set him aside and give his votes to some other candidates] and I have come to ask Your Eminence's counsel, having nothing before my eyes but the good of the Church in the current most solemn circumstances.' I replied, 'If at the beginning of the next session, the divergence remains, though there is good reason to hope it is ending, I shall make to Your Eminence a negative signal that shall tell Your Eminence not to read the exhortation.' "[982]

And so it came about. Cardinal Gasparri made the negative signal when, during the ninth ballot, two of Serafini's electors went over to Della Chiesa and in the tenth ballot, the decisive one, the archbishop of Bologna reached the precise quorum of thirty-eight votes, to Serafini's eighteen: exactly two-thirds of the votes.

In this case, it was necessary to verify whether the elected candidate had voted for himself or for another. If in fact, he had given it to himself, his vote would be null and void and, lacking the majority, the ballot would have to be repeated. To enable the verification, every ballot slip had on the back a number and a motto which the elected had to identify in the case of a precise two-thirds majority. Opening Cardinal Della Chiesa's slip, it was verified that his vote had

[982] *Memorie del card. Gasparri,* in AA.EE.SS., *Stati Ecclesiastici,* 1934, Pos. 515, P.O., fasc. 529, f. 60.

been correct. The election was considered valid. Cardinal Serafino Vannutelli, assisted by Cardinal Agliardi, approached the newly elected with the Gospel in his hands. The entire assembly was in religious silence. Giacomo della Chiesa was still a simple cardinal, but when he answered the ritual question of the cardinal dean with "*accepto*" he became the supreme pontiff of the Catholic Church. Mercier wrote, "Up to that moment he was a cardinal: the Church, by means of the Sacred College, offered him the possibility of becoming the successor of Peter. By pronouncing the word *accepto* the divine mission was accomplished."[983]

The conclave had lasted four days, from August 31 to September 3, 1914, with ten ballots, four per day. As Gasparri recalled, "This election made an impression because it had been the tradition that, for a cardinal to assume the Chair of Peter he had to have under his belt a certain number of years in the cardinalate, whereas the archbishop of Bologna had been a cardinal for little more than three months; in truth, the fact that a man would become pontiff after only one hundred days of the cardinalate is unique in the annals of the Church."[984]

Benedict XV

Of the three cardinals from the United States, only John Murphy Farley of New York took part in the conclave of 1914, being already in Europe.[985] Gibbons and William H. O'Connell, who had left Boston on the ship *Canopi* on August 20, the same day news of the death of Pius X had arrived, arrived in Naples on September 3. Without waiting for the train, O'Connell rented a car and headed at breakneck speed toward Rome.[986] But when he arrived at Velletri, they heard the bells ringing out the election of the new pope.[987] If O'Connell had participated in the conclave,

983 "Notes du cardinal Mercier," p. 222.

984 *Memorie del card. Gasparri*, in AA.EE.SS., cit., ff. 60–61.

985 John Murphy Farley (1842–1918), an Irishman who became a naturalized American citizen, metropolitan archbishop of New York from 1901, was made a cardinal by Pius X in the consistory of November 27, 1911.

986 William Henry O'Connell (1859–1944), formerly bishop of Portland, Maine (1901), was metropolitan archbishop of Boston from August 30, 1907, until his death. Pius X made him a cardinal in the consistory on November 27, 1911. Due to the long transatlantic voyage, he arrived late to the two conclaves of 1914 and 1922, but participated in the conclave that elected Pius XII in 1939.

987 Cf. Dorothy G. Wayman, *Cardinal O'Connell of Boston: A Biography of William Henry O'Connell, 1859–1944,* Farrar, Straus and Young, New York 1955, pp. 172–176; and Gerald P. Fogarty, "La Chiesa negli Stati Uniti nella grande Guerra e a Versailles" [The Church in the United States During the Great War and at Versailles], in Antonio Scottà (ed.), *La Conferenza di pace di Parigi fra ieri e domani (1919–1920),* Rubbettino, Soveria Mannelli 2003, pp. 212–213.

according to his biographer Dorothy Wayman, he would certainly have followed the indications of Merry del Val and followed the fully "Roman" line of action. O'Connell was in fact bound in friendship to Merry del Val since the time he had been rector of the North American College and Merry del Val the president of the Pontifical Academy of Ecclesiastical Nobles and, in his *Memoires*, remembers him as "my dear old friend of former times."[988] In 1906, Merry del Val had arranged his nomination as auxiliary bishop of Boston with the right to succession.[989]

Benedict XV, just like Leo XIII and Pius X, gave the first blessing from the loggia within the basilica, above the main entrance. Dalla Torre recalls that "his slim figure seen up there seemed even slimmer and his face, always pale, seemed made of wax. He responded to the thundering acclamation with that smile that hinted of melancholy which he often wore."[990] "One can say with all due respect," wrote Cardinal O'Connell, "that the new pope had very little in his physical appearance that might recall the majesty of Leo XIII or the sweet amiability of Pius. No, one could not fail to feel a sentiment of profound compassion for this fragile pontiff, who seemed almost crushed under the great tiara that represented the burdens of a triple kingdom."[991] O'Connell was struck by his lack of physical attractiveness and hobbled bearing.[992] Msgr. Della Chiesa certainly did have an ungainly physique that reminded some of that of Giacomo Leopardi.[993]

After the election, Crispolto Crispolti described the new pontiff, "of a tenacious will, acute and ready intelligence, witty, dismissive, brief and rapid in his words, vivacious in his gestures, with a gaze both penetrating and fleeing behind his gold spectacles."[994] According to Carlo Falconi, one of the characteristics that most struck those who approached Della Chiesa was the complete absence in him of any "unction" whatsoever. The man wore his priestly garb, but "in his general behavior and, above all in his words, never recalled, or almost never, only when necessary, the priest or bishop."[995]

988 William O'Connell, *Recollections of Seventy Years*, Houghton Mifflin Company, Boston 1934, p. 229.

989 James Gaffey, "The Changing of the Guard: The Rise of Cardinal O'Connell of Boston," *Catholic Historical Review* 59 (1973), pp. 228–237 (pp. 225–244).

990 Dalla Torre, *Memorie*, pp. 45–46.

991 O'Connell, *Recollections of Seventy Years*, pp. 339–340.

992 Ibid., p. 240.

993 Danilo Veneruso, "La contrastata ascesa di Giacomo della Chiesa verso il pontificato" [The Controversial Ascent of Giacomo della Chiesa to the Pontificate], in Letterio Mauro (ed.) *Benedetto XV. Profeta di pace in un mondo in crisi*, Minerva Edizioni, Bologna 2008, p. 349.

994 Crispolto Crispolti, "Benedetto XV," *L'Illustrazione Italiana* 37 (September 13, 1914), p. 238.

995 Falconi, *I Papi del ventesimo secolo*, p. 118.

Despite this absence of solemnity, he was a pious man who had exercised scrupulously and diligently his pastoral activities as archbishop of Bologna. Della Chiesa had been one of the closest collaborators of Cardinal Rampolla as his personal secretary in Spain and as his minutes keeper in the Secretariat of State, where he had stayed for fourteen years.[996] His mother expressed her regrets with Rampolla for this delay in his career advancement and received this reply: "Just have a little patience: your son will take only a few steps, but they shall be big ones."[997] On April 23, 1901, Rampolla nominated Della Chiesa substitute in the Secretariat of State and, if the former had been elected pope, would probably have nominated the latter secretary of state.[998] The election of Pius X blocked his ascendancy, but Msgr. Della Chiesa continued to frequent the men of the old Leonine guard, in particular, besides Rampolla himself, Cardinal Ferrata and Msgr. Gasparri. During his deposition at the process of beatification of Merry del Val, the canon Francesco Rossi Stockalper stated that "Msgr. Della Chiesa saw in Cardinal Rampolla the pope who should have been and thus did not look kindly upon the servant of God (Merry del Val) in the role of secretary of state. Msgr. Della Chiesa often came out with expressions such as, 'But Cardinal Rampolla would not have done it like that!' But the Servant of God, though aware of this, never complained and continued to treat Msgr. Della Chiesa kindly."[999]

Under Pius X, the two "section heads" of Rampolla's Secretariat of State, Gasparri and Della Chiesa, remained at their posts until 1907, when they were both substituted within the span of a few months. "Their simultaneous termination from the Secretariat of State seemed to seal their friendship and bound them indissolubly for the future," wrote a biographer of Gasparri.[1000] The former, given the merits he had acquired as secretary of the commission for the codification of

[996] Klaus Unterburger, "Da minutante a sostituto della segreteria di Stato" [From Desk Clerk to Substitute Secretary of State], in Cavagnini and Grossi (eds.), *Papa Giacomo della Chiesa nel mondo dell' "inutile strage,"* vol. 1, pp. 61–67; J.-M. Ticchi, "Rampolla, Della Chiesa, Benedetto XV," in ibid., pp. 85–94.

[997] Falconi, *I Papi del ventesimo secolo*, p. 120.

[998] Cf. Ticchi, *Rampolla, Della Chiesa, Benedetto XV*, pp. 85–94. Both Rampolla and Della Chiesa had studied at the Capranica College. They performed their offices with the apostolic nuncio in Madrid before both working in the Secretariat of State.

[999] *Processus informativus ordinarius*, p. 141. Francesco Rossi Stockalper de la Tour of the Barons of Duin (1876–1957), auditor to the nunciature in Vienna, was detested by the Archduke Ferdinand, who stated that as long as he was in Vienna the Curia would be poorly informed (Pastor, *Tagebücher*, p. 574).

[1000] Francesco Maria Taliani, *Vita del cardinal Gasparri, segretario di stato e povero prete [The Life of Cardinal Gasparri, Secretary of State and Poor Priest]*, A. Mondadori, Milan 1938, p. 126.

canon law, was made a cardinal on December 16, 1907, while Della Chiesa was nominated archbishop of Bologna on October 8, 1907, substituting the deceased Cardinal Svampa. The diocese of Bologna and the nunciature of Spain were vacant contemporaneously and Pius X, as he later told Msgr. Parolin, called for Msgr. Della Chiesa to ask him, "Do you prefer the care of souls or Diplomacy? Because the see of Bologna and the nunciature in Spain are both vacant." And Msgr. Della Chiesa replied, "The care of souls, Holy Father." And so Pius X replied, "I shall consecrate you myself; if you had chosen the nunciature of Spain I would have had the secretary of state consecrate you."[1001]

Della Chiesa narrated the episode in a somewhat different manner, making it clear that he would have preferred the nunciature in Madrid to the archdiocese of Bologna. According to Msgr. Alberto Serafini, the nomination as archbishop of Bologna was for Cardinal Della Chiesa "like a bucket of ice-cold water over my head (he told me verbatim and I've never forgotten it)."[1002] He accepted it, nevertheless, without batting an eye. The archdiocese of Bologna was, according to an ancient custom, a titular cardinalate see, but Msgr. Della Chiesa had to wait seven more years for the red biretta, which came during the consistory of May 26, 1914, Pius X's last. His great protector and friend Cardinal Rampolla had died six months earlier and according to Crispolti, "on the eve of the close of the consistory he seemed the least *papabile* of the non-*papabili*."[1003] No one could have foreseen that, one hundred and one days after his admission to the *porporati*, the Sacred College would have made him pope.

From the very beginning, Benedict XV manifested his determination to change the orientation of the Pius pontificate, returning to the "Rampollian" line of governance. On September 3, he named Cardinal Domenico Ferrata secretary of state who, despite his bad health, accepted the appointment. To the Italian prime minister, Antonio Salandra,[1004] who before the conclave had asked him for a prediction, Borgo Police Commissioner Bertini had replied, "Ferrata

[1001] *Pii Papae X. Positio*, p. 157. On the nomination of Msgr. Della Chiesa to the archdiocese of Bologna cf. also Antonio Scottà, *Giacomo della Chiesa arcivescovo di Bologna (1908–1914)*, Rubbettino, Soveria Mannelli 2002, pp. 84–87.

[1002] Mons. Alberto Serafini, *Processus Informativus Ordinarius, Sessio* LIV, vol. 2, p. 413.

[1003] Crispolto Crispolti, "Benedetto XV," p. 239.

[1004] Antonio Salandra (1853–1931), exponent of the liberal-conservative wing, was prime minister from March 21, 1914, to June 18, 1916. Cf. Federico Lucarini, *La carriera di un gentiluomo. Antonio Salandra e la ricerca di un liberalismo nazionale (1875–1922) [The Career of a Gentleman. Antonio Salandra and the Quest for a National Liberalism]*, Il Mulino, Bologna 2012.

pope and Della Chiesa secretary of state."[1005] The results were backward, but the bond between the two cardinals was indestructible.

The pope immediately showed himself firm and demanding with his collaborators: "Capable navigator in the world of curial craftiness," writes Andrea Tornielli, "he controlled every aspect of the life of the Holy See and it was his habit to draw up a report card with grades given at the end of each month to the director of the *L'Osservatore Romano*, Count Giuseppe dalla Torre, and to the editors of the Vatican newspaper."[1006]

Secretary of the Holy Office

Cardinal Merry del Val was granted forty-eight hours to have the Borgia apartments ready for Cardinal Ferrata and transfer his belongings to the lodgings of the archpriest. This episode profoundly struck Msgr. Eugenio Pacelli who, before the conclave of 1939 that elected him pope, had all his belongings quickly packed up, convinced that he would have to leave the rooms he occupied as secretary of state.[1007] When asked the reason for such haste, he replied, "I remember that this is what happened upon the death of Pius X. His secretary of state Cardinal Merry del Val was not given the time to collect his things and his archives. I would not like to experience the sufferings of that man."[1008]

Cardinal Pizzardo[1009] remembered being quite impressed by the humility with which Merry del Val abandoned the rooms he had been using, "to be reduced to a modest apartment in Santa Marta."[1010] "I shall soon be going to my new residence," wrote Merry del Val to Msgr. Broadhead, "the house of the archpriest of St. Peter's, in the Basilica square." Then a touching note about Pius X, "Joe, my heart is fairly broken. I can't get over it. I realized how much I loved him when he had gone. You see, my life was one with him in everything and he was indeed a saint."[1011]

1005 Bertini, *Ai tempi delle guarentigie*, p. 248.

1006 Andrea Tornielli, *La Stampa*, September 1, 2011.

1007 Andrea Tornielli, *Pio XII. Eugenio Pacelli un uomo sul trono di Pietro [Pius XII. Eugenio Pacelli, a Man on the Throne of Peter]*, Mondadori, Milan 2009, p. 62.

1008 Ibid., p. 293.

1009 Giuseppe Pizzardo (1877–1970) was substitute secretary of state from 1921 to 1929, when he was named secretary of the Congregation of Extraordinary Ecclesiastical Affairs, remaining in that post until 1937. Consecrated bishop in 1930, he was made a cardinal by Pius XI in the consistory of December 13, 1937.

1010 *Processus Informativus Ordinarius, Sessio* XCIII, vol. 2, p. 565.

1011 Buehrle, *Merry del Val*, p. 176; Forbes, *Merry del Val*, p. 116.

After the conclave in which he had not been able to participate, Cardinal O'Connell remained in Rome, and recalled, "Understanding well the situation, I dared, immediately after the election of Pope Benedict XV, to say something to my dear old friend Cardinal Merry del Val: a word of hope and kindness. His only reply was, 'I tried to do my best in the role I had the honor to play for eleven difficult and demanding years. I am all too happy now to be relieved of a tension that I doubt I could have endured any further. I shall leave the Vatican without regrets and the tranquility of Santa Marta will be a welcome relief.' And then he added with a pathetic smile that I can still see today, '*Non habemus hic manentem civitatem*' [Here we have no lasting city; Heb 13:14]. I embraced him with affection and admiration that had grown through all the years in which I had the privilege of his friendship."[1012]

On October 10, 1914, the new secretary of state Cardinal Ferrata died after a brief illness in his residence on the Ara Coeli. On October 13, Benedict XV nominated as his primary collaborator Cardinal Pietro Gasparri.[1013] From then on, for the next fifteen years, under two popes, he would be the dominus and the guarantor of the Vatican's ecclesiastical politics. When they walked next to each other through the great Vatican halls, "Della Chiesa, small and contorted like an olive tree, seemed to lean on Gasparri."

The Prefect Bertini recalls Gasparri in this way: "Born in Visso in Norcia, in the land of Spoleto, he bore in his strong limbs the tenacious stamp of his mountains and because his brothers and their ancestors were country merchants and traders of sheep, he was not offended if they called him the 'Sheep Seller' Cardinal."[1014] An untiring worker, throughout the entire pontificate of Benedict XV he held in his fist the Vatican's politics.

On October 14, 1914, the new pope named Cardinal Merry del Val secretary of the Holy Office.[1015] Benedict XV reserved the same treatment for Pius X's secretary of state as Pius X had reserved for Leo XIII's: a treatment in both

[1012] O'Connell, *Recollections of Seventy Years*, p. 342.

[1013] Msgr. Giuseppe De Luca recalls that Pietro Gasparri was defined by many as "the Giolitti of the Church, a man of great expertise, but a man of his trade" ("La figura del card. Pietro Gasparri," in *Il cardinale Pietro Gasparri*, Pontifical Lateran University, Caccia, Rome 1969, p. 69).

[1014] Bertini, *Ai tempi delle Guarentigie*, p. 286. "A Sheep Seller" is what Senator Giulio Andreotti called him in a meeting with Domingo Merry del Val according to the latter.

[1015] AAS, VI, 6 (October 16, 1914), p. 525. The secretaries of the Congregation of the Holy Office, named the Sacred Inquisition until 1908, and the Congregation for the Doctrine of the Faith after 1965, were six: Mariano Rampolla del Tindaro, Domenico Ferrata, Rafael Merry del Val, Donato Raffaele Sbarretti, Giuseppe Pizzardo, and Alfredo Ottaviani.

cases that was most honorable, since the Holy Office, charged with safeguarding the purity of the faith, was the first and most important congregation of the Curia. Merry del Val was the first non-Italian to occupy this post, as he had been as secretary of state.

Rafael Merry del Val was also named a member of various dicasteries of the Curia over the following years: of the Congregation of the Consistory on May 14, 1915; of the Propagation of the Faith on December 14 that same year; of the new congregation *Pro ecclesia orientali* on November 29, 1916; and of the Congregation of Seminaries and Universities on March 11, 1919.

On November 3, 1914, responding to Fr. Frédéric Rouvier who rejoiced over his nomination to the Holy Office, Merry del Val wrote, "Only with great reluctance did I surrender to His Holiness' supplications and accept the heavy responsibility he wished to entrust to me, because I felt a great need to rest and recollect after the years of incessant fatigue and enormous responsibilities. And what can I tell you of the pain that oppresses me and that I shall carry with me my whole life? I lost the Holy Pontiff and Father to whom I gave without reserve all the powers of my soul and whom I loved as one can love only once in one's life. God will look over his Church, but my personal loss is irreparable."[1016]

The room where Merry del Val lived in Santa Marta seemed like a monk's cell. The only ornament was a portrait of Our Lady of Sorrows above his bed and a large photo of Pius X with his autographed dedication. He slept on the old student's bed he had used his entire life, painted black, without springs, with a hard pallet and wool mattress. His apartment included a little dining room and two rooms for guests, one of which was reserved for his secretary Canali.

One of the most important nominations Pope Benedict made was that of his old friend Baron Carlo Monti as unofficial "intermediary" with the Italian government.[1017] On September 6, 1914, just three days after his election, Benedict XV indicated to Prime Minister Salandra that Monti was the one who could

[1016] Letter of Merry del Val to Rouvier, November 3, 1914, in Archives Jésuites, *Dossiers personnels Rouvier,* box 1.

[1017] Baron Carlo Monti (1851–1924) studied at the National College and then at the State University of Genoa along with Giacomo della Chiesa. In 1908, he became general director of the Worship Foundation, dependent on the Ministry of Justice of the Italian State. In 1924, the Holy See purchased from his widow, Baroness Maria Lucchesi, the *Diary* and the Archive of Baron Monti. The *Diary* is preserved in the Historical Archive of the Second Section of the Secretariat of State (documents of an institutional nature in the State Central Archive, the Interior Ministry, the General Directory of the Worship Foundation); the personal and confidential papers from the years 1914–1924 are in the Vatican Apostolic Archive, Religious Foundation (Carte C. M.).

be a confidential liaison on both banks of the Tiber regarding urgent questions of particular importance. Salandra consented and Monti began to frequent the Vatican regularly as a sort of unofficial *charge d'affairs.* As Pollard observes, Monti had the ideal positioning to carry out this task, being general director of the office for Affairs of Worship in the Ministry of Justice, addressing all the questions that had to do with relations between the Church and the Italian state.[1018] During the next seven years of the pontificate, Baron Monti was received in audience by the pope 175 times.

Also among Benedict's first nominations, on September 5, 1914, were Monsignors Camillo Caccia Dominioni, Alberto Arborio Mella di Sant'Elia, Rodolfo Gerlach, and Giuseppe Migone as secret chamberlains to His Holiness. Two days later, he nominated Msgr. Vittorio Amedeo Ranuzzi de'Bianchi as majordomo of His Holiness; Msgr. Riccardo Sanz de Samper as master of His Holiness' chamber, and Msgr. Luigi Misciattelli as vice-prefect of the Sacred Apostolic Palaces and Palatine Prelate; all of them, except the last one, belonging to his entourage.

Benedict XV seems to have confided to Baron Monti that one of the first things he intended, in agreement with Secretary of State Ferrata, was to remove Msgr. Nicola Canali from the office of substitute secretary of state, which Canali had received in 1907 instead of Msgr. Della Chiesa himself.[1019] Della Chiesa was amazed how an "undoubtedly capable person, intelligent and with such lordly manners" like Merry del Val could suffer the influence of Canali, whom he defined as "coarse and boorish."[1020] Canali did not have the allure of Msgr. Merry del Val, but remained ever devoted to him. After announcing to him his removal, the pope proposed to Canali a nunciature of the highest level, which could have opened the path to becoming a cardinal. Msgr. Canali, however, refused the offer to the surprise of the pontiff, and despite his insistence, stated that he preferred to remain in Rome as a simple collaborator to Cardinal Merry del Val. And so he did. But when Msgr. de Samper was promoted to majordomo of His Holiness and the post he had previously occupied as secretary of the Ceremonial

1018 John F. Pollard, *Il Papa sconosciuto. Benedetto XV (1914–1922) e la ricerca della pace [The Unknown Pope. Benedict XV and the Search for Peace]*, San Paolo, Milan 2001, pp. 90–91.

1019 *La conciliazione ufficiosa. Diario del barone Carlo Monti, "incaricato d'affari" del governo italiano presso la Santa Sede (1914–1922) [The Unofficial Conciliation. The Diary of Baron Carlo Monti, "Charge d'Affaires" of the Italian government to the Holy See]*, ed. A. Scottà, 2 vols. Libreria Editrice Vaticana, Vatican City 1997. *Diario 1916*, p. 93.

1020 Ibid., p. 91.

Congregation was left vacant, this dignity was entrusted to Msgr. Canali to allow him to remain at the side of Merry del Val.[1021] In Canali's place as substitute secretary of state, the pope nominated one of his trusted men, Msgr. Federico Tedeschini,[1022] while maintaining (at least until 1917) Msgr. Eugenio Pacelli as undersecretary of state for Extraordinary Affairs.

Benedict XV and the First World War

In the meantime, the war was raging. The death of Foreign Minister Antonio di San Giuliano on October 16, 1914, according to historians, represented for Italy "one of those events that had incalculable consequences."[1023] Prime Minister Salandra proposed to the King appointing to the Foreign Ministry Baron Sidney Sonnino, a representative of the historical right, of Jewish origins though an Anglican in practice.[1024] Nominated foreign minister on November 5, Sonnino was in favor of neutrality during his first months, but in February 1915, changed policy and began pushing Italy toward intervening in the war. The Italian government opened secret negotiations with both the Central Powers and with the Entente, conditioning the decision to intervene, as Salandra said, on the "sacred egoism" of Italian interests.

In masonic circles, the war was seen as an act of national solidarity and as an instrument of self-redemption for the nations. Catholics, like the rest of the country, were divided in interventionist and neutrality camps.

Those who opposed the war, like Msgr. Giovanni Volpi, bishop of Arezzo,[1025] perhaps the most intransigent of the neutralist bishops, were

1021 *Processus Informativus Ordinarius Sessio* CXIII, vol. 3, pp. 803–804.

1022 Federico Tedeschini (1873–1959), ordained a priest in 1896, entered the Secretariat of State under Rampolla in 1900. On March 31, 1921, he was named apostolic nuncio to the Kingdom of Spain and on the following April 30 received the title archbishop of Lepanto, receiving episcopal consecration from the hands of Benedict XV in the Sistine Chapel on May 5, 1921. He was made a cardinal by Pius XI in the consistory of March 13, 1933, and reserved *in pectore*; his name was published in the consistory of December 16, 1935. He remained in Spain with the title of pro-nuncio until June 10, 1936. Pius XII also named him archpriest of the patriarchal Vatican Basilica and major datary.

1023 Gian Enrico Rusconi, *L'azzardo del 1915. Come l'Italia decide la sua guerra [The Wager of 1915. How Italy Decided on its War]*, Il Mulino, Bologna 2009, p. 106.

1024 Baron Sidney Sonnino (1847–1922), after having been prime minister (1906 and 1909–1910), signed the Pact of London (1915) as foreign minister.

1025 Giovanni Volpi (1860–1931), made titular bishop of Dionisiade and auxiliary of Lucca in 1897, was transferred to Arezzo on November 14, 1904. Called to Rome in 1919, he was promoted to the titular archbishopric of Antioch in Pisidia and named canon and vicar of the Basilica of St. Mary Major. He was a supporter of the *Sodalitium pianum* (*Pii X Disquisitio*, p. 234). Since 2000, his remains lie next to those of St. Gemma Galgani in Lucca, as he had requested.

targeted by masonic attacks.[1026] According to Romolo Murri and Luigi Sturzo, founder of Christian Democracy in Italy, the war was promoted as a "powerful purifier" destined to elevate "the value of divine and eternal principles of morality, law, and religion."[1027]

The attitude of the vast majority of bishops was not at variance with that of the Popular Union, which was the nucleus of Catholic Action at the time, and which had at its head in Count Giuseppe dalla Torre. Catholics obeyed the laws, collaborated with local government authorities in facing the demands and difficulties of civil life, and contributed to the work of assistance connected to the state of belligerence.[1028] Giuseppe dalla Torre, thirty years old, enrolled voluntarily as an officer of an artillery unit.

Dalla Torre recalled the words of Benedict XV addressing Cardinal Achille Ratti after his election: "They want to condemn silence. The Vicar of Christ ought not to invoke peace. They will not succeed in sealing my lips. Woe if the Vicar of the Prince of Peace were to remain mute in the hour of the tempest!"[1029]

From his very first public discourse as pontiff, Benedict XV began a tenacious operation of diplomacy in an attempt to convince the great powers to resolve the international questions through negotiation.[1030] In his apostolic discourse *Ubi primum* of September 8, 1914, the pontiff implored all the children of the Church, especially the Lord's ministers, "that they continue, insist, and make every effort both privately with their humble prayers and publicly with frequent supplications, to implore God, arbiter and lord of all things, to remember His

1026 Caterina Ciriello, "Benedetto XV, la guerra e le posizioni dei vescovi italiani" [Benedict XV, the War and the Positions of Italian Bishops], *Anuario de Historia de la Iglesia* 23 (January–December 2014), pp. 52–53 (pp. 41–60).

1027 Emilio Gentile, *L'Apocalisse della modernità [The Apocalyspe of Modernity]*, Oscar Mondadori, Milan 2014, pp. 211–212.

1028 Alberto Monticone, "I vescovi italiani e la Prima guerra mondiale," in G. Rossini (ed.), *Benedetto XV, i cattolici e la Prima guerra mondiale*, pp. 627–659.

1029 Dalla Torre, *Memorie*, p. 30.

1030 Cf. Rossini, *Benedetto XV, i cattolici e la Prima guerra mondiale*; Francis Latour, *La papauté et les problèmes de la paix pendant la première guerre mondiale*, L'Harmattan, Paris-Montréal 1996; Gabriele Paolini, *Offensive di pace. La Santa Sede e la Prima guerra*, Polistampa, Florence 2008; Antonio Scottà, *Papa Benedetto XV. La Chiesa, la Grande Guerra, la pace (1914–1922)*, Edizioni di Storia e Letteratura, Rome 2009; Roberto Morozzo della Rocca, "Benedetto XV e la Prima guerra mondiale," *Annali di Scienze Religiose* 8 (2015), pp. 31–44; Botrugno (ed.), *Inutile strage*; Gabriele Rigano, "Un così necessario dissidio. La Santa Sede e la Conferenza per la Pace: politica religiosa, questione romana e diplomazia internazionale (1914–1919)" [Such a Necessary Disagreement. The Holy See and the Peace Conference: Religious politics, the Roman Question and International Diplomacy], *Storia e Politica. Annali della Fondazione Ugo La Malfa* 32 (2017), pp. 104–134.

mercy and remove the scourge of wrath with which He administers justice for the sins of the nations!"[1031]

On November 1, 1914, in his encyclical *Ad beatissimi,* which set forth the program of his pontificate, Benedict XV stated that the true cause of the "most disastrous war"[1032] was the disappearance from state legal systems of the norms and practices of Christian wisdom, which alone "contained the peace and stability of institutions" and in whose absence civilization was in peril: "the absence from the relation of men of mutual love with their fellow men; the authority of rulers is held in contempt; injustice reigns in relations between the classes of society; the striving for transient and perishable things is so keen, that men have lost sight of the other and more worthy goods they have to obtain."[1033]

In this his first encyclical, after having proposed a return to the spirit of the Gospel, Benedict XV renewed the protest against the status quo created after the occupation in 1870 of Pontifical Rome, but in a more resonating manner than his predecessors. This statement placed in relief the pope's intention to reexamine, on the international level, the Roman Question in the future Peace Conference. On this point, his position resembled that of Cardinal Rampolla, who had always fostered the hope of recovering through diplomatic means the temporal power of the pope.

Article 15 of the Pact of London[1034] demanded that the powers of the Triple Entente [of Great Britian, Russia, and France] "support Italy in opposing any eventual proposal of admission of a representative of the Holy See in the peace negotiations at the end of the present war."[1035] Despite this, the Holy See was counting on the Peace Conference that would inevitably be held at the end of

1031 Benedict XV, Encyclical *Ubi primum,* September 8, 1914, in AAS 6 (1914), pp. 501–502.

1032 Benedict XV, Encyclical *Ad beatissimi apostolorum principis,* November 1, 1914, no. 30, https://www.vatican.va/content/benedict-xv/en/encyclicals/documents/hf_ben-xv_enc_01111914_ad-beatissimi-apostolorum.html.

1033 Ibid., 5.

1034 Formally known as the Treaty of London, this secret agreement of April 26, 1915, aimed at inducing Italy to join World War I on the side of the Entente powers in return for significant territorial gains to Italy, particularly in the Austro-Hungarian Empire.

1035 Roberto Pertici, *Chiesa e Stato in Italia. Dalla Grande Guerra al nuovo Concordato (1914–1984),* Il Mulino, Bologna 2009, p. 43. Cf., more generally, Italo Garzia, *La Questione Romana durante la Prima guerra mondiale,* ESI, Napoli 1981; G. B. Varnier, "Il pontificato di Benedetto XV (1914–1922) e l'inizio di una nuova era nei rapporti tra la Santa Sede e l'Italia," [The Pontificate of Benedict XV and the Beginning of a New Era in Relations Between the Holy See and Italy], in *Aequitas sive Deus. Studies in honor of Rinaldo Bertolino,* Giappichelli, Turin 2011, vol. 2, p. 1107. The minutes of the discussion held on March 29, 1917, are published by F. Margiotta Broglio, "March 1917: uno stato per il Papa" [March 1917: A State for the Pope], *Limes* 3 (1993), pp. 110–122.

the war, regardless of which side was to win it, to place the Roman Question on the international level.

The Congregation for Extraordinary Affairs held a particular assembly in 1915 during which they confronted the theme of the war and its consequences. Cardinal Gasparri requested Cardinal Merry del Val's opinion on the Roman Question. Merry del Val submitted a fifteen-page typed memo[1036] on November 6, 1915, in which he stated that the solution to the controversy with the Italian State should be "a territorial solution, in other words, the possession of Rome with an extension of territory sufficient for ensuring the independence of the pope and his communication with the Catholic world and to render his sovereign liberty beyond debate and visible to the eyes of all."[1037]

Given that such a solution was at the moment impracticable, he had to emphasize the urgency through the work of the Catholic episcopate in this direction. The conclusion was that "from the European Congress or on the occasion of the same, it would be truly necessary and of the greatest advantage to obtain a public and worldwide statement proclaiming: 1) that the current situation of the Roman pontiff is unacceptable, nor can it be considered normal or definitive; and 2) that the Roman Question is of interest to all nations."[1038]

Cardinal Merry del Val did not hide his estimation that it would be difficult to obtain this result, but considered it possible that some governments, perhaps just a few (among them Bavaria, Spain, and Colombia) might make simultaneous declarations to this effect at the Congress or outside of it.

The Allies (Triple Entente) often accused the pope of being under the influence of the Triple Alliance (Central Powers), but the simple fact is that, unlike the Austrian and German empires, the powers of the Entente had very few official contacts with the Holy See. France had interrupted diplomatic relations in 1904. Russia sent an extraordinary representative during the first weeks of the war, while Great Britain did so in December of 1914. Despite this, the Holy See was represented neither in St. Petersburg nor in London. Germany and the Austro-Hungarian Empire, on the other hand, had much closer ties with the Vatican. The apostolic nuncio of Vienna reported to the Austrian ambassador to the Holy See. Although the pope had a nuncio in Munich, and not

1036 AAV, *Spoglio cardinale Domenico Jacobini*, busta 3, fasc. 81, ff. 1–15.

1037 Ibid., f. 2.

1038 Ibid., f. 12.

in Berlin, the Germans were doubly represented in the Vatican. Bavaria was represented by Baron Otto von Ritter von Grünstein[1039] and Prussia by Otto von Mühlberg.[1040] Germany was therefore the only nation to have two diplomatic corps to the Holy See.

On December 17, 1914, Prince Bernhard von Bülow arrived in Rome as Kaiser Wilhelm II's extraordinary envoy.[1041] An intense diplomatic clash was played out during the winter of 1915 between Bülow and the ambassador of the French Third Republic, Camille Barrère, legate of the Grand Orient who pushed for Italy's entrance into the war on the side of the Entente.

Pressure from the street began to grow, incited by a lively minority of interventionists at the head of which were the poet Gabriele D'Annunzio and Benito Mussolini, who had left his role as director of the socialist daily *Avanti* to establish, in November 1914, *Il Popolo d'Italia,* financed by French Quay d'Orsay and some Italian industrialists interested in increasing military expenditures by entering the war.[1042]

Foreign Minister Sonnino, for his part, played both sides unscrupulously. On April 26, 1915, when Italy was still fundamentally allied with Austria and Germany, he entered the Treaty of London unbeknownst to the Italian parliament. This secret agreement between Italy and England committed Italy to entering the war within a month alongside the Powers of the Entente.[1043] The Sonnino government committed Italy to entering the war without even having consulted the head of the joint chiefs of staff of the army, Count Luigi Cadorna, who learned of Italy's obligation to join the battlefield alongside the Entente Powers just twenty days before the fateful date.[1044] During the night of May 23, the Italian army, composed of 1,058,000 foot soldiers and 31,000 officers,

1039 Baron Otto von Ritter von Grünstein (1864–1940), beginning in 1909, was extraordinary envoy and plenipotentiary minister of Bavaria to the Holy See and from 1920, representative of the Free State of Bavaria, with its See in Lugano.

1040 Otto von Mühlberg (1843–1934) was extraordinary minister of Prussia to the Holy See from 1907 to 1919.

1041 Prince Bernhard von Bülow (1849–1929), ambassador in Rome during the 1890s, then foreign minister and Reich chancellor from 1900 to 1909, married Maria Beccadelli of the princes of Camporeale, daughter of Lady Laura Acton, the second wife of the statesman Marco Minghetti. In 1906, he purchased Villa Malta, at Porta Pinciana, today belonging to the Jesuits, making it the center of their intense diplomatic activity.

1042 Renzo De Felice, *Mussolini il rivoluzionario: 1883–1920,* Einaudi, Turin 1995, pp. 302–303.

1043 Mario Toscano, *Il Patto di Londra. Storia diplomatica dell'intervento italiano, 1914–1915,* Zanichelli, Bologna 1934.

1044 Giorgio Petracchi, *1915. L'Italia entra in guerra,* Della Porta Editori, Pisa 2015, p. 207.

crossed the Piave River to reach the border with Austria. Of these, 650,000 would never return.

On May 8, *L'Osservatore Romano,* recalling the Austrian concessions that had come to the aid of Italian aspirations, implored Italy not to succumb to a sinister occult power, with a clear reference to the role of Freemasonry in the development of events.[1045] At noon that day, the "Supplication" to the Virgin Mary composed by Bartolo Longo was recited for the first time by Benedict XV and his closest collaborators.[1046]

Meanwhile, September 27, 1915, a few months after Italy joined the hostilities, a powerful explosion in a munitions depot in the port of Taranto destroyed the left side of the armored ship *Benedetto Brin,* which sank along with half of its crew: 456 sailors died. On August 2, 1916, in the same port of Taranto, another explosion gutted the armored ship *Leonardo da Vinci,* dragging 249 sailors to the bottom. The government conducted a thorough investigation that brought to light the so-called Gerlach Case, implicating possible responsibilities in the Vatican.

The Gerlach Case

Rudolf von Gerlach began his career as a young petty officer in the Bavarian Army.[1047] Around 1906, at the age of twenty, he left the army to move to Paris with a ballerina.[1048] In 1907, his family sent him to Mexico City where he converted to Catholicism under the influence of the local archbishop. After his return to Germany, he studied philosophy and theology in Freiburg, and was ordained

1045 "Nell'attesa angosciosa," *L'Osservatore Romano,* May 8, 1915.

1046 Bartolo Longo (1841–1926), founder and benefactor of the Sanctuary of the Blessed Virgin Mary of the Rosary of Pompei, was beatified by John Paul II on October 26, 1980.

1047 On Rudolf von Gerlach (1886–1945), cf. Hartmut Benz, *Prälat Rudolf von Gerlach: Gewogen — und für zu leicht befunden (Teil 1),* "Römische Quartal Schrift für Christliche Altertumskunde und Kirchengeschichte," 116/3–4 (2021), pp. 255– 279; David Alvarez, *Spies in the Vatican: Espionage & Intrigue from Napoleon to the Holocaust,* University Press of Kansas; Annibale Paloscia, *Benedetto fra le spie. Negli anni della Grande guerra un intrigo tra Italia e Vaticano, [Benedict among the Spies. In the Years of the Great War, Intrigue Between Italy and the Vatican],* Editori Riuniti, Rome 2007; F. Latour, "Un espion du Kaiser au Vatican," *Guerres mondiales et conflits contemporains* 232 (2007), pp. 129–141; Giovanni Fasanella, Antonella Grippo, *1915,* Sperling & Kupfer, Milano 2014, pp. 131–164. Cf. the material preserved in AAV, Secr. State, *Guerra (1914–1918),* fasc. 10, fol. 174r and in AA.EE.SS., III, *Italia,* Pos. 894, ff. 323–328 and Pos. 903, f. 331.

1048 In his *Memoires* on March 11th, 1917, Gerlach stated he had never been a Bavarian official, but an "Offizieraspirant" in Saarburg in Alsace (AA.EE.SS., Italia 1917, Pos. 894, fasc. 324, f. 480). He did not say, however, that he could not continue his military career "because he was not considered suitable and because he had committed several careless mistakes," as testified by Msgr. Giuseppe Marchetti Selvaggiani (AA.EE.SS., Italia 1917, Pos. 894, fasc. 325, f. 60).

a priest in the nunciature in Munich by the papal nuncio in Bavaria, Frühwirth. With the aid of the bishop of Trent, Celestino Endrici,[1049] he was admitted to the Academy of Ecclesiastical Nobles, and thanks to the support of influential benefactors, among whom the archbishop of Bologna, Giacomo della Chiesa, who was taken by his attractive ways and diplomatic abilities, climbed rapidly in the ecclesiastical hierarchy.[1050]

In 1914, after the death of Pius X, he accompanied Della Chiesa to the conclave that ended with the latter's election to the papacy. The very day of his enthronement, the new pope nominated him to the role of secret chamberlain, despite having been discouraged by Cardinal Merry del Val, who was familiar with the extravagant and unedifying lifestyle that the priest was leading in Rome. Count Francis de Salis,[1051] representative of the British government, in a report sent to London, wrote that "there seem to be very few doubts about the fact that he was a swashbuckler without scruples. Cardinal Merry del Val warned the pope against him before the conclave of 1914 had even ended, and his opinion was supported by Msgr. Zonghi,[1052] the rector of his college, as well as by Msgr. Maglione,[1053] the nuncio in Switzerland at the time who had worked with the Secretariat of State."[1054]

Gerlach entered the pope's closest entourage: he was the head chamberlain and controlled all who had access to Benedict in the papal antechamber. But above all, he was the pope's counselor in German, Austrian, and Swiss affairs. When, in April 1915, the leader of the Catholic Center Party, Mathias Erzberger,[1055] arrived in Rome, Gerlach became the intermediary between the politician and the Secretariat of State, creating in this way a parallel diplomacy to that of the German and Austrian diplomatic representatives to the Holy

1049 Celestino Endrici (1866–1940) was bishop (1904) and later archbishop (1929) of Trent.

1050 Paloscia, *Benedetto fra le spie*, pp. 27–28.

1051 Sir John Francis Charles, Count of Salis-Soglio (1864–1939), was the extraordinary envoy and plenipotentiary minister in the Netherlands (1896–1908) and to the Holy See (1916–1922).

1052 L'arcivescovo Giovanni Maria Zonghi (1847–1941) was president of the Pontifical Ecclesiastical Academy from 1914 until his death.

1053 Luigi Maglione (1877–1944), after having worked in the Secretariat of State, was nuncio in Switzerland. He was made a cardinal by Pius XI and was named secretary of state by Pius XII in 1939.

1054 *Anglo-Vatican Relations, 1914–1939: Confidential Annual Reports of the British Ministers to the Holy See*, ed. Thomas E. Hachey, G. K. Hall, Boston 1972, p. 19.

1055 On Mathias Erzberger (1875–1921), leader of the left wing of the German Center Party, cf. *Erlebnisse im Weltkrieg*, Deutsche Verlags-Anstalt, Stuttgart-Berlin 1920; Carlotta Benedetti, "Le carte Erzberger," in *Dall'Archivio Segreto Vaticano*; Various texts, essays and inventory, Vatican Secret Archive, Vatican City 2014, pp. 3–103.

See.[1056] Erzberger was also in close contact with Baron Franz von Stockhammern, who in September 1914 was assigned to the Bavarian legation in Rome with the task of gathering information and financing pro-German propaganda.[1057] The English minister to the Holy See, Sir Henry Howard,[1058] was informed by his sources that Stockhammern usually organized private meetings with influential exponents of the Curia at the Hotel de Russie.[1059] When the war broke out, the German and Austrian embassies to the Holy See were transferred to Switzerland where Stockhammern continued to hold the strings of a spy network that saw in Gerlach one of its main collaborators.

The German prelate's attendance upon German and Austrian diplomats attracted the attention of Italian authorities. Beginning in 1914, the general director of Public Security of the Interior Ministry, Giacomo Vigliani,[1060] activated the police commissioner of the Borgo, Bertini, in collecting information about Rudolf Gerlach who, according to some notifications that had reached the prime minister, was pointed out as an agent of Austro-German espionage. Foreign Minister Sidney Sonnino wrote in his *Diary* that, according to the British ambassador in Rome, James Rennell Rodd, Gerlach was "one of Germany's most dangerous agitators."[1061]

Italian counter-espionage considered Gerlach to be involved in sabotage activities that had led to the sinking of the two ships of the Italian Navy. For this reason, already on May 29, 1915, the head of the prime minister's cabinet transmitted the following order to police headquarters: "Msgr. Gerlach, a German subject, known for spying in favor of the Austro-Hungarian Empire, resides to this day in the Vatican. He must be arrested the moment he sets foot outside the Vatican."[1062]

1056 Cf. Stefano Trinchese, "I tentativi di pace della Germania e della Santa Sede nella I Guerra Mondiale: l'attività del deputato Erzberger e del diplomatico Pacelli (1916–1918)" [Attempts at Peace by Germany and the Holy See During the First World War: The Activity of Deputy Erzberger and the Diplomat Pacelli], *Archivum historiae pontificiae* 35 (1997), pp. 225–255.

1057 Franz Xaver von Stockhammern (1873–1930) worked in Bern beginning in 1915 and was placed at the service of the Reich Chancellor for special charges.

1058 Sir Henry Howard (1843–1921) was extraordinary envoy and plenipotentiary minister in the Netherlands (1896–1908) and to the Holy See (1914–1916). Cf. Angelo Martini, "L'invio della missione inglese presso la Santa Sede all'inizio della Prima guerra mondiale" [The Sending of the English Mission to the Holy See at the Beginning of the First World War], *La Civiltà Cattolica* 118 (1967), q. 2797, pp. 330–344.

1059 Sir Henry Howard, *Diario*, cit. in Alvarez, *Spie in Vaticano*, p. 110.

1060 Giacomo Vigliani (1862–1942), three times Director General of Public Security in the Interior Ministry, between 1911 and 1922, was named senator for life in 1920.

1061 Sidney Sonnino, *Diario 1914–1916*, Laterza, Bari 1972, p. 136.

1062 ACS, MI, DGPS, UCI, buste 4–5, f. 63.

When the Italian authorities informed the Holy See of their suspicions, Benedict XV and Cardinal Gasparri, his secretary of state, indignantly rejected the accusations and made no investigations into the matter. Cardinal Merry del Val, who had his own informers, asked that the question be thoroughly investigated,[1063] but was blocked by Gasparri and the substitute secretary Tedeschini.[1064] In December 1916, Baron Monti confirmed to the pope the existence of an order for the arrest of Gerlach, kept on hold by the government, and that it would be prudent to send Gerlach out of Rome as soon as possible.[1065] In the end, Benedict conceded. On January 4, 1917, Monti wrote in his diary that he had "arranged everything regarding the departure of Msgr. Gerlach with commander Vigliani, general director of public security."[1066] On the evening of January 6, 1917, Gerlach left the Vatican heading for Switzerland, furnished with a passport issued by the Swiss embassy.

The scandal broke out immediately after, and on February 22, 1917, an investigative commission unveiled the existence of a network of spies making use not only of Gerlach but also of Giuseppe Ambrogetti, personal secretary and treasurer of Benedict XV.[1067] The commission remanded the verdict to the judgment of the Territorial Military Tribunal of Rome. On March 1, 1917, Secretary of State Gasparri requested Gerlach to shed "full light" on "the charges that appear most serious and would lead one to conclude that Your Lordship, abusing the position His Holiness entrusted You and the safety conferred by Italian laws, has stained yourself with the crime of treason to the harm of the nation that hosted you."[1068] Gerlach replied to him on March 11, with a long and impassioned memo,[1069] which Cardinal Gasparri forwarded on March 19 to Baron Monti, feigning to have welcomed the German Monsignor's claims.[1070] According to what Monti wrote in his diary on May 19, "The Holy Father holds that there is proof neither of treason nor of espionage and

1063 Cf. an informational note of the UCI in ACS, MI UCI, busta, 23, f. 84. Bertini to the prefect of Police in Rome, November 25, 1914, A4, Espionage, Gerlach, busta 3, f. 39.

1064 Tedeschini to the president of the Military Tribunal, May 17, 1917, AAV, Secr. of State, rubr. 244, f. 99.

1065 Monti, *Diario 1916*, December 28, pp. 137–138.

1066 Ibid., January 4, 1917, p.3.

1067 Giuseppe Ambrogetti, participating secret chamberlain, became secretary and economic clerk under Benedict XV who made him Knight Commander of Pope St. Sylvester.

1068 AA.EE.SS., *Italia 1917*, Pos. 894, fasc. 324, ff. 40–41.

1069 Ibid., ff. 31–34.

1070 Ibid., fasc. 326, ff. 3–6.

that therefore, Gerlach should not be condemned because the condemnation would be unjust: moreover, to be completely thorough, there should be absolution for insufficiency of evidence."[1071]

Tried for contempt of court, Rudolf von Gerlach was accused of espionage on behalf of Germany and the Austro-Hungarian Empire and of having financed "defeatist" associations and newspapers. He was also suspected, but not accused, of having been an accomplice in 1915 and 1916 in the sabotage of the two Italian warships. Msgr. Tedeschini, vice-secretary of state, testified on his behalf, while Gerlach proclaimed his innocence from Switzerland.[1072] The sentence was given on July 3, 1917. Gerlach was condemned to life in prison, although the military tribunal excluded any responsibility on the part of the Holy See.[1073]

The pope never believed in the guilt of his collaborator, thus arousing spiteful voices. He wrote an affectionate letter to him on July 4, 1917, in which he reassured him of his "old, unchanged affection" and confirmed the absolute certainty of his "profound innocence."[1074]

Despite this, on April 29, 1924, a few years after the death of Benedict XV, Gerlach sent the Holy See a "menacing letter" in which he threatened to publish documents he had taken with him to Switzerland that could have compromised Benedict XV and the Holy See. Secretary of State Gasparri appointed the Capuchin Fr. Cölestin von Deggendorf to get in touch with Gerlach to foil the threat.[1075] The meeting took place in the castle of Kuttenplan of Count Walter Berchem-Haimhausen.[1076] Gerlach accepted not to publish the documents and asked to be laicized. He abandoned the priestly life and adopted a worldly style of life. He disappeared, although it seems he died in 1945 in Great Britain, where he lived under a false name, collaborating with His Majesty's secret services.[1077]

1071 Monti, *Diario 1917*, January 4, 1917, pp. 52–53.

1072 Tedeschini to the president of the Military Tribunal, May 17, 1917, AAV, Secr. State, Guerra 1914–1918, rubr. 244, f. 99, in Alvarez, *Spies in the Vatican*, p. 118.

1073 Cf. the sentence of life imprisonment in AAV, S.d.S., rubr. 244, fasc. 9, p. 135.

1074 Monti, *Diario*, p. 125; Paloscia, *Benedetto fra le spie*, pp. 152–154.

1075 AA.EE.SS., Report of Fr. Cölestin von Deggendorf, in *Italia 1917*, Pos. 894, fasc. 328, ff. 20–24. Fr. Cölestin Schwaighofer von Deggendorf O. F. M. (1863–1934) was a theologian and consultor to several Roman Congregations.

1076 Count Walter Berchem-Haimhausen (1880–1967), diplomat and officer, was arrested by the Gestapo for having participated in the Putsch against Hitler on July 20, 1944, but was able to escape.

1077 Alvarez, *Spies in the Vatican*, p.121; Paloscia, *Benedetto fra le spie [Benedict Among the Spies]*, pp. 160– 161.

The War Years

Baron Monti's diary refers to hearsay that the apartment of Cardinal Merry del Val in Santa Marta was called "the Little Vatican" because it was considered to be the center of discontent toward Benedict XV. Historians who document these voices neglect, however, the service that Merry del Val rendered to Benedict XV, above all as secretary of the Holy Office and archpriest of St. Peter's Basilica, as well as the pope's high regard for him.

The life of Merry del Val was intense and regulated. "My programme this week," he wrote an old friend, "was as follows: Monday, Congregation for Oriental Churches; Tuesday, Congregation of Rites; Wednesday, Holy Office; Thursday, Consistorial; Friday, Audience; Saturday, Holy Office; and, as one has to go prepared to these meetings, my time and powers are fully absorbed."[1078]

Romans and foreigners flocked to St. Peter's not only for the beauty of the ceremonies, but also to admire the solemnity of his person. "Anyone who ever had the privilege of seeing the Cardinal's majestic figure at the altar raising his hand to impart a blessing or heard his high and solemn voice in the chant of the sacred liturgy, could never forget it," recalled the director of the Vatican Museums, Bartolomeo Nogara.[1079] The writer Anel Bonnard, describing the Office of *Tenebrae* on Holy Wednesday celebrated in the apse behind the High Altar of St. Peter's, wrote that "the cardinal's bearing was admirable. He sustains the entire solemnity of the ceremony on his own; while the canons cough, blow their noses, chatter among themselves, and the seminarians cannot resist looking back at the galleries, he is not distracted for a moment, never raising his eyes from his book."[1080]

Cardinal Canali told that an English gentleman, John Fellowes, converted to Catholicism by Merry del Val, delayed making his renunciation because of some doubts he still had on the Real Presence of Jesus in the consecrated Host. "But during the feast of Corpus Domini, after having seen and admired

[1078] Buehrle, *Merry del Val*, p. 206; Forbes, *Merry del Val*, p. 131.

[1079] "Il cardinale Merry del Val," *L'Illustrazione Vaticana* 11 (1931), pp. 27–32; cited in Dal-Gal, *Merry del Val*, p. 58. Bartolomeo Nogara (1868–1954), Italian archaeologist and philologist, was the director general of the pontifical museums and galleries. On January 9, 1925, Card. Merry del Val named him director of the Petrine Museum.

[1080] Anel Bonnard, *Rome*, Hachette, Paris 1931, p. 40. Abel Bonnard (1883–1968), novelist and essayist, was a member of the French Academy and then Minister of National Education in the collaborationist Vichy government.

how, with great recollection and spirit of faith, Cardinal Merry del Val carried the Blessed Sacrament into St. Peter's Basilica, he decided to abjure, thinking that if a man of such worth and high dignity displayed so much ardor of faith and profound piety, he could have no doubt about the Real Presence of Jesus in the Eucharist."[1081]

During the war, the cardinal received news of his father's death in San Sebastian, Spain, on August 29, 1917, at the age of eighty-six. His thoughts went to his aged mother. "I dream of going to England soon," he wrote to Msgr. Broadhead in May 1919, "but I fear it may only be a dream this year. I want to meet my old Mother, now eighty years of age, whom I have not seen for five years, and my brother, from whom I have been separated for over sixteen. If we could arrange a meeting in England, I might get a few days at Ushaw, e.g., in September. But travelling is still a problem and public events may prevent my going any distance from Rome."[1082]

In April of the same year, he wrote a nun in England, "We can live for God only to the extent that we die to this world and to ourselves; and this is the only true life, which is in Him, and it is eternal."[1083]

One of the most profound sufferings for Cardinal Merry del Val during the long war of 1914–1918 was the fate of his youth from Trastevere who were called to arms. They left in 1915 accompanied by the blessing of their "Angel of Mercy" or "St. Raphael," as they called him, who exhorted them to fulfill their duty as Christians and as soldiers.[1084] The cardinal followed them individually for four continuous years, comforting them and helping them wherever they were, in the trenches, in the backlines, or in prison camps. In 1917, he secretly sold in London one of his pastoral rings to be able to help them materially as well as spiritually.

After the war, he visited the battlefields, seeking the places were the fighting had been most intense and tenacious. On Col di Lana, or "Hill of Blood," a mountain of two thousand meters altitude on the border between the Kingdom of Italy and the Austro-Hungarian Empire, Merry del Val wandered, gathering the unburied bones of the fallen and blessing the cemeteries covered with crosses.

[1081] *Processus Informativus Ordinarius, Sessio* CXI, p. 679. The wife of John Fellowes, after Cardinal Merry del Val's death, came to Rome and established a foundation to provide electrical lighting of his tomb, candles, and a daily Mass to be celebrated on a nearby altar.

[1082] Buehrle, *Merry del Val*, pp. 204–205; Forbes, *Merry del Val*, pp. 130–131.

[1083] Ibid, p. 135.

[1084] Dal-Gal, *Merry del Val*, p. 160.

THE PEACE CONFERENCE

On Sunday, May 13, 1917, in the Sistine Chapel, Benedict XV elevated Msgr. Eugenio Pacelli to the dignity of archbishop with the title of archbishop of Sardi *in partibus* and nominated him apostolic nuncio to Bavaria. Attending the ceremony were Cardinals Merry del Val, Gasparri, Vannutelli, and Frühwirth of the pontifical court, as well as numerous bishops representing the diplomatic corps and Roman patricians.

That same day, Our Lady appeared to three shepherd children in Fatima, entrusting them with a message for humanity. Benedict XV did not know of this message, which shed supernatural light on the terrible events of 1914–1918.[1085] He was certainly informed, however, of the magnificent miracle of the sun that occurred in the Cova da Iria on October 13, 1917.[1086]

The exhaustion of the belligerents, the horrors of war, and the uncertainty of final victory had spread proposals and hopes for peace beginning in the winter of 1916 and the first months of 1917, in both camps. Even the Holy See undertook an intense diplomatic effort, though without concrete results. At the end of May 1917, attempts at a "separate peace" with France and England, promoted by Emperor of Austria Karl I, through the mediation of his brother-in-law Prince Sixtus of Bourbon-Parma, fell through.

Since 1915 Benedict XV had insisted on the necessity of beginning peace negotiations, but on August 1, 1917, with his exhortation *Dés le dèbut*, he again invited the heads of the belligerent powers to open discussions of peace capable of putting an end to the "useless slaughter."[1087] The pope proposed the

1085 The canonical diocesan process begun in 1922 by the bishop of Leiria, José Alves Correia da Silva (1872–1957), concluded in 1930 with the promulgation on April 14 of his pastoral letter in which he officially allowed the veneration of Our Lady of Fatima. The Holy Office was not directly involved concerning the apparitions of Fatima and the relative veneration. In 1932, there appeared the book *The Wonders of Fatima* by Fr. Luigi Gonzaga de Fonseca S. J. (1878–1963), professor at the Pontifical Biblical Institute in Rome (Propaganda Mariana, Casale Monferrato 1932) which was the first serious work on the subject.

1086 The journalist Avelino de Almedia (1873–1932), editor in chief of *O Século*, the socialist daily paper of Lisbon, who had up to that moment ridiculed the events, wrote in his newspaper on October 15, 1917, "The immense crowd turned towards the sun, that shone from behind the clouds at its zenith. The star seemed like a disk of dark silver and it was possible to gaze at it without the least difficulty. It did not burn or blind. One might have said an eclipse was taking place. But then a colossal shout arose from the spectators and from those standing near one heard shouts of 'Miracle, miracle! Wonder, oh wonder!'"

1087 Benedict XV, Exhortation *Dès le début. Aux chefs des peuples bélligérants*, August 1, 1917, https://www.vatican.va/content/benedict-xv/fr/apost_exhortations/documents/hf_ben-xv_exh_19170801_des-le-debut.html.

mediation of the Holy See to this effect. "The fundamental point must be that the moral force of law takes over from the material force of arms. Thus, a just accord of all for the simultaneous and reciprocal decrease of armaments according to norms and guarantees is to be established, to a degree necessary and sufficient for maintaining the public order of each individual state; and in substitution for weapons, the institution of arbitration with the greatest pacifying function, according to the norms to be agreed upon and the sanctions to be established against the state that refuses to submit the international questions to arbitration or to accept its decisions."[1088]

The idea of a tribunal of arbitration to resolve international conflicts was fully in line with the views expressed by Leo XIII and Cardinal Rampolla, but the initiative did not have the results the pope had expected. The Italian government feared that the Holy See might obtain, in an international forum, the reopening of the debate on the Roman Question. Minister Sonnino had forced the inclusion into the Pact of London a clause which, in exchange for Italy's entrance into the war, excluded the Holy See from every representation in the end of the conflict.[1089]

In February, revolts broke out in Russia that led to the abdication of Czar Nicholas II and to a profound regime change. In October, the Bolshevik Party of Lenin and Trotsky took power in Russia, establishing a bloody "dictatorship of the proletariat." On December 1, 1917, the Stefani Agency broadcast a telegram dated St. Petersburg, November 28, 1917, in which, following the publication of secret documents by the Bolshevik government, the Pact of London was brought to light, foretelling the opposition of Italy to any diplomatic move by representatives of the Holy See in view of a peace accord.[1090] Discouraged, Benedict XV made no further attempts for the remainder of the

1088 Ibid., p. 973. On the note of the belligerent powers of August 1917, cf. M. de Leonardis, "San Pio X, Benedetto XV: i loro tentativi di pace nel contesto politico europeo" [St. Pius X, Benedict XV: Their Attempts at Peace in the European Political Context], in Botrugno (ed.), *Inutile Strage*, pp. 41–47.

1089 Enrico Serra, "La Nota del 1 agosto 1917 e il governo italiano: qualche osservazione," [The Note of August 1, 1917 and the Italian Government: Several Observations], in Giorgio Rumi (ed.), *Benedetto XV e la pace — 1918*, Morcelliana, Brescia 1990, pp. 49–61.

1090 For a detailed reconstruction of the controversies aroused by the news, cf. Historicus (Arturo Colletti), *Dalla Triplice Alleanza al Patto di Londra (20 maggio 1882–26 aprile 1915) [From the Triple Alliance to the Pact of London (May 20, 1882 — April 26, 1915)]*, Tip. Lemurio, Acquapendente 1920, pp. 100–120. Freemasonry declared itself openly against the participation of the Holy See, in the person of Grand Master Nathan. Cf. Gian Biagio Furiozzi, *Massoneria e politica*, Morlacchi, Perugia 2012, pp. 115–123.

conflict, but set the objective of the participation of the Holy See in the future Peace Conference, which seemed an ideal occasion to internationalize the Roman Question, still open between the Holy See and Italy.[1091]

In October 1918, the Congregation for Extraordinary Ecclesiastical Affairs, following the advice of Cardinal Merry del Val, decided to appoint Cardinal Mercier, the Belgian primate, as spokesman for a request of the worldwide episcopate in favor of the liberty and independence of the papacy, to be presented to the Peace Conference by means of this declaration: "Catholics of the world, dissatisfied with the condition in which the Holy See currently finds itself, invite the powers to declare that they take interest in the situation of the Roman pontiff, August Head of millions of their subjects, and that, concerned to ensure peace among peoples in the best possible manner under this aspect as well, desire that the person of the pope be always respected and safeguarded, and the full independence of his spiritual governance over the Catholics of every nation guaranteed."[1092]

On November 4, 1918, with the armistice of Villa Giusti, the Austro-Hungarian Empire capitulated. The German capitulation followed on November 11. In January 1919, the Peace Conference assembled in Paris with the task of reconstructing Europe after the profound disasters of the long conflict. Three empires — the Austrian, Russian, and Turkish — were suppressed.

An Italian delegation, guided by Prime Minister Vittorio Emanuele Orlando,[1093] along with his foreign minister, Sidney Sonnino, participated in the conference. The pope sent Msgr. Cerretti to Paris where he had a meeting

1091 Cf. I Garzia, *La Questione Romana durante la Ia guerra mondiale [The Roman Question During the First World War]*, Edizioni Scientifiche Italiane, Naples 1981, pp. 164–168; Giuseppe Maria Croce, "Le Saint-Siège et la Conférence de la paix (1919). Diplomatie d'Église et diplomaties d'État," *Mélanges de l'École française de Rome, Italie et Méditerranée* 2 (1997), pp. 793–823; Latour, *La papauté*, pp. 221–237; Americo Miranda, "Il papa non "ammesso tra le grandi potenze." Benedetto XV e l'esclusione della Santa Sede dalla Conferenza di pace di Parigi" [The Pope Not "Admitted among the Great Powers." Benedict XV and the Exclusion of the Holy See from the Peace Conference in Paris], *Rivista di Storia e Letteratura Religiosa* 25 (2009), pp. 341–367; Riganò, "Un così necessario dissidio," pp. 104–139.

1092 Hand written manuscript of the discussion, AA.EE.SS., III, Rs, Session 1224, November 3, 1918. Merry del Val held that too much should not be requested, but neither too little. According to the former secretary of state, receiving a negative response from the Peace Conference was the equivalent of burying the question forever: for this reason they should ask for a minimum that could not be refused. Cf. Riganò, "Un così necessario dissidio," p. 125.

1093 Vittorio Emanuele Orlando (1860–1952) was prime minister from October 30, 1917 to June 23, 1919.

with Orlando in June with the aim of setting in motion a solution to the Roman Question.[1094] The Vatican representative submitted to Orlando a memo prepared by secretary of state Gasparri, but Vittorio Emanuele III had no intention at that moment of modifying the laws regulating relations between Italy and the Holy See.

The principles and criteria for reestablishing peace in Europe and the world were those enunciated in American President Wilson's "Fourteen Points." In them were expressed generous aspirations of solidarity, freedom, and the self-determination of the nations. Benedict XV was not able to add his contribution to the elaboration of the Peace Treaty, but Wilson's Fourteen Points given to the American Senate were not antithetical to his pontifical exhortation of August 1, 1917.[1095] In the encyclical *Pacem, Dei munus pulcherrimum* of May 23, 1920, the pope seemed to accept, though with some reservation, the collaboration of the nascent League of Nations.[1096]

Benedict XV and Modernism

In his first encyclical *Ad beatissimi apostolorum*, after having illustrated the great merits for the Church of his predecessor, of which "grateful posterity will preserve the memory," Benedict XV outlined his program of governance, exhorting: "We must devote our earnest endeavors to appease dissension and strife, of whatever character, among Catholics.... There is no need of adding any qualifying terms to the profession of Catholicism: it is quite enough for each one to proclaim 'Christian is my name and Catholic my surname,' only let him endeavor to be in reality what he calls himself."[1097] This passage was read as a condemnation of anti-modernist Catholics who defined themselves "integralists."

However, the pope renewed "in its broadest extension" the condemnation of the "monstrous errors of 'modernism,' which our predecessor rightly declared to be 'the synthesis of all heresies.'"

[1094] Cf. Bonaventura Cerretti, "La soluzione della Questione romana nelle conversazioni fra l'on. Orlando e mons. Cerretti a Parigi nel giugno del 1919" [The Solution to the Roman Question in the Conversations between Hon. Orlando and Msgr. Cerretti in Paris in June 1919], *Life and Thought* (June 1929), pp. 401–417; Latour, *La papauté*, pp. 244–251.

[1095] Benedict XV, Exhortation *Dès le début*, pp. 254–259.

[1096] Benedict XV, Encyclical *Pacem, Dei munus pulcherrimum*, May 23, 1920, in AAS, 12 (1920), pp. 209–218.

[1097] Benedict XV, *Ad beatissimi apostolorum*, nos. 20, 22, 24.

> Since this plague is not yet entirely stamped out, but lurks here and there in hidden places, we exhort all to be carefully on their guard against any contagion of the evil, to which we may apply the words Job used in other circumstances: "It is a fire that devoureth even to destruction, and rooteth up all things that spring" (*Job* xxxi. 12). Nor do we merely desire that Catholics should shrink from the errors of modernism, but also from the tendencies or what is called the spirit of modernism. Those who are infected by that spirit develop a keen dislike for all that savors of antiquity and become eager searchers after novelties in everything: in the way in which they carry out religious functions, in the ruling of Catholic institutions, and even in private exercises of piety.[1098]

No practical consequences came of these declarations of principle, however. Four months after the death of Pius X, Msgr. Eudoxe Mignot,[1099] archbishop of Albi, and one of the initiators of modernism,[1100] presented to Cardinal Ferrata, secretary of state of the newly elected Benedict XV, a *Memorial* in which he ferociously attacked the movement of anti-modernist reaction promoted by Pius X and invited the Holy See to assume a policy of "reconciliation" with modernists.[1101] His suggestions were, in part, received thanks to the pragmatism of Cardinal Gasparri, Ferrata's successor as secretary of state, which earned the title of "Third Party" along the line followed by Benedict XV and his secretary of state, between modernists and anti-modernists.

On March 12, 1915, the director of the Christian Democrat newspaper *Düsseldorfer Tagblatt*, Heinz Brauweiler,[1102] a representative of the "Cologne School" defending inter-confessionalism among Christian unions, denounced to the German authorities in occupied Belgium the existence of a secret

1098 Ibid., no. 25.

1099 Eudoxe-Irénée Mignot (1842–1918), bishop of Fréjus in 1890 and archbishop of Albi in 1899, was the friend and protector of Loisy and Marc Sangnier. Cf. Louis- Pierre Sardella, *Msgr Eudoxe Irénée Mignot (1842–1918). Un évêque français au temps du modernisme*, Cerf, Paris 2004.

1100 The beginnings of modernism, according to Loisy, dated back to a meeting on November 22, 1893, between himself, Msgr. Eudoxe Mignot, and von Hügel (*Mémoires*, vol. 1, p. 293).

1101 The memorial, published during the period of "Mouvement des idées et des faits" between January and May 1924, can be found reproduced in an appendix to Nicolas Fontaine (Louis Canet), *Saint-Siège, "Action française" et "catholiques intégraux,"* Librairie Universitaire J. Gamber, Paris 1928, pp. 121–137. The text was probably edited by the vicar general of Mignot, Fr. Louis Birot (1863–1936).

1102 Heinz Brauweiler (1885–1976) was editor in chief of the *Düsseldorfer Tagblatts* and later director of the daily *Der Stahlhelm*. Cf. Poulat, *Intégrisme et catholicisme intégral*, pp, 33–36, 524–535.

international organization guided by Msgr. Benigni who, under the pretext of defending Catholicism, was said to have orchestrated a violent anti-German campaign on behalf of France. Brauweiler succeeded in obtaining from the German military government an order for the search of a Flemish member of the *Sodalitium pianum*, the Belgian lawyer Alphonse Jonckx from Ghent, resulting in the confiscation of documents he had imprudently kept in his files.[1103] The search took place on May 18, 1915, and was conducted by a German military police commissioner aided by Brauweiler and the Dutch Camilian priest Hubertus Höner.[1104]

The sequestered documents were deposited in the Abbey of Ruremond in the Netherlands, but later ended up in the hands of the Jesuits of the magazine *Etudes*, and were published in the anonymous memorial *Une Société secrete*, by the historian Fernand Mourret, who distributed them to his Roman contacts.[1105]

On November 25, 1921, Cardinal Sbarretti[1106] of the Congregation of the Council, who had treated the affairs of the *Sodalitium* under Pius X, asked Msgr. Benigni, on behalf of Benedict XV, to disband the organization. On December 1, Benigni announced the dissolution of the *Sodalitium* set for December 8, 1921.[1107] This time its closure was definitive.

Merry del Val and the Holy Office

Cardinal Merry del Val had made profitable use of Msgr. Benigni's services to the Holy See, with the full approval of Pius X. But at the moment in which the new pope decreed the dissolution of the *Sodalitium pianum*, he decided that the battle against modernism would have to be conducted in a different manner, something the Anglo-Spanish cardinal was able to do effectively in his role as

1103 Alphonse Jonckx (1872–1953) was a Belgian jurist and journalist, a member of the *Sodalitium pianum*, and exponent of the Flemish Party (1907–1937).

1104 Hubertus Höner (1871–1920) was a Dutch Camillian Father who played a decisive role in the dissolution of the *Sodalitium pianum*. On the papers of Ghent, cf. Poulat, *Intégrisme et catholicisme intégral*, pp. 11–45.

1105 Fernand Mourret (1854–1938), a Sulpician priest, was a Church historian of modernist tendencies.

1106 Donato Raffaele Sbarretti Tazza (1856–1939) of Spoleto, alumnus of the Roman Seminary, was ordained in Rome in 1879. In 1900, he became bishop of San Cristóbal de La Habana, Cuba, and was named apostolic delegate in Canada (1902–1910). Recalled to Rome, he was named secretary of the Congregation of Religious (1910). Made a cardinal by Benedict XV in the consistory on December 4, 1916, he succeeded Merry del Val as secretary of the Congregation of the Holy Office.

1107 Cf. Dieguez, "Una specie di massoneria nella Chiesa," pp. 437–439.

secretary of the Holy Office, which he governed for fifteen years from 1914 until his death in 1930.[1108]

Following the reform of Pius X, the renewed Congregation of the Holy Office was kept in first place among the various Roman congregations and was later even granted the title "Supreme," deriving from the fact that it was presided over by the pope himself. In its jurisdictional sphere, it handled the defense of the doctrine on faith and morals, the cases against heresies, and all other types of crimes that bear the suspicion of heresy (for example, celebration of the Mass and the hearing of confessions by those who had not yet received priestly ordination, sexual solicitation by priests in confession, divination, sorcery, curses, and so forth).

Under Cardinal Merry del Val's governance, the Holy Office fought for the maintenance of the anti-modernist oath instituted by the encyclical *Pascendi*. Despite the fact that the current secretary of state had ensured that the anti-modernistic *professio fidei* would not be inserted into the *Code of Canon Law* due to its transitory character,[1109] a decree of the Holy Office on March 22, 1918, approved by the pope, established that "since the spread of the modernist virus has in no way ceased, the prescriptions must remain valid and binding until the Apostolic See decides otherwise in this matter."[1110]

An illuminating case was that of Ernesto Buonaiuti who, writing to his modernist friend Houtin on September 17, 1914, defined the election of Card. Della Chiesa as "the indication of an ecclesiastical government . . . which is the perfect antithesis of Pius X's regime."[1111] These expectations were disappointed, however, thanks to the nomination of Merry del Val to the Holy Office, who would place the modernist historian under observation. On the weekend of April 14,

[1108] During the fifteen years that he governed the Holy Office, Merry del Val was accompanied by three different assessors: Donato Sbarretti (1856–1939) until 1916; Carlo Perosi (1868–1930) until 1926; and Nicola Canali (1874–1961), who remained in that post until 1935. Merry del Val's successor, Donato Sbarretti, remained in the office until 1938, with the help of Msgr. Alfredo Ottaviani (1890–1979) beginning in 1936, in the role of assessor. All of these became cardinals.

[1109] G. Vian, "Il modernismo durante il pontificato di Benedetto XV, tra riabilitazioni e condanne" [Modernism During the Pontificate of Benedict XV, Between Rehabilitations and Condemnations], in Cavagnini and Grossi (eds.), *Benedetto XV*, vol. 1, p. 466.

[1110] Suprema Sacra Congregatio S. Offici, *Decretum circa consilia a vigilantia et iuramentum antimodernisticum*, in AAS, vol. 10 (1918), p. 136. Cf. "Dichiarazione della Sacra Congregazione del S. Offizio circa il Modernismo" [Declarations of the Sacred Congregation of the Holy Office regarding Modernism], *La Civiltà Cattolica* 69, no. 2 (1918), pp. 174–175.

[1111] Letter of Buonaiuti to Houtin of September 17, 1914, in "Carteggio Houtin- Buonaiuti," *Fonti e Documenti* 1 (1972), p. 131.

1915, immediately after the nomination of Buonaiuti as professor of history of religion at the University *La Sapienza* in Rome, the Holy Office asked the university's cardinal vicar to convoke Buonaiuti and, on behalf of the Holy Father, to beseech him strongly to heed the obligation of keeping strictly to the teaching of the Catholic Church. The Holy Office suggested, furthermore, that a person of absolute confidence in the vicar's office should attend an entire semester of his lectures to verify his orthodoxy.[1112]

On June 5, 1916, the Congregation of the Index decided to add to the Index of prohibited books Buonaiuti's *Magazine of the Science of Religion,* which had already been condemned by the Holy Office for its modernist ideas. The decision was accompanied by the suspension from the priestly office of the prelates who made up the editorial board of the magazine: besides Buonaiuti, there was Nicola Turchi,[1113] Primo Vannutelli,[1114] and Bacchisio Raimondo Motzo.[1115]

Cardinal Gasparri, as Buonaiuti recalled in his *Memoirs,* did all he could to readmit the four priests to the exercise of their ministry: "Returning today to the memories of the strenuous discussions of those days, it makes me think that in our case a subtle, but meticulous and heated duel was transpiring between the former secretary of state (Merry del Val) locked in his cloister of the Holy Office and the secretary of state at the time (Gasparri), working to make our ecclesiastical re-integration his personal victory."[1116] Carlo Falconi writes that "the most clever jurist suggested an interpretation of the anti-modernist oath

1112 ADDF. S.O. *Rerum Variarum* 1915, n. 15.

1113 Nicola Turchi (1882–1958), a classmate of Buonaiuti at the Roman Seminary and his inseparable friend, retired progressively to the private life, dedicating himself to teaching history of religion at the University of Rome.

1114 Primo Vannutelli (1885–1945) came from a family that had already given two cardinals to the Church in the brothers Serafino and Vincenzo. Ordained in 1909, he lived until his death in the Oratory of St. Philip Neri at the Chiesa Nuova in Rome. Cf. Federico Battistretta, *Trittico eretico. Sentieri interrotti del Novecento religioso. Ernesto Buonaiuti, Primo Vannutelli, Ferdinando Tartaglia [Heretical Tryptic. Interrupted Paths of the Religious 1900s. Ernesto Buonaiuti, Primo Vannutelli, Ferdinando Tartaglia]*, Millenia, Novara-Milan 2005; and F. Ricossa, "Un "profeta" modernista. Il testamento di don Primo Vannutelli" [A Modernist "Prophet." The Testimony of Fr. Primo Vannutelli], *Sodalitium* 64 (2010), pp. 14–22. A modernist disbeliever until his death, denying the divinity of Jesus Christ and the Church, the Roman priest theorized the necessity of not leaving it, awaiting its inevitable historical transformation.

1115 Bacchisio Raimondo Motzo (1883–1970), ordained priest in 1905, was one of the collaborators of *Journal of the Science of Religion* of Buonaiuti. He abandoned the priesthood in 1905 and married the pedagogist Cecilia Dentice d'Accadia (1893–1891).

1116 Buonaiuti, *Pellegrino di Roma*, pp. 150–151.

that completely satisfied the four scholarly priests," "as a simple disciplinary assent to the authority of the Church."[1117]

The suspension *a divinis* was revoked by Benedict XV after the four priests made their anti-modernist oath in his private chapel on July 13, 1916.[1118] "After this sacrilegious comedy of the oath," noted Benigni, "Buonaiuti remained an hour with Gasparri and said he admired the cardinal's open-minded ideas (!). Evidently Gasparri persuaded them to take the oath in his hands and with the inflection he gave to it, in agreement with their understanding of it."[1119]

In his memoirs, Buonaiuti speaks with high esteem and deference for Gasparri, affirming that toward 1918–1920 he met with the secretary of state several times a week."[1120] According to Falconi, "The explanation of such an unusual relationship can be found most likely in the plan the cardinal was toying with to entrust Buonaiuti with the direction of the Vatican Press Office, perhaps also with the aim of distracting him from his research as a scholar of the history of Christianity."[1121] What is certain is that Buonaiuti was always able to depend on Cardinal Gasparri, who twice came to visit him when he was in the hospital fighting for his life. But if in 1916, Gasparri succeeded in directing him along the path of escaping the condemnation of the Holy Office, over the coming years these stratagems were no longer sufficient.

In 1919, Buonaiuti founded a new journal, *Religio*, which came to an end in 1921. In its third edition, published in December 1920, there appeared just one article by him, "The Fundamental Experiences of Paul," containing several phrases that denied the Real Presence of Christ in the Eucharist. The attempt at "recovery" carried out by Gasparri in 1921 in the Roman clinic where Buonaiuti lay in grave danger of death, fell into a void.

In January 1921, Merry del Val welcomed a visit from Fr. Alfredo Buonaiuti, Ernesto's brother, and confided that he had often reprimanded his brother for

1117 Falconi, *I Papi del ventesimo secolo*, p. 150.

1118 Guido Verucci, *L'eresia del Novecento [The Heresy of the 1900s]*, Einaudi, Turin 2010, p. 73. Cf. L. Bedeschi (ed.), "Il processo del Sant'Uffizio contro i modernisti romani" [The Trial of the Holy Office Against the Roman Modernists], in *Fonti e documenti* 7 (1978), pp. 7–18, 51–55, 58–60. Cf. furthermore F. Parente, *Ernesto Buonaiuti*, Istituto Enciclopedia Italiana, Rome 1971, pp. 46–47. On Gasparri's intervention in the affair cf. L. Bedeschi, *Buonaiuti, il Concordato e la Chiesa*, Il Saggiatore, Milan 1970, pp. 77–79.

1119 AAV, *Fondo Benigni*, 2, f. 242.

1120 Buonaiuti, *Pellegrino di Roma*, pp. 150, 189.

1121 Falconi, *I Papi del ventesimo secolo*, p. 151.

his philosophical ideas.[1122] But his sibling replied, "You understand nothing should leave him in peace," because "his ideas will be accepted in thirty to forty years."[1123] Instead, with a decree on January 14, 1921, the Holy Office declared Ernesto Buonaiuti excommunicated and suspended *a divinis*, putting an end to the ambiguity of an ecclesiastical situation that coexisted with his activity of demolition of the Church's dogmas.[1124]

The Birth of the Popular Party

In 1918, the Popular Union of Italian Catholics addressed to Cardinal Gasparri a long memorandum in light of the upcoming political elections, to face "the masonic block, official socialism, and the democratic block" with "a political organization with its own name and responsibility."[1125]

On January 18, 1919, the program of the new Italian Popular Party (PPI)[1126] was published under the title of *Appeal to the Free and the Strong*, founded by Fr. Luigi Sturzo. The new party found its *trait d'union* with the Holy See in Carlo Santucci, a personal friend of Cardinal Gasparri.[1127]

In June 1919, the Orlando government collapsed and Vittorio Emanuele III called upon Francesco Saverio Nitti to succeed him.[1128] Just days before the elections in November 1919, for the first time with universal male suffrage and a law of proportionality, the Holy Penitentiary officially abolished the *non expedit*. The Italian Socialist Party and the Italian Popular Party succeeded in running their candidates everywhere under their respective symbols of the hammer and sickle, and the shield with a cross, winning majorities.

1122 Alfredo Buonaiuti (1875–1933), brother of Ernesto, was parish priest of Settecamini (Rome), on Via Tiburtina.

1123 AAV, *Spoglio Merry del Val*, busta 5, n. 634–636, January 17, 1921, *Visita di don Alfredo Buonaiuti [Visit with Fr. Alfredo Buonaiuti]*, n. 634. In Merry del Val's estimation, Fr. Alfredo Buonaiuti seemed a "simpleton"(ibid, n. 634).

1124 AAS, vol. 13 (1921), p. 46.

1125 AAV, AES, Italia III, Pos. 953–954, fasc. 345, c. 48.

1126 On the Popular Party cf. Gabriele De Rosa, *Il Partito popolare italiano*, Laterza, Rome-Bari 1979; Franco Bruno, *Il dibattito sulla denominazione del partito di ispirazione cristiana [The Debate over the Denomination of the Party of Christian Inspriation]*, Salvatore Sciascia, Caltanissetta-Rome 1993.

1127 The attorney Carlo Santucci (1849–1932), a noble of Velletri, was a close collaborator of Cardinal Gasparri in his work on the reform of the *Code of Canon Law*. He was later the president of the Bank of Rome (1916–1923) and senator of the Kingdom since 1919.

1128 Francesco Saverio Nitti (1868–1953), numerous times minister and prime minister from 1919 to 1921, became an opponent of fascism in political exile, and then deputy of the Constitutional assembly (1946), and senator of the Republic.

La Civiltà Cattolica dedicated to the Popular Party an article by Fr. Enrico Rosa, whose text was desired and reviewed personally by Benedict XV.[1129] The article placed in evidence the lacunae of the new Catholic party, above all the non-confessional choice.[1130] To correct these errors, following pontifical indications, Fr. Rosa gave his support to the birth of a "right wing"[1131] within the PPI, though it did not have a long life.

On September 6, 1920, the Catholic weekly *Parola del popolo* published a pastoral letter by Cardinal Tommaso Pio Boggiani, archbishop of Genoa, heavily criticizing the new party because it did not embrace in its entirety the Catholic program of the renovation of society. "The battles of God," wrote the archbishop, "must be fought in God's name, never in the name of a party, whatever might be the title that distinguishes it."[1132] Furthermore, the prelate insisted that "those Catholics who take the battlefield in public and political life with the program of reestablishing the social order on Christian foundations, must absolutely proclaim with full voice, defend with all their strength and see triumph insofar as is possible the principles of the Gospel, or risk jeopardizing their objectives."

This was also the position of Cardinal Merry del Val, who remained ever faithful to the line of *cattolici deputati, non deputati cattolici.*

Over the course of the following years, Italy was to suffer an economic and moral crisis that afflicted especially the middle class and those with a fixed income. Strikes followed, while continuous confrontations took place in parliament

1129 Enrico Rosa S.J. (1870–1938) entered the Society of Jesus in 1886, was ordained in 1900, and took final vows in 1904. In 1905 he began collaboration with *Civiltà Cattolica* of which he was director from 1915 to 1931. About him, cf. Ambrogio Fiocchi S.J., *P. Enrico Rosa S.J. scrittore della "Civiltà Cattolica" (1870–1938)*, La Civiltà Cattolica, Rome 1957.

1130 Enrico Rosa S.J., "Programmi nuovi di partiti vecchi. Il partito popolare italiano e il suo 'Programma della Nuova Italia'" [New Programs for Old Parties. The Italian Popular Party and its 'Program for a New Italy'], *La Civiltà Cattolica* 70 (1919), vol. 2, p. 107.

1131 Silvio Tramontin, "La formazione dell'ala destra nel partito popolare italiano" [The Formation of the Right Wing in the Italian Popular Party], in *Modernismo, fascismo, comunismo. Aspetti e figure della cultura e della politica dei cattolici nel '900*, Il Mulino, Bologna 1972, pp. 453–478; Giovanni Sale S.J., *Popolari e destra cattolica al tempo di Benedetto XV [Popular Party and the Catholic Right in the Time of Benedict XV]*, Jaca Book, Milan 2005.

1132 Tommaso Pio Card. Boggiani, *L'Azione Cattolica e il Partito Popolare Italiano*, Tipografia Arcivescovile, Genoa 1920, p. 24. Cardinal Tommaso Pio Boggiani (1863–1942), assessor of the Consistorial, was consecrated on October 16, 1908, as bishop of Adria, and nominated in January 1912 archbishop of Edessa and apostolic delegate to Mexico, where he lived until 1914. Returning to Italy, he participated as secretary of the Sacred College in the conclave in September 1914 and was named apostolic administrator and later archbishop of Genoa from 1919 to 1921. He was made a cardinal by Benedict XV on December 4, 1916, and named chancellor of Holy Roman Church by Pius XI in 1933.

between populists and socialists. On June 15, 1920, the king recalled the Giolitti government in the midst of "a red biennial" characterized by sit-ins in the fields and the factories and by a series of violent actions against exponents of the bourgeois, the clergy, and above all, veterans of war. Their slogan insisted that the Russian Communist Revolution be brought to Italy. Giolitti, the old politician from Piedmont, was incapable of confronting the sit-ins in the northern factories proclaimed by the unions under pressure from Communist groups of the "New Order" inspired by Antonio Gramsci.[1133]

Gramsci himself, an attentive observer of the Bolshevik revolution, considered collaboration between Communists and the Catholic Popular Party to be necessary. "Democratic Catholicism," he wrote in his journal, "can do what Communism cannot: it amalgamates, orders, vivifies, and will then commit suicide.... The Populists are to socialism what Kerensky is to Lenin."[1134]

The Last Phase of the Pontificate

In his encyclical *Pacem Dei munus pulcherrimum* of May 23, 1920, Benedict XV denounced the existence of a "framework of misery" that continued to oppress humanity four years after the conclusion of the conflict. "For if in most places peace is to some extent established and treaties signed, the seeds of former enmities remain; and you well know, Venerable Brethren, that there can be no stable peace or lasting treaties, though made after long and difficult negotiations and duly signed, unless there be a return of mutual charity to appease hate and banish enmity." [1135]

Benedict's strong political sensibility was accompanied by sincere personal piety, which he manifested by honoring great figures who illuminated the Church such as St. Margaret Mary Alacoque,[1136] St. Boniface,[1137] St. Joan of Arc,[1138] St. Jerome,[1139] St. Ephrem the Syrian,[1140] St. Francis of Assisi,[1141] and

1133 Antonio Gramsci (1891–1937) was among the founders, in 1921, of the Communist Party of Italy, performing the role of secretary from 1924 to 1927.

1134 A. Gramsci, "I popolari," in *L'Ordine Nuovo (1919–1920)*, Einaudi, Turin 1954, p. 286.

1135 Benedict XV, *Pacem Dei munus pulcherrimum*, May 23, 1920, no. 1, https://www.vatican.va/content/benedict-xv/en/encyclicals/documents/hf_ben-xv_enc_23051920_pacem-dei-munus-pulcherrimum.html.

1136 Benedict XV, Discourse *Non va lungi*, January 6, 1918; Bull *Ecclesiae consuetudo*, May 13, 1920.

1137 Benedict XV, Encyclical *In hac tanta*, May 14, 1919.

1138 Benedict XV, Bull *Divina disponente*, May 16, 1920.

1139 Benedict XV, Encyclical *Spiritus Paraclitus*, September 15, 1920.

1140 Benedict XV, Encyclical *Principi Apostolorum*, October 5, 1920.

1141 Benedict XV, Encyclical *Sacra propediem*, January 6, 1921.

St. Dominic Guzmán.[1142] In the last phase of his pontificate, at the urging of Cardinal Gasparri, he undertook a series of diplomatic negotiations with the Nation States. The speech delivered for the consistory *In hac quidem* on November 21, 1921, in which the pontiff declared his willingness to establish with governments "new pacts that are more appropriate to the changed political circumstances," is considered the point of departure of what, under Gasparri's guidance, would become the concordat policy of the Holy See under Pius XI.[1143]

The pontificate of Benedict XV was shorter than even he had imagined it would be. On the morning of December 27, 1921, the pope went to celebrate Mass in the hospital for infirm priests, as was the papal custom, next to the little church of St. Martha. Stepping out, he caught a cold that progressed to bronchitis, which was the beginning of his ill health, announced officially by *L'Osservatore Romano* on the evening of January 18. The next day, his condition grew worse, such that the Holy See communicated to the Italian government that the health of the Holy Father was in danger. From that day, the pontiff suffered alternating moments of crisis and calm. At 2 a.m. on January 21, he was administered Extreme Unction. Benedict XV asked to receive privately Cardinal Gasparri, to communicate to him his last will. Finally on the morning of Sunday, January 22, he passed away.

"This pope leaves us without ever having known him; nothing, I mean, which is not biographical news, but the intimate side of his thought, the beating of his heart," wrote Renato Simoni shortly after his death for *Illustrazione Italiana*.[1144] The writer continued,

> Pius X placed before us his Christian joy and his Christian sufferings. We could imagine his private life; his days and his evenings; his words and his prayers. Giacomo della Chiesa stood in the shadows of his intentions, and seemed dry and taciturn. But before dying, he gave us a sign of himself that we shall remember. He was already exhausted by his illness; he was already speechless; in the drowsiness that precedes the supreme sleep and is already part of it. A cardinal said to him,

1142 Benedict XV, Encyclical *Fausto appetente*, June 29, 1921.

1143 Benedict XV, Discourse *In hac quidem*, November 21, 1921, in AAS (1913), pp 521–524.

1144 Renato Simoni (1875–1952), known also under the pseudonym *Turno and The Nobleman Vidal*, was a journalist, theater critic, and successful comedy writer.

> "Holiness, bless the world that so longs for peace." Then the pontiff summoned his poor weak body, raised himself on his bed, and three times traced in the air, with his quickened, majestic hand, the pacifying sign of the cross.[1145]

His body was dressed in the papal habit and exposed to the faithful before being buried in the Vatican Grottoes in front of the tomb of his predecessor. Expressing a widely felt sentiment, Cardinal Baudrillart noted in his diary, "His death moved me less than that of Pius X, even though his politics and behavior were for us a source of less embarrassment and difficulty; but he did not give that impression of the supernatural that we felt with Pius X. We felt mostly the diplomat and politician."[1146]

The pontificate of Benedict XV lasted nearly eight years. Half of these were wrapped in the flames of the Great War. The pope's efforts to put an end to the conflict were unsuccessful, and equally uncertain seemed his efforts at reconstructing a new international order.

Everyone considered the pontificate of Benedict XV a period of transition, and at his death, a decisive battle unfolded between the different currents that coexisted within the Catholic Church. In those years, while everything around him was changing, Rafael Merry del Val exerted himself in remaining faithful to the spiritual inheritance of Pius X, continuing its work, above all the anti-modernist battle.

1145 Nobleman Vidal (Renato Simoni), "Benedict XV," *L'Illustrazione Italiana*, January 29, 1922, p. 114.

1146 Card. Alfred Baudrillart, Note of January 22, 1922, in Paul Christoph (ed.), *Les Carnets du Cardinal Afred Baudrillart, January 1, 1922–April 12, 1925*, Éditions du Cerf, Paris 2001, p. 66.

6

Secretary of the Holy Office Under Pius XI

The Two "Parties" on the Eve of the Conclave

The election of a pope is an event that can change the history of the world. In January 1922, after the sudden passing of Benedict XV, all international attention was turned to the Vatican in light of the imminent conclave. A French diplomat, François Charles-Roux, recalled how in Rome at that moment, "everything extraneous to the event in the Vatican passes into the second row; everything is relegated to the background, internal and external politics. The attention is absorbed by what is happening behind a closed window in St. Peter's Square and what will happen afterward."[1147]

After the death of Cardinal Francesco Salesio della Volpe, Benedict XV had not ensured that a new Chamberlain of the Holy Roman Church was elected. His functions were therefore carried out by Secretary of State Gasparri in his role as prefect of the Sacred Palaces. The custodian of the conclave was Prince Ludovico Chigi Albani della Rovere. On January 21, he was appointed by Cardinal Gasparri to assume the functions of internal policing belonging to the role of Marshal of the Conclave that was the right of his family.

In a confidential report sent to London on October 25, 1922, Count Francis de Salis described the existence in the Sacred City of two parties that could be defined, according to their different perspectives, as "religious" and "reactionary" on the one hand, and on the other, "political" and "progressive." These denominations, however imprecise, dated back to the preceding century and had not lost their relevance to the times. "Zealots and Politicians," he wrote, "were the Old Roman names."[1148]

[1147] François Charles-Roux, *Souvenirs diplomatiques. Une grande ambassade à Rome. 1919–1925*, Arthème Fayard, Paris 1961, pp. 156–157. François Charles-Roux (1879–1961) was counselor to the French Embassy in Italy from 1916 to 1924 and from 1932 to 1940 ambassador to the Holy See.

[1148] De Salis, *Anglo-Vatican Relations*, pp. 13–14. The term "zealous cardinals" was used under Pius VII to indicate the cardinals who opposed the line of accomodation towards Napoleon pursued by the secretary of state Ercole Consalvi (1757–1824). The expression is nevertheless prior to this. Cf. "Cardinali

While at the conclave of 1914, the traditional distinction between religious and political was superimposed by that of the different nationalities due to the war that had just exploded, at the conclave of 1922, the two tendencies presented themselves in a more distinct manner. The secretary of the Holy Office, Rafael Merry del Val, supported by Cardinals Boggiani and De Lai, was the leader of the "religious" or "zealots" defined as "fundamentalists" by their adversaries; the secretary of state, Gasparri, supported by Cardinals Maffi and Ratti, was the point of reference for their opponents. The former took its inspiration from the religious and theological vision of Pius X; the latter followed the "political" school of Leo XIII and Benedict XV.[1149]

Msgr. Umberto Benigni, perhaps the most attentive of the many observers, also saw the "two opposing tendencies" being Merry del Val on one side, and the trio Gasparri-Maffi-Ratti on the other.[1150] The founder of the *Sodalitium pianum* clarified, "The tendency until now personified in Benedict XV and today headed by the PPI (Italian Popular Party) and by the White International (Christian-Socialists) has its candidates: Cardinal Gasparri as its preference, Maffi and Ratti as its probables."[1151]

Pietro Gasparri, seventy-nine years old, born in Ussita in the Marche, of a wealthy farming family, after receiving his training in the Roman Seminary of the Apollinare, lived for a long period in Paris as a professor at the *Institut Catholique*, and espoused the Rampollian line of *ralliement* and of the possibile validity of Anglican ordinations.

For this reason, Pius X had distanced him from the Secretariat of State, sending him off to a no-less-important position as head of the reform of the *Code of Canon Law*, which had earned him the cardinalate, according to the ancient formula *promoveatur ut amoveatur*. Benedict XV, also a disciple of Cardinal Rampolla, made him his secretary of state.

Giovanni Spadolini defined him "more sensible to events than to ideas, realistic with a note of Guicciardini," "capable of being extremely pliant as well as astute, in the service of a goal that he deems essential."[1152]

---

zelanti e fazioni cardinalizie tra Sei e Settecento" [Zealous Cardinals and Cardinalate Factions in the 17th and 18th Centuries], in Gianvittorio Signorotto and Maria Antonietta (eds.), *La corte di Roma tra Cinque e Seicento "teatro" della politica europea*, Visceglia, Bulzoni, Rome 1998, pp. 139–165.

1149 Msgr. Primo Principi, *Informatio*, p. 115.

1150 AAV, *Fondo Benigni*, busta 59, f. 81.

1151 Ibid., f. 82.

1152 Spadolini, *Il cardinale Gasparri e la questione romana*, pp. 25, 56.

Msgr. Benigni considered Gasparri the official candidate of France,[1153] describing him in this way:

> Gasparri, Pietro: a worthy canonist, but he sees everything, beginning with religion, from the juridical and legal point of view. Very liberal and also very skeptical. He was the one who pushed the policies of Benedict XV to the point of granting every concession, from the French *Cultuelles* to the Italo-Papal conciliation. A man of talent, but not of judgment. Very avid for money and indulgent in nepotism. Can be a candidate of the PPI, of the French *cultuellistes*, etc. at the conclave, but will not succeed because he will arouse the resentment of some and the diffidence of others.[1154]

Equally precise was the portrait this Umbrian prelate gave of Cardinal Rafael Merry del Val. "Merry del Val. Anglo-Spaniard, once chamberlain of Leo XIII, delegate in Canada, president of the Academy of Ecclesiastical Nobles, cardinal secretary of state to Pius X, archpriest of St. Peter's, secretary of the Holy Office. A man of great talent and experience, moderate by tendency, reactionary by reflection; of a timid and uncertain character despite appearances. Highly esteemed by many prelates. Hypothetically *papabile* in the case of an election of a foreigner. He would resume the policies of Pius X but in a very attenuated way."[1155]

There were divergences between Merry del Val and Benigni, but considering how biting and often unflattering the pen of Benigni was, it becomes clear that his judgment of Pius X's secretary of state was positive, especially when compared to that of other cardinals of the same intransigent line, like De Lai, who had also been one of the main protectors of the *Sodalitium pianum*: "Under Pius X, he was quite reactionary in the anti-modernist struggle, but then conceded to keep his post. Little substance, impressionable, violent, changeable. Little esteemed as a man of governance. Very industrious. Very ambitious to the point of intrigue. Not *papabile*."[1156]

1153 AAV, *Fondo Benigni*, busta 59, f. 95, "Highly confidential note" of January 26, 1922: "The official candidate of the French Embassy is Cardinal Gasparri."

1154 AAV, *Fondo Benigni*, busta 59, f. 44.

1155 Ibid., f. 52. ASMAE, *Fondo Benigni*, busta 23. Describing the Sacred College at the beginning of 1919, he defined him briefly: "Pius X. *Papabile*" (AAV, *Fondo Benigni*, busta 59, f. 52). It is interesting to notice that in the Archive of the Spanish Embassy to the Holy See, there is a telegram from the ambassador in Madrid repeating verbatim Benigni's judgment. Cf. Urbano Muñoz, *El cardenal secretario de Estado Merry del Val*, vol. 2, p. 308. This confirms the influence which Benigni continued to exercise.

1156 AAV, *Fondo Benigni*, busta 59, f. 71.

De Lai's candidate was Merry del Val, but De Lai, as a strategist, was to become the weak link, not the strong one, in the list of those opposing Gasparri in the conclave, which included Cardinals Billot,[1157] Boggiani,[1158] and Oreste Giorgi,[1159] the latter being the only one Benigni considered *papabile*.

In the ranks of their opponents, Benigni marked down Achille Ratti as *papabile*: "Well known in Poland, he is the candidate of the PPI and the White International along with Pisano Maffi and Gasparri. Of the three, most bets are on Ratti."[1160] In a confidential note of January 23, he indicated Ratti as the true candidate of Gasparri's party,[1161] a surprising analysis when considering that Ratti was unknown to the majority of cardinals.

The cardinal archbishop of Malines, Désiré Mercier, was also considered one of the *papabile* and he himself, on the eve of the conclave, considered his election a possibility.[1162] Gasparri had gone to see him and told him that at all costs they must avoid electing "a second integralist" after Pius X, and that he, and those who shared his way of thinking, were very disturbed by the efforts of Merry del Val in favor of Cardinal La Fontaine,[1163] the patriarch of Venice.[1164]

And yet Merry del Val himself was still a strong candidate. Msgr. Francesco Roberti,[1165] a witness at the beatification process, told how, as the

1157 "Réactionnaire d'Action française. Très bon théologien, mais pas d'expérience, très nerveux et impressionable" (AAV, *Fondo Benigni*, busta 59, f. 66). Louis Billot (1846–1931), of the Society of Jesus, taught dogmatic theology at the Gregorian from 1885 to 1910. Made a cardinal by Pius X on November 27, 1911, he renounced the dignity on September 19, 1927. About his life, cf. Henri Le Floch C. S. SP., *Le cardinal Billot lumière de la théologie*, Beauchesne, Paris 1947; Peter J. Bernardi, "Louis Cardinal Billot, S.J. (1846–1931): Thomist, Anti-Modernist, Integralist," *Journal of Jesuit Studies* 8 (2021), pp. 585–615.

1158 "De l'école de Pie X, il veut la réforme religieuse de l'Église et le moins possible de politique. Homme très ferme, mais calme et pondéré. Pas papable; mais il sera entendu au Vatican" (AAV, *Fondo Benigni*, busta 59, f. 68).

1159 Oreste Giorgi (1856–1924) was made a cardinal by Benedict XV in the consistory of December 4, 1916. "Homme de talent, de caractère, solide. Conservateur moderé. Très estimé dans les deux camps. Papable, quoique on n'en parle pas, et peut être surtout pour cela" (AAV, *Fondo Benigni*, busta 59, f. 47).

1160 Ibid., f. 56.

1161 Ibid., f. 88.

1162 Aubert, "Le cardinal Mercier aux conclaves de 1914 et 1922," p. 193.

1163 Pietro La Fontaine (1860–1935), from Viterbo, was bishop in Calabria, before becoming secretary of the Congregation of Rites (1910–1915) and being nominated patriarch of Venice and made cardinal by Benedict XV in 1916. Cf. Domenico Sparpaglione, *Il cardinale Pietro La Fontaine patriarca di Venezia*, Paoline, Alba 1951.

1164 Aubert, "Le cardinal Mercier aux conclaves de 1914 et 1922", p. 195.

1165 Francesco Roberti (1889–1977) was undersecretary of the Congregation for Catholic Education (1931), secretary of the Sacred Congregation of the Council (1946), and prefect of the Supreme Tribunal of the Apostolic Signatura (1959). John XXIII made him a cardinal on December 15, 1958.

conclave approached, Cardinal Basilio Pompili told him that "he had guessed all the last pontiffs and made it clear that the future pope would be Card. Merry del Val. One of those present observed that he was not Italian and the cardinal replied, 'But I believe no one understands the current situation of the Church like Card. Merry del Val.'"[1166] Another witness at the beatification process, Msgr. Primo Principi, reported that Pompili had told him, "We shall have a pope on Saturday and he shall be one of the youngest."[1167] In fact, Rafael Merry del Val was fifty-seven at the time. The Belgian ambassador Eugène Beyens, who had met with him during those days of pontifical interregnum, wrote, "I met Cardinal Merry del Val in Brussels when his father represented the government of King Alfonso XII of Spain. At the time, he was a handsome young man, silent and meditative, a student with an ardent religious vocation. In the little building where he lives as archpriest of St. Peter's, behind the basilica, I found a man in the flower of his years and already white-haired, with profound, magnificent eyes, whose cordiality tempered his Spanish gravitas. He spoke kindly to me of the relationship between our two families, explaining the complicated mechanism of the conclave and said only, 'We are about to sacrifice a victim; we shall send him to live and to die in the prison of the Vatican.'"[1168]

The Most Embattled Conclave of the Century

The conclave that was beginning would be the longest of the century, "one of the most embattled in history," as Cardinal Gasparri wrote with a bit of exaggeration.[1169]

On the eve of the conclave, Benigni noted, "The predictions are still very uncertain. The party of Benedict XV will try to save itself with a pope from its own (Ratti, Maffi, Gasparri), but the opposition on the right has a good third option, at least. So, there should be a pope of compromise, unforeseeable: perhaps an Italian from the provinces."[1170] Benigni clarified that the Popular Party and the White International had placed its veto on Merry del Val, Boggiani, and De Lai. For Merry del Val they even added a veto to his nomination as secretary

[1166] *Processus Informativus Ordinarius*, vol. 1, *Sessio* XLVII, p. 307, deposition of Msgr. Francesco Roberti.

[1167] Ibid, *Sessio* XLIX, p. 317, deposition of Msgr. Primo Principi.

[1168] Baron Beyens, *Quatre ans à Rome 1921–1926*, Librairie Plon, Paris 1934. Baron Eugène Beyens (1855–1934) was Belgian ambassador in Rome from 1921 to 1926.

[1169] According to Msgr. Primo Principi, *Informatio*, p. 115.

[1170] AAV, *Fondo Benigni*, busta 59. f. 65.

of state under the future pope.[1171] Meanwhile, Benigni, who was fighting the Gasparri regime, proposed at this point a "Plan for the Catholic Defense of the Conclave," according to which Cardinals Boggiani and Billot would present at the first ballot the candidacy of Card. Merry del Val:

> In this way, from the very first ballot, his name would have the highest possible number of votes so that in the second ballot one could hope for the arrival of additional votes sufficient to obtain the necessary number. Moreover, it seemed opportune that this proposal be made declaring that it must be above all a statement of principle in deference to the true interests of the Church, so that if the vote had turned out in their favor, God would be praised; otherwise it would give the impression of an attempt at victory followed by a defeat. In the event that the vote was not successful, the cardinals who had followed their lead could then negotiate with Cardinals Merry, Boggiani, and Billot to choose a candidate acceptable to them and to the more moderate members of the other side, in other words, a last vote that could save at least a continuation of the regime by now terminated.[1172]

As in the preceding conclave, we are able to follow events thanks to the *memoirs*, cited previously, of the Cardinal Archbishop of Vienna, Gustav Piffl, and other indiscretions.[1173] There were fifty-three cardinals locked inside the conclave on the evening of Thursday, February 2, 1922: thirty Italians and twenty-three foreigners of the sixty who had the right to be present. Every cardinal was accompanied to his cell by a Noble Guard; then, intoning the *Veni Creator*, the electors processed to the Sistine Chapel where they made their ritual oath.

Every morning there were two votes and two every afternoon. On February 3, the first exploratory ballot took place: Merry del Val was immediately in the lead with twelve votes, followed by Maffi with ten, Gasparri with eight, Ratti with five, La Fontaine with four and Van Rossum with four. This first result, and those that followed, displayed, according to Cardinal Piffl, "the

1171 "Precisioni. Lunedì sera 23 gennaio" [Clarifications. Monday Evening, January 23], AAV, *Fondo Benigni*, busta 59, f. 91.

1172 AAV, *Fondo Benigni*, busta 59, ff. 79–80. It is not clear who Benigni's true candidate was, suggesting Maglione as secretary of state. AAV, *Fondo Benigni*, busta 59, f. 81.

1173 Cf. Lorenza Lullini, "Il conclave del 1922 e il ritorno del papa Pio" [The Conclave of 1922 and the Return of the Pius Pope], in Cavagnini and Grossi (eds.), *Benedetto XV*, vol. 2, pp. 1051–1119.

existence of two tendencies: 1) the reappearance of old integralists guided by Merry del Val; 2) the continuation of the policy of Benedict XV, for which the candidate was Gasparri."[1174]

The matchup was extremely intense, and it seemed it would end in favor of the "intransigent" or "Pius" party for its fidelity to Pius X, but during the seventh ballot on Saturday, February 4, when it appeared obvious that Merry del Val would not be able to obtain the necessary two-thirds majority, his votes shifted to La Fontaine, who obtained twenty-two against Gasparri's twenty-four. Nevertheless, that evening, Piffl noted in his diary that there was little chance that Gasparri would get the twenty-eight votes needed, and "tomorrow we might see the election of La Fontaine."[1175]

Pietro La Fontaine was a cardinal whom everyone appreciated for his human and spiritual qualities. Nominated bishop of Cassano Jonio in Calabria in 1906 by Pius X, he had faced with efficiency the situation in his diocese after the earthquake of December 1908. From 1907 to 1909, the years of the modernist crisis, he had been appointed by the pope to carry out apostolic visits in seminaries in Benevento and Liguria, and in the diocese of Massa Marittima, Pisa, Volterra, Malta, and Gozo, distinguishing himself for his goodness and determination. On February 28, 1915, Benedict XV promoted him to patriarch of Venice and on December 4, 1916, made him a cardinal. He was appreciated by the intransigent party, though opposed for this reason by the more liberal wing of the Sacred College.

On Sunday, Gasparri's decline was accentuated, his votes reduced to nineteen from twenty-four and then to sixteen, but the votes for La Fontaine diminished as well, going from eighteen to eight, while the name of the old Cardinal Granito di Belmonte unexpectedly emerged with eight votes, a candidacy with little hope of success. In this situation of stalemate, the liberal party played its cards more astutely than the intransigent party. Gasparri had his votes transferred to the archbishop of Milan, Achille Ratti, who over the course of the day went from eleven votes to fourteen, then to twenty-four and finally to twenty-seven. The cardinal dean, Vincenzo Vannutelli[1176] who, like Gasparri,

1174 Liebmann, "Les conclaves," p. 50.

1175 Ibid.

1176 Msgr. Benigni defined cardinal Vincenzo Vannutelli "plein de talent et de ruse, vide de scrupules. Avide de plaisirs et de l'argent. Libéral et concessionaire par scepticisme. Peu estimé pour tout cela" (AAV, *Fondo Benigni*, busta 59, f. 62).

was an adversary of the intransigent party, suggested to Cardinal Mercier to go to his friend Gasquet, one of La Fontaine's electors, and convince him to transfer his vote to Ratti. According to Aubert, Mercier was to have played the "scientific card" on the erudite Gasquet: the Church needed a man of science, and Ratti, formerly prefect of the Vatican Library, was that man.

Like Della Chiesa in the preceding conclave, Cardinal Ratti had donned the *porpora* for less than a year. Unlike Benedict, XV however, he was unknown to most. Among the few who knew him well from the days when he was prefect of the Vatican Library was Cardinal Gasparri, who had considered making him his preference in case his own candidacy failed. Gasparri moved with much dissimulation, such that only later would De Lai, the director of the strategy of the intransigents, realize that the great protector of Ratti was precisely Gasparri.

According to Gasparri, De Lai went to Cardinal Ratti to assure him his group's votes if he, once pope, would not reconfirm Gasparri in the role of secretary of state, but Ratti had refused him bluntly. Gasparri then accused De Lai and Merry del Val of having incurred excommunication *latae sententiae* for having sought to condition the results of the voting.[1177] The accusation, however, was utterly devoid of foundation. Conclaves have always been a place of negotiations among cardinals, and it was entirely reasonable that De Lai would have communicated to Ratti that a group of cardinals was ready to vote for him, but was restrained by fear that Cardinal Gasparri, whom they held in low esteem, might continue to hold the office of secretary of state.

According to the reconstruction of Ambassador Francesco Taliani in his biography of Gasparri, based on confidences of the cardinal, "There were those who said they supported the candidacy of Ratti on the condition that Gasparri would formally renounce his appointment as secretary of state under the new pontiff. And Gasparri immediately committed himself to what was asked of him, joyfully, without expressing the least reservation, and placed in the hands of an independent cardinal, Giorgi, his explicit declaration."[1178]

Cardinal Gasparri, according to Taliani, was to go back on his words by order of the new pope, betraying his written declaration. "Thus it was that

[1177] Spadolini, *Il cardinale Gasparri e la questione romana*, p. 259; *Animadversiones*, pp. 57–58.

[1178] Taliani, *Vita del cardinal Gasparri*, pp. 165–166. The Marquis Francesco Maria Taliani de Marchio (1887–1968) was an Italian ambassador and author of historical and diplomatic works.

Gasparri, an unprecedented example in the history of the Church, was able to give two pontiffs his collaboration as secretary of state."[1179]

In fact, Ratti, during the first ballot on Monday, February 6, went from twenty-seven to thirty votes, while La Fontaine lost four. During the following scrutiny, the fourteenth of that extenuating conclave, the shift occurred: Achille Ratti obtained forty-two votes, six more than needed for the two-thirds majority, while Pietro La Fontaine decreased to nine votes.

Achille Ratti[1180] thus became the successor to Benedict XV. The cardinal dean Vannutelli placed the fisherman's ring on his finger and asked him, "*Quomodo vis vocari?*" The newly elected replied: "It was under Pius X that I took my first steps in my ecclesiastical career. Pius IX called me to Rome. Pius is a name of peace. Desiring to consecrate my efforts to the work of world pacification, to which my predecessor Benedict XV dedicated himself, I choose the name Pius."[1181]

The Election of Achille Ratti

The bells of St. Peter's rang at length, and echoing them, all the bells of Rome, to greet the new Roman pontiff. Pius XI confirmed Cardinal Pietro Gasparri as secretary of state and, following his suggestion, decided to impart his blessing from the external loggia of St. Peter's Basilica, thus breaking a tradition inaugurated by Leo XIII after the taking of Rome.

At 12:43 on February 6, 1922, Pius XI appeared in the central loggia of St. Peter's as the Pontifical Armed Corps presented their arms under a slight drizzle. The royal troops, lined up in front of the flight of stairs, rendered the new pope their homage amid the ovations of the crowd and the waving of handkerchiefs. The pope, waving his arms, smiling, was surrounded by the entire Sacred College. Pius XI, wearing the mantle and red hat, imparted his triple blessing to the kneeling faithful filling the square. This gesture expressed the preeminent objective of the new pontificate: putting an end to the Roman Question and affirming the political role of the Holy See on the international field.

1179 Ibid., p. 167.

1180 Achille Ratti (1857–1939) was pope under the name of Pius XI from February 6, 1922, to February 10, 1939. About him cf. Luigi Salvatorelli, *Pio XI e la sua eredità pontificale [Pius XI and his Papal Legacy]*, Einaudi, Turin 1939; Jean Daujat, *Pie XI, le Pape de l'Action catholique,* Téqui, Saint-Céneré 1995; Y. Chiron, *Pie XI,* Via Romana, Paris 2013; *Pio XI e il suo tempo*, ed. F. Cajani, Acts of the Convention, 4 vols, I Quaderni della Brianza, 2000, 2002, 2004, 2006: including the acts of four conventions of studies promoted by the International Center of Studies and Documentation on Pius XI in Desio.

1181 Aubert, "Le cardinal Mercier aux conclaves de 1914 et de 1922," p. 231.

The evening of that solemn day, the Marshal of the Conclave, Ludovico Chigi Albani, communicated to the *Agenzia Stefani* of Rome the following declaration:

> His Holiness Pius XI, with all the reservations in favor of the inviolable rights of the Church and the Holy See, which he has sworn to uphold and defend, has imparted his first blessing from the external Loggia in St. Peter's Square, with the particular intention that the blessing itself be directed not only to those present in St. Peter's Square, not only in Rome and in Italy, but to all the sundry nations and all the peoples, and imparts to all the wish and the proclamation of this universal pacification for which all so ardently long.

As had occurred in 1914, Cardinal William O'Connell of Boston, accompanied by the other American cardinal, Dennis Dougherty,[1182] reached the Vatican too late, about half an hour after the election. Going to Gasparri, the prelate from Boston protested not having received, either through apostolic delegation or directly, any news concerning the worsening conditions of Benedict XV's health, lamenting the fact that there was not even an effort to postpone by several days the opening of the conclave.[1183] Tied to Merry del Val by a solid friendship, O'Connell would in fact have certainly supported the strategy of the "intransigent" group, just as Cardinal Dougherty would have. Their votes would not have changed the outcome of the election, but the deplorable fact remained that for the second consecutive time the leaders of the American Church were not able to take part in a conclave.

Msgr. Giulio Mancini mentioned that he had met Cardinal Merry del Val, who immediately after the conclave left the Vatican to return to his apartment in Santa Marta.[1184] The Cardinal was quite joyful and said to him, "The danger lasted but a short time. Except for the first night, I slept quite peacefully."[1185]

On Sunday, February 12, the solemn coronation was celebrated in St. Peter's Basilica. The ceremony was to begin at 8:30 a.m., but by 6 a.m. the Basilica was already filling with a crowd calculated at around forty thousand people.

[1182] Dennis Dougherty (1865–1951), archbishop of Philadelphia from 1918, was made a cardinal by Benedict XV on March 7, 1921.

[1183] Cf. Wayman, *Cardinal O'Connell of Boston*, pp. 178–181.

[1184] Msgr. Giulio Mancini (1880–1943), domestic prelate, was chaplain of the Pontifical Gendarmerie.

[1185] *Processus Informativus Ordinarius, Sessio* XLIX, vol. 1, p. 211, deposition of Msgr. Primo Principi.

Cardinal archpriest Merry del Val awaited the papal cortege at the entrance, surrounded by the canons of St. Peter's. The procession that slowly reached the doors of the basilica was opened and closed by the Swiss Guards. After the penitentiaries of St. Peter in white chasubles, there processed the mitered abbots, the bishops, archbishops, patriarchs, and cardinals. Immediately after them came the princes who assisted at the threshold, Fr. Marcantonio Orsini, and the secret chamberlains of the cape and sword, in their sixteenth-century costumes of black silk. Pius XI, wearing a great white cape with gold stitching, was seated on the *sedia gestatoria*, carried by grooms in red damask. His appearance, embodying the majesty of the Church, was greeted by immense applause. The pope was surrounded by the Swiss Guards with their long shinny swords resting on their right shoulders, as two secret chamberlains in red cowls with white ermine furs held the *flabella*.[1186]

At a certain moment during the procession, a ceremonial genuflected three times before the pontiff, lit waddings stuck into silver rods and, while the flame was burning, slowly pronounced the words, "*Pater Sancte, sic transit gloria mundi*!" (Holy Father, thus does human glory pass). Then began the Pontifical Mass and at the end, the cortege, after having crossed the basilica once again, climbed the *scala regia* and reached the loggia above the portico of St. Peter's. The pope climbed upon a throne and a choir sang the ancient hymn, *Corona aurea super caput eius.* As dean of cardinals, Vannutelli placed on the pontiff's head the gem-studded tiara, pronouncing the words: "Receive the tiara adorned with three crowns and know that you are the father of princes and kings, the ruler of all the earth, the vicar of our Savior Jesus Christ, to whom be honor and glory forever and ever. So be it."

Then the pope looked out from the external loggia, opened his arms, raising them toward heaven and blessed the packed crowd, while the pontifical troops performed the papal hymn and the king's troops saluted with the royal fanfare.

From the gallery reserved for diplomats, François Charles-Roux observed "this enormous mass of spectators and of the faithful contemplating the splendor of the pontifical Mass,"[1187] whereas an American journalist defined the ceremony "even more dazzling and more colorful than that of the coronation of the

[1186] The *flabello* was a large fan of ostrich and peacock feathers used in papal ceremonies when the pope sat on the *sedia gestatoria*.

[1187] Charles-Roux, *Souvenirs diplomatiques*, p. 159.

King of England."[1188] The Belgian ambassador Beyens wrote in his diary, "The pope's procession is the symbol of a unaltered tradition, the image of a court that has been perpetuated and renewed far from revolutions, and to which none of the imperial courts that shone with ephemeral splendor before 1914 could be compared."[1189]

That evening there was a great meal at the French Embassy at which five French cardinals participated, as well as the archbishop of Westminster, Francis Bourne, and the archbishop of Malines, Désiré Mercier. The latter sat next to Cardinal Billot, who told him "that he was unhappy with the election of Cardinal Ratti."[1190] For the second time since the death of Pius X, the "Pius" or intransigent party had been defeated.

Cardinal Merry del Val wanted to be the first to lay at the feet of the newly elected pope the homage of his "unconditional fidelity and obedience" together with "the expression of immense joy that fills our hearts in seeing the venerable person of Your Holiness rise to the Chair of Peter.... Called by God to govern his Church, in times so turbulent and full of threats, while the faith of Christ is ignored by many and opposed, while the Gospel of love is forgotten by many and not infrequently despised, our gaze is raised trustingly to you, Blessed Father, to you, heir today of the divine promises, Teacher of truth, secure Guide and supreme Pastor of the mystical flock."[1191]

THE PERSONALITY OF PIUS XI

Achille Ratti was born in Desio, Lombardy, on May 31, 1857, to a family of bourgeois entrepreneurs who for many generations exercised the art of spinning and weaving silk. According to Cardinal Carlo Confalonieri,[1192] who was his private secretary, he never abandoned the concrete and reflexive spirit of a small Lombard entrepreneur, although he spent most of his life in the library, first as a professor and prefect at the Ambrosiana in Milan and then as prefect

[1188] Thomas Morgan, *A Reporter at the Papal Court. A Narrative of the Reign of Pope Pius XI*, Longmans, Green and Co., New York 1937, p. 47. Thomas B. Morgan (1885–1972) was the Roman correspondent for the *United Press* between the two World Wars.

[1189] Beyens, *Quatre ans à Rome*, p. 94.

[1190] Aubert, "Le cardinal Mercier aux conclaves de 1914 et 1922," p. 206.

[1191] Archive of the Postulation, ff. 498–500.

[1192] Carlo Confalonieri (1893–1986), personal secretary of Pius XI (1922–1939) alongside Msgr. Diego Venini, later became bishop of Aquila (1941), secretary of the Congregation of Seminaries (1950), prefect of the Congregation of Bishops (1958), and dean of the Sacred College.

of the Vatican Apostolic Library.[1193] This appointment did not prevent him from practicing in a systematic way his love for mountain climbing, which he considered a metaphor of life. Among his achievements, in 1899 he crossed Monte Rosa over the Zumstein and the ascent of Monte Bianco in 1900, taking a new route on the descent.[1194]

"At sixty, Achille Ratti was still hidden behind his books,"[1195] recalled Cardinal Confalonieri, who was close to him. The nomination in 1911 to vice-prefect of the Vatican Library, as assistant to Fr. Ehrle,[1196] whom he succeeded in 1914, opened to Ratti the door to new perspectives. On April 25, 1918, Benedict XV entrusted him with the difficult task of apostolic visitor to the vast territory of Poland and Lithuania, threatened by the Soviet Army. On March 30, 1919, Msgr. Ratti recognized the Polish State on behalf of the Holy Father; on June 6 he was promoted to apostolic nuncio; and on October 28, consecrated titular archbishop of Lepanto.

In the twenty-five months he spent in Poland, the new bishop demonstrated energy and courage, staying in Warsaw even when, in 1920, the Bolshevik troops besieged the capital, and almost all the other diplomatic missions dispersed. All seemed lost, but on August 16, 1920, in an epic battle at the gates of the city that went down in history as the "Miracle of the Vistula," Polish troops led by Marshall Pilsudski[1197] stopped the advance of the Red Army. The memory of those events remained so impressed on the nuncio that, once elected pope, he wanted the chapel in the Papal Palace at Castel Gandolfo to be frescoed with paintings telling the story of the Miracle of the Vistula.[1198]

1193 Carlo Confalonieri, *Pio X visto da vicino [Pius X Close Up]*, S.A.I.E, Turin 1957, pp. 89–90. Cf. also Carlo Puricelli, *Un papa brianzolo. Le radici culturali di Achille Ratti, Pio XI [A Pope from Brianza. The Cultural Roots of Achille Ratti, Pius XI]*, Editore NED, Milan 1991.

1194 In the mountaineering context, his name is associated with a peak of over 2,800 meters above Valle d'Aosta, a refuge in Val Venosta, and not a few exploits: a "first" on Punta Dufour del Rosa and, above all, a "first" on Monte Bianco known as "Via del Papa" or "Via Ratti-Grasselli." Cf. Domenico Flavio Ronzoni, *Achille Ratti. Il prete alpinista che diventò papa [Achille Ratti. The Mountaineering Priest who Became Pope]*, Bellavite Editore, Missaglia (Lecco) 2009.

1195 Confalonieri, *Pio X visto da vicino*, p. 15.

1196 Franz Ehrle (1845–1934), a German Jesuit, was prefect of the Vatican Apostolic Library from 1895 to 1914. He was made a cardinal by Pius XI in December 1922 and named librarian and archivist of Holy Roman Church in 1929. Cf. In Vian, "Una illustre successione alla Biblioteca Vaticana: Achille Ratti," in *Mélanges Eugène Tisserant*, vol. 8, Vatican City 1964, pp. 373–439.

1197 Jòzef Pilsudski (1867–1935), after having fought in the First World War with a Polish legion incorporated into the Austro-Hungarian army, in 1918 was elected commander of the army. In 1926, he took power through a military coup.

1198 Concerning the "Miracle on the Vistula," cf. Adam Zamoyski, *Warsaw 1920: Lenin's Failed Conquest of Europe*, Harper Press, London 2008. Concerning the apostolic visit and the nunciature in Poland

In 1921, Msgr. Ratti was nominated cardinal and archbishop of Milan, but he was to govern the diocese for just a few months. No one had thought that on February 6, 1922, he would become the new pontiff with the name Pius XI.

When elected, Achille Ratti was sixty-five years old and, according to the English *charge d'affaires* in the Vatican, Ogilvie-Forbes, to those who approached him he gave the impression of a teacher. "Just replace the zucchetto and the white habit with the toga of the doctor in letters and behold a professor in scholastic lore of Victorian England."[1199] Behind his round spectacles, with thick glass lenses, his eyes scrutinized his surroundings with curiosity and concealed from his interlocutor a demanding and imperious character.

Sweetness did not belong to Pius XI's temperament. Expressions of exasperation, of wrath, of indignation were often on his lips. Jean-Dominique Durand has dedicated a fine essay to "The Style of Governance of Pius XI," explaining that the pontiff wanted to be informed about everything, concerned himself with every detail, and exercised his authority through the assiduous consultation of his collaborators with whom he stayed in close contact, even if he often did not follow their counsel.[1200] The salient trait of his pontificate was, as observed Giovanni Coco, "a governing activity both strong and at times authoritarian that did not fear moving even in open opposition to the thought of some authoritative cardinals."[1201] The strategy of turning separately to the opinion of individual cardinals without convoking a plenary session became over the course of his pontificate a privileged weapon for overcoming the opposition of the Sacred College.[1202] Cardinal Confalonieri remembered that Pius XI held that "he, the pope, was sufficient for commanding. He allowed himself to take no one's hand, considering dicasteries and curial officials as executors of superior dispositions."[1203]

---

of the future Pius XI, cf. *I Diari di Achille Ratti*, Vatican Secret Archive, Vatican City 2015, 2 vols.

1199 Cit. in Anthony Rhodes, *Il Vaticano e le dittature 1922–1945*, Mursia, Milan 1973, p. 27. Sir George Arthur Drostan Ogilvie-Forbes (1891–1954) was *chargé d'affaires* to the Holy See from 1930 to 1932.

1200 Jean-Dominique Durand, "Lo stile di governo di Pio XI," in *La sollecitudine ecclesiale di Pio XI alla luce delle nuove fonti archivistiche [The Ecclesiastical Solicitude of Pius XI in Light of New Archival Sources]*, ed. Cosimo Semeraro, Libreria Editrice Vaticana, Vatican City 2020, pp. 44–60.

1201 Giovanni Coco, "L'anno terribile del cardinale Pacelli" [The 'Terrible Year' of Cardinal Pacelli], *Archivum historiae pontificiae* 47 (2009), p. 154.

1202 Ibid., p. 159.

1203 Confalonieri, *Pio XI visto da vicino*, p.172.

The Politics of Pius XI

The year of Pius XI's election was that of the "March on Rome." In 1919, Benito Mussolini founded in Milan the *Fasci Italiani di Combattimento* (Italian Fasces of Combat), which in 1921 became the National Fascist Party.[1204] During the elections of May 15, 1921, Giolitti allied with Mussolini and the nationalists, giving rise to a "national block" that won the majority of seats against the Popular and Socialist Parties.[1205] Giolitti governed until July 1921, when he ceded his post to Ivanoe Bonomi, but the liberal State, born in the *Risorgimento*, showed itself incapable of facing the profound social crisis of the post-war period.[1206] The violence of the extreme left grew, and the country was on the precipice of civil war. Prime Minister Luigi Facta succeeded Bonomi on February 26, and asked the king to reinstate legality.[1207] But Vittorio Emanuele III refused to sign the state of emergency, and on October 30, Benito Mussolini received the charge to form a new government, which was to be the longest in the history of united Italy, lasting until July 25, 1943.

On October 31, 1921, more than fifty thousand black shirts with flags, banners, and pennants marched from Villa Borghese to the Altar of the Patria. The parade reached the Quirinale where the king watched from the royal balcony with General Diaz and Admiral Thaon di Revel, the two protagonists of victory in 1918, watching beside him for three hours as swarms of airplanes twirled about the sky.

On November 4, the fourth anniversary of victory,[1208] Mussolini and all the new ministers went to the Altar of the Patria in Piazza Venezia to kneel before the remains of the Unknown Soldier. The unknown soldier had been transferred the year before by a special train from Aquileia to Rome as a symbol of the silent sacrifice of 600,000 fallen soldiers in the war.

[1204] On the origin and evolution of fascism, besides the monumental work by Renzo De Felice, cf. F. Perfetti, *Lo Stato fascista. Le basi sindacali e corporative,* Le Lettere, Florence 2010, pp. 13–70; Emilio Gentile, *Storia del partito fascista. Movimento e milizia, 1919–1922,* Laterza, Rome-Bari 2021. Concerning the "March on Rome": Domenico Fisichella, *Dal Risorgimento al Fascismo. 1861–1922,* Pagine, Rome 2019, pp. 336–361.

[1205] The National Block obtained 19.1% of the vote in the national elections and a total of 105 deputies, of whom 35 were fascists and 20 of the Italian National Association.

[1206] Ivanoe Bonomi (1873–1951), a socialist politician, between July 4, 1921, and February 26, 1922, was the prime minister, interior minister *ad interim,* and minister of foreign affairs. A Freemason of high degree, he was a member of the Supreme Council of the *Gran Loggia d'Italia* from 1924–1926.

[1207] Luigi Facta (1861–1930) was the last prime minister before fascism, from February 26 to October 27, 1922.

[1208] The last major Allied offensive of World War I occurred at the Battle of the Sambre on November 4, 1918, followed by the Armistice a week later.

Pius XI and his secretary of state followed the events attentively and received the new government benevolently. "This movement," declared Secretary of State Gasparri on November 11, "has become a necessity. Italy was moving toward anarchy and the king has acted wisely, since commanding soldiers to shoot was equally harmful."[1209] Mussolini, for his part, repudiated the anticlericalism of his youth on September 5, 1921, and declared, "Rome, beyond being the capital of Italy, is to be considered the capital of an immense spiritual empire. If nationalism were to utilize the strength of Catholicism for the aim of national expansion, I believe it could draw great benefit from it."[1210]

While fascism reached out to Catholics, the pontiff proclaimed, in his encyclical *Ubi arcano*, of December 23, 1922, the need to establish "the peace of Christ in the Kingdom of Christ" and encouraged the "holy battle" of "that whole group of movements, organizations, and works so dear to our fatherly heart which passes under the name of Catholic Action."[1211]

Pius XI gave Catholic Action a rigidly centralized structure, placing it under the control of the ecclesiastical hierarchy, and assigning it the tasks of moral and spiritual education.[1212] According to the pope's intentions, it was to be the principal instrument for establishing the authority of the Church in public life, in complete obedience to the directives of the Holy See.[1213] With the October Revolution in Russia and the subsequent birth of communist parties in various parts of the world, the dismemberment of Austria, the foundation of new nation states, the advent of fascism in Italy and Nazism in Germany, and the religious persecutions in Russia, Mexico, Spain, and Germany, Pius XI found himself in the crosshairs of advancing anti-Christian forces. He entrusted to Catholics the task of re-Christianizing society, extending and increasing the Kingdom of Christ with the encyclical *Quas primas* of December 11, 1925.[1214]

1209 G. Sale, *Fascismo e Vaticano, prima della Conciliazione [Fascism and the Vatican, Before the Conciliation]*, Jaca Book, Milan 2007, p. 10.

1210 Benito Mussolini, *Opera omnia*, ed. Duilio Susmel, La Fenice, Florence 1951–1963, vol. 15, p. 187.

1211 Pius XI, Encyclial *Ubi arcano*, December 23, 1922, nos. 54–55, https://www.vatican.va/content/pius-xi/en/encyclicals/documents/hf_p-xi_enc_19221223_ubi-arcano-dei-consilio.html.

1212 Mario Casella, *L'Azione Cattolica nell'Italia contemporanea (1919–1969)*, Ave, Rome 1992.

1213 Cf. Mario Bendiscioli, *La politica della Santa Sede. Direttive, origini, realizzazioni (1918–1938) [The Politics of the Holy See. Directives, Origins, and Realization]*, La Nuova Italia, Florence 1939; F. Margiotta Broglio, *Italia e Santa Sede dalla Grande Guerra alla Conciliazione. Aspetti politici e giuridici, [Italy and the Holy See from the Great War to the Conciliation. Political and Juridical Aspects]*, Laterza, Bari 1966; R. Pertici, *Chiesa e Stato in Italia. Dalla Grande Guerra al nuovo Concordato (1914–1984), [The Church and State in Italy. From the Great War to the New Concordat]*, Il Mulino, Bologna 2009.

1214 Pius XI, Encyclical *Quas primas*, December 11, 1925, AAS, 17 (1925), pp. 593–610.

To reach this objective, the pope turned to a political strategy begun under his secretary of state Gasparri during the pontificate of Benedict XV, consisting in dealing directly with political interlocutors of every tendency. The instrument of the new ecclesiastical policy was the concordat, eighteen of which were to be stipulated over the course of his pontificate.[1215]

Pius XI was convinced that concordats with totalitarian regimes would contribute to the apostolic activity of the Church in a more efficacious manner than could Catholic political parties, from which he retracted his support. On July 1, 1924, Don Sturzo resigned as secretary of the Popular Party and in October of the same year left for London and then for New York.

The concordat policy was extremely flexible, as demonstrated by the attitude toward the *Cristeros* in Mexico, who did not receive the full support they had expected; as concerned Spain (where the Holy See supported the Republicans for five years, beginning in 1931); but also in regard to the situation in Russia, where Msgr. d'Herbigny, president of the Pro Russia Commission, was the unbiased architect of the Holy See's first *Ostpolitik*.[1216]

Perhaps only toward the end of his pontificate did Pius XI perceive the depth of the ideological and persecutorial dimensions of totalitarian regimes. The two encyclicals of 1937, *Divini Redemptoris*[1217] and *Mit brennender Sorge*,[1218] both of profound doctrinal substance, marked the threshold of awareness that Nazism and communism, the "twin enemies" of the twentieth century, were not

[1215] Nikolaus Hilling spoke of *Konkordatsinflation* in the pontificate of Pius XI, cf. "Die Konkordatsfrage," *Archiv für Kirchenrecht* 110 (1930), pp. 121–135. Ten concordats were signed under Pius XI: Latvia (1922), Bavaria (1924), Poland (1925), Romania and Lithuania (1927), Italy and Prussia (1929), Baden (1932), Austria and the Germanic Empire (1933); an eleventh was signed with Yugoslavia (1935) though not ratified; also signed were the *modus vivendi* with Czechoslovakia (1927) and with Ecuador (1937) as well as a series of conventions (cf. *Raccolta di concordati su materie ecclesiastiche tra la Santa Sede e le autorità civili [Collection of Concordats on Ecclesiastical Matters Between the Holy See and Civil Authorities]*, vol. 2, 1915–1954, ed. Angelo Mercati, Vatican City 1954). Cf. also Rhodes, *Il Vaticano e le dittature*; F. Margiotta Broglio, "La politique concordataire du Vatican vis-à-vis des États totalitaires," *Relations Internationales* 27 (1981), pp. 319–342.

[1216] Michel-Joseph Bourguignon d'Herbigny (1880–1957), a French Jesuit, was named rector of the Pontifical Oriental Institute and the Pontifical Commission for Russia by Pius XI. On February 11, 1926, he was secretly consecrated bishop by the pope, who entrusted him with the mission of creating a clandestine hierarchy for the Catholic Church in the Soviet Union during the persecutions of the 1920s. On relations between Pius XI and d'Herbigny, cf. Léon Tretjakewitsch, *Bishop Michel d'Herbigny S. J. and Russia: A Pre-Ecumenical Approach to Christian Unity*, Augustinus Verlag, Würzburg 1990.

[1217] Pius XI, Encyclical *Divini Redemptoris* on atheistic Communism, in AAS, 29 (1937), pp. 65–106.

[1218] Pius XI, Encyclical *Mit Brennender sorge* on the situation of the Catholic Church in the German Reich, in AAS, 29 (1937), pp. 145–167.

expressions of pure force with which one could negotiate, bending them to one's own interests, but ideological visions incompatible with that of the Church and with which no other attitude was possible than open hostility.

The Holy Office and the Buonaiuti Case

During the pontificate of Pius XI, as under that of Benedict XV, Cardinal Merry del Val carried out with zeal his role as secretary of the Holy Office, the "Supreme" Congregation presided by the supreme pontiff. Through its doctrinal interventions, it often distanced itself from the policies of the secretary of state. In fact, Rafael Merry del Val and Pietro Gasparri not only had two different personalities, but incarnated two divergent visions of pastoral and political action of the Church in the face of the challenges of the modern world.[1219] For this reason, the party that found its inspiration in Pius X continued its opposition to Gasparri until his substitution with Pacelli on February 7, 1930. Cardinal Baudrillart wrote in his diary, "In the Vatican, a knife fight is being waged against Gasparri, and Merry del Val is leading the charge."[1220]

The "Buonaiuti Case" was exemplary in this regard. In his pragmatism, Gasparri was convinced he could "recover" Buonaiuti. Merry del Val held, instead, that it was necessary to arrest his intellectual influence within the Catholic world, as Buonaiuti was not retracting his positions. Pius XI started by employing the Holy Office in carrying out its task of safeguarding the faith. On March 28, 1924, Buonaiuti was again excommunicated, and all his writings were placed on the Index, expressing "inability to tolerate any further without grave scandal and harm to the faith this subtle and continuous demolition of the Faith by a Catholic priest who insists on wanting to appear as such."[1221]

The day before the excommunication, Buonaiuti requested an audience with Cardinal Merry del Val, whom he defined "an enigmatic and sinister

[1219] Marie Levant, "Gasparri, Merry del Val et le gouvernement de Pie XI," in François Jankowiak and L. Pettinaroli (eds.), *Les cardinaux entre Cour et Curie. Une élite romaine, 1775–2015*, École française de Rome, Rome 2017, pp. 307–320.

[1220] Note of August 13, 1923, in Christoph (ed.), *Les Carnets du Cardinal Afred Baudrillart, 1 janvier 1922 — 12 avril 1925*, Éditions du Cerf, Paris 2001, p. 565. Alfred Baudrillart (1859–1942), a priest with the Oratory, was professor and then rector of *Institut Catholique* in Paris from 1907 until his death. Bishop of Imeria in 1921, then archbishop of Melitene (1928) and cardinal in 1935, he was elected to the *Académie Française* in 1918. Beginning on August 1, 1914, Baudrillart kept a diary of the main events of his day until his death.

[1221] AAS, 16 (1924), p. 159. Decree of the Holy Office on March 26, 1924, "Condemnationes sac. Ernesti Buonaiuti eiusque operum omnium."

figure,"[1222] contrasting his "haughty and vain presumption" to the "burly and ever-so-slightly unrefined figure of Pietro Gasparri, though illuminated and redeemed by a profundity of gaze, smiling and good-natured."[1223] It was Msgr. Carlo Perosi, a secretary of the Holy Office, who received him, however,[1224] saying, in light of the censure about to be issued, "It is precisely your teaching that has provoked the measure that will be promulgated tomorrow. You are incorrigible and your teaching from the chair is aimed at disturbing consciences."[1225]

In January 1925, Buonaiuti was deprived of his use of ecclesiastical garb and finally, on February 25, 1926, the Holy Office issued against the priest the decree of excommunication that defined him as *vitandus* (banned): "With the decree of Wednesday, March 26, 1924, the priest Ernest Buonaiuti was inflicted with excommunication, the condemnation of all his books and writings, and the prohibition to write, hold conferences, and teach in public schools, in matters pertaining to religion … the Pontiff Maximus declares with the present Decree the above-mentioned priest Ernesto Buonaiuti excommunicated nominally and personally and, according to the disposition of ca. 2258, para 2, expressly banned, with all the consequences of law."[1226]

Cardinal Merry del Val's anti-modernism was never flinching. On May 13, 1923, Pius XI had beatified Cardinal Robert Bellarmine of the Society of Jesus.[1227] The following year, the pope sent Merry del Val as his representative to the hundredth anniversary of the restoration of the Pontifical Gregorian University. On May 13, during the pontifical Mass celebrated in remembrance of this anniversary, Merry del Val recalled the majestic figure of Blessed Bellarmine as an exemplary defender of the faith and combatant against heresies:

1222 Buonaiuti, *Pellegrino di Roma*, p. 49.

1223 Ibid., p. 149.

1224 Carlo Perosi (1868–1930), brother of the illustrious composer don Lorenzo Perosi, beginning in 1915 was consultor and in 1916 assessor of the Holy Office. Pius XI elevated him to the rank of cardinal in 1926. In 1928, he was named secretary of the Consistorial Congregation.

1225 Buonaiuti, *Pellegrino di Roma*, pp. 206–207.

1226 Cf. J. M. de Bujanda, *Index Librorum Prohibitorum 1600–1966*, Librairie Droz, Geneva 2002, p. 174. With the decree of June 17, 1944, the Holy Office condemned the *Opera et scripta omnia* of Buonaiuti, as it had already done in 1924 and 1925. In 1931, Buonaiuti was also stripped of his university chair for having refused to make the oath prescribed by the fascist government. Regarding this case cf. Broglio, *Italia e Santa Sede*, pp. 171–180.

1227 Robert Bellarmine (1542–1621), after his beatification in 1923, was canonized in 1930. On September 17, 1931, Pius XI proclaimed him a Doctor of the Church.

> Against the deadly heresies of his time, Blessed Bellarmine was an unvanquished and dreaded combatant; and we can hold for certain that if God has desired to delay until our day the definitive glorification of this renowned paladin of the Catholic Church, He has done so that He might offer us his example to follow in combating errors, old and new, that we must confront in the present age.... Today, the oscillation of thought is immediately exalted as progress, and these innovators, stumbling in the darkness of the most specious sophisms, construct nothing but destroy everything, raising problems they are incapable of resolving.... May new defenders of the truth arise in all fields of knowledge, and following in the footsteps of the great master, Blessed Bellarmine, may they know how to dissipate the shadows of error with the power of their genius and the depth of their studies; may they know how to illustrate the luminosity of the immutable doctrine, always true, of the Church of Christ, and at the same time cooperate tenaciously in the salvation of souls following the edifying example of his virtues. May they be learned, but above all holy: "*qui ad iustitiam erudiunt multos fulgebunt quasi stellae in perpetuas aeternitates*" [those who turn many to righteousness, will shine like the stars for ever and ever; Dan. 12:3]."[1228]

Padre Pio and the Holy Office

A more complex case was that of Padre Pio,[1229] the man of the stigmata from Gargano, whom the Church today venerates as a saint. Francesco Forgione, whose religious name was Pio da Pietrelcina, was a Capuchin friar who lived in the convent of San Giovanni Rotondo in the Diocese of Manfredonia. It was there that he received the permanent stigmata on September 20, 1918, during a vision of Jesus Crucified who said to him, "I join you to my Passion." This phenomenon and the fame of sanctity of this friar created a movement of devotion throughout Italy with an impressive flow of faithful to San Giovanni Rotondo. The presence

1228 Cenci, *Merry del Val*, p. 810; Archive of the Postulation, ff. 546–554.

1229 Padre Pio of Pietrelcina, born Francesco Forgione (1887–1968), received the stigmata on the night of August 5, 1918. He was beatified in 1999 and canonized in 2002 by John Paul II. Cf. Ferdinando da Riese, *Padre Pio da Pietrelcina, crocifisso senza croce, [Padre Pio of Pietrelcina, Crucified Without a Cross]*, Edizioni Padre Pio da Pietrelcina, San Giovanni Rotondo 1984; Gerardo di Flumeri, *Il Beato Padre Pio da Pietrelcina*, Edizioni Padre Pio da Pietrelcina, San Giovanni Rotondo 2001; Luigi Peroni, *Padre Pio da Pietrelcina*, Borla, Roma 2002; P. Marcellino Iasenzaniro, *Padre Pio. Profilo di un Santo*, Edizioni Padre Pio da Pietrelcina, San Giovanni Rotondo 2009; Angelo Maria Mischitelli, *Padre Pio. Un uomo un santo [Padre Pio. A Man, A Saint]*, Sovera, Rome 2015.

of Padre Pio disturbed, however, the climate of moral laxity in which the diocese was immersed due to the immoral conduct of its archbishop, Pasquale Gagliardi,[1230] and of some of his collaborators.[1231] In order to rid themselves of this cumbersome Capuchin, the archbishop and these priests accused him of being a corrupter of women and of having invented the supernatural manifestations, using nitric acid to procure the wounds.

Msgr. Gagliardi had important friendships in Rome from his time as a student in the Capranica College and the Gregorian. The supporters in his campaign against Padre Pio were Cardinal De Lai, prefect of the Consistorial Congregation; Msgr. Carlo Perosi, brother of the more renowned musician and assessor of the Holy Office;[1232] and above all, Fr. Agostino Gemelli, a psychiatrist turned Franciscan who later became the founder and rector of the Catholic University of Milan.[1233]

Cardinal Merry del Val and Fr. Agostino Gemelli had met in 1907 when Pius X's secretary of state was helping the young, scholarly Franciscan free himself from the temptation of modernism. Gemelli recalled being disturbed by the publication of *Pascendi* and having almost decided to leave religious life. He went for an audience with Pius X who advised him to speak with Don Guanella and with Cardinal Merry del Val.[1234] The secretary of state, with great supernatural affection, exhorted him to persevere and to continue his studies.[1235] In 1918, Merry del Val invited him to collaborate with the Holy Office, entrusting him various cases to examine. Gemelli recalled that once, concerning miracles to which the Franciscan raised objections, Merry del Val told him, "We make saints and you unmake them." Gemelli was disconcerted by these playful words,

1230 Pasquale Gagliardi (1859–1941), alumnus of the Capranica College and the Gregorian, ordained a priest in 1883, was named archbishop of Manfredonia and perpetual administrator of Vieste by Leo XIII in 1897. In 1922, he was named assistant to the papal throne by Pius XI, but in October 1929 was transferred to the titular archbishopric of Lemnos, returning to his residence in Tricarico where he was born and eventually died.

1231 In particular, the archpriest Giuseppe Principe (1872–1950), parish priest of San Giovanni Rotondo, and the canon Domenico Palladino (1890–1977), both of the archdiocese of Manfredonia.

1232 Giuseppe Pagnossin, *Il calvario di padre Pio [The Calvary of Padre Pio]*, Tip. M. Suman, Conselve 1978, vol. 1, pp. 161–162.

1233 Agostino Gemelli (1878–1959) grew up in an agnostic, positivist setting. He returned to the practice of the faith and in November 1903 entered the Franciscan Order and took vows on December 23, 1904. He was later the founder (1921) and rector of the Catholic University of the Sacred Heart of Milan.

1234 Don Luigi Guanella (1842–1915), founder of the Daughters of St. Mary of Providence, was proclaimed a saint by Benedict XVI in 2011.

1235 *Processus informativus ordinarius, Sessio* XCVI, vol. 2, p. 577.

but the cardinal replied that he ought to continue his scientific investigations with the same scrupulosity, reserving the final judgment to his superiors.[1236]

Despite his conversion, the approach of the Franciscan physician-philosopher to mystical phenomena remained positivistic and scientistic. In 1920, Fr. Gemelli accepted to go to San Giovanni Rotondo at the behest of the bishop of Foggia, Msgr. Salvatore Bella, probably in agreement with Msgr. Carlo Perosi. He met with Padre Pio only for a few moments on April 19, with the intention of examining the stigmata. But the ecclesiastical authorities had decided the previous year that any examination of the friar's wounds would be carried out only with the written authorization of the Holy Office, which Gemelli did not possess. Padre Pio therefore refused to show him the stigmata. Although he had not examined the Capuchin, that same day Fr. Gemelli sent Msgr. Perosi an initial report in which he stated that he considered the stigmata to be somatic manifestations of a hysterical nature. Much more in depth were the reports sent by Dr. Giorgio Festa on November 10, 1919, and on August 31, 1920, to the Holy Office.[1237] As documented by Fr. Flavio Peloso, Fr. Gemelli had in fact already been to San Giovanni Rotondo in 1919, in disguise, playing, as he himself wrote, "the comedy of the doctor convinced and converted for having had the luxury of observing, seeing, and verifying."[1238] Gemelli's report had, nevertheless, the character of a personal initiative and not of an official report requested by the Holy Office.[1239]

The one who did receive the appointment of the Holy Office to conduct an investigation into Padre Pio was the future cardinal Raffaele Carlo Rossi, a Carmelite who had been named bishop of Volterra several years earlier, a pious and learned religious who, after a detailed investigation, came to the

1236 Ibid., p. 576.

1237 Giorgio Festa (1860–1940) was a physician from Rome who, at the behest of the Minister General of the Capuchin friars, twice visited Padre Pio and, in 1925, operated on his inguinal hernia. Concerning him, cf. *Misteri di scienza e luci di fede. Stigmate del padre Pio da Pietrelcina [Mysteries of Science and Light of Faith. The Stigmata of Padre Pio of Pietrelcina]*, Ferri, Rome 1938.

1238 Thus wrote Fr. Gemelli in in a detailed report to the Holy Office of thirteen typewritten pages with signed corrections, dated April 6, 1926. Cf. ADDF S. O., *Devotiones Variae, P. Pio da Pietrelcina,* 255/19, VIII, 131, pp. 1–13. The text is dated April 6, 1926, and was registered on May 7, 1926, as a note in the margin reports.

1239 Flavio Peloso, "Padre Agostino Gemelli disse il vero: visitò le stimmate di Padre Pio da Pietrelcina" [Fr. Agostino Gemelli Spoke the Truth: His Visit to the Stigmata of Padre Pio of Pietrelcina], *Bulletin of the Archive of the History of the Catholic Social Movement in Italy* 51 (2016), pp. 71–86. "Gemelli: wanted to receive an official mandate of the Holy Office to examine Padre Pio. But that mandate never arrived." (Francesco Castelli, "L'imputato Gemelli è assolto," [The Indicted Gemelli Acquitted], *L'Osservatore Romano,* May 5th, 2021).

opposite conclusion to that of Fr. Gemelli.[1240] In January 1922, Msgr. Rossi presented the Holy Office with his assessment: a text of 123 pages with 27 documents, in which Padre Pio was defined "a good friar," excluding Fr. Gemelli's thesis of "self-stigmatization," and affirming that "one cannot say how the extraordinary nature of what is happening to the person of Padre Pio comes about, but it certainly does not come from diabolical intervention nor through deceit or fraud."[1241] "The future will tell," wrote the Inquisitor of the Holy Office, "what today cannot be read in the life of Padre Pio da Pietrelcina."[1242]

On June 2, 1922, the Congregation of the Holy Office[1243] sent to the Minister General of the Capuchins a letter signed by Cardinal Merry del Val communicating that the cardinal inquisitors had concluded that Padre Pio needed to remain "under observation." "To this effect," it stated, "it is first of all necessary and indispensable to avoid every peculiarity and commotion regarding his person and for this reason he should be reduced in everything to the practices of the common life of the other religious."[1244]

In support of the resolution of May 31, 1923, the Holy Office emanated a *declaratio*, according to which, in light of the investigation carried out, it could not definitively establish the supernatural nature of the events concerning Padre Pio ("*non constare de eorundem factorum supernaturalitate*") and exhorted the faithful "to conform themselves in their way of acting to this declaration."[1245] The resolution was communicated to the Capuchin provincial by means of a

1240 Raffaele Carlo Rossi (1876–1948), Discalced Carmelite, was consecrated bishop of Volterra by Benedict XV in 1920. He was later assessor of the Consistorial Congregation (1923–1930), titular archbishop of Thessalonica (1923–1930), superior of the Missionaries of San Carlo (1930–1948), made a cardinal with the titular church of Santa Prassede on June 30, 1930. In 1976, the cause for his beatification was introduced. Fr. Francesco Castelli, pp. 277–284, expresses this opinion: "Balance, culture, holiness of life, gifted with governing abilities, perspicacity and wisdom, these were the characteristics of his life and of this investigation" (*Padre Pio sotto inchiesta. L' "autobiografia" segreta [Padre Pio Under Investigation. The Secret "Autobiography"]*, Ares, Milan 2008, p. 277.

1241 ADDF, *S.O. Devotiones Variae, P. Pio da Pietrelcina*, n. 1, fasc. 1–2 (1919–1923), Report on the visit by Msgr. Raffaele Carlo Rossi (1921), p. 45.

1242 Ibid., p. 2. The complete text of his official opinion is reproduced in Castelli, *Padre Pio sotto inchiesta*, pp. 103–274.

1243 In 1922, the prefect of the Holy Office was Pio XI, Cardinal Merry del Val was the secretary, and Msgr. Carlo Perosi was assessor. The commissioner was Fr. Alessando Lottini O.P.M.; the cardinal "inquisitors" were: De Lai, Pompili, Gasparri, Van Rossum, Sbarretti, Frühwirth, Billot, Lega, and Giorgi.

1244 The text of the deliberation is found in Pagnossin, *Il calvario di padre Pio*, vol. 1, pp. 142–143.

1245 AAS, 15 (1923), p. 356. Text of the Declaration, in Pagnossin, *Il calvario di padre Pio*, vol. 1, pp. 175–176, reproduced in *L'Osservatore Romano*, July 5, 1923.

letter on June 15, in which the Curia General was given the order to prohibit Padre Pio from celebrating in public and carrying out any written activity of spiritual direction.[1246] On July 24 there was another warning in which the faithful were asked to abstain absolutely from all relations, even epistolary, for reasons of devotion, with Padre Pio."[1247]

However, when San Giovanni Rotondo learned that the transfer of the religious to another monastery was also foreseen, there was an outright popular uprising led by the mayor, Francesco Morcaldi.[1248] On August 17, the Holy Office gave the order to delay the transfer, while in San Giovanni Rotondo a group of people took the initiative and gathered documents and testimony in defense of Padre Pio and to reveal the corruption of the personalities accusing him.

Emanuele Brunatto and Merry del Val

At this point, a unique personality entered the scene, the young Emanuele Brunatto.[1249] Born in Turin in 1892, after having led a wayward and disorderly life, in 1922 he was converted by Padre Pio, who accepted him as a spiritual child. He became a devout disciple and lived for many years in San Giovanni Rotondo, creating an association with Mayor Morcaldi to prove the innocence of Padre Pio and the corruption of those denigrating him. Brunatto, whom Padre Pio called "the Policeman" for his investigative gifts, organized a full "counter-espionage" organization, consisting in stakeouts, stalking, photographs of documents acquired at a high price, and even incursions into private dwellings. Coming to Rome in June 1925, he brought with him two "voluminous dossiers" and met with Don Luigi Orione

1246 Pagnossin, *Il calvario di padre Pio,* vol. 1, p. 182.

1247 AAS, 16 (1924), p. 368.

1248 Francesco Morcaldi (1889–1976) was mayor of San Giovanni Rotondo from 1923 to 1927, from 1954 to 1958, and from 1962 to 1965.

1249 Emanuele Brunatto (1892–1965), born in Turin, and actor and fashion impresario, was converted by Padre Pio. He lived in the monastery of San Giovanni Rotondo from 1920 to 1925. His body was buried on September 26, 2020, in the cemetery of San Giovanni Rotondo in front of the old chapel of the Capuchin Friars where the parents of Padre Pio lie in rest as well. Cf. his autobiographical book *Padre Pio. Mon Père spirituel*, Éditions de L'Orme Rond, Fontenay sous Bois 2012, edited by his son François. Cf. also Francobaldo Chiocci, *L'uomo che salvò Padre Pio: vita avventurosa e morte di Emanuele Brunatto [The Man Who Saved Padre Pio: The Adventurous Life and Death of Emanuele Brunatto]*, Adnkronos Libri, Rome 2003; Edoardo Misuraca, *Brouillon. Il manoscritto di Emanuele Brunatto... cinque anni accanto a Padre Pio [Rough Draft. The Manuscript of Emanuele Brunatto… Five Years Next to Padre Pio]*, Youcanprint, Lecce 2023. Misuraca published Brunatto's manuscript furnished with the publication of nearly all the accessory documentation used in the writing of *Lettera alla Chiesa [Letter to the Church]* (1929) and *Gli anticristi nella Chiesa di Cristo [The Antichrists in the Church of Christ]*, Aldana, Paris 1933.

in his house in Via delle Sette Sale.[1250] After having consulted the documents, Don Orione advised Brunatto not to give them to anyone, but to make copies of them to submit to the attention of the cardinals of the Holy Office, of whom he gave Brunatto the list. Taking his leave, he said to him, "You are fighting a good and holy battle. Trust in the Lord."[1251] Following Orione's instructions, he met with many ecclesiastics and left a copy of his dossier with each of them.[1252]

"Cardinal Merry del Val," recalled Brunatto, "received me in his residence in Santa Marta, in the Vatican. He had a youthful face, under a halo of white hair, black eyebrows, clean gaze, full of light. A great lord, bearing the *porpora* with natural majesty, the man with whom I was about to cross swords seemed to have come out of one of David's portraits."[1253]

The secretary of the Holy Office listened attentively to him, examined the documents he presented, and heard his summations patiently. Brunatto relates having said during the interview: "Eminence, the faithful, who know only a part of the documents on the extraordinary events I am presenting to you, cannot understand how the Holy Office could have declared that the events attributed to Padre Pio da Pietrelcina are not of a supernatural nature." The cardinal replied, "The Holy Office never said this. In the communications of the Holy Office, it says '*non constat*,' which means 'we have not ascertained.'" "And yet, Your Eminence, the meaning is clear from what follows. The faithful have been exhorted to have no contact, not even epistolary, with the aforementioned Padre Pio; and this, it seems to me, is a condemnation." "No, Mr. Brunatto, the Holy Office has not condemned Padre Pio. When the Supreme Congregation wants to condemn a priest it suspends him *a divinis*. Now, this is not at all the case with Padre Pio and furthermore, you have misinterpreted the text: the warning of the Holy Office exhorts the faithful not to have contact with Padre Pio *devotionis causa* [out of devotion]. Do not forget, finally, that all saints during their lives have had trials, and even harsh ones at times."[1254]

1250 "It was Sunday," recalled Brunatto. Don Orione "held a meeting outdoors for a crowd of collaborators and benefactors. He had a pure gaze, firm voice and a simple and sublime harmony, with a touch of cunning that rendered him irresistible" (Misuraca, *Brouillon*, p. 39).

1251 Gerardo Saldutto, *Un tormentato settennio (1918–1925) [A Seven-Year Torment]*, Edizioni Padre Pio da Pietrelcina, San Giovanni Rotondo, p. 196.

1252 Brunatto met Cardinals Gasparri, Merry del Val, Pompili, Sbarretti, De Lai, Lega, Van Rossum, Silj, Billot, Msgr. Carlo Perosi, and the Jesuits Enrico Rosa and Pietro Tacchi Venturi.

1253 Misuraca, *Brouillon*, p. 41.

1254 Flavio Peloso, *Don Orione e Padre Pio da Pietrelcina nel decennio della tormenta (1923–1933) [Don Orione and Padre Pio da Pietrelcina During the Tormented Decade]*, Jaca Book, Milan 1999, p. 461; Misuraca, *Brouillon*, p. 42.

These words reassured Brunatto, but above all they can help us to understand the position of the Holy Office, which did not intend to take punitive measures with respect to the Capuchin of San Giovanni Rotondo, but simply to evaluate prudently the unique case of the first priest in history to receive the stigmata.[1255] The formula *non constat de supernaturalitate* is ambiguous in the sense that it confirms neither the supernatural origin, nor a non-supernatural origin of the phenomenon, and is different from the clearly negative phrase: *constat de non supernaturalitate.* The Congregation of the Holy Office behaved in a cautious manner, therefore, taking into consideration not only the phenomenon as such, but also the context in which it occurred and the possible repercussions on the religious and civil settings.[1256] The timeline of the Holy Office was not that of the impetuous Brunatto, and so the enterprising youth, seeking to precipitate the situation, decided to give to the press the scandalous material he had collected. The volume came out in 1926 under the title Padre Pio da Pietrelcina, but was placed on the Index by the Holy Office for not having first obtained the *imprimatur.*[1257] The Vatican acquired almost all the copies, and the book never entered circulation.

The documents presented by Brunatto were, nevertheless, unassailable, and Merry del Val, who did not cater to the enemies of Padre Pio, requested an investigation into the diocese of Manfredonia. "Thanks to the resolute attitude of the Cardinal Secretary of the Holy Office," recalled Brunatto, "the apostolic visitor was nominated in the person of Msgr. Bevilacqua, a prelate of singular perspicacity and rectitude, who worked energetically in his investigation with no tolerance for pressures or interference of any sort."[1258]

Msgr. Bevilacqua, then responsible for discipline in the vicariate of Rome, was named apostolic visitor for the entire diocese of Manfredonia.[1259] He asked Merry del Val for Brunatto's assistance in his investigations. Together they went to San Giovanni Rotondo, residing in the home of Maria Pyle, an American

1255 St. Francis of Assisi was a friar but was never ordained a priest.

1256 F. Castelli, *Padre Pio e il Sant'Uffizio (1918–1939). Fatti, protagonisti, documenti inediti [Padre Pio and the Holy Office. Facts, Protagonists, and Unpublished Documents]*, Edizioni Studium, Rome 2011, p. 133. cf. idem, *Padre Pio sotto inchiesta: L'autobiographia Segreta [Padre Pio Under Investigation: The Secret Autobiography]*, Ares, 2008, pp. 105–255.

1257 E. De Rossi (pseudonym of Emanuele Brunatto), *Padre Pio da Pietrelcina*, Giorgio Berlutti Editore, Rome 1926.

1258 Brunatto, *Gli anticristi*, p. 42.

1259 Msgr. Felice Bevilacqua (1876–1936) of Valdagno (Vicenza) was assistant in the Chancery and later apostolic protonotary in 1933.

woman devoted to Padre Pio who was fighting the same battle.[1260] The apostolic visit, conducted in a discrete manner from March 26 to April 5, 1927, confirmed the accusations of Brunatto. Msgr. Gagliardi was forced to resign, the canon Palladino was suspended *a divinis*, and the archpriest Prencipe was incriminated for immorality and false testimony. Padre Pio continued, however, to suffer canonical restrictions and Msgr. Bevilacqua, inexplicably, was removed from the assignment, and the Holy Consistorial Congregation, directed by Cardinal De Lai, named Msgr. Giuseppe Bruno as the new apostolic visitor to continue with the investigation.

More Scandals in the Vatican

After the success of the investigation into the archdiocese of Manfredonia, Cardinal Merry del Val and Secretary of State Gasparri convinced Pius XI that, before the next cardinalate nominations, a number of sensitive investigations were needed into high level prelates in the Roman Curia, and that the right men to lead it would be Msgr. Bevilacqua and Emanuele Brunatto.

During pontifical ceremonies, the Holy Father was flanked on his right by the Master of Chamber and on his left by His Holiness's majordomo, prefect of the Sacred Palaces.[1261] Until 1928, these appointments were filled by Msgr. Camillo Caccia Dominioni[1262] and Msgr. Ricardo de Samper[1263] respectively.

Pius XI had been the private tutor in Milan of the counts of Caccia Dominioni and wanted to elevate to the *porpora* Msgr. Camillo Caccia Dominioni, but heavy doubts about his moral standing weighed upon him. Moreover, if he

1260 Adelia Maria McAlpin Pyle (1888–1968), from a wealthy American family, was a close collaborator in Europe of Maria Montessori until, in 1923, she met Padre Pio, became a Third Order Franciscan, and settled in San Giovanni Rotondo, building a house on the hillside near the Capuchin monastery. Cf. Dorothy M. Gaudiose, *Maria l' "Americana." La vita di Mary Pyle all'ombra di padre Pio [Maria "The American." The Life of Mary Pyle in the Shadow of Padre Pio]*, San Paolo, Cinisello Balsamo (Milan) 1995.

1261 A chapter of Brunatto's book is dedicated to "His Excellency the Majordomo of the Prefect of the Sacred Apostolic Palaces," Ricardo de Samper (pp. 52–58) and another to "the Master of the Chamber of His Holiness," Camillo Caccia Dominioni (pp. 59–63).

1262 Camillo Caccia Dominioni (1877–1946), of Lombard nobility, studied at the Academy of Ecclesiastical Nobles and was ordained by the cardinal of Milan, Andrea Ferrari. Benedict XV named him participating secret chamberlain (1915) and Master of the Chamber (1921). He was confirmed in this role on February 2, 1922, by Pius XI, who made him a cardinal on December 16, 1935.

1263 Ricardo Sanz de Samper y Campuzano (1873–1954), born in Bogotá (Colombia), studied at the Academy of Ecclesiastical Nobles, was ordained in 1898, and later entered the pontifical family of Leo XIII. A participating secret chamberlain during the pontificate of Pius X, he was named Master of Chamber by Benedict XV (1914) and majordomo and prefect of the Sacred Palace by Pius XI, until he was suspended from these roles.

made Caccia Dominioni a cardinal, the pope would have had to do the same for Msgr. de Samper, whose scandalous life had made him, according to Brunatto, "the legend of Rome,"[1264] but whose reaction the pope feared. "Powerful by virtue of the secrets of three out of four pontiffs whom he had served, intelligent and wealthy, he seemed unmovable at the summit of the court hierarchy, blocking the advancement of those of a lower level, and especially of Msgr. Caccia Dominioni, a man particularly dear to the pontiff's heart."[1265]

Msgr. Alberto Serafini, a prelate who did not love Cardinal Merry del Val, in his deposition at the process of beatification, certified that the latter sought in vain to discourage Benedict XV from promoting Msgr. de Samper to Master of Chamber, to avoid opening the path to his promotion to higher dignities within the Church.[1266] De Samper was notoriously tied by close friendship to another controversial personality, Msgr. Alfredo Peri-Morosini,[1267] apostolic administrator of Lugano. On November 8, 1926, Merry del Val received a letter from Edouard Diricq of Lausanne, an attorney to the Countess Peri-Morosini, sister of Msgr. de Samper, in which he explicitly denounced an intrigue organized by the same de Samper and Msgr. Peri-Morosini (brother and brother-in-law of his client), with the complicity of a certain "Cesario," perhaps Cesare Bertini, police chief in the Borgo.[1268] Merry del Val asked Brunatto for a memorandum on the rumors going around Rome about de Samper, with the aim of presenting it to the Holy Father. The memo was submitted to Pius XI who was stunned and asked Merry del Val to order an investigation to find juridical proof of his majordomo's guilt.

1264 Brunatto, *Gli anticristi*, pp. 52–53. David I. Kertzer, *Il patto col diavolo. Mussolini e papa Pio XI. Le relazioni segrete fra il Vaticano e l'Italia fascista [The Pact with the Devil. Mussolini and Pope Pius XI. The Secret Relations Between the Vatican and Fascist Italy]*, Rizzoli, Milan 2014, pp. 101–104.

1265 Brunatto, *Gli anticristi*, p. 53.

1266 Serafini, *Processus informativus ordinarius, Sessio* LXIV, vol. 2, p. 410.

1267 Alfredo Peri Morosini (1862–1931), born in Lugano to the attorney Giacomo Peri and the Countess Carola Morosini, studied at the Academy of Ecclesiastical Nobles, became a secretary in the nunciature in Paris (1891), then apostolic administrator in the Canton of Ticino from 1904, and was consecrated bishop of Arca of Armenia on April 17, 1904, by Cardinal Merry del Val. The accusations against his moral conduct by some exponents of the Curia, supported by some conservative politicians such as the Swiss attorney Giuseppe Motta (1871–1940), gave rise to a trial for immoral conduct. Despite being acquitted, he submitted his resignation from the office of Apostolic Administrator and returned to Rome where he was named consultor of the Sacred Congregation for Extraordinary Ecclesiastical Affairs. In 1926, he was deposed from his ecclesiastical office and suspended *a divinis*. The newspaper *Resto del Carlino* reported on September 3, 1916, along with the news of his resignation, that of the dismissal from the Curia of Msgr. Ricardo de Samper.

1268 AAV, *Spoglio Merry del Val*, busta 6, ff. 716–718.

Merry del Val appointed Brunatto to investigate into Msgr. Camillo Caccia Dominioni as well.[1269] Cardinal Gasparri, for his part, saw in Brunatto a possible instrument to strike Msgr. Benigni, whom he presented as "an ominous man, totally corrupt, clever," who "possessed important documents of state with which he kept in check the Holy See and fought the Jesuits."[1270] Brunatto, though not entirely convinced, accepted the appointment: "I had no possibility to choose: to obtain justice in San Giovanni Rotondo, to liberate Padre Pio, I could not refuse Cardinal Merry del Val and Gasparri to take up the investigations into Caccia and de Semper, and these in turn were subordinated to the investigation into Benigni."[1271]

To undertake these numerous investigations, Brunatto requested a written warrant, given a few days later on December 19, 1927. He began his research with his customary diligence, and in the case of Msgr. Benigni, it ended up in a dead end, as displayed by the fact that there exists no trace of a canonical trial or a disciplinary trial of any sort against him, despite the hopes of Cardinal Gasparri and Fr. Enrico Rosa.[1272] The immorality of Monsignors de Samper and Caccia Dominioni was, on the other hand, proven and documented, but their respective fates were different.

Samper was expelled from the Curia and Msgr. Serafini attributed to Merry del Val his "catastrophe."[1273] Caccia Dominioni was defended before the Holy Father by Gasparri and Fr. Rosa. When, in May 1928, the scandal erupted involving Msgr. Caccia Dominioni, it was precisely Fr. Rosa who calmed the waters, asking Brunatto to close both eyes.[1274] To keep Caccia Dominioni far away until the scandal had subsided, the pope sent him as his representative to the Eucharistic Congress in Australia.

Meanwhile, Brunatto did not forget his principal pursuit. He thought of publishing another book about the enemies of Padre Pio, under the form of a *Letter to the Church*. In the first months of 1929, he stipulated a contract with an editor in Leipzig, *Spamerske Buchdruckerei*, to print a thousand copies of the

1269 In a report to the Foreign Ministry of September 27, 1929, one reads that Msgr. Caccia Dominioni "is accused with great scandal of pederasty. A most serious incident that occurred last year attributing to him this infamous accusation." (ASMAE, busta 7, f. 1, *Santa Sede, 1919–1930, Informazioni. Monsignor Caccia Dominioni,* September, 1929). Cf. also Kertzer, *Il patto col diavolo,* pp. 102–103.

1270 Misuraca, *Brouillon*, p. 85.

1271 Ibid., p. 87.

1272 Ricossa, "In difesa di mons. Umberto Benigni," pp. 123–124.

1273 Serafini, *Processus informativus ordinarius, Sessio* LXIV, vol. 2, p. 410.

1274 Brunatto, *Gli anticristi*, pp. 68–70.

book, cosigned by the attorney Francesco Morcaldi.[1275] In the end, at the request of Morcaldi, the draft of the text was never published, but when the more acute phase of persecution against Padre Pio began in 1931, Brunatto decided to collect in a "white book" the history of the events in San Giovanni Rotondo and in 1932 submitted to the Parisian publisher Aldana a new dossier under the pseudonym John Willoughby, with the title *Antichrists in the Church of Christ.*

Finally, on July 14, 1933, Padre Pio's forced isolation was lifted by the Vatican, and Brunatto, having obtained his aim, decided not to put the book on the market.

Brunatto had sought to penetrate "into the heart of this lavish court that ignobly exploits the immortal glory of the martyrs, of the confessors, and of the humble *oranti* who have sacrificed their entire existence to the divine light of the Naked Crucified One."[1276] The picture that emerged from his investigations was foul, but Jesus Christ himself had likened the Church to a field in which both good grain and weeds grow together. The presence of the weeds, for some the object of scandal, is actually a mark of the true Church, which ever since the beginning has discovered within itself offenses against faith and the purity of morals. Distinct from the personal holiness of its members, who at times were also great sinners, there is however an ontological holiness of the Church,[1277] which is always present in all its fullness, even in periods of greater misery recorded throughout history. "The proof that the Church is a divine institution," said Don Orione to Francesco Morcaldi, "is precisely that she continued to triumph, despite the fact that many of those who should have sustained and served her, did all they could to undermine her foundations."[1278]

The Conversations of Malines

In 1920, Anglican bishops, united for their conference at Lambeth Palace, London, launched an "Appeal to all Christians" to undertake an "ecumenical movement" among Christian churches. Within the Anglican church, Lord Halifax was still active despite his eighty years of life and had not renounced his Anglo-Roman project, scuttled in 1896 after the encyclical *Apostolicae curae* by Leo XIII.

[1275] The volume consisted in 431 pages with the photographic reproduction of 281 documents that formed the basis on which the Msgr. Bevilacqua's visit was carried out.

[1276] Brunatto, *Gli anticristi*, p. 52.

[1277] *Sainteté, Note de l'Église*, DTC, vol. 14 (1939), col. 847–860.

[1278] Peloso, *Don Luigi Orione e padre Pio*, p. 71.

Halifax reestablished contact with his old friend Fr. Portal, and together they took the initiative to hold a number of unofficial meetings between Anglicans and Catholics. Portal's biographer wrote, "In 1893 [Halifax] allowed himself to be pushed forward by the enthusiastic and impatient Portal; in 1921, on the contrary, he was the one who had to pester and pursue Portal, who was full of reservations."[1279] The initiative needed the support of a Catholic prelate, and Halifax found his man in Cardinal Mercier, the archbishop of Malines. Riding in the powerful Rolls-Royce convertible of the English lord, the two old "unionists" arrived in Malines on October 19 to ask the cardinal to promote several private meetings between Anglicans and Catholics with the aim of setting in motion a reunification movement for the two Churches. The cardinal accepted and suggested that Lord Halifax write a memorandum that would serve as the framework for their discussions. The meetings took place between 1921 and 1926 and were known as the "Conversations of Malines"[1280] since they took place in the home of the archbishop of Malines who sponsored the talks.

Only after having set in motion the discussions with a letter on April 3, 1922, did Cardinal Mercier inform Secretary of State Gasparri, requesting the approval of the Holy See.[1281] Régis Ladous writes, "One year earlier, in his supplication to Benedict XV, Mercier had declared he had never undertaken anything without the formal approval of the Holy See. And behold him, now, dialoging with three heretics without having asked or received any authorization."[1282]

The theme was profoundly divisive. On July 4, 1919, the Holy Office had renewed the prohibition of Pius IX (1864) of participating "in conferences either public or private organized by non-Catholics proposing as their objective promoting union among the groups which proclaim themselves Christian."[1283] But the

1279 Ladous, *Monsieur Portal et les siens*, p. 420.

1280 The conversations were held over four separate sessions, all presided by Cardinal Mercier, on December 6–8, 1921; June 14–15, 1923; December 7–8, 1923; and March 19–20, 1925. Cf. R. Aubert, "Les Conversations de Malines. Le Cardinal Mercier et le Saint-Siège," *Bulletin de la Classe des Lettres et des Sciences Morales et Politiques* 3 (1967), pp. 87–159, now in *Le cardinal Mercier (1851– 1926). Un prélat d'avant-garde*, ed. Jean-Pierre Hendrickx, Jean Pirotte, and Luc Courtois, Presses Universitaires de Louvain, Louvain 1994, pp. 393–452; Étienne Fouilloux, *Les catholiques et l'unité chrétienne du XIXe au XXe siècle. Itinéraires européens d'expression française*, Le Centurion, Paris 1982, pp. 125–158; Bernard Barlow, *"A Brother Knocking at the Door". The Malines Conversations 1921– 1925*, Canterbury Press, Norwich 1996.

1281 AA.EE.SS., *Stati Ecclesiastici*, Pos. 312, P.O., fasc. 66, ff. 3–5.

1282 Ladous, *Monsieur Portal et les siens*, p. 421.

1283 Decretum *De Partecipatione catholicorum societati "ad procurandam christianitatis unitatem,"* in AAS, 11 (1919), p. 309.

death of Benedict XV and the election of Pius XI favored a new climate, and Gasparri was personally in favor of the initiative. The historian John A. Dick, who dedicated his doctoral dissertation to the conversations of Malines,[1284] recalled that in Rome two groups were squaring off: "a group in favor of the conversations, symbolized by Cardinal Pietro Gasparri, the pope's secretary of state, and a group hostile to the conversations, symbolized by Cardinal Merry del Val, secretary of the Holy Office and previously secretary of state under Pius X."[1285]

On April 11, 1922, Gasparri communicated to Mercier the full approval of the Holy Father[1286] and on November 25, 1922, informed the Belgian cardinal that the pope authorized and blessed the meetings.[1287] This approval, however, was of a private and confidential character, and the meetings themselves were to remain so as well. Mercier, wanting to publicize the initiative, insisted on obtaining the official support of the pope, but on February 10, 1924, the secretary of state confirmed to the cardinal that he considered this solution inopportune.[1288] On January 18, 1924, in a pastoral letter dedicated to *Les conversations de Molines*, Mercier explained to the priests and faithful of his diocese that these were not about official negotiations, but private meetings. Through his letter, however, he rendered them public, though not official, making the situation even more confusing. The most significant event during the fourth conversation was the reading by Mercier of a text entitled *L'Eglise Anglicane unie non absorbie*, whose author was the Benedictine liturgist Fr. Lambert Beauduin, founder of the Monastery of Chevetogne in Amay-sur-Meuse, in which the monks had to "de-Romanize" themselves and open themselves to "dialogue" with the Anglicans and the schismatic Orthodox.[1289] The influence of this document on the Belgian clergy was profound, as recalled by Cardinal Suenens. "Our generation was marked by the 'Conversations of Malines' during which Cardinal Mercier read the famous Memorandum of the Benedictine Fr. Lambert

1284 John A. Dick, "Cardinal Merry del Val and the Malines Conversations," *Ephemerides Theologicae Lovanienses*, fasc. 4 (December 1986), pp. 333–355.

1285 Ibid, p. 334.

1286 AA.EE.SS., *Stati Ecclesiastici*, Pos. 312, P.O., fasc. 66, f. 7. According to Mercier, since the moment of his election, Pius XI had shown himself favorable to the meetings that had already gotten underway under the previous pontificate, stating: "J'ai une foi illimitée dans la bonne foi de ceux qui ne sont pas des nôtres dans notre Église catholique" (Aubert, *Le cardinal Mercier, 1851–1926*, pp. 398–399).

1287 Ladous, *Monsieur Portal et les siens*, p. 422.

1288 AA.EE.SS., *Stati Ecclesiastici*, Pos. 312, P.O., fasc. 68, f. 4.

1289 Cf. Louis Bouyer, *Dom Lambert Beauduin (1823–1960). Un homme d'Église*, Casterman, Paris 1964, pp. 133–135.

Beauduin, the future founder of the ecumenical monastery of Amay, on the Anglican Church, annexed but not assimilated."[1290]

The concerns of Merry del Val over the unfolding of the conversations of Malines were more than justified, based on the information he was receiving from his correspondents in London, Msgr. James Moyes[1291] and Fr. Francis Woodlock[1292] of the Jesuit church on Farm Street.

Moyes had contributed thirty years earlier to the document of Leo XIII against Anglican ordination, and now, in an article in *The Tablet,* October 7, 1922, he reported on the affinity between Anglican doctrine and that of the Oriental and Greek Church on transubstantiation, through the formula of the "non-definition."[1293] Moyes agreed with Merry del Val on the danger of a "neo-modernism that would nullify all the dogmas and aim at uniting all people on the basis of a mere religious sentiment. This movement is strong and profound in this country and in America."[1294]

In a letter to Fr. Woodlock on July 3, 1925, Merry del Val wrote that the error behind all the drafts of "reunion" was the "branch theory," according to which "there are three Churches, the Greek, the English, and the Roman, which form the Catholic Church, even though unfortunately divided." He did not understand how Catholics could speak of "a *reunification* with the English Church of today, because that Church, if one can truly call it a Church, was never united to the Catholic Church. It has always been a new institution, with

1290 Léo Suenens, *Souvenirs et espérances,* Fayard, Paris 1991, p. 62.

1291 Among the papers of Merry del Val conserved in the archives of the Secretariat of State, there is a packet dated January 18, 1921, that collects "Important documents concerning the so-called 'Anglican Catholics' in the heart of the Protestant Church of England, with useful notes written by Rev. Msgr. Moyes, theologian of the Cathedral of Westminster, most competent in the matter, who was a member of the Pontifical Commission for the Question of Anglican Ordinations" *(Spoglio Merry del Val,* busta 7, ff. 955–958).

1292 Francis Woodlock (1871–1940), ordained a priest in 1902 with the Society of Jesus, was a professor of philosophy in their houses in Leeds and Stonyhurst, and then was sent to the church in Farm Street where he was director until his death of the *Farm Street Solidarity.* Titles by him include *Constantinople, Canterbury and Rome* (1923) and *Modernism and the Church of Christ* (1925).

1293 Moyes, "The Great Eastern Church and Transubstantiation," *The Tablet,* October 7, 1922, p. 453 (pp. 453–455).

1294 AAV, *Spoglio Merry del Val,* busta 7, f. 954. In a letter of February 11, 1925, Msgr. Moyes pointed out the role of Fr. Gordon George, a young priest residing in Villa Lascaris, Fiesole. "He seems to have assumed recently the mischievous role of Portal in 95;" he acts like "a propagandist of the Malines movement, and as an officier de liason between all concerned," "whether he is doing so on his own initiative, or under the influence of Rome or Malines, your Eminence will be in a better position to judge than I am" (ibid., n. 962). He sent similar information to Fr. Woodlock to whom, on July 28, the cardinal replied: "Mr. G. G. is a most unreliable person.... His knowledge of Catholic doctrine is most limited" (*Papers Woodlock,* SJ/142/3/10. Letters-Cardinal Merry del Val, Farm Street Archive).

different, heretical doctrines, different and invalid ordinations in our sense of that word, and a different and invalid constitution."[1295]

A few days later, on July 9, Lord Halifax gave a programmatic discourse in Albert Hall in London, in which he repeated the thesis of Fr. Beauduin, according to which reconciliation with Rome was not to be understood as "the absorption of the Church of England into the Church of Rome, but rather the union of the two Churches under the primacy of the successor of St. Peter, which is quite another thing."[1296] Fr. Woodlock wrote to Merry del Val that Lord Halifax's speech "was a deplorable misunderstanding of the situation. He emphasized the possible disciplinary concessions that could be hoped for and then said, 'One must remember that reconciliation with Rome does not imply any denial of the historical claims of Canterbury.'"[1297]

Afterward, Fr. Woodlock published in the journal *Etudes* the complete text of Lord Halifax's intervention, adding his commentary in which he explained that "the common error of the Anglo-Catholics is what impedes the same Lord Halifax from entering the Roman Church. He invoked the acknowledgment of papal supremacy as a privilege of divine right, but because he is totally convinced he is already a Catholic because he is Anglican, he remains in the official Church of England and desires that all Anglicans do the same, working for the 'reunion of bodies.' Only these last words contain a false doctrine. There can be no reunion of bodies that were never united before."[1298]

The insurmountable hurdle remained that of Roman primacy and of the presumed Anglican episcopal ordinations. At the end of July 1925, Merry del Val wrote to Woodlock expressing his hope that Cardinal Bourne and the English bishops would take the opportunity "to make a clear declaration and get rid of this false doctrine," recalling that Leo XIII intended that his pronouncement on Anglican ordinations was to be "irreformable for all ages."[1299]

Gasparri encouraged the pan-Christian project secretly, but the turning point came at the meeting on December 5, 1925, in Rome between Cardinal

1295 Letter of Merry del Val to Fr. Woodlock, July 3, 1925, in *Papers Woodlock*, SJ/142/3/10. Letters-Cardinal Merry del Val, Farm Street Archive.

1296 Viscount Halifax, *Reunion and the Roman Primacy*, A. R. Mowbray, London and Oxford 1925, p. 35.

1297 Francis Woodlock S.J., Letter to Merry del Val, July 10, 1925, in AAV, *Spoglio Merry del Val*, n. 1008.

1298 Francis Woodlock S.J., "A propos des 'conversations de Malines,'" *Études* 184 (July–September 1925), p. 309 (pp. 304–310).

1299 Letter to Merry del Val from Fr. Woodlock, July 28, 1925, in *Papers Woodlock*, SJ/142/3/10. Letters-Cardinal Merry del Val, Farm Street Archive.

Bourne and Pius XI, in which the English primate explained, using historical and theological arguments, his opposition to the ecumenical meetings. The pope was now to tip the scales. With Mercier seriously ill, the position of Pius XI began diverging ever more from that of his secretary of state, as had happened in 1895 between Leo XIII and Cardinal Rampolla, also on the question of Anglican ordinations.

On January 23, 1926, Cardinal Mercier died. Just a few months later, on June 19, 1926, Fr. Portal passed away as well. The fifth conversation of Malines took place October 11–12, 1926, under the direction of Msgr. Jozef-Ernest Van Roey, the new archbishop of Malines, but the situation had changed.[1300]

On March 13, 1927, the secretariat of state communicated to Cardinal Van Roey through the Belgian nuncio that "the meetings held by the dearly departed Cardinal Mercier are now considered as being part of the movement of union of the different Protestant confessions with the Roman Church and therefore the Holy Father deems that they have ceased to be opportune and in fact desires that they be interrupted."[1301]

Less than a year later, on January 6, 1928, Pius XI published the encyclical *Mortalium animos*, condemning with clarity the false ecumenical movement.[1302] On January 21, *L'Osservatore Romano* announced that there would be no more conversations in Malines.

Some days later, on January 24, Cardinal Merry del Val wrote Fr. Woodlock, "I thank God for the encyclical.... It was a tormented work and I nearly despaired of obtaining the objective amidst the confusion of those who raised the uproar, the incapacity of many to understand the situation, and the ignorance of the facts."[1303]

1300 Jozef-Ernest Van Roey (1874–1961) succeeded Cardinal Mercier as metropolitan archbishop of Malines and Belgian primate. He was made a cardinal by Pius XI on June 20, 1927.

1301 AA.EE.SS., *Stati Ecclesiastici*, Pos. 312, P.O., fasc. 70, f. 63.

1302 Pius XI, Encyclical *Mortalium animos de vera religionis unitate fovenda*, January 6, 1928, in AAS, 20 (1928), pp. 5–16.

1303 Letter of Merry del Val to Woodlock, January 24, 1928, in *Papers Woodlock*, SJ/142/3/10. Letters-Cardinal Merry del Val, Farm Street Archive. In the letter, Merry del Val returned to criticize the letter of the now deceased Cardinal Mercier to the Archbishop of Canterbury of October 25, 1926: "With all respect I consider Card. Mercier's letter to Canterbury deplorable. He writes on equal terms as from Church to Church, which is censured in the Encyclical, and the '*ut unum sint*' is expressed on the apparent basis that our Lord's Prayer has still to be heard and fulfilled: as if the Church were not one from the beginning."

Merry del Val and the Encyclical *Mortalium Animos*

The encyclical *Mortalium animos* was promulgated soon after the first *World Conference on Faith and Order* in Lausanne (August 3–21, 1927) and the negative response of the Congregation of the Holy Office to the doubt whether it was licit for Catholics to participate in pan-Christian conferences.[1304] This encyclical can be considered the most important pontifical act on the doctrinal level since *Pascendi.*[1305] It struck at the roots of the false notions of unity proposed by those who interpreted the words of Christ "that they all be one ... one flock and one shepherd" (Jn 17:21; 10:11) as though "Christ Jesus merely expressed a desire and prayer, which still lacks its fulfillment."[1306]

Pius XI stated that by natural law and divine positive law, the only true religion is the Catholic Christian religion, and that Jesus founded but one Church as a visible and sovereign society, destined to gather into its bosom all men. Against the false ecumenism of the so-called pan-Christians, the pope reiterated that true union is not possible except through the return of dissidents to the true Church and by accepting the primacy of St. Peter and his successors. "Let, therefore, the separated children draw nigh to the Apostolic See, set up in the city which Peter and Paul, the Princes of the Apostles, consecrated by their blood; to that See, we repeat, which is 'the root and origin whence the Church of God springs' (St. Cyprian, Epist. 48.3); not with the intention and the hope that 'the Church of the living God, the pillar and ground of the truth' (1 Tim 3:15) will cast aside the integrity of the faith and tolerate their errors, but, on the contrary, that they themselves submit to its teaching and government."[1307]

Cardinal Merry del Val entrusted to his young and talented collaborator Msgr. Ernesto Ruffini the task of drafting the report that led to the papal document.[1308] It was the same Ruffini who composed the first version of the encyclical. The research by Johan Ickx in the Vatican Secret Archive has documented that Merry del Val "was behind the scenes the true author *par excellence*

[1304] AAS, 19 (1927), p. 278.

[1305] As defined by *Corriere della Sera*, January 14, 1928.

[1306] Pius XI, *Mortalium animos,* no. 7, https://www.vatican.va/content/pius-xi/en/encyclicals/documents/hf_p-xi_enc_19280106_mortalium-animos.html.

[1307] Ibid., no. 12.

[1308] Ernesto Ruffini (1888–1967), named bishop in 1925, was made the secretary of the Congregation for Seminaries and Universities in 1928, then prefect and later rector of the Pontifical Lateran University. He was named archbishop of Palermo on October 11, 1945, and made a cardinal in 1946 by Pius XII. From 1924 he was the substitute for the censure of books at the Holy Office and consultor of the supreme Congregation of the Holy Office and of the Biblical Commission.

of the preparatory work for the encyclical *Mortalium animos*,"[1309] an encyclical that was entirely "a question of the Holy Office. There it was thought out, written, corrected, and promulgated, and everything took place as if it were a most confidential internal matter," as the researcher Manuela Barbolla confirms.[1310]

Pius XI's encyclical meant to strike not only the Conversations of Malines between Catholics and Anglicans, but also the birth of a "German High Church" intending to conflate the main Christian confessions into one ecumenical Church: Catholicism, Protestantism, and the Greek Orthodox Church. After the condemnation of the works of the modernist theologian Josef Wittig,[1311] Merry del Val wrote to the apostolic nuncio in Germany, Eugenio Pacelli, on July 30, 1926, requesting news and an update on the issue.[1312] On November 15 of the same year, the nuncio in Berlin sent to the secretary of the Holy Office a detailed forty-seven page report on the High Ecumenical Church and on the situation in Germany.[1313] After having consulted its advisers, the Holy Office asked the opinion of the cardinal inquisitors. The discussion that followed led, on Ash Wednesday, March 16, 1927, to the formulation of the decision that was then submitted to the attention of Pius XI regarding the timeliness of promulgating a papal encyclical. The next day the pope approved the decisions taken by the cardinals.

In a note from 1927,[1314] dedicated to the movement of the so-called High Ecumenical Church and its periodical *Una Sancta*, Merry del Val wrote,

> If one reflects on the uncontestable influence of errors creeping everywhere, of dogmatic liberalism and modernism in all its forms, the question assumes today great importance and one must recognize in it a grave danger. The campaign of our adversaries is most insidious

[1309] Johan Ickx, "L'enciclica *Mortalium animos* (1928): sfide storiografiche in base al nuovo materiale archivistico della Santa Sede" [The Encyclical *Mortalium animos* (1928): Historiographical Challenges Based on New Archival Material of the Holy See], in Semeraro (ed.), *La sollecitudine ecclesiale di Pio XI*, p. 328 (pp. 313–320).

[1310] Manuela Barbolla, "La genesi della *Mortalium animos* attraverso lo spoglio degli Archivi Vaticani," *Rivista di Storia della Chiesa in Italia* 64 (2012), p. 512.

[1311] Josef Wittig (1879–1949) was professor of ecclesiastical history and exponent of German modernism. Several of his works were condemned by a decree of the Holy Office in July 1929. Refusing to retract his positions, he was excommunicated in 1926.

[1312] ADDF, S.O., *Rerum Variarum*,1927, n. 28, f. 11/5.

[1313] Ibid., f. 17–40.

[1314] AAV, *Spoglio Merry del Val*, busta 7, f. 1012, *High Ecumenical Church Periodical "Una Sancta,"* ff. 1–7. The three following citations are all from this same source.

> and grows daily even among Catholics, as they toy with a vague sentiment of fraternal understanding and universal pacification that confounds doctrinal error with the charity that is proper toward those who profess it, quite often in good faith. The concept of revealed and immutable dogma is being increasingly lost, along with the concept of the divine constitution of the one true Church of Christ, visible and indefectible.

The cardinal emphasized an error that, in his opinion, had not been sufficiently highlighted by the other consultants of the Holy Office:

> Our Lord's words are invoked ad nauseam: '*Ut unum sint . . . fiet unum ovile et unus pastor*,' but in the sense that in no way has this prayer of the Divine Savior been fulfilled, and that this unity of doctrine and rules — the characteristic note of the one, true, visible Church of Christ — has never existed nor does it exist on the face of the earth. It is an objective to be attained. Desirable and perhaps to be hoped for in a distant future, but which in reality has never been achieved.
>
> None of these, however, when speaking of union or reunion, thinks in the least of a submission to the magisterium and governance of the pope and the Roman Church, as the one flock of Christ; on the contrary, they reject it scornfully, unless the pope were to change doctrine, and to this end they are willing to negotiate. The fundamental error which I mentioned, of the non-existence of one visible Church, with the absolute unity of faith, of sacraments, and of episcopal governance with the Vicar of Christ at its head, is at the root of all the attempts, congresses, and movements promoted by non-Catholics to reunite the churches and all Christianity.

At the beginning of May 1928, the news spread that the so-called Anglo-Catholics were organizing a pilgrimage to Lourdes. On May 14, Merry del Val sent a confidential letter to Msgr. Alexandre Poirier,[1315] Bishop of Tarbes and Lourdes, in which he implored him to abstain "from favoring that pilgrimage in any way and not to allow its participants, presuming it were to arrive, to participate, at least collectively or as a group, in Catholic ceremonies, making it clear that they are

[1315] Alexandre Philibert Poirier (1866 – 1928), ordained a priest in 1890 and named chaplain of Saint-Louis-des-Français in Rome (1896), on August 24, 1927, became bishop of Tarbes and Lourdes.

considered a Protestant sect, as they are in reality."[1316] The cardinal reminded him that the main representative of the "so-called Anglo-Catholics" was Lord Halifax, "a pious man but full of illusions that caught unawares the good faith of Card. Mercier in Malines and that of many others outside of England. The Holy Father has put matters in order with the encyclical *Mortalium animos* of January 6, 1928, and has publicly and formally debunked Lord Halifax's statements concerning the Conversations of Malines."[1317]

The full return of England to the purity of the Catholic faith, with neither contamination nor compromise, remained a constant goal of Merry del Val's activity. On the morning of May 8, 1925, Cardinal Bourne of Westminster and 1,200 English pilgrims gathered in the vast nave of St. Peter's to participate in the Holy Mass celebrated by the cardinal. At the end of the ceremony, Merry del Val delivered a discourse in which he recalled the bond between Rome and England: "You are the sons of saints and martyrs and belong to the 'Dowry of Mary.' The Catholic faith that you so faithfully profess reached your lands through the initiative and zeal of St. Gregory the Great, the Apostle of England. It is the faith of St. Augustine of Canterbury, of St. Anselm, St. Thomas Becket, of the blessed martyrs John Fisher and Thomas More, of Cuthbert Maine, Edmund Campion, and of a legion of others. It is the faith transmitted through the great Councils of the Church, reaffirmed solemnly at the Council of Trent and the Vatican Council. You know well that this doctrine so explicitly proclaimed cannot be attenuated in any way, nor reconsidered or modified for any consideration: the sacrosanct formulas of that doctrine say clearly what they mean and signify clearly what they say. They are and will remain immutable, because they are an expression of eternal truth. It is the faith of your forefathers to which, in conformity with your traditional hymn, you will be faithful unto death."[1318]

The "Friends of Israel"

In February 1926, through the initiative of a young Dutch Jew, Francisca van Leer,[1319] and Fr. Antonio van Asseldonk, procurator general of the Canons of

[1316] ADDF, S.O., *Rerum Variarum*, 1928, n. 20, f. 1.

[1317] Ibid.

[1318] Cenci, *Merry del Val*, p. 277.

[1319] Francisca van Leer (1892–1953), born into a Jewish family, after having participated in the German Spartacus League, converted to Catholicism and proposed to develop relations between Catholics and Jews. In 1926, she founded the Association *Amici Israël* and the newspaper *De Stem van Israel* (The Voice of Israel).

Santa Croce,[1320] there began in Rome an international association for the promotion within the Catholic Church of an attitude favorable to the Jews and to Israel, Priestly Opus Friends of Israel. The association, whose original vocation was to pray for the Jews and to develop an apostolate aimed at their conversion, gathered in its ranks nearly two thousand priests, two hundred bishops, and eighteen cardinals, among whom were Merry del Val, Van Rossum, Frühwirth, Pompili, and Rossi, all members of the Holy Office, as well as Secretary of State Gasparri.[1321]

Matters changed when the Congregation of Rites was asked to suppress the words *perfidis* and *perfidiam*[1322] in the prayers *Pro Judaeis* of Good Friday and the reestablishment of the genuflection accompanied by the words *Oremus, Flectate genua, Levate* in the rubric that dated back to the Roman Missal of 1570. The case was entrusted to the erudite abbot of the Benedictine monastery of St. Paul Outside the Walls in Rome, Fr. Ildefonso Schuster. On January 20, 1928, he made known to the Holy Office that he considered the request justified from the point of view of the tradition of the Roman liturgy.[1323] The question passed then to the Holy Office, which appointed the papal theologian Marco Sales to evaluate the matter.[1324] Fr. Sales, on the contrary, criticized the dossier presented by the Friends of Israel, both due to the "unseemly" character of the

[1320] Antonio van Asseldonk (1892–1973) was Superior General of the Canons of Santa Croce.

[1321] Laurence Deffayet, "*Amici Israël*. Le raison d'un échec. Des éléments nouveaux apportés par l'ouverture des archives du Saint-Office," *Mélanges de l'École française de Rome* 117 (2006), p. 833 (pp. 831–851). Cf. also idem, "Pie XI et la condamnation des Amis d'Israël (1928)," in Jacques Prévotat (ed.), *Pie XI et la France. L'apport des archives du pontificat de Pie XI à la connaissance des rapports entre le Saint-Siège et la France*, École française de Rome, Rome 2010, pp. 87–102; Menahem Macina, "Essai d'élucidation des causes et circonstances de l'abolition, par le Saint-Office, de l'Opus sacerdotale Amici Israël (1926–1928)," in *Juifs et chrétiens, entre ignorance, hostilité et rapprochement (1898–1998)*, Travaux et Recherches de l'Université, Lille 2003, pp. 87–110.

[1322] "Oremus et pro perfidis Judaeis ut Deus et Dominus noster auferat velamen de cordibus eorum; ut et ipsi agnoscant Jesum Christum, Dominum nostrum. Omnipotens sempiterne Deus, qui etiam judaicam perfidiam a tua misericordia non repellis: exaudi preces nostras, quas pro illius populi obcaecatione deferimus; ut, agnita veritatis tuae luce, quae Christus est, a suis tenebris eruantur." This was the invitatory of the prayer of the eighth solemn oration of the Good Friday liturgy as it appeared in the Roman Missal 1570. The words *perfidis* and *perfidiam* had the meaning of "nonbelievers," without injurious intentions. They were abolished at the behest of John XXIII, with the reform of the Missal in 1962.

[1323] Alfredo Ildefonso Schuster (1880–1954), Benedictine monk, in 1918 became the abbot of St. Paul Outside the Walls in Rome. He was named archbishop of Milan by Pius XI and made a cardinal in 1929. He was beatified by John Paul II in 1997.

[1324] Marco Sales (1877–1936), a Dominican theologian and exegete, after having taught at the Angelicum (1909–1911) and at the Theological Faculty of Freiburg (1912–1925), was named Master of the Sacred Apostolic Palaces on October 12, 1925. In this role he was also theological consultor of the Holy Office.

request and due to the theological audacity of the form, concluding his evaluation with a *Nihil esse innovandum*: nothing should be changed.

The question worsened when, at the beginning of 1928, a seventy-page booklet was published under the title *Pax super Israel,* in which the promoters of the association explained their true political and ideological program in detail, which did not consist in welcoming the "conversion" of the Jewish people, but in attaining "peace" between the Church and Israel.[1325] This peace was to be realized by eliminating from the liturgy all those expressions and elements that might sound anti-Jewish and by avoiding every form of "antisemitism." In Catholic settings, there was to be no more talk of Jews as "God killers," and the concept of "conversion" was to be renounced because this expression sounded hateful to the ears of the Jews.[1326]

Cardinal Merry del Val immediately opened an investigation into the booklet, attending to the matter himself. Events precipitated when, on February 23, 1928, the Central Committee of the Friends of Israel organized in Rome a meeting to confront these issues. Four days later, on February 27, in a meeting of the Holy Office, Merry del Val definitively rejected any modification of the Good Friday liturgy and proposed the dissolution of the Central Committee of the association, unless the association accepted to be reduced to a simple union of prayer for the conversion of the Jews.[1327]

On March 7, 1928, Merry del Val presented the cardinal consultors a detailed evaluation of the case. After having declared "entirely unacceptable and I will also say nonsensical" the request for the suppression of the prayer *pro perfidis Iudaeis* in the Good Friday liturgy, he defined the work of the Association of the Friends of Israel "reprehensible and harmful;" in fact, "this work falls more or less within the framework of inter-confessionalism and religious indifferentism."[1328]

The following day, during the usual audience with the secretary of the Holy Office, it was Pius XI himself who took up the case. The pope approved

1325 *Pax super Israel,* Rome 1928. Cf. ADDF, S.O., *Rerum Variarum,* 1828, n. 2, f. 1 16/2.

1326 H. Wolf, *Il Papa e il diavolo. Il Vaticano e il Terzo Reich [The Pope and the Devil. The Vatican and the Third Reich],* Donzelli, Rome 2008, pp. 93–94.

1327 Letter from Card. Merry del Val, March 7, 1928, S. Uffizio, S.O. 125/28. Cf. Deffayet, "Amici Israël: les raisons d'un échec," pp. 841–842.

1328 *Votum* of Card. Merry del Val for the plenary assembly of cardinals *Feria Quarta,* March 7, 1928, in ADDF, S.O., *Rerum Variarum,* 1828, n. 2, f. 1/20. Text in Deffayet, "Pie XI et la condamnation des Amis d'Israël," in Prévotat, *Pie XI et la France,* p. 101.

the proposal of the cardinals, adding several caveats. On March 9, he convoked Merry del Val again in audience to discuss further the "serious question" of the Friends of Israel. On March 25, 1928, a decree of the Holy Office appeared that disbanded the Association, condemning at the same time "modern antisemitism."[1329] One reads in the document:

> The Catholic Church, which has always considered the Jews as the people that, until the coming of the Divine Savior, was the depository of the divine promises, and despite its successive blindness, in fact precisely because of it, has always prayed for the Jewish people, has protected it against unjust persecutions and, just as it condemns all forms of hatred between peoples, so condemns in particular hatred against the people who were originally the People of God, a hatred that today is commonly referred to as antisemitism. Nevertheless, given that and considering that the above-mentioned work the 'Friends of Israel' has adopted attitudes and expressions not in conformity with the traditional sense of the Church, which also the Holy Liturgy expresses, the Eminent Fathers have decreed the dissolution of said association and the ceasing of all related publications.[1330]

According to Wolf, "in this passage for the first time modern antisemitism was rejected by the doctrine of the Church."[1331] "This appears to be noteworthy in fact, insofar as no one could have foreseen at that moment either the rise to power of National Socialism in Germany … or the antisemitic turn of Italian Fascism at the end of the 1930s."[1332]

In the proceedings that led to the dissolution of the Friends of Israel, the secretary of the Holy Office had assumed the most resolute positions. He underlined, among other things, that the association must be placed "more or less in the framework of interconfessional and religious indifferentism," which just a few weeks earlier Pius XI, in the encyclical *Mortalium animos*, had condemned, denouncing precisely its theological roots, buried in dogmatic relativism and indifference in the religious field.

[1329] Holy Office, *Decretum de consociatione vulgo Amici Israel abolenda*, in AAS, 20 (1928), pp. 103–104.

[1330] Ibid., p. 104.

[1331] Wolf, *Il Papa e il diavolo*, p. 120.

[1332] Ibid.

Fr. Schuster retracted unconditionally his position. Fr. Van Asseldonk, secretary of the association, convinced he had received a special vocation for Israel, left his congregation without authorization and in August of 1928 went to Haifa in Palestine, where he lived in civilian clothes in a little apartment he shared with Francisca van Leer.[1333] "The adventure that had begun under the best of auspices two and a half years earlier, concluded quite miserably and its main protagonists played no further role in the nascent pro-Semitism between the two wars."[1334]

Merry del Val and the Index of Prohibited Books

The compilation of lists of prohibited books is a traditional practice of the Church. But it was only after the invention of the printing press that the lists of forbidden books became ever more frequent, also due to the fact that the spread of Protestantism came about especially by means of books.[1335]

In 1515, Leo X published the bull *Inter sollicitudines*[1336] by which he introduced the rule that every text committed to print must first receive the approbation of religious authorities. In the sixteenth century, various lists of forbidden books were published and then collated in the one *Index* of Paul IV, printed with a decree of the Inquisition on December 30, 1558.[1337]

Welcoming the request by the Council of Trent, Pius IV revised the Index and updated it with the constitution *Dominici gregis custodiae* on March 24, 1564.[1338] St. Pius V confirmed the rules and established the Congregation of the Index, destined to become a permanent organization of the Church's

1333 Deffayet, "Amici Israël: les raisons d'un échec," pp. 846–847.

1334 Ibid., p. 848.

1335 Cf. De Bujanda, *Indice dei libri proibiti [Index of prohibited books]*, in DSI, vol. 2, pp.775–780; idem, *Index des livres interdits*, 10 vols., Centre d'Études de la Renaissance-Librairie-Droz, Sherbrooke-Genève 1984–1996; Franz Heinrich Reusch, *Der Index der verbotenen Bücher: Ein Beitrag zur Kirchenund Literaturgeschichte*, Cohen, Bonn 1883–1885, ristampa Scientia Verlag, Aalen 1967. Cf. also Fr. Louis Petit, *L'Index, son histoire, ses lois, sa force obligatoire*, Lethielleux, Paris 1888; B. Neveu, *L'erreur et son juge; remarques sur les censures doctrinales à l'époque moderne*, Bibliopolis, Naples 1993; H. Wolf, *Storia dell'Indice. Il Vaticano e i libri proibiti*, Donzelli, Rome 2006.

1336 *Bullarium Romanum*, vol. 5, pp. 623–624.

1337 *Index auctorum, et librorum...*, Antonio Blado, Rome 1558.

1338 *Bullarium Romanum*, vol. 7, pp. 281–282. This Index, which became the model for all the later revisions, consisted of two parts: the first contained ten rules by which the categories of prohibited books were established according to natural law or general law; the second gave in alphabetical order the catalogue of books proscribed by special decree. The first five rules concerned books stained by heresy. The last five rules foresaw the interdiction of obscene and immoral books, with the exception of the classics of antiquity, prohibited only to the very young, and condemned books on magic, necromancy, judicial astrology, and Jewish cabal.

governance. The tasks of the congregation were to evaluate all published books, draft from time to time an Index of prohibited books, and oversee the application of these lists. The jurisdiction of the Index extended to all countries of the Catholic religion and to all the baptized, including the members of the highest levels of the hierarchy. Under Pius X numerous consultors were members of the Congregation, chosen from diocesan and religious clergy, theologians, and canon lawyers, among whom (according to ancient Church law) were the Master General of the Dominicans, the Master of the Sacred Palaces, and a theologian belonging to the order of the Franciscan Conventuals. Besides these, various officers of the Congregation were "qualifiers," a particular category of consultant (not to be confused with the consultors) chosen among the most eminent and renowned theologians and canon lawyers residing in Rome. These were called upon to express and present their written opinion to be submitted to the examination of the consultors concerning the degree of error of a book or of a doctrine, referred to the judgment of the Congregation.

In his motu proprio *Alloquentes* of March 25, 1917, Benedict XV decreed the suppression of the old Congregation of the Index as an autonomous organism, reincorporating it into the Holy Office. In the same document, the pontiff lightened the duties of Holy Office by removing from its jurisdiction all matters regarding the use and concession of indulgences, transferring them entirely to the Apostolic Penitentiary, except for the doctrinal examination of new prayers and devotions.

Thus, the Index of prohibited books came to depend directly on the Holy Office directed by Cardinal Merry del Val who, already in his role as secretary of state beginning in 1903, was frequently in contact with the Congregation of the Index, and carryied out an important role, as we have seen, in the condemnation of Alfred Loisy.

The "Instructions" of the Holy Office on Mystical-Sensual Literature

In the decadent climate in Italy in the final years of the nineteenth century, Gabriele D'Annunnzio had inaugurated a literary genre that expressed an aggravated sensuality, in the name of an individualistic and pagan-leaning conception of life.[1339] The plots of all Gabriele D'Annunzio's novels (except for one: *The Maidens of the Rocks*) are "based on sinful relationships." This was one of the main accusations the Sacred Congregation of the Index brought against him in its three decrees on May 8, 1911, condemning his *Omnes fabulae amatoriae*, the *Omnia opera dramatica* and the *Selected Writings*.

The novelist Guido da Verona, though not sharing D'Annunzio's literary pretensions, followed in his footsteps by advocating his rejection of bourgeois morality and the search for morbid and often blasphemous pleasures.[1340] Da Verona had become Italy's most widely read author during the 1920s. His novel *Mimì Bluette, Flower of My Garden* narrates the life of a young lady, at first a prostitute, then a successful ballerina, who then commits suicide for love. It sold 20,000 copies in one year, and by 1922 had reached 300,000 copies, an impressive run for that time. Even more transgressive was the 1920 title *Undo your Braid, Mary Magdalen*, a sentimental, erotic story, set in the sacred town of Lourdes.

Merry del Val assigned the drafting of a final evaluation on *Undo your Braid, Mary Magdalen* to Cardinal Gaetano De Lai. His judgment given on April 14 was explicit: "This is certainly a wretched book. In it one finds pages of such noxious sensuality that one cannot read them. Others are derisive, skeptical, sparring with the most sacred matters.... Thus, a most dangerous book. If the others by da Verona are like this, a comprehensive condemnation is needed."[1341]

1339 Gabriele D'Annunzio (1863–1938) dominated Italian literature in the early 1900s, creating "Dannunzianism" understood to be the cult of the form and the exaltation of the passions of the soul and the pleasure of the senses. Cf. Matteo Brera, "Gabriele D'Annunzio e la Santa Sede. Il processo e la condanna del 1911 nei documenti della Congregazione dell'Indice" [Gabriele d'Anunzio and the Holy See. The Trial and Condemnation of 1911 in the Documents of the Congregation of the Index], *Quaderni del Vittoriale* Nuova serie 8 (2012), pp. 27–43; idem, "Il Poeta, il Papa e il Dittatore. L' "Opera omnia" di Gabriele D'Annunzio all'Indice e i difficili rapporti tra Stato e Chiesa all'ombra del Concordato" [The Poet, the Pope and the Dictator. The *Opera omnia* of Gabriele d'Anunzio on the Index and the Difficult Relations Between State and Church in the Shadow of the Concordat], *Quaderni del Vittoriale* Nuova serie 9 (2013), pp. 43–67; *Novecento all'Indice. Gabriele D'Annunzio, i libri proibiti e i rapporti Stato-Chiesa all'ombra del Concordato [1900s on the Index. Gabriele d'Anunzio, the Prohibited Books and Church-State Relations in the Shadow of the Concordat]*, History and Literature, Rome 2016.

1340 Guido da Verona, pseudonym of Guido Verona (1881–1939), was a novelist of vast renown in Italy during the years after the First World War. Some scholars give as certain his death by suicide (cf. Enzo Magrì, *Guido da Verona, l'ebreo fascista*, Pellegrini, Cosenza 2005, pp. 115). On his condemnation, cf. Brera, *Novecento all'Indice*, pp. 101–116.

1341 ADDF, S.O., *Censurae Librorum* 1913–1921 c. 2.

On April 20, 1920, the group of cardinals met and elaborated the nucleus of the decree of condemnation of Guido da Verona's *Opera omnia*.[1342] Two days later, the assessor of the Holy Office informed Benedict XV of the cardinals' deliberation. The pope approved their proposal of condemnation and rendered it effective, placing on the Index all the author's works, who in his novels "makes a religion of sensuality and carries that sensuality even into the temple, making it blasphemous."[1343]

The trial of the so-called mystical-sensual literature was of broader scope. The case originated in 1917 from the denunciation brought to the Holy Office by the lawyer Raymond Hubert,[1344] against Léon Bloy and other French authors belonging to the school of the so-called *Renouveau catholique*.[1345] The Holy Office concerned itself at length with this problem, entrusting to its consultors and consultants the study of these authors. The procedure passed through three final examinations in 1919, 1920, and 1921.[1346] The final report was entrusted to two French consultors highly esteemed by Cardinal Merry del Val: the Jesuit Frédéric Rouvier[1347] and the Dominican Albert Marie Janvier.[1348]

On May 3, 1927, the Holy Office condemned this literary genre with the Instruction *Inter mala*,[1349] which affirmed, among other things, "That among

1342 Decree of April 23, 1920, in AAS, vol. 12 (1920), pp. 158–159.

1343 Giovanni Casati, *The Index of Prohibited Books*, part 3, Casa Editrice "Pro Familia," Milan-Rome 1939, p. 391. De Bujanda, *Index Librorum Prohibitorum*, p. 915.

1344 Raymond Hubert (1886–1966) was a Swiss attorney. *Léon Bloy et le prétendu Renouveau catholique*, Frey & Trincheri, Nice 1917.

1345 ADDF, S.O., *Rerum Variarum*, 1927, n. 31, *Rinnovamento letterario in Francia, [Literary Renewal in France]*. Hubert denounced three generations of French writers: the "masters" (Charles Baudelaire, Paul Verlaine, Arthur Rimbaud), the "middle generation" (such as Léon Bloy) and finally, that of the so-called "Catholic renewal" (Edward Montier, Paul Claudel, Robert Vallery-Radot, François Mauriac). Cf. Jean Calvet, *Le Renouveau catholique dans la littérature contemporaine*, Plon, F. Lanore, Paris 1927.

1346 Cf. ADDF, S.O., *Rerum Variarum*, 1927, n. 31, containing the verdicts of the consultors and consultants. Cf. Jean-Baptiste Amadieu, "L'instruction de 1927 sur la littérature mystico-sensuelle," in Prévotat (ed.), *Pie XI et la France*, pp. 315–345.

1347 Frédéric Rouvier (1851–1925) was a Jesuit author of numerous books and pamphlets, some dedicated to Freemasonry, under the pseudonym E. d'Avesnes. He carried out his apostolate in Lyon, distinguishing himself for his apologetic works, together with his confrere Antonin Eymieu (1861–1933). Among his numerous works: *La Révolution maîtressed'école* (1880), *Les Anges sur la terre* (1891), and *La Franc-Maçonnerie et les projets Ferry* (reprinted in 2017).

1348 Albert Marie Janvier (1860–1939), a Dominican, was a theologian and preacher, close to *Action française*. Cf. André Laudouze, *Dominicains français et Action française*, Les Éditions Ouvrières, Paris 1989, pp. 73–88.

1349 AAS, 19 (1927), pp. 186–189. Holy Office, *Istruzione ai vescovi e agli ordinari sulla letteratura mistico-sensuale [Instructions to Bishops and Ordinaries on the Mystical-Sensual Literature]*. The Italian text, published by *L'Osservatore Romano* on May 11, 1927 is available today in the appendix to Brera, *Novecento all'Indice*, pp. 308–311.

the most nefarious evils corrupting Christian morals entirely in our age and which greatly harm the souls redeemed with the Most Precious Blood of Jesus Christ is above all to be enumerated the literature that fosters the sensual passions, lust, and a certain type of lascivious mysticism. Of this character are mainly novels, short stories, dramas, and comedies: all these writings are multiplying today in an incredible manner and spreading every day, far and wide."

The document of the Holy See placed in relief "the grave harm inflicted upon souls by this flood of books, as fascinating as they are immoral," "that go through the hands of all with amazing rapidity." "Novels much worse than others usually produced, dreadful as it is to say, dare to justify noxious sensuality with sacred things, uniting indecent loves with a sort of piety toward God and with a religious mysticism that is obviously false."

According to the Instruction of the Holy Office, "Anticipating therefore the spread of this sensual literature that every year inundates almost every nation, this Supreme Sacred Congregation of the Holy Office, responsible for safeguarding faith and morals, with apostolic authority and on behalf of the Holy Father, prescribes all ordinaries to do what is possible to remedy this urgent, serious evil. In fact, it belongs to them, constituted pastors in the Church of God by the Holy Spirit, to keep watch with lively diligence over what is printed and published in their respective dioceses."[1350]

A new condemnation of Gabriele D'Annunzio followed this provision, extended on June 27, 1928, to the *Reliqua opera*, after the government had decided to make a national edition of all his works.[1351]

In the audience to the Lenten preachers on February 20, 1927, Pius XI stigmatized "the literary apotheosis of an author, many of whose books are already expressly condemned by the Church and many others of which stand condemned in themselves," urgently requesting the preachers to make known "to the many poor souls" the poison in the works of D'Annunzio, and to recall to the minds of Christians "the duty to beware of these in conformity with common moral sense and the condemnation of the Church."[1352]

[1350] ADDF, S.O., *Censurae librorum 1928, Procedimento a carico dell'*Opera Omnia *di Gabriele D'Annunzio [Censurae librorum 1928, Injunction Against the Opera Omnia of Gabriele D'Anunzio]*. Cf. the documents reproduced in the appendix to Brera, *Novecento all'Indice*, pp. 293–334.

[1351] De Bujanda, *Index Librorum Prohibitorum*, p. 265.

[1352] *Discorsi di Pio XI*, ed. Domenico Bertetto, vol. 1 (1922–1928), SEI, Turin 1960, pp. 762–765.

If Italian literature boasted its most renowned personality in Gabriele D'Annunzio, in the field of philosophy, its two main representatives were Benedetto Croce and Giovanni Gentile.

The fact that in those years the *Opera Omnia* of all these authors had been placed on the Index shows how far the world of Italian culture was from the teaching of the Church.[1353] But it shows as well the courage of ecclesiastical authorities in condemning every school of thought opposed to the Magisterium, challenging the Fascist regime that found in Giovanni Gentile its philosopher and in Gabriele D'Annunzio its "High Priest."

On June 7, 1929, Cardinal Merry del Val signed the preface to a new edition of the Index of prohibited books, the last one published by the Holy Office.[1354] The secretary of the Holy Office expressed the following:

> The Holy Church throughout the centuries has endured great persecutions, gradually multiplying the heroes who sealed with their blood their Christian faith; but today, a much more terrible battle is stirring hell, as devious and delicate as it is deleterious, and it is depraved publishing. No other danger more serious than this threatens the integrity of faith and morals, and thus the Church never ceases to awaken Christians to this threat. Irreligious and immoral books are often written in an attractive style, they often treat subjects that stoke the carnal passions or flatter the pride of man's spirit, always with studied tactics and captiousness of every genre in their aim of capturing the minds and hearts of incautious readers; it is therefore natural that the Church, as a prudent mother, with her opportune prohibitions, warn the faithful that they might not draw to their lips the facile chalices of this poison. Not out of fear of the light, therefore, does the Holy See prohibit the reading of certain books, but out of the zeal by which God has inflamed it and which does not tolerate the loss of souls, teaching the same experience that man, fallen from original justice, is heavily inclined to evil and thus has extreme need for protection and defense. At any rate, the extent to which the repression of

1353 The condemnation of the *Opera omnia* of Croce and Gentile, established by the Holy Office on June 20, 1934, was ratified by Pius XI the following day. Cf. Guido Verucci, *Idealisti all'Indice. Croce, Gentile e la condanna del S. Uffizio [Idealists on the Index. Croce, Gentile, and the Condemnation of the Holy Office]*, Laterza, Bari-Rome 2006.

1354 *Index of Prohibited Books.* Revised and published by order of His Holiness Pius XI, Tipografia Poliglotta, Vatican City 1929.

> corrupt publications is necessary for the public good and how it agrees perfectly with proper freedom, have been displayed above all in recent times even by the most civil governments which, to safeguard the law or the tranquility of order, have had recourse even to preventative censure, a severity unknown in the Church.

The last edition of the Index dates from 1948 and remained in force with new additions until its suppression in 1966.

The Condemnation of *Action Française*

In France, the question of the legal and canonical *associations cultuelles* remained suspended since the papacy of Benedict XV. The law of 1905 remained unmodified by parliament, but was "reinterpreted" by the executive. On January 18, 1924, Pius XI published the encyclical, *Maximam gravissimamque.*[1355] Accepting a compromise with the French government, he declared the *associations diocésaines* (which replaced the *associations cultuelles* condemned by Pius X) to be "permitted" "as an experiment."[1356] Cardinal Merry del Val tried to "express with the greatest reverence" to Cardinal Gasparri his "profound conviction to the contrary," already contained in one of his *votum* of July 23, 1922, saying that the pontifical decision ended up approving "the inauspicious law" of 1905, which remained integrally in force."[1357]

The victory of the left-leaning block in the elections of May 11, 1924, confirmed Merry del Val's concerns. Prime Minister Herriot announced in June 1924 to the French parliament the suppression of the embassy to the Holy See and the integral application of the laws regarding religious congregations.[1358] The Herriot administration did not last long, however, and his successor Briand announced to the Chamber, in April 1925, that he intended to maintain the embassy to the Vatican, inaugurating a climate of greater détente, expressions of which were found in

1355 Pius XI, Encyclical *Maximam gravissimamque. De Consociationibs Diocesanis in Gallia,* January 18, 1924, in AAS, 16 (1924), pp. 12–18, 19–24.

1356 Following two governmental proposals, brought to fruition by Minister Poincaré in March 1929, the ecclesiastical property confiscated by the state that had not already been destined to other uses was restored to the diocesan worship associations, and permission was given to the Missionary institutes to use the property of the disbanded congregations for missionary institutes outside of the metropolitan area.

1357 AAV, *Spoglio Merry del Val,* busta 6, f. 663. Note of January 6, 1924.

1358 Édouard Herriot (1872–1957), socialist, was on several occasions minister and prime minister (1924–1925, 1926, 1932). After World War II he was president of the National Assembly (1947–1954).

the two agreements between France and the Holy See on December 4, 1926, concerning the liturgical honors rendered to French representatives in the Far East.[1359]

It was in this context that the *Action française* question was set, an issue that agitated the French Catholic world for a decade. *Action française* was a journal founded in 1899 by a group of intellectuals of various cultural backgrounds, who saw in the monarchy the possibility for returning to the political and social order subverted by the French Third Republic. The undisputed leader of the movement was Charles Maurras, a writer and journalist from Provence, formed in the positivist school of Auguste Comte.[1360] In 1907, the *Institut d'Action française* was created as a counter-university, publically opposing the Enlightenment spirit of the universities, and in 1908, the journal *Action française* became a combative daily newspaper in which Maurras proposed, in the formula *politique d'abord*, the idea of a counterrevolution founded on the political platform of "organizational empiricism."

Maurras's theories on the practical level of consequences, as well as his doctrinal premises, appeared much closer to those of the papal Magisterium than were the theories of liberal Catholics. *Action française* supported Pius X, denouncing the danger of modernism: this earned it the support of some champions of French anti-modernism such as the Benedictine Jean-Martial Besse,[1361] the former Jesuit Emmanuel Barbier,[1362]

[1359] AAS, 19 (1927), pp. 9–12.

[1360] Charles Maurras (1868–1952), admitted to the *Académie française* in 1938, during the German occupation in WWII became one of the advisors to Marshall Pétain, until 1942. Arrested in September 1944, he was condemned for life for collaboration, but in 1952 was released due to his poor health. Reconciled with the Catholic Church, he dedicated a book to *Le Bienheureux Pie X, sauveur de la France* (1953). About him, cf. Y. Chiron, *La vie de Maurras*, Perrin, Paris 1991; Jean Madiran, *Maurras*, Nouvelles Éditions Latines, Paris 1992; Bruno Goyet, *Charles Maurras, une biographie critique*, Presses de Sciences Po, Paris 2000. For a general presentation of *Action française*, cf. J. Prévotat, *L'Action française*, Presses Universitaires de France, Paris 2004. Works of fundamental reference: Eugen Weber, *Action française*, Stanford University Press, Stanford 1962; Victor Nguyen, *Aux origines de l'Action française*, Fayard, Paris 1991. Bibliography until 2002 in Alain de Benoist, *Charles Maurras et l'Action française. Une bibliographie*, Éditions BCM, Niherne 2002.

[1361] Jean-Martial Besse (1861–1920) entered the Benedictines of Solesmes (1881) and was ordained a priest (1886) in the abbey of Ligugé, where he spent most of his life. Besides his studies of the monastic tradition, cf. on him *Église et Monarchie* (1910); *L'Église et les libertés modernes. Le Syllabus* (1913); *Les religiones laïques* (1913).

[1362] Emmanuel Barbier (1851–1925), ordained in 1882 with the Jesuits, was rector of the College of St. Ignatius in Paris and later of the College of Saint-Joseph in Poitiers (1895–1901), then regional chaplain of the *Association Catholique de la Jeunesse française* (1902–1904). In 1905, he asked to leave the Society of Jesus to dedicate himself more freely to this controversy and was incardinated into the diocese of Poitiers with permission to reside in Paris where he published *Les idées du Sillon. Étude critique* (1905); *Les erreurs du Sillon* (1906); and *Cas de conscience: les catholiques français et la République* (1906). His *opus magnum* is the *Histoire du catholicisme libéral et social en France du Concile du Vatican à l'avènement de SS. Benoît XV* (1870–1914), in 5 vols. (1923–1924).

and the Dominican Thomas Pégues.[1363] Pius X himself, receiving a renowned French writer and musician, Camille Bellaigue, defined Maurras "a fine defender of the faith."[1364] The main opposition to *Action française* came from the setting of Catholic Democrats embodied in *Sillon*, which denounced some of Maurras's writings to the Holy Office with the accusation of agnosticism and immorality. The Congregation of the Index, on January 29, 1914, condemned five works of the French writer.[1365] Although Pius X ratified the condemnation, applying to Maurras's books the formula *damnabiles non damnados*, he decided not to promulgate it in the *Acts of the Holy See*.[1366] Although aware of the limits of Maurras's thought, the pope considered the political struggle of *Action française* against the anticlerical Republic to be beneficial for the Church and for this reason considered it his duty to postpone the promulgation of the decree. In May 1915, Benedict XV also decided to postpone the promulgation of the decree of condemnation, of which all trace seemed to have been lost in the Holy Office.[1367]

The attitude of the Holy See changed with the policy of *apaisement* toward the Third Republic under Pius XI. Pius XI decided to exhume the condemnation of 1914 because *Action française* represented an obstacle to this policy, and he showed his concern over the growing influence of the movement over Catholic youth in France. The pope decided to strike the movement with a condemnation, but wanted the offensive to be launched by the French episcopate and not by Rome. Many bishops were approached, but only the elderly

[1363] Thomas Pègues (1866–1936), Dominican, was a professor at the Angelicum (1909–1921), then rector of studies at the monastery of Saint-Maximin (1921–1927), which he had to leave after the condemnation of *Action française*, which he frequented, to retire to Italy living near Pistoia (1927–1935) and then Minerva (1935–1936).

[1364] This episode is narrated by Camille Bellaigue in his *Pie X et la France*, Nouvelle Librairie Nationale, Paris 1916. On the three audiences of Pius X with Camille Bellaigue, cf. Prévotat, *Les catholiques et l'Action française*, pp. 158–161.

[1365] On January 2, 1914, the Congregation of the Index declared that the five books by Maurras (*Chemin de Paradis, Anthinea, Les amants de Venise, Trois idées politiques, L'avenir de l'intelligence*) and the journal *L'Action française* directed by him merited condemnation.

[1366] On the question, besides the fundamental study by J. Prévotat, *Les catholiques et l'Action française. Études de deux condamnations romaines*, Fayard, Paris 2001 ; cf. Lucien Thomas, *L'Action française devant l'Église. De Pie X à Pie XII*, Nouvelles Éditions Latines, Paris 1965; Michael Sutton, *Nationalism, Positivism and Catholicism: The Politics of Maurras and French Catholics*, Cambridge University Press, London 1982; André Ladouze, *Dominicains français et Action française*, Les Éditions Ouvrières, Paris 1989; Philippe Prévost, *Autopsie d'une crise politico-religieuse. La condamnation de l'Action française 1926–1939*, Librairie canadienne, Paris 2008; idem, *La condamnation de l'Action française, une affaire politique*, C.E.C., Paris 2009; Y. Chiron and E. Poulat, *Pourquoi Pie XI a-t–il condamné l'Action française ?*, Éditions BCM, Niherne 2009.

[1367] Prévotat, *L'Action française*, p. 59.

Cardinal Andrieu,[1368] archbishop of Bordeaux, offered his willingness to take the initiative.[1369] On August 27, 1926, the Cardinal from Bordeaux published in his diocesan bulletin, *L'Aquitaine,* a letter in which he denounced Maurras's doctrines and those of his collaborators, going so far as to accuse them of paganism and atheism: "They make reference to God and yet they consider God un-knowable and nonexistent.... They substitute our moral laws with a pagan social organization in which the state is everything and the individual is nothing."[1370] On September 5, *L'Osservatore Romano* reproduced the letter on the front page and on September 8, Pius XI wrote to Cardinal Andrieu to thank him publicly.[1371]

The interventions of Cardinal Andrieu and Pius XI aroused an immediate reaction from the militants of *Action française.* One of the more authoritative among them, Count Bernard de Vésins, president of the *Ligue d'Action française* in Bordeaux, replied in a letter to Pius X, "On behalf of the thousands of members of the League, practicing, devout Catholics, we humbly place at the feet of Your Holiness a solemn protest of our complete faith in the dogmas of the Catholic Church and of our submission to its Head." [1372]

As the controversy increased, the definitive word from Pius XI was pronounced during his address to the secret consistory, *Misericordia Domini,* on December 20, 1926. In this document, the pope stated, "It is not allowed in any way for Catholics to take part in the activities and, in a certain sense, in schools that place the interests of political parties above religion and make the faithful serve the former.... Neither is it permissible for Catholics to support, sustain, or read journals directed by men whose writings, deviating from our dogmas and from our moral doctrine, cannot escape blame."[1373]

The response to this allocution came in the article *Non possumus* published on December 22 in the daily *L'Action française.* "In the situation France finds itself

1368 Pierre-Paulin Andrieu (1849–1935) was named bishop of Marsiglia (1901) by Leo XIII and archbishop of Bordeaux (1909) by Pius X, who in the consistory of December 16, 1907, made him a cardinal.

1369 "Il ne le fait par sa propre initiative. L'ordre vient de Rome" (Chiron, *Pie XI,* p. 265).

1370 "Réponse de S. Em. le cardinal archevêque de Bordeaux à une question posée par un groupe de jeunes catholiques au sujet de l'Action française," in Prévotat, *Les catholiques et l'Action française,* pp. 675–677.

1371 Pius XI, Letter to Cardinal Andrieu, September 5, 1926, in Prévotat, *Les catholiques et l'Action française,* pp. 678–679.

1372 Count Bernard de Vésins (1869–1951), militant monarchist, was one of the cofounders of the daily *L'Action française* in 1908, and president from 1919 to 1930 of the *Ligue d'Action française.*

1373 Official text in AAS, 18, December 31, 1926, pp. 513–524.

in, the act of assassinating *Action française* is not purely or primarily a religious action. It is above all a political action.... Favoring this action would be a betrayal.... Rejecting it, we cannot cease to be good Catholics; obeying it, we would cease to be good Frenchmen. We will not betray our fatherland: *Non possumus*."

Maurras admitted to having compromised his own position with this act of rebellion, even if the condemnation had already been decided.[1374] One of the reasons for the resistance and the controversy aroused by the condemnation was, as observed Prévotat, "the awkwardness with which the affair had been handled."[1375]

On December 31, 1926, a decree of the Congregation of the Holy Office was promulgated condemning the five works of Charles Maurras included in the decree of Pius XI in 1914, adding to them another two works and the daily newspaper *L'Action française*.[1376]

The decree bore a double date: "January 29, 1914, and December 29, 1926," to highlight the continuity between the two pontiffs, Pius X and Pius XI. In the text of the Holy Office, the censure against the works was not accompanied by censure against the people involved in them, as distinct from what had happened with modernism. Nevertheless, in March 1927, Rome decided to refuse the sacraments (Baptism, Penance, Communion, Matrimony, and funerals) to whomever subscribed to or read *L'Action française*. In 1936, funeral rites were even refused to the historian Jacques Bainville, who had been nominated to the French Academy just a few months before his death.[1377] Émile Poulat remarked, "Here is where the drama was consumed: the faithful who insisted on reading the newspaper were not excommunicated, but were treated with maximum severity as public sinners, deprived of the sacraments and of funeral services."[1378]

1374 "La prise à partie de Rome, avec ce "non" dit en face, est ce qui compromit et faussa notre position. Une polémique empoisonnée, empoisonneuse devait s'ensuivre, et pourtant, ce que nous étions accuses de déchirer, ce que nous semblions déchirer, nous déchirait nous-memes" (C. Maurras, *Le Bienheureux Pie X, sauveur de la France,* Plon, Paris 1953, pp. 140–141).

1375 Prévotat, *L'Action française*, p. 67. Poulat also speaks of "*impardonable maladresse*" (*Le Saint-Siège et l'Action française*, p. 58).

1376 AAS, 1926, pp. 538–539. To the five works condemned by Pius X, Pius XI added *La politique religieuse* and *Si le coup de force est possible* by Maurras. In 1939, after the signing by the board of directors of *Action française* of a declaration of submission, the sanctions concerning the journal were lifted by Pius XII. Cf. Decree of the Holy Office of July 10, 1939; reply of the Sacred Penitentiary of July 24 of the same year. The condemnation of Maurras's works listed on the *Index* remained in effect.

1377 Jaques Bainville (1879–1936) was a brilliant monarchist journalist and historian, elected in 1935 to the French Academy. Among his works are: *Histoire de France* (1924), *Napoléon* (1932), *La IIIe République* (1935).

1378 Poulat, *Le Saint-Siège et l'Action française*, p. 24.

The condemnation of *Action française* was accompanied by intense controversy. On January 29, 1927, Italian Interior Minister Luigi Federzoni[1379] reported in his diary of having learned from the writer Piero Misciattelli[1380] of the explanation given in the Vatican for the condemnation of *Action française*: "In the final period of his nunciature in Paris, the nuncio stumbled into an unfortunate amorous affair, with bothersome consequences from which he was saved by Mr. Briand. But the latter does not bestow favors for free. As the nuncio was departing for Rome, where he was to receive the cardinalate, it is said that Briand beseeched him to obtain the repudiation of *Action française*. Nor would the nuncio have been capable, not wanting to lose the *porpora*, of refusing the request of the cunning Aristide."[1381]

On March 25, the news was confirmed to Federzoni from Count di Bonvouloir, claiming that one evening "the nuncio was surprised in a nightclub in Montmartre in a very delicate situation." Briand had immediately reassured him that "the matter would be kept silent; but in return I shall request his hide."[1382] The nuncio in question was Msgr. Bonaventura Cerretti,[1383] nuncio to Paris from 1911 to 1926 and a determining factor in the condemnation of Maurras.[1384]

[1379] Luigi Federzoni (1878–1967), member of parliament beginning in 1913, was Minister of the Colonies and Interior Minister, senator (1928), and president of the Senate (1929–1939) and of the *Accademia d'Italia* (1938–1943). He was a member of the Gran Consiglio of fascism, and on July 25, 1943, adhered to the Grandi agenda, for which he was condemned to death in absentia by the Tribunal of Verona. After Liberation, he was condemned to life in prison by the High Court of Justice in 1945 and given amnesty in 1947.

[1380] Marquis Piero Misciattelli (1882–1937) studied, among other things, Sienese history and art and Medieval literature, especially mystical literature (*Idealità francescane*, 1909; *Mistici senesi*, 1911). He established in Siena (1926) the journal *La Diana* and the *Cattedra cateriniana* at the university. His mother Aurora had as her spiritual director Cardinal Merry del Val.

[1381] Luigi Federzoni, *1927. Diario di un ministro del fascismo [Diary of a Minister of Fascism]*, Passigli, Florence 1993, p. 60. According to a note by Msgr. Benigni of March 17, 1924, the Italian foreign minister had identified the presumed lover of Msgr. Cerretti as a political agent, a "certain Annie Basily" (ASMAE, Fondo Benigni, busta 13, n. 88, *Vicende affare B. Cerretti-Annie Basily*).

[1382] Ibid., p. 143. Jules Achard of the counts of Bonvouloir (1874–1930) married Bianca Colonna of Stigliano (1887–1944) in 1905.

[1383] Bonaventura Cerretti (1872–1933) worked for the Secretariat of State (1900–1904), before becoming an apostolic delegate in Mexico, auditor in Washington (1906–1914), titular archbishop of Corinth (1914), and secretary for Extraordinary Ecclesiastical Affairs (1917). In 1919, he was in Paris during the Peace Conference and in 1921 was named nuncio in France, staying in this post until April 1925. On December 24 of the same year, he was made a cardinal by Pius XI. Cf. Giuseppe De Luca, *Il cardinale Bonaventura Cerretti*, Storia e Letteratura, Rome 1971; Vittorio De Marco, *Un diplomatico vaticano all'Eliseo. Il cardinale Bonaventura Cerretti, 1872–1933*, Edizioni di Storia e Letteratura, Rome 1984, in particular pp. 80–155 on the nunciature in France; Fiorentino.

[1384] Chiron, *Maurras*, p. 340.

From the archival documents, it turns out that already two years earlier the Italian government and the Holy See had been informed of voices that were circulating around nuncio Cerretti. According to a note by the political police, October 10, 1925, "Cardinal Merry del Val defines him as a man without scruples. It seems that Msgr. Cerretti is in some manner under the sway of the French government, due to certain letters brought to him while he was in the home of a Russian lady."[1385] Cardinal Gasparri was convinced that these were malicious voices and exchanged harsh letters with the archbishop of Aix, Maurice-Louis-Marie Rivière,[1386] who was accused of having been one of the agents who had contributed to their circulation.[1387] Msgr. Rivière denied the accusations, but on April 3, 1926, Msgr. Cerretti took leave from Briand and returned to Rome.

In 1930, new testimony and documents were produced against the cardinal, making a great impression on the pope.[1388] When Cerretti passed away, a note by the political police, dated May 9, 1933, described his life as "morally and politically, individually and socially, depraved," to the point that it "made him the cancer of the Sacred College."[1389]

This news would tend to give credence to those who consider the papal intervention to have been of a political nature. On the other hand, if it is true, as observed Prévotat,[1390] that according to Pius XI the condemnation concerned the naturalist and pagan foundations of the *politique d'abord* mentality, it is equally true that the condemnation was situated in the context of what has been defined a second *ralliement* of the Holy See with the French Third Republic. The most balanced assessment was proposed by the theologian Victor-Alain

1385 ACS, *Segreteria particolare del Duce. Carteggio riservato*. Busta 127, Report of October 10, 1925. The text is reported, with a different placement, also by P. Scoppola, *La Chiesa e il fascismo. Documenti e interpretazioni [The Church and Fascism. Documents and Interpretations]*, Laterza, Bari 1971, p. 150. Another report of July 23, 1928, reports that "a cardinal said that there are two unscrupulous cardinals in the Sacred College: Gasparri and Cerretti. One stays put and makes money; the other gets out of the way and makes money. Both are without a conscience of any sort: this explains why they always manage to stay afloat" (ACS, *Segreteria particolare del Duce. Carteggio riservato*, The Duce's Private Secretary. Confidential Papers, Busta 127, Report of July 23, 1928).

1386 Maurice-Louis-Marie Rivière (1859–1930) was named bishop of Périgueux by Benedict XV in 1915 and, in 1920, archbishop of Aix.

1387 The papers are inserted into AA.EE.SS., *Francia*, 1923–1926, Pos. 514, P.O., fasc. 4.

1388 ACS, *Polizia politica, Fascicoli Personali, 1927–1944 [Political Police, Personal Folders]*, 284, "Bonaventura Cerretti," note of April 10, 1930. According to a following note of May 1, 1930, "it seems that against Cardinal Cerretti new elements have been gathered which prove his libertine conduct in Paris" (ibid.).

1389 ACS, *Polizia politica, Fascicoli Personali, 1927–1944*, 284 "Bonaventura Cerretti," note of May 9, 1930.

1390 Prévotat, *Les catholiques et l'Action française*, p. 68

Berto, claiming that Pius XI did not admit the principle of the *politique d'abord,* neither in the order of values, nor on the level of execution, holding that Catholics should commit all their strength to Catholic Action, subordinated to the hierarchy, a different position from that of St. Pius X and Cardinal Merry del Val.[1391] In this sense, the condemnation was not "doctrinal" but rather of a "pastoral" character.

In reality, after the condemnation of *Action française,* a campaign was inaugurated against intransigent Catholics, those faithful to the spiritual and doctrinal legacy of Pius X. This campaign gave rise to the volume *Saint-Siège, "Action française" et "Catholiques intégraux"* (1928), written by Nicolas Fontaine, a pseudonym of Louis Canet, a government functionary of modernist leanings and executor of Loisy's will.[1392] Canet established a regrettable connection between what he defined "integral Catholicism" and the integralist nationalism of *Action française.* The attempt was to extend the condemnation of Pius XI to those intransigent Catholics who, following Pius X, had attempted to halt the penetration of modernism within the Church.

Father Le Floch and Cardinal Billot

Canet took aim at two ecclesiastical personalities: Cardinal Billot and Fr. Henri Le Floch, who had always distinguished themselves for their anti-modernist stances. Canet, who was defined "the last Gallican," detested these two exponents of a "Roman" Catholicism incompatible with his ideological position. In

1391 Victor-Alain Berto, *Une opinion sur l'Action française,* Éditions BCM, pp. 10–11. The article originally appeared in *Itinéraires* in April 1968 (pp. 72–82). Fr. Victor-Alain Berto (1900–1968) studied at the French Seminary (1904–1927), was ordained in 1926, carried out his ministry in Brittany, and was among the foudners of the journal *La Pensée Catholique* in 1946, in which he published numerous essays. A concise biography can be found in *Notre Dame de Joie. Correspondance de l'abbé V.–A. Berto prêtre. 1900–1968,* Éditions du Cèdre, Paris 1989, pp. 11–48. His contributions to *La Pensée Catholique* and to the work of the Council are gathered in *Pour la Sainte Église Romaine. Textes et documents de V.A. Berto prêtre. 1900–1968,* Éditions du Cèdre, Paris 1976.

1392 Louis Canet (1883–1958), functionary of Quay d'Orsay, where he directed the office of religious affairs, was the executor of the will of Loisy and the author, under the pseudonym of Nicolas Fontaine, of *Saint-Siège, "Action française" et "Catholiques intégraux"* (Librairie Gambier, Paris 1928). "A une autre époque, il eut été volontiers gallican. D'esprit, il était jansséniste" (P. Prévost, *L'Église et le ralliement,* EC, Paris 2010, p. 135). Cf. Bruno Neveu, "Louis Canet et le service du conseiller technique pour les affaires religieuses du ministère des Affaires étrangères," *Revue d'histoire diplomatique,* avril–juin 1968, pp. 134–180; Fabrice Robardey, "Louis Canet et l'Alsace: le double service de l'Église et de l'État (1918–1927)," in Prévotat (ed.), *Pie XI et la France,* pp. 53–72; Robert A. Graham, "L'ultimo gallicano del Quai d'Orsay. La nostalgia di Louis Canet (1883–1958)," *La Civiltà Cattolica* q. 3373, 142/I, 05/05/1991, pp. 13–22; Luc Perrin, "Autour d'un portrait de Louis Canet," *Revue des sciences religieuses* 91/1 (2017), pp. 3–11.

his accusation, he wrote that "one of the main centers [of resistance to the condemnation of *Action française*] was in Rome, in the French Seminary of Santa Chiara, fueled by the arguments of Cardinal Billot and by the intrigues of Fr. Le Floch."[1393]

The French Seminary of Santa Chiara had been directed since 1904 by Fr. Henri Le Floch, consultor of the Holy Office beginning in 1918, and highly esteemed by Cardinal Merry del Val.[1394] Like Cardinal Billot, Le Floch was an admirer of *Action Française,* although he saw its limits. He sought to defend it until its condemnation, and then bowed to the will of the Holy Father. After the address to the secret consistory of December 20, Le Floch requested of his students "the sacrifice of all discussions."[1395] On December 27, he expressed himself clearly in these words: "The solemn words of the pope have condemned *Action française*. From now on, everything is clear and no one can take refuge in ambiguity."[1396]

Le Floch was accused of having had in his hands the dossier concerning the condemnation of Maurras and of having retained it to block or postpone the ruling of Pius XI.[1397] The pontiff had given orders to Msgr. Canali, the assessor of the Holy Office and custodian of the archives, to find the documentation of the condemnation of Maurras from 1914, but his search was laborious and the decree of Pius X was found only several days after the adress to the secret consistory of December 20. Pius XI seemed to allude to it, stating on January 5, 1927, "It is clear that we would have used quite different procedures if the documents we are promulgating had been in our possession; but it was only after the day of the consistory that they came into our

1393 Canet, *Saint-Siège, Action française et "Catholiques intégraux,"* p. 93. Canet's resentment had ancient roots. When he viciously attacked Benedict XV with an anonymous article published in the *Revue de Paris* under the title "La politique de Benoît XV" (October 15 and November 1, 1918), Fr. Le Floch replied with a volume published by Téqui, entitled: *La politique de Benoît XV. Réponse aux articles anonymes de la Revue de Paris* (Téqui, Paris 1919).

1394 Henri Le Floch (1862–1950), ordained in 1886 in the Congregation of the Holy Spirit, of which he became the Superior General (1923–1927), directed the French Seminary in Rome for over twenty years until 1927, when, following the condemnation of *Action française,* of which he was a sympathizer, Pius XI forced him to leave Rome. For a profile on him, cf. in V.–A. Berto, *Pour la Sainte Église Romaine*, pp. 113–144. Cf. also Paul Airiau, "Henri Le Floch, recteur du Séminaire français (1904–1927)," in P. Levillain, P. Boutry, Yves-Marie Fradet (eds.), *150 ans au coeur de Rome, Le Séminaire français 1853–2003*, Karthala, Paris 2004, pp. 103–118.

1395 *Carnets personnels du P. Le Floch*, recopied by Édith Crosnier, Kersaint-Landunvez (Finistère), n. 19, December 21, 1926.

1396 Cit. in Prévotat, *Les catholiques et l'Action française*, p. 332.

1397 Ibid., pp. 338–339.

possession ... We lacked positive documents, they were lacking until the last hour, and only after repeated searches, made following the indications suggested by the habits of a past life spent mostly among books and documents, were they finally found."[1398]

The accusation was unjust and rash, and Cardinal Merry del Val intervened in defense of his collaborator. After an article published in *La Croix* on October 26th, 1927, Merry del Val wrote on November 1 to Fr. Le Floch,

> I am profoundly saddened by the news you gave me and my soul is disgusted by the hateful calumny hurled against you. I am particularly indignant about the behavior of your most recent aggressor (Msgr. Durand),[1399] about his boldness and his false and ridiculous insinuations. All that you have said is true. All that has been said is false. You have always been perfectly correct and scrupulous as a consultant of the Holy Office, where you have rendered important services which we have fully appreciated. The documents in question were not contained in the volume in your possession and which you returned immediately. You are in no way involved in the matter under discussion. No one, furthermore, has hidden, lost, or refused anything: everything is clear, known, and easily demonstrable. You did well to communicate with the right people: you must defend your honor and demand reparation. I hope justice will be served.[1400]

Merry del Val knew the issue thoroughly, and his letter is so categorical that it absolves Fr. Le Floch completely from the calumny brought against him.[1401] But the cardinal was accused in turn for having defended Le Floch in order to cover himself.

The accusation then extended to Cardinal Billot,[1402] closely tied both to Le Floch and to Merry del Val. The French cardinal was considered the most

[1398] Pius XI, Chirograph to Card. Andrieu of January 5, 1927, in AAS, 19 (1927), p. 6.

[1399] Léon Durand (1878–1945) was bishop of Orano from 1920.

[1400] AA.EE.SS., *Francia,* 1926–1941, Pos. 648, P.O., fasc. 211. Letter of Card. Merry del Val to Fr. Le Floch, November 1, 1927 (copy). Cardinal Dubois submitted the letter to the Holy Father during the audience of February 20, 1928.

[1401] L. Thomas, *L'Action française devant l'Église*, pp. 204–208.

[1402] Regarding the "Billot case," cf. Prévotat, *Les catholiques et l'Action française*, pp. 480–486; and above all the reconstruction by Msgr. Sergio Pagano, "Dalla porpora al chiostro. L'inflessibilità di Pio XI verso il cardinale Louis Billot" [From the Cardinalate to the Cloister. The Inflexibility of Pius XI Toward Cardinal Louis Billot], in Jean-Pierre Delville and Marko Jakov (eds.), *La Papauté contemporaine*, Vatican Secret Archive, Vatican City 2009, pp. 395–410.

eminent Thomist of his time, but also a man of great piety and purity. One of his admirers, Robert Havard de la Montagne, described him in this way: "Those who knew him well recognized in him the priest of Jesus Christ, pious, detached, candid; candid in the sense of purity, of brilliance, of candor, of his entire soul revealed through his corporal trappings."[1403] Billot and Le Floch, he added, had in common "their theological treasure, the disapproval of the same errors, and a great benevolence toward people.... Their courtesy and their good graces were the effect of an elegance nourished by Christian charity that distinguishes between the malice of sin and the infirmity of sinners."[1404]

The progressive theologian Marie-Dominique Chenu, who detested the "Roman School," compared the Romanism of Cardinal Billot to the Romanism of Cardinal Merry del Val in conducting the policies of the Holy See. Under St. Pius X, according to Chenu, Billot had been an executor of the "policies" of the "reactionary Merry del Val."[1405]

What he could not forgive in both was their role in the condemnation of modernism under Pius X.

From the very beginning of *Action française*, Billot had followed the movement with sympathy and made no mystery of having an opinion about it similar to that of Pius X, to whom he owed his *porpora*. On October 26, 1911, Pius X had written to Fr. Franz Xavier Wernz, Superior General of the Jesuits, to communicate to him his intention of making Fr. Louis Billot a cardinal: "I know that, according to their Rule, the fathers of the Society of Jesus not only must not aspire to, but also must refuse, all dignities. To remedy this circumstance, I grant all the necessary dispensations, imploring Your Most Reverend Paternity and the Rev. Fr. Billot not to insist on being exempted. I point out, furthermore, that if in the days of St. Ignatius the cardinalate was a dignity held in high honor in the profane world as well, today it is rather a cross, and he who accepts it and carries it with holy resignation increases his merits in paradise."[1406]

Sixteen years later, during the secret consistory of December 19, 1927, Pius XI announced that the eminent Cardinal Louis Billot had renounced the

1403 Havard de la Montagne, *Chemins de Rome*, p. 148.

1404 Ibid., p. 149.

1405 Bernardi, *Louis Cardinal Billot*, pp. 596–597.

1406 *Carte Pio X. Scritti, omelie, conferenze e lettere di Giuseppe Sarto [The Papers of Pius X. Writings, Homilies, Conferences, and Letters of Giuseppe Sarto]*, ed. A. M. Dieguez, Vatican Secret Archive, Vatican City 2010, p. 456.

sacred *porpora* and had returned to the "simple life" of a Jesuit "to retire to a house of the Society of Jesus as a humble religious to prepare for his death."[1407]

Pius XI was, in fact, profoundly irritated when he discovered that, in autumn 1926, after the condemnation of Cardinal Andrieu, Cardinal Billot had written a letter to the author Léon Daudet expressing his support for *Action Française*.[1408] On December 6, Billot had a tempestuous meeting with Cardinal Gasparri who wanted to push him to rectify publicly his ideas, or to resign as a cardinal. Billot replied to the secretary of state and repeated some months later to the Superior General of the Society of Jesus, Wlodimir Ledóchowski,[1409] that, if in matters of a political nature the pope did not allow a cardinal to have divergent opinions from his own, he was willing in all tranquility to renounce the cardinalate rather than renounce his convictions.

The high prelate was summoned to the Vatican on September 13, 1927, by Pius XI. The audience was brief and Billot left the room without his zucchetto, ring, and pectoral cross. His resignation was officially accepted by the pope on the twenty-first of that month. Louis Billot died a simple Jesuit priest on December 18, 1931, at the age of eighty-five in the Jesuit house in Galloro, outside Rome.

He wrote: "I have always responded, orally and by writing, to all who have consulted me about the line of action to take, that not only should they carefully avoid everything that might have the appearance of insubordination or rebellion, but also to make the sacrifice of their own particular ideas to conform themselves to the orders of the sovereign pontiff. Personally, I have been the first to adhere to this rule."[1410]

Merry del Val and Pius XI vis-à-vis *Action Française*

Cardinal Merry del Val, the secretary of the Supreme Congregation of the Holy Office and former secretary of state under Pius X, could allow himself to be quite frank in his language with Pius XI, and did not fail to make known to the pontiff his opinions in the *Action française* case, in an extremely

[1407] AAS, 19, December 22, 1927, pp. 438–439. Cf. *La Civiltà Cattolica*, q. 1855, October 1, 1927, p. 78.

[1408] Léon Daudet (1867–1942), a writer and journalist, was one of the leaders of the movement *Action française*. He was the author of *Souvenirs des milieux littéraires, politiques, artistiques et médicaux* (1914) and *Le stupide XIXe siècle* (1922).

[1409] Wlodimir Ledóchowski (1866–1942), a Jesuit, born into a Polish aristocratic family and nephew of the cardinal primate of Poland Mieczyslaw Ledóchowski, succeeded Fr. Franz Xavier Wernz as the Superior General of the Society of Jesus on February 11, 1915.

[1410] Henri du Passage, "Réponse à une calomnie," *Études* 210 (1932), pp. 491–492.

respectful though resolute manner. He himself narrated this in a thorough, five-page report drafted after an audience with the pope on February 23, 1927.[1411] "His Holiness begins by saying that given the most serious nature of the matter he wants to speak to me directly because he intends to take full responsibility for his actions." The topic of the meeting was Merry del Val's criticism of the way in which Pius XI was conducting the *Action Française* case, without consulting the cardinals. Since "the pope became agitated as he spoke with such emphasis and passion that they could neither respond nor open their mouths," Merry del Val told him, "If Your Holiness will not allow me to speak, I can only keep silent." "No, speak at will," replied the pope, but when the cardinal attempted to give his explanations, Pius XI "grew heated and in an agitated voice repeated: do not go down that path, do not go down that path, it is false, it is colossal, etc."

"I replied that I believed that a cardinal could speak and express his thought with a colleague or with a bishop who requested explanations, but that if he was to be gagged, this was another matter. Another fit of rage by H.H."

Merry del Val attempted to say that he knew well the question of *Action Française* because as "a former secretary of state of Pius X, who had lived those things and spoken constantly with the pope, he too had some authority to acknowledge the pope's thought," but Pius XI, without responding to this, stated "that it was better to err on the side of the pope," adding, "I do not err, I have heard all the voices and I know what I have done."

"To this I replied that I was immensely sorry for having caused him pain, but that he could do as concerns me whatever he believed best." "I could have submitted my resignation, but this seemed something done '*ab irato*' or out of spite and would have serious consequences. I limited myself to saying that I didn't think I deserved such a severe judgment." "'Do not say severe, say true,' exclaimed the pope and continued speaking excitedly," accusing him of having spoken ill of him to the French writer Camille Bellaigue. Merry del Val tried to protest, but was bowled over by an avalanche of words. "There was no way to reason, so I kept silent." He concluded, "The pope treated me like a schoolboy."[1412]

[1411] AAV, *Spoglio Merry del Val*, busta 6, n. 731. The archive preserves Cardinal Gasparri's letter, the note from the audience, the outline of the letter, and Bellaigue's retraction of an injurious phrase towards Pius XI which was supposedly written by Merry del Val (n. 730–736).

[1412] AAV, *Spoglio Merry del Val*, busta 6, n. 732.

These excesses of anger by Pius XI were quite common. In a confidential report of November 22, 1929, the Italian ambassador to the Holy See, De Vecchi, informed Foreign Minister Dino Grandi[1413] of having had on November 15 a turbulent audience with Pius XI over the relationship between Fascism and the Holy See, in which the pope "went off in a rage raising his voice, cutting me off as I tried to speak.... The pope gesticulated wildly, rising to his feet, agitating and pronouncing words and phrases that were less than ... diplomatic."[1414]

In any case, the final word belonged to the pope. Since Pius XI had accused Merry del Val of having told the writer Camille Bellaigue that the pope was "stubborn like a mule," the cardinal immediately wrote his French friend to beg him to send the pope a denial of this claim.[1415] The following day, Cardinal Merry del Val, "profoundly grieved for the displeasure caused to Your Holiness," renewed his apologies, writing Pius XI, "Your Holiness shall have the certainty that now and always you will find in me a filially obedient servant and unconditionally subservient." The incident was considered closed by the pope.[1416] Nevertheless, on April 26, 1927, Cardinal Gasparri communicated to Merry del Val the pope's decision to "permit, in serious cases and for grave reasons, the reading of the periodical *Action française*."[1417]

After the death of Cardinal Merry del Val and Pius XI, the question of *Action française* was reconsidered by Pius XII, who assigned the Holy Office the task of reexamining the case. Among those who insisted on the revocation of sanctions was the assessor of the Congregation of the Holy Office, Nicola Canali, the old secretary of Merry del Val, elevated to the *porpora* in 1935. In his opinion, echoing the thought of Merry del Val and Pius X, Canali stated, "Most of the directors of *Action française* are neither anti-Catholic nor amoral, but all of them admit the doctrine of the Church in its fundamental demands as the basis of their activity, even political activity. And in the past, *Action française* even had a teaching chair on the Syllabus."[1418] "One must say that the cause of

1413 Dino Grandi, Count of Mordano (1895–1988), was member of the Grand Council of Fascism from 1923, undersecretary of the Interior (1924–1925) and foreign undersecretary (1925–1929), foreign minister (1929–1932), and finally ambassador in London (1932–1939).

1414 ASMAE, busta 7, fasc, 1, *Holy See, 1919–1930*. Report of Ambassador De Vecchi to Minister Dino Grandi of November 22, 1929.

1415 AAV, *Spoglio Merry del Val*, busta 6, n. 733.

1416 Ibid., n. 735.

1417 ADDF, *Censura Librorum, Action française*, n. 1168, 1926, I. 1–21.

1418 Ibid., *Circa la revoca della condanna dell'Action française. Voto del cardinal Canali*, p. 6.

the Church today is better served by this prohibited journal than in the hands of certain other journals, approved and encouraged by certain ecclesiastical authorities, that foster liberalism, communism, and strikes, to the point of placing France in immediate danger of civil war: journals such as *Aube*, *Esprit*, and *Temps Présent*."[1419]

The assessor of the Holy Office then criticized Cardinal Verdier[1420] and the other French bishops who opposed the annulment of the condemnation, highlighting that in France, "religious persecution, though in an underhanded manner, has never ceased." "When do we ever hear from the bishops a word of protest, especially concerning the grave question of the schools, in such a way that, it is painful to say, in many circumstances the bishops seem to have become '*canes muti*'?"[1421] "What is certain is that if *Action française* is to be freed from this censure, it will be an immense relief for a great number of French Catholics who are obediently silent, awaiting the hour of liberation: and in this way the Holy See could affirm once more the wise maxim of leaving Catholics free rein in political matters, while demanding they remain united in religious matters."[1422]

Thirteen years after the condemnation by Pius XI, his successor Pius XII revoked the ruling against *Action française*. On June 19, 1939, a declaration of submission was made by the members of the board of directors of the movement and on July 10, 1939, a decree of the Holy Office raised the prohibition against the newspaper and abolished the canonical sanctions against the members of *Action française*.[1423]

Cardinals Tedeschini and Merry del Val

Among the many enemies Cardinal Merry del Val had during his life, one of the most malicious was Monsignor (and later cardinal) Federico Tedeschini,

1419 Ibid., p. 11.

1420 Jean Verdier (1864–1940), of the Company of Priests of St. Sulpice, was named archbishop of Paris and cardinal by Pius XI in 1929.

1421 *Circa la revoca della condanna dell'Action française. Voto del cardinal Canali*, p. 12.

1422 Ibid., pp. 14–15.

1423 AAS, 9, July 10, 1939, pp. 303–306. Text in Prévotat, *Les catholiques et l'Action française*, pp. 709–710. The decree of December 29, 1926, was not abolished: the seven works of Maurras and the journal *L'Action française* remained condemned, but only within the chronological limits imposed by Pius X (from December 29, 1926, to July 10, 1939). Cf. the documentation concerning the annulment in ADDF, *Censura libri, Action française*, n. 1168, 1926, I, 1–21.

who had been a collaborator of his at the Secretariat of State during the pontificate of Pius X.

Federico Tedeschini was born in Antrodoco, in the diocese of Rieti, on October 12, 1873.[1424] Ordained a priest in 1896, in 1900 he entered the Secretariat of State as a clerk in the service of Msgr. Della Chiesa, who became his protector. The same Della Chiesa, rising to the papal throne in 1914 with the name Benedict XV, nominated him substitute secretary of state. Tedeschini enjoyed the pope's complete trust, as he demonstrated by acting on his behalf in the thorny Gerlach affair.

On March 31, 1921, Benedict XV named him apostolic nuncio to the King of Spain and on May 5, consecrated him bishop of the Sistine Chapel with the title of archbishop of Lepanto.[1425] Tedeschini remained in the Spanish capital until June 1936, five weeks before the beginning of the civil war.[1426] His diplomatic mission had lasted nearly sixteen years and was the longest of any pontifical representative in Spain in modern times.

The public controversy concerning some aspects of the nuncio's lifestyle, as well as his somewhat eccentric dealings with some lords of the Madrid aristocracy, the assassination attempt he suffered,[1427] and the automobile

[1424] In *Fondo Benigni*, busta 47, ff. 12–15 there is an anonymous typewritten note dated "Aquila, March 31, 1917," according to which the Tedeschini brothers "enjoy in their native town (Antrodoco) the traditional reputation of a clan of scarce moral rectitude" (f. 13); and "Msgr. Tedeschini and his brothers are capable of anything" (p. 14). In particular, the economic fortunes of one of the brothers, Costantino, a vendor of salt and tobacco, "undoubtedly derives from his brother the Monsignor by way of political and financial intrigues, that is to say, through dubious political and financial relations that they leave to most competent among them to sort out the kinks in Rome" (f. 15).

[1425] V. Cárcel Ortí, "Instrucciones del Cardenal Gasparri al Nuncio Tedeschinien 1921," *Revista Española de Derecho Canónico* 48 (1991), pp. 455–482; Id., "La nunciatura de Federico Tedeschini en Madrid durante la monarquía (1921–1931)," *Archivum historiae pontificiae* 45 (2007), pp. 97–184; Id., "La Repubblica spagnola nel diario del nunzio Tedeschini 1931–1936," *Archivum historiae pontificiae* 50 (2012), pp. 95–140; V. Càrcel Ortí, *Pío XI entre la República y Franco. La angustia de un Papa ante la tragedia española,* BAC, Madrid 2008. The articles by Msgr. Cárcel Ortí ignore Tedeschini's responsibility, whereas José Ramón Rodríguez Lago goes more in depth in "La batalla eclesial por Madrid (1923–1936). Los conflictos entre Eijo Garay y Federico Tedeschini," *Hispania sacra* 64 (January–June 2012), pp. 205–222; idem, "Las claves de Tedeschini: la política vaticana en España (1921–1936)," *Historia y política* 38 (2017), pp. 229–258. Cf. also Ramiro Trullén Floría, *Religión y política en la España de los años treinta. El nuncio Federico Tedeschini y la Segunda República,* Institución "Fernando el Católico," Zaragoza 2012; Alfredo Verdoy, "Vicente Cárcel Ortí, Diario de Federico Tedeschini," *Estudios Ecclesiasticos* 95, 373 (2020), pp. 457–468.

[1426] Tedeschini stayed in Spain as nuncio until December 16, 1935 (the date on which his nomination to the cardinalate was made public, although it had been decided *in pectore* on March 13, 1933), then as pro-nuncio until the nomination of his successor on June 4, 1936.

[1427] A note sent by Minister Grandi to ambassador De Vecchi on July 14, 1929, concerning Msgr. Tedeschini, spoke of his ambiguous relations with "a wealthy, elderly lady of the luxurious Spanish

accident that involved him in August 1933, contributed to fostering suspicion and rumors about him.[1428] But the real problem that made its way to Rome was the open hostility he displayed toward three personalities who "incarnated, in contrast to the diplomacy and political prudence represented by the nuncio, the hard line of the Church toward the government of the Republic:"[1429] the archbishop of Madrid-Alcalá, Leopoldo Eijo y Garay; the cardinal of Toledo, Pedro Segura y Sáenz;[1430] and the archbishop of Trazona, later cardinal of Toledo, Isidro Gomá y Tomas.[1431]

Between Cardinal Segura and Cardinal Merry del Val there was a deep affinity of spirit. In a meeting that took place several days before his death, Merry del Val addressed Segura with the following words:

> I am about to tell you something, Pedro, that might surprise you, although you too are a cardinal as I am. I have spent my entire life here in the Roman Curia and I believe I have the authority to tell you this. After the time spent at the Holy Office, and having been the secretary of state for an entire pontificate, I have reached the following conclusion. There are two elements in the Church, the divine and the human. As for the divine aspect, I have tried to do the little I have been able to do. I would give my life for this a thousand times over.

---

aristocracy, for whom he soon became advisor, treasurer, and spiritual father" and sustained that the person responsible for the attempt on Tedeschini's life in the garden of the Royal Palace in Madrid had been the nephew of this wealthy lady who accused the cardinal of having swindled his aunt. (ASMAE, busta 7, fasc. 1, *Santa Sede, 1919–1930*. Note "Tedeschini" July 14, 1929).

1428 Cf. Lago, "Las claves de Tedeschini," p. 235; Verdoy, "Diario de Federico Tedeschini," pp. 464–466; and more in general, A. Nogueira Lousado, *Bajo el látigo de Tedeschini*, Industrias Gráficas Aribau, Barcelona 1934. In August 1933, the automobile in which the nuncio was travelling crashed into a tree near Miranda del Ebro. Tedeschini was accompanied by his driver, his valet, and three women: the former marquise of Almoguer, Carmen Masana; Miss Maria Magdalena de Ubagón y Castellana; and a young woman said to be the nuncio's niece.

1429 Verdoy, "Diario de Federico Tedeschini," p. 461.

1430 Pedro Segura y Sáenz (1880–1957), titular bishop of Apollonia and auxiliary of Valladolid (1916), then bishop of Cáceres (1920) and Burgos (1926), was transferred to the metropolitan see of Toledo on December 19, 1927, taking possession of it on January 23, 1928. The Interior Minister of the republican government expelled him from Spain on June 15, 1931. As of December 31, 1931, he lived for six years in Rome, dedicating his ministry to the poor, especially in the neighborhood of Trastevere. He was nominated to the metropolitan see of Seville on September 14, 1937. Cf. G. Coco, "Dai sacri canoni al diritto internazionale: il caso Segura tra la Santa Sede e la Spagna repubblicana" [From the Sacred Canons to International Law: The Case of Segura Between the Holy See and Republican Spain] in *Fede e diplomazia*, p. 162.

1431 Isidro Gomá y Tomás (1869–1949), bishop of Trazona (1927), was promoted to the primate see of Toledo by Pius XI on April 2, 1933 and made a cardinal in the consistory on December 16, 1935.

> But as for the human side, my dear Pedro, how miserable it is. Nevertheless, we must move forward if this is God's will.[1432]

Professor Plinio Corrêa de Oliveira recalled a meeting between Cardinal Segura and Pius XI that revealed the Spanish cardinal's freedom to speak his mind. "Cardinal Pedro Segura, whom I met in Spain in 1950, told me of his personal conversation with Pope Pius XI. A man of incredible robustness, the pope boasted of never having been ill. With a respectful smile, Cardinal Segura replied, 'Then Your Holiness does not have the mark of predestination!' In the face of the pontiff's stupor, he continued, 'There are no predestined who have never been seriously ill, at least during one period of their lives. Suffering is necessary for salvation.' Days later, Pius XI had a serious cardiac problem. From his sickbed, he wrote a note to the Spanish cardinal, 'Eminence, now I have the mark of the predestined!'"[1433]

During the consistory of December 19, 1927, Pius XI made Msgr. Segura y Sáenz the primate of Toledo and at the same time elevated him to the cardinalate. On December 23, in the Matilde Chapel, Cardinal Merry del Val received from the hands of Pius XI the sacred pallium to be bestowed upon the new primate of Spain.

Tedeschini, who cultivated republican and progressive friendships in Spain, attacked those who opposed this political vision, above all Eijo Garay and Segura. He circulated rumors about archbishop Eijo Garay saying that he was the stepbrother of Cardinal Merry del Val.[1434] According to Tedeschini, the cardinal's father had an illegitimate child, Eijo Garay, by a maid in the Spanish embassy to the Holy See, and the cardinal was facilitating his career for this reason. Of all the accusations leveled against Cardinal Merry del Val, the accusation of nepotism was not the worst, but it was the most insidious because it was disseminated for years in hushed tones and then launched by Fr. Frédéric Raurell, who complained about the fact that during the beatification process,

[1432] The meeting is mentioned in Leopoldo Duran, *Graham Greene: Friend and Brother*, Harper Collins, London 1994, p. 103, and was reproduced by Vik van Brantegem on his blog *Korazym.org* on August 29, 2023.

[1433] Plinio Corrêa de Oliveira, *Lourdes e la sofferenza cristiana*, February 6, 1965, https://www.pliniocorreadeoliveira.info/IT_650206_lourdes_sofferenza_cristiana.htm.

[1434] On Leopoldo Eijo y Garay (1878–1963), bishop of Tuy (Galizia) in 1914, then of Vitoria in 1917, and archbishop of Madrid-Alcalá from 1922 until his death, cf. Santiago Mata, *Leopoldo Eijo Garay, la pasión por la unidad*, Amanecer, Madrid 2014.

Cardinal Federico Tedeschini was not heard despite his "abundant knowledge on the person of Merry del Val."[1435]

Cardinal Leopoldo Eijo y Garay was naturally aware of these rumors, given that during his deposition at the beatification process he presented himself as the "legitimate son" of Leopoldo and Generosa and stated, under oath, that he had "no bond of consanguinity" with Merry del Val, whom he had met in 1893 when the seminary in Seville sent him to study at the Spanish College in Rome.[1436]

Tedeschini's statements are also contradicted by the facts. Leopoldo Eijo y Garay was born on April 11, 1878, in the home of Mr. Francisco Tapia in Vigo, Spain, where his mother, named Generosa, worked as a maid. Rafael Carlos Merry y del Val in 1878 was a diplomat in Belgium and arrived in Rome as ambassador to the Holy See in 1893, when Leopoldo was fifteen.[1437] Furthermore, Generosa Garay, the presumed mother, had never been to Rome. Thus, the malicious rumors turn out to be unsupported by any documentation.

What is true is that Cardinal Merry del Val, who attentively followed the religious life of the Spaniard, always supported Eijo y Garay, whom he had met when the latter was in Rome finishing his ecclesiastical studies as a student at the Pontifical Spanish College and then at the Gregorian University.

On May 28, 1914, when Pius X proclaimed him bishop of Tuy, Leopoldo Eijo y Garay was the youngest bishop of his time, having just turned thirty-six. On March 22, 1917, he was nominated bishop of Vitoria by Benedict XV, a diocese that at the time included the lands of the three Basque provinces, and on December 14, 1922, was named bishop of Madrid-Alcalá by Pius XI. After having assumed this office on June 26, 1923, he made his solemn entrance into the Spanish capital on July 1, 1923, where he remained for forty years, without ever becoming a cardinal. Nevertheless, on July 21, 1946, Pope Pius XII granted him the personal title of patriarch of the West Indies, which has been granted to no one else after him. His ecclesiastical career was certainly encouraged by Secretary of State Cardinal Merry del Val, who considered him "the purest glory of the Spanish College in Rome," but no document exists that

[1435] Frederic Raurell, "Un cardinale e tre conclavi: Merry del Val," *Laurentianum* 50 (2003), pp. 292–296. Fr. Raurell also reports on oral testimony he gathered from the Jesuit historian Miguel Battlori and Giacomo Martina, both with modernist leanings.

[1436] *Informatio*, p. 400 (pp. 400–413).

[1437] Domingo Merry del Val pointed this out astutely in his Introduction to *Rafael Merry del Val, 150 anni dalla sua nascita*, pp. 64–65.

might prove his kinship.[1438] Even without documentation, if this kinship were true, the four popes who promoted Eijo y Garay would most certainly have known about it, especially Pius X, who would definitely not have favored the ecclesiastical career of the young man had he not been convinced of his merits. Furthermore, for an accusation to be plausible, it must be established not only on the existence of proof that confirms it, but also on the personal credibility of the accuser. In this case, the evidence is nonexistent: could Cardinal Tedeschini be considered a credible ecclesiastical personality?

The main responsibility Tedeschini had during his ecclesiastical career was that of nuncio in Madrid. His mission showed itself to be disastrous, however, due to a lack of farsightedness that led him to ignore the danger represented by the revolutionary forces in Spain, but also due to the aversion he had toward the most valorous defenders of the Spanish Church, beginning with Cardinal Primate Pedro Segura y Sáenz.

On April 23, 1931, Pius XI summoned the first session of the Congregation of Extraordinary Ecclesiastical Affairs to confront the "Question of Spain" and, in particular, the disagreement that had arisen between the nuncio Tedeschini and Cardinal Segura.[1439] Other meetings followed in June and September. In the plenary session of September 15, Cardinal Raffaello Rossi noted the "distressing impression drawn from an attentive reading of the nuncio's reports."[1440] Cardinal Segura may have committed errors, he observed, "but that this had led the nuncio to allow himself to make pronouncements in official reports, and not just once, *lapsus calami*, but habitually, with regard to a Prince of the Church, in the insolent and vulgar terms with which Msgr. Tedeschini embellished his writings, this is absolutely beyond the rules, I shall not say of diplomatic correctness, but of every elementary norm of Christian charity and civilized manners."[1441] Cardinal Rossi then offered a collection of excerpts of Tedeschini's phrases against the Spanish Cardinal: Segura's conduct, according to the nuncio, is "that of an ignoble animal and of an unworthy priest;" "he is a nefarious man of whom all the abuses, all the aggressions, all

[1438] Llaquet de Entrambasaguas, "El Cardenal Merry del Val," p. 188. V. Cárcel Ortí, "Intervención del cardenal Merry del Val en los nombramientos de obispos españoles (1903–1914)," *Archivum historiae pontificiae* 32 (1994), pp. 287–288.

[1439] AA.EE.SS., *Rapporti delle Sessioni,* vol. 86. Session 1335. Report of the meeting on April 23, 1931.

[1440] AA.EE.SS., *Rapporti delle Sessioni,* vol. 86, Session 1344, print 1223. *Spagna. Situazione religiosa,* p. 20.

[1441] Ibid., p. 21.

the iniquities are camouflaged and masked under a disguise that is the most abominable of all: sanctity;" "he is ambitious, intriguing, and overbearing;" "his adherence to the Holy See is false and diabolical;" "naive, irresponsible, and drunk on power."

"All this," commented Cardinal Rossi, "from the pen of a nuncio, is most serious, concerning a cardinal whom other reputable personalities consider a man of piety and zeal. I do not think that these copies can remain in the acts of the Secretariat without them being tied to a word of rebuke, in the form that the case and the circumstances might prudently suggest."[1442]

The Cardinal Secretary of State Pacelli himself defended Cardinal Segura from the accusations of Tedeschini, observing that if they were true, they would have been used by the anticlerical Spanish government, "instead, no one has said anything, which proves that the matter is unheard of."[1443]

In a meeting on December 12, 1931, just after the approval of the anti-religious laws in Spain, Cardinal Boggiani spoke of "most serious consequences of the irrational capitulation" of the nuncio and "his policy of numbing prelates and Catholic faithful,"[1444] accusing him of allowing himself to be "dominated by his personal rancor" against Cardinal Segura.[1445] Cardinal Lauri[1446] intervened in turn during the meeting, stating, "How can the nuncio participate in the blasphemies and evil laws? It is a humiliation for him and for the Holy See."[1447]

Tedeschini had an irascible and vindictive character and lacked the equilibrium that characterized those whom he opposed. Fr. Raurell deplored the fact that the cardinal was not called upon to testify at the process of beatification of Merry del Val. But it was most likely Tedeschini himself who declined, as did another adversary of Merry del Val, the nephew of Cardinal Gasparri,

[1442] Ibid., pp. 21–22.

[1443] Ibid., p. 27.

[1444] AA.EE.SS., *Rapporti delle Sessioni*, vol. 86, Session November 12, 1931, session 1345, print 1225, p. 3.

[1445] Ibid., pp. 4–5.

[1446] Lorenzo Lauri (1864–1941), named archbishop of Ephesus by Benedict XV, was substitute apostolic nuncio in Peru (1917) and nuncio in Poland (1921). Made a cardinal by Pius XI in the consistory of December 20, 1926, he was a consultor to the Holy Office.

[1447] AA.EE.SS., *Rapporti delle Sessioni*, vol. 86, Session of November 12, 1931, session 1345, print 1225, p. 18.

Msgr. Filippo Bernardini[1448] who refused to testify, responding with disdain to the insistence of the postulator of the cause.[1449]

A historian cannot ignore that the value of testimony is determined by the credibility of the one testifying. And the credibility of Cardinal Tedeschini, to the historian, seems objectively scarce.

Pontifical Legate in Assisi

While Pius XI acted with great severity toward *Action française*, he was much more benevolent in his attitude toward Italian fascism. This can be explained by the fact that the concordat policy of the Holy See sought interlocutors in governments of any ideological tendency. In his youth, Benito Mussolini had been intensely anticlerical, but once he came to power he proclaimed on several occasions his respect for religious values and his intention of reaching an agreement with the Holy See. From the very beginning, he made a series of provisions favorable to the Church: restoring the cross in the Colosseum;[1450] restoring military chaplains in the army; restoring the crucifix on the walls of courtrooms and classrooms; instituting obligatory religious instruction in elementary schools; rendering more onerous the penal sanctions against offenses to Catholic religion and clergy.[1451] Both the *duce* of fascism and the head of the Catholic Church were searching for an agreement that would regulate the "Roman Question" begun by the invasion of the Savoy Monarchs on September 20, 1870.

On January 20, 1923, there was a first secret meeting between Mussolini and Cardinal Gasparri in the home of Senator Carlo Santucci in Via del Gesù. The apartment had two entrances in different streets in which the two personalities entered respectively. The meeting did not go beyond a pronouncement

1448 Filippo Bernardini (1884–1954) was the youngest of three prelates related to Cardinal Gasparri, among whom his nephew Enrico Gasparri (1871–1946) and his first cousin Augusto Silj (1846–1926). Born in Pieve of Ussita, he lost his father when young and was raised by his uncle, Cardinal Pietro, his mother's brother. Ordained a priest on March 12, 1910, he taught canon law in Rome at Sant'Apollinare and was at the same time secretary to his uncle Cardinal. From 1914 to 1933 he lived in Washington, D.C., where he taught canon law at *Catholic University*. He was then named apostolic delegate in Australia by Pius XI and consecrated titular archbishop of Antioch in Pisidia on May 21, 1933. Named apostolic nuncio of Switzerland on October 10, 1945, he later became the secretary of the Congregation of Propaganda Fide on January 15, 1953.

1449 *Informatio*, pp. 420–422.

1450 The cross had been placed there in 1675, but in 1874 was substituted with a statue of *Roma triumphans*, holding in its fist a lance instead of the cross.

1451 Cf. Alberto Guasco, *Cattolici e fascisti. La Santa Sede e la politica italiana all'alba del regime (1919–1925) [Catholics and Fascism. The Holy See and Italian Politics at the Dawn of the Regime]*, Il Mulino, Bologna 2013.

of the goodwill of both sides, however.[1452] The event that marked the public thaw between the Holy See and fascism was in 1926, the historic celebration of the seventh centenary of the death of St. Francis of Assisi.

Merry del Val had already been the pontifical representative in Assisi in 1920 on the occasion of the first centenary of the rediscovery of St. Francis's remains. Benedict XV had granted him the use of the papal throne and, after the solemn Pontifical Mass, the cardinal addressed the Umbrian catechetical congress recalling the commitment of Pius X, Benedict XV, and Pius XI against the religious ignorance of the time. His second visit to Assisi as pontifical legate to Pius XI was to have a quite different significance.

The papal delegation, guided by the secretary of the Holy Office, left Rome officially on October 3, in a special train provided by the Italian government.[1453] Along the route, at the stations of Orte, Terni, and Spoleto, a military band received the Vatican representatives with the playing of the Royal March. Upon entering Assisi, Merry del Val was greeted by a twenty-one-canon salute, as he met with the Minister of Public Instruction Pietro Fedele,[1454] who kissed his ring and said with an emotional voice, "Eminence, I bring you the homage of the government, of the king, and of its head."[1455]

The religious celebrations in the papal basilica were exceptionally solemn and the words of Merry del Val (who was made an honorary citizen of Assisi) had an international resonance. On October 4, in the Hall of the Palazzo dei Priori, the cardinal celebrated St. Francis, "the highest glory of Assisi and of Italy," stating, "I have lived many years, nearly my entire life, here in Italy, a sign that, if you allow me to say, I have acquired the right to call it my second homeland. You, Lord Mayor, with such kind and considerate thoughtfulness have sealed this pact with the high honor of offering me honorary citizenship in this city. I am profoundly grateful for this consideration, which I shall always remember with profound gratitude."[1456] He went on to say, "Let us not reduce our

1452 Scoppola, *La Chiesa e il fascismo*, p. 63.

1453 The pontifical mission was composed of Msgr. Francesco Faberi and Msgr. Giovanni Bressan, canons in the Vatican; Marquis Giovanni Battista Sacchetti, major herald of the Sacred Apostolic Palaces; and Count Antonio Cagiano de Azevedo, secret chamberlain of the cloak and sword; and the cardinal's court.

1454 Pietro Fedele (1873–1943), professor of Medieval and modern history at the University of Rome, was Minister of Public Instruction from 1925 to 1928.

1455 Cenci, *Merry del Val*, p. 509.

1456 Discourse of Cardinal Rafael Merry del Val for the seven hundredth anniversary of the death of St. Francis of Assisi in *Spoglio Merry del Val*, busta 8, f. 1068.

joyous celebrations to a mere manifestation of temporary enthusiasm that dissolves with the final ringing of our bells and dies with the glow of the last torch. No, let us return to God, as Francis desires. May his seraphic, austere spirit inflame our hearts, disseminate in our minds his radiant light, crush the resistance of every rebellious will and come, come to give us once again peace in justice and love."

Then, after having thanked the bishop and the civil and military authorities, Merry del Val said, "My thanksgiving goes out also to those who hold the reins of the Italian government and with clear vision of the reality of matters, have desired that religion be respected, honored, and practiced. Visibly protected by God, he has wisely raised up the fate of the nation, increasing its prestige throughout the world."[1457]

The king's minister spoke in turn in the following words: "May the divine blessing from the height of the Apostolic See that has descended upon Italy through you be the bearer of good, the propitiation of rebirth, not only social and economic but also moral and spiritual, of the Italian people, to which the national government and its illustrious head are inclined with all their powers."[1458]

It was the first time since 1870 that a minister of the Kingdom of Italy encountered a direct representative of the pope and that greetings of peace were expressed in official discourses. Three years later, the day on which the Conciliation between the Holy See and Italy was signed, the *Corriere della Sera* defined the meeting in Assisi "a luminous date for the Roman Question."[1459]

Toward Conciliation

On the evening of October 4, 1926, just a few hours after Merry del Val had given his discourse, Mussolini wrote to the constitutional lawyer Domenico Barone asking him to undertake with the greatest secrecy an exploratory negotiation with the Vatican to study the possibility of resolving the Roman Question.[1460] On August 8 of the same year, the lawyer Francesco Pacelli,[1461] brother of the

[1457] Cenci, *Merry del Val*, p. 511.

[1458] Ibid., p. 512.

[1459] Paolo Romano, "La Questione Romana e il Fascimo," *Corriere della Sera*, February 11, 1929.

[1460] Christopher Duggan, *Il popolo del duce. Storia emotiva dell'Italia fascista [The People of the Duce. Emotive History of Fascist Italy]*, Laterza, Rome-Bari 2013, p. 124.

[1461] Francesco Pacelli (1874–1935), attorney, brother of Eugenio Pacelli, was chosen by Pius XI to lead the negotiations that led to the Lateran Pacts (1926–1929), receiving for this achievement the title

future Pius XII, met with Barone[1462] for the first time, initiating the negotiations that would lead three years later to the resolution of the conflict.

The frequent meetings between Barone and Pacelli were at first informal and later official, though always secret. On November 24, 1926, the consistorial lawyer submitted to Barone a first draft of the agreement. Three days later, the pope sent with him Msgr. Francesco Borgongini Duca, secretary of the Congregation for Extraordinary Ecclesiastical Affairs, to write a draft concordat.[1463] Both were bound to strict secrecy under penalty of severe sanctions.

The negotiations lasted thirty months, until November 18, 1928, when all the cardinals of the Curia were summoned to the apartment of Secretary of State Gasparri, who announced as promised the stipulation of an agreement between the Holy See and the Kingdom of Italy. Merry del Val expressed his satisfaction "when [he] understood that Mussolini had consented to recognize the full sovereignty of the pope over a territory that would be considered as a true State."[1464] On the other hand, the cardinals remained perplexed for having been excluded from the negotiations on a theme as important to the future of the Church as this.[1465]

Finally, on February 11, 1929, Cardinal Gasparri, minister plenipotentiary of Pope Pius XI, and Benito Mussolini, head of the Italian government, signed the agreement that created the Vatican City State and established, after fifty years, a new relationship of collaboration between the church and state

---

of marquis. Cf. Francesco Pacelli, *Diario della Conciliazione. Con verbali e appendice di documenti [Diary of the Conciliation. With the Minutes and Appendix of Documents]*, ed. Michele Maccarrone, Vatican City 1959. Cf. AA.EE.SS., Pos. 702, P.O. 1926–1927.

1462 Domenico Barone (1879–1929) was an Italian magistrate, negotiator of the Italian part of the Lateran Pacts during the years 1926–1928.

1463 Francesco Borgongini Duca (1884–1954), secretary of the Congregation of Extraordinary Ecclesiastical Affairs, participated in the signing of the Lateran Pacts and on June 30, 1929, was the first apostolic nuncio to Italy, an office he held until Pius XII made him a cardinal in the consistory of January 12, 1953.

1464 AA.EE.SS. *Italia,* Pos. 702, P.O., vol. 2, f. 305. According to Marcello Staglieno, there were in reality two, absolutely secret, working commissions: an official one (desired by Gasparri) and an unofficial one (desired by Mussolini), both equally important. Taking part in the former were Domenico Barone and Francesco Pacelli, subject to the directives of Secretary of State Gasparri. Participating in the second commission were Cardinal Rafael Merry del Val, Cardinal Pio Tommaso Boggiani, Fr. Paolo De Töth, Arnaldo Mussolini, and Fr. Pietro Tacchi Venturi (1861–1956), who was the true *spiritus absconditus* of the entire operation for he was the hinge between the two so-called commissions (Marcello Staglieno, *Arnaldo e Benito. Due fratelli [Arnaldo and Benito. Two Brothers]*, Mondadori, Milan 2004).

1465 Merry del Val to Pius XI, March 2, 1929, in AES, *Stati Ecclesiastici,* Pos. 407, P.O., fasc. 290, ff. 29–30.

in Italy.[1466] In the great hall of the popes in the Lateran Palace, on a table covered in a blue-red cloth, three documents composed on three parchments were set out: the Financial Convention, the Treaty, and the Concordat, which altogether constituted the Lateran Pacts.

The Financial Convention quantified a sum of 1,550 million notes that Italy committed itself to pay the Holy See as reparations for the damages suffered by the Vatican due to the events of 1870.

In the Treaty, Italy recognized the sovereignty of the Holy See on the international level and its exclusive jurisdiction of the Vatican.

The Concordat ensured the Church the free exercise of spiritual power and the public exercise of worship. The Catholic religion was declared the "state religion," religious instruction was introduced in all schools, and religious marriage was given civil recognition.

These articles objectively constituted the self-limitation of the regime and, in this respect, a success for the Church. The Pope was convinced that fascism and Catholicism, sharing the same enemy, could find a convergence and that fascism was reducible to an "instrument" of Providence, in the conviction that it was destined to evolve in the sense of an ever-greater subordination to the ecclesiastical hierarchy. In fact, the Concordat made it impossible for fascism to become an effectively totalitarian regime, even though it did not mark, as many had hoped, the beginning of a Catholic restoration in Italy and in Europe.

For his part, the pontiff officially recognized the Kingdom of Italy, closing the profound wound that had impeded Catholics from having a place in the state that emerged from the *Risorgimento*.[1467] Renzo De Felice observed that, in

[1466] The Lateran Pacts were ratified on May 27, 1929, n. 810 (Text in Scoppola, *La Chiesa e il fascismo*, pp. 161–189). Cf. R. De Felice, *Mussolini il fascista*, Einaudi, Turin 1968, vol. 2, pp. 382–436; Mario Casella, *Stato e Chiesa in Italia dalla Conciliazione alla riconciliazione (1929–1931). Aspetti e problemi nella documentazione dell'Archivio Storico Diplomatico del Ministero degli Affari Esteri [Church and State in Italy from Conciliation to Reconciliation (1929–1931). Aspects and Problems in the Documentation of the Historical Diplomatic Archive of the Ministry of Foreign Affairs]*, Congedo Editore, Galatina (Lecce) 2005; L. Carboni, "I Patti Lateranensi," in Barbara Jatta (ed.), *1929–2009. Ottanta anni dello Stato della Città del Vaticano [1929–2009. Eighty years of the Vatican City State]*, Vatican City 2009, pp. 73–88; G. Coco, *Il Labirinto romano. Il filo delle relazioni Chiesa-Stato tra Pio XI, Pacelli e Mussolini (1929–1939) [The Roman Labyrinth. The String of Relations Between Church and State from Pius XI, Pacelli and Mussolini]*, 2 vols., Vatican Secret Archive, Vatican City 2019.

[1467] On the Roman Question, besides the texts cited in the previous note, cf. A. Martini, *Studi sulla Questione romana e la Conciliazione*, Edizioni 5 Lune, Rome 1963; P. Scoppola (ed.), *Chiesa e Stato nella storia d'Italia. Storia documentaria dall'Unità alla Repubblica*, Laterza, Bari 1967; Margiotta Broglio, *Italia e Santa Sede*; Spadolini, *Il cardinale Gasparri e la questione romana*; G. B. Varnier, *Gli ultimi governi liberali e la Questione romana, 1918–1922*, Giuffrè, Milano 1976; I. Garzia, *La Questione*

the Lateran Pacts, Mussolini won a victory, perhaps the most complete and important in his entire political career, which from one day to the next, increased his prestige throughout the entire world.[1468]

Msgr. Francesco Borgongini Duca was nominated nuncio to Italy and Count Cesare Maria De Vecchi di Val Cismon,[1469] *quadrumvir* of the March on Rome, became the first Italian ambassador to the Holy See on June 17, 1929. De Vecchi made a round of visits to cardinals to form an impression of their judgment on the achievement of Conciliation between church and state.[1470] Not all of them showed their enthusiasm, however, for the manner in which the "Roman Question" was resolved.

According to the *Memoires* of the *quadrumvir*, published by Luigi Romersa in 1983, "there were two 'blocks' in the Vatican, one consisting of those favorable and the other of the dissatisfied, who criticized the Concordat and naturally the pope who had signed it. The criticism was varied, of course: some was bland and respectful, other was implacable and even poisonous. I must say, however, that in the College of Cardinals there were more in favor than against, but it must also be added in all truth that the adversaries expressed themselves with a previously unheard-of violence."[1471]

From the very beginning, De Vecchi harbored malevolent sentiment toward Merry del Val, the figure who most represented the intransigent cardinals, who criticized the way the agreement between the Vatican and the fascist regime was reached. "In his discourse to professors and students at the Catholic University of the Sacred Heart, Pius XI said that to obtain the Conciliation, 'we

romana durante la Prima guerra mondiale, Edizioni Scientifiche Italiane, Naples 1981; R. Pertici, *Chiesa e Stato in Italia.*

1468 De Felice, *Mussolini il fascista*, vol. 2, p. 382.

1469 Cesare Maria Luigi De Vecchi (1884–1959), one of the "*quadrumviri*" of the March on Rome, was governor of Somalia (1923–1929), ambassador to the Holy See (1929–1935), Minister of National Education (1935–1936), and governor of the Aegean Islands until 1940. He was nominated Senator of the Kingdom (1924) and granted the title of count by Val Cismon (1925) and for this was condemned to death *in absentia* by the Social Republic at the trials in (1944). After the war, he was condemned (1947), *in absentia*, by the Italian Republic to a light sentence. Cf. Cesare Maria De Vecchi di Val Cismon, *Il quadrumviro scomodo. Il vero Mussolini nelle memorie del più monarchico dei fascisti [The Troublesome Quadrumvir. The True Mussolini in the Memoires of the Most Monarchical of the Fascists]*, ed. Luigi Romersa, Mursia, Milan 1983.

1470 During his "diplomatic tour," De Vecchi met with the cardinal dean Vannutelli, Cardinal Gamba, archbishop of Turin, and with cardinals Sbarretti, Ragonesi, Scapinelli, Granito Pignatelli di Belmonte, Ehrle, Merry del Val, Perosi, Frühwirth, Boggiani, Laurenti, Bisleti, Nasalli Rocca, Pompili, Sincero, Ceretti, Lega, Capotosti, Lauri, and Verde.

1471 De Vecchi, *Il quadrumviro scomodo*, p. 141.

needed a mountain-climbing pope, a pope who was accustomed to facing the most arduous ascents.'"[1472] "The phrase did not escape Merry del Val's attention, who, in his conversations with me, said, 'We can clearly see that the Concordat was made by a mountain-climber!' He paused and then added, 'Quite right, it is a Concordat made with his feet!'"[1473]

It seems improbable that an observant diplomat like the cardinal, accustomed to weighing every word, would have let himself go in a biting one-liner while speaking with an official representative of the Italian government who was as loquacious as was De Vecchi. "The cardinal's quip," continued De Vecchi, "was not extinguished within the walls of the Vatican, but rapidly scaled them and spread throughout Rome, becoming the daily bread of certain subtle and gossipy environments in the Capital." But who was spreading them if not De Vecchi himself? Nothing emerged during the process of beatification against the cardinal, not even in the most critical depositions, like that of Msgr. Alberto Serafini, always ready to give credence to rumors and gossip. It would be more logical to think that the words that De Vecchi attested to having heard with his own ears were attributed to Merry del Val by some wicked tongue in Rome. De Vecchi concluded, "Disheartened and concerned, I sought to inform Cardinal Gasparri and begged him to refer the matter to the pontiff. The cardinal looked at me and, stretching out his arms, responded in a disconsolate tone, 'The Holy Father knows. He is profoundly saddened and did not hesitate to reprimand these sacrilegious mouths.'"[1474] Cardinal Merry del Val's name does not seem to have appeared among those reprimanded.

On March 7, 1929, Cardinal Gasparri, on behalf of Pius XI, thanked Merry del Val for the congratulations he expressed on March 2, "for having brought to term the long and serious conflict between the Holy See and the Italian state." "Confiding in the assistance of Divine Providence, I unite my prayers to those of Your Holiness, that the Lord might bless the results of the accords concluded and that everything be for the advantage of the Church, Italy, and the Catholic world, and according to the ardent desire of Your Holiness that it might contribute to making universal peace more stable and extend the Kingdom of Christ in

[1472] Pius XI, Discourse *Vogliamo anzitutto*, February 13, 1929, to professors and students of the Catholic University of the Sacred Heart, in AAS, 21 (1929), p. 113.

[1473] De Vecchi, *Il quadrumviro scomodo*, pp. 141–143.

[1474] Ibid., p. 143.

every Nation."[1475] As early as 1904, in the *Livre Blanc* of the Holy See, published on the occasion of the visit of President Loubet to the Quirinale, Cardinal Merry del Val had stated that to guarantee the independence of the pope with respect to Italy, "no other path has been found than that of its own and independent territory."[1476] But the way in which the agreements had been conducted, without consultation with the College of Cardinals, had left the cardinal, and other *porporati* close to him, perplexed.

No lack of respect toward the pope was ever manifested in public by Cardinal Merry del Val, however, or by other cardinals. The Catholic Church is not a totalitarian regime, and tolerates within it differences of opinion, expressed with great liberty even, as long as the principle of authority on which the Mystical Body of Christ rests is not placed publicly in discussion.

The Twilight of Cardinal Gasparri

The Lateran Pacts represented a success for Cardinal Gasparri, but also the beginning of his rapid decline.[1477] On April 27, 1929, there appeared in *Il Popolo di Trieste* a long article by Guido Pallotta in which he celebrated the political activity of Cardinal Gasparri, "the only statesman still in power in the world since the outbreak of the Great War."[1478] In reality, the cardinal's decline was already underway, as Carlo M. Fiorentino amply documents in the vast chapter he dedicates to "The Twilight of Cardinal Pietro Gasparri" in his work *In the Shadow of Peter.*[1479] The expectations of the Holy See and of the world suffered a chill after the two speeches pronounced by Mussolini to parliament on May 13–14 for the ratification of the Treaty, and in the Vatican, Gasparri was accused of an excess of condescension toward Mussolini. Furthermore, the Lateran Pacts were seen differently by Gasparri and Pius XI. The former understood the Conciliation above all as the stipulation of an international treaty between two sides, which should have a separate life from the Concordat, while the latter desired that the

[1475] AAV, *Spoglio Domenico Jacobini*, busta 3, fasc. 3.

[1476] De la Brière, *Les luttes présentes de l'Église*, Sixième série 1920–1924, Beauchesne, Paris 1924, p. 193.

[1477] A. Guasco, "Pietro Gasparri e il fascismo," in Pettinaroli and Valente (eds.), *Il cardinale Pietro Gasparri*, Heidelberg University Publishing, Heidelberg 2020, online publications of DHI Rome, pp. 93–113; Carlo M. Fiorentino, *All'ombra di Pietro. La Chiesa Cattolica e lo spionaggio fascista in Vaticano 1929–1939 [In the Shadow of Peter. The Catholic Church and Fascist Espionage in the Vatican]*, Le Lettere, Florence 1999, pp. 41–83.

[1478] Guido Pallotta, "Pietro Gasparri, il grande cardinale," *Il Popolo di Trieste*, April 27, 1929.

[1479] Fiorentino, *All'ombra di Pietro*, pp. 41–83.

Treaty and Concordat be tied by an indissoluble bond, according to the formula "*simul stabunt aut simul cadent* [they will stand together or fall together]."[1480]

During these years, Mussolini had strengthened the information service of the Italian government, making use especially of two press offices that existed for about twenty years: that of the Ministry of Foreign Affairs and that of the President of the Council of Ministers, both of which, beginning in 1927, came to depend on the Division of Political Police.[1481] The State Archive preserves ample documentation consisting of a series of files under the headings of prelates in the Curia, as well as some laymen in the service of the Holy See.[1482] There were dossiers reserved for Cardinal Merry del Val and his secretary Msgr. Nicola Canali, who was defined as a "very high profile figure in the Vatican ecclesiastical world insofar as he is the shadow of Cardinal Merry del Val."[1483] Among the prime minister's informants were most certainly Msgr. Umberto Benigni and the journalist Francesco Zanetti,[1484] "one of the best informed people on Vatican affairs and knowledgeable of the most obscure behind-the-scenes information"[1485] of which the State Archive preserves several autographed reports. Msgr. Benigni also placed his network of information

1480 AAS, XXI (1929), p. 305. Cf. the chirograph of Pius XI to Cardinal Gasparri, AA.EE.SS., *Stati Ecclesiastici*, Pos. 214, fasc. 13, ff. 20–26.

1481 The two offices later fused into the Press Office of the Head of the Government, which in September 1934 assumed the dignity of Undersecretariat of State, directly dependent on the head of the Government, then (in June 1935) was elevated to the Ministry of the Press and Propaganda, and then to the Ministry of Popular Culture. Cf. Mauro Canali, *Le spie del regime*, Il Mulino, Bologna 2004; Claudio Maria Mancini, *L'Archivio della Direzione Generale per la Stampa Estera del Ministero della Cultura Popolare nell'Archivio Storico-Diplomatico del Ministero degli Affari Esteri. Appunti di una prima ricerca [Archive of the General Direction for Foreign Press of the Ministry of Popular Culture in the Historical-Diplomatic Archive of the Ministry of Foreign Affairs. Notes of Initial Research]*, MAECI, Rome 1922.

1482 Carlo Maria Fiorentino was the first to study these files in his *All'ombra di Pietro*, with a fine reconstruction of the political climate in the Vatican immediately after the Lateran Pacts.

1483 ACS, *Polizia politica, Fascicoli Personali, 1927–1944*, busta 227, "Canali Msgr.," note of November 16, 1929. "Canali deserves full consideration thanks to his firm and decisive character and for his proven seriousness" (ibid.).

1484 Francesco Zanetti (1870–1938) was chief editor of *L'Osservatore Romano*. According to Fiorentino, he was tied to Cardinal Merry del Val by a bond of devotion and friendship (*All'ombra di Pietro*, pp. 23–26).

1485 ACS, Polizia politica, *Fascicoli personali 1926–1944*, busta 1747, "Zanetti, chief Francesco," note of March 18, 1933. It was probably Zanetti who, on November 16, 1929, reported that Canali "continues to carry out through his Monsignor confidant, relations with Msgr. Benigni, the historian and most learned diplomat" and "entirely deplores the fact that the latter no longer frequents the Vatican, the Secrtariat of State and other pontifical dicasteries" (ACS, Polizia politica, *Fascicoli Personali, 1927–1944*, busta 227, "Canali, Msgr.," note of November 16, 1929).

at the service of the Press Office of the Ministry of Foreign Affairs.[1486] A memo of February 14, 1926, to the Police Chief Francesco Crispo Moncada gave this efficacious portrait of the Umbrian prelate: "Poor, shabby in his dress, closed for hours and hours in his modest apartment, possessing only books, journals, and files (he has been working for years on a voluminous historical study), Msgr. Benigni immediately reveals to his interlocutors his acute intelligence, prodigious and diversified culture, and a political and unscrupulous spirit. His judgments of men and matters are usually precise, always biting, and nearly without any reservations of formal courtesy.... As a politician, he seems too passionate and too doctrinaire for positions of leadership and responsibility, and this, perhaps, united to his corrosive spirit and his unscrupulousness approaching cynicism, must have greatly contributed to his being kept far from Church governance."[1487]

Beginning in September 1929, news of the imminent removal of Cardinal Gasparri from the charge of secretary of state began to circulate, while in a notice from the Political Police transmitted to the Ministry of Foreign Affairs it was written that "the prestige of Cardinal Merry del Val was growing in the bosom of the Sacred College."[1488]

The reasons for Gasparri's decline dated back to a growing diffidence on the part of the pope toward his collaborator's politics that were too pro-fascist, but also, as observed Fiorentino, to the symptoms of his intellectual, psychological, and perhaps spiritual decline, that seemed to render him ever more skeptical and indifferent to the problems of the Church.[1489]

On September 17, Gasparri wrote the pope from Ussita, "I have not forgotten (and how could I have?) what Your Holiness told me last July, if I'm not mistaken, namely that especially given the probable struggle with the fascist government in defense of Catholic Action, Your Holiness considered opportune that others take my place; and neither have I forgotten how I replied, namely that for some time I have been under the persuasion that this same

1486 From the network of information, active from 1923 to 1927, it turns out that the head of this office was the journalist Pietro Mataloni (1899–1966), nephew of Msgr. Benigni. Cf. Margherita Bettini Prosperi, "Le carte di Umberto Benigni," *Clio* 2 (1992), pp. 289–300; C. M. Mancini, *Il Fondo Benigni dell'Archivio Storico del Ministero degli Affari Esteri*, Historical Diplomatic Archive, Rome 2016.

1487 ACS, MI, DPGS, AAGG, *Atti Speciali (1898–1940)*, busta 4, fasc. 33.

1488 Note, Rome, July 14, 1929, in ASMAE, Political Affairs 1919–1930, Holy See, busta 7, fasc. 1.

1489 Fiorentino, *All'ombra di Pietro*, p. 47.

opportunity might be in the interests of the Church, although for different reasons than those indicated by Your Holiness."[1490]

On November 23, 1929, Pius XI recalled to Rome Msgr. Eugenio Pacelli, nuncio in Berlin, the man he was relying on to succeed Gasparri. His aristocratic profile resembled that of Merry del Val, who had served for a decade under Pius X. Pacelli's return and his promotion to the cardinalate, publicized on December 5, did not surprise the Curia circles, which saw in that move his coming nomination to secretary of state.[1491] Gasparri saw it as a victory of the "Pius party" opposed to him and seemed to have welcomed his successor with a "pathetic scene," reprimanding him for having come to oust him.

Police informer "35" reported on December 18, 1929, a conversation with Msgr. Canali during which the assessor of the Holy Office and faithful collaborator of Cardinal Merry del Val had confided to him that the chosen candidate to succeed Cardinal Gasparri as secretary of state was Cardinal Pacelli who, "for the aims of this pontiff and the current circumstances, is probably the most suitable."[1492] Pacelli "represents the true secretary of state, with full approval of the Italian government thanks to his reflection of his brother's personality, the expert negotiator of the Conciliation; being always obsequious toward everyone, he has been accepted by the Sacred College; fully accepted by the pope who will ensure that all Pacelli's full talents be put to use."[1493] Cardinal Cerretti's name was also mentioned, although according to Msgr. Canali, "Cerretti is compromised because he is too devoted to the French government, because he is the recognized adversary of the fascist government, because he is too much discussed in matters of morality, etc."[1494]

On January 23, 1930, Mario Missiroli's[1495] book *Give to Caesar: Mussolini's Religious Policy, with Unpublished Documents* was placed on the Index by the Congregation of the Holy Office.[1496] It was one of the last acts signed by

[1490] AA.EE.SS., *Stati Ecclesiastici, 1934*, Pos. 515, fasc. 543, f. 5.

[1491] Coco, *L'anno terribile del cardinale Pacelli*, p. 179.

[1492] ACS, Polizia politica, *Fascicoli Personali, 1927–1944*, busta 227, "Canali, Msgr.," note of December 18, 1929. The text of the note is also reproduced in the appendix of Fiorentino, *All'ombra di Pietro*, pp. 242–243

[1493] Ibid., p. 242.

[1494] Ibid.

[1495] Mario Missiroli (1886–1974) was "prince journalist," director under various political regimes of four newspapers: *Il Resto del Carlino*, *Il Secolo*, *Il Messaggero*, and the *Corriere della Sera*.

[1496] De Bujanda, *Index Librorum Prohibitorum*, p. 623. "A sophistic and paradoxical book of audacious exaggerations and heretical aberrations, especially as concerns the rights of the Church and the supreme authority of the Roman Pontiff and the exercise thereof" (Casati, *L'Indice dei libri proibiti*, p. 263).

Cardinal Merry del Val. Several weeks before, on November 30, the *Corriere della Sera* had published a review in praise of the book, signed by parliamentarian Lando Ferretti, whom the newspaper presented as "Chief of the Press Office of the Head of the Government."[1497] The nuncio in Italy, Borgongini Duca, communicated the same day to Foreign Minister Dino Grandi that the article contained "affirmations and judgments that the Holy See can in no way tolerate."[1498] Mussolini himself responded to this complaint, in the absence of the minister, on December 1, clarifying that the article had been written by Ferretti in his role as collaborator of the newspaper, without any intention "of harming the interests of the Holy See or the authority of the supreme pontiff."

On December 2, as he transmitted the letter of the head of the government to the nuncio, Foreign Minister Dino Grandi declared his "disapproval of all the publications of any sort that can in some way disturb the peaceful and cordial relationship established between the Holy See and the Italian state based on the Lateran Accords."[1499]

On February 11, 1930, on the first anniversary of the signing of the Lateran Pacts, Cesare Maria De Vecchi offered a grand reception at the Italian embassy, at which were present cardinals, the entire diplomatic corps accredited with the Holy See, and much of the Roman aristocracy. At 6 p.m., in the presence of all the cardinals, De Vecchi vested Cardinal Gasparri with the collar badge of the Supreme Order of the Most Holy Annunciation, the highest honor given by the House of Savoy, rendering the cardinal a "cousin to the King." It was the first time since 1850 that a cardinal secretary of state had received such an honor.

The following day, February 12, a letter was published in *L'Osservatore Romano* in which the pope communicated that Cardinal Eugenio Pacelli would succeed Gasparri and assured the secretary of state of having arranged "a convenient abode" that would allow him to spend "a well merited and not idle rest."[1500] Pius XI granted Gasparri in perpetual use a small residence in the Baths of Titus

1497 Lando Ferretti (1895–1977), fascist parliamentarian in 1924, president of CONI, was called upon in 1928 to direct the Press Office of the Head of the Government.

1498 Letter or Msgr. Borgongini Duca to Foreign Minister Dino Grandi, November 30, 1929, in ASMAE, busta 7, fasc, 1, *Santa Sede, 1919–1930, Incidente con la Santa Sede per un articolo dell'on. Lando Ferretti [Holy See, 1919–1930, Incident with the Holy See over an Article by Hon. Lando Ferretti].*

1499 Ibid.

1500 On the resignation of Gasparri, cf. G. Coco, "Eugenio Pacelli: cardinale e Segretario di Stato (1929–1930)," in Marcel Chappin, G. Coco, and S. Pagano (eds.), *I "Fogli di udienza" del cardinale Eugenio Pacelli Segretario di Stato [The "Audience Papers" of Cardinal Eugenio Pacelli Secretary of State]*, vol. 1 (1930), Vatican City 2010, pp. 39–143.

on the Colle Oppio near the Colosseum. "He went sadly, almost hiddenly: with rude frankness, he denied the news that had been circulated by his admirers that he had been the one to ask Pius XI to free him from the honor and the burden. He added: But I thank the pope from the depths of my heart. It's high time to implore God's pardon and mercy."[1501]

On February 9, 1930, Eugenio Pacelli took possession of the office of secretary of state on the first floor of the Apostolic Palace in the Vatican. To Gasparri's old friend Cardinal Granito di Belmonte, it seemed that Gasparri lost his mind, so intense was his grief at having been expelled from his old office.[1502]

Gasparri died on November 18, 1934, and his funeral was celebrated in the Church of St. Ignatius in the presence of civil authorities representing both the sovereign and the government. The absolution of the corpse was imparted on behalf of the pope by Cardinal Granito di Belmonte.

After resigning as secretary of state in February 1930, Cardinal Gasparri planned, announced, and wrote his autobiography. In reality, his *Memoires* never saw the light of day, giving rise to a legend that lasted decades. When he died, the *Memoires* were requisitioned along with the other papers pertaining to the Holy See, and deposited in the Archive of the Secretariat of State.[1503] It seems Msgr. Domenico Tardini was right when, according to Msgr. De Luca, he defined Gasparri's *Memoires* as "the intellectual suicide of the poor cardinal, for appearing in them was not the man of broad and strong ideas, but of minute and pathetic particulars."[1504]

1501 Taliani, *Vita del cardinal Gasparri,* p. 263.

1502 Fiorentino, *All'ombra di Pietro,* p. 56.

1503 His *Memorie,* published in part by Giovanni Spadolini, are preserved in the Historical Archive of the Section for Relations with States of the Secretariat of State: AA.EE.SS., *Stati Ecclesiastici,* Pos. 515. Angelo Martini advances serious reservations about the *Memorie,* which do not allow for a precise and complete reconstruction of his personality and "are not sufficient for definitively reconstructing his actions or establishing his religious and political thought." "Le memorie del card. Gasparri e la loro presentazione," *La Civiltà Cattolica* q. 2943 (February 3rd, 1973), p. 267 (pp. 259–267). Cf. also the observations of Luca Carboni, "Le 'Memorie' del cardinale Gasparri e la 'Storia documentata della Conciliazione.' Vicissitudini archivistiche di una fonte storica sopravvalutata" [The "Memorie" of Cardinal Gasparri and the "Documented History of the conciliation." Archival Vicissitudes of an Overestimated Historical Source], in Pettinaroli and Valente (eds.), *Il cardinale Pietro Gasparri,* pp. 19–34.

1504 Carlo Felice Casula, *Domenico Tardini (1888–1961): l'azione della Santa Sede nella crisi fra le due guerre [Domenico Tardini: The Work of the Holy See in the Crisis Between the Two Wars],* Studium, Rome 1988, p. 84 and 453.

A Cardinal in the Dolomites

On the eve of his sixty-fifth birthday, Rafael Merry del Val was a well-built man, with a high forehead, receding hairline, and the profound and meditative gaze of a thoughtful man of action, "a thinker who sees things from the heights of philosophy and theology; a man of action with his gaze fixed on reality, who can scrutinize the depths of people, things, and events."[1505] His amiable features, those of a lord, put all his interlocutors at ease, from the humble youth in Trastevere to the most illustrious guests in the Vatican basilica, such as the King Alfonso XIII of Spain and King George V of England.[1506] Trastevere and the Vatican were the geographical poles of his daily life.[1507] When he was nominated secretary of state and cardinal, he had promised his Trastevere youth that he would not abandon them and did not cease visiting them every day, walking there from his residence in the Vatican. Merry del Val took pleasure in recalling when, on the last Sunday of October, 1928, he celebrated with them his patronal feast day and the twenty-fifth anniversary of his cardinalate, telling them, "I have the consolation of believing that I have never failed in honoring my promise made twenty-five years ago."[1508]

The colorful neighborhood of Trastevere is the symbol of *romanità* (Romanness), and the polyglot cardinal felt he was above all a Roman like them, despite the blood of many nations that flowed in his veins. But his *romanità* was above all supernatural: love for a city that is not only the geographical center of Christianity, but the place where the ultimate truths necessary for salvation of man are safeguarded, as well as the most profound values of western civilization. In *romanità*, which embodies the perfection and quintessence of the Church,[1509] the personality of Cardinal Merry del Val found its harmonious equilibrium.

From 1903 until the cardinal's death, he left Italy only on a few occasions. In 1927 he returned after many years to England, fully disguised, to see his relatives and visit Ushaw College. There he embraced his old companion Msgr. Broadhead and, following the custom in use among alumni, he planted a pine

1505 Corrêa de Oliveira, *A Altivez é harmonioso complemento da humildade*, p. 7.

1506 In May 1923, King George V and Mary of England visited the Vatican Basilica privately, and fifteen days later, in the full splendor dictated by protocol, the sovereigns of Belgium as well. In November of the same year, King Alfonso XIII and Queen Vittoria of Spain came to Rome.

1507 Cf. Orietta De Filippis, "Rafael Merry del Val. Il cardinale che amò Trastevere," *Lazio ieri e oggi* 9 (September 2013), pp. 274–277.

1508 Deposition by Card. Canali, in *Processus informativus ordinarius, Sessio* CXII, vol. III, p. 692.

1509 Cf. Msgr. Rudolf Michael Schmitz, "Che cos'è la Romanità," in *Gricigliano. Rivista del seminario San Filippo Neri-Istituto di Cristo Re Sommo Sacerdote*, 2020, p. 5.

tree on the college grounds, to which a plaque was affixed. The cardinal also visited Birmingham where Denis Sheil awaited him, the younger brother of Laura Sheil, wife of his uncle Pedro Juan Zulueta, rector of the Oratory; as well as Oxford, where he was the guest of his cousin Francis de Zulueta, who taught there.[1510] From the Castle of Upbrooke where he was the guest of another cousin, Count Alfonso de Torre Diaz, he visited the majestic Benedictine Abbey of Buckfast in Devonshire.

In Italy as well, the cardinal often traveled incognito, dressed as a simple priest, to avoid being given the honors of his rank. He loved visiting sanctuaries, such as Loreto, Genazzano, Pompei, and Montevergine. During the summer holidays, he would make brief stops in Tyrol, Austria, and in Switzerland. But the place he chose most often to renew his strength, consumed as it was by his intense work, was Arabba in the Dolomites, a typical village at 1,600 meters above sea level, between the Pordoi and Falzarego Passes, where he sojourned every summer from 1924 to 1929.

The parish priest of Arabba, Fr. Angelo Frena, recounted his days there in the mountains.[1511] The cardinal arrived by car from Rome, after having stopped in Riese, the birthplace of Pius X, hosted by the pope's nephews, Ermenegildo and Petronilla Parolin.[1512] He would always stop in recollection at the sanctuary of the Cendrole, where the young Giuseppe Sarto had venerated the image of the Virgin of Pardon smiling sweetly upon the Child Jesus resting in her lap.[1513] As soon as he arrived in Arabba he would go to the parish church to adore the Blessed Sacrament, offering Him the days he would

[1510] Francis de Zulueta (1878–1958), son of Pedro Juan de Zulueta y Wilcox and Laura Sheil, *regius professor* of civil law at Oxford from 1919 to 1948, was a close friend of J.R.R. Tolkien (1892–1873), and godfather of his daughter Priscilla. Cf. Lorena Atzeri, "Francis de Zulueta (1878–1958): An Oxford Roman Lawyer Between Totalitarianisms," in Kaius Tuori and Heta Björklund (eds.), *Roman Law and the Idea of Europe*, Bloomsbury Publishing, London 2019, pp. 53–72.

[1511] Don Angelo Frena (1886–1967), born in Colle Santa Lucia, ordained in Brixen in 1912, chaplain in Cortina d'Ampezzo during the First World War, was parish priest in Arabba (1924–1939) and then of San Cassiano in Val Badia (1939–1961). He wrote a fine book of prayers and hymns for the faithful: *Laudate Dominum. Preghiere e canti per il popolo*, Officina Grafica Fratelli Amprimo, Turin 1949. Cf. his letters of September 19, 1953, in AAV, *Spoglio Merry del Val*, n. 1363, f. 25 and n. 1368, f. 31; Cenci, *Merry del Val*, pp. 481–485.

[1512] In 1903, just days after the election of Cardinal Sarto to the Papal throne, the house where the Pontiff was born began to receive visitors. The structure was purchased in 1897 by Anna Sarto, the sister of Pius X, with the approval of all the siblings. At her death, the house passed in inheritance to another sister, Maria, who donated it to the city of Riese in 1924.

[1513] The cardinal's visits to Riese are registered: August 2, 1924; August 9, 1925; August 17, 1926; and August 1 1929.

spend in the Dolomites. Arriving at the *Hotel Posta,* where he always stayed, the entire town would come out to greet him. The most important event for him was the celebration of the Holy Mass in the little seventeenth-century church of Sts. Peter and Paul in the center of Arabba. A marble plaque in the church remembers him in the words, "Cardinal Rafael Merry del Val, pilgrim to the land of Pius X, from the marvelous Dolomites, here looked into the horizon of God, sacrificed on the altars of Arabba, accepted by God and by his people. August 1924 — 1925 — 1926 — 1929."

The cardinal, in his cassock and mountaineer's cap, walking-stick in hand, loved to climb the highest peaks that remind man of his destiny in Heaven. "A photograph depicts him thus: book in hand, his cassock slightly windblown, cap with a visor, in studded boots, conversing with an old friend, all 'with the composure and seriousness for which he was admired in St. Peter's.'"[1514] The ski lift did not yet exist that today takes one from Passo Pordoi to Mt. Sass Pordoi, when on August 26, 1926, Merry del Val reached Piz Boé during an excursion of many hours, climing over a thousand meters to the highest point of the Sella Massif, where at three thousand meters above sea level one enjoys a spectacular panorama extending from the Marmolada to the Austrian Alps. Contemplating this wonder of creation, the cardinal intoned with his powerful voice the *Gloria in excelsis Deo* as an act of adoration and glorification of the greatness of the Creator. He wrote in one of his notebooks, "I consecrate every beat of my heart, every breath, every word, and every movement of my soul and my body to You, my God, desiring nothing else but that my whole self should sing to You a long hymn of praise, of expiation for my sins, and of thanksgiving for Your benefits."[1515]

Another note shows us the measure of the intensity of his spiritual life:

> I promised God by His grace not to begin any action without reminding myself that He is witness to it; that He works with me and gives me the means for doing it; never to terminate any action without the same thought, offering it to God as something that belongs to Him; and, if during the course of the action the same thought were to come to mind, to stop for a moment and renew the desire to please only Him.[1516]

1514 Msgr. Alberto Canestri, *Un missionario in porpora. S. Em. il cardinale Merry del Val [A Missionary Cardinal. His Eminence Cardinal Merry del Val]*, Missionary Union of the Clergy in Italy, Rome 1934, p. 32.

1515 Merry del Val, *Pensieri ascetici*, p. 113.

1516 Ibid.

Merry del Val was appointed by the pope to preside over the international congresses of the League of Catholic Women in 1922 and 1925, alongside Princess Fanny von Starhemberg.[1517] In October 1925, the sixth congress of the organization was held in Rome during the Holy Year, with the theme "The dangers that threaten the family and with it all society." The cardinal welcomed them "in this homeland of the soul . . . wherein one feels closer to the heavenly homeland," reminding the Catholic women gathered in Rome from around the world that "to woman belongs above all the sublime mission of defending the family, which is so intimately bound to the fate of human society, in such a way that, if one perishes, the other is necessarily dragged to ruin."[1518]

In May 1925, Rafael Merry del Val celebrated his episcopal jubilee. The anniversary fell on May 6 but was saddened by news of his mother's death, which occurred just days before, on May 1.[1519] The last time he had seen Donna Josefina, she had asked her priest son to hear her general confession, as had the mother of St. Francis de Sales. The cardinal was not able to dissuade her. He listened and gave her absolution.

The ceremony of his episcopal jubilee was thus delayed to June 25 and was celebrated in St. Peter's Basilica in the presence of a host of cardinals and representatives of the Roman Curia. Responding to the affectionate greeting of Msgr. Salvatore Talamo,[1520] the dean of the chapter, who praised the exemplary way in which he carried out his offices, the cardinal said, "I have sought, insofar as I have been able, to correspond to the ardent desire of our glorious and holy pontiff Pius X, namely that of maintaining the decorum and splendor of the Sanctuary and of ensuring that the splendor of the material edifice might not lack the visible example of an edifying clergy in its spirit of piety and priestly virtue."[1521] But to a pious lady, Stella Wood, whom he had

[1517] Franziska von Starhemberg (1875–1943), born Countess Larisch von Moennich, married Prince Ernst Rüdiger von Starhemberg (1861–1927) in 1898. She founded the Austrian *Katholische Frauenorganisation* and was a protagonist in Austrian political life. Their son Ernst Rüdiger von Starhemberg (1899–1956) was a conservative politician, vice-chancellor to Engelbert Dollfuss, and leader of the group *Heimschutz*.

[1518] Cenci, *Merry del Val*, pp. 797–798. Complete text, pp. 793–800.

[1519] The cardinal suffered from not being able to be with his mother on her sick bed. "This has been a great sorrow to me; yet it is a joy to have a real sacrifice to offer to the Sacred Heart," he wrote to his uncle Francisco de Zulueta (Archive of the Postulation, f. 1109).

[1520] Msgr. Salvatore Talamo (1854–1932), dean of the Vatican Chapter and secretary of the Roman Academy of St. Thomas, was one of the main promoters of Scholastic philosophy in the nineteenth and twentieth centuries.

[1521] Cenci, *Merry del Val*, p. 549.

converted to the Catholic faith, who had expressed to him how moved she was by the magnificent and impressive ceremony, he responded: "That ceremony made me think of my funeral at which, in all probability, those cardinals will be present."[1522] "The more we advance in years, the more Our Lord detaches us from this earth, breaking the bonds that draw us to this passing and ephemeral life, and preparing us for the happy and eternal life," as he wrote to another spiritual daughter.[1523]

Ellin Craven Learned, an American journalist, was converted in 1926 during a trip to Rome while attending Mass celebrated by the cardinal.[1524] "Afterward, when he carried the Blessed Sacrament to the altar of repose, I could [see] as he passed, the holiness of his face. As people streamed out to follow the procession, I hastened out, followed, knelt, and adored at the Chapel of the Blessed Sacrament, and knew that I could never go back to the Episcopal Church."[1525] On that occasion, Ellin Learned approached the cardinal, who assured her he would pray for her by name every day during the celebration of the Holy Sacrifice.

On May 17, 1927, Ellin Learned received Confirmation and for the first time Holy Communion from the one to whom she owed her conversion. Several days later, on the feast of the Ascension, the new convert attended a Mass celebrated in St. Peter's by the pope, in the presence of the cardinal archpriest of the Basilica. "More and more was I impressed by his manner, so quiet and composed, and his erect, motionless figure whether standing, or seated, never turning, never leaning ungracefully, as others do, always straight, and best of all, always recollected, and with eyes and attention fixed on the book in his hand."[1526]

The cardinal wrote her in turn from Arabba on August 11, 1928, "Distance counts for nothing in the spiritual life, for there is always the Communion of Saints and we are always united in the Blessed Sacrament and at the same altar. The intercourse of prayer brings us all together on both sides of the grave, in time and in Eternity."[1527]

1522 Ibid., p. 557; Dal-Gal, *Merry del Val*, p. 145.

1523 Merry del Val, *Pensieri ascetici*, p. 83.

1524 Ellin Craven Learned, *The Etiquette of New York Today*, F. A. Stokes, New York 1906; *Everybody's Complete Etiquette*, F. A. Stokes, New York 1923; *Finding the Way*, Parish Visitors of Mary Immaculate, New York 1940.

1525 Buehrle, *Merry del Val*, p. 243.

1526 Ibid., pp. 260–261.

1527 Ibid., p. 262; Archive of the Postulation, ff. 616–617. On the back of the envelope: "August 11, 1928. Distance does not matter in the least."

On October 24, Cardinal De Lai died, after having watched his activity diminish to that of a mere figurehead. Along with Merry del Val and Vives y Tutó, De Lai had been one of Pius X's closest collaborators in times long gone. On October 27 of the same year, Merry del Val wrote a spiritual daughter, "How the years have flown by. It is difficult for me to realize how old I am. Forty years a priest, twenty-five a bishop, and twenty-three a cardinal: and how different my life has been from what I had hoped and prayed it would be! May God's will be done."[1528]

In one of his meditations, the cardinal had said,

> *Venit ergo ad Simonem Petrum, et dicit ei Petrus: Domine tu mihi lavas pedes? Respondit ei Jesus: Quod ego facio, tu nescis modo, scies autem postea* [John 13:6–7]. Let us pause here a moment to consider these words of the Savior. They are words that will not pass away: *Verba autem mea non transibunt.* They are words that Our Lord would like to repeat to our souls, if we wish to listen to them. When we have some ardent desire and we remain disappointed and are tempted to grumble, Jesus reprimands us with great compassion, saying: *Quod ego facio, tu nescis modo, scies autem postea.* Perhaps tomorrow everything will be explained and you shall know why I did not grant your request, and that I give you something better. And in any case, at the moment of death, and before the judgment seat of God, you shall understand how I acted toward you, you shall be happy and will bless me.[1529]

Rafael Merry del Val was, in the eyes of the world, a man full of glory and honors. During those years he was cardinal archpriest of St. Peter's Basilica, secretary of the Congregation of the Holy Office, prefect of the Fabric of St. Peter's, and member of the following congregations: the Consistorial Congregation, the Congregation for the Eastern Church, the Congregation for the Council, the Congregation for the Propagation of the Faith, the Congregation of Rites, the Ceremonial Congregation, the Congregation for Extraordinary Ecclesiastical Affairs, and the Congregation of Seminaries and Universities. He was also a member of the Pontifical Commission for Biblical Studies, the Cardinals' Commission for the Administration of the Patrimony of the Holy See,

[1528] Letter of October 27, 1928, in Cenci, *Merry del Val*, p. 389.

[1529] AAV, *Spoglio Merry del Val*, busta 8, f. 1119.

president of the Pontifical Academy of the Catholic Religion, and cardinal protector of twenty-nine religious institutes.[1530] These were not honorary positions, but responsibilities he carried out with all the commitment he could muster, amidst deep affliction, which was a characteristic of the spiritual life and which he saw reflected in the image of the Our Lady of Sorrows before which he prayed in his chapel.

He commissioned Fr. Rouvier, his esteemed collaborator in the Holy Office, to write a manual on the great merits of Christian pain and suffering, which was published in 1923 under the title, suggested by the cardinal, *Savoir souffrir*.[1531] Merry del Val gave many indications to the French priest, who wanted to publish it under the name of His Eminence, or at least to dedicate it to him.[1532] The cardinal did not permit his name to appear in any way in the book, but only wanted to see himself in the words: "We do not know the suffering, the sadness, the bitterness, the misfortunes that await us, distributed silently along the path of our lives,"[1533] but we know that suffering cannot be eliminated from the life of man. Trials, disappointments, tribulations, and deceit constitute the drama of the life of every Christian. And yet, "just as the dew descends and fecundates the furrows opened deeply by the plow in the viscera of the earth, so in the open furrows of pain in the depths of the soul grace often accumulates with greater force to render it fecund."[1534]

In the meantime, what Renzo De Felici defined "the years of consensus" of the fascist regime were beginning, approved by the Holy See and by the Savoy monarchy.[1535] On January 11, 1930, Fr. Lorenzo Rocci wrote in his diary, "immense celebrations in Rome this week for the marriage of Umberto of Savoy and Maria José of Belgium: the archbishop of Pisa, Card. Maffi, blessed the nuptials in the Pauline Chapel of the Quirinale. Everyone, especially Catholics, have great hopes in the Prince who claims he is very religious."[1536] That same day, informer "35" of the political police noted, "The

1530 Cf. Roy-Lysencourt, *Merry del Val*, pp. 61–62, with a list of the religious communities of which he was the protector.

1531 Frédéric Rouvier, *Savoir souffrir*, Desclée de Brouwer, Bruges, 1923.

1532 Cenci, *Merry del Val*, p. 425.

1533 Rouvier, *Savoir souffrir*, p. 147.

1534 Ibid., p. 78.

1535 Renzo De Felice, *Mussolini il duce. Gli anni del consenso. 1929–1936*, Einaudi, Turin 1974.

1536 Vittorio Capuzza, *Lorenzo Rocci S.J. Diario (anni 1880–1933)*, Bibliotheka, Rome 2021, p. 558. Lorenzo Rocci (1864–1950) of the Company of Jesus, was one of the leading scholars of Greek language and literature in the 1900s.

pope, and all the dignitaries of the pontifical court with him, were profoundly fond of and satisfied by the sincere piety and fervent attachment to the person of the Vicar of Christ and of religion, demonstrated by the venerable young couple and by all the other Savoy princes."[1537] A short note a few days earlier had communicated, "The King has confessed to his Grand Squire and to the other high dignitaries of court, that the personage with whom he most willingly conversed, because of his lordly manner, was that man of spirit and the perfect diplomat: Card. Merry del Val."[1538]

Cardinal Merry del Val was not deceived by totalitarian regimes. He was concerned about the expansion of communism throughout the world and studied communist strategy,[1539] anticipating the analysis that Pius XI would later develop in the encyclical *Divini redemptoris* of March 19, 1937. But the conversion of England dominated his thoughts and his prayers. On January 3, 1930, Merry del Val sent a letter to the rector of Bede College, Msgr. Charles L. Duchemin,[1540] in which he confirmed his zeal for the conversion of England, recognizing that "much has been done and there is every reason to hope that, under your wise direction, the College will make further progress."[1541] Several days later, he wrote to Fr. Woodlock, relating to him that there had been a solemn meeting of all the cardinals of the Holy Office, in the presence of the Holy Father, "the meeting we call a *Feria V*, a bit like an ecumenical Council and an '*ex cathedra*' definition. I suppose there exists no more solemn form of procedure." During the meeting, which lasted more than two hours, "the cardinals were unanimous in declaring the ordinations to be absolutely invalid." Merry del Val concluded the letter suggesting that Fr. Woodlock read the pamphlet *Catholic Orders and Anglican Orders* by the Jesuit Hornyhold, as "an excellent summary of the entire question," [1542] and study the Protestant author Dyson Hague's *The Story of*

[1537] ACS, Polizia politica, *Fascicoli Personali, 1927–1944*, busta 227, "Canali, Msgr.," note of January 11, 1930.

[1538] Ibid., busta 228, "Merry del Val, Raffaele," December 7, 1929.

[1539] Murphy, *Spiritual Writings*, p. 17.

[1540] Msgr. Charles L. Duchemin (1886–1965) was rector of the Bede College for thirty-three years from 1928 to 1961.

[1541] *Processus informativus ordinarius*, vol. 2, Doc. 161.

[1542] Vincent Hornyhold (1849–1922) was a Jesuit historian and spiritual writer, author of the study *Catholic Orders and Anglican Orders*, which the cardinal held in high esteem, congratulating the author with a card on January 24, 1919.

the English Prayer Book, which confirmed the Catholic thesis on Anglican ordinations.[1543]

One year earlier, on December 15, 1929, the cardinal had attended the beatification of the English martyrs, killed in hatred of the Faith during the seventeenth and eighteenth centuries.[1544] Among the last works he read, according to what he wrote a friend in January 1930, was a *Life of Blessed Philip Howard*.[1545] On February 15, 1930, the evening of the triduum in honor of the English Martyrs, he had gone to the church of the Jesuits, reciting on his knees the rosary in the midst of the crowd of faithful. The cardinal was feeling the weight of his responsibilities, but was in no way a tired or weary man. "Seeing him walking down the alleyways of Rome, agile and quick, erect in stature, accompanied by Msgr. Canali, or seeing him during the long functions in St. Peter's without giving the least sign of fatigue, or hearing his witty and sharp conversation, one would say that he was born to reach healthily and vigorously a ripe old age without infirmity. No one would have thought of a demise so immature and sudden."[1546]

1543 Dyson Hague, *The Story of the English Book of Common Prayer: Its Origin and Developments: With Special Chapters on the Scottish, Irish, American and Canadian Prayer Books*, Longmans, Green and Co., London 1926. Dyson Hague (1857–1935) was a Canadian Evangelical pastor, author of various works of a historical and theological nature.

1544 On December 8, 1929, the decree on martyrdom was promulgated, followed by the beatification on December 15. Fifty-four were beatified by Pope Leo XIII in 1886 and another nine in 1895. Two of these, John Fisher and Thomas More, went on to be canonized by Pius XI in 1935. On October 25, 1970, Paul VI canonized forty of the above-mentioned martyrs, eleven of whom belonged to the group of blessed from 1886 and twenty-nine to that of 1929. On November 22, 1987, Georg Haydock and eighty-four companions were beatified by Pope John Paul II. Cf. Celestino Testore S.J., *Il primato spirituale di Pietro difeso dal sangue dei martiri inglesi [The Spiritual Primacy of Peter Defended by the Blood of the Enlgish Martyrs]*, Soc. Tip. Macioce & Pisani, Isola del Liri 1929.

1545 Cecil Kerr, *The Life of the Venerable Philip Howard: Earl of Arundel and Surrey*, Longmans, Green and Co., London 1926. Philip Howard (1557–1595), XX Count of Arundel, was imprisoned in the Tower of London, where he died in 1595. He is venerated as a martyr and was beatified by Pius XI on December 15, 1929, and canonized by Paul VI on October 25, 1970, among the Forty English and Welsh Martyrs.

1546 Cenci, *Merry del Val*, p. 576.

7

The Mystery of a Death and the Secret of a Life

The Sickness and Death of Cardinal Merry del Val

On the morning of Saturday, February 22, while presiding at the Congregation of the Holy Office, Cardinal Merry del Val received news of the death of Cardinal Perosi, the brother of the choir director of the Sistine Chapel. Perosi, who had received his cardinal's beret in 1926, was sixty-one and since 1916 had been an assessor of the Holy Office. Merry del Val was greatly affected and went immediately to visit his deceased friend's corpse, arranging for it to be exposed in the chapel of the Congregation. The funeral was set for February 26 in the Basilica of San Carlo al Corso.

On the morning of Monday, February 24, the cardinal rose as always before 6 a.m., and after his meditation, celebrated the Holy Mass. In the afternoon, after having recited Vespers and Compline, and after his usual visit to the Blessed Sacrament in his private chapel, he went out on foot with Msgr. Canali to the Association of the Sacred Heart in Trastevere, where for over thirty years he had carried out his pastoral ministry. Canali recalled that the cardinal was in fine health and that he had even had to ask him to slow his pace.[1547]

Returning home before the evening prayers, Merry del Val confided to Canali that he had a little visceral disturbance. The next morning, Tuesday, although the pain had not passed, he wanted to receive Msgr. Caccia Dominioni who, on behalf of the Holy Father, was bringing him the gift of a ring, in memory of the baptism he had administered two days earlier to his grandniece Maria Pia Persichetti-Ugolini.[1548] His last act was a letter to Pius XI, written in his own hand, on the morning of Tuesday, February 25, to thank him for the precious gift.

That afternoon he showed signs of a slight fever and the pontifical physician, Dr. Aminta Milani, was called, who diagnosed him with a form of appendicitis,

[1547] Cenci, *Merry del Val*, p. 579.

[1548] Maria Pia Persichetti-Ugolini was the daughter of the Marquis Edoardo Persichetti-Ugolini and Maria Luisa Ratti, niece of Pius XI.

mild for the moment, but that the matter should be kept under surveillance.[1549] Dr. Milani had the cardinal visited by Dr. Giuseppi Bastianelli, who after having examined him, confirmed the diagnosis of his colleague.[1550] The Spanish nursing nuns, the Servants of Mary, were called to give him nocturnal assistance. He had been close to them for years, and just the previous year they had assisted him during a heavy bout of influenza. At 6:30 a.m., on Wednesday, February 26, Msgr. Pescini, one of Pius XI's two personal secretaries, who was very close to Merry del Val, received a telephone call from Msgr. Canali, who with a very emotional voice asked him to come to Santa Marta, because the Cardinal had a fever and was in intense pain. Pescini rushed there and, sitting next to His Eminence, had the impression that he was "invaded by a certain apprehension, ably repressed by the perfect self-control so typical of him, and which had rendered him so sublime during moments of anguished struggle."[1551]

Dr. Milani was called once more, and in agreement with Dr. Giuseppi Bastianelli, decided to consult the latter's brother, the surgeon Raffaele Bastianelli, despite the contrary opinion of Msgr. Canali.[1552] Milani went in person to Bastianelli's clinic in Viale Regina Margherita, communicating to the surgeon who was busy with an operation, that during the night, Merry del Val had worsened.[1553] It seemed to him a case of acute appendicitis, and he invited the doctor

[1549] Aminta Milani (1877–1944), professor of clinical pathology and head surgeon at the Ospedali Riuniti, was pontifical physician since 1928 and director of the health services of the Vatican. He was succeeded by Prof. Riccardo Galeazzi Lisi.

[1550] Giuseppe Bastianelli (1862–1959), professor of medical semeiotics at the University of Rome, has often been confused with his younger brother Raffaele (1863–1961), a surgeon. The father of both was Giulio Bastianelli (1824–1904) from Umbria, primary physician at the Santo Spirito Hospital in Rome. In 1895, he took part in the Committee for the solemnization of the twentieth anniversary of the liberation of Rome, promoted by Freemasonry.

[1551] Report of Msgr. Pescini, in Cenci, *Merry del Val*, pp. 582–583.

[1552] Msgr. Canali proposed the name of another surgeon, but Prof. Milani insisted on Bastianelli (Cenci, *Merry del Val*, p. 581). Prof. Raffaele Bastianelli operated in his clinic situated in Viale Regina Margherita 277 and, until 1927, in the first pavilion of Polyclinic Umberto I, but never had a university chair. He was a surgeon to the Royal House (1893), the head surgeon at the Ospedali Riuniti of Rome (1896–1927), general director of the Regina Elena Institute for the study of tumors (1931–1950), and senator of the Kingdom of Italy (1929). In 1932, he commemorated at the Medical Academy of Rome the Roman surgeon Vincenzo Montenovesi (1849–1931), a leading exponent of Freemasonry of the Italian Symbolic Rite ("Commemorazione del prof. Vincenzo Montenovesi," in Luigi Pozzi (ed.), *Bulletin and Acts of the Royal Medical Academy of Rome*, LVIII, Roma, 1932, p. 4).

[1553] The reconstruction of Card. Merry del Val's last hours is based above all on the testimony of Msgr. Giuseppe Pescini (*Informatio*, pp. 430–435); of Prof. Raffaele Bastianelli (*Informatio*, pp. 240–242); and of Mother Maria Ester Di Giusto (*Processus informativus ordinario*, Sessio CIII, vol. 2, pp. 617–620, *Informatio*, pp. 248–250).

to come to the Vatican to see if it merited a surgical intervention. Bastianelli continued to operate, asking Dr. Milani to update him further. Later that morning, while the surgeon was beginning a second operation, Milani telephoned him warning that his temperature had increased and that the cardinal's condition was worsening. At this point, Bastianelli invited a nurse, Mother Ester Maria Di Giusto, of the Institute of the Franciscan Missionaries of Mary, to coordinate the preparations in the event the operation were to be necessary.[1554]

Meanwhile, trying to show composure, Msgr. Pescini asked the cardinal if he wished to receive Communion, to which he replied calmly though without giving Pescini time to finish his question, "I believe so, yes, I was thinking, I want to receive Communion." His usual confessor, Fr. Alisiardi, was called from the Jesuit church and, arriving at Santa Marta, administered the sacraments of Penance and the Eucharist.[1555] During these hours, the cardinal was lovingly assisted by the Spanish nursing nuns. Sr. Rosario Porron Zabalza, of the Servants of Mary,[1556] who had already assisted him during the illness the previous year, testified, "I cannot recall in all my life having met a priest as mortified as he was and with such self-control as he had. I was greatly edified."[1557] The patient, she recalled, had burned lips but never asked for anything that might bring him refreshment and, although burning with fever, if we took his temperature, never asked what it was.[1558] Around 1 p.m., Dr. Bastianelli arrived at Santa Marta accompanied by Dr. Ernesto Boni and Enrico Bardellini, his assistants. The surgeon visited the cardinal, submitting him to a long interrogation, and judged that the operation would be needed.[1559] Bastianelli informed Merry del Val of his decision, although the latter asked the doctor not to use chloroform. "I would prefer to suffer rather than be chloroformed."[1560] In fact, Dr. Bastianelli

1554 Maria Ester Di Giusto (1879–1964) of the Franciscan Missionaries of Mary, born Maria di Giusto, was born in Tarcento, worked from 1915 in the clinic of Bastianelli as a nurse nun in charge of the operating room. In 1938, she became head nurse.

1555 Celestino Alisiardi (1847–1931) entered the Society of Jesus in 1889 and made final vows on February 2, 1900. He was a member of the Roman Province residing in Via degli Astalli and was also confessor to Pope Pius XI.

1556 The *Siervas de María Ministras de los Enfermos* were a religious institute founded in Madrid in 1851 by St. Soledad Torres Acosta (1826–1887), beatified by Pius XII in 1950 and canonized by Paul VI in 1970. On June 16, 1927, Merry del Val gave the blessing of the new church in Rome of the religious in Via Antonio Musa.

1557 Sr. Rosario Porron, *Processus Informativus Ordinarius, Sessio* LX, vol. 2, p. 376 (pp. 375–378).

1558 Ibid.

1559 Ibid., *Sessio* C, vol. 2, pp. 602–603.

1560 *Informatio*, p. 129.

discussed with Dr. Milani what would be the best way to apply anesthetics and opted for general anesthesia using ether.

When Dr. Milani communicated to the cardinal that they would use a general anesthetic, "his hand trembled slightly and then he mumbled: 'Go ahead,'"[1561] testified Sr. Rosario, adding, "At that moment he gave himself more entirely to God than he ever had before to carry out his divine will and understood the possibility of what was indeed to take place shortly."[1562]

The cardinal went on his own feet to the operating room that had been set up in Santa Marta, though doubled over in pain. It was about 3 p.m. The general anesthetic was given by means of a mask over his face. Besides Dr. Bastianelli and Dr. Milani, the two assistants, Boni and Bardellini, were also present as well as Sr. Ester Di Giusto, who administered the surgical instruments.

Sr. Ester Di Giusto recalled that "when Dr. Bastianelli was about to remove the appendix he gave a cry, 'His blood isn't circulating, get rid of the mask and start artificial respiration!'"[1563] They laid him on his back and began artificial respiration. According to Sr. Ester, "seeing that he was not breathing at all, despite the artificial respiration, the doctor made a tracheotomy to allow him to breath better. Despite this, after three-quarters of an hour applying artificial respiration, he gave no signs of life. He had died."[1564] Dr. Milani left the operating room with his hands in his hair murmuring in a choked voice, "His Eminence isn't breathing."[1565] The sister added, "We were all left petrified and utterly forlorn. I can still see Dr. Bastianelli trembling with pain, as was Dr. Milani, and I broke down and cried."[1566] Msgr. Giulio Mancini ran to the chapel, took the holy oils and, with the help of Msgr. Pescini, administered Extreme Unction to the cardinal who lay inanimate on the bed.

Msgr. Cenci wrote, "The Lord had arranged that this great Servant of his might terminate his generous earthly life in such an extraordinary way, with an effusion of blood and a wound to his neck inflicted after death, outside his most modest bed, as if to testify that his arduous existence, full of tribulations, born

1561 Sr. Rosario Porron Zabalza, *Processus Informativus Ordinarius, Sessio* LX, vol. 2, p. 377.
1562 Ibid.
1563 Sr. Ester Di Giusto, *Informatio*, p. 250.
1564 Ibid.
1565 Pescini Report, in Cenci, *Merry del Val*, p. 585.
1566 Ester Di Giusto, in *Informatio*, p. 250; *Processus Informativus Ordinarius*, p. 620.

always with virtue that can be called heroic, had been terminated with the exterior expression of a martyrdom of blood."[1567]

Cardinal Merry del Val often said he "wanted to fall asleep in this life and wake up in Paradise," recalled Fr. Giovanni Borboni, his collaborator at the Holy Office.[1568] "Our life is the tree, our death is its fruit. *Non est arbor mala faciens fructum bonum* [no evil tree brings forth good fruit; Luke 6:43]," the cardinal had written in his spiritual notes.[1569] "Therefore, we must not hope or desire to know long in advance the hour of our death; but we are allowed to desire and pray that in our last sickness, if we die of that sickness, a false hope of healing might not deceive us, but that in union with our Savior we might know that our time has come."[1570]

Doubts and Suspicions Concerning the Cardinal's Death

On February 27, 1930, *L'Osservatore Romano* published the following news: "Yesterday, Wednesday, at 3:30 p.m., fortified by all the comforts of Our Holy Religion and by a special Blessing of the Holy Father, the archpriest of the Patriarchal Vatican Basilica, secretary of the Supreme Congregation of the Holy Office, prefect of the Sacred Congregation of the Fabric of St. Peter's, Cardinal Raffaele Merry del Val presented his good soul to God." That same day, an informant of the state police communicated, "Cardinal Merry del Val is no more! He died during an operation on his appendix, suddenly, lightning-quick. When the dismayed Msgr. Canali gave us the news, we could not believe it, but going immediately to Santa Marta, we had to accept this most disheartening reality. The cardinal was dead and seemed to be sleeping. Nothing in his appearance suggested a violent, rapid, or implausible death."[1571]

The news left those who had recently met with the cardinal stunned, for they had found him in the fullness of his physical and intellectual strength. The cause of Rafael Merry del Val's death was attributed to a cardiac arrest, which seemed inexplicable to many, given the excellent state of health the cardinal was in. Many wondered what the true causes might have been for such a sudden

1567 Cenci, *Merry del Val*, p. 586.

1568 Deposition of Msgr. Giovanni Borboni, in *Informatio*, p. 95.

1569 AAV, *Spoglio Merry del Val*, busta 8, f. 1117.

1570 Ibid., f. 1172.

1571 ACS, Polizia politica, *Fascicoli Personali, 1927–1944*, busta 228, "Merry del Val, Raffaele," note of February 27, 1930.

passing, ascribed to the unfortunate outcome of a simple appendix operation, performed by a surgeon of recognized fame as was Dr. Raffaele Bastianelli.

Another note put out by the police stated, "a serious accusation is circulating tenaciously in settings of the Holy See against the honorable Dr. Bastianelli, which we must take account of with great prudence on the informative level. According to this accusation, the capable surgeon had killed His Eminence Cardinal Merry del Val, no less. It states that the operation should have gone well but that the administering of chloroform too abundantly sent the secretary of the Supreme Congregation of the Holy Office to the next life.... The suspicion of such an egregious error seems to have been communicated to the pope, who was quite dismayed and stricken. The entourage of the Secretariat of State is maintaining strict silence concerning this 'incident'; but despite this, the serious accusation against the renowned surgeon is circulating everywhere in the Holy See."[1572]

On March 6, the police noted, "From direct sources, it seems that the fatal event that caused the syncope of Cardinal Merry was suffocation for which the gravest of responsibilities weighs upon Bastianelli." The surgeon was not careful to prevent the anesthetized patient from "swallowing his tongue," dying of suffocation.[1573]

Yet another note, on March 25, communicated that "the pope wants an investigation to be undertaken to establish the cause of death of Cardinal Merry del Val, given the insistent rumors going around inside and outside the Vatican, that the poor cardinal was barbarously killed by the malpractice and error of the doctors. The matter is most sensitive and secret, nor from such an investigation will they be able to obtain any serious and conclusive result. On trial and under accusation are Dr. Milani, the cardinal's physician, as well as Hon. Bastianelli, called to perform the surgery, too late, upon the illustrious patient."[1574]

In this note, the hypothesis is made that the golden dentures the cardinal had in his mouth were not seen, and that the patient had swallowed these teeth as soon as the chloroform had taken effect, and that the surgeon was forced to abandon the operation on the appendix and immediately begin

1572 ACS, Polizia politica, *Fascicoli Personali, 1927–1944*, busta 228, "Merry del Val, Raffaele," note of February 27, 1930.

1573 Ibid. Note of June 8, 1930.

1574 Ibid. Note of March 6, 1930. On April 9, the informer stated that "the pope has requested a complete and precise report on the commemoration of the facts of the deceased."

operating on the trachea to avoid suffocation. "Thus, it seems obvious that there was so much confusion in the overlapping operations that the poor cardinal died asphyxiated."[1575]

In early June, another Police notice announced that Dr. Boni, the anesthetist of the medical team, "Bastianelli's personal assistant for over fifteen years," had died "suddenly."[1576] According to Msgr. Canali and others (following the indiscretions gathered by the police informants), he had, in fact, killed himself. Again, according to the cardinal's secretary who continued to blame the doctors, the pressure not to insist further in verifying the account came from Msgr. Giuseppi Pizzardo, "protector" of the other doctor present, Dr. Milani, once a member of the close circle of "the pope's doctors."[1577]

The last note in the dossier on Merry del Val found in the government Central Archive, of August 30, 1933, states that "the true cause of the death of Merry del Val" was purported to be "suffocation."[1578]

Interrogated during the process of beatification, Dr. Raffaele Bastianelli was not able to explain the cardiac arrest that occurred during the operation, but excluded categorically that death had been caused by "suffocation due to a foreign body, namely the dentures."[1579] Luigi Nardini, president of the Association of the Sacred Heart in Trastevere, asserted that "due to the general anesthesia he was suffocated by his tongue and not by the dentures descending into his throat as was said and publicized, because he did not have removable dentures, but just

1575 Ibid. In a note of August 30, 1933, the informant communicated that "the true cause of the death of Merry del Val was suffocation because he swallowed his dentures which remained lodged in his throat." This thesis, which was shown to be unfounded, was taken up by Alessandro Visani, in "La misteriosa morte del cardinale Merry del Val nelle carte della polizia politica fascista" [The Mysterious Death of Cardinal Merry del Val in the Papers of the Fascist Political Police], *Giornale di storia* 7 (2011, online). Yet the cardinal had neither dentures nor gold teeth.

1576 "Dr. Boni, who was for 15 years the anesthetist assistant to Bastianelli, after the tragic death of Card. Merry del Val, is said not to have died suddenly, but rather, according to Msgr. Canali and others, to have committed suicide." (ACS, Polizia politica, *Fascicoli Personali, 1927–1944*, busta 228, "Merry del Val, Raffaele," note of June 8, 1930).

1577 ACS, Polizia politica, *Fascicoli Personali, 1927–1944*, busta 228, "Merry del Val, Raffaele," note of April 13, 1930.

1578 Ibid. Note of August 30, 1933.

1579 "It was a cardiac arrest" (Di Giusto, *Processus Informativus Ordinarius, Sessio* CIII, p. 620). "Absolutely excluded that it was due to suffocation by means of a foreign body, namely the dentures" (Ibid., *Sessio* C, p. 604). "I am not able to establish which factor above all determined in this case what occurred. Medicine and surgery have long known and with ever greater precision that the arrest of the cardiac function and of breathing can come about in the course of even a simple operation without being able to identify the causes" (ibid.).

one molar with a lead filling, according to the declarations his dentist gave me by telephone."[1580]

Certainly, his death was caused by asphyxiation during the general anesthetic. Msgr. Pescini attributed the cause of death to an excessive dose of ether used during the anesthesia.[1581] According to another witness, Fr. Raffaele Taucci of the Servites, "it was said that his death came about through suffocation due to the surgeon's negligence."[1582] Msgr. Alberto Serafini as well stated that "insofar as I have heard, his death was the consequence of an absurd distraction by the medical staff."[1583]

A police note of April 3 claimed that Msgr. Canali had said to an informant, "I shall never tire of shouting that H.E. Merry del Val was assassinated!" And since the informant looked at him astonished, Msgr. Canali repeated, "Yes, assassinated. Because the professional skill of Dr. Bastianelli and his assistants cannot be doubted, one has the right to say that their error was homicide, however involuntary it might have been."

Domingo Merry del Val, who met with Cardinal Canali in the 1950s, recounted that the cardinal's old secretary repeated on numerous occasions: "Your uncle was assassinated." Other highly placed personalities in the Vatican told him the same thing. Fr. Muñoz Urbano as well, one of the cardinal's most serious scholars, refers to an oral tradition claiming that Merry del Val was assassinated during the operation by one of the doctors, a Freemason, through an excessive dose of anesthesia. Muñoz Urbano defines this oral tradition "open to future investigation."[1584]

To frame this problem, one can establish a parallel between the death of Cardinal Merry del Val and that of John Paul I, Albino Luciani, which occurred in the Vatican on the night of September 28, 1978, after only thirty-three days of his pontificate.[1585] The sudden death of the pope, with a hasty diagnosis of

1580 Luigi Nardini, *Processus Informativus Ordinarius,* Sessio LXXXIV, vol. 2, p. 528.

1581 Testimony of the architect Giuseppe Sartor, in *Informatio,* p. 34.

1582 Fr. Raffaele Taucci, *Processus Informativus Ordinarius,* Sessio XCVII, vol. 2, p. 584.

1583 Alberto Serafini, *Processus Informativus Ordinarius,* Sessio LVIII, vol. 2, p. 445. We know that similar errors are more common than we might believe. When Leo XII, on February 10, 1829, died after an operation, a murderous accusation was hurled at the surgeon: "On February 10 a rare event has occurred! A wild lion was murdered by an ass!"

1584 Muñoz Urbano defined this oral tradition as "*abierta a futuras investigaciones.*" (*El cardenal secretario de Estado Rafael Merry del Val,* vol. 1, p. 132).

1585 On Albino Luciani (1912–1978), pope by the name of John Paul I for thirty-three days, from 27 August to 29 September 1978, cf. C. Siccardi, *Giovanni Paolo I. Una vita per la fede,* Paulines, Milan 2011, in particular pp. 188–192, on his death.

myocardial infarction and a number of contradictions in the official communications of the Holy See, stoked from the very beginning a great number of doubts and suspicions, such as that of a renowned Catholic intellectual, Carlo Bo, who petitioned in *Corriere della Sera* on October 1, 1978, that an autopsy be done on the pontiff, something the Vatican did not grant.[1586] Later, a British investigative journalist, David Yallop, published a best-seller in which he hypothesized that John Paul I had been assassinated by poisoning.[1587] Yallop pointed to Cardinal Secretary of State Jean Villot, a man who deviated into masonic circles, as hypothetically responsible for his death.[1588]

The Vatican rejected Yallop's theses with all too much certainty, although it is true that the English journalist's book insinuates doubts without offering any documented certainties. It cannot be excluded that Villot was the indirect cause of John Paul I's death, if it is true, as affirmed his secretary Fr. Diego Lorenzi, that on the evening before his death there had been an intense verbal clash between Villot and the pope. After this tempestuous meeting, the pope showed signs of having chest pain which eventually led to his death. It seems, however, that the last person to have had contact with the John Paul I was not Cardinal Villot but Cardinal Baggio, who had a dispute with the notoriously cardiopathic pope.[1589]

The death of Cardinal Merry del Val occurred half a century before that of John Paul I, when the curtain of secrecy that surrounded everything that happened in the Vatican was thick and impenetrable and the mass media had not yet rendered society "transparent" as it had in the 1970s. There is no doubt, however, that the suspicious elements regarding the death of Merry del Val are much greater than those that surround the death of John Paul I. Both cases deal with the premature passing of relatively young men, both in a good state of health. But in the case of John Paul I, his own secretary excluded the possibility of homicide, while the secretary of Merry del Val spoke

[1586] Carlo Bo (1911–2001) was an Italian literary critic. In 1939 he became professor of French language and literature at the University of Urbino, of which he was the rector from 1950. From 1984 he was made a senator for life of the Italian Republic.

[1587] David Yallop, *In God's Name: An Investigation into the Murder of Pope John Paul I*, Bantam Books, Toronto 1984.

[1588] Jean Villot (1905–1979), auxiliary bishop of Paris (1954) and archbishop coadjutor with the right to succession of Lyon (1959), participated in the Second Vatican Council as an undersecretary. He was later promoted archbishop of Lyon and made a cardinal by Paul VI in 1965. In 1969, he became secretary of state and the following year, Chamberlain of the Holy Roman Church.

[1589] This is suggested by the report given to Rome by Cardinal Gagnon, Fr. Charles T. Murr, in *Murder in the 33rd Degree: The Gagnon Investigation into Vatican Freemasonry* (2022).

explicitly of assassination, a term that can naturally be understood broadly. Indeed, it is common to say that a surgeon "killed" a patient, when the latter dies because of his malpractice.

Was the cause of death of Merry del Val truly an inexplicably unsuccessful operation, despite the competence and expertise of the surgeon? How was it possible that a luminary of the medical profession like Bastianelli was "distracted"? There are errors that ruin the career of a doctor. After such an enormous mistake, Bastianelli's career should have been over, and yet he continued having great success. How can one not notice the contrast between the undiminished fame of Bastianelli and the sudden end of the anesthetist Boni, if it is true that he committed suicide? If it had been an error on the part of Boni, is it possible that the anesthetist would have gone so far as killing himself? And in this case, would it not have been logical to leave a few lines explaining his error and declaring that he did not want to outlive the man he had killed involuntarily or at someone's orders? Or can we surmise that the death of Boni was not voluntary? That perhaps he too was killed? Naturally, these are only hypotheses, but the historian cannot exclude them *a priori*.

Yallop attributed the death of John Paul I to his secretary of state Villot and Freemasonry. By the same logic, one might attribute the death of Merry del Val to the secretary of state under Pius XI, Pietro Gasparri, who notoriously detested Merry del Val and feared his election as future pope.[1590] Dr. Bastianelli was an old friend of Cardinal Gasparri. Pius XI's secretary of state did recall this friendship with Bastianelli in his *Memoires,* dating back to when the young doctor transferred to Paris to finish his studies, when Gasparri was working there in the nunciature.[1591] It is likewise possible that the doctor was tied to masonic circles, since his father, Giulio Bastianelli, was a notable representative of Freemasonry in Perugia. It is certain, at any rate, that Merry del Val had many enemies after the Conciliation, as well as being considered a *papabile*.

All of this evidence does not prove that the cardinal was assassinated, but it might justify a historical and academic investigation that has been lacking until now and that some of the Merry del Val family have been requesting. At the symposium held in Rome on October 1, 2015, during which Pope Francis received 150 members of the family, the grandnephew of the cardinal, Domingo

[1590] A Police note of July 5, 1929, defined Cardinal Gasparri the "open and irrevocable adversary of Merry del Val" (ASMAE, busta 7, fasc, 1, *Santa Sede, 1919–1930*).

[1591] AA.EE.SS., *Stati Ecclesiastici,* 1934, Pos. 15, P.O., fasc. 527, pp. 47–48.

Merry del Val, publicly requested an investigation into "whether it was true that he was intentionally killed on the operating table, as sustained by illustrious people, but above all to seek the motive!"[1592]

In the days that followed the death of Rafael Merry del Val, the Marquis Alfonso, his older brother, was requested by the Vatican to express opposition to an autopsy, saying that "incalculable harm has been done to the Church and to the family, but no scandal will be able to remedy this loss." This was and has remained the position of the Holy See. On February 15, 2016, Prof. Philippe Roy-Lysencourt, research director of the symposium on Cardinal Merry del Val, submitted to Pope Francis a request to carry out the autopsy. Roy-Lysencourt made known that he had been in touch with a renowned pathologist who declared his willingness to do the autopsy, in a double evaluation with an Italian colleague, if permission were to be granted by the Holy See.[1593] The request has never received a response.

In his article in *Corriere della Sera* in 1978, concerning the death of John Paul I, Prof. Carlo Bo rightly wrote, "The Vatican palaces or underground are no longer the theater of criminal actions that were once abundantly exploited by certain polemicists and a sort of popular and coarse literature. For this very reason, that the windows of that house might be ever more limpid, one cannot understand why it was decided not to proceed with any sort of scientific investigation, in other words, why an autopsy was not performed.... To know what the pope died of is a legitimate fact that is purely historical, belonging to our visible history and does not touch in any way the spiritual mystery of his death."[1594]

The least one can say is that Merry del Val died because of a tragic error, of which the anesthetist Ernesto Boni and the surgeon Raffaele Bastianelli bear the responsibility. The former died of suicide, it would seem, in 1930, while the latter died at ninety-eight in 1961, taking to his tomb the truth regarding the death of Cardinal Rafael Merry del Val, which still remains one of the many unsolved mysteries in the history of the Church.

1592 Domingo Merry del Val (ed.), Conclusion, *Rafael Merry del Val. 150 anni dalla sua nascita*, p. 273.

1593 The person indicated was Philippe Charlier, professor at the University of Paris and director of the laboratory of forensic anthropology, who specialized in ancient human remains. Prof. Philippe Roy-Lysencourt communicated that the necessary finances were available for carrying out the scientific investigation, assuring that it would not cause any alteration of the cardinal's body, the physical integrity of which would be perfectly preserved.

1594 Carlo Bo, "Perché dire no all'autopsia?" [Why refuse the autopsy?], *Corriere della Sera*, October 1, 1978.

Posthumous Homage

In the days following the death of the cardinal, a long procession of homages were offered to his corpse, while the funeral was postponed to March 3 to allow the cardinal's brother Alfonso Merry del Val, ambassador in London, to be present.

The morning of Monday, March 3, the Vatican basilica was packed. The funeral procession processed through the two rows of pontifical gendarme that rendered him their honors. The side of the transept called Sts. Processus and Martinianus was draped in mourning, with a broad black swath lined with gold that descended along the altar wall. The funerary bier on which the coffin lay was surrounded by the traditional hundred candelabras in wrought iron, with candles of pure beeswax and four flares. At the foot of the coffin was placed the red galero.[1595] The Mass was officiated in a solemn manner by Msgr. Agostino Zampini,[1596] vicar general for the Vatican City, in the presence of almost the entire Sacred College residing in Rome,[1597] the pontifical family, a large representation of the diplomatic corps to the Holy See, and the Roman aristocracy, but above all by an unexpected throng of the faithful, gathered to give their final homage to the deceased cardinal.

After his death and over the following months, the press from around the world remembered with admiration the figure of Cardinal Merry del Val, shedding light on his ecclesiastical career and the human, political, and diplomatic talents that had made him one of the most outstanding men of his time.

The *Corriere della Sera,* in an ample article titled "The Man and the Statesman," after having summarized his dazzling career, wrote that "one can say of the superb work that Cardinal Merry del Val carried out as secretary of state that it grows ever greater with the passage of time and constitutes one of the most glorious pages in the history of the Church." Outside of Italy, the *New York Herald,* in an article on February 28, 1930, entitled "A Prince of the

1595 Cenci, *Merry del Val,* p. 604. The galero is a broad-brimmed, flat-crowned, red hat with tassels, traditionally worn by Roman Catholic cardinals.

1596 Agostino Zampini (1858–1937), of the Hermits of St. Augustine, was consecrated bishop by Cardinal Merry del Val on January 6, 1911, in the Basilica of Sant'Agostino in Rome. He was sacristan of the Apostolic Palaces and in this role, during the night of August 19, 1914, administered Viaticum and Extreme Unction to the dying Pius X. After the Lateran Pacts, he was the first vicar general of the Holy Father for the Vatican City.

1597 Present were Cardinals Pompili, Granito di Belmonte, Sbarretti, Boggiani, Pietro Gasparri, Enrico Gasparri, Van Rossum, Frühwirth, Locatelli, Scapinelli di Léguigno, Cerretti, Sincero, Capotosti, Lauri, Lépicier, Pacelli, Laurenti, Ehrle, and Verde (Cenci, *Merry del Val,* p. 605).

Church," defined him "a marvelous example of that strength that the Catholic Church still possesses and that it has always possessed," comparing him "to some of the great ecclesiastical figures and men of the world of times past": "Merry del Val was an example, and a conspicuous example of that capacity that the Catholic Church still possesses and has possessed all throughout her history, to attract to herself some of the greatest minds and some of the greatest capacities, in organization and in politics, in every age." Similarly, *El Debate* of Madrid, on February 27, 1932, wrote of him, "The life of Merry del Val has all the vigorous, energetic, precise traits of the exception. Even without knowing his works, one could estimate by the very aversion of the enemies of the Catholic Church, the traits of this man of such extraordinary personality."

In his will, the cardinal left as his universal heir the Congregation for the Propagation of the Faith, nominating as the executor of his will his "dearest and most faithful friend" Msgr. Nicola Canali.[1598] The cardinal manifested his desire to be buried in the Vatican Grottoes,[1599] "as close to Pius X as possible."

Fr. Javierre expressed in the following terms the symbiosis that existed between St. Pius X and Merry del Val: "The pontiff and his secretary of state acted with an impressive communality of viewpoints; they followed common objectives and evaluated together the methods for doing so. With two diverse temperaments and two personal histories that were very different, an impetuous vein filled with a higher force charged their spirits with identical resonances. If it is true that the universe revolves in music, it must be said that the conjunction of the stars produced in the souls of Pius X and Merry del Val the same harmony."[1600]

Pius XI granted Merry del Val's request. In a letter of March 24, 1930, to Camillo Serafini (1884–1952), the first governor of the Vatican City from 1929 to his death, Secretary of State Pietro Gasparri communicated that Pius XI, "recognizing the desire expressed by the defunct Cardinal Merry del Val in his will to be interred in the crypt of the Vatican basilica, as close to the tomb of the supreme pontiff Pius X as possible, has deigned to arrange that this desire be carried out."[1601]

1598 Archive of the Postulation, ff. 602–606. He left all his worldly possessions to the Propagation of the Faith to be used for missions in poor lands; Dal-Gal, *Merry del Val*, pp. 48, 163.

1599 Ibid., ff. 895–898.

1600 Javierre, *Merry del Val*, p. 173.

1601 In AA.EE.SS., *Stati ecclesiastici*, year 1929–1939, Pos. 408, fasc. 3, f. 70.

Cardinal Merry del Val was buried in the Vatican Grottoes in front of the tomb of the Cardinal Duke of York,[1602] who had also been archpriest of St. Peter's. On his tomb was cut the same inscription that the cardinal had indicated in his will: "*Da mihi animas, coetera tolle.*"[1603]

> Everything for God, only for him our efforts, our actions, our sufferings, our soul and our body, now and always, docile without reservations to his most holy will: *Da mihi animas, coetera tolle.*[1604]

This inscription did not fail to arouse amazement. It seemed to summarize the profound aspirations of a missionary, but how could it fit a man who had spent the last twenty-eight years, the most decisive of his life, closed in the Vatican collecting appointments and honors? In reality, Rafael Merry del Val had always been above all a man of the Church, and the Church has as its supreme mission the glory of God and the salvation of souls. Merry del Val's thirst for souls was not only the profound desire that the greatest number of souls possible be saved, but that the greatest number of souls called to salvation become saints. The supreme will of God is not only salvific but also sanctifying. No one knows how many souls Merry del Val directed and led to sanctity, but many of his spiritual sons and daughters have left moving testimonies.

"Thus disappeared in the sacred shadows of the Vatican Grottoes," wrote Cardinal Eugenio Pacelli, "the venerable figure of the most zealous Cardinal Merry del Val, reposing to the cry of '*Da mihi animas, coetera tolle*' next to the great pontiff for whom he was a most faithful and indefatigable minister; while the gaze of his thoughtful image still turns toward the Vatican basilica whose precious marbles and restored pavements conserve the witness of his piety and munificence."[1605]

1602 Henry Benedict Stuart, Duke of York (1725–1807), the last of the Stuarts, made a cardinal in 1747, was bishop of Frascati (1761), then vice-chancellor of the Holy See; at the death of his brother Charles (1788), he claimed his hereditary right to the English throne, proclaiming himself king with the name Henry IX. In 1803, he became dean of the Sacred College and bishop of Ostia and Velletri. He is buried in the Vatican Grottoes with the name Henry IX.

1603 The source of the motto is Genesis: "*Dixit autem rex Sodomorum ad Abram: Da mihi animas, cætera tolle tibi*" [Then the king of Sodom said to Abraham: "Give me the persons; but take the goods for yourself"] (Gen 14:21).

1604 *Processus Informativus Ordinarius, Sessio*, p. 12.

1605 Cardinal Eugenio Pacelli, Preface to Cenci, *Merry del Val*, p. XII.

Among the papers of the process of beatification of Cardinal Merry del Val preserved in the Apostolic Archive, of great importance is a document signed by Fr. Celestino Alisiardi, his confessor, of June 21, 1930, in which he testified,

> For many years I had the blessing of knowing intimately the Eminent Cardinal Merry del Val who made use of me as his confessor, and I always knew him as a pious man, of great integrity, delicate conscience, zealous, a true model of a priest, a bishop, and a cardinal. He confessed unfailingly every Saturday: every day he attended to his spiritual life, his meditations, prayers, examination of conscience, etc. He possessed true love of God and his neighbor, burned with the greatest love for the Church, and was most dear to the Holy Father Pius X who chose him as his secretary of state. Hence, I am certain that the above praised cardinal is saved and enjoys great glory in Heaven.[1606]

This declaration is the testimony of sanctity by one who, like no other, knew the soul of the cardinal through his regular, frequent confessions.

Secretum Meum Mihi

Rafael Merry del Val's old friend Fr. Denis Sheil recalled his motto: "*Secretum meum mihi.*"[1607] Count Giuseppe dalla Torre testified,

> The cardinal was by nature and character extremely reserved: his unquestionable and recognized gifts of intelligence and culture, for example, could be guessed, but he never manifested them ostentatiously, much less flaunted them. So too with his intimate sentiments and his private life. Likewise, it seems to me, and much more so, the same can be said of his interior life. If his sanctity is recognized, I believe it will be that of a Contardo Ferrini,[1608] a very interior sanctity with a scrupulous modesty toward itself, as if, were it to reveal itself, it would loose its perfume before God, as if it had an innocent conviction of having nothing

[1606] AAV, *Spoglio Merry del Val*, busta 9, f. 1680.

[1607] *Processus Informativus Ordinarius*, p. 378; *Informatio*, p. 379.

[1608] Contardo Ferrini (1859–1902) was a professor of Roman law and a Third Order Franciscan, beatified on April 13, 1947. Cf. M. Invernizzi, *Il Beato Contardo Ferrini (1859–1902). Il rigore della ricerca, il coraggio della fede [Blessed Contardo Ferrini. The Rigor of Research, the Courage of Faith]*, Piemme, Casale Monferrato 2002. Cardinal Merry del Val was postulator of Ferrini's cause of beatification and had a portrait of him in the parlor of his apartment in Santa Marta.

extraordinary to it that might be of example to its neighbor or at any rate, that it nourished the fear of men's praise, so dangerous if merited, or of adulation. Something of this nature is to be found in those who are hermits in spirit and can be called *humility* to a heroic degree. In other words, the virtue that is at the heart and summit of holiness."[1609]

Cardinal Canali affirmed that the spiritual characteristic of the cardinal was "hidden humility." He explained, saying, "Honestly, in the hagiography of the saints we find that many of them practiced humility, but it is not easy to find one who desired, and was able to hide, a true and sincere humility under the apparent mantle of a comfortable and honored life, as the Servant of God did."[1610] For this reason, "when he appeared in religious ceremonies he was the prince of the Church, but when he retired to the intimacy of his private life he was the humble and poor priest of God."[1611]

He slept on an iron bed of metal slats and a straw mattress, was frugal in his meals, and his cassocks were threadbare and mended. After his death, moreover, it was learned that Cardinal Merry del Val, like Charles Borromeo, wore a hairshirt under his cassock. In the bottom drawer of his desk, among his personal objects, were found two instruments of penance:[1612] a discipline with little iron tips nearly consumed by long use and two hairshirts with a thick weave of knitted irons.[1613] Cardinal Canali was more surprised and amazed than others by this, because having had thirty years of familiarity with the cardinal he had never noticed these instruments of penance. Canali also collected a number of depositions under oath that confirm the existence of this secret of his virtue and mortification.[1614]

1609 *Processus Informativus Ordinarius*, *Sessio* XXXI, vol. 1, p. 211; *Informatio*, p. 71.

1610 Ibid., *Sessio* CXII, vol. 3, p. 675.

1611 Ibid., Testimony of Madre Augusta Klottenberg, *Sessio* XX, vol. 1, p. 167.

1612 In 1952, Fr. Giovanni Battista Janssens (1889–1964), Superior General of the Society of Jesus (1946–1964), sent to his confreres a letter on "continual mortification," in which he contrasted the positions of the *nouvelle théologie*, that tended to exclude reparatory and impetratory penances and wrote that fasts, flagellations, hairshirts and other asperities must remain hidden from men according to the rule of Christ (Mt 6:16–18), but must be taught and inculcated to the young Jesuits up to the third year of probation (*DIP*, vol. 7, col. 472).

1613 Dal-Gal, *Merry del Val*, p. 176; Cenci, *Merry del Val*, pp. 441–445. "As soon as the Servant of God died, Msgr. Canali was called and saw in his drawer the hairshirt used by the Servant of God with nails a finger-long and full of dried blood. I learned that the Spanish Catechism Sisters, while cleaning his room, found drops of blood on the floor" (Evangelina Caymari, *Informatio*, p. 12).

1614 Cenci, *Merry del Val*, pp. 440–445. On the spirituality of Card. Merry del Val, cf., among others, Alberto José González Chaves, "La espiritualidad del cardenal Rafael Merry del Val," in Domingo Merry del Val (ed.), *Rafael Merry del Val, 150 anni dalla sua nascita*, pp. 227–251 and the introduction by Harriet Murphy to *El ángel del Vaticano: Escritos espirituales del Cardenal Merry del Val*, Nuova Eva, Madrid 2021.

The life of Rafael Merry del Val was a constant meditation on humility. He wrote:

> Jesus prepared for his own death with an act of humility: by washing the feet of his disciples. Every act of humility is an excellent preparation for death. Above all, one should understand the utility of the humble confession of one's sins, of true contrition, and of every act of penance and mercy that unites humiliations with charity. St. Augustine, shortly before his death, reread the penitential Psalms and said he would not like to die on a day he had not made some act of penance. Thus, it is always useful to confess the sins of one's past life. *Sciens quia omnia dedit et Pater in manus* [Knowing that the Father had given all things into his hands; John 13:3]. Unfortunately, it so happens that honors produce within us the effect of inebriating our mind and rendering us stupid with pride. Twice in the same Psalm we read, *Homo cum in honore esset, non intellexit* [In his riches, man cannot discern; Ps 49:21, Grail translation].... Thus, Jesus leaves us a precious warning, namely, that when we are in places of honor, we have a special need to lower ourselves.[1615]

In the discourse he gave in Assisi in 1926 on the humility of St. Francis, Merry del Val explained that humility is above all truth:

> It is the conscience illuminated, the candid and felt recognition of our nothingness, and this nothingness of ours is an incontrovertible reality, an undoubtably certain truth that in vain the amateurs of the world seek to ignore, and this reality constitutes the immutable basis of the relationship between creature and the Creator and therefore the basis of religion.... We have being, the soul, the body, but all this we receive from God and for this reason we are dependent on Him by necessity.... Toward God we can conceive incontestable duties, not rights, since we have no right even to our existence.... This is the truth that no human philosophy or aberration of our mind and no perverse rebellion can ever change; and it is for this reason that in Sacred Scripture the humble are declared blessed and wise, and the proud unhappy and foolish.... The path to Paradise is but one, narrow and rough as the

[1615] AAV, *Spoglio Merry del Val,* busta 8, f. 1141.

> Divine Master has said, and it is no other than the path of humility. "Learn from me for I am meek and humble of heart."[1616]

Humility is not only the foundation of all the other virtues but is the one that draws nearest to God. "The humble soul seeks nothing but God: when it has found God and His glory, this suffices. God cannot raise Himself up above Himself; the humble soul does not seek to raise itself above the others. This is what the Child Jesus teaches us so eloquently from [the] moment He was in the crib."[1617]

The humility to which Merry del Val exhorted his listeners can be found in the purest tradition of Christian spirituality. St. Benedict refers to the twelve degrees of humility,[1618] taken up by St. Thomas as well.[1619] For St. Ignatius, the third degree of humility has its foundation in the actions of Christ and leads Him to the heroism of the cross: "He who wishes to come with me, must suffer with me, for following me in suffering he will follow me in glory" (n. 95.5). As observed by Fr. Roothan, the first and second degree of humility "comprehend perfect indifference and presuppose the most absolute fight against the rebellion of the flesh, of the senses, and of self-love and worldliness; but the third degree of humility is content neither with indifference nor combating the rebellion, but continually undertakes to fight against (*agere contra*) any inclination of nature, solely to more fully imitate and resemble Christ."[1620]

How can we not notice in the final part of Cardinal Merry del Val's famous Litany of Humility the expression of St. Ignatius of Loyola's third degree of humility?

> *That others may be loved more than I,*
> *Jesus, grant me the grace to desire it.*
> *That others may be esteemed more than I,*
> *Jesus, grant me the grace to desire it.*
> *That, in the opinion of the world, others may increase and I may decrease,*
> *Jesus, grant me the grace to desire it.*

1616 Archive of the Postulation, ff. 593–605.

1617 Discourse on humility of December 28, 1924, to the Confraternity of the Sacred Heart, in Cenci, *Merry del Val*, p. 411.

1618 *Rule of St. Benedict*, ch. 7, PL vol. 103, col. 837.

1619 St. Thomas Aquinas, *Summa Theologiae*, II-IIae, q. 161, a 6.

1620 Giovanni Filippo Roothan S.J., *Annotazioni*, in St. Ignatius of Loyola, *Spiritual Exercises*, Editrice Ancora, Milan 1967, p. 223.

That others may be chosen and I set aside,
Jesus, grant me the grace to desire it.
That others may be praised and I go unnoticed,
Jesus, grant me the grace to desire it.
That others may be preferred to me in everything,
Jesus, grant me the grace to desire it.
That others may become holier than I, provided that I may become as holy as I should,
Jesus, grant me the grace to desire it![1621]

The Mysticism of Abandonment to Divine Providence

It would be reductive, however, to limit the cardinal's spiritual life to the ascetical dimension, when it seems to have reached the mystical level.

Some theologians have sought to separate the ascetical from the mystical, reserving to the latter the gift of contemplation. In reality, as Fr. Garrigou-Lagrange explained, it would be wrong to imagine the two as separate, just as it would be erroneous to think that the first phase is entirely human and the second entirely divine. The spiritual life knows no distinctions between asceticism, as an ordinary means reserved to many, and mysticism, as an extraordinary means reserved to but a few: it is predominantly one, and leads to the heights of perfection.[1622]

One of the cardinal's last writings was dated February 6, 1930. In the introduction to a book that collected the discourses to priests given by Pius X on the occasion of his priestly jubilee, Merry del Val explained the necessity of "living according to supernatural principles, seeing things from the supernatural point of view and being guided in our thoughts, words, and actions by considerations of a supernatural character."[1623]

1621 In his discourse to apostolic nuncios, June 13, 2019, Pope Francis proposed as a "sort of dialogue" the litanies of humility by Card. Merry del Val, reproducing them from the agency *Correspondenza Romana*, cited in the last note of his discourse. https://www.vatican.va/content/francesco/fr/speeches/2019/june/documents/papa-francesco_20190613_nunzi-apostolici.html.

1622 On the unity of the spiritual life, cf. Réginald Garrigou-Lagrange, *Christian Perfection and Contemplation According to St. Thomas Aquinas and St. John of the Cross*, trans. Doyle, Herder, St. Louis 1942, pp. 23–42; Amato Dagnino, of the Saverian Missionaries, *La vita interiore secondo la Rivelazione, studiata dalla teologia e insegnata dalla Chiesa [The Interior Life According to Revelation, Studied in Light of Theology and Taught by the Church]*, Edizioni Paoline, Milan 1960, pp. 28–41.

1623 Archivio della Postulazione, ff. 367–370.

> St. Augustine tells us how we can attain that. By means of the purity of our actions offered to God, continuous prayer throughout the day becomes possible. *In Innocentia operum tuorum, praepara te ad laudandum Deum tota die.* God does not ask for our words, but our hearts. *Non verba quaerit a te Deus, sed Cor.* Not that the great Doctor of the Church excluded vocal prayer; to the contrary: *Cum potes ore lauda.* But he goes on to say: *Cum non potes, corde lauda, corde benedici, corde in aram conscientiae victimas sacras impone.* Give praise with the lips when you are capable of doing so; if you cannot, then praise and bless Him all the more frequently and constantly, and place the sacred holocaust on the altar of your heart. These holocausts are the renunciations that we must impose on ourselves almost every hour of the day, with the aim of preserving ourselves from sin and safeguarding our sacred office. And this constitutes habitual prayer.[1624]

The constant teaching of Merry del Val was this: "Strive for holiness within your own state in life. Be at peace wherever God has put you and do His holy will. Never look beyond your own life."[1625]

Circumstances are "the messengers of the Good God," and so we must go out to meet them "with great elasticity," which consists in being completely ready to change one's way of acting according to the indications of the divine will.[1626] We must abandon ourselves to the will of God, he exhorts, for "the will and the love of God are one and the same thing, they are the basis of the dispositions of Divine Providence."[1627] "Desiring everything that God does, doing everything that God wants ... this is what can draw us near to the Heart of Our Lord." "Let us reflect often that there is not an instant of the day, nor a circumstance in our life, that is not permitted or desired by God, so that we might make use of it to show Him our love."[1628] Theologians define this conformity to the will of God as "holy abandonment."[1629]

Among the books that Merry del Val recommended, especially to converts to the Catholic faith, were two classics: *Abandonment to Divine Providence* by

1624 Ibid.

1625 Testimony by Lady Viola Symes, in Dal-Gal, *Merry del Val*, p. 122.

1626 *Pensieri ascetici*, pp. 14–16.

1627 Ibid., p. 84.

1628 Ibid., p. 20, p.41.

1629 Royo Marin and Jordan Aumann, *Theology of Christian Perfection*, Priory Press, Dubuque 1962, pp. 502–508; Adolfo Tanquerey, *Compendio di teologia ascetica e mistica, [Compendium of Ascetical and Mystical Theology]*, tr. it., San Paolo, Cinisello Balsamo (Milan) 2018, pp. 242–252, n. 476–498.

Fr. Jean-Pierre Caussade[1630] and *Holy Abandonment* by Fr. Vital Lehodey.[1631] The secret of holiness, taught Caussade, is abandonment to the will of God in the present moment. "Would to God that kings, and their ministers, princes of the Church and of the world, priests and soldiers, the peasantry and labourers, in a word, all men could know how very easy it would be for them to arrive at a high degree of sanctity. They would only have to fulfil the simple duties of Christianity and of their state of life; to embrace with submission the crosses belonging to that state, and to submit with faith and love to the designs of Providence in all those things that have to be done or suffered without going out of their way to seek occasions for themselves."[1632] The will of God, explains Fr. Vital Lehodey, is the "universal principle of being, of life, and of action. Everything is done according to its behests, nothing happens independently of its decrees; there is no effect but proceeds from it as from its first cause, nor any motion which it does not originate as prime mover. And consequently, there is no event, whether small or great, which does not reveal some volition of the divine good-pleasure."[1633]

All the saints have lived in this spirit of abandonment, fulfilling the divine will, however it manifested itself, from moment to moment, without allowing themselves to be dismayed by unforeseen setbacks and without concern for their future. Merry del Val wrote, "We must accept willingly and with complete submission the dispositions of Providence, seeing in everything the will of God."[1634]

Abandonment to Divine Providence is not passivity or inaction, but active cooperation of a human will with the divine will. It is only when we have fulfilled our duty that we can truly abandon ourselves to the divine will, however mysterious it may appear. To Margherita de Colmar,[1635] the foundress of the community *Parva Domus Pacis*, which found itself in serious difficulty, the cardinal said, "Lean

[1630] Jean-Pierre de Caussade (1675–1751), Jesuit, was author of *Abandonment to Divine Providence*, published in 1861 by Fr. Henri Ramière. The original critical text was presented by Fr. Michel Olphe-Galliard S.J. (Paris 1966).

[1631] Vital Lehodey (1857–1948), Cistercian, was abbot of the monastery of Bricquebec and author of spiritual writings, among which *Le saint abandon* (1909). Cf. Michel Niaussat, *Frère Vital ou le triomphe de la grâce: Suivi de Autobiographie originale de Dom Vital Lehodey*, Desclée de Brouwer, Paris 2007.

[1632] Jean-Pierre de Caussade, *Abandonment to Divine Providence*, 3rd. ed. trans. E. J. Strickland, Catholic Records Press, Exeter 1921, section 3, p. 5.

[1633] Dom Vital Lehodey, *Holy Abandonment*, M. H. Gill, Dublin 1954, p. 8.

[1634] Merry del Val, *Pensieri ascetici*, p. 22.

[1635] Margherita de Colmar (1888–1968), born in France into a noble family, carried out in Rome her apostolate of charity. There she founded and directed from 1925 to 1957 the *Parva Domus Pacis*, which welcomed children from the surrounding countryside, offering them instruction and vocational preparation, through the help of young teachers who offered their service freely.

on Our Lord and go forward with trust as long as you can. God asks nothing more. The success of the endeavor matters little; what matters is to do what God wants, how He wants, as long as He wants."[1636] "God blesses what He gives us to do," he wrote to Princess Fanny Starhemberg. "He does not bless, or blesses less, what we undertake on our own beyond the strength He gives us, which usually is the most visible indication of His will. It is useless to throw the net to the wrong side of our boat; we shall work all night without catching anything; let us throw out our net under His direction and we shall catch in abundance."[1637]

This doctrine, as explained by Fr. Garrigou-Lagrange, is very consoling, since it follows that "in the life of the just, every deliberate act that is not sinful is at the same time morally good and meritorious, whether it is easy or difficult, small or great."[1638] This is the "secret and hidden wisdom of God" of which St. Paul speaks (1 Cor 2:7). Ascetic and mystic are not two different and incommunicable paths, but the sole itinerary of the man who draws near to God. Union with God, in which the complete perfection of Christian life consists, is the fruit of the ascetical effort by man's will and of his docile abandonment to the action of the Holy Spirit.[1639]

The entire perfection of Christian life is found in the mysterious equilibrium between active fidelity to one's daily duties and confident abandonment to divine grace, which manifests itself in the unforeseen events that it brings us in every moment of the day. "This union of faithfulness and abandonment," observes Fr. Garrigou-Lagrange, "allows us to perceive what must be the union of asceticism, that insists on fidelity or conformity to the will of God, and mysticism, which places the accent on abandonment."[1640]

The Cyrene of Four Popes

Some who consider the figure of Cardinal Merry del Val consider him a man blessed by fortune, due to the circumstances that promoted his prestigious ecclesiastical career.[1641] There have also been those like Cardinal Gasparri who defined

1636 Cenci, *Merry del Val*, p. 350.

1637 Letter to Princess Fanny Starhemberg of June 18, 1923, in Cenci, *Merry del Val*, p. 527.

1638 R. Garrigou-Lagrange, O. P., *La Providence et la confiance en Dieu*, Les Éditions Militia, Montréal 1953, p. 263.

1639 R. de Mattei, *Breve Trattato sulla Divina Provvidenza*, Edizioni Fiducia, Rome 2022, p. 123.

1640 Garrigou-Lagrange, *La Providence et la confiance en Dieu*, p. 237.

1641 One of the first of these was the historian Maximilian Claar (1873–1938), in "Das Staatssekretariat Merry del Val (1903–1914)," *Zeitschrift für Politik* 20, 1931, pp. 30–42, which defined him from his childhood "*ein Kind des Glucks gewesen*," "a fortunate child" (p. 30), attributing to him the dream (he never had) of becoming archbishop of Toledo and primate of Spain (p. 31).

Cardinal Merry del Val a man of "limitless ambition,"[1642] incapable of admitting that his prestigious appointments were due only to chance circumstances. Gasparri was an eminent canon lawyer, but was incapable of comprehending that there exist mysterious designs of Divine Providence that move history against the will of its protagonists. The success that was imputed to Merry del Val, as if by a fault, was for him the ruin of his missionary dream, and the silent cross of his life was precisely that of being where he did not want to be.

The Church must one day declare whether Cardinal Merry del Val was a saint only in the private sphere or if, on the contrary, he heroically exercised the virtues in his function as secretary of state, just as St. Pius X exercised them in the role of visible head of the Church. A distinguished theologian, Fr. Victor-Alain Berto, was convinced of this.[1643] He wrote, "I am certain, as a private theologian, that Cardinal Merry del Val will be beatified for having exercised heroically his role as secretary of state."[1644] Fr. Berto referred to the decisive testimony of Pius XII, who was a direct collaborator of Cardinal Merry del Val and who desired his process of beatification, saying, "That Cardinal Merry del Val had the complete trust of Pius X is a fact no historian can ever obscure; that he was worthy and remained worthy of it was the solemn testimony of Pius XII."[1645]

Cardinal Pacelli, Merry del Val's successor in the double office of secretary of state and archpriest of the Vatican Basilica, in a discourse he pronounced before his tomb on June 9, 1931, recalling the extremely close collaboration of Cardinal Merry del Val with Pius X, stated:

> These two great souls have encountered each other in the joy of God, as we rightly trust, in the reward for the union of their work, while their names shall be preserved by history enthralled in the radiance of the light of truth and peace which the Roman pontiff spread throughout the world in the first decades of this century.[1646]

1642 Deposition of Msgr. Primo Principi, in *Informatio*, pp. 112–113; *Animadversiones*, p. 57. Gasparri's judgment is taken up by several pro-modernist historians like Fr. Annibale Zambarbieri, according to whom the "dazzling" career of Merry del Val was prepared by an attentive ecclesiastical politics (*Modernismo e modernisti*, p. 131).

1643 Victor-A. Berto, "À la mémoire du serviteur de Dieu le cardinal Raphael Merry del Val," *La Pensée Catholique* 26 (1953), p. 46 (pp. 42–46).

1644 Berto, *Pour la Sainte Église Romaine*, p. 106.

1645 Ibid., p. 105.

1646 Cenci, *Merry del Val*, p. 743.

And during the discourse for the beatification of Pius X on June 3, 1951, Pius XII said, "Pius X, assisted by the great soul of his most trusted secretary of state, Cardinal Merry del Val, gave proof of that enlightened prudence that is never lacking in the saints, even when in its application it contrasts, painfully yet unavoidably, with the deceitful postulates of human and purely terrestrial prudence."[1647]

In a letter from Milan, February 12, 1934, professor of canon law Orio Giacchi,[1648] wrote, "It seems to us … that one of the strongest reasons why the figure of the holy cardinal ought to be better known, loved, and in the near future, one might be able to invoke his intercession at the throne of God is this: he displayed what even many Catholics fail to see, namely that the Roman Curia, in its appearances not unlike other splendid earthly courts, is on earth the great center of the spiritual world, and that many of the souls that make up the Curia are saints, enlightened not only by the grace of their station, but also by the interior light that the Lord gives His elect. Who better than a cardinal, secretary of state first, secretary of the Congregation of the Holy Office later, and in times that are much like our own, to show this to the world, Catholic or not?"[1649]

Among the many testimonies concerning Cardinal Merry del Val's reputation of sanctity that are preserved in the Vatican Archives in the dossier on his cause of beatification, there is a letter sent by Prof. Plinio Corrêa de Oliveira, prior of the Third Order of Carmel of St. Paul.[1650] On July 16, 1952, during one of his visits to Rome, Oliveira wrote the following: "The passing of time, which slowly places every personality in its true historical perspective, is working to make better known and understood the extraordinary personality of Cardinal Merry del Val. To the eyes of a growing number of historians, to men of thought and of action, the great cardinal is already seen as the personification of piety, wisdom, and strength, thanks to the aid of accurate historical criticism. In Brazil, thanks to the efforts of the great bishop of Campos, Msgr. Antonio de Castro Mayer, the number of people who know and venerate the memory of the

[1647] Pius XII, Discourse of June 3, 1951, in *Discorsi e radiomessaggi*, vol. 13, p. 131.

[1648] Orio Giacchi (1909–1982) was professor of canon law at the Catholic University of Milan. Cf. Giacchi, "Il cardinale Raffaele Merry del Val," *Vita e Pensiero* 5 (May 1933), pp. 288–295.

[1649] AAV, *Spoglio Merry del Val*, busta 9, f. 1723.

[1650] Plinio Corrêa de Oliveira (1908–1995) was a Brazilian scholar and man of action, founder of the Brazilian Society for the Defence of Tradition, Family and Property in 1960, and author of numerous works, among which *Rivoluzione e contro-Rivoluzione* (1959), reprinted in various languages innumerable times. On him, cf. R. de Mattei, *Il crociato del secolo XX. Plinio Corrêa de Oliveira [The Crusade of the 20th Century. Plinio Corrêa de Oliveira]* Piemme, Casale Monferrato 1996.

unforgettable secretary of state of Blessed Pius X is growing considerably. Visiting Rome, I perceived not without profound emotion, kneeling at the tomb of Cardinal Merry del Val, the surge of profound veneration that he arouses in visitors who visit his tomb, with recollection and trust, to ask God that the halo that shines over the head of Pius X may also shine one day over the head of the man who was rightly called his Cyrene."[1651] The Marquise Aurora Misciattelli,[1652] who received spiritual direction from Cardinal Merry del Val and who for over thirty years recorded every ascetical thought and spiritual suggestion received from him, wrote in a memo preserved in the Vatican's Apostolic Archive: "I can positively assert that I know that Cardinal Merry del Val offered his life for that of Pius X. Having intuited this from one of his observations, I asked him and he told me, 'Yes, I offered it.' And we spoke about it several times after that."[1653]

Simon of Cyrene is the one who came to the aid of Jesus Christ on the way to Calvary, bearing His cross. Rafael Merry del Val desired to lighten the suffering of Pius X, the pope to whom he was intimately bound, to the point of offering his life for him. In every pope he served over the course of half a century, he saw the Vicar of Christ and sought to be his humble Cyrene. This was his silent cross, but it was also the complete fulfillment of the mission God had assigned him.

1651 AAV, *Spoglio Merry del Val*, busta 9, n. 1355, f. 17, *Le Cyréné.*

1652 Aurora Dimitrievna Buturlin (1860–1944) was born into a Russian noble family transferred to Florence in 1817. There she married the Marquis Francesco Misciattelli delle Ripe (1853–1918) in 1880, with whom she had three children: Piero (1882–1937), Olga (1883), and Lydia (1890).

1653 AAV, *Spoglio Merry del Val. Dichiarazione della M.sa Aurora Misciattelli n. C.ssa Boutourline*, n. 1982, p. 5.

Index of Names

G

H

L

M

Q

R

S

T

About the Author

Roberto de Mattei is a Catholic historian who has taught in several Italian universities. Between 2003 and 2011, he served as vice president of the National Research Council, the highest Italian scientific institution. He is president of the Lepanto Foundation and editor of the magazine Radici Cristiane and the news agency Corrispondenza Romana. He has authored thirty-five books, including *The Second Vatican Council: An Unwritten Story,* which was translated into eight languages; *Love for the Papacy & Filial Resistance to the Pope in the History of the Church*; *Saint Pius V*; *The Meaning of God's Providence in Our Lives*; *The Paths of Evil*; and *The Church in Storms*. He has received many awards, including membership in the Order of St. Gregory the Great from the Holy See for his service to the Roman Catholic Church. He is married with five children.

Sophia Institute

Sophia Institute is a nonprofit institution that seeks to nurture the spiritual, moral, and cultural life of souls and to spread the gospel of Christ in conformity with the authentic teachings of the Roman Catholic Church.

Sophia Institute Press fulfills this mission by offering translations, reprints, and new publications that afford readers a rich source of the enduring wisdom of mankind.

Sophia Institute also operates the popular online resource CatholicExchange.com. *Catholic Exchange* provides world news from a Catholic perspective as well as daily devotionals and articles that will help readers to grow in holiness and live a life consistent with the teachings of the Church.

In 2013, Sophia Institute launched Sophia Institute for Teachers to renew and rebuild Catholic culture through service to Catholic education. With the goal of nurturing the spiritual, moral, and cultural life of souls, and an abiding respect for the role and work of teachers, we strive to provide materials and programs that are at once enlightening to the mind and ennobling to the heart; faithful and complete, as well as useful and practical.

Sophia Institute gratefully recognizes the Solidarity Association for preserving and encouraging the growth of our apostolate over the course of many years. Without their generous and timely support, this book would not be in your hands.

www.SophiaInstitute.com
www.CatholicExchange.com
www.SophiaTeachers.org

Sophia Institute Press is a registered trademark of Sophia Institute.
Sophia Institute is a tax-exempt institution as defined by the
Internal Revenue Code, Section 501(c)(3). Tax ID 22-2548708.